The Archaeology of Islam in Sub-Saharan Africa

This book is the first comprehensive study of the impact of   -Saharan Africa. Timothy Insoll charts the historical background as we‾   archaeological evidence attesting to the spread of Islam across the Sudan, Eth   , Eastern Africa, Southern Africa and Nigeria, surveying a time span from the nmediate pre-Islamic period through to the present. He also analyses in detail the syncretism which has occurred between Islam and African traditional religions, and looks at the processes – *jihad*, trade, missionary activity, prestige – by which Islam spread. This book will be of great relevance to scholars and students, as well as to all those interested in Africa, archaeology, religion and Islam.

TIMOTHY INSOLL is Lecturer in Archaeology at the School of Art History and Archaeology of the University of Manchester. His previous publications include *Islam, Archaeology and History: The Gao Region, Mali* (1996), *The Archaeology of Islam* (1999), *Urbanism Archaeology and Trade* (2000) and *Archaeology and World Religion* (2001).

CAMBRIDGE WORLD ARCHAEOLOGY

The Cambridge World Archaeology series is addressed to students and professional archaeologists, and to academics in related disciplines. Most volumes present a survey of the archaeology of a region of the world, providing an up-to-date account of research and integrating recent findings with new concerns of interpretation. While the focus is on a specific region, broader cultural trends are discussed and the implications of regional findings for cross-cultural interpretations considered. The authors also bring anthropological and historical expertise to bear on archaeological problems and show how both new data and changing intellectual trends in archaeology shape inferences about the past. More recently, the series has expanded to include thematic volumes.

Books in the series
A. F. HARDING, *European Societies in the Bronze Age*
RAYMOND ALLCHIN AND BRIDGET ALLCHIN, *The Rise of Civilization in India and Pakistan*
CLIVE GAMBLE, *The Palaeolithic Settlement of Europe*
CHARLES HIGHAM, *Archaeology of Mainland South East Asia*
SARAH MILLEDGE NELSON, *The Archaeology of Korea*
DAVID PHILLIPSON, *African Archaeology* (second revised edition)
OLIVER DICKINSON, *The Aegean Bronze Age*
KAREN OLSEN BRUHNS, *Ancient South America*
ALASDAIR WHITTLE, *Europe in the Neolithic*
CHARLES HIGHAM, *The Bronze Age of Southeast Asia*
CLIVE GAMBLE, *The Palaeolithic Societies of Europe*
DAN POTTS, *The Archaeology of Elam*
NICHOLAS DAVID AND CAROL KRAMER, *Ethnoarchaeology in Action*
CATHERINE PERLÈS, *The Early Neolithic in Greece*
JAMES WHITLEY, *The Archaeology of Ancient Greece*
PETER MITCHELL, *The Archaeology of Southern Africa*

CAMBRIDGE WORLD ARCHAEOLOGY

THE ARCHAEOLOGY OF ISLAM IN SUB-SAHARAN AFRICA

TIMOTHY INSOLL
University of Manchester

CAMBRIDGE
UNIVERSITY PRESS

PUBLISHED BY THE PRESS SYNDICATE OF THE UNIVERSITY OF CAMBRIDGE
The Pitt Building, Trumpington Street, Cambridge CB2 1RP, United Kingdom

CAMBRIDGE UNIVERSITY PRESS
The Edinburgh Building, Cambridge, CB2 2RU, UK
40 West 20th Street, New York, NY 10011–4211, USA
477 Williamstown Road, Port Melbourne, VIC 3207, Australia
Ruiz de Alarcón 13, 28014 Madrid, Spain
Dock House, The Waterfront, Cape Town 8001, South Africa

http://www.cambridge.org

First published 2003

Printed in the United Kingdom at the University Press, Cambridge

Typeface Trump Medieval 10/13 pt.   *System* LaTeX 2_ε [TB]

A catalogue record for this book is available from the British Library

ISBN 0 521 65171 9 hardback
ISBN 0 521 65702 4 paperback

This book is dedicated to my parents, Pamela, and the late Antony Insoll

CONTENTS

ILLUSTRATIONS

ACKNOWLEDGEMENTS

Various people have assisted me in writing this volume, and a debt of gratitude is owed to the following, but above all to my wife Rachel and my daughter Freya, for their patience in allowing me to absent myself from long periods of family life. Numerous colleagues have also been of assistance, and many thanks are extended to the following: to Paul Lane for kindly copying photos from the archive of the British Institute in Eastern Africa, Peter Robertshaw for answering various bead-related queries, and David Phillipson for kindly supplying illustrations. Eric Ross is also gratefully acknowledged for providing a copy of a paper in advance of publication, as are Detlef Gronenborn, Richard Helms, Randi Haaland and Adria LaViolette. Anne Haour must also be thanked for providing an extremely useful annotated bibliography and photocopies of otherwise unobtainable articles. John Sutton also kindly provided copies of hard-to-obtain references.

Similarly, I am grateful to Patrick Darling for providing copies of his unpublished conference papers, Detlef Gronenborn for providing offprints, Derek Welsby, John Alexander and David Edwards for answering queries on the Sudan, as well as Pam Rose and Pierre de Maret for supplying obscure references. A special vote of thanks is also due to Peter Shinnie for providing me with several envelopes of photographs from his own archives, his generosity has been exceptional. Pamela Insoll and Rachel MacLean are also thanked for their assistance with some of the illustrations, as are likewise the staff of the Gten Photographic Unit in the University of Manchester, Derek Trillo, Anne Perrott and Michael Pollard. The Egypt Exploration Society is thanked for allowing access under the auspices of John Alexander to the Qasr Ibrim archive in Cambridge, and the staff of the Griffith Institute in Oxford are also thanked for helping me to find the Newbold Archive. Finally, a grateful acknowledgement is also due to the Series Editor, Norman Yoffee, and the two anonymous readers of the manuscript who pointed out its many shortfalls and steered the volume back on course. All remaining errors and shortfalls are obviously my own.

Funding for parts of the research which form the basis of this volume was provided by St John's College, Cambridge, the British Institute in Eastern Africa, the McDonald Institute, Cambridge, the British Academy and the University of Manchester. I am most grateful for the assistance provided. The officers of the British Institute in Eastern Africa, especially John Sutton, the former director, must also be thanked for providing a hospitable base in which some of the library work was completed. Finally, I am most grateful to His Highness Shaikh Salman bin Hamad al-Khalifa, the Crown Prince of Bahrain, for arranging the funding for the period of research leave in which this volume was completed – a period during which I also tried to juggle the excavation of parts of Bahrain, hopefully not too unsuccessfully.

Every effort has been made to trace copyright holders. The author and publisher would like to apologise in advance for any inadvertent use of copyright material, and thank the following individuals and organisations who have kindly given their permission to reproduce copyright material. For illustrations: **cover, 6.12** Professor Pierre de Maret; **2.3–2.5, 2.10–2.12, 2.14, 2.16, 4.3, 4.5, 4.7–4.9, 4.12, 4.15–4.16, 4.20–4.22, 8.5** British Institute in Eastern Africa; **3.4** Kegan Paul Ltd; **3.7–3.10, 5.6, 6.4–6.5, 6.15, 7.11** Professor Peter Shinnie; **3.12, 4.14, 5.16** Dr Rachel MacLean; **4.2** James Currey Publishers; **4.4** Professor Felix Chami; **4.10** Dr Richard Helm; **5.2, 5.5, 7.9** Cambridge University Press; **6.3** Dr Detlef Gronenborn; **6.14** University of Wisconsin Press; **7.4** Professor Christopher DeCorse; **7.5** Professor Susan Keech McIntosh; **8.2, 8.4** Dr David Phillipson.

CHAPTER I

THE ARCHAEOLOGY OF ISLAM IN SUB-SAHARAN AFRICA: AN INTRODUCTION

Aims and objectives

This volume aims to examine the archaeology of Islam in Africa south of the Sahara. Yet this simple statement masks a great deal of complexity, for it suggests that the archaeology of Islam in sub-Saharan Africa is the residue of one uniform faith from the Cape to Timbuktu. This, however, is not the case: great diversity is evident, and although key recurring elements might be preserved (as are discussed in some detail below) African Islam has been subject to historical process. Such historical process was described by Ray (1976:176) as 'a history of several phases and types of religion...a history of developing orthodoxy and of developing synthesis...the result was not a confused syncretism, but a variety of new religious and cultural syntheses which bear the unique character of sub-Saharan Islam'. The importance of this paraphrased quote is that it emphasises the plural character of Islamic development within Africa – one Islam as structured by the requirements of faith (see below), but numerous local interpretations thereof once the core prerequisites were fulfilled.

This multiple interpretation has resulted in the creation of the archaeological record that is the focus of this study; its further aims are to provide an introduction to the richness and diversity of Islamic material culture in sub-Saharan Africa in all its many forms, from mosques and tombs through to trade goods – beads, glazed pottery and glass. Such monuments and archaeological material are found across the continent from the fringes of the Sahara in the north to the shores of the Indian Ocean in the far south. This is also an archaeological record which has been neglected to date as regards an attempt at synthesis. This is perhaps somewhat unsurprising, as Africa south of the Sahara is a vast area, frequently more dissimilar than similar and only, in many respects, unified for the purposes of this study by its geographical borders, i.e. the fact that it is bounded to the north by the barrier of the Sahara and on its other sides by ocean. Yet, conversely, it is equally surprising that the archaeology of Islam has never been considered in great detail – for the impact of Islam has been of fundamental importance in much of the continent, and has been felt on many fronts, not only ideologically, but also economically and socially. This is important, for as Brenner (1993a:59) notes, the creation of identity, both Muslim and non-Muslim (the latter also a subject with which this volume is concerned), 'are formulated through the appropriation and reassortment of various elements or building blocks which may be religiously significant, but are also socially, politically and economically motivated'. The archaeology of Islam in sub-Saharan Africa is thus not only the residue of explicitly religious process; for, to quote an oft-cited phrase, Islam must be seen as more than a religion, it is a way of life, with all the attendant material culture implications which such a statement implies.

This is because the study of Islam in sub-Saharan Africa is not merely of religion – it provides a point of entry into the study of other institutional systems, allowing a consideration of concomitant changes in, for example, society, economy and politics. Therefore, along with the introduction of Islam in sub-Saharan Africa there are many changes in the material record in the continent south of the Sahara, and in many respects the archaeology of Islam in sub-Saharan Africa is really the archaeology of sub-Saharan Africa in the last millennium, the effects were so widespread and profound. Given these changes in sub-Saharan Africa in the last millennium, we are allowed a focus on what changed and thus must consider, to an extent, the nature of the societies and belief systems prior to Islam, and also how these survived in whole or in part and in a variety of associations with Islam.

Yet manifestations of Islamisation might be various. Within religious belief there might be a shift in emphasis from a pantheon of deities to a more immediate relationship with a single God. Economically, local trade networks could be tied into the Muslim world economy. Socially, material changes might be manifest in house types, settlement patterns, diet and funerary customs. Politically, the adoption of Arabic, of literacy and of new forms of administration could result in great change. These possibilities for change are manifold, and various aspects of this process can be traced in the archaeological record. But equally, as will be considered below, the presence of a Muslim or Muslim community might leave only an ephemeral material imprint (Insoll 1999a). Complexity, both in process and in the concepts that are to be explored in this volume, has to be recognised from the outset. This is something also remarked upon by Mervyn Hiskett (1994:184) in a study of the history of Islam in Africa, who likens the process of studying Islam in the continent to looking through a kaleidoscope, whereby 'no sooner does one pattern emerge then a thought, a forgotten factor or a sudden reservation intervenes and the whole pattern changes'.

Complexity acknowledged, it has also to be recognised that we are concerned with several key processes which it is useful to define at the outset. Critical among these is a term already used, 'Islamisation', which according to Levtzion (1979c:7) refers to religious change, though it is useful for our purposes here to use the term to refer both to religious and the frequently accompanying cultural change. This, perhaps, is of lesser importance with reference to Levtzion's research focus, that of historical sources and process, but needs to be admitted where the focus rests upon material culture as well. A second and differing term is 'Islamism', which according to Rosander (1997:4) is focused upon *shari'ah* (Islamic law), with Islamists conceiving 'of Islam as an ideology, a total mode of life'. Islamism as defined by Rosander, and as considered here, refers to the reform of African Islam, something which has occurred periodically (especially more recently), with as its stated aim the 'purification' of African Islam 'from local or indigenous African ideas and practices as well as from Western influences' (Rosander 1997:1). A further term to be encountered is 'Arabisation', which is in fact of little relevance outside a few contexts in the continent south of the Sahara. Arabisation literally refers to the Arabising of society – culturally, ethnically or ideologically – and is of importance in parts of the Nilotic Sudan as we will see in chapter 3, and in areas of the East African coast, as described in chapter 4. Similarly, the terms 'orthodox', 'popular' or 'syncretic' will be utilised with reference to religious practice. These are considered at greater length at the end of this chapter.

Thus having considered something of the aims and objectives of this study it is also worthwhile considering how these are going to be fulfilled. Essentially, a multi-source approach has to be adopted in evaluating the archaeology of Islam in sub-Saharan Africa, as each of the available sources of evidence has its limitations. Archaeological evidence devoid of the supporting interpretative props of historical sources, when they are available, can appear dry and lifeless. Fortunately for the purposes of interpreting the archaeology of Islam in sub-Saharan Africa the relevant historical source documents, written primarily in Arabic, are increasingly available in translation, facilitating their wider circulation and utilisation (see for example Freeman-Grenville 1962; Cuoq 1975b; Levtzion and Hopkins 1981; Hamdun and King 1994; and the 'bio-bibliographical' volumes edited by Hunwick and O'Fahey 1994, 1995, 1998), a trend which it is hoped will continue. Where the Arabic sources leave frequent gaps, in central Africa, for example, early explorers', travellers', and missionaries' accounts can be exploited, while oral history can also prove extremely useful in tracing Islamisation across the continent. However, as with archaeological interpretation devoid of supporting sources, the use of historical sources in isolation is not unproblematical. The sources might provide us with the basic chronological framework of Islam in sub-Saharan Africa, yet we must also turn to archaeology to begin to reconstruct the diverse social, political and economic effects of conversion to Islam, and the direct and indirect impact of the religion upon the peoples of the continent south of the Sahara. The archaeology of Islam is here foregrounded because, as in other forms of historical archaeology, there is the possibility that what we can learn from material culture not only complements and supplements the historical record, but also may contradict what we think we know from history.

A certain interdependence of sources is therefore evident, and the historical and archaeological evidence is also supplemented by anthropological, ethnographic, linguistic and architectural data. As Levtzion (1979c:5) notes, many sources exist for studying the processes of conversion to Islam: historical texts, inscriptions, names, and even dreams (for this latter unusual source of evidence see Jedrej and Shaw 1992) – the whole conspiring to enrich our understanding of the archaeology of Islam in Africa south of the Sahara. For it is with people that we are concerned and with dynamic ongoing processes of religious conversion. This adoption of a multi-source approach is made more essential as the processes we are observing in the archaeological record, the spread and acceptance of Islam, are very much alive and ongoing today in many areas of sub-Saharan Africa. Furthermore, a multi-source approach is necessary as it is somewhat presumptuous to assume 'that any *one* discipline will provide a universal key to unlock all the secrets of religion(s)' (Sutherland 1991:32). These are issues which this author has considered elsewhere (Insoll 2001), where it was suggested that the multi-source umbrella offered by approaches such as those encompassed within the history of religions (see Sharpe 1986) might be a useful methodological step forward for archaeological approaches to complex phenomena such as Islam, in recognising diversity, and in approaching the material sympathetically.

Geographical and temporal frameworks

The establishment of a methodological framework is a necessary step in approaching the diverse material incorporated within this study. A geographical division of the material has also proven essential, and for the purposes of discussion the continent south of the Sahara has been divided into seven regions. These are: Ethiopia and the Horn of Africa; the eastern or Nilotic Sudan (the modern republic of this name); the East African coast; the western Sahel; the central Sudan (Sudan here refers to the vegetation belt); the West African Sudan (as before) and forest; and finally, east-central and southern Africa **(figure 1.1)**. Undeniably, any such division is in certain respects unsuitable, and its use does not mean that each region was a self-contained and isolated entity, as the archaeology testifies to the various contacts that took place over vast distances across the continent. These regions were frequently interconnected, as will become apparent.

This pattern of geographical progression was chosen in approaching the material as it broadly follows the chronological pattern of the initial spread of Islam, a process which begins on the Red Sea coast and in Nubia, the former area the earliest zone of Muslim contact from the very beginnings of Islam in the seventh century (and considered in chapters 2 and 3). By the late eighth to early ninth centuries Islam had spread to parts of the East African coast (for simplicity the CE (Common Era), BCE (Before Common Era) dating system has been adopted, and all dates are CE unless otherwise specified), and almost contemporaneously in the late ninth to early tenth centuries to the western Sahel.

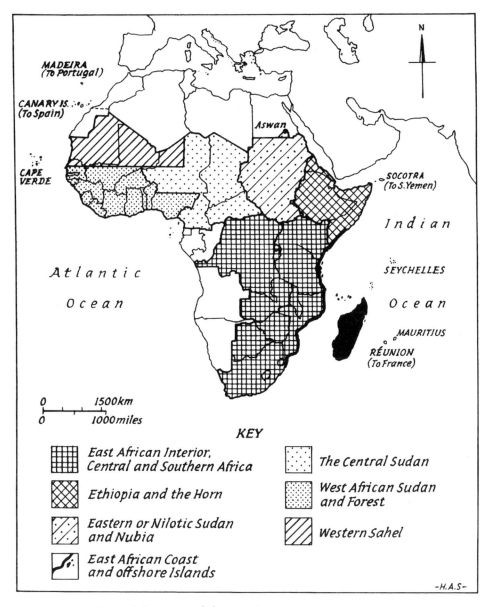

Figure 1.1 The subdivisions of the continent

Subsequently, in the eleventh century, the first tangible evidence for Islamisation is found in the central Sudan, while in the West African Sudan and forest this evidence dates from the twelfth century. Finally, on the other side of the continent, in east-central and southern Africa, the spread of Islam was much later, dating from the mid-seventeenth century in parts of the Cape, but elsewhere largely from the the nineteenth century. Discussion commences with

Ethiopia and the Horn of Africa, for it encompasses part of the Red Sea coast, the importance of which during the early Islamic period has already been referred to, but also because the connections between Ethiopia and parts of Arabia have a substantial pre-Islamic history.

It must also be noted here that reduction to a simple chronological framework such as that just provided is unacceptable, and it has to be realised that dynamic processes of Islamic conversion were incorporated within this historical process. Equally, the notion that a uniform suite of Muslim material culture was laid out in each of the geographical regions from the date just defined must be dismissed. On the contrary, the pattern that exists can be likened to a mosaic with some pieces the residue of Muslim communities, others followers of traditional religion, or perhaps of another world religion such as Christianity, all possibly coexisting and, with regard to the first two, frequently intermixing. For example, the western Sahel from the tenth century, the date of the earliest archaeological evidence for the presence of Muslims, cannot be thought of as completely Muslim at that point in time; it was a mosaic of different religious elements. Even today it cannot be argued that it is wholly Muslim. We are observing the residue of long-drawn-out processes rather than of a 'single act of conversion' (Levtzion 1979c:21).

The archaeology of Islam in each of the regions just defined is also a continuation of the Iron Age archaeology. It is not suddenly separated out by dint of being created by Muslims or Muslim communities. Thus this study slots into the pre-existing archaeological context, as only in a few rare instances could it be thought of as the archaeology of foreign imposition, it is African Iron Age archaeology. The pre-Islamic background was crucial in dictating the degree of Islamisation, the types of relationship entered into with Muslims by non-Muslims, the rate of Islamic conversion, and the impact of Islam upon the various societies that existed. Hence to neglect material pre-dating the arrival of Islam as unnecessary permits only an incomplete understanding of subsequent developments. However, it must also be acknowledged that this study must by its very nature privilege the Islamic element in the archaeological record, and also undeniably more so with regard to the 'religious' element of this material culture – though having said this, this study should be considered as part of the series in which it is conceived, other studies considering the non-Muslim context in much greater detail. Similarly, this study is also concerned with the residue of an African religion, Islam being as much an African religion as are traditional religions (this is considered below). For the undenied success of Islam in Africa was because 'it appropriated and had been appropriated' (Eaton 1993:303) by Africans (figure 1.2). The quote just used in fact refers to processes of Islamic conversion in Bengal, but it applies equally to the African situation. Islam in Africa is African Islam, albeit of diverse character, and this is reflected in the archaeology.

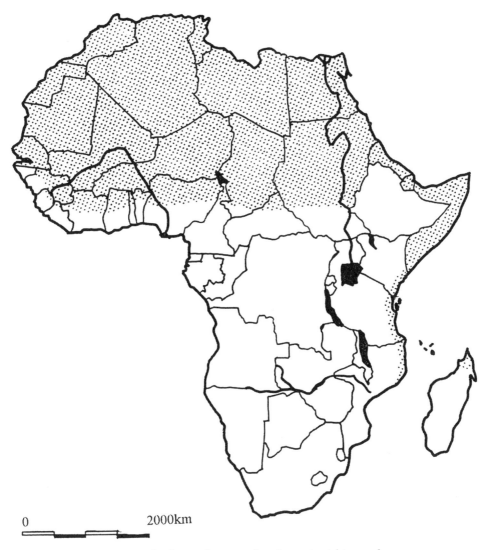

0   2000km

Figure 1.2 Areas in which Muslims predominate in Africa today

A history of research

This study should also be placed within the context of past research, where it has already been noted that a synthesis of the archaeology of Islam in sub-Saharan Africa does not exist. A similar situation pertains to relevant anthropological studies: much excellent and detailed research has been completed (see for example Goody 1971b; Holy 1991; Mitchell 1956), but no overall review exists, in part due to the difficulty in compiling such a volume or volumes. The nature of the anthropological evidence perhaps precludes its viable summary, in comparison to archaeological or historical data. Alternatively, this might be due to the fact that, to quote Morris, anthropology texts 'largely fo-cus on the religion of tribal cultures and seem to place an undue emphasis on its more exotic aspects' (1987:2). So-called tribal religions are split up into phenomena – myth, witchcraft, magic etc. – whereas in contrast, as Morris also notes (1987:3), world religions are treated according to a quite different theo-retical framework whereby they are classified as discrete and distinct entities, such as 'Buddhism' or 'Islam', with these classifications provided by historians rather than anthropologists. Besides this synthetic archaeological and anthro-pological lacuna (other than a basic introductory article on the archaeology by this author: see Insoll 1996a), the literature on Islam in Africa is vast, and only a selective consideration can be supplied here, focusing upon more widely available works.

In general, the relevant study of Islam in Africa at a regional or continen-tal level has predominantly been one of historical synthesis and survey with attention paid to archaeological evidence, if at all, only in passing. Spencer Trimingham could be regarded as the doyen of such approaches, certainly as regards Anglophone scholarship, with his series of detailed regional studies of Islam in Africa (1949, 1952, 1959, 1962, 1964), along with one continental overview (1968). These are still invaluable sources as starter works for orienting oneself with regional developments and the 'classical' texts of scholarship on Islam in sub-Saharan Africa. However, it should be borne in mind that these are also dated in content, and old-fashioned in style and approaches. Trimingham perceives Africa as marginal to the Islamic world, evident in comments such as 'the adoption of Islam brought little change in the capacity of Africans to con-trol the conditions of their existence for they were in touch but in a peripheral way with the developed civilizations of other Islamic peoples' (1968:1–2). This is the opposite of the implicit premise in this study that Africa was an integral part of the Muslim world. Trimingham also speaks of the spread of Islam as if it is a depersonalised amorphous entity 'penetrating' (1968:37) the continent. No allowance for the individual is given, and though group dynamics are obvi-ously significant in the conversion process, individual decision making cannot be excluded either.

Further, what could be termed 'old-fashioned' studies of Islam in sub-Saharan Africa (in English), are provided by the volumes *Islam in Tropical Africa* edited by I. M. Lewis (1966, 1980b), and *Islam in Africa* edited by J. Kritzeck and W. H. Lewis (1969). Yet these cannot be criticised in the same way as Trimingham's work. Lewis's volume, for example, is a landmark study, admittedly not so much for the series of regional historical surveys of Islam in Africa that are provided, but rather for the introductory study by Lewis (1980a) which con-siders in detail the factors underpinning conversion to Islam and the interplay between Islam and traditional religions. Francophone equivalents (this empha-sis on English and French literature reflects the author's linguistic capabilities, not the complete literature on Islam in Africa) of these general historical syntheses are provided by the volumes written by, among others, J. C. Froelich (1962) and Joseph Cuoq (1975a). Cuoq's volume differs from those just described in that although he employs a similar pan-continental emphasis, a gazetteer-type format is utilised in an attempt to place Muslims 'dans leur communauté concrète actuelle' (1975a:8). Similarly, dated regional syntheses in French, comparable to those already noted for Trimingham, also exist, but these are usually more circumscribed in geographical focus or subject (see for example Marty 1917; Chailley et al. 1962; Monteil 1964). The latter study is certainly still of interest in drawing together a number of strands including a history of Islamisation in West Africa imaginatively entitled 'les Fétiches ont Tremblé', and a reference to Shehu Ahmadu's comment on hearing the Bambara guns during the opening of his *jihad* in Masina in 1818 (Fisher and Rowland 1971:220; see chapter 7).

A general observation that can be drawn from comparing Anglophone and Francophone studies of Islam in Africa is, continental syntheses aside, that the regional focus very much reflects spheres of interest and colonial subdivisions. Colonial process is also sometimes manifest much more overtly in the archaeology of Islam in sub-Saharan Africa through the interpretations proposed by archaeologists of the colonial period. These are issues which will be reviewed in the following chapters, but as Robertshaw (1990:93) notes in a general context, 'many of the theories that buttressed colonial ideology have been overturned and replaced by models emphasising indigenous innovation and development'. Within Francophone West Africa, for example, the origins of the great 'medieval' empires, which were among the first polities to be exposed to Islam in sub-Saharan Africa, were sought outside Africa. Individuals such as Maurice Delafosse (1922) argued that Ghana was 'founded and ruled by Judeo-Syrians from the fourth to eighth centuries AD' (de Barros 1990:161), and foreign origins were sought, be they of 'Jews, Yemenites, Arabs' (Holl 1990:300). Colonial focus in this region was upon the capitals of the empires, sites that could be tied to Arab texts, and the civilising effects of Islam were promoted. Holl (1996:193) describes how French colonial scholarship served to provide data up the chain of command, allowing those at the top to use this for grand interpretation 'of the historical precedence and superiority of white people over black natives, thus reinforcing their *mission civilisatrice*'.

The excesses of these Delafosse-type interpretations might have been diluted over the subsequent years of colonisation in West Africa, but notions of backward locals and innovative foreigners persisted, frequently tied to a civilising Islamic input. The influential French archaeologist Raymond Mauny (1961:390), for instance, drew parallels between settlements such as Koumbi Saleh, the reputed capital of the empire of Ghana, and the neighbouring trade centre of Tegdaoust, also in Mauritania, and the manner in which European cities were superimposed next to the medinas of the colonial Maghreb. Consciously or subconsciously, archaeologists of the colonial period were thereby justifying their own presence. Colonisation had occurred before, thus they were only continuing a long tradition. Similar processes are evident elsewhere in the continent – on the East African coast, for example (see chapter 4). In general there was, as Trigger (1989:138) succinctly notes, 'a significant but complex relationship between archaeology and the colonial setting in which it was practiced in Africa'. But such processes of colonial justification can hardly be said to be unique to the interpretation of Islamic archaeological remains in Africa, or indeed to African archaeology in general. Chakrabarti (1997) has recently reviewed such processes with regard to Indian archaeology, while in a more general context such issues have been examined by Kohl and Fawcett (1995), Stone and Molyneaux (1994) and Pels (1997).

More recently, a wealth of excellent studies of Islam in Africa have been written. These, however, seem to have changed in focus in comparison to earlier works, with emphasis now upon specific subject areas or regions, rather than a pan-continental emphasis. Exceptions are provided by Mervyn Hiskett's (1994) historical survey of Islam in Africa, which follows a traditional vein of scholarship, and which is drawn upon in the following pages, and the similar but much larger study by Levtzion and Pouwels (2000), which is likewise a useful volume. More characteristic of contemporary scholarship are studies such as Brenner's (1993c) edited volume looking at Muslim identity in sub-Saharan Africa. Brenner also reviews various relevant contemporary currents in scholarship, where he notes (1993b:12) that, importantly, African Muslims are now organising their own conferences on Islam in Africa such as that held in Abuja (Nigeria) in 1989. These, he argues, are creating a vision of Africa as unified through Islam which will ultimately 'become increasingly competitive with the other "Africas" which are projected in the African discourse', the geo-political Africa of pan-Africanists, the Africa of the diaspora, and of 'Black Africa' (1993b:17). Again this notion of multiple voices is not unique to scholarship on Islam in Africa, but its recognition shows that scholarship on the subject has come of age.

Such more nuanced approaches are also manifest in other recent studies. Rosander and Westerlund (1997), for example, consider, as the title of their edited collection implies, the concepts of 'tradition' and 'modernity' within African Islam, encapsulated in the ongoing conflict between the processes of Islamism and popular religious tradition. Conversion processes have also been the focus of some attention, most notably by Nehemia Levtzion (1979a; Levtzion and Fisher 1986), and again by Sanneh (1997), while debate has also been recently initiated over the nature of African Islam. Ross (in press), for instance, has criticised the 'persistent tendency in the authoritative literature to view Africa as being outside of normative Islam'. What exactly is normative or orthodox Islam is debatable in itself (and is considered further below), but Ross is right in critiquing the former emphasis in scholarship whereby Africa was not usually 'considered as a contributing source – as an active ingredient – in the construction of Islam', it is seen as passive, 'simply receiving Islam' (in press). These are points already isolated with regard to sentiments expressed by Trimingham, and Ross is adding a further element to scholarship on Islam in Africa. Diverse themes are also increasingly being explored within recent Francophone scholarship, as exemplified by Coulon's (1983) study of Islam as counter-culture in Africa and its role in power negotiations in society.

Thus far emphasis has been upon studies of Islam in Africa which, if they deal with it at all, only touch upon archaeological evidence. This might seem strange within a study concentrating upon the archaeology of Islam in sub-Saharan Africa, but it does in fact make sense. Various regional archaeological syntheses of pertinent data exist, either wholly or partly concerned with Islam, but these are reviewed and utilised within the following chapters, and it would be merely repetitious to include such a discussion here. Having said this, it is worthwhile noting that relevant archaeological research did not start until comparatively late in many regions of Africa. This might not be so in Francophone West Africa, for reasons already described, but was certainly true of elsewhere in the continent where emphasis was upon the Stone Age and hominid origins at the expense of Iron Age studies. Reasons for this were various, as Kense records (1990:142), and included the perception that research on the Iron Age might carry political undertones, linking in turn to points already made about colonial approaches. Appropriate archaeological research was therefore, comparatively, a later development, as on the East African coast, where it largely began following the establishment of the British Institute in the region in 1959 (Robertshaw 1990:88). The institute itself has not been immune from criticism, perhaps unfairly, as having a 'European-dominated agenda, colonial setting, European membership' (Schmidt 1996:129). Today, there is cause to be much more positive, as increasingly Iron Age archaeology, including that focusing on Islamic material, is being completed by indigenous scholars pursuing their own research agendas, exemplified by Felix Chami (1998) on the East African coast, Ayele Tarekegn in Ethiopia (1998), or Tèrèba Togola (1996) in the western Sahel.

Yet once initiated, the quantity of relevant archaeological research has similarly varied across the continent. Some areas can be said to have been more privileged than others – the East African coast, for example – while other equally important regions have been almost wholly neglected, such as large areas of the central Sudan. The reasons for this imbalance in archaeological research are many. These include, admittedly as viewed from an overseas perspective, the perceived importance of the region, the visibility of the archaeological remains, the ease of working in a particular area (civil strife, logistics etc.), the presence of research centres such as the British Institute in Eastern Africa, or the existence of research initiatives such as the Swedish (SAREC) funded Urban Origins in Eastern Africa project, which can facilitate archaeological fieldwork in many ways. Therefore it has to be acknowledged that the apparent lack of archaeological remains in one region need not necessarily mean that the people there were not exposed to Islamic influences, but rather may be a reflection of a lack of archaeological research.

Islam: an introduction

As well as considering the context of scholarship in which this study is placed, it is also necessary to introduce the two main elements with which we are concerned, Islam and African traditional religions, and their corresponding material manifestations; firstly, Islam.

Origins

Briefly summarised, Islam ('submission' to the will of God) originated in the Arabian Peninsula when the Prophet Muhammad (b. *c.*570; d. 632) began to receive his first revelations from God, via the Angel Gabriel, in about 610. Initially, Muslim converts were few, but by 615, Muhammad could be regarded as the leader of a community (Lapidus 1988:25). This community was established in Mecca (contemporary Saudi Arabia), but owing to difficult conditions there, Muhammad and his followers moved to Medina in 622 (also in Saudi Arabia), in an event known as the *hijrah* or migration, and forming Year One of the Muslim calendar (1 AH, *al-hijrah*). With this move the formal establishment of the Muslim community, *ummah*, can be considered to have taken place. Conflict with the non-Muslim Meccans continued until an armistice was signed in 628, and in 630 the Muslim occupation of Mecca was completed. In 632 the Prophet died in Medina, where he was buried (Lapidus 1988; Waines 1995, Insoll 1999a).

The progress of Islam in its first century was swift; Muslim power in Arabia was rapidly consolidated, and under the successors to Muhammad, the Khalifahs or Rightly Guided Caliphs, the Muslim armies spread into and conquered Palestine, Iraq, Syria, large parts of Iran, and Egypt between 633 and 650. These initial conquests were shortly followed by others under subsequent dynasties; between 674 and 715, a Muslim Central Asian frontier zone was established with the conquest of Transoxania, and by the end of the first quarter of the eighth century, the conquest of the Maghreb (North Africa) and al-Andalus (Islamic Spain) was complete (Lapidus 1988). Thus Islam was established in the Arabian Peninsula across the Red Sea from Africa, north of the Sahara in parts of the Maghreb and in Egypt, all three areas bordering or adjacent to parts of sub-Saharan Africa with which we are concerned.

Teachings, components and obligations

The precepts and principles of the Qur'an, regarded by Muslims as the immutable word of God, form the basis of the Islamic faith. The Qur'an (lit. recitation or reading) was revealed to the Prophet Muhammad via the Angel Gabriel in the form of verses, which are arranged in 114 chapters or *surah*. Second only to the Qur'an as the source of *shari'ah* (Islamic law) are the Prophet's sayings and doings, the *hadith* (traditions), which were transmitted by either, or both, oral and written methods from their original source. Six major collections of *hadith* are recognised by almost all Muslims as genuine. These, in chronological order, were compiled by: al-Bukhari (d. 870); Ibn al-Hajjaj (d. 875); Ibn Maja (d. 887); Abu Dawud (d. 889); al-Tirmidhi (d. 892); and al-Nasa'i (d. 915). Together these form the *sunnah*, the way of the Prophet, which should form the example as to how to lead one's life for all Muslims (Gibb and Kramers 1961). The *shari'ah* is the law of Islam, which by its origins and nature is sacred in character. Besides the Qur'an and *hadith*, the other two main roots of the law are analogy through reasoning, *ijtihad*, and consensus, or *ijma*.

The essential principles of the Islamic faith as contained in the Qur'an and *shari'ah* are the Five Pillars of Islam, which are the requirements for believers. The first is the credo, or *shahadah*, 'There is no god but God and Muhammad is the Prophet of God', which is the expression of absolute monotheism. The second is ritual prayer five times a day in the direction of Mecca (*salat*). The third is the fast (*sawm*) in the tenth month of the lunar year, Ramadan. The fourth is *zakat* (alms), that is, giving between 2.5 and 10 per cent of one's wealth to the needy. The fifth is *hajj*, making a pilgrimage to Mecca at least once in one's life if one has the necessary means to achieve this. Within sub-Saharan Africa, often this was not the case, and many alternative pilgrimage centres developed, examples of which will be considered in the following chapters where necessary.

Fortunately, the Five Pillars lend themselves to archaeological recognition and are key criteria to the archaeological recognition of a Muslim community both in general (see Insoll 1999a) and in sub-Saharan Africa. The general categories of evidence which might allow the material recognition of a Muslim community are varied and are described in further detail below. But specifically with regard to the Five Pillars, archaeological evidence indicating their existence could include: for the *shahadah*, inscriptions in many different media; *salat* by the mosque and other places of prayer; alms-giving by inscriptions and through the system of endowments (*waqf*) by pious and wealthy individuals of buildings such as hospitals, mosques, religious schools etc.; *hajj* by pilgrims' hostels, routes, wells, milestones etc. It is only *sawm* that will be unlikely to be recognised archaeologically. Each of these categories of evidence, theoretically at least, should be present in sub-Saharan Africa, and their archaeological visibility is assessed in the following chapters.

Muslim groups in sub-Saharan Africa

Different approaches in interpreting the *shari'ah* led to the emergence of four legal schools – the Hanafi, Maliki, Shafi'i and Hanbali – which are named after the scholar-jurists who founded them, and which were largely consolidated by the tenth century. All the four legal schools are Sunni, meaning the adherents of *sunnah*, and these dominate in Africa south of the Sahara. The four Sunni legal schools differ in how they interpret points of the law, which is the domain of learned men (*ulama*), and administered by the religious judges (*qadi*). But it should be noted that the existence of a class of learned and legal men does not equate with that of a priesthood, which does not exist in Islam (excluding, perhaps, Shi'ah Islam). Even the imam, here meaning the leader of congregational prayer, can be 'any respectable Muslim, sufficiently versed in the technique of *salat*' (Gibb and Kramers 1961:165). Interestingly, a correlation between the school of law present and the geographical diffusion of Islam has been made. To quote Eaton (1993:130), 'in the Islamic World generally, converted populations have tended to adopt the school of law adhered to by the carriers of Islam in their region'. This is of significance for our purposes, and assists in establishing Islamisation processes in sub-Saharan Africa and elsewhere.

The Shi'ah, numerically the second most dominant group in Islam, developed their own laws, but these differ little from orthodox Sunni law (Schacht 1964:16; Halm 1991). Shi'ism has been defined as 'the general name for a large group of very different Muslim sects, the starting point of all of which is the recognition of Ali as the legitimate caliph after the death of the Prophet' (Gibb and Kramers 1961:534). Essentially, the core Shi'ah beliefs do not diverge substantially from Sunni ones: the Qur'an is central, the Five Pillars are the same; as Akbar Ahmed (1988:57) notes, 'the Sunni ideal also holds for the Shi'ah'. However, it is in the position of the imamate, or religious leadership, that the real difference lies, as in the Shi'ite view, the Caliphate became corrupted through the wrong succession. Ali was the first Imam designated by the Prophet, followed by a line of twelve or seven Imams, depending on tradition. The majority 'Twelvers' believe 'that the Twelfth Imam (last seen in 873) was the *Mahdi* or "guided one" and is still alive, though hidden, waiting for God's instruction to appear and establish the kingdom of God on earth' (Bruce 1995:82; and see Momen 1985). The 'Seveners' stop the line at the seventh Imam, Isma'il, and are thus known as Isma'ilis.

Within sub-Saharan Africa these differences are largely meaningless, as only small numbers of Shi'ah are found in parts of the continent south of the Sahara, with the Isma'ilis of East Africa forming the most important community. This community is almost wholly of Asian origin and is in turn subdivided, with a useful introduction to these Isma'ili groups being provided by Amiji (1969). The Isma'ili Khojas are centralised 'around the person of their living Imam' (Amiji 1969:145), the Aga Khan, and are set apart from other Muslim groups through some of their practices. For example, *zakat* comes first rather than the more orthodox fourth or fifth in their prioritising of the Five Pillars of Islam. Similarly, they lack mosques in the strict sense of the definition (see below) but have *jamat khanas* (assembly halls) which include a special prayer room containing a portrait of the Aga Khan at one end, and 'the devotees pray squatting on the floor facing the portrait of the Aga Khan' (Amiji 1969:153). They are also set apart by other features of belief and practice. A second important Isma'ili group found in East Africa are the Musta'lian Isma'ilis or Bohras. They have a concealed Imam, who is represented on earth by the Dail Mutlaq, 'the absolute summoner'. The Bohras accept the Five Pillars but, according to Amiji (1969:163), add another: 'ritual cleanliness'.

Many other offshoots of Islam also exist, but are of little relevance in sub-Saharan Africa. An exception, however, is provided by the Kharijites, who are in turn divided into a number of sub-groups, the Nukkarites, Sufrites and Ibadis. The Kharijites have been described as espousing 'intransigent idealism' (Waines 1995:106), and were democratic in outlook, believing that anyone could be elected head of the Muslim community, if they possessed the right qualifications. The Ibadis are the most important for our purposes, surviving to this day in Oman, and in parts of North and East Africa. However, the relevant background history to the Ibadis is provided later where the significance of this movement is considered in its appropriate regional contexts. Similarly, other features of Islam such as Sufism (religious orders, usually of a mystical nature), which are popular in parts of sub-Saharan Africa, are discussed later.

Material manifestations of Islam

It should also be noted that to briefly summarise the material manifestations of Islam, i.e. literally what might signify the former presence of a Muslim or Muslim community in the archaeological record, is difficult to achieve with brevity. Thus for further detail the reader should consult Insoll (1999a), though elements are further expanded upon in the following chapters.

The mosque

A convenient starting point in establishing the archaeology of Islam is provided by the mosque, and the criteria that define a mosque are simple: 'a wall correctly oriented towards the *qiblah*, namely the Black Stone within the Ka'bah in Mecca. No roof, no minimum size, no enclosing walls, no liturgical accessories are required' (Hillenbrand 1994:31). Prayer itself occurs at four levels: individually five times a day; congregationally at noon on Friday; communal (village or town prayer) at festivals; and at the level of the entire Muslim world. Material manifestations of these prayer requirements are: firstly, the prayer rug and a simple *masjid* or prayer hall; secondly, the *jami* or Friday (congregational)

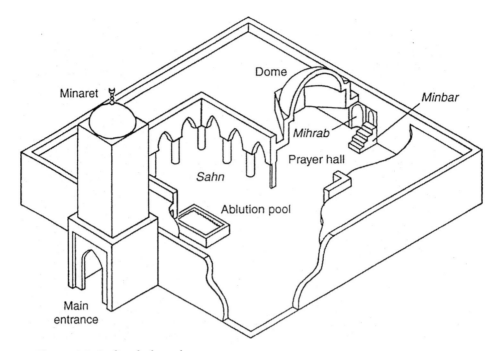

Figure 1.3 Stylised plan of mosque components

mosque; and thirdly, the *musalla* (place of prayer) – a common term, but sometimes used specifically to denote a place of prayer used at festivals. A physical embodiment of the fourth level of prayer does not exist, but pilgrimage to Mecca, or *hajj*, can perhaps be seen as what Dickie terms 'a congregation of all the Muslims of the World' (1978:35). The actual act of prayer is also reflected in the form of the mosque, with the rectangular shape of the mosque sanctuary, the *haram*, reflecting the need to pray in rows parallel to the *qiblah*, the wall facing Mecca **(figure 1.3)**.

Various features might be incorporated in a mosque which could aid its archaeological recognition. Primary among these and related to the question of orientation is the physical marker of the direction of prayer, the *mihrab*, an almost universal feature which is built into, or as a salient from, the *qiblah* wall, and forms the focus of the mosque sanctuary. From in front of the *mihrab* the prayers are led by the imam, and although almost always a niche in form, it can be decorated in many ways. Other features include the *minbar*, a flight of sometimes movable steps placed next to the *mihrab*, from which the imam preaches a sermon at Friday prayers. Another is the minaret, which has been called the 'Symbol of Islam' (Bloom 1989). It is usually a tower, attached to or near the prayer hall containing a staircase leading to a balcony for the *muezzin* to make the call to prayer. To these could be added an enclosed courtyard (*sahn*) attached to the sanctuary containing an ablutions area. Washing prior to prayer is obligatory, and thus a fountain, tap or a pot of water should be provided for the use of worshippers. The entrance to the courtyard and thence to the sanctuary could also be of significance, a marker between the sacred and the profane. A number of other features may or may not be present: a screened area for women; a raised and screened enclosure (*maqsura*) for the ruler or Imam; Qur'an stands and chests; and a *dikka*, a platform formerly used by the *muezzin* to transmit responses to the prayers to the congregation before the advent of loudspeakers (Gibb and Kramers 1961; Kuban 1974; Dickie 1978).

The Muslim burial

The Muslim burial is another primary category of evidence, but one which, because of understandable prohibitions on disturbing such sites, is largely theoretical in importance. Throughout the Muslim world an essentially uniform funerary rite should be employed, and should be straightforward, unostentatious and simple (Hastings 1911:501). This should entail the corpse being washed and perfumed immediately following death, and then being enveloped in the shroud or grave clothes. Burial is rapid, and the stretcher or bier is carried to the place of burial by men, followed by the funeral procession (**figure 1.4**). The corpse is lifted out of the bier and placed in the grave (a coffin is not usually used), the head in the direction of the *qiblah*, so that it lies on its right side with the face toward Mecca (sometimes supported in this position by bricks, or by a narrower grave-shaft). The grave itself should be reasonably shallow to allow the deceased to hear the *muezzin*'s call, but also deep enough to allow the corpse to sit up for its interrogation by the angels Munkar and Nakir and thus gain entry to paradise. Only the place where the head of the deceased is laid may be commemorated with a marker stone or piece of wood. However, in reality great variety with regard to grave markers is found, according to the Islamic legal school or sect followed and geographical area (Gibb and Kramers 1961:89–90, 515–17; Hastings 1911:501–2; Dickie 1978:44–6; Simpson 1995:241–2, 244–5). Needless to say, many exceptions to these rites occur. Among the Shi'ah, for example, Rogers (1976:130) records that the corpse was sometimes buried with the feet in the direction of Mecca (and see Insoll 1999a:172–3). However, it is above ground that complications arise, and ideals and reality diverge, for it is the means of commemorating the dead – the funerary monument – that is subject to great variability, and this applies equally to sub-Saharan Africa.

The domestic and community environments

Further possibly important material manifestations of Islam are provided by the traditional domestic (house, tent) and community (settlement) environments. Obviously, the concept of privacy was not invented by Muslims (see

Figure 1.4 Muslim burial stretcher, Kizimkazi mosque, Zanzibar

Insoll 1999a:64), but domestic space is referred to in both the Qur'an and the *hadith*, where the sacrality of the house is indicated, and strict rules to maintain domestic privacy are outlined (see Petherbridge 1978; Campo 1991). The primary and overriding concern is with privacy and the protection and seclusion of women (in certain cultural contexts referred to as purdah) and the sanctity of the family. To achieve this, physical space is often segregated into two spheres, be it in two halves of a tent, within a single or double courtyard, or spread over several palatial complexes. The private area is for family life, including the harem or women's quarters, which is the arena for domestic activities and from which all men except immediate male relatives (husbands, sons, brothers) are usually excluded. The second area forms a male-communal sphere usually referred to within the literature as 'public' or 'semi-public', and which can include a reception room or rooms, or area where guests (usually male) are entertained, and possibly separate men's living quarters. Numerous permutations are possible, and many devices can be used to ensure privacy.

Within the traditional courtyard house, the dominant permanent type which might be encountered archaeologically, privacy can be further maintained through a deliberate inward orientation of space. Exterior windows, which are usually few, are above street level, to avoid views inward, and the exterior walls are usually austere and undecorated and entered by a single door; a second (women's) door is sometimes present. Angled entrance-ways are employed to deny the passer-by a view into the interior of the house, and guest rooms are placed close to the entrance so the family quarters are left undisturbed (al-Azzawi 1969). Allied with the social requirements that Muslim domestic architecture might aim to satisfy, cultural and environmental factors must also be considered, and it is perhaps best to define traditional Muslim domestic architecture as a mix of varying local cultural, religious, social and environmental factors. Such concerns are also manifest in structures built both by nomadic pastoralists and sedentary agriculturists in less durable materials. The fact that such people frequently live in shelters constructed of ephemeral materials – cloth, skin or reeds, for example – does not mean that they were excluded from structuring their domestic space according to Islamic custom (see, for example, Feilberg 1944; Faegre 1979; Banning and Köhler-Rollefson 1992).

The Muslim community environment, be it city, town, village, hamlet or camp, also functions in a socially important manner within Muslim life, and can be archaeologically recognisable as such. Certainly the Muslim city has in the past provided a convenient unit of study, and – based upon a limited number of examples, mainly drawn from North Africa and the Near East – wide-ranging generalisations were made as to the overall character of the Muslim city everywhere. These studies were one of the first manifestations of the Orientalist approach, whereby the structure of the city was defined in terms of religious requirements (and often linked with the erroneous assertion that Islam can only flourish in an urban environment, as exemplified by a point made by Levtzion, 'because it is in the urban milieu that one can fully practice the Muslim way of life' (1979c:15)), and a similar form was said to exist from Morocco to Indonesia. This process of the creation of a stereotypical Muslim city has been examined by a number of scholars (Bonine 1977; Abu-Lughod 1987; Haneda and Miura 1994). The stereotype which was created comprised a standard kit of elements, such as the *medinah*, or central urban entity, within which was the *casbah* or walled citadel, a city within the city containing the ruler's residence, mosque, barracks, stores etc. The *medinah* would be walled with several gates, and perhaps surrounded by *rabad* or *rabat* – outer suburbs. The inhabitants lived in distinct quarters according to ethnic or economic background in groups of courtyard houses connected by winding alleyways and narrow streets, supposedly characteristic of the 'oriental' or Islamic city. The *medinah* would also contain a number of core elements: the Friday mosque, other local mosques, *suq* or *suqs* (markets) arranged spatially according to the goods sold, baths, hostels for travellers, schools, shops, cemeteries perhaps (usually outside the city), and all the other prerequisites of urban life.

Although such a checklist-type approach does not work in identifying a Muslim settlement, it is possible to identify a Muslim settlement archaeologically. However, by no means can the aforementioned suite of traits be expected to be encountered everywhere (if anything, questions of scale will rule this out, as a village will obviously not have all the facilities of the city). Secondly, some of these features are very rare in sub-Saharan Africa – *hammams* (baths), for example, though prevalent in North Africa, are absent in the western Sahel, and in most of the other regions discussed. Which components are present and how they are manifest will vary, as will the structuring principles behind both the development and form of the Muslim settlement, and even within Africa south of the Sahara great diversity is evident in the form of the Muslim settlement.

Diet

Muslim diet should also be structured by religious law, and in theory this should also provide another category of evidence which might indicate the existence of a Muslim community archaeologically. Issues of non-observance must be acknowledged, and differences between the Islamic schools of law recognised, but in general terms a number of binding rules exist. Three categories of food exist: *halal*, that which is lawful; *haram*, that which is prohibited; and *makruh*, that which is reprehensible, but which is not subject to the degree of prohibition as *haram*. Alcohol, spilt blood, pork, dogs, excrement, carrion and the milk of animals whose flesh is not eaten are forbidden, and a complex body of laws regulates in great detail which food is considered lawful and when exceptions concerning consumption can be made. Similarly, slaughter is subject to religious law, and an animal must be killed facing the *qiblah*, the name of God invoked and its throat cut (see Pellat 1971:304–9; Gibb and Kramers 1961:431–2, 556).

To the archaeologist studying a faunal assemblage it might theoretically be possible to identify the remains generated by a diet structured according to these Muslim dietary laws. Pertinent questions which might be asked could include:

1. Are certain species absent in faunal assemblages, pigs and dogs for example, and is this a result of dietary avoidance?
2. Is a *halal* diet noticeable, i.e. through special butchery patterns, cut marks on bones, body parts and offal left over?
3. Are slaughter patterns different among herds owned by Muslims, as opposed to those of other religious groups?
4. Is the composition of a 'Muslim herd' different, and can this be recognised archaeologically?

Yet unlike the mosque or Muslim burial, it is difficult to advance beyond theory in considering the archaeological recognition of Muslim diet, for when it is tested against archaeological data it is apparent that to answer questions such as those posed above, an 'ideal' faunal assemblage is required, well preserved and numerically abundant (see Insoll 1999a:96–9). More complex even is the recognition of the vegetable component of the Muslim diet. This is not subject to dietary law as is flesh and associated products, and thus cannot begin to be an archaeological indicator of a Muslim community in the same way, as staple food crops often remained unchanged in regions to which Islam spread. Botanical remains might, however, indicate the spread of crops associated with the Muslim world. Crops such as rice, sugar cane and wheat were widely diffused, but obviously they do not take on a Muslim identity. Rather, at a precise point in time they can be said to be culturally associated with Islam, as al-Hassan and Hill (1992:212–13) discuss.

Miscellany

Numerous other elements of Muslim life could be manifest in the archaeological record. These range from seemingly humble items such as a seal ring denoting Muslim identity through to the residue of a pilgrimage route crossing the central Sudan. Feasts and festivals, pilgrimage and travel, education and health, personal possessions and dress, magic, and war – each of these can be used in many different ways to create the overall religious, and in turn social, identities, and can be of great importance in reconstructing Islamisation processes in their entirety. More detail on the possible significance of these categories of material is provided where required in the following discussion.

Art and calligraphy

Similarly, art objects which might be identified as Islamic or items decorated with calligraphy in Arabic could also signal the presence of Muslims or of Islamisation in the archaeological record. However, this statement covers a wide range of techniques, which can be applied in myriad contexts, and rendered in equally diverse materials, and aspects of this subject are also considered later (and see the box on Arabic).

Arabic

The Arabic script is used in Muslim communities across sub-Saharan Africa (and here it should be noted that script is being referred to, not the language, as other languages can be and are rendered in the Arabic script, including Swahili and Hausa). The importance of writing is stressed in the Qur'an, where it is thought to be of divine origin (Schimmel 1990), and although the Arabic script existed at the time of Muhammad, he was illiterate (this latter point is disputed by other scholars; see, for example, Guillaume 1954:57). His pronouncements were written down on any available material, and the first Qur'an was assembled during the reign of 'Uthman, the third Caliph, in the mid-seventh century. The sacred character of writing encouraged its spread, and since the language in which God's message was transmitted was Arabic, the Arabic script took precedence over all others.

   The two dominant styles of Arabic script are Kufic and cursive. Kufic, which originated in Kufah (Roman 1990:ix), is angular in appearance and was used for copying Qur'ans and extensively in inscriptions on buildings and tombstones **(figure 1.5)**. Kufic inscriptions are almost without exception in Arabic, and various regional styles developed. The style declined in usage after the eleventh century, when it either begins to be found in coexistence with cursive scripts or is replaced altogether by cursive (Schimmel 1990:25). Cursive scripts, which are more rounded and easier to use, were developed in Mecca and Medina, and were of use for everyday purposes. They coexisted with Kufic from the very beginning of Islam, but it was not until the thirteenth to fourteenth centuries that the multitude of cursive scripts which had developed were systematised into six styles: *thuluth, riqa, naskh, tauqi, muhaqqaq* and *rihani* (Schimmel 1990:22).

African traditional religions: an introduction

Islam has been briefly introduced, and it is necessary to do the same for African traditional religions, as it is these that Islam replaced, or more usually fused with. African traditional religions are also in many ways much more misrepresented than Islam, being misconceived as religions little removed from witchcraft and lacking any formal structure. They have also often been

Figure 1.5 Forms of Kufic script

presented as not definable as true religions. This is indicated by sentiments expressed by the Victorian explorer Richard Burton, who notes that the African had 'barely advanced to idolatry' and 'had never grasped the ideas of a personal Deity, a duty in life [or] a moral code' (R. Burton 1864:199, cited in Kirby 1994:60). Burton's opinions on African religion fit into a standard pattern of scholarship eloquently described by Evans-Pritchard as comprising

a reference to cannibalism, a description of pygmies (by preference with a passing reference to Herodotus), a denunciation of the inequities of the slave trade, the need for the civilizing influence of commerce, something about rainmakers and other superstitions, some sex (suggestive though discreet), add snakes and elephants to taste; bring slowly to the boil and serve. (1971:144, cited in Ray 1976:3)

But what then are African traditional religions? They are not ancestor worship, animism or paganism (Mbiti 1975:17), terms which are either derogatory or reduce African traditional religions to a simplistic level. In fact, relevant studies of African traditional religions are numerous (see, for example, Mbiti 1975; Parrinder 1976; Ray 1976; Ranger 1991; Hackett 1996), but misconceptions still persist. Hunwick (1989:176), for example, describes African traditional religions as 'ethno-specific polyspiritual systems operating within a micro-cosmic environment', and continues, arguing that 'the advent of Islam opened up for communities in tropical Africa a macrocosm which took them not merely beyond the confines of village or tribal society, but incorporated them into a vaster pan-Islamic cultural system and into a world economy' (Hunwick 1989:177). Now although the latter part of this statement is difficult to fault with regard to incorporation within a wider economic system, it is the notion of the microcosmic ethno-specific elements that various scholars would disagree with, including this author, because this in effect breaks African traditional religions down into small pieces, and in so doing appears to deny the existence of any element of similarity in religious belief or practice. In contrast, a degree of similarity in African traditional religions both appears to have existed in the past and still exists today, even if perhaps only unintentionally, across vast areas of the continent.

However, introducing such a notion of similarity implies that we can talk of an African traditional religion rather than a group of religions. The degree to which an African traditional religion, as opposed to a group of African traditional religions, exists has been the subject of much debate (see, for example, Mbiti 1975; Clarke 1991; van Beek and Blakely 1994). Religious similarities are manifest in belief and in elements of ritual behaviour, the two most common types being associated with animal sacrifice and rites of passage (Ray 1976:78), but more importantly, as Zahan (1970:4) notes, in 'man's attitude towards the invisible, through the position which he feels he occupies in creation, and through his feeling of belonging to the universe'. The end result of this is, to quote Zuesse (1991:171), that African traditional religions do 'genuinely exhibit an astonishing uniformity of emphasis which make of them merely local variations on a few axiomatic themes, to a much greater degree certainly than we find in Christianity or others of the world religions such as Hinduism'. Yet although similarities might be evident in African traditional religions, the plural is still preferable to the singular, as the latter creates artificial simplicity. African traditional religions are complex phenomena and subject to differing historical development and differing development of religious ideas.

A further element of importance in African traditional religions for our purposes here is the fact that the acknowledgement, prior to Islam, of the existence of one God has to be recognised in some cases. Mbiti, for example, makes the somewhat sweeping statement that 'all African peoples believe in God' (1975:40), and then provides a list of names for God which exist in African languages (see also Mbiti 1970). This universal approach is erroneous, but similarly Ray (1976:50) also describes the existence of the high god among some ethnic groups – the creator god, as exemplified by Kwoth the Nuer supreme god, or Olurun the Yoruba one (see Evans-Pritchard 1956; Idowu 1962). However, Ray (1976) also argues that the supreme God is at the apex of a variety of dimensions which exist in African traditional religions – monotheistic, polytheistic and pantheistic. The complexity of African religions is thus explicitly signalled, as is the inappropriateness of assuming that African traditional religions are merely composed of devotion to a host of spirits but lacking a figure comparable to the one God, Allah. Such a concept evidently existed in certain instances and, implicit in numerous creation myths, pre-dated Islam. Therefore, as I. M. Lewis (1980a:61) indicates, the pre-existing high god could easily be assimilated with Allah, as with the Galla and Somali god Waq, the Nupe Soko, the Swahili Mungo and the Mossi Winam. It was when attempts were made to integrate the lower tiers of spirits within an Islamic framework that problems frequently emerged.

Thus in various instances a high god existed with, below, these lesser tiers of intermediary spirits through which God could be approached. These are classified by Mbiti (1975) into nature spirits, in turn subdivided into sky and earth spirits, as well as human spirits – composed of the long dead and the recently dead. Offerings could be made to all or none of these, for 'reverence to the intermediary beings is reverence to God' (Zuesse 1991:175). Living human intermediaries could also have an important role, as oracles, priests, diviners, or even as divine kings, the latter functioning in a parallel God-like role and often approached through intermediaries themselves (Zuesse 1991:177). Thus divine kings were often remote and inaccessible, with prohibitions upon watching them eating, speaking to them directly, or even meeting their gaze (Mbiti 1975:161–3). Complexity in ritual practice is again evident, but common strands persist, with sacrifice and rites of passage isolated as examples of these. Religious practice was concerned with many things, as Ranger (1991:109) notes: relationships, as manifest in cults of land; ancestors; and alien or asocial spirits – but also with morality and the abstract. Ritual practice could be at a communal level, with each sacrifice functioning as 'a re-creation of the group's solidarity, every rite of passage a reforging of the corporate life' (Ray 1976:17). These rites would commonly take on a threefold structure, sacrifice involving 'consecration, invocation-immolation, communion-purification' and rites of passage 'separation, transition, and reincorporation' (Ray 1976:79, 91). Sacrifice functioned to perpetuate life (de Heusch 1985:202), rites of passage to 'give form and meaning to human events' (Ray 1976:91).

Alternatively, God could be approached directly through prayer, even individually, and again debate exists as to quite how much African traditional religions were a communal, as opposed to individual, phenomenon (Mbiti 1975; Zuesse 1991; Ray 1976; Ranger 1991). This too is important for our purposes, for a preadaptation to communal religion as well as the similarities in religious belief and practice that existed across large areas of the continent prior to the arrival of Islam in Africa cannot but have helped to secure the popularity of Islam in Africa, with Islam meshing with pre-existing religions in many ways rather than necessarily confronting them. Yet having presented a picture of the similarities that exist in African traditional religions, it must also be recognised that, to repeat, complexity is evident as much as are any broad generalities in ritual and belief might be within these structures. Traditional religions in general are not ahistoric and unchanging; the non-literate context of traditional religions means, according to Clarke (1991:63), that they have 'been more flexible and tolerant of change than those excluding, literate religions or religions of the book'. African traditional religions were subject to change and must be treated as historical phenomena as much as any other religions (Ranger 1991:107), and archaeology is again well placed to investigate these changes.

Material manifestations of African traditional religions

As with Islam a distinct and rich body of material culture can indicate the existence of African traditional religions, and an important point to note in this respect is that a strict dividing line between the archaeology of Islam and that of traditional religions cannot always be drawn. This is something that is readily apparent once the archaeological record is considered, for the integration of elements of pre-Islamic religions within a Muslim framework is a recurring feature, and something which can leave recognisable material traces, as is considered in the following chapters. Although this is examined later, it is also useful to introduce the archaeology of African traditional religions here, and in general the material legacy of traditional religions is varied and could include a variety of categories of evidence, but as with many aspects of African archaeology this is a subject that still awaits a detailed consideration. An exception to this is provided by a brief review written by de Maret (1994), who interestingly seems to equate traditional religions with prehistory, a somewhat limited stance, as much can also be learnt about traditional religions in proto-historical and historical archaeological contexts as well.

De Maret (1994) considers the archaeological evidence for traditional religion under the headings of rock art, burial rituals, monuments and linguistics, and undoubtedly these are all important but broad categories. Shrines alone, for example, could fall within the first three of de Maret's posited headings and covers a wide range of material, ranging from formalised 'built' complexes such as the Yoruba shrines unearthed in Ife (Eyo 1977), providing evidence contrary to Zahan's (1970:18–19) statement that Africa lacked the materials, techniques and political centralisation necessary to build 'temples', through to no less important natural shrines: sacred groves, trees, watercourses, pools, rocks etc.

(see, e.g., Mbiti 1970). A continuity in the importance of sacred space is also a recurring feature indicating either the appropriation of the old or its more peaceful
integration within Islamic tradition **(figure 1.6)**. This is something considered
by I. M. Lewis (1980a:63), who provides various examples indicating its material visibility, as in Sierra Leone where Temne village mosques were frequently
built in sacred groves, or in Somalia where the tomb of a Muslim saint, Sharif
Yusuf al-Kawneyn, was built beside a hill said 'to contain the mortal remains' of
a non-Muslim 'magician chief'. Other examples are provided later illustrating
this aspect of religious continuity/appropriation as seen through archaeological
evidence.

Settlement structure might also indicate traditional religious beliefs, and this
could fall under de Maret's heading of 'monuments'. Examples of cosmological
influence on settlement patterning are indeed described later. Overt cosmological patterning is perhaps something that might be expected to have disappeared
with Islamisation – in many instances it does, in others it need not, and again
this is something considered further below with regard to archaeological evidence. Similarly, evidence for sacrifice might also survive, material difficult
to slot into de Maret's (1994) schema, but also found after conversion to Islam
has occurred. Sacrifice can take many forms and involve animate or inanimate
offerings. The centrality of the chicken within West Africa provides an example
of a sacrificial animal which has recently been pursued from an archaeological
perspective (MacDonald 1995), and one which assumes the title of 'universal
sacrificial animal' (Zahan 1970:34) across Africa for a variety of reasons. Yet
it is one among numerous species that could be of significance within an archaeological faunal assemblage (see Simoons 1981 for a detailed consideration
of others), while human sacrifice crosses the divide into de Maret's category of
'burial rituals'. This latter type of sacrifice, contrary to the often florid beliefs
of the Victorian explorers of Africa, was comparatively rare. Where practised,
it was often in times of stress, as among the Bambara of Mali where an albino
was sacrificed 'when the king had governmental difficulties, the victim was
cut in half, at the stomach...His cries, gestures and excrement were believed
to transmit a *nyama* (vital force) which could do away with the difficulty the
king faced' (Dieterlen 1951:95, cited in de Heusch 1985:165). In summary, the
examples just described – shrines, settlement patterns and sacrifice – are just
a few of the material manifestations of traditional religion; others exist, and
these will be referred to where necessary in the ensuing discussion.

The social dynamics of conversion

Previously, the utility of traditional religions in Africa as a means of compre-
hending existence and as a mechanism for building and ensuring continuity in
communal relationships was emphasised. Based upon the obvious success and
longevity of traditional religions in the continent it could then be asked: why

Figure 1.6 Dogon circumcision place still in use even though many Dogon have converted to Islam

did people convert to Islam? And how has the religion spread so widely in the continent? Can apparent similarities be seen in the spread of Islam in many areas of the continent and among different socio-economic groups? These are issues that have been considered in Africa by historians, anthropologists and scholars interested in religious studies (see, e.g., Trimingham 1959; R. Horton 1971, 1975; Fisher 1973a, 1985; Thorold 1987), but less frequently by archaeologists, perhaps because such models cannot be applied uniformly. Complexity is again evident both in the reasons that can be suggested to explain why people converted to Islam and in the models that can be advanced to explain this phenomenon in sub-Saharan Africa, in part as any general rules are often overruled by the fact that religion is very much an individual experience (Geertz 1968). We are attempting to set a course between what van Beek and Blakely (1994:3) describe as the 'Scylla of universal categorization (ethnocentrism in disguise) and the Charybdis of extreme relativism'.

A second important factor is that we are also endeavouring to unravel very complex processes from limited archaeological data, made more difficult by the fact that even the term 'conversion' does not adequately define what occurred. These difficulties are voiced by Ray (1976:184) when he makes the point that 'it would be misleading to speak of the process of Islamization as a process of "conversion" from African belief to orthodox Islamic religion. A gradual blending took place between African and Islamic elements, making a new configuration which assumed different forms in different areas.' However, it is not necessary to be unduly pessimistic; rather, it is useful to look firstly outside Africa at conversion processes elsewhere to see if patterns in religious conversion can be seen which might be helpful for our purposes.

The 'expression of cultural meaning from one cultural system into a different cultural system' (van Beek and Blakely 1994:3), i.e. the spread of religious traditions such as Islam in contrasting areas of the world, has been well examined, and the key issue that arises is that of complexity in both process and result. In the Indian subcontinent, for example, Sufism assisted in the spread of Islam and a pragmatic approach was adopted by Muslim teachers in adopting Hindu and Buddhist practices as a means of spreading Islam, 'so far as they did not compromise essential Islamic precepts' (Nizami 1989:75). Conversion to Islam in a more specific area of the subcontinent, Bengal, has also recently been examined by Eaton (1993). Instead of models invoking, besides Sufism, the usually posited explanatory devices of Muslim immigration, conversion by the sword or acceptance of Islam because of patronage or as a way of escaping the Hindu caste system, Eaton proposes a three-phase conversion model of 'inclusion', 'identification' and 'displacement'. This is a model which allows for gradual religious change and, importantly, assimilation of older elements within the process as well, thus broadly comparable to the processes of Islamic conversion in much of sub-Saharan Africa, being also long drawn out, and inclusive of older elements. Of significance for our purposes here, Eaton presents archaeological evidence attesting to all three phases. This is exemplified by the fusion within the 'inclusion' and 'identification' phases of local Hindu and Muslim notions of God, as indicated through inscriptions such as 'when the Arabic name Allah was used interchangeably with the Sanskrit Niranjan' (Eaton 1993:269), also reminiscent of the assimilation of Allah with pre-existing high gods in parts of Africa referred to earlier. This is a model which, as we shall see, is best suited to some of the African data.

Elsewhere conversion patterns can be more varied. In Turkey, for example, Norton (1989:84) describes how 'various categories of converts existed' as did various conversion processes. Ménage (1979:62–3) isolates four dominant strands of Islam in Anatolia: orthodox Sunni Islam of the Hanafi school, mysticism, Ghazi Islam of the warriors and Islam as interpreted by the Dervishes. Some people, such as soldiers taken into the army, abandoned the old ways fully and accepted orthodox Islam. Others, such as the nomad and semi-nomad Turkomans who were heavily influenced by a shamanistic background, took to Sufism and associated religious brotherhoods 'with strong heterodox elements and distinct traces of Shamanism' (Ménage 1979:85). Similar patterns are evident in Indonesia (Ricklefs 1979; Kratz 1989), with orthodox and mystical Islam both prevailing, as referred to by the terms used for the followers of the two religious traditions – *santri* and *abangan* in Java, for example (Geertz 1960). Importantly, the latter, the followers of the more mystical religious tradition, are 'no less convinced personally of their own religious sincerity' (Kratz 1989:137). Complexity in conversion patterns and processes can be seen to be evident worldwide. How then is one to make sense of this within sub-Saharan Africa without resorting to the recipe concocted by historians to describe conversion processes as outlined by Bulliet (1979:30), whereby 'historians often mix one part *cuius regio, eius religio* with another part "pagan survivals" and flavour the amalgam with a pinch of missionary zeal, a bit of new-convert fanaticism, and a generous dollop of economic motivation'?

In effect, no one model is satisfactory to explain conversion to Islam in sub-Saharan Africa. A mosaic of processes, factors, reasons and results exist – and comparable, unfortunately, to the pattern Bulliet condemns. Yet within Africa and elsewhere phased patterns of conversion to Islam have frequently been identified and/or proposed, and it is useful to look at these models briefly to see whether they have any utility as explanatory devices. The three dominant models that have been developed to explain conversion to Islam (and Christianity) in Africa are those of Trimingham (1968), R. Horton (1971, 1975 and see 1993) and Fisher (1973a, 1985). These models have in turn have been further analysed and summarised by, among others, Thorold (1987) and Clarke (1989).

Trimingham (1968:43) uses the terms 'germination', 'crisis' and 'reorientation' to describe the stages he suggests were involved in converting to Islam in Africa. This is evocative language, with stage one being the preparatory phase of contact and involving aspects of Muslim material culture – such as amulets and dress, perhaps – being adopted, but without traditional religious systems being unduly disturbed. This is fair enough, and is frequently supported by archaeological and historical data, though the second phase, that of 'crisis', is more contentious. This involves the assimilation of elements of Islamic practice such as prayers and food prohibitions alongside a continuation of traditional religious practice with an accompanying 'weakening of the indigenous culture', leading to a 'crisis' developing. In reality the existence of such crises are not supported by any data: what actually occurs is the development of popular Islamic traditions. The third of Trimingham's phases, that of 'reorientation', is defined as involving the communal cults losing power at the expense of the Muslim 'clergy'. Again, this is a generalisation describing a situation (excluding the inappropriate use of the term 'clergy' in a Muslim context) which can occur but which is by no means universal.

Similar concepts are proposed by Fisher (1973a, 1985) though in a more refined manner and less evocatively phrased. Fisher also proposes three stages of conversion to Islam in Africa: firstly, quarantine, being when the religion is confined to a specific group, such as traders; secondly, mixing, when conversion to Islam among the local population occurs along with the mixing of Muslim and traditional beliefs and practices; and thirdly, a phase of reform, literally a wave of Islamic reform, perhaps represented by *jihad* or holy war. In total this model has been described as seeing 'Islam as moving inexorably toward an anti-syncretic telos' (Shaw and Stewart 1994:16). Fisher's model has more utility than Trimingham's but is still subject to the same faults, in that it is not universally applicable. The circumstances outlined might fit in certain contexts, such as among the Yao of Malawi, as indicated by Thorold (1993, and see chapter 8 below), but not in others. It has also been criticised for overvaluing 'the influence of Islam as a transcendental spiritual force and underestimates the significance in conversion of traditional religious beliefs and institutions' (I. M. Lewis 1980c:viii).

A third major model, albeit largely concerned with Christianity, is that developed by R. Horton (1971, 1975) who suggests that the basic African cosmology is a two-tiered structure, 'the first tier being that of the lesser spirits and the second that of the supreme being. The lesser spirits underpin events and processes in the microcosm of the local community and its environment, while the supreme being underpins events and processes in the wider world or macrocosm' (Thorold 1987:19). This two-tier structure, as has been outlined, is quite correct, but other aspects of the model contain faults. For example, Horton suggests that prior to the growth of trade and states (and the imposition of colonial rule), the microcosm prevailed in people's daily lives, but following these developments the macrocosm impinged and the microcosm broke down. With the growing importance of the macrocosm, this led 'to an elaboration of the concepts and practices concerned with the supreme being, and the weakening of those associated with lesser spirits. This increasing prominence of the supreme being in the basic cosmology paves the way for the success of Islam and Christianity in Africa' (Thorold 1987:18–19). As Clarke (1989:184) notes, this 'suggests that there exists an interdependence between patterns of belief and patterns of social organisation and that shifts of emphasis or changes of belief are more than anything else a response to changes in social organisation'. This is again a generalisation which is not supported by the archaeological (and other) data.

Thus far the two-phased models of Trimingham and Fisher, and Horton's tiered model, appear to be of little utility in reconstructing the social dynamics of conversion to Islam in sub-Saharan Africa. The primary reason for this is that they are too general to explain such complex and diverse phenomena within such a wide geographical area. Similar criticisms have been made of a three-phase model proposed to explain conversion processes in the Malay–Indonesia archipelago (Kratz 1989:126), whereas Eaton's (1993) three-phase model referred to earlier, which was developed to explain conversion to Islam in Bengal, is much more successful, for it is concerned with a more culturally unified and smaller geographical area. In summary, we are left with the realisation that these general all-encompassing models are not particularly effective, though equally it has to be acknowledged that conversion to Islam can be a phased process involving different stages of incorporation and assimilation, and this is sometimes evident in the archaeological record, as will be discussed in the following chapters.

Similar issues of complexity and diversity are apparent when an attempt is made to evaluate the possible factors underpinning conversion (trade, war, literacy, magic etc.), and any potential differences in conversion rates between the various socio-economic groups (nomads, traders, sedentary agriculturists, town dwellers) which might have been affected. What might be of great significance as a factor aiding the spread of Islam in one area of the continent can be of little importance in another. One recurring factor of importance, however, is trade. Trade acted as the stimulus for, and agent of, the spread of Islam throughout much of the continent (see for example Levtzion and Fisher 1986). This trade took many different forms – local, inter-regional and long distance – undertaken by traders ruthlessly seeking slaves, gold and ivory for international markets, or peacefully acquiring commodities such as kola nuts for local ones. It was also conducted by many different people, both foreign merchants such as the Arab traders of the western Sahel and indigenous merchant groups such as the Mande of the western Sudan. Trade could also function as the agency through which ideas, including religious ones, were transmitted, through for example traders being accompanied or followed by religious teachers and holy men (Levtzion 1986a), creating what Levtzion (1986b:12) has termed 'lines of communication' linking Muslims far and wide. Alternatively, holy men unconnected with trade could serve as agents of Islamisation, as with the wandering *fuqara* of the Funj and Darfur kingdoms in the Nilotic Sudan, multi-functional individuals who acted as 'part missionary, politician, charlatan, mystic, and magician' (O'Fahey 1979:199).

Warfare, in comparison, was in general a much less important factor in the spread of Islam in sub-Saharan Africa. Conversion by the sword did undoubtedly occur, but supposed instances of its occurrence, when re-examined, can be shown to be overexaggerated, as with the reputed forced conversion by the Almoravids of the population of the capital of the kingdom of Ghana in the western Sahel in the mid-eleventh century (Conrad and Fisher 1982, 1983, and see chapter 5 below). *Jihad* was not of great significance in much of sub-Saharan Africa until the nineteenth century when a wave of nomadic Fulani-led reform swept the western and central Sudan (Levtzion 1986b). Other factors of seemingly little significance could in fact have been of much greater importance in encouraging conversion to Islam. Belief in the magical powers of this new religion, or of the Arabic script, could be a contributing factor, for example. Numerous instances of this exist across the continent, as among the Yao, where initially the Qur'an functioned 'as a sort of fetish, a source of power rather than doctrine' (Thorold 1993:84). Similar processes are charted on the other side of Africa by Green (1986) in the Kong region of the Ivory Coast where amulets and magical services were the first elements of Dyula (Mande) culture accepted by the local people.

Literacy in Arabic, both with its possible magical importance as indicated by the production of amulets or charms in a pre-literate context (and equally in literate contexts) and its obvious administrative benefits, could encourage conversion to Islam. Related to this is the power of the Qur'an itself, which also has to be acknowledged as 'immortal and unchallengeable – written scripture' (Eaton 1993:291). With the success of Islam, as Sanneh (1994:24) notes, 'founded on the perpetuation of the sacred Arabic', Islamic learning and literacy could be wholeheartedly encouraged and adopted by local rulers, as among some of the Fur sultans of the Nilotic Sudan (O'Fahey 1979:204), or access to it restricted until the implications of the new religion had been properly considered, as in the western Sahel, both dimensions which are further explored later. Conversion to Islam could be encouraged by rulers, as in parts of West Africa, though equally no direct connection between ruler and the transmission of Islam need exist as, I. M. Lewis (1980a:33) states, Islam spread as easily among 'the acephalous Muslim Somali' and many other 'uncentralised' groups in Eritrea and the eastern Sudan. Finally, the factor of genuine belief is impossible to approach archaeologically, linked as it is with the numinous (Otto 1950), irreducible element that underpins religion. Complexity is again evident, and patterns discernible in one area need be of no significance in another.

Similarly, isolating general patterns in the pace of conversion to Islam among different socio-economic groups is equally difficult. Frequently, for example, there is a posited correlation between nomadic groups and early conversion to Islam, as indeed by this author previously for the western Sahel (Insoll 1996b, and see chapter 5 below). Suggested reasons for this include the ease of worship Islam enjoys (no formal clergy etc.), and through nomads' exposure to Muslim-dominated trade, as guides for instance (Trimingham 1959), or because Islam acted in nomad societies as a means 'towards tribal cohesion and solidarity' (Trimingham 1968:40). Unfortunately, such general assumptions are not warranted across the continent, where in certain areas nomads might be early converts to Islam, as in the western Sahel or the Horn of Africa, but in others remain wholly unaffected, as in East Africa. Likewise, general observations that town-dwellers were also often keen converts to Islam, as the religion has been said to appeal to the urban mind for being universalistic in outlook, and thus has the power to bring together the different ethnic groups that frequently make up the population of the major settlements in sub-Saharan Africa (Trimingham 1959), are not universally applicable. Likewise, proposing a tardiness for conversion to Islam among sedentary agriculturists across the continent for reasons such as the impermeability of their ancestral bond with the soil are also simplistic. Such explanations are convincing in some areas, such as parts of West Africa (Bravmann 1974; Dramani-Issifou 1992), but do not work everywhere. It seems that universalising models, convenient as they might be in beginning to approach the complexities of religious conversion, are not in the end suitable for describing such a diverse range of local circumstances and factors.

The nature of Islam in sub-Saharan Africa

What then is the nature of Islam in sub-Saharan Africa? Can we really reconstruct the archaeology of Islam in sub-Saharan Africa? The important point is that Islam in Africa is an African religion, obviously derived from outside but then adapted in many different ways to suit many different contexts. Though the core elements of belief might remain the same, within Islamic practice in sub-Saharan Africa 'there exists diversity, represented by different ways of life – nomad and sedentary, town- and country-dweller – ethnic, cultural and geographical factors, elements of non-observance, and varying interpretations and creeds' (Insoll 1999a:11). What has occurred is that Islam in sub-Saharan Africa has been popularised, but even this is a difficult term to define, for as Hinnells (1995:386) notes, 'there is no single definition of what constitutes popular religion'. The blending of older traditions with Islam has occurred in many instances, what is usually referred to as syncretism – a term which is used here but which has been criticised for implying 'inauthenticity' or 'contamination' of a 'supposedly "pure" tradition' (Shaw and Stewart 1994:1). Yet without labouring the point, setting up such an opposition is unnecessary; value judgements should be laid aside and the position here follows that of Levtzion (1979b:216) when he makes the point 'I accept as Muslim every individual who regards himself (themselves) as Muslim'. Syncretic or non-syncretic, Islam in sub-Saharan Africa is diverse in character, and this is now taken as a given. Our task henceforward is to chart this diversity in the archaeological record, for as was stated at the start of this chapter, the study of Islam in sub-Saharan Africa allows an entry into looking at change in a variety of areas – in economy, society or political systems – a study process facilitated by a multi-source approach, beginning with the earliest area of Muslim–African contacts in Ethiopia and the Horn of Africa.

CHAPTER 2

AKSUM TO ADAL: ETHIOPIA AND THE HORN OF AFRICA

Introduction

The first region to be considered is that of Ethiopia and the Horn of Africa, and it is perhaps best to describe this region as 'one of immense geographical, and other, contrasts' (Richard Pankhurst 1998:6), contrasts which are evident in environments, population, religions and archaeology. This is also an area within which are encompassed the modern nation-states of Ethiopia, Eritrea, Somalia and Djibouti (figure 2.1; the Somali coast south of Mogadishu is included in chapter 4 for reasons described below). Contrast is certainly evident in the climate of the region, which is extremely varied – from the baking hot lowland plains along the Red Sea coast where temperatures can reach 50°C to the highlands of Ethiopia, where freezing night-time temperatures are not uncommon in the winter months (figure 2.2). This climatic and environmental variety is largely due to altitude, which varies considerably, from the Danakil depression up to 120 m below sea level to the high mountains of the Ethiopian highlands, 4600 m above (Phillipson 1998).

The vegetation is equally varied, reflecting the altitudinal and climatic differences, from the sparse desert vegetation in much of the arid lowlands through grassland and various types of woodlands, temperate, tropical alpine, and even rainforest (Phillipson 1998:11–13). Within these varied environments are found an equally diverse population living by a variety of economic practices. Numerous ethnic groups are represented, from the nomadic Somali, Afar and Beja of the coast and the lowlands to the Amhara, Tigreans and other mainly sedentary agriculturist groups of the higher altitudes. This is also a region where, uniquely in sub-Saharan Africa, plough agriculture was practised in the northern and central highlands, while ensete or false banana and other root-crop cultivation prevailed in the southern highlands (Richard Pankhurst 1998:7). Similarly, even in the lowlands, diversity is evident. Although pastoralism might prevail over the bulk of the area, substantial pockets of sedentary and semi-sedentary cultivators are found, as in the inter-river region between the Juba and Shabelle rivers in Somalia, where 'grain, cotton and fruit' are produced (Arnoldi 1986:18). In fact, 25 per cent of the population of Somalia are agriculturists living by seasonal rain-fed agriculture or more permanently where riverine irrigation is possible (Cassanelli 1986:67).

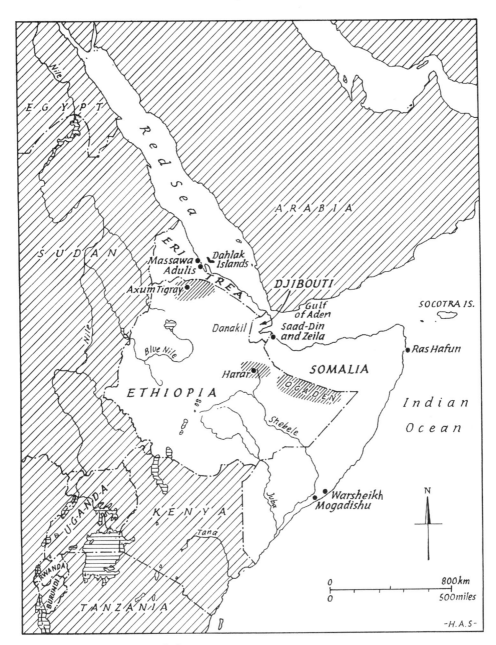

Figure 2.1 Ethiopia and the Horn

This is also a region which had been exposed to world religions before the growth of Islam, through the existence here of both Christianity and Judaism. The latter is described by Phillipson (1998:20) as sharing 'a common ancestry with modern Judaism, whilst not being Jewish in the sense commonly

Figure 2.2 The Eritrean highlands

attributed to that term today'. Both these religions have a long history in many parts of the Ethiopian highlands, and the existence of these other world religions in this region is of significance for our purposes. Firstly, for their impact upon Islam, for all these world religions are not necessarily impermeable entities. This is because of various factors, but a dominant one can be singled out, again as Phillipson notes (1998:15), because 'socio-political differentiation is largely a matter of an individual's sense of identity'. Interchange and influence between Muslims and Christians has occurred, as also between Christianity and Judaism (Ullendorff 1956). Conversion and reconversion has also taken place, and conflict was not always 'incessant, and inevitable', as the process of interfaith relations in this region is often portrayed (see H. Ahmed 1992:18 for a discussion of this).

Secondly, the existence of other world religions is of importance for how they have affected the study of Islamic history and archaeology. This is because, unfortunately, the existence of a Christian tradition in Ethiopia and Eritrea has frequently led to their being considered, at least in the highlands, as wholly Christian entities. Such a perspective is wrong, as many Muslims are found in the region, and besides their indisputed predominance in the coastal lowlands, they are also, along with groups of followers of traditional religions, scattered throughout the highlands as well. Indeed, the varied and scattered nature of Muslims in this region is reflected in the diversity of Islamic schools found, and something described by Trimingham (1971a:6) as 'an aspect which distinguishes Islam of the region from other parts of Africa'. These include adherents of the Maliki school in parts of Eritrea (an influence from the Nilotic Sudan), Shafi'i among the Galla and Somali (an influence from Arabia), and Hanafi on the Eritrean coast and in parts of the Ethiopian interior (the Turkish and Egyptian legacy). This stands in contrast to the other usually 'mono-legal' regions of sub-Saharan Africa (as will be shown), and testifies to the diversity already remarked upon for many aspects of culture and environment in Ethiopia and the Horn.

These people have left an extensive archaeological legacy which remains largely unstudied, as Islamic archaeology in Ethiopia and the Horn has been almost completely neglected to date. Whereas in contrast, in Eritrea and Ethiopia at least, much attention has been focused upon early man (Johanson and Edey 1990), megaliths (Joussaume 1980; Anfray 1990:215–57), the archaeology and material culture of Christianity (Buxton 1947, 1971), or that of Aksum (Munro-Hay 1991; Phillipson 1997, 1998). Hussein Ahmed sums up such perspectives when he makes the point that 'the history of Islam in Ethiopia has at best been viewed only in relation to the history of the Christian kingdom and, at worst, as an unpleasant episode in an otherwise glorious national history' (1992:45). However, it should be noted that such a bias is not of relevance as regards Somalia or Djibouti, where Christianity was never of importance, and where the large-scale absence of any relevant archaeological research (or of archaeological research in general) is more due to overall neglect and political circumstances.

The pre-Islamic background

Prior to examining the archaeological and other evidence for early Islam in Ethiopia and the Horn it is necessary, for reasons outlined in chapter 1, to place this evidence within context by looking at aspects of the pre-Islamic picture especially with regard to international contacts and other world religions.

Saba and D'MT

Contacts across the Red Sea between the cradle of Islam, the Arabian Peninsula, and Ethiopia pre-dated the rise of Islam by several centuries, as the pre-Aksumite remains of the fifth–fourth centuries BCE in the northern highlands of Eritrea and Ethiopia attest (Anfray 1968, 1990). Nevertheless, long before this the wider region was known to the ancient world, especially to Pharaonic Egypt, as Punt, defined by Phillips (1997:438) as 'a generalised area within the eastern coastal regions of the modern Sudan south of modern Port Sudan, Eritrea and northern-most Ethiopia, or somewhat further inland'. This is admittedly vague, but the description was applied between c.2500 and 600 BCE to this area, which was known as a source of ivory, and was the focus of various Egyptian expeditions sent to obtain ivory and war elephants (Richard Pankhurst 1998:14–17). However, material evidence for these possible early Egyptian–Punt contacts is lacking, for items of Egyptian provenance found in either Ethiopia or Eritrea and dating from before the Ptolemaic period are unknown (Phillips 1997:439). In fact, the bulk of objects of Egyptian provenance date from the Aksumite period, i.e. after the first century CE (Phillipson 1998:24).

In contrast, archaeological evidence testifying to South Arabian contacts is much more abundant. These contacts between South Arabians and Ethiopia appear to have a substantial time depth stretching back as far as the eighth century BCE, as indicated by excavations of sites with an 'unmistakable South Arabian appearance' (Munro-Hay 1991:61). A key site indicating these contacts is Yeha in Ethiopia (Anfray 1972, 1973), where the remains of a pre-Aksumite temple sanctuary built of dressed sandstone and dating from the fifth–fourth centuries BCE was found. This parallels structures in South Arabia, and Ross (in press) describes how the Yeha sanctuary 'preserves to this day a ruined cube similar in size (12 × 12 × 15 m), though not in orientation to Mecca's Ka'ba'. Similarly, at Gobochela, another rectangular temple structure was recorded, where 'incense altars of South Arabian type still lay on a sort of raised bench in this "temple"' (Munro-Hay 1991:199). These, according to Stuart Munro-Hay (1991:196), were sanctuaries which were dedicated (as appears to be indicated by inscriptions found on altars) to worshipping South Arabian gods such as Nuru the dawn-god, and Astar or Venus. These deities continued, in some cases, to be worshipped in the pre-Christian Aksumite period as well.

Other material with South Arabian affinities which has been recorded at over thirty sites in Ethiopia and Eritrea (Phillipson 1998:44) includes inscriptions, altars, tombs, stelae and even secular structures – the remains of what Munro-Hay (1991:66) has termed a 'Sabaean-influenced Ethiopian population'. Saba, with its capital at Marib, was one of five kingdoms which flourished in South Arabia, beginning in the first millennium BCE. The others were Qataban, with its capital at Timna; Hadramaut, with its capital at Shabwa; Ma'in, with its capital at Qarnaw; and finally Ausan (Doe 1971; Daum 1987). The evidence, including the sudden appearance of features such as monumental stone architecture, writing and sculpture in the archaeological record of 'some highland areas of Tigray and Eritrea' has been interpreted by Phillipson (1998:42) as attesting to the strong connections that were maintained with South Arabia. This point has to be agreed with, and it further appears that the two sides of the Red Sea might also have been linked politically under the polity known as D'MT, perhaps pronounced Daamat, as recorded in 'unvocalised inscriptions' (Phillipson 1998:45). Yet by the latter part of the first millennium BCE this South Arabian-influenced kingdom had disappeared, and a little-understood period in Ethiopian proto-history begins prior to the rise of Aksum.

Aksum and northern Somalia

The Aksumite kingdom grew from origins which are only just beginning to be reconstructed, with what appears to be a 'Proto-Aksumite Phase' (Fattovich 2000:91) between the fourth and second centuries BCE, before the full development of Aksum in the first century CE. Aksum was also, like its predecessors, centred in the northern Ethiopian/Eritrean highlands, and flourished in the first seven centuries of the first millennium CE. Again strong contacts across the Red Sea with South Arabia were maintained, and besides the extensive trade contacts that existed it would also appear that the Aksumites exercised political control over parts of southern Arabia in the third, and certainly in the fourth and sixth centuries (Phillipson 1998:42). This would appear to be indicated by, for example, King Ezana making use in the fourth century of the title 'king of Saba and Himyar' (Munro-Hay 1996:408). This was a reference to two South Arabian kingdoms, one of which has already been mentioned, the other kingdom, Himyar, with its capital at Zafar, being a somewhat later development in the second to first centuries BCE (Doe 1971).

Undeniably, trade was a major factor in both the growth and prosperity of Aksum, at both international and more local levels. Aksumite overseas trade was directed via the Red Sea port of Adulis, south of Massawa on the Eritrean coast, and some 170 km in a straight line from Aksum (Phillipson 1998:58). Excavation has been undertaken at this site, and the remains of what was interpreted as a gold workshop were recorded (Paribeni 1907, cited in Munro-Hay 1991:235). This included gold rods, ashes, a stone mould, amphorae and gold earrings. An elephant tusk was also reportedly found along with marble fragments of church furniture, such as screen fitments, which when the marble was analysed indicated they were sourced from a range of places, and included 'Proconnesian marble, presumably from the imperial workshops near

Constantinople' (Munro-Hay 1996:412). Excavations have also been completed, but are largely unpublished, at the Aksumite site of Matara in Eritrea (Anfray 1967), where a human skeleton still wearing shackles was found, a probable (and rare) indicator of slavery (Phillipson 1998:55). Slaves were a major export from Aksum, as recorded by Kosmas Indikopleustes in the sixth century (Munro-Hay 1996:407).

In this respect we are fortunate in having a few historical sources to provide details on trade commodities missing in the archaeological record. Sources such as the *Periplus of the Erythraean Sea*, an anonymous Greek source written, probably, in the first century also provide data on trade routes and the ports involved. This lists ivory as an export from Adulis, tortoiseshell from the neighbouring Dahlak islands, and slaves from Avalites (modern Zeila), also on the coast of the Horn (Schoff 1995:66, 73), and along with the Dahlaks, a site which will be referred to again below. Imports included cloth, brass and iron, glass vessels and beads, and oils, spices and wines (Munro-Hay 1996). However, these sources are few in number, and as M. Horton (1996a:446) notes, there is a 'lacuna in historical evidence' between the *Periplus* and the *Geography* of Ptolemy until the Arab sources of the ninth century (with a couple of exceptions such as the writings of Kosmas Indikopleustes already referred to).

Yet it is at the site of Aksum itself that the bulk of trade-related evidence has been found – perhaps unsurprisingly, as this was the capital of the kingdom. Recent excavations at Aksum have provided a variety of evidence for trade, variously dating from the first to sixth centuries (Munro-Hay 1989; Phillipson 1995, 1998; Phillipson and Reynolds 1996). Items of diverse provenance were recovered from many areas of the Old World. These included a piece of cast iron of probable Chinese origin of third-century date (Phillipson 1998:67), as well as glass vessels of Egyptian origin (Morrison 1989b) **(figure 2.3)**, glass beads from India (Morrison 1989a), Roman-produced African red slip-ware, glazed pottery of possible Sasanian provenance from southern or central Iraq, amphorae from the eastern Mediterranean, and metal bowls of probable Meroitic origin from the Sudanese Nile valley (Phillipson and Reynolds 1996; Phillipson 1998). A hoard of Indian Kushana coins were also recovered from the monastery of Debra Damo dating from the 220s and 'found in an Aksumite style box' (Phillips 1997:451).

Besides tangible trade goods, the international contacts maintained by the people of Aksum also meant that they were exposed to ideas, including religious ones. King Ezana, a ruler who has been previously referred to, was, according to tradition, the first Aksumite convert to Christianity, in 330. This was achieved, again according to tradition, by a Syrian monk, Frumentius, a missionary of the Coptic church – an event that began a connection with the Patriarchate in Alexandria which lasted until 1951, as the Ethiopian Archbishop was appointed from there until that point in time (Phillips 1997:453). Ezana's

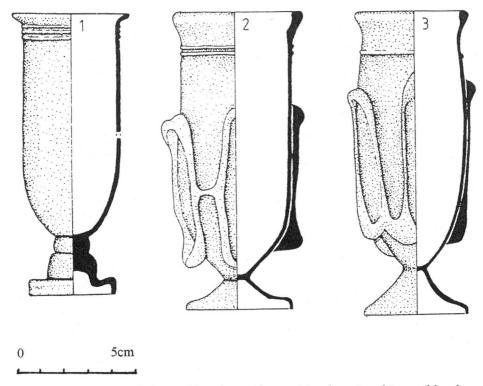

0   5cm

Figure 2.3 Imported glass goblets from Aksum. Numbers 2 and 3 possibly of
Egyptian origin

conversion to Christianity is also a process signalled materially, as, for example, on coinage, with the replacement of the sun and crescent symbols by the
cross (Munro-Hay 1991). Yet it should be noted that the process of Christianisation of the bulk of the population of Aksum was not instantaneous. On
the contrary, as Phillipson (1998:112) notes, this was long drawn out, with the
religion not becoming widespread in the countryside until the fifth century,
and again associated with another momentuous event, the arrival of the 'nine
saints', a group of 'Greek-speaking missionaries' (Richard Pankhurst 1998:36)
who founded churches in the countryside. Prior to this (and probably for some
time later, albeit perhaps less overtly), people persisted in their traditional beliefs, centred on divine kingship, sacrifice and making offerings (as indicated
by the incense burners frequently found), and as a whole 'based largely but not
exclusively on deification of the sun, moon and stars' (Phillipson 1998:114).

Participation in international trade was not solely confined to the inhabitants of Aksum. Similarly, to the south-east along the coast of Somalia, archaeological evidence indicating the existence of international trade before
the development of Islam has been found. At Ras Hafun, for example, possibly to be identified with the classical port of Opone, sherds of Parthian

and early Sasanian wares were recorded. This site has been interpreted as a stop-over point for sailors involved in trade along the East African coast who were awaiting monsoonal changes (M. Horton 1996a:450). Variously over time these individuals, as the archaeological material indicates, had contacts with Red Sea ports under Ptolemaic and Roman control, and subsequently with Gulf and South Asian ports (Smith and Wright 1988:139–40). Matching sailors' camps have been recorded at Daamo, possibly to be identified with Aromaton Emporion (M. Horton 1996a:449) and Heis, also in northern Somalia. At the latter, Egyptian millefiori glass dating from the mid-first century CE was recovered (Stern 1987), along with Roman red slip-ware and amphorae fragments (M. Horton 1996a).

Ras Hafun

Ras Hafun was excavated by the late Neville Chittick (1976), under the auspices of the British Institute in Eastern Africa of which he was director. It is described as 'the easternmost point in Africa' (Chittick 1976:122) and consists of a 25-km-long massif of rock rising from the sea which is connected to the northern Somali mainland by a spit of sand. On each side where it meets the headland there are well-protected anchorages which have been utilised since antiquity. Two sites were recorded by Chittick, the main and west sites. The main site on the south side of the headland was indicated by a spread of pottery covering some 1.3 ha and included features such as post-holes, and two rectangular stone cairns **(figure 2.4)**. Pottery recovered indicated a date range of between the second and fifth centuries, and in the earlier phases the 'most common origin' for the pottery was from South Asia and Mesopotamia/Iran (Smith and Wright 1988:125). Among the features recorded at the west site were piles of sandstone blocks which were 'identified as a structure with multiple rooms surrounding a courtyard' (M. Horton 1996a:449). Finds from this site included a large midden of *Murex Virginius* shells, 'which may have been collected for its dye' (M. Horton 1996a: 449). The pottery from the west site was earlier than that at the main site, and dated from the first century BCE–first century CE. It did not, however, indicate to the same extent the identity of the mariners who prepared their meals there, though it appeared that they 'regularly provisioned at ports in the Nile sphere' (Smith and Wright 1988:124). Both these sites were feasibly interpreted as stop-over points for ships' crews involved in 'pre-Islamic voyaging along the coast of Eastern Africa' (Smith and Wright 1988:138).

The importance of this detailed pre-Islamic background is that it indicates that Ethiopia and the Horn maintained extensive pre-Islamic international contacts,

Figure 2.4 Grave at Ras Hafun

indirectly or directly via indigenous or foreign merchants (the mechanisms are still largely unclear), with Persians (Sasanians), Arabs, Romans and Indians. Aksum and its predecessors were in contact with South Arabia and shared similar religious beliefs and other aspects of culture. Thus seen in this light Islam can be viewed not as something wholly foreign to this, the first area of Muslim contacts in sub-Saharan Africa, but as forged, in part, in the same cultural milieu.

The early Islamic period (seventh–tenth centuries)

The historical evidence – Aksum, Muhammad and Arabia

The close relations that had been enjoyed intermittently across the Red Sea charted thus far continued in the immediately pre- and early Islamic periods, but materially there is very little to indicate these. However, information derived from historical sources is useful in indicating the extent of contacts, both peaceful and otherwise. For example, it is recorded in a biography of the Prophet

Muhammad by Ibn Ishaq (d. c.772) that an Abyssinian general with a large force of men and elephants was defeated by divine intervention when he threatened to take Mecca, his soldiers being killed by smallpox and stones dropped by birds (Guillaume 1954:21–2). This coincided, 'so it is said, with the birth of the Prophet Muhammad' (Sutton 1989:3). More peaceful mentions of contacts also exist. Muhammad's grandfather reputedly 'visited Aksum frequently on business' (Richard Pankhurst 1998:39), while the first *muezzin* in Islam, Bilal, who had the role of calling the faithful to prayer, was a freed slave of Ethiopian origin. Bilal was also the bearer of the Prophet's lance, according to tradition given by an Ethiopian ruler to a companion of the Prophet, and in turn to Muhammad (Miles 1952:164–5; Munro-Hay 1991:93–4). This was used in the first years of Islam to indicate the direction of prayer prior to the development of the *mihrab*, or fixed niche indicating the direction of prayer (see chapter 1), the use of which spread from the early eighth century (Insoll 1999a:31).

It has also been suggested that the Prophet Muhammad's nurse, Baraka Umm Ayman, was of Ethiopian origin, and that the many Ge'ez (an Ethiopian Semitic language) words in the Qur'an indicate 'that Muhammad himself acquired some of that language from the Ethiopians of Mecca' (Erlich 1994:5). The validity of the last statement is difficult to test and their existence in the Qur'an is probably more due to, as Guillaume notes (1954:62), the trade and other contacts that existed between the inhabitants of Mecca and Medina and those of Aksum. Hitti (1974:106), for instance, argues that the Qur'anic references 'to the sea and its tempests (surahs 16:14, 10:23–4, 24:40), which are characterized by unusual clarity and vividness, are an echo of the active maritime intercourse between al-Hijaz and Abyssinia'. These relations must have been cordial, as in 615 the reigning Ethiopian ruler, or *Najashi*, offered asylum to persecuted members of the early Muslim community in Mecca. This was a mere five years after Muhammad began to receive his first revelations from God (Lapidus 1988:25), again reflecting the intertwining between parts of sub-Saharan Africa and the early Muslims which existed from the very first. Ultimately, two waves of exiles sought refuge at Aksum – initially a small group of fifteen in 615, which included Muhammad's son-in-law and future successor 'Uthman ibn 'Affan (Richard Pankhurst 1998:40), followed by a second *hijrah* (migration) of 101 individuals a couple of years later. The latter group did not return until 628 (H. Ahmed 1993:207; Munro-Hay 1996:409).

More controversial is the notion that one of the kings of Aksum, Ashama, actually converted to Islam and exchanged a series of letters with the Prophet – a claim made by one of the Prophet's biographers, ibn Hisham (H. Ahmed 1992:22). This is obviously of fundamental importance in assessing the role, history and material legacy of Islam in Africa, as it would mean that the head of this Christian state was a Muslim, and would also make Aksum the first Muslim-ruled state in sub-Saharan Africa. However, as Ahmed (1992:22) notes, the conversion is usually dismissed out of hand by non-Muslim scholars, with the letters regarded as fakes, while both Arab and Ethiopian Muslim scholars frequently accept it. Unfortunately, the archaeological evidence can add nothing to this issue either way, and at present this question remains unsettled.

Nevertheless, if such a conversion to Islam occurred, reconversion to Christianity by one of Ashama's successors must also have taken place. Christianity certainly continued in Ethiopia and, interestingly, an Ethiopian ruler is portrayed as one of six rulers 'overcome by the advance of Islam' in a painted fresco at the eighth-century palace of Qusayr Amra in Syria. Here the Ethiopian ruler is portrayed alongside, among others, the Sasanian ruler and the king of the Visigoths (Talbot Rice 1993:26–7). Whether this painting, which has been dated to the Umayyad period (some time between 710 and 750), indicates the subordination of these rulers, as Talbot Rice seems to think (1971:24, 1993:26–7), or 'the family of kings', the predecessors of the Muslim rulers as major rulers of the world, as Erlich suggests (1994:11), is unclear. This example does, however, illustrate that the study of Islam in sub-Saharan Africa, archaeological and historical, is not somehow sterile, but is in many instances of significance in the contemporary world, where, as was noted in the last chapter, religious conversion is ongoing, and relationships between believers of different religious traditions are constantly being renegotiated.

Other historical references exist which appear to indicate the African–Arabian interaction just before and immediately after the development of Islam but, as with the conversion of King Ashama, it is sometimes difficult to separate myth and reality. This is amply indicated by assessing whether there is any veracity in the suggestion that the Ka'bah at Mecca, the holiest shrine in Islam and focal point of all the mosques in the world, was built in 608 by an Aksumite, Bakum, of wood from a shipwreck, resulting in a stone- and wood-layered building typical of Aksumite architecture (Munro-Hay 1996:409). This has fundamental implications for African–Arabian contacts, but whether it is true (which is unlikely) is impossible to assess (it is also wholly contradicted by other sources, for example Richard Burton (1964 [1893]:322), admittedly no great lover of Africans and a romanticiser of the Arabs, who relates that Bakum was a Greek merchant who provided ships' timbers to re-roof the eighth Ka'bah). This is firstly because the Ka'bah has been much rebuilt and all traces of this original structure have probably disappeared; secondly because of the improbability of conducting an examination of the Ka'bah; and thirdly because of the controversy of assigning such an attribution. As with the possible conversion of King Ashama to Islam, Aksumite origins for the Ka'bah are extremely sensitive **(figure 2.5)**.

The communities of African origin found along the Arabian shore of the Red Sea form a more visible and less controversial African legacy in Arabia. The pre-Islamic relationship between parts of Ethiopia and South Arabia has already

Figure 2.5 Aksumite capital used in the congregational mosque in Sana'a,
Yemen

been described. Inscriptions in South Arabian have been found in the region,
referring to the existence of Habashat (Ethiopians) in areas where 'the population [is] of unmistakably African origin nowadays' (Serjeant 1966:26). Serjeant
also mentions a much later historical source, a reference by Abu Makhramah

writing *c*.1500, who describes how people from both Mogadishu and Zeila were living in Aden, 'and says in fact most of the inhabitants are Abyssinians (Hubush) and Barabir' (Serjeant 1966:31). Thus both the considerable time depth of some of these communities and their substantial numbers would appear to be indicated by the historical and epigraphic evidence.

These communities continue to exist today. They are also attested archaeologically, as along the Saudi coast, where survey in the Djayzan area of the South-Western Province recorded 'unusual circular, conical structures with thatched roofs' (Zarins et al. 1981:33). These were roughly dated to the last 300 years, and according to the investigators, 'with their artifacts and cemeteries appear to have African affinities' (Zarins et al. 1981:33). Besides the huts, the ploughs found in the Tihama also resemble those found on the African side of the Red Sea, as do some items of basketry, other utensils and string beds. Furthermore, sorghum predominates as the major crop grown in this region, as well as pearl millet, both described by Zarins and al-Badr (1986:38) as 'demonstrably of African origin'. Similar architecture to that found on the Red Sea coast of Saudi Arabia continues to be utilised further south on the Tihama plain on the coast of Yemen. Serjeant has remarked how he noted 'African huts', and whole villages, Arabic speaking, 'but completely African in appearance' (1966:27). The crudely described 'huts' are in fact roundhouses built of brushwood or reeds which are then coated with mud. They have been described as 'African building in Arabia – a cultural drift phenomenon parallel to the continental drift which is the explanation given by historical geology for the physiography of the Tihama, a piece of Africa in Arabia' (G. R. H. Wright 1987:205).

The archaeological evidence – the Red Sea, piracy and slavery

More substantial archaeological evidence for contacts during the crucial early Islamic period is to be found midway between the African and Arabian coasts on the Dahlak islands in the Gulf of Massawa, off the coast of Eritrea. Here, on this arid group of islands, among the first direct archaeological evidence we have for the presence of a Muslim community within the Horn of Africa was found. However, prior to the rise of Islam the Dahlak islands were controlled between the third and sixth centuries by the Aksumite kingdom, and before this point in time are perhaps to be identified with the 'Elaia' of some classical sources (e.g. Artemidorus, *c*.100 BCE), as well as the 'Alalaios' of the *Periplus*, recorded as a source of tortoiseshell (Tedeschi 1969:50). Following the decline of Aksum in the late sixth–seventh centuries they became a centre of piracy, a fact which was to have direct implications for their Islamisation. The reasons for the decline of Aksum itself are not certain and could be attributed to a variety of possible factors: environmental degradation (soil erosion) in the Aksum region; internal rebellion; loss of international trade routes, especially those in the Red Sea following Persian occupation of South Arabia in the late sixth

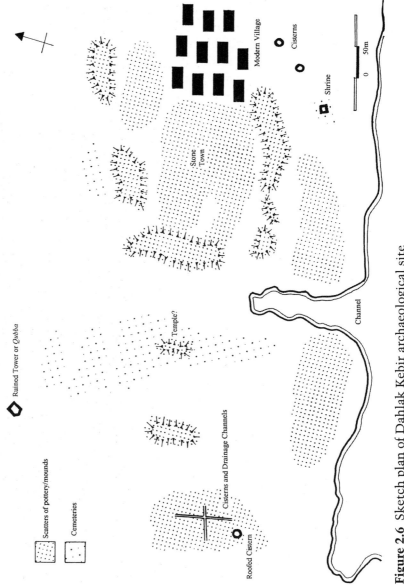

Figure 2.6 Sketch plan of Dahlak Kebir archaeological site

century; or the growth of Islam itself (Richard Pankhurst 1998:41; Munro-Hay 1996:412).

What is more certain is that the Dahlaks' role as a pirate base hampered the trade of the early Muslim state. For example in 702–3, 'Abyssinian' pirates were recorded as having attacked Jeddah (Tedeschi 1969:52), and as a reaction to this the Dahlaks were occupied in the early eighth century by Muslim naval forces. From this point in time the islands could be considered as Islamised – that is, all traces of Aksumite influence were expunged, though traces of these remain for the archaeologist. These include the remains of an Aksumite building near Gimhile in the north-east of Dahlak Kebir, the largest of the 220 or so islands that make up the group. This structure is described as being composed of a rectangular podium of stone blocks some 1 m in height and 11.5 × 7.5 m in dimensions, around which were scattered fragments of spiral carved marble columns (Puglisi 1969:37–8). The function of this structure, if indeed it is Aksumite, is unknown, though the remains of a similar structure, again with spiral marble columns, were recorded at the settlement of Dahlak Kebir, on the island of the same name (Insoll 1997a), and this too appears to be pre-Islamic.

References to Muslim control of the islands are lacking prior to the tenth century when it is recorded that they had been used as a place of political exile known as 'the island of thorns' (Tedeschi 1969:52). It is also known that in the tenth century the islands were linked with Yemen through a tributary arrangement with Zabid. By the late eleventh–early twelfth centuries they were apparently autonomous and home to an independent Muslim sultanate. This polity lasted some time; Maqrizi, writing in the fifteenth century, records that in 1393 'the Egyptian Sultan received from the sovereign of the Dahlaks several elephants' (Tedeschi 1969:60). The Dahlak islands were also, besides their political and prison role, a major centre of trade. A key centre appears to have been Dahlak Kebir, the possible Aksumite settlement already referred to. Here extensive archaeological remains testify to its former importance. These include cemeteries, a multi-period settlement, extensive cisterns and water collection systems, and what appears to be a port area (Insoll 1997a) **(figure 2.6)**. Of especial significance are a group of over 200 Arabic funerary inscriptions on basalt, incised or carved in relief in both Naskhi and Kufic script, and which date from between 911 and 1539 (Oman 1974) **(figure 2.7)**. These have been well studied (Bassat 1893; Wiet 1951; Oman 1974), and have provided information on the sultanate of Dahlak, as, for example, by a reference on a stele dated to 1093 to a Sultan al-Mubarak, apparently the name of a sovereign of the Dahlaks in the late eleventh century (Tedeschi 1969:63). One individual was even commemorated by four stelae, 'a case unique in the epigraphy of Dahlak Kebir and also in Islamic epigraphy' (Oman 1974:259).

Besides the inscribed tombstones, the remains of standing *qubba* (domed) tombs also exist at Dahlak Kebir. These are built of dressed coral and were

Figure 2.7 Muslim tombstone, Dahlak Kebir

formerly rendered with plaster, traces of which remain. They are undated but appear on the basis of construction similarities to be connected with the extensive stone town (Insoll 1997a). One of these *qubba* tombs stands in what Puglisi (1969) describes as the Farsi (Persian) cemetery. It is also noteworthy that some of these tombs, though semi-derelict, continue to be of religious significance to the mixed Afar and Dahlakin population inhabiting the islands today. This is indicated by numerous pieces of rag tied to one of the structures, and the remains of incense burners and burnt offerings scattered around the interior, and immediate proximity, of the tomb (Insoll 1997a). These practices were also mirrored close by on the mainland, or rather immediately offshore on Sheikh Sa'id (Green Island) near Massawa (Eritrea). Here, the remains of another saint's tomb were recorded in which were found the remains of incense burners and offerings, including a sacrificed desiccated sheep, all concentrated within the *mihrab* (Insoll 1996c) **(figure 2.8)**. The function of the offerings is not certain, but obtaining blessings for safety in trading and fishing expeditions is a major factor underlying these ritual practices (C. Hillman, pers. comm.). The importance of both shrines and the cult of saints was a significant feature throughout this region (I. M. Lewis 1994, and see below).

The trade role of the Dahlaks has already been mentioned. The Muslims took over the remnants of dying Aksumite commerce and injected new vitality

Figure 2.8 Sacrifice remains in a *mihrab*, Massawa

(Phillipson 1998). Yet quite how significant was Red Sea trade in the early Islamic period has been the subject of some debate. M. Horton (1987b:350) has argued that it did not become important until Fatimid control of Egypt began in 969, following a post-Aksumite lull. This, however, appears to be contradicted by archaeological evidence from certain locations, as with the recovery of T'ang ceramics from Aqaba in Jordan indicating international commerce right up the Red Sea prior to this point in time (Whitcomb 1988, cited in Hourani et al. 1995:129). Controversy over trade routes aside, trade from the Dahlak islands was in a variety of commodities, though we lack information on many of these. The importance of tortoise shell in the Aksumite period has been described as indicated by the *Periplus* (Schoff 1995), and slaves were of importance in the Islamic period. Essentially, the patterns evident in the Aksumite period – namely, the export of slaves and raw materials, and the import of finished goods – appears to have continued.

Archaeological evidence for slavery is generally elusive (Insoll 1996b:73), though a possible indication of its former importance on the Dahlak islands might be attested by the presence of so many rock-cut water cisterns. Puglisi (1969:45) has suggested that they were built 'in the interests of the merchants who were trading in slaves'. It is certainly correct that the number of cisterns is far in excess of the requirements of the population today (Insoll 1997a:385). The slave trade was concentrated at several points on the coast, and it is possible that the clustering of cisterns at certain port sites in the arid coastal plain and on the offshore islands could indicate participation in the slave trade, as well as consumption of the water they contained by the local free population. Besides Dahlak Kebir, cisterns have been recorded at Massawa and Kutto in Eritrea, Saad-Din, an island close to Zeila in Somalia, and at various sites in the Nilotic Sudan (Salt 1967 [1814]:169; Burton 1987 [1894]:51; Richard Pankhurst 1975:91, and see chapter 3). Usually, these cisterns are very well made, cut from the coral, roofed over and supported by columns, and rendered watertight with internal coatings of plaster **(figure 2.9)**.

Puglisi (1969) also suggests that 3,000–4,000 slaves passed through Dahlak Kebir each year. A sizeable transient slave population en route from the African mainland would fulfil the excess cistern capacity. It was noted earlier that slaves were recorded as an export from the wider region, specifically from Avalites (Zeila) in the *Periplus*, and demand certainly increased during the Islamic period to meet labour requirements for the households and farms of the Persian Gulf region and Arabia (Insoll 1998b:239). Puglisi's suggested figure is quite substantial and is probably to be preferred to Lovejoy's (1983:24) more conservative estimate of pre-1600 slave exports from the Red Sea region of only 2,000 per year, with 5,000–10,000 in total exported annually from sub-Saharan Africa. This figure would appear too low, though equally it has to be admitted that reliable statistics are impossible to reconstruct.

Figure 2.9 Cistern entrance, Dahlak Kebir

The Zanj revolt

The scale of slave exports, at least from the Eastern African coast, would appear to be indicated by the Zanj revolts. The Zanj (a generic term for slaves from eastern Africa) were employed in large gangs of between

500 and 5,000 workers preparing the ground for cultivation in the salt flats of southern Mesopotamia (Freeman-Grenville 1975:117), an occupation which exposed them to extreme privations and harsh conditions. As a reaction to this they revolted several times, possibly in 694 (there is a question mark over whether the revolt was by the Zanj or the Zull, 'cattle-keeping immigrants from Sind' (Hourani et al. 1995:146)), in 765, and again between 869 and 883. This latter revolt has been considered the most serious (Afolayan 1998:713), and included the occupation and sacking of Basra in Iraq by the Zanj. It has been estimated that this revolt involved between 100,000 and 300,000 slaves, and as an action has been described as the 'greatest protest movement by African slaves in the Islamic World' (Afolayan 1998:713). It was eventually suppressed by an army of 50,000 soldiers.

The importation of finished objects is somewhat better attested at Dahlak Kebir, and this provides some information on possible trade partners (Insoll 1997a:386–7). Numerous monochrome glass trade beads of types ubiquitous across the continent have been recorded, along with fragments of multi-coloured chevron-decorated glass bracelets of types similar to examples known at Aden, a major centre of production (**figure 2.10**). Others were similar to examples recovered from Qusayr al-Qadim in Egypt, where they have been dated to the thirteenth–fourteenth centuries (Insoll 1997a; Whitcomb 1983). Sherds of undated Chinese blue-and-white wares, celadon (green wares) and white wares have also been recorded at Dahlak Kebir, as were sherds of sgraffiato wares (Insoll 1997a). These are all types of trade ceramics found along the coasts of both the Red Sea and Indian Ocean, the latter as far south as Mozambique (see chapter 4). The Chinese wares are described later, but sgraffiato, produced in Mesopotamia and the Persian Gulf, is generally dated to the ninth–twelfth centuries, though later production continues in Egypt, and has been defined as 'slip painted ware' either decorated with incised or carved designs (Philon 1980:283). Decoration can be floral, epigraphic or geometric in red, buff or sandy fabric with either a transparent or transparent green or mustard-coloured glaze. Common forms include bowls and plates (Philon 1980).

The bulk of the trade goods, cursorily dated as they are, appear to date from the time when the Dahlaks were an independent sultanate. This declined in the latter part of the fifteenth century and was in part due to the Portuguese rounding the Cape of Good Hope, and an accompanying decline in Red Sea trade (see below and chapter 4). The Sultan of the Dahlaks was for a time even a tributary to the Portuguese, and the last reference to an independent Sultan of the Islands is made in 1541 (Tedeschi 1969). The arrival of the Ottomans in the Red Sea (see below) was of further significance to the islands' inhabitants, but the process of decline was inexorable, and when visited by James Bruce in

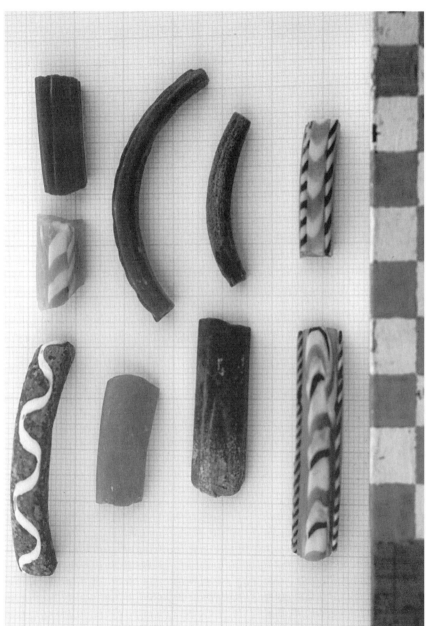

Figure 2.10 Glass bracelet fragments from Dahlak Kebir

1769, Dahlak Kebir was reduced to a collection of 'miserable huts' (Tedeschi 1969:73).

The spread of Islam (tenth–fourteenth centuries)

From the coast to the interior

Until the tenth century, Muslims were largely confined to the coast, and off-shore islands such as Dahlak Kebir. From this date, trade, allied with pros-elytisation, were the vital factors in the spread of Islam away from coastal areas. An example of this process is provided by considering the trade route which led ultimately from the Dahlak islands into the interior of Eritrea and Ethiopia. Muslim communities grew up along these interior trade routes – communities that, until the tenth century, were tributary to the Christian population (Hiskett 1994:137). Various pieces of archaeological evidence indi-cate an inland Muslim presence from this point in time. For instance, in the Quiha area of Tigre in Ethiopia several engraved basalt stelae bearing inscrip-tions in Arabic have been recorded, dating from the eleventh–twelfth centuries (Schneider 1967; Anfray 1990:156–7). These are similar to the examples already described from the Dahlak islands, though the Tigrean stelae possibly com-memorate local converts to Islam (Schneider 1967:117), rather than merchants from the coast.

Evidence in all probability linked to these same trade routes has also been discovered at the Christian monastery of Debra Damo. This inaccessible site in northern Tigre, where access is only gained via a rope climb up a 17 m ascent controlled from the monastery itself (Phillipson 1998:128–31), has al-ready been mentioned in connection with Aksumite trade. Several fragments of Islamic textiles were recorded here, including a piece bearing an inscription embroidered in red with the name of the Abbasid Caliph al-Mu'tamid and a date of 891, as well as a poorly preserved fragment identified as a late Fatimid piece of eleventh-century date. Various coins from the Muslim world including Umayyad and Abbasid issues (AH 78–331) were also found (Mordini 1957:75–7).

This example is of importance for two reasons. Firstly, it indicates the exten-sive commerce which 'Éthiopie Chrétienne maintenait du VIIIe au XIIe siècle' with Egypt and elsewhere in the Muslim world (Mordini 1957:76). Secondly, this example is also instructive in indicating that the presence of goods origi-nating from the Muslim world need not be indicative of an accompanying ac-ceptance of the religion. Relations between Christians and Muslims might have fluctuated, but trade contacts were frequently maintained, often via Muslim merchants. In fact, Richard Pankhurst (1998:72) refers to a mutual dependency which existed between Muslims and Christians, with Muslim coastal traders and caravans handling 'a large part of the commerce of the interior', individuals who 'at times acted as commercial agents for the Christian kings'. The existence of mutually incompatible blocs of Islam and Christianity has thus been shown to be, largely, an unlikely and infeasible scenario. This was because economic and other relations existed (as also discussed in the next chapter with regard to the Christian Sudanese Nile kingdoms).

To the south a further trade route led from the port of Zeila into the north/central Horn. Zeila is mentioned as early as 891–2 by Yaqut (Richard Pankhurst 1985:54). Salt, gold, ivory, slaves and skins travelled to the coast, while weapons, metalwork, cloth, glass and glazed pottery were traded into the interior (figure 2.11). This route was of equal importance in the gradual process of disseminating Islam away from the coast, an area which, Hiskett (1994:137–9) argues, was sufficiently Islamised by the tenth century to be considered part of the *dar al-Islam*, literally 'the abode of Islam'. Importantly, Abdi (1992:10) argues that this area of the Somali coast was exposed to the influence of Islam even earlier, 'si bien qu'à l'époque du Prophète Mahomet et surtout après sa mort, les côtes Somalies servirent de refuge aux vaincus de la guerre des Khalifats'. Similarly, I. M. Lewis (1994:140) suggests that this northern area of the coast felt the effects of Muslim influence 'very soon after the Hejira', which fits in with the evidence already described for the Dahlak islands. He further dates the origins of the Adal sultanate to the ninth–tenth centuries on the basis of historical mentions such as those by Ibn Hawqal and al-Istakhri in the second half of the tenth century.

Zeila, the Muslim end of the trade route, is also described in its heyday of the mid-fourteenth century by Ibn Battuta, an unparalleled source of information on Islam in Africa during the mid-fourteenth century. Ibn Battuta has been rightly described as 'the greatest of the pre-modern travellers' (Hamdun and King 1994:1). Born in 1304 in Tangier in Morocco, he travelled throughout the Muslim world, through Arabia, the Near East, Iran and Central Asia, India, and even on to China (Gibb 1993). He also travelled extensively in sub-Saharan Africa, and besides visiting the Horn, also travelled across the Sahara to the western Sahel and down the East African coast. He died in about 1370. Zeila is described by Ibn Battuta as being inhabited by 'blacks', followers of the Shafi'i school, who kept large numbers of sheep and goats. His description thus indicates both the indigenous nature of the city, as indicated by the composition of its population, and, by implication through the presence of the livestock, the existence of nomads in its vicinity. He also describes Zeila as 'a big city and has a great market but it is the dirtiest, most desolate and smelliest town in the world. The reason for its stink is the quantity of fish and the blood of the camels they butcher in its alleyways' (Hamdun and King 1994:15). Five hundred years later, when visited by Richard Burton, Zeila was much smaller, containing only a dozen stone houses and approximately 200 thatched ones, alongside six mosques and a saint's tomb, the whole surrounded by a coral and rubble wall with five gates. It was still a centre of caravan trade to the interior, as well

Figure 2.11 An incense tree in Somalia. Incense was a further crucial item of
international trade

as functioning as the port for the sultanate of Aussa, Harar and the whole of southern Ethiopia (Burton (1987) [1894]:16).

Substantial settlement remains have been recorded at Zeila, and on the neighbouring island of Saad-Din. Curle (1937:316) describes Zeila as covered in the remains of its former splendour. These included sherds of Chinese celadon and blue and white wares, both together ascribed a thirteenth–sixteenth centuries date range (Mathew 1956:51), and 'Arab' glazed pottery and glass (otherwise undescribed). At Saad-Din, further sherds of unspecified Chinese porcelain (twelfth–fifteenth centuries), the remains of houses and an associated cistern were recorded clustering in the south-western corner of the island (Curle 1937:316, 325; Mathew 1956:51). To these features can be added Burton's (1987 [1894]:51) description of a cemetery, saint's tomb, and traces of rock-cut channels leading to cisterns on the island. The destroyed nature of much of the archaeology at Zeila, and its reduced state, commented on by Burton, are in all probability due to its later chequered history. It was besieged by Christian Ethiopian forces in the early fifteenth century and its defender, Saad Din, he of the island, was killed (Curle 1937:325; Richard Pankhurst 1998:75). Zeila was also burnt by a Portuguese fleet under Lopez Suarez Alberguiera in 1516, and was seized by the Ottomans in the following year, who followed this by establishing a customs house there (Curle 1937:325).

The evidence for trading voyages farther along the Somali coast in the classical period has already been discussed, and this was a coastline also dotted with Muslim trading communities. Communities split into two nominal zones, with the area north of Mogadishu known to the Arabic geographers as 'Barbar' or 'Berbera', possibly equating with the land then inhabited by the Somali (H. S. Lewis 1966), while south of Mogadishu was the land of 'Zanj' (Chittick 1971:112). This distinction is followed here, with the discussion of the Islamic archaeology on the southern Somali coast being included in chapter 4 – i.e. that concerned with the East African coast. North of Mogadishu little information on the archaeology of the coast exists. During the course of Chittick's (1976:122–6) survey of the region, previously mentioned, the base of a Sasanian Islamic jar possibly dating from the seventh–tenth centuries was collected at the Ras Hafun Main Site. Similar, but later, trade ceramics, including fourteenth-century celadons and fifteenth-century Islamic monochrome wares, were collected at other sites on the coast. Otherwise, the Islamic archaeological remains which have been recorded are much later in date, as with the nineteenth-century mosque at Warsheikh, or a mosque of similar date which Chittick (1976) refers to at the site of Abai Dakhan.

The exception to these patterns is provided by Mogadishu, the origins and development of which have been investigated in some detail (Chittick 1971, 1976, 1982; Jama 1990; Broberg 1995). Conflicting dates as to the foundation of the city exist. I. M. Lewis (1994:140) suggests that along with Brawa, Mogadishu was founded in the tenth century. Jama (1990:107) similarly refers to a tradition that records the immigration of a group of Arabs from the Persian Gulf who supposedly founded both cities at the same date. However, he discounts this tradition on the basis of epigraphic evidence, namely a tombstone of a woman which was found in Mogadishu dated to c.720 CE. This is an important piece of evidence also referred to by Abdi (1992:122), who mentions that it commemorates one Fatima binti Cabdi Samad bin Yaquut. He also refers to another stele of 138 AH (752 CE), commemorating an El Haajiya binti Maxamed Midqaani. Unfortunately, the current whereabouts of either are not mentioned.

Chittick, who excavated in Mogadishu, is more cautious. Based upon his excavations near the congregational mosque in Hamar Weyne, part of the old town (figure 2.12), he suggests that Mogadishu was founded in the late twelfth century, and peaked in the thirteenth–fourteenth centuries (Chittick 1982). Chittick's excavations also uncovered sherds of sgraffiato ware, probably of Persian Gulf origin, of twelfth-century date, as well as black-on-yellow pottery which was probably produced in the vicinity of Aden (as also widely found on the East African coast and given a similar provenance; see chapter 4), and is given a fourteenth-century date. A number of dated tombs (thirteenth–fourteenth centuries) were also recorded, as were three mosque inscriptions, including one of 1238 on the congregational mosque (Chittick 1982:54–60) (figure 2.13). More recently, rescue excavation at the site of a mosque in Shangani quarter found that the mid-eighteenth-century mosque that was being demolished overlay six earlier structures dating back to the the early thirteenth century (Broberg 1995:119–20).

The indications are also that the medieval town was of some considerable extent, as Chittick (1982:48) further refers to remains of the old city, Hamar Jajab, 'smashed-up Hamar', being found some 4 km west of Hamar Weyne. A variety of evidence was thus uncovered which attests to the importance of Mogadishu as the pre-eminent anchorage on this part of the Somali coast. It is, however, probable that Chittick is being overcautious as regards the foundation date of Mogadishu, as Jama (1990:108) suggests that Chittick stopped – because of safety concerns – his excavation prior to reaching the earlier basal levels, which he places at 10 m depth. This depth of deposits was due to the continual process of raising floor levels to keep pace with those of the alleys outside as they were filled with building debris and rubbish (Broberg 1995:116). In summary, a tenth-century foundation date for Mogadishu, as indicated by the tradition (and that is excluding the tantalising evidence of the early stelae) would not appear at all unreasonable. As Broberg (1995:121) notes, the inhabitants of the Shangani quarter had already established international trade contacts by the eleventh century, thus allowing the suggestion to be made that the city had been founded some time before.

Also of importance for the information it provides to supplement the archaeological data is the description of Mogadishu by Ibn Battuta, who visited the city in 1331. He records that 'it is a town endless in size', of 'powerful

Figure 2.12 Swahili type doorway, Hamar Weyne, Mogadishu

Figure 2.13 *Mihrab* of the congregational mosque, Mogadishu

merchants', where numerous sheep and camels are slaughtered every day, and where a 'famed' cloth was manufactured which was exported as far as Egypt. Cloth was also imported from various places, and both Egypt (otherwise unspecified) and Jerusalem are named (Hamdun and King 1994:16–21). This picture of cosmopolitan international trade is supported by the results of Chittick's work, in the ceramics found and also in the inscriptions recorded, commemorating people from Persia, the Hadramaut, and the Hejaz (1982:53). Ibn Battuta also describes the government of Mogadishu as 'a fully Islamic state'. Various categories of Muslim functionary were in place including a *qadi, wazirs, sharifs* and *amirs*, and from Ibn Battuta's description it is evident that formal dispute procedures were also in operation for both matters relating to Islamic law (*shar'iah*) and those of a more general nature. Previous systems had disappeared, to be replaced by effective Muslim administration, thus providing a direct example of the social impact of Islam within sub-Saharan Africa, and most importantly of Muslim systems utilised within an indigenous context.

A further source of evidence from the region are several thousand coins which have been 'collected' from this area of the Somali coast, the majority from the vicinity of Mogadishu. These predominantly date from between 1300 and 1700 and, though they lack contextual data, provide information on the local dynasties, and on inter-regional and Indian Ocean trade. Twenty-one local rulers were represented on copper, silver and billon issues. These coins also appear to have been exported, as a copper coin of Sultan Ali ibn Yusuf dating from the fifteenth or sixteenth century was recovered from the site of Julfar in Ras al-Khaimah (United Arab Emirates) (Lowick 1985:5). Interestingly, the title 'sultan' is missing from one of the Mogadishu coins dating from 1322–3, thus immediately antedating Ibn Battuta's visit, but is apparently present on later issues (Freeman-Grenville 1963:187). Besides the local issues, various sultans of Kilwa in Tanzania (see chapter 4) are represented, including Ali ibn al-Hasan and al-Hasan ibn Sulaiman. More far-flung connections are attested by a 'rare T'ang dynasty' (Freeman-Grenville 1963:199) coin, and several Song dynasty issues (960–1279) also from China (Freeman-Grenville 1963:196). These latter finds correlate with an abundance of Chinese export ceramics found along the East African coast dating from the Song period. This was a time when Chinese trade with other areas in the Indian Ocean increased considerably, and China became, as Duyvendak notes, 'sea-minded' (1949:15).

Chinese contacts with Africa

The earliest accounts of Africa appear in Chinese literature during the T'ang period (618–906). By the mid-ninth century Canton was home to a substantial Muslim trading community, and the first African slaves were brought to China between the eighth and tenth centuries, awakening Chinese interest in the wider world. For example, a late ninth-century compendium of various kinds of knowledge, the *Yu-Yang-Tsa-Tsu*, mentions Po-Pa-li, which is probably a reference to the coast of Somalia (Wheatley 1975b:284). Trade with Africa at this time was still limited and indirect, but increased considerably during the subsequent Song period (960–1279). Large quantities of Chinese ceramics dating from this period are found on the coasts of the Horn and East Africa, with rare sherds in West Africa as well (Insoll 1998d, in press c, and see chapter 4 below). The chief historical source on Song knowledge of Africa is the *Chu-Fan-Chih*, or 'Gazetteer of Foreigners' compiled in 1225 by Chao-Ju-Kua (Wheatley 1975b:287). This refers to ivory, rhinoceros horn and ambergris being obtained from Africa. In contrast, during the subsequent Yuan period (1280–1368), little interesting information on Africa is to be found in Chinese sources. Apparently, however, Mogadishu was trading actively enough with China in the late thirteenth century to attract the attention of Kublai Khan, the Mongol Yuan ruler who conquered southern China and put an end to the Song dynasty (Snow 1988:19).

With the subsequent resumption of native Chinese rule during the Ming period (1368–1644), it was decided that prestige needed to be reinforced overseas (Wheatley 1975a:90). China entered a new era of contacts with East Africa in particular. Raw materials were required by the imperial court and new outlets needed for goods such as ceramics; Africa could supply these (Snow 1988:23). Direct contacts were also initiated for the first time. In 1418 a Chinese fleet commanded by a Muslim Chinese eunuch, Zheng He (Cheng Ho) reached the East African coast, followed by subsequent visits in 1421–2 and 1431–3 (Snow 1988). These voyages were documented in the *Wu-Pei-Chih* charts based on the collated logs of the vessels (Wheatley 1975b:289). Commercial and diplomatic contacts were briefly maintained, but a combination of circumstances led to a renewal of Chinese insularity in the late fifteenth–early sixteenth centuries and an accompanying loss of interest in international seafaring and Africa. As Filesi (1972:72) notes, the legacy of these contacts, direct and indirect, is very little, 'apart from some coins, some porcelain and some fragments of Chinese pottery [*sic*], the sporadic maritime contacts of former times, and in particular those organized with such eclat by Zheng He, have left few visible traces'.

A final piece of evidence which is of interest from Mogadishu is a stone phallus which was recorded in the Shangani area of the city, another early area of settlement. This, even in the mid-1980s, was bespattered with offerings, and its ascribed function varied from symbolising the visit of the prophet Nebi Khadar, 'l'objet de nombreux contes et superstitions parmi les Somalis' (Abdi 1992:89), to its acting as a fertility symbol for sterile women. The phallus would certainly appear to be a material symbol of what Abdi describes as a fertility cult, one of a number of cults which continue to exist among some of the Somali, a people largely Islamised since the eleventh century (Abdi 1992). Yet, as was noted in chapter 1, the two – traditional religious expression and Islam – need not sit uneasily together but are more usually seamlessly integrated, as we will see throughout this volume. This process is something I. M. Lewis (1994:102) similarly refers to, what he calls a 'Cushitic substratum' of Somali Islam, and manifest in the Islamisation of older religious elements such as sacrificial offerings made 'at former shrines of Cushitic spirits' (I. M. Lewis 1994:103), sacrifices which are made to various entities, to the sky god Waq, to ancestors or to Muslim saints. The stone phallus is a material representation of religious integration or syncretism (see Shaw and Stewart 1994) as already described in chapter 1. More practically, it might also be significant in understanding the so-called pillar tombs of the East African coast, which are considered in chapter 4.

Stone towns of the interior

By the twelfth century, Islamic conversion among the nomadic population in the hinterland surrounding coastal centres such as Zeila and Mogadishu was well advanced. With the pastoralist Somali for example, the rise of influential Muslim families/clan groups began as early as the tenth century, with the lineage ancestors within this 'elaborate system of clans and lineages' soon being transformed into Muslim saints (I. M. Lewis 1986:139). Little information is to be found in the historical sources describing Islamisation of the interior, in part – again as regards the Somali for instance – because their language was not written down 'to any appreciable extent' before 1950 (Andrzejewski 1986:35). Secondly, as H. Ahmed (1992:23) notes, because the contemporary sources that do exist, such as al-'Umari (1301–49), repeat what their predecessors say and deal only with the coast, thus having 'limited value as far as developments taking place in the Muslim interior are concerned'. However, archaeological evidence attests to this gradual process of Islamisation in the interior, as from Zeila and the other Red Sea ports, camel caravans traversed the desert to the highlands. These caravans travelled between a chain of permanent settlements, situated on the hills which studded the Ogaden and Danakil desert plains and along the Arusi and Harar highlands. Once the 'mountain shoulders' of Shoa and southern Wollo were reached the loads were then transferred from camel to mules and donkeys (Kidane and Wilding 1976:16).

Various of these abandoned settlements have been surveyed, but they still await excavation. Wilding (1980:379) describes the sites as sharing several characteristics, being set at *c*.1800–2000 m above sea level and built on heavily defended hilltops usually near good grazing and a water supply. They tended to cover an area less than 1,000 m^2 and contained remains of houses built of wattle and daub. Similar patterns are described by Azaïs and Chambard (1931) **(figure 2.14)**. Notable is the defensive location of many of these settlements – the frequent hilltop situation and infilling of gaps left in any available natural

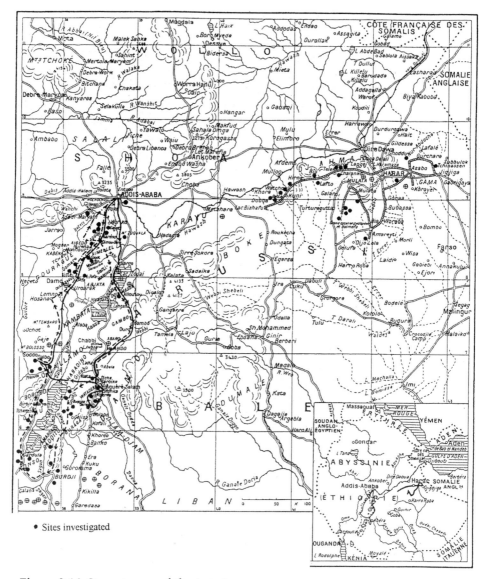

Figure 2.14 Stone towns of the interior

defences with dry-stone walling, sometimes with provision also made for grazing. Though varying in size, the permanence of the architecture is also a recurring feature as indicated by various structures, besides the houses already remarked upon. These include abandoned stone-built mosques, as for example at Amareyti or Derbiga, mosques constructed of cut stone which had been plastered. Interestingly, the latter mosque at Derbiga, though ruined, continued to be of religious significance to elements of the local population, as indicated by incense burners left in the *mihrab* (Azaïs and Chambard 1931:49), thus similar to the evidence already described from Dahlak Kebir.

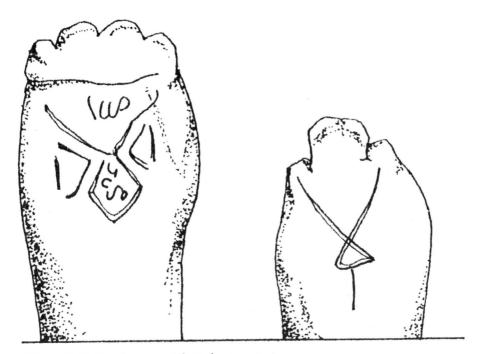

Figure 2.15 Tombstone with Kufic inscription

Further Muslim settlements have been identified in north-eastern Shoa (Ethiopia), the transshipment point already referred to. Here, mosques, inscriptions in Arabic and other remains stretch from the southern Wollo mountain fringe to Afar, with a significant concentration of sites in the heart of the former sultanate of Ifat, around the town of Shoa-Robit. The settlements of Gozie, Rasa, Asberi and Weissiso-Nora are all described by Tilahun (1990), and similar features to those just described for the hilltop trade-connected centres are found. At Asberi, for example, the remains of a large mosque were recorded, some 30 m in length by 27.5 m width, and built with stone walls 1.8 m thick. Cemeteries with Arabic inscriptions, unfortunately undated, were also noted by Tilahun, including a stele opening with the *Bismallah*, 'There is no God but God and Muhammad is the Messenger of God', and also referring to a 'king and a son of a king' (Tilahun 1990:310) – an inscription of obvious historical, but as yet uncertain, importance.

Other groups of stelae from elsewhere in this region have also been recorded, some bearing dates. Ravaisse (1931) describes eighteen inscriptions, the majority from Harar and Shoa, including four from south of Addis Ababa at Munessa near Lake Zuwai. These were re-analysed by Huntingford (1955:230) who makes the point that they all seem to have been 'in or near recognizable Moslem [sic] cemeteries'. Two of these inscriptions from Baté are in a fine Kufic script and date from c.1000; the others are more crudely made and date from around the thirteenth century **(figure 2.15)**. Schneider (1970) adds to this group with three

Figure 2.16 Mosque columns, Abasa

further crudely engraved stelae dating from the twelfth to thirteenth centuries. The patterning of the stelae varies, with some being connected with caravan trade, while others were recorded at a distance from the trade routes, as with the stele from Heyssa (Huntingford 1955:232). The latter, perhaps, are grave markers of Muslim missionaries who are known to have wandered widely throughout the whole region (see below), or of their converts.

The Shoan settlements are also interpreted as being linked with trade networks directed to the coast, and are undated, though Tilahun (1990:314) suggests an attribution to a period of 'strong Islamic influence' between 896 and 1415. Who they were founded by is unclear. Local tradition ascribes them to Arab settlers, including members of the Quraysh, the Prophet's tribe. However, this is more probably an instance of the Islamising of tradition, a recurrent feature in both Ethiopia and the Horn and across the continent. Braukämper (1984b:150) refers to another common claim of descent in this region, to one Isma'il Djabarti, an eleventh-century Islamic missionary with a shrine near Hadaftino in northern Somalia. This, if correct, would mean that 'millions of Cushitic speaking people were descendants of this one person' (Braukämper 1984b:150). Similar claims are evident in the western Sahel, on the opposite side of the continent, where the origins of the Songhai, a major ethnic group in the region (see chapter 5), are frequently ascribed to the arrival of two brothers from the Yemen (Rouch 1953:170), though this latter tradition provides an example of the Arabising of origins, a similarly recurring phenomenon in African Muslim historiography, with both Islamising and Arabising frequently being seen as a way of constructing authentic Muslim 'pedigrees'. This is something also reflected in the use of early Muslim imagery or replicas of early Muslim material culture which are found occasionally in sub-Saharan Africa, as described in chapter 4 with reference to the site of Kilwa.

Investigation of a further group of inland stone towns was completed in the 1930s. These thirteen ruined lowland towns on the borders of northern Somalia and Ethiopia are well described by Curle (1937), and again similarities with the other settlements in the region are apparent. The principal towns of Amud, Abasa, Au Bare and Gogesa were situated at over 1,000 m above sea level and contained over 200 houses each, built with stone walls, and ranging from a single room to multi-roomed courtyard houses. Niches were cut in the walls for storage, and they were roofed with brushwood laid over wooden rafters. The mosques were more 'ambitiously planned' (Curle 1937:319) **(figure 2.16)**, the one at Amud containing a separate antechamber with a 2 m-deep cistern for ablutions. Coffee beans, grinding stones, and camel, sheep and goat bones, were also recovered. These are of significance, for there is a general absence of data on dietary remains in this region, and in the description Curle (1937:324) provides, he mentions two of the often-stated dietary signifiers of Muslim identity in this region, coffee and camels (see box). Other small finds included locally made burnished brown and black wares, as well as imported glass trade beads in blue, yellow and white, carnelian beads, multi-coloured glass bracelet fragments and quantities of Chinese ceramics. The latter were described by Mathew (1956:51) as including good-quality celadons with a fine grey fabric and sea- or blue-green glaze. He suggests that these date from the thirteenth to sixteenth centuries.

Diet and religion in Ethiopia

Hopefully without stating the obvious, faunal and botanical remains can be of especial significance, not only in Ethiopia and the Horn, but elsewhere in sub-Saharan Africa – and indeed the world – in signifying religious conversion and identity (Insoll 1999a:95–100, 2001). However, frequently, the required archaeological material is lacking and anthropological and historical sources have to be utilised for relevant interpretative data. An example of this within Ethiopia is provided by Braukämper's (1984a) study of possible dietary factors underlying conversion to Islam and Christianity among both nomadic and sedentary members of the Hadiya ethnic group. Based upon his observations, Braukämper argued that Christianity did not appeal to the nomadic population of the lowland Rift Valley, as it involved much fasting and abstinence from meat – up to 150 days a year. This was interpreted as an unattractive proposition to nomads, who consumed meat or livestock products as a major part of their diet; hence they converted to Islam. In contrast, abstinence from meat was not a factor of great importance to the sedentary highland Hadiya, who as ensete cultivators consumed only a small amount of animal protein as part of their diet (Braukämper 1997:323). Braukämper (1984a:432) further suggests that alcohol was also of significance in his model of Hadiya religious conversion, with the sedentary cultivators accustomed to the production and consumption of alcoholic beverages, whereas nomads were not. Thus Islam with its general prohibition on alcohol did not appeal to the agriculturist Hadiya.

Braukämper's model is interesting, but perhaps too idealistic, as exceptions to his proposed patterns could be found. Social histories of alcohol in Africa exist (Akyeampong 1991) which indicate that Muslims of course drink, but he is generally right in stating that 'dietary rules... have a decisive impact on cultural orientation, which people seek either in Christianity or in Islam' (1984a:442). Certainly the role of diet in perceptions of religious identity in Ethiopia is apparent in other sources. J. Bruce (1964 [1790]:48) commented in the late eighteenth century on the 'abundance of flesh' at Gondar though he 'could not touch a bit of it, being killed by Mahometans, as that communion would have been looked upon as equal to a renunciation of Christianity'. Nesbitt (1955:80) also refers to having to shoot two of each prey, one for the Christians and one for the Muslims during his travels in the Danakil depression in 1928, for neither would touch it if expected to share. Furthermore, Ethiopian Christians will not touch camel meat. It has become a Muslim 'cultural symbol' (Insoll 1999a:102), whose consumption in parts of the Muslim world has come to be regarded 'as almost an Islamic rite, and a sort of profession of faith' (Simoons 1981:87). For similar reasons, because of its perceived association with Muslims, coffee was likewise avoided by Ethiopian Christians until the end of the nineteenth century (Rita Pankhurst 1997:528), as was the narcotic leaf qat, both indigenous species to this region (Weir 1985; Hattox 1991). Thus religious identity was literally spelt out in what was consumed.

The historical significance of these settlements varies. Some, because of the absence of historical sources and excavation, are little understood; others can be more clearly placed within their historical framework. The Shoan sites and stelae, for example, are the remains of the Muslim states of Shoa (or Shawa) and Ifat. Shoa was founded, according to tradition, in 896, and was the first inland Ethiopian Muslim polity. Initially it was probably tributary to the Christian state, but by the 1280s it had been absorbed by the sultanate of Ifat (Huntingford 1955:230; Erlich 1994:26). Ifat in turn was one of seven Muslim sultanates recorded by al-'Umari as existing in Ethiopia in the first half of the fourteenth century. This was a period of trade-related conflict between Christians and Muslims, specifically over 'trade to the coast' (Richard Pankhurst 1998:73), but possibly also over control of the goldfields of Enarya and Damot on the south-western edge of Christian Ethiopia (Sutton 1997:238). Conflict was periodically intense, and in 1415 Christian forces advanced through the Danakil as far as Zeila, 'the most easterly point apparently ever reached by the Ethiopian empire, which soon thereafter began to contract' (Richard Pankhurst 1998:75). Based upon the evidence just described it would seem reasonable to conclude that trade activities and the spread of Islam into the interior would appear to be loosely interconnected, as indicated by the distribution of many of the sites. Further connected with this would have been proselytisation by Muslim religious teachers and holy men, in processes already described in chapter 1, all factors also connected with the Islamisation of the nomad population as well, as will now be considered.

The nomad factor

A frequently posited, though equally erroneous, correlation between nomads and early conversion to Islam has already been referred to in chapter 1. Nevertheless, in parts of the Horn of Africa such a correlation would appear more warranted. Yet charting this process using archaeological evidence is frequently difficult owing to the ephemeral nature of much nomad material culture (Cribb 1991; Insoll 1999a:46–7) (**figure 2.17**). The historical framework might be

Figure 2.17 Nomad camp and Muslim tomb, Somalia

reasonably clear, but supporting archaeological evidence can be elusive. Among Somali pastoralists, for example, we know that Sunni Islam of the Shafi'i school was already well established by the eleventh century, and today 'Somali culture is permeated by Islam', but 'at the same time, and in no way detracting from their commitment to Islam, Somali culture and society strongly affect the character and modalities of the local style of Muslim life' (I. M. Lewis 1986:139). Thus the types of patterns outlined in chapter 1, such as the popularisation of Islam, are also found among the Somali. However, examining the Islamisation of the Somali and the development of popular Islamic traditions among them is difficult using archaeological evidence, though ethnographic and anthropological evidence can be utilised to supplement this.

The 'local style of Muslim life' just referred to is manifest in different ways, such as in the large-scale absence of veiling and seclusion among nomad Somali women, a frequent correlate of nomad life evident elsewhere, as among the Tuareg and Tedu of the central Sahara (Nicolaisen 1963; Faegre 1979). This stands in contrast to the more evident privacy concerns of the coastal Somali, reflecting the feasibility of their maintenance in a sedentary as opposed to nomad lifestyle (Campo 1991). This factor was reflected in the different shelter types found: portable collapsible hut structures among the nomads; and *arish*, rectangular huts, among the coastal Somali. The latter were described by I. M. Lewis (1994:87) as internally divided, with women sharing a common room at the rear. Privacy concerns, as outlined in chapter 1, are more easily upheld in these fixed structures – whereas among nomads, on the move for large periods of the year, it is not feasible to maintain seclusion of women in quite the same way, either through the veil or within the domestic environment. Veiling thus reflects more than religious orthodoxy, but also social and economic lifestyle and status. Yet although diversity might be manifest in veiling and domestic architecture, all Somali, nomad or sedentary, follow orthodox Muslim burial rites (I. M. Lewis 1994), as also outlined in chapter 1.

In contrast, the burial practices of the Afar, a related nomad group in the region, are much more varied. The Afar, sometimes referred to as the Danakil, inhabit a largely inhospitable territory encompassing the coastal strip south of Massawa in Eritrea (including Djibouti), the Danakil depression, and parts of the Somali–Ethiopian borderlands (Thesiger 1935). The single fertile district within their lands, Aussa on the Awash river, gave rise to a sultanate of the same name in the sixteenth century (Thesiger 1998). We are indebted to I. M. Lewis (1994) for providing data on Afar Islam, and he makes the point that 'Islam has not yet acquired anything like as strong a hold over the nomadic population of Dankalia as it has among the Somali' (1994:172). In the main towns such as Tadjoura, cosmopolitan orthodox Muslim communities are found, but in the country, 'l'astronomie, l'astrologie, la devination ou "kaloan" mais aussi le culte des ancêtres, de la nature, des arbres et des maigres cours d'eau, paraissent très présents' (Jacob 1997:186). Formerly, this integration of traditional religious belief with Islam which characterises nomad Afar religion was much maligned. For example, Salt describes the Danakil as professing Islam, 'of which, however, they know little more than the name; they have neither priests nor mosques in their country' (1967 [1814]:177). Trimingham (1952:171) also refers to the laxity of Danakil Muslim practice.

However, to state, as Salt did, that the Afar/Danakil lacked mosques is erroneous. Jacob (1997:186), for example, describes Afar mosques formed of rock outlines with a *mihrab* composed of a single large stone. Outline mosques were a common component of Muslim nomad material culture, and found also in parts of Arabia, for example (Cole 1975:127). Where nomad Afar material culture does differ is in respect of funerary monuments. Wilfred Thesiger (1935:10–11, 1998:137), who travelled along the Awash river to Aussa, provides a description of these **(figure 2.18)**. They included the *dico*, an orthodox Muslim grave with head- and footstones, which along with with a walled variant, the *kabare*, are found where Muslim influence is strong, as along the coast (I. M. Lewis 1994:171). In the interior preference was for either rough stone cairns, *waidella*, or *das*, stone circles of various configurations with a single entrance and the burial in the centre. These were tombs which were finished with a line of upright stones indicating the deceased man's victims.

All these tombs were built by Muslims but the 'Cushitic' element of Afar religion evident in these tombs is much more noticeable in the interior than on the coast. This indicates, according to I. M. Lewis (1994:172), the continuation of a 'cult of the dead', something which is understandable within the wider context, again as Lewis relates, where the sky god Waq is easily identified with Allah, and where wandering Muslim holy men are often 'identified with pre-Islamic Cushitic priests' (I. M. Lewis 1994:172). In other words, what is again evident is the meshing of Islam with traditional Somali religion. Furthermore, it can also be suggested that what is being indicated is analogous to what Eaton (1993) would refer to in a Bengali context as 'identification', or perhaps even the preceding phase of 'inclusion' – the latter whereby local and Muslim religious figures are fused, as with Krishna and Muhammad in Bengal (Eaton 1993:270).

The expansion, retrenchment and stabilisation of Islam (the late fourteenth century onwards)

Adal and Harar – city of saints and missionaries

The development of the sultanate of Shoa, the subsequent development of Ifat and its contemporaries and the occupation of Ifat by Christian forces have already been mentioned. Ifat in turn was absorbed by Adal in the last quarter of the fourteenth century (Hiskett 1994:140). The centre of the sultanate of Adal was Harar, an important city which will now be considered. Harar has

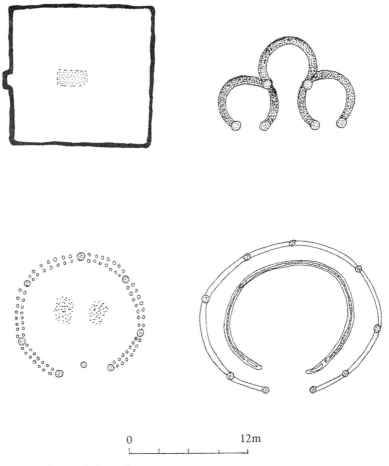

0   12m

Figure 2.18 Types of Danakil tombs

been referred to as the 'Timbuktu' of Ethiopia (source unknown), as a similar centre of scholarship and synonym for the remote prior to the arrival of the first European visitors (namely Richard Burton in 1854, see R. Burton 1987 [1894]). Harar is also an Islamic centre of great significance within the region, and Braukämper (1984b:149) describes Islam as having a 'foothold in the Harar plateau' from the tenth–eleventh centuries. This 'foothold' was derived from trade with Zeila, and by the thirteenth century Islam was the majority religion in the Harar plateau (Braukämper 1984b).

The origins of Harar itself remain unclear: its foundation date is uncertain, though various suggestions have been made. Azaïs and Chambard (1931:3) refer to a local tradition ascribing its foundation to Arabs from the Hadramaut in the seventh century. This is almost certainly a further instance of Islamising/Arabising of tradition in the vein of that described with regard to the Songhai previously. Hecht (1987:2) mentions a 'Harari claim' of tenth-century

origins, while Richard Pankhurst (1985:49) suggests that the city was founded
in the early sixteenth century by Sultan Abu Bekr owing to its good position commanding coast-to-interior trade routes. He further suggests that it
replaced an earlier centre, Dakar, an opinion supported by Braukämper, who
notes that it replaced the former Muslim centres of Funyan-Bira and Dakar in
1521 (1984b:146). What then can be made of this evidence? Essentially, it is
certain that Harar as it stands today dates largely from the eighteenth century
onwards (Hecht 1987:1), that it has been extensively rebuilt, and that it almost
certainly stands upon the site of various earlier settlements perhaps dating back
to the tenth century (or before). These earlier origins (pre-sixteenth century) are
further supported by the foundation dates of some of the mosques in the city,
which M. Horton (1994:197) suggests can be placed in the thirteenth century,
thereby agreeing with the date cited earlier for majority Islamisation in the
wider Harar area. Excavation is required, however, to establish a more reliable
chronology.

The lack of archaeological data is in part compensated for by good architectural information reflecting various useful studies which have been completed
(see for example Wilding 1976; Hecht 1982; A. M. Ahmed 1990). The city wall,
for instance, has been the focus of study. This structure, known locally as the
djugel, was originally constructed of granite, sandstone and dry mortar in the
mid-sixteenth century by Nur ibn Mujahid to counter Oromo incursions into
Harar (Hecht 1982:58; A. M. Ahmed 1990:321). Five gates were initially included, with two subsequently added, each of which corresponded with one
of the five quarters in the city after which they were named. In the local language, CeyCinan, these were Assum Bari, Argob Bari, Suqutat Bari, Badro Bari
and Asmadiri Bari (A. M. Ahmed 1990:323) **(figure 2.19)**. This subdivision into
quarters served both to define the community within and as a marker within
local sacred geography. The latter function was reflected in the number of quarters, five, reflecting the Five Pillars of Islam, and also mirrored in the names
of the quarters, Badro Bari commemorating, for example, the battle of Badr,
'the decisive victory scored by the Prophet and the Ansar over the non-Muslim
Meccans in 624' (A. M. Ahmed 1990:324). The name 'Asmadiri' possibly reflected the fact that this quarter was famous for producing wandering 'vagrant
missionaries' (A. M. Ahmed 1990:324).

The missionaries of Harar are described by R. Burton (1987 [1894]:165) thus:
'they carried dressed goatskins, as prayer carpets, over their right shoulders dan-
gled huge wooden ink bottles with *lauh* or wooden tablets for writing talismans,
and from the left hung a greasy bag, containing a tattered copy of the Koran and
a small ms. of prayers'. This type of missionary was also crucial in propagating Islam, not only in Ethiopia but in many areas of sub-Saharan Africa, but
went largely unrecorded and unremarked. They were the footsoldiers of Islam,
who served to spread the religion in a manner more effective than that ever
achieved, for example, by actual soldiers or *jihad* (see, e.g., Levtzion 1986a for a

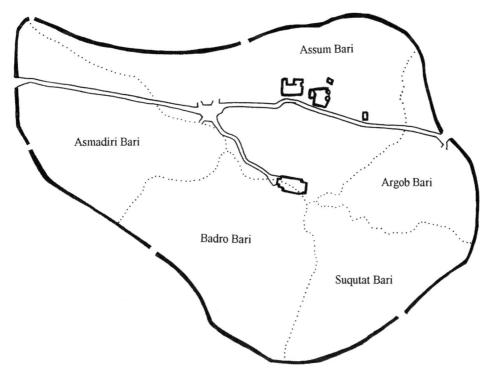

Figure 2.19 Plan of Harar

discussion of their role). The five quarters of Harar were in turn subdivided into sub-quarters and neighbourhoods, serving both administrative purposes and as markers of social identity. The latter role is exemplified by the fact that these *lasims* or neighbourhoods, comprising groups of families in adjacent houses, were 'often named after a Muslim shrine or an old tree' (Hecht 1982:57). As there were originally eighty-six mosques in the city (M. Horton 1994a), there was no shortage of focal points for this purpose.

The five-fold subdivision evident in the city is also represented within the traditional Harari house, an intentional effect by the designers 'in as much as they sought the total of each to correlate with the Five Pillars of Islam' (A. M. Ahmed 1990:331). The basic plan of the traditional Harari house, which has also been well studied, conforms with the idealised house described in chapter 1. Access is gained through a single entrance, often with a screened-off women's area on the second floor, while the ground floor functions for the reception of guests. The main reception room used for these purposes, the *gidir gar*, is in turn subdivided over half the floor space into a 'series of raised platforms' or *nedaba*. Each of these has a clearly defined function, with the *suteri nedaba*, the highest and most intimate, 'the exclusive province of the father and his wife and highly respected guests by invitation' (Wilding 1976:31). The houses are usually

built of stone and mortar, finished inside and out with plaster (Hecht 1982:62).
Furnishings were formerly sparse, and niches built into the walls of the *gidir gar*
were used for storing and displaying personal possessions (see Insoll 1999a:80–1
for similar examples). Interestingly, the shape of the niches was significant,
with the two rectangular niches (out of eleven) in the *gidir gar* theoretically
reserved for books, especially the Qur'an, and their rectangular shape serving
to remind the individual of 'death' and the 'grave' (Hecht 1982:65).

The importance of Harar as a centre of trade has already been signalled (see
Richard Pankhurst 1985), a fact supported by the large numbers of coins, both
minted in the city and from elsewhere recovered in Harar (see Zekaria 1991).
These date from as early as 1218, increasing in number in the sixteenth century,
but with the majority dating from the eighteenth–nineteenth centuries. Besides
its trade role, Harar was more famous as a centre of religion, being known as
'the town of saints' (Foucher 1994:71), the '*Madinat al-awliya*' (Braukämper
1984b:155), with over 150 saints' shrines in and around Harar known, giving
an idea of their density. In fact, a tradition exists (not based, it should be noted,
on any known *hadith*) that the Prophet Muhammad while on his Night Journey
saw a bright spot shining on the earth, which, according to Harari interpretation, 'could but mean the city of Harar' (Foucher 1994:71). The shrines themselves vary and are defined by Braukämper (1984b:156) as being any 'man-made
sanctuary', and sometimes associated with a natural object such as a tree or
pool. This is a further recurring element within sub-Saharan Africa, and something, perhaps, that can be linked with pre-Islamic notions of sacred sites as
described in chapter 1. The saints they are associated with are also graded
into hierarchies, of local, regional and more widespread importance. An example of the latter is provided by the shrine of Abd al-Kadir al-Djilani in south-
west Harar. Abd al-Kadir was a Sufi saint of great significance who founded
the Kadiriyya brotherhood and who lived in Baghdad between 1077 and 1166.
He is also credited with having forty lives, hence the existence of his shrine
in Harar as well (Braukämper 1984b:158).

In general, the emphasis upon the cult of saints in the Harar region, throughout Ethiopia and the Horn and, indeed, in many other parts of sub-Saharan
Africa is, in the words of I. M. Lewis (1986:140), because 'saints provide the
hope of direct mediation between man and the Prophet and ultimately God,
and trust in them is to some extent a reflection of a sense of human impotence
and spiritual inadequacy'. The individual, by visiting the saint's shrine, could
partake of the saint's *barakah*, the numinous essence of the saint, and hopefully obtain blessings, solutions and cures for numerous purposes (see Insoll
1999a:183–4). Saints can assume the role of an intermediary with God, with
the existence of intermediaries isolated as a feature of traditional African religion (see chapter 1), and thus perhaps also signalling an element of continuity as well. Saints also stand in contrast, along with Sufism, to what Gellner
has described as the Islam led by the *ulama*, the Muslim learned class of the
cities, 'puritanical, unitarian, individualist' Islam (1981:159). Saints function,

as Foucher (1994:72) succinctly puts it, as 'figures and religious models suitable for adapting the religion and the culture'.

Similarly, through this process sanctuaries of the old religion could be transformed into Muslim ones, thus facilitating the fusion of traditional religions and Islam, a process which has already been referred to in Mogadishu and among the Afar, something which has also been suggested as analogous with the phases of 'inclusion' and 'identification' in Bengal (Eaton 1993). Foucher describes further such shrines in and around Harar including the Sherif Huddun rock where incense is constantly left burning, 'to dissipate bad influences and attract good ones' (1994:75). Pilgrimage sites also sometimes developed with rites and perceptions of importance parallel to those of Mecca, both in this region, as with the ceremonies surrounding Sheikh Hussein's tomb on the Goba plain (Trimingham 1952:253), and elsewhere in sub-Saharan Africa. Furthermore, visiting Islamic saints' shrines in this region was not confined to Muslims alone, but could also be undertaken by Christians 'seeking health and material prosperity' (H. Ahmed 1992:21) – thus again reinforcing the notion that exclusivity of religious traditions is usually not the case, but rather that interrelations on various levels exist (Insoll forthcoming).

World powers – the Ottomans and Portuguese

The absorption of Ifat by Adal was of great significance, and the last years of the fifteenth century saw an intensification of Christian–Adal conflict. This was again trade related but with the addition of a new dimension – that of obtaining firearms. The history of this period is summarised by Richard Pankhurst (1998:81–93), who describes how the Christian empire was subjected to a series of raids led by the Muslim raider Mahfuz in the 1490s. Mahfuz was killed in 1517, but more significant events were to occur. This was the renewal of conflict under Ahmad ibn Ibrahim al-Ghazi, better known as Ahmad Gragn, or 'Ahmad the left handed'. Gragn took power in Adal and control of Harar, a base from which he launched a series of raids beginning in 1527 and documented in the *Futuh al-Habasha*. The progress of his successful campaigns, including those in Shoa in 1529, Amhara in 1531 and Tigre in 1535, was nothing short of meteoric, a process aided by his use of firearms acquired via the Ottomans (Erlich 1994:31). An empire was 'carved out' (Hiskett 1994:141), for by 1540 virtually the whole of the country was conquered (Erlich 1994).

Part of Gragn's success might be attributable to the fact that he added a *jihad* element to his campaigns and adopted the title Imam. He was also, as Richard Pankhurst (1998:88) notes, 'passionately interested in conversion', converting large numbers of Christians to Islam (many of whom reconverted following his ultimate defeat). Gragn succeeded in uniting 'around Harar and under the banners of *jihad* all of Islam of southern Ethiopia' (Erlich 1994:30). However, Gragn's successes were relatively short lived. A new power in the region was to prove his downfall – the Portuguese, who, under the leadership of Christopher

Figure 2.20 Mosque and tomb of Sheikh Hammali, Massawa

da Gama, defeated Gragn's forces at the battle of Wayna Dagna in 1543, leading to the collapse of Adal, and a battle in which Gragn was killed 'probably by a shot from a Portuguese musket' (Richard Pankhurst 1998:92–3). The Portuguese had been called upon for assistance by the Ethiopian ruler, a development which can ultimately, but indirectly, be traced back to the momentous rounding of the Cape of Good Hope by Vasco da Gama in 1498 (M. Horton 1987b:357). Although they saved Christian Ethiopia, the Portuguese did not long remain in the Horn, for the arrival of one world power in Ethiopia heralded the arrival of another, a Muslim one: the Ottomans.

The Ottomans were a Turkish dynasty of Oghuz origin founded in the late thirteenth century. Significant Ottoman power developed in the mid-fourteenth century following the military occupation of the European side of the Bosphorus and subsequent territorial expansion both in Europe, the Near and Middle East, parts of northern Africa, and the Red Sea region. The Ottomans survived, albeit in a reduced form, until just after the First World War (van Donzel 1994:331). The first real Ottoman contact with the Red Sea coast of the Horn occurred in 1557 when a contingent of Ottoman troops was disembarked at Massawa under the command of Ozdemir Pasha, 'already Beylerbey of Yemen' (Tedeschi 1969:71). Ottoman occupation of parts of the region was to last some three centuries, but it was always a province of secondary importance, where Turkish control was largely limited to the control of ports such as Massawa, and to customs, 'which gave a small income' (Tedeschi 1969:71). However, marginal as their thoughts on their Ethiopian possessions might have been, Ottoman influence can be seen in the archaeological and architectural legacy, which is beginning to be studied.

Massawa, a port on the Eritrean Red Sea coast, provides a useful case study illustrating this. Massawa assumed the role of pre-eminent port for this stretch of Red Sea coast, a duty formerly occupied by Adulis and Dahlak Kebir, as has been described. This was in part due to the fact that Massawa or, more specifically, Port island, was in a good defensible position close to the mainland, and again a preoccupation with the provision of fresh water through the presence of the ubiquitous tanks or cisterns can be seen, with forty-nine being recorded by a Portuguese visitor in 1520 (Richard Pankhurst 1975:90). In the seventeenth century the principal building on Massawa was the Turkish governor's palace, with the ground floor containing the customs offices and a warehouse for goods, and the upper floor accommodation. In the following century, Bruce describes Massawa island as being divided into three parts – one-third cisterns, one-third houses and one-third for the dead (Richard Pankhurst 1975:92). Besides various historical descriptions, an inventory of standing monuments, including Ottoman ones, has recently begun (C. Hillman, pers. comm.). Notable among the buildings recorded is the mosque and tomb of Sheikh Hammali, a large complex founded in the second half of the sixteenth century comprising a mosque, courtyard, minaret and *qubba* tomb for the saint **(figure 2.20)** (Cresti 1994).

Ottoman interests also extended to the mainland. The remains of an Ottoman settlement at Hergigo (Arkiko) close to Massawa still stand (Insoll 1996c). Another important centre was at Debarwa, 30 km south of Asmara. This site was intermittently occupied by Ottoman forces who established a fort there from the mid- to late sixteenth century, and it was an important point on the coastal–interior trade routes (Richard Pankhurst 1985:68–9). Bruce also describes Debarwa in the late eighteenth century as being divided into two parts, a higher and lower town. Muslims inhabited the upper section, and Christians the lower (Richard Pankhurst 1988:119). This pattern of dual settlements was replicated elsewhere in the highlands at this time, as at Gondar (Richard Pankhurst 1979), with Muslims frequently being tolerated in Christian towns as they controlled foreign trade, and because trade as a Muslim profession carried social stigma in Christian eyes (H. Ahmed 1992:20).

Dual settlements were also a feature elsewhere in sub-Saharan Africa, as in the western Sahel (see chapter 5), and also beyond Africa. Dolukhanov (1996:189), for example, records how 'paired settlements' were a characteristic feature of 'early urban development' in eastern and northern Europe as evident in dual Slav and Viking settlements. Richard Pankhurst (1988:116–18) relates how Muslim and Christian roles were clearly delineated in these Ethiopian twin settlements, and that Muslim merchants dealt in cloth and 'large goods' and Christians in provisions and 'cheap things'. This pattern of 'Functional coexistence' (Erlich 1994:42) was one which was to continue and largely characterised Muslim–Christian (and Jewish) relationships to the present day. It again indicates that the picture of coexistence between Muslims and Christians evident when the Aksumite king offered shelter to members of the early Muslim community, described at the start of this chapter, appears not to have been an isolated incident. Though the relationship between the members of the two religious traditions has frequently been one of conflict, equally, their centuries-old proximity is not insignificant in less violent terms as well.

Summary and conclusions

The material considered within this chapter has indicated, if anything, the plural character of Islamic development within sub-Saharan Africa. Two other points specific to this region are also immediately apparent: firstly, the existence of another world religion, Christianity, as a significant contributing factor to the history of Islam in the region; and secondly, the early contacts, many centuries before the rise of Islam in the case of D'MT, which were maintained between both sides of the Red Sea. In more general terms, it is also evident that there is frequently not so much a change in religious belief as a successful fusion of old and new. It exemplifies what was considered in the last chapter, i.e. as eloquently outlined by Eaton (1993:303), the 'appropriation' of the inhabitants of the region by Islam, and its simultaneous appropriation by them. This can be seen, as for example among the Somali, in the replacement of intermediary spirits by saints, the replacement of the sky-god by Allah, the incorporation and 're-branding' of pre-Islamic shrines, and likewise with rain-making practices and ancestor cults. Materially, Islamisation might be apparent, even allowing for the vagaries of the evidence and relevant research which has been completed, yet this is far from uniform. Mosques and burials signify religious change/fusion, but other elements can remain little changed. It is the residue of a long-drawn-out process (Levtzion 1979c), and as was noted, also in the introductory chapter, the dividing line between the archaeology of Islam and that of traditional religion cannot always be easily drawn.

Approaching the question of why people converted to Islam without falling into the trap of 'palaeopsychology' (Fritz 1978) is difficult. It is safe to assume that the reasons for this are as varied as the evidence that indicates Islamisation itself. The agents of conversion are somewhat easier to speak of, but again these are varied. Trade recurs, usually allied with proselytisation, hard work by holy men and missionaries, as outlined by Levtzion (1986a). The cult of saints was obviously also significant, as was Sufism in certain circumstances. Yet the inadequacies of phased models such as those of R. Horton (1971, 1975) and Fisher (1973a, 1985), discussed in chapter 1, can again be seen, in contrast to the more human model developed by Eaton (1993). The required clear patterns are not evident, because in reality they do not appear to exist. Diversity is certainly the theme for this region – diversity in peoples and environments, diversity in the Islamic legal schools found – and a theme which extends into the next region to be considered, the Nilotic Sudan.

CHAPTER 3

THE NILOTIC SUDAN

Introduction

Christianity has been important in parts of the Nilotic Sudan, but, unlike Ethiopia, it has disappeared as a living faith in the Sudan leaving the material remains of its legacy for the archaeologist to interpret. One of the primary reasons for the abandonment of Christianity in parts of the Nilotic Sudan, notably Nubia, was the encroachment of Muslims – through a variety of processes, both peaceful and warlike. This occurred via different routes – through the eastern desert, down the Nile valley, and from the Red Sea coast (Hasan 1966; Holt and Daly 1988). Similarly, as with the Horn of Africa, the inhabitants of parts of the Nilotic Sudan were in contact with Muslims from an early date. In Nubia, as already noted, initial conflict between Muslims and Christians in the mid-seventh century eventually gave way to several centuries of uneasy truce – a truce exemplified by the *baqt* or treaty concluded between the two parties, which uniquely defined Nubia as the *dar al-mu'ahada*, 'the abode of pact or guarantee', in contrast to the usually defined spheres of the *dar al-harb*, 'the abode of war', and the *dar al-Islam*, 'the abode of Islam' (Hasan 1966:115). Early contacts were also evident on the Red Sea coast, where Muslim trading communities appear to have been resident from as early as the mid-eighth century. Elsewhere in the Nilotic Sudan contacts between Muslims and followers of other, largely traditional, religions were much later – and in some cases Islamisation, as we shall see, is ongoing.

A dominant reason behind the staggered nature of Islamisation in the Nilotic Sudan is the vast size of the region, an area which for the purposes of discussion here is defined as approximating the boundaries of the modern Republic of the Sudan. This is the largest country in Africa, covering over 2,500,000 km^2, and the size of the country is reflected in the mosaic of environments, and of ethnic and cultural groups, found. In the north are deserts, with the Nubian desert lying between the Nile and the Red Sea coast, itself demarcated by the Red Sea hills which mark the eastern flank of the Rift Valley. To the west of the Nile are further deserts, the Libyan and Bayuda. South of these deserts are shrub steppes with grazing for livestock such as camels and goats. To the south-west, in Kordofan, further grazing areas are found in this area of thorny savannah steppe. Further south are areas of more open flat savannah, before a vast area of swamps is reached – the apt name for which, Sudd, is derived from the Arabic *sadd*, literally meaning 'block' (Trimingham 1949:2–3). Other areas and environments of significance to the discussion here include the hills of Darfur in the west of the country, the Nuba hills of Kordofan and the savannah forests of the Zande kingdoms of the southern Bahr al-Ghazal in the far south-west of the country, as well as the Gezira (Arabic *jazirah*, 'island' or 'peninsula' (Holt and Daly 1988:2)), a peninsula between the White and Blue Niles, which was the 'granary' of Sennar, the Funj capital, and is now an important area for cotton cultivation (McHugh 1994:34).

Inhabiting this diverse range of environments is an equally diverse range of ethnic and cultural groups. Sedentary cultivators predominate along the Nile utilising the waters of the river through irrigation. In parts of the western and southerly regions where rainfall is more abundant, agriculturists are also found – Nuba, Fur, Zaghawa etc. – frequently interspersed with pastoralist groups, such as the Arab groups who emigrated many centuries ago from Egypt and the Kababish, described by Holt and Daly (1988:7) as a 'synthetic' ethnic group, 'formed from diverse elements by a common way of life', as reflected in their name which is derived from the Arabic '*ka Sh*' – 'ram'. The Baqqara, another pastoralist group, could similarly be defined, with their name derived from the Arabic '*baqar*' – 'cow' (Holt and Daly 1988). Other non-Arab pastoralists also exist, Muslim Beja of the Red Sea hills region, or followers of traditional religions in the south, groups only recently influenced by Islam, such as the Nuer.

Throughout this vast country flow the tributaries of the Nile. The White Nile, flowing from Lake Victoria, is joined by its tributaries the Bahr al-Ghazal and the Sobat, and the Blue Nile, which collects waters from the Ethiopian highlands and joins with the White Nile at Khartoum (Trimingham 1949:1). The Nile itself is subdivided by five chains of cataracts (six if southern Egypt is included), which, when the river's winding course is taken into account, has in fact encouraged 'more direct routes across the desert' (Welsby 1996:11), routes such as the Bayuda road, rather than river transport along great stretches of the Nile. It would also be reassuring to say that the Nile lends an essential unity to the archaeology of Islam within the region, but, as is probably apparent from the diversity already described, it does not. Many different interpretations of Islam are evident – from that of Darfur, which is permeated with traditional religious practices and very much central Sudanic in character, to the reforming Islam of the Mahdist state in the second half of the nineteenth century. The geographical and ethnic diversity just described is thus reflected in the archaeology of Islam, and discussion can be conveniently divided into three sections **(figure 3.1)**. In the east is the Red Sea coast and Beja country; in the centre, Nubia and the Nile region, stretching from Egyptian Nubia south to the Ugandan border and encompassing southern Sudan; and finally Darfur in the west.

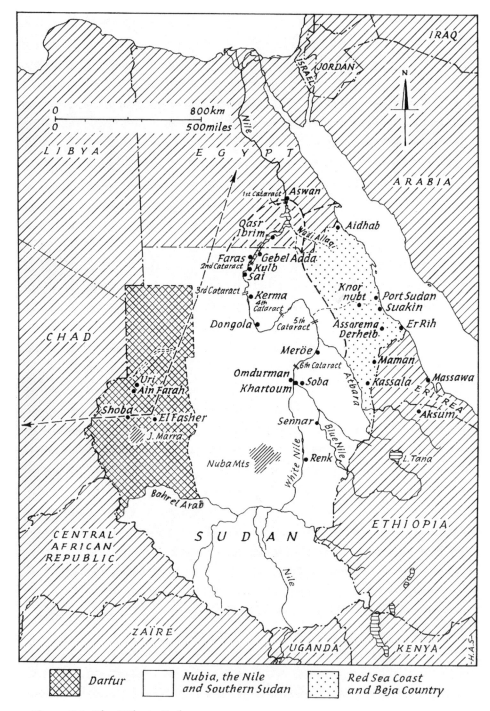

Figure 3.1 The Nilotic Sudan

Besides the convenience of being able to geographically divide the archaeology of Islam in the Nilotic Sudan, the variety of material found in this area, besides providing a general overview of Islamic archaeological remains in the region, also allows a range of case studies to be considered in detail. The fundamental importance of pilgrimage to Muslims, as one of the Five Pillars of Islam, has already been noted in chapter 1, and on the Red Sea coast of the Sudan one of the major pilgrimage ports of the medieval period flourished, Aidhab. This allows an insight into the archaeology of *hajj* in sub-Saharan Africa. The interaction between Muslims and Christians in Nubia has already been alluded to. It is equally possible to examine this archaeologically through the Islamisation of material culture. This process has already been referred to in chapter 1, as well as with regard to Christian–Muslim relations in Ethiopia in the last chapter, and in Nubia many continuities in material culture are also indicated. The break with previous traditions following conversion to Islam is not necessarily profound, as recent scholarship is illustrating, and this will be discussed.

However, having noted this point about cultural continuity, a further factor has to be considered within the archaeology of Islam in the Nilotic Sudan, that of Arabicisation as well as Islamisation. This too was discussed in chapter 1, where the point was made that outside the East African coast, it was only really a factor of importance in the Nilotic Sudan. In this respect it is important to note that what is being described as Arabicisation is a more thorough process of cultural replacement than that seen elsewhere in sub-Saharan Africa, where the term 'Arabising' has been used, as with regard to Somali and Songhai origins described in the last chapter. Manger, for example, who considers the process of Arabicisation in some detail, makes the point that it involves factors such as the replacement of local language by Arabic (1994:27), something he describes with regard to the Nuba, but which could equally apply to the Berti of Darfur (Holy 1991), or many other ethnic groups in the Nilotic Sudan.

Quite why it is of such significance in the Nilotic Sudan is due to a variety of reasons: ethnic politics and interrelations, notions of belonging, and because of the overriding threat of enslavement which was of periodic importance to many ethnic groups. As McHugh (1994:10) notes, 'identification with an Arab lineage was not a choice – it was the only choice. It was the badge of membership in the community of Muslim Arabs. In theory, adhering to Islam and being an Arab are entirely separate, yet in practice (in the Nilotic Sudan) there has been a fusion between them.' It is this issue of choice that sets the Nilotic Sudan apart from elsewhere in sub-Saharan Africa, including the East African coast, and this issue of Arabicisation will be considered below with reference to the Nuba. Finally, it is also possible to approach the processes of conversion to Islam through archaeological evidence with regard to the Funj kingdom of Sennar and the successive dynasties of Darfur, helped by the fact that this evidence can be considered alongside the limited available historical sources.

The pre-Islamic background

The pre-Islamic background in the Nilotic Sudan is one of some complexity and one which defies adequate synthesis in comparison to that which was attempted in the last chapter. Yet it is also important to emphasise that the degree of detail comparable to that provided on Aksum and its antecedents is unnecessary for the Nilotic Sudan. This is because the latter was not directly connected to the Arabian Peninsula in the same way, nor did it play such a major role in the shaping of Islam from the very beginnings of the religion. However, this is not to deny the Nilotic Sudan a past of equal significance to that of Ethiopia and the Horn. It had one, and in Nubia, for example, are found the remains of some of the earliest states in sub-Saharan Africa. This was a process which began with a period of Egyptian control during the Pharaonic Middle Kingdom, i.e. from the first quarter of the second millennium BCE, when several forts were built around the second cataract on the Nile (W. Y. Adams 1977). The subsequent succession of polities that occurred in Nubia is unnecessary to list here (but see Connah 1987 for a useful summary), though it should be noted that states such as Kerma, Napata, Meroë and the 'X-Group' or Ballana culture were indigenous foundations (the Christian kingdoms are considered below). They were subjected to varying degrees of influence from the north (see Edwards 1996; Török 1997; Wildung 1997).

These states prospered through trade with the Near East and Mediterranean world. This is something Welsby (1996:12) notes with regard to Kerma, for example, a state whose development in the third millennium BCE was spurred on by 'a rich source of materials to the south and of a massive consumer market to the north'. Exports from the south included gold, ivory and slaves, trade commodities of recurring importance in many parts of the continent during the later Islamic period. In return, manufactured goods were imported into the Nubian kingdoms – pottery, bronze and silver metalwork – and foodstuffs such as wine and olive oil (Welsby 1996), again broadly paralleling the patterns of later Islamic trade here and elsewhere in sub-Saharan Africa. Ideas and goods flowed along this 'corridor', as the middle Nile valley has been called (W. Y. Adams 1977), but the lack of archaeological evidence for influences extending beyond this corridor further into the Nilotic Sudan would certainly suggest, to quote Graham Connah (1987:25), that, 'on the basis of present evidence, it does indeed seem that the Nubian corridor, in spite of its impressive social developments, was a cultural cul-de-sac'.

The Red Sea coast and Beja country

The Red Sea coast

The earliest Islamic archaeological remains in the Nilotic Sudan are found on the shore of the Red Sea. These date from the mid-eighth century and match the types of site found further south on the same coast already noted in chapter 2.

Similarly, as with the Muslim trade centres on the Red Sea coast in Eritrea, the more northerly coastal trade centres in the Nilotic Sudan are physical testimony to trade patterns stretching far back into antiquity. Egyptian and Roman merchants had long had trade centres on the northern part of the Red Sea coast at sites such as Ptolemais Theron and Berenike (M. Horton 1987b; Hinkel 1992). Berenike, for example, has recently been the focus of archaeological excavation (Sidebotham and Wendrich 1998), and the cosmopolitan nature of this trading centre situated some 260 km east of Aswan on the Egyptian Red Sea coast was amply attested. Home to people from Nubia, the Nile, Arabia and South Asia, it was inhabited between the third century BCE and the sixth century CE, when its role was assumed by Er Rih and Aidhab in the Sudan. It was both a manufacturing centre (of glass, beads and metalwork) and a trade emporium, indicated for instance by fine wares imported from India. A further important site, actually in the Sudan itself (between Suakin and Er Rih), and which might also have been a centre of classical trade, is Akik. Crowfoot (1911:534) describes various remains he recorded there, including a large block of carved stone decorated with 'cyma, dentils, and fillet' and of 'Hellenistic rather than Roman age', along with Muslim tombs, and a monumental stele, 2.25 m high and mounted on a square plinth 4.95 m across. However, apparently this site has not been subsequently reinvestigated, so its classical provenance remains uncertain.

Trade, as on the coast of the Horn of Africa, was again fundamental during the Muslim period, and the primary reason for the presence of Muslims on the Red Sea coast. Nevertheless, it is also correct to say that in their initial phases of occupation the trade centres and ports that were established on the coast were largely divorced from the interior. These centres served as feeder stations for Red Sea trade, transshipping products from the Indian Ocean and Persian Gulf on their way to Egypt, and vice versa, as well as serving as collection points for products from the interior for addition to the trade networks (Hourani et al. 1995). Little direct influence was exerted on the interior. It was only later, with the growth in the Muslim community in the interior of the Nilotic Sudan, and with the expansion in east–west connections across the Sudanic belt, that the coastal traders became more closely connected with the interior through, for example, the slave trade and pilgrim traffic across the Red Sea, via Jeddah, to Mecca (Holt and Daly 1988). However, even at the beginning of the twentieth century the outlook of the Red Sea traders appears to have continued to be directed seaward. This is seemingly indicated by a point made by J. W. Crowfoot about the inhabitants of the port of Suakin, who notes that their 'interests are concerned with other Red Sea ports or even with Aden, Bombay and Mombasa almost more than with the mainland immediately behind them, which is held by nomads distinct in race and language and customs' (1911:528).

Among the earliest of the Muslim trade centres recorded on the Red Sea coast of the Sudan is the site of Badi on the southern tip of Er Rih or al-Rih island, some 210 km south of Port Sudan. This site, according to historical sources, appears to have been occupied from the mid-seventh century (Hebbert 1935:308). The first historical mention of Badi, a reference to the expulsion there of one Abu Mihjan al-Thagafi in 637 by Caliph Umar ibn al-Khattab (Kawatoko 1993b:189), also indicates that, like the Dahlak islands, it was initially used as a penal colony or place of exile. It would, however, appear to have fairly rapidly assumed an important trade role, a function it continued to maintain until the late twelfth century. Yaqut, for instance, described Badi in the eighth century as trading with the interior, a source of ivory and ostrich shell which was exchanged for 'medicines, perfumes and combs' (Crowfoot 1911:543). These interior contacts also appear to be indicated by a further mention by Yaqut that the people of Badi spoke the language of Ethiopia, al-Habashat (Nawata 1997:310), which might be a reference to Beja perhaps, and indicating a language of trade besides Arabic. The extent of conversions to Islam by the inhabitants of the interior at this time is, however, wholly unknown. More certain is that interior products were supplemented with those of the Red Sea, such as pearls, coral and tortoiseshell. A further commodity of importance was operculum, as indicated by thousands of empty mollusc shells from which it was collected, littering Er Rih island. The reason for its collection was that it is material which 'emits a pleasant smell when burned', and it is used in the manufacture of perfumes to this day (Nawata 1997:313).

Various other remains testify to the former prosperity of Badi, a settlement which, besides having a similar penal role to that of Dahlak Kebir, is also very similar in layout to the latter with a central area of coral walls and houses, backed by a chain of middens up to 10 m in height. North and east of these mounds are areas of cisterns, of various types, and described as covering an area about 'twice the size of the residential region' (Crowfoot 1911:543), likewise showing a similar preoccupation with conserving adequate supplies of drinking water in this arid region (figure 3.2). Further parallels between the two sites extend to the cemetery locations, which are similarly placed at a distance beyond the cistern area. These similarities are perhaps not surprising, as Badi is described in historical sources as being of equal importance to both Zeila and the Dahlak islands in the tenth–eleventh centuries (Kawatoko 1993b:189). This was a period of significance, again according to Kawatoko (1993a:203), because it correlates with the Fatimid transfer of their capital from Tunis to Cairo in 969 and the subsequent growth in importance of the Red Sea region as 'a main passage from the Indian Ocean to the Mediterranean' – a fact which will also seen to be of possible importance on the East African coast (see chapter 4). Equally, Crowfoot's (1911:546) assertion that this boom period at Badi correlates with a peak in activity in the gold mines of the Wadi Allagi region (see below) is also convincing as an explanation for the variety of archaeological evidence found at the site dating from this period.

Several excavations have been completed at Badi. Crowfoot excavated one of the middens and recorded 'the bones of domestic animals, shells, potsherds, glazed earthernware, and glass' (1911:543). Hebbert (1935) similarly excavated

Figure 3.2 Cistern types at Badi

a courtyard house built of coral blocks bonded with lime mortar and measuring
$c.25$ m^2. This structure comprised a main building on one side of the courtyard,
and subsidiary ones on the other, with a cistern in the centre – an architectural
style characteristic of the Red Sea coast and similar to structures also encountered on the East African coast, as will be described. Detail on small finds
is sparse, but these included the stone from a signet ring, an onyx measuring
12 mm $\times$ 10 mm $\times$ 2 mm and inscribed with a tree bearing fruit. More recent
excavations in a large structure in the centre of the site and on the western slope
of one of the mounds uncovered a variety of evidence indicating participation
in international trade as indicated in the historical sources. Among these were
fragments of Chinese whitewares and celadons of the tenth to twelfth centuries,
glass from Iran or Iraq, monochrome glass trade beads in yellow, blue and ver-
milion glass, and two glass weights, including one of transparent pale green
glass, bearing traces of Kufic script and possibly of Fatimid origin (Kawatoko
1993a:209).

Concrete testimony to the former presence of a Muslim community at Badi
was also provided by burials and fragments of tombstones found. Excavation of
a couple of graves 'brought to light the skeletons of men looking towards Mecca
in the most orthodox position of hopeful resignation' (Crowfoot 1911:545).
Crowfoot also recorded twenty-four stele fragments, although many of the inscriptions at Badi were rendered indecipherable through age (being carved on
coral). Three could be read and provided dates of 997, 1015 and 1037 (these were
of hardier black and grey felsite), with epigraphy similar to that of the Dahlaks
and Aswan of comparable age. These inscriptions followed a standard pattern,

beginning with the *Bismallah* and followed by a quotation from the Qur'an. Surnames which were recorded included one, 'El Mansi', meaning 'the forgotten', that is still in use in Egypt, while another appeared to indicate the presence at Badi of a family from South Arabia (Crowfoot 1911). Other inscriptions paralleling the Kufic epigraphy of the Dahlak islands bore dates of 997, 1015, 1036 and 1046 (Kawatoko 1993b:197).

The significance of Badi as a trade centre is thus well indicated by the archaeological evidence, especially for the tenth–eleventh centuries when it was probably influenced by events to the north in Egypt and through proximity to the gold mines in the Beja lands. The parallels with Dahlak Kebir are also striking: in settlement layout, in material present and in the funerary epigraphy found. Yet Badi was in the end only one of many trade centres which dotted the shores of both the Red Sea and Indian Ocean coast of East Africa. Many of these trade centres exhibit a similar range of material culture, but Badi is significant here, for it is still one of the earliest sites providing evidence for the presence of Muslims in the region. Yet it has to be remembered that their numbers would have been small and, at least until the mid-ninth century, they would have been largely confined to their coastal enclaves, again mirroring patterns further to the south.

Badi declined in the twelfth century for reasons which remain unclear; a lack of water, a shift in trade patterns and events in the interior, all are possible. What is certain is that the Red Sea coast of the Sudan was not abandoned but that trade shifted elsewhere on the coast. This is customary of a pattern in these coastal sites, defined by Crowfoot (1911:547) as a 'tendency of sites to shift slightly round a common centre in obedience to external conditions' – something apparent throughout sub-Saharan Africa, as with the sites of north-western and north-eastern Madagascar, for example (see chapter 4). Primary among the second set of trade centres was Aidhab, situated north of Badi and close to the modern Egyptian border. It prospered through general Red Sea trade in spices, pearls and Chinese porcelain, and in Egyptian commodities such as cotton, dates, sugar and glass (Paul 1955:64). But Aidhab also flourished through proximity to the Wadi Allagi gold mines (see below) and served as their port from the mid-tenth century (Hinkel 1992:56). This was a function supplemented by pilgrim traffic, as Aidhab was located in an ideal position to benefit from this business owing to its location opposite Jeddah, the port for the Holy Places of Mecca and Medina. Aidhab was thus economically multi-functional, but of especial importance was this *hajj* traffic.

Aidhab, like Badi, has been the focus of various archaeological investigations. These, besides providing information on the trade function of Aidhab, have also provided evidence for pilgrimage. The settlement covered about 1.5 km² and is situated on a coral ridge. It was divided into three distinct zones; the port itself; an area of coral houses linked with the port; and an area covered with ceramic scatters which was interpreted as the former site of nomad encampments (**figure 3.3**). Specific evidence interpreted as indicating the numbers of

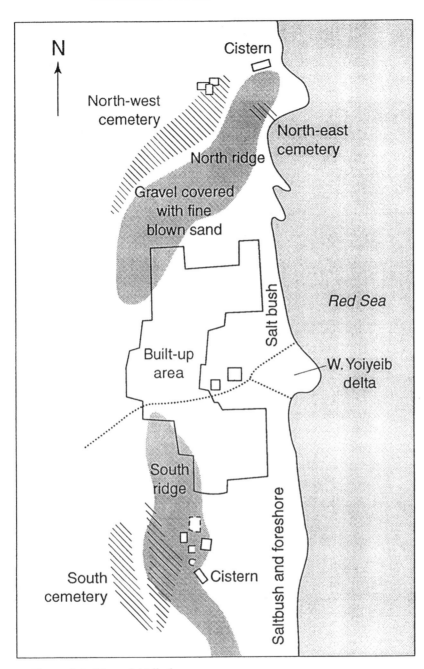

Figure 3.3 Plan of Aidhab

pilgrims who had passed through Aidhab included cisterns and wells (surprisingly few in number in comparison to Badi and Dahlak Kebir, for example) and, more significantly, extensive cemeteries – way beyond the needs of the local community. These were interpreted as 'ample reminder of the appalling death rate among the pilgrims' (Paul 1955:67). One of the cemeteries included what appears to have been a non-Muslim zone of burial, recognisable through grave orientation, and interpreted as the burial place of Jews or Coptic Christians (Elisséeff and El Hakim 1981:41).

Trade-related evidence which has been reported from Aidhab includes celadons whose quality 'is remarkable' (Paul 1955:68), along with green and blue glass from Egypt. Glazed pottery from Morocco or Islamic Spain has also been recovered from trial excavations at the edge of the town in an area used by caravans heading to Aswan and the interior of the Sudan (Elisséeff and El Hakim 1981:31). These sherds could be interpreted as brought by pilgrims from the far west of the Muslim world rather than indicating trade, as their presence is otherwise anomalous in this region. Though these wares are undated, black-on-yellow pottery from Yemen, similar to that from the Horn of Africa described in the last chapter, has also been excavated and ascribed a fourteenth-century date. Other dated wares found include Ch'ing Te-chen Chinese porcelain, Lung-ch'uan celadons, and coarse light green, and better quality white-on-blue marvered glass from Egypt, all of comparable date (Kawatoko 1993a:206).

Strong Egyptian connections are therefore indicated in the archaeological material as well as in the historical sources. Aidhab was connected to the Egyptian pilgrimage route to Mecca, which grew in importance after the land route through Sinai was closed by the Crusaders in the twelfth century (F. E. Peters 1994:90–1). Besides Egyptian pilgrims, this route also served the needs of pilgrims from the Maghreb, from Islamic Spain (as the sherds described above might indicate), and also any pilgrims who might have made the journey across the savannahs from the western Sahel and the western and central Sudan at this time. It is likely, however, that the numbers of West African pilgrims following this direct east–west route would have been low prior to its fully opening up in the sixteenth century (McHugh 1994). Instead, pilgrims from these areas of Africa would probably have travelled north across the Sahara and then along the coast of North Africa, as the Malian ruler Mansa Musa did in the mid-fourteenth century (Levtzion 1973, and see chapter 7 below). However, there is no reason to disbelieve that these African pilgrims on completing their arduous journey to the coast of the Nilotic Sudan would not have joined ships at Aidhab en route to the Arabian shore of the Red Sea.

By all accounts Aidhab was an unpleasant place, because of both the heat and the predations of the surrounding Beja inhabitants. Maqrizi described the inhabitants of Aidhab in the late fourteenth century as 'beasts, wild animals rather than men, and those pilgrims who survived the rigours of their treatment, and they were few, were as men rescued from the grave' (Paul 1955:66).

M. Horton (1987b:354) adds detail and mentions how the pilgrims were fleeced 'for everything they were worth...the poorer pilgrims were not uncommonly suspended by their testicles, in order to adduce additional payments'. In this context, perhaps the lack of cisterns noted earlier was a mechanism for charging higher prices for what water there was available. This dislike of Aidhab evident in the historical sources begins at an early date when, according to Paul (1955:64), the Persian poet Nasr-i-Khusraw made an enforced stay there in 1080, and throughly disliked the experience. However, the picture presented of Aidhab has varied somewhat. Ibn Battuta, who visited the port in the mid-fourteenth century, though not exactly glowing in his description, is neither unduly negative, describing Aidhab as 'a large town', 'well supplied' from Egypt, with Beja, 'black-skinned people', as its inhabitants. Ibn Battuta's main complaint was that the ships used for pilgrimage had been sunk in an ongoing conflict between the sultan of the Beja and the Turks (Gibb 1993:68–9). This latter act is thus reminiscent of the earlier sacking of the town by the galleys of the Crusader Renaud de Chatillon, Lord of Kerak, in 1183 (Paul 1955:65). Christian hands were not, however, responsible for the ultimate demise of Aidhab, which was eventually destroyed in 1426 by the forces of the Mamluk sultan Bars Bey as a punishment to its inhabitants for plundering a caravan carrying gifts to Mecca. However, by this time the gold mines of the Wadi Allagi were exhausted and trade had already largely shifted again, this time to Suakin (Paul 1954:76).

Aidhab thus provides an archaeological indicator of pilgrimage, much as Badi is representative of early Muslim trade. The third Red Sea trade centre that will be considered has just been mentioned, Suakin. This is a port which is also representative of the period of later Ottoman control, and thus important in this respect, as further evidence for this external power in sub-Saharan Africa, a power whose influence in the region has already been described in the last chapter. Although especially important as the major port on the Red Sea coast of the Sudan during the Ottoman period (Greenlaw 1995), Suakin is also of some antiquity. It is recorded historically as being on the route the family of the murdered Caliph Marwan took on their flight south from Egypt to Aksum in 750 (Bloss 1936:279). This suggests the presence of a Muslim community at Suakin, or at least a population amenable to Muslims, at an early date. Furthermore, it again indicates the hospitable nature of the rulers of Aksum to Muslims, a fact remarked upon previously. Suakin also developed as something of a rival to Aidhab in the twelfth century, eventually took over its role – as already noted, following the latter's destruction – and was controlled for a period by the Funj kingdom before becoming an Ottoman Turkish possession in the early sixteenth century (Hinkel 1992:57). From this point, as Greenlaw notes (1995:13), 'Suakin was, almost without interuption, under Turkish authority'. The Turks made it one of their major bases, improved the port facilities, and used it for their invasion of Yemen in 1629. It continued to be an important port up until

1902 when it was superseded by Port Sudan, 60 km to the north, thus continuing the cycle of use and disuse of these Red Sea ports which has been charted back into the pre-Roman period.

The abandonment of Suakin as a working port has left it as something of an open-air museum, albeit a poorly conserved one, with the 'remains of a small Turkish town built between the sixteenth and twentieth centuries' (Greenlaw 1995:8) standing on Suakin island and the neighbouring mainland. This fact has intrigued scholars, and fortunately a couple of detailed studies of the architecture have been completed (Matthews 1953; Greenlaw 1995; and see N. Lewis 1938 for photographs). The archaeology has been less well investigated, and little is known of its role prior to the Ottoman period. An exception is provided by Chittick's (1981) description of a cistern on Condenser island, one of the three islands in the Suakin lagoon. This structure, a roughly circular cistern *c*.6 m in diameter with a slightly domed roof supported by four circular columns, is, according to Chittick, possibly of Roman date. This observation was based upon the types of bricks and mortar used, 'unlike those observed elsewhere in the Sudan, and perhaps suggesting' that this is a relic of the trade of the classical world in the Red Sea (Chittick 1981:183). This is quite plausible and merits future investigation.

However, as stated, information derived from archaeology on the earlier medieval role of Suakin does not as yet exist. The later medieval town is built in what is described as the 'Red Sea style' (Matthews 1953), characteristic of architecture found until recently on both sides of the Red Sea in coastal towns such as Jeddah, Hodeidah and Massawa. The architects of the Red Sea style have 'always turned to the sea and sailors for inspiration and materials' (Matthews 1953:66). Dominant among the latter is the use of coral – madrepore – blocks of *Porites solida*, cut from the seabed when wet, thus easy to work, and then allowed to harden in the sun (M. Horton 1987b:359, 1994a). These would then be used to construct walls of roughly shaped blocks finished with lime plaster, with more carefully hewn coral being used for features such as doorheads (Matthews 1953). This construction style was also adopted by the Swahili on the East African coast (see chapter 4). Java teak obtained via the sea trade and mangrove poles from the East African coast were also utilised, as timber was largely lacking in this arid region. The buildings that were constructed were ideal for the extremes of climate in the region. They addressed both environmental factors and social concerns over the privacy of women and family life. This dual function was illustrated through the design of the *mashribiyya*, for example. Cooling breezes were obtained through the use of these slatted and grilled wooden balconies which were inserted at intervals in the walls, but they also served to allow women to observe the world beyond without themselves being seen (Oliver 1987:120–3, Insoll 1999a:64).

The overall design of the houses in Suakin and the other Red Sea ports also served this dual function through the use of the courtyard as a central feature.

This served to capture breezes and allow the structuring of social space over one or more floors (see Insoll 1999a). Typically, the reception area for male guests would be on the ground floor by the main entrance, with the family rooms on the upper floors, served by a second entrance. Furnishings would be sparse and in many ways similar to those already described in chapter 2 for the guest and family rooms in the houses of Harar. Alcoves for storage were cut into the walls; rugs, trays and cushions would be dotted around, with a coffee stove always present in the room used for entertaining male guests (Matthews 1953; Greenlaw 1995). Over 200 of these houses survived until fairly recently in Suakin, including two owned by descendants of the Prophet himself, house numbers 66 and 93 in the island settlement.

Besides the houses, a variety of other structures were also preserved largely as abandoned, though many are now in a perilous state. The information that was recorded prior to their complete disintegration gives an insight into the workings of this Ottoman port. Among these structures was the vast *wakala*, or caravanserai, a unique building within sub-Saharan Africa, being built on three floors and encompassing a central quadrangle of 40 m^2 **(figure 3.4)**. Within this courtyard could be accommodated, in the words of Greenlaw (1995:76), 'a large caravan of up to one hundred camels'. Also provided, as is characteristic of a caravanserai, which is a structure found across the Muslim world (see Sims 1978; Petersen 1994), were both quarters for the merchants and safe storage for their goods. The *wakala* was built by a leading merchant of Suakin, Shennawi Bey, in 1881, only a few years before the end of the working life of the port.

The buildings of Suakin were the culmination of the architectural styles developed in sites such as Dahlak Kebir, Badi and Aidhab, where coral was used and courtyard houses built. They were less grand than those at Suakin, but the Suakin architecture gives us an insight into what might have been added to the groundplan or wall stubs that survive at these earlier sites (Insoll 1998e). Yet even Suakin, as already mentioned, was to be eclipsed by the demands of modern trade. This, as Greenlaw (1995:78) notes, was a demise ultimately wrought by 'railways, steamships and modern dockyards'. It brought the culmination of pre-modern economic life for this series of Red Sea ports whose roots stretched back to the early years of Islam – and in some instances before, as we have seen.

The Beja

In direct contrast to the cosmopolitan inhabitants of the coastal trade centres were the Beja, nomadic pastoralists who occupied the country between the Nile and the Red Sea, from Aswan almost as far as Massawa in Eritrea. These people, the Blemmyes of the Roman period (Paul 1954:1), traded with Nubia, Aksum and the coast. They were not, however, initially at least, under their cultural and political influence, as indicated by Maqrizi's comment (1364–1442) that they were 'troublesome and aggressive' (Vantini 1975:623). The Beja very

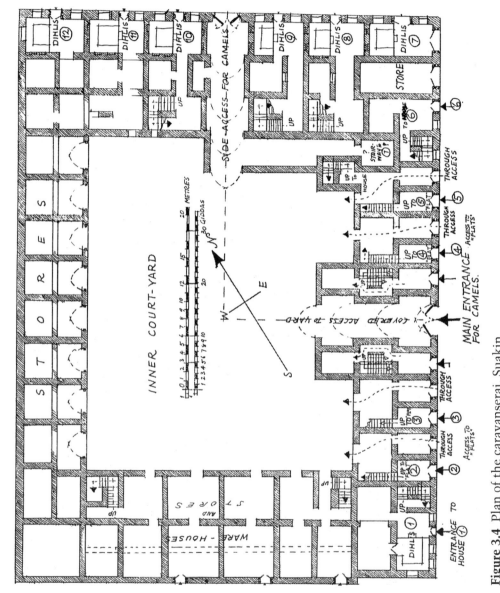

Figure 3.4 Plan of the caravanserai, Suakin

much exhibited their own character as the descriptions of their activities in and around Aidhab, cited above, indicate. Furthermore, as regards Islamic conversion among the Beja, at first glance the connection between trade and Islam, and nomads and early Islamic acceptance, outlined in chapter 1 would again appear to be apparent – but in this instance such an association does not work.

The coast of the Nilotic Sudan might have been home to Muslim communities from the mid-eighth century, but the interior, across most of the lands inhabited by the Beja, was not. Quite when Muslim contacts with the Beja began is not clear. Paul (1954:64) suggests that there was a slow infiltration of small numbers of Muslim Arabs into Beja lands from the mid-seventh century onwards, i.e. soon after the conquest of Egypt (see below). Archaeological evidence for the presence of some Muslims in Beja territory at a reasonably early date has been found at Khor Nubt, 90 km inland from Suakin. This comprised Muslim burials with inscribed tombstones bearing dates ranging from the mid-eighth to early tenth centuries (Paul 1954:68; and see Bloss 1936; Gridden 1954). These stelae are described by Kawatoko (1993b:198) as the earliest Arabic tombstones found in the Sudan. Quite why a Muslim community should have been present at Khor Nubt is unclear, but as Paul notes (1954), the settlement, according to the epigraphic evidence, had a life of over 150 years. Perhaps, as Hinkel (1992:207) argues, it was the centre of a Beja chief, as may be indicated by the remains of an undated mosque, rubbish mounds, well shaft, and ruined settlement also found.

Thus it would appear that some Muslims were in Beja lands, or some Beja were Muslims, from an early date, but Beja–Muslim relations were not always peaceful. Conflict with Muslim forces occurred on many occasions, and raids were launched by the Beja against Upper Egypt. Indeed, following one such raid, the Beja were defeated by a punitive force sent against them by the Caliph al-Mu'tasim in 831 (W. Y. Adams 1977:553). Following this defeat a treaty was imposed upon the Beja – not the first, but a much stricter one than those that had gone before. As Hasan (1966:117) notes, it 'shows a marked increase in Muslim influence in the region' and indicated that 'the Beja country from Aswan to the border between Badi and Massawa became the property of the Caliph'. Among other things, this treaty opened up the Beja lands for free passage to Muslims, though the relationship between the Beja and the Egyptian Arabs continued to be somewhat fraught, as indicated by a further Beja raid in 854, which reached as far north as Esna in Egypt, leading to another punitive mission and Beja defeat in a battle near Jebel Zabara (Paul 1954:68).

Conflict aside, it is also undeniable that over this time larger numbers of Beja were increasingly converting to Islam. This occurred both through a combination of contact with Muslim traders and with migrating Arab groups moving south from Egypt in search of new grazing lands. Possibly it also occurred because Muslims benefited from the matrilineal succession system in the Beja area (and elsewhere in the Nilotic Sudan), which meant that children of marriages with Beja chiefs became rulers (Hasan 1966:117–19; Hiskett 1994:67). This system was abandoned after the majority of the Beja converted to Islam in the fourteenth–fifteenth centuries (Paul 1954:78–9). Thus in this instance a variety of factors are responsible for the Islamisation of the Beja. It is not satisfactory to invoke a simple correlation between their being nomads, and thus Islam appealing to them for its ease of worship, for example, as might be evident elsewhere. Nevertheless, Beja adherence to Islam has been classified as patchy. Hinkel (1992:49) describes them as not showing 'much devotion to the obligations of Islam' – something evident, he argues, in popular practices such as cults of possession spirits (the Zar cult – described below), Muslim festivals being held at the tombs of important ancestors, and the use of human media to avert evil and cure sickness. These features, however, are popular both elsewhere in the Nilotic Sudan and other regions of sub-Saharan Africa, as has and will be described, and the Beja are not particularly special in this respect.

This popularisation of Islam by the Beja, as referred to by Hinkel, is evident materially. An example is provided by certain types of tomb which have been recorded. These include tower tombs, which have been described as 'local variations' of the Muslim *qubba* (domed tomb) (Newbold n.d.), as well as various circular and 'fishtail'-shaped tomb structures (Madigan 1922; Crowfoot 1922; Paul 1952). These tombs are found in the Red Sea hills and litoral, and Hinkel (1992:77), for example, lists twenty-three sites where tower tombs have been found, to which he ascribes a date of the late thirteenth–early fourteenth centuries. These tower tombs vary in size and shape. At Assarema Deraheib, for instance, they were built of dry-stone slabs in three stages with a flattened dome at the top and 'battlements at the four corners. The best-preserved example at this site measures 5 m in height and 6.6 m² at the base, diminishing to 3 m² at the top of the third tier' (Crowfoot 1911:549). The circular and other low-lying tombs also varied. Madigan (1922:81) describes one as built of dry stone and of 5 m diameter and 1 m height with a circular hole *c*.1.2 m in the centre. These were said by the locals not to be graves, but upon excavation were found to be just such. They were also interpreted as Muslim, as indicated by the orientation (sometimes careless) of the corpse, but also by the orientation of the monuments themselves, described as 'oriented on the direction of Mecca' and thus the 'tombs of Muslims' (Crowfoot 1922:85).

Some of the tombs do, or did, function as places of pilgrimage, being thought in many instances to contain the remains of saints. This functional interpretation was supported at some of the tower tombs by the clustering of other tombs around the central main structure, or the presence of prayer places nearby, as at Asafra (Hinkel 1992:180). This clustering, based on parallels elsewhere, was so that the deceased might partake of the *barakah* of the saint. Newbold (n.d.) further describes how the tower tombs at Deraheib Baanet and Deraheib Meisa were visited by local Beja groups and sacrifices offered at them at specific times during the seasonal round. This is reminiscent of the patterns already remarked upon for Ethiopia and the Horn. It is further evidence for *ziyarah*, the practice of visiting saints' and holy men's tombs, individually or in a group, which is found in many areas of the Muslim world (Insoll 1999a:113–14), and which was mentioned previously.

Besides punitive missions, inter-group contacts and intermarriage with occasional Muslim settlers, the Beja were brought into contact with the Muslim world through coastal trade, as already noted, but also through the presence in their lands of gold mines, as well as emerald mines in the Nubian desert. The emeralds were obtained, according to al-Ya'qubi (872–91), from two mountains called al-'Arus and al-Khasum (Vantini 1975:76). The whole area, which has had a long history of exploitation, was known to the Arab geographers as *bilad al-ma'din*, 'the land of the mines' (Holt and Daly 1988:16). Gold-mining activities in part of the region, the Wadi Allagi, are thought to have had an extensive history prior to the Muslim period, for it is believed to be the mining site represented on the Turin Papyrus dating from the fourteenth century BCE. Strabo (c.63 BCE–21 CE) also describes the mining operations in detail, and refers to the use of convict labour in the mines (Newbold unpublished). As Welsby (1996:12) notes, the gold mines 'acted as a magnet to the rulers of the north for three thousand years'. After a hiatus in working, possibly due to a lack of water or upheaval associated with the Muslim conquest of Egypt, gold mining in the Wadi Allagi was restarted in the ninth century, with possibly Badi, and certainly later Aidhab, serving as their ports. Gold production was interrupted in 854 by a Beja massacre of the Arab inhabitants of the mines, a further factor leading to the punitive mission already described, with production only restarting in 878 (Paul 1954:68,72; and see Castiglione and Castiglione 1998 for a summary of the historical sources).

The remains testifying to the millennia of gold working in the Nubian desert vary, and have recently been surveyed and test-excavated (Sadr et al. 1993, Castiglione and Castiglione 1998; Castiglione et al. 1998). This research led the investigators to make the point that 'the vast majority of archaeological remains recorded in the Nubian Desert are of the Medieval Period, and most of these are Islamic remains' (Sadr et al. 1993:116). These included graves of various types (e.g. low gravel mounds with head- and footstones, oval gravel mounds ringed by uprights and simple mounds with no embellishments), so-called 'medieval Aswani ceramics' (Sadr et al. 1993). Other features recorded included the remains of settlements inhabited by the miners (dispersed scatters of circular and rectilinear dry-stone structures, and nucleated apartment-style blocks of rooms) and the areas in which they processed the gold-bearing ore. Besides these features, the mosques used for their prayers were also surveyed (Sadr et al. 1993:123–35; Castiglione et al. 1998:43).

The Wadi Allagi was also focused upon during the recent investigations, with one site, Deraheib or Berenice Pancrisia (Castiglione et al. 1998:47), found to be of especial importance. This site stretched for 8 km along the Wadi Allagi

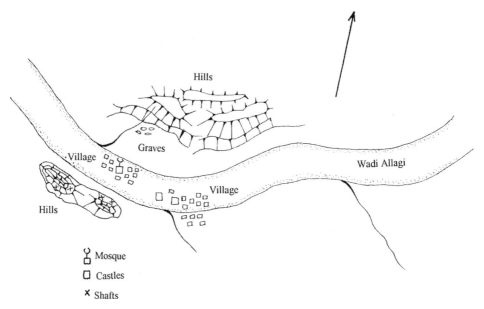

Figure 3.5 Plan of Deraheib

(Castiglione and Castiglione 1998:24). This was a site also investigated by D. N. Newbold over sixty years previously, and he describes the workings as consisting of numerous excavations made into two of the hills in the vicinity, alongside areas where the pounded rock was washed to extract the gold dust (Newbold n.d.) **(figure 3.5)**. The gold was extracted via shafts up to 50 m in length, 'in which wooden props were used to support any weaknesses in the adit' (Paul 1954:29). According to al-Hassan and Hill (1992:237) adit mines are a useful technique for finding and following quartz veins in which the gold is found. Following the extraction of the ores it is probable that they would have been dressed by crushing and milling, sifting and washing (al-Hassan and Hill 1992). Strabo describes earlier mining operations in the region in some detail and refers to the rock being broken up with stone mortars in iron pestles, with the poundings being further ground and washed by women (Newbold n.d.). Numerous grinding stones, as well as places used for washing the ore, the *'table de lavage'*, have been recorded at the site (Castiglione and Castiglione 1998: fig. opp. p. 40). The washing places from Deraheib seem similar to those recorded at other gold-mining sites in the Muslim world. As, for example, in the Negev area of southern Israel where in the Wadi Tawahin, 'the millstone wadi', small low-walled work stations for processing quartz ore to extract gold were recorded dating from the eighth to tenth centuries (Gilat et al. 1993).

The remains of two villages, presumably for the workers, were also recorded at the Deraheib site by Newbold (n.d.), as well as two stone-built castles **(figure 3.5)**. One of these was two storeys in height with gateways, towers and bastions at the corners, 'and a maze of rooms inside' (Newbold n.d.). The presence of the castles obviously indicates the importance of the site, and the need for defence in what were unsettled times. The villages themselves were composed of stone-built houses, along with a mosque and a cemetery. These are elements of the site also recently reinvestigated, and it was found that the Islamic-period occupation was distinguished by buildings built of schist rather than the granite of preceding periods (Castiglione and Castiglione 1998:23). Numerous potsherds were also recorded, including examples with green glaze described by Newbold (n.d.) as 'Chinese like Aidhab', indicating contacts with the Red Sea ports from which the mines were supplied. Rose (n.d.) also provides information on the ceramics recovered from the recent investigation of Berenice Pancrisia. These included Aswani wares of various types, as well as glazed and unglazed wares, produced in Fustat, also in Egypt.

The Beja thus provide another dimension to the archaeology of Islam in the Nilotic Sudan and one that stands in contrast to the trade centres of the Red Sea coast. This further emphasises the picture of diversity that exists within the archaeology of Islam in the Nilotic Sudan which was remarked upon at the start of this chapter. Equally, the archaeology of this region also differs from that of Nubia, its neighbour to the west, the next area to be considered.

Nubia, the Nile and southern Sudan

Nubia

Contacts between Christian Nubians and Muslim Arabs, both peaceful and aggressive, began almost immediately after the conquest of Egypt by Muslim forces. This was a campaign with an attractive prize, the Byzantine Egyptian province, whose allure included, as described by Lapidus (1988:39), 'her position as the granary of Constantinople, her proximity to the Hijaz, important naval yards, and a stategic location for further conquests in Africa'. It was a location obviously well suited as a launch pad for further campaigns into Nubia further south on the Nile. Thus the invasion of Egypt began under the initiative of the Arab general 'Amr b. al-'As in 641, a campaign which was largely complete by 643 (Lapidus 1988). However, this was not followed by the swift capture of Nubia as well. On the contrary, as already noted at the beginning of this chapter, relations between Muslims and Christian Nubia were maintained for several centuries under a specific treaty, owing to the military defeat of the Muslims by the Nubians. However, prior to looking at the treaty obligations, it is necessary to look at Nubia itself in a little more detail.

In Nubia statehood, as has also been described, was well advanced long before the appearance of Islam, or before the Christianisation of the region. In fact, Edwards (1999:96) makes the point that the 'scale of political integration achieved during the medieval period, never matched that of the earlier Kushite state'. The Christian kingdoms of Nubia thus differed from their predecessors as well as continuing the line of political authority previously described. Christian Nubia was first divided into three kingdoms, and later into two. The initial three kingdoms were Alwa, Makuria and Nobadia, though at an 'uncertain' date (possibly before the Muslim–Nubian treaty was signed, as the silence in this document as regards Nobadia appears to suggest it had disappeared by the mid-seventh century (Zarroug 1991:16)) the two northern kingdoms, Nobadia and Makuria, fused into one, Makuria, with its capital at Dongola (Holt and Daly 1988:15). Alwa, with its capital at Soba, continued as a separate political entity. The Christianisation of Nubia appears to have been achieved by the late sixth century. In Alwa, for example, the Byzantine bishop and church historian John of Ephesus records that the king converted in 580 (Welsby and Daniels 1991:7), with the Nubian church as a whole defined by W. Y. Adams (1996:24) remaining 'simply a territorial extension of the Coptic Orthodox Church of Egypt'.

Essentially, Christianity acted as a block to the Muslim conquest of Nubia for several centuries. But this was not achieved without political compromise, as evidenced by the aforementioned treaty signed between the Muslims and Nubians. The events that led to the signing of the treaty were precipitated by a Muslim invasion of Nubia in 652 and a decisive Nubian victory before the walls of Dongola. This was a victory which, according to Spaulding (2000:117), meant that 'for most of six centuries thereafter the Nubian authorities were able to impose their own terms upon relations with the Islamic world'. The effectiveness of the Nubian archers is well indicated by this description of the fighting by Ibn al-Khordadhbeh (c.885): 'the Muslim horsemen, led by him ('Uqba ibn Nafi) entered Nubia, but were met by the "pupil-smiters", and many (Muslims) lost their eyes' (Vantini 1975:69). The implementation of the treaty led to several centuries of largely peaceful contacts, commercial and otherwise, between Muslims and Christians. From the Nubian side, the best-known element of their treaty obligations were the annual delivery of 400 slaves, the *baqt*, to the Muslims at al-Qasr, about 10 km from Aswan, while in return the Muslims supplied them with certain foodstuffs and cloth (Hasan 1966; Vantini 1975). Thus another dimension to Muslim–Christian relations is indicated, adding to those already described in the last chapter, but again showing a certain degree of interdependence, albeit prescribed by treaty.

This was to change in the mid-thirteenth century, as although the first 'substantial Islamic political entity' (Hiskett 1994:68), the Banu Kanz, had been established south of Aswan in the eleventh century, this act did not have the impact on the Christian kingdoms that the events of the mid-thirteenth century did. What occurred at this date was that the Mamluks came to power in Egypt. One of the primary consequences of Mamluk rule for Nubia was that a breakdown in relations between the Mamluks and various nomadic Arab groups in Egypt led to the latter moving into parts of the Nilotic Sudan. These included Kordofan and the Gezira, and the effects were to further Islamisation and increase pressure on the Nubian kingdoms (Hasan 1966:122; Trimingham 1968:22–3). Allied with this was the defeat of the army of Makuria at Dongola by Mamluk forces in 1276 and the installation of a Nubian puppet prince, Shakanda, on the throne (Holt and Daly 1988).

Mamluks

In 1250 the existing Ayyubid dynasty in Egypt was 'overthrown by a rebellion of one of its own Mamluk or slave regiments' (Lapidus 1988:354). The last Ayyubid ruler was killed and replaced by a Mamluk officer, Aybeg. Mamluk rule lasted until the Ottoman conquest of the region in 1517, and the Mamluk era was renowned for its 'slave-military system' (Lapidus 1988:355). This meant that, theoretically at least, no one could be a member of the elite unless they were of foreign slave origin, usually Turkish or Circassian. The reason for this was that the Mamluks were raised and trained as property of the state and served the state accordingly with a great degree of loyalty. Mamluk military effectiveness was well illustrated by their military expedition into Nubia to install the Nubian prince Shakanda in 1276. A force composed, according to the Arab sources, of horsemen, regular and irregular soldiers, grenadiers and flame throwers defeated the Nubians at Dongola, in the process killing or taking prisoner 'ten thousand' (Vantini 1975:498). These captives were sold for 110,000 dirhems. The net result of the Mamluk expedition was that Shakanda was successfully installed on the throne in Dongola and the *jizyah* or poll tax was imposed upon the populace, as non-Muslims, but protected Peoples of the Book.

Thereafter, archaeology certainly attests to the disappearance of the Christian kingdoms. Yet prior to looking at the evidence for this it is useful to note a couple of points concerning Islamic archaeology in Nubia. This is a subject which has been reviewed by W. Y. Adams (1987), who, besides usefully dividing the region for the purposes of study into three Islamic cultural zones, also makes an important point, namely, that Islamic archaeology has been neglected in Nubia because its 'defining criteria' are 'almost negative: no monumental architecture, no religious texts or pictures, no carving, no fancy decorated pottery', making sites hard to identify 'and unrewarding to excavate' (Adams 1987:327). The latter point can certainly be disagreed with, but the former would appear to be largely correct. A paucity of material culture, as evident in a decline in the finds of bronze and glass (Adams 1987), would appear to characterise much of the post-medieval (as the Islamic period is sometimes called in Nubia) archaeology. However, this should hardly be a valid reason for neglecting Islamic archaeology, but it seems to have functioned as such, with money and resources invested in earlier more 'profitable' periods. Yet besides a paucity of material (though mosques and Muslim burials appear), a certain degree of continuity is also evident. This is something McHugh (1994:4) comments on with reference to Adams's work: that the latter 'sees little cultural and economic change from the late Christian period and even concludes that the Christian and Islamic eras can be regarded as a single phase in Nubia's cultural development'. Again this is a factor indicating that the archaeology of Islam in sub-Saharan Africa is largely one of continuity rather than of sudden imposition.

One site where change is certainly evident is at Qasr Ibrim, in part because it was home to a foreign (Bosnian) Ottoman garrison. Although not actually in the modern Republic of the Sudan (it is in fact situated in Egyptian Nubia, some 220 km south of Aswan (Alexander 1988:73)), it must be included on account of its importance. Qasr Ibrim also survived the flooding that has destroyed much of the archaeology of this part of the Nile during the building of Lake Nasser and the Aswan High Dam, and thus has been the focus of archaeological investigation since 1964 by the Egypt Exploration Society (see Plumley 1970; Alexander and Driskell 1985; Alexander 1988; W. Y. Adams 1996). In total the occupation sequence at the site covers a period of over 3,000 years, serving in its Muslim incarnation as an Ottoman frontier post between about 1560 and 1811 (Alexander 1988, 1994). This was a post which was initially garrisoned by Ottoman Janissary troops of Bosnian origin, for it was situated on a frontier zone where Ottoman authority ended (subsequently in the late sixteenth century this frontier was extended to Sai island further to the south (discussed below)) (see Alexander 1996, 2000). The Janissaries were elite troops recruited from slaves, often captured Christian boys from the Balkans who subsequently converted to Islam. Their effectiveness is illustrated by the fact that in the mid-eighteenth century, records show that the Ottoman state maintained over 113,000 Janissaries in total (Nicolle 1995:9).

Exceptional preservation of organics, including numerous Turkish and Arabic documents, has allowed detailed reconstruction of the life of the Ottoman garrison, and a clear differentiation can be made from the preceding Christian levels based on a variety of evidence. Qasr Ibrim was Christianised from around 500 CE, and by the eighth century it had become incorporated into the kingdom of Makuria, with its function described by Alexander (1988:81) as 'primarily a religious centre with a cathedral church, the largest in the region'. Irrigation agriculture was practised in the proximity of Qasr Ibrim and it was on the trade route to Egypt, with commodities such as slaves, dates, hides and cotton being exported north and finished items such as glazed pottery imported in return. Trade in this area of Nubia between Muslims and Christians was unrestricted, and excavations in the Christian levels provided evidence for this trade including ceramics from Lower Egypt along with a few sherds 'possibly Syrian or Anatolian, and a few sherds of Chinese Ming porcelain' (W. Y. Adams 1996:209).

However, relations between Christians and Muslims were not always amicable, for in about 1173 Qasr Ibrim was attacked by Muslim forces led by Shams ed-Dawla, and the cathedral and its library were ransacked (Frend 1996). This is a raid which is linked by Alexander (1988:83) in its wider context with the European holy wars, the Crusades, which interrupted the existing Muslim–Christian relationship in the Nile valley. The result of the raid was that the columns of the cathedral were toppled, and because material for reroofing was lacking it was left open with the burned manuscripts being buried (W. Y. Adams 1996:253). These, and other manuscript materials which have been preserved, have proved invaluable. They included physical evidence for the *baqt*, 'an exchange of letters between the eparch at Ibrim and the emir at Aswan' (Frend 1996:312) unearthed in a stone cist in a building interpreted as the governor's palace, and insisting from the Muslim perspective 'on the payment of tribute accepted by the Nubians' (Frend 1996). Besides the cathedral and the documents uncovered, the Christian community at Qasr Ibrim was also indicated by numerous small finds, such as crucifixes, palm crosses, fragments of icons and amulets (W. Y. Adams 1996). Even more spectacularly its presence was attested by the body of a bishop, Timotheus, found along with his testimonial letters from Gabriel IV, Pope of Alexandria (1370–8) (Frend 1996:308).

Although occupation continued after Shams ed-Dawla's raid, Qasr Ibrim appears to have been reduced in size. Frend (1996:310) suggests that when the Ottoman garrison arrived in the sixteenth century it 'must have found an abandoned or practically abandoned site'. However, occupation was immediately recommenced and much information can also be gained on this period of Muslim occupation as well. Again, the documents found are useful, and several thousand in Turkish and Arabic have been found (Hinds and Sukkout 1986; Hinds and Menage 1991). These included routine items relating to administrative matters such as pay dockets and commercial documents, as well as legal documents for land ownership (W. Y. Adams 1987:332), and also the contents of various Muslim amulets, which would have served a variety of functions – for protection from disease or attack, for example (Insoll 1999a:125).

Small finds were also informative. Numerous personal possessions such as pens, knives, shoes, bracelets, combs and locks were found, some of these of similar types to items recovered from the preceding Christian levels (see W. Y. Adams 1996) **(figure 3.6)**. Imports included Turkish tiles, Chinese porcelain and brick tea, as well as a 'magnificent silk Ikat pall' from Central Asia, possibly imported via Turkey (N. K. Adams 1990:12). Men's clothing found indicated that they wore cotton or linen trousers under a gown, the *galabiyah*, with a small round cap on the head and a turban to finish the costume. Women's dress was similar, a gown and trousers, with over this a *milayah*, 'large enough to wrap totally around the body, covering the head and touching the ground' (N. K. Adams 1990:8). Yet, as expected, differences were also evident, and the Muslim occupation levels lacked the obvious religious paraphernalia of the Christian

Figure 3.6 Personal objects from Qasr Ibrim

levels such as the palm crosses, iron and bronze crucifixes, and icons described previously.

The exceptional preservation at Qasr Ibrim also meant that many dietary remains survived. The general picture obtained in terms of the species present was broadly similar to other Nubian farming villages dating from the previous Christian period, with the bones of cattle, sheep and goat found, and wheat and barley winnowed on site (W. Y. Adams 1987:331). However, Simoons (1994:42) makes the point that one of the reputed first acts of the Muslims following the raid of 1173 was to kill 'all seven hundred pigs found in the community', and that pig-keeping in Nubia was 'abandoned' following the demise of Christianity. Certainly, the sorghum remains recovered during the excavations proved informative in setting the two communities apart. What was apparent was that the bicolor variety of sorghum ceased to be cultivated, though the cultivation of the durra variety continued when the change from Christian to Muslim occupation occurred in the sixteenth century. This was interpreted as due to the fact that the bicolor was more suited to the making of beer, and 'so the Islamic prohibition of the consumption of alcohol may be one possible reason for this' (Rowley-Conwy 1989:135). Several crops usually associated with the Islamic 'agricultural revolution' (Watson 1983), for example, sorghum, cotton and durum wheat, were also found in levels dated to well before the period of Muslim occupation, namely between 0 and 550 CE. This further indicated, according to

Rowley-Conwy (1989:137), that certain developments could have been disseminated from Nubia by Muslims (rather than brought in), or were developments which covered a wider area in the pre-Islamic period than known previously.

W. Y. Adams (1987:330) makes the point that by the seventeenth century Qasr Ibrim, initially a military outpost, with 80 houses, a garrison of 200, and 40 guns in the sixteenth century (Alexander 1988:86), was more like an ordinary town and commercial centre, 'albeit a fortified one'. Noticeable changes in how domestic architecture was configured were also evident between the Christian and Muslim phases of occupation. Characteristic double-courtyard houses were built in stone during the Ottoman occupation, with a clear subdivision into distinct male and female areas, forming recognisable public and private domains (N. K. Adams 1990). These certainly indicated a changed social pattern from that of the previous Christian and pre-Christian settlements, and have been interpreted as being built to conform to an Islamic model (Alexander 1988), as outlined in chapter 1. Later, in the seventeenth–eighteenth centuries, the site became more crowded and a degree of poverty was evident, reflected in a change in the domestic architecture with doorways blocked and partitions subdividing up the larger houses (W. Y. Adams 1987:331). Although pre-Ottoman buildings were not reused except as a source of building materials (N. K. Adams 1990:4), the cathedral was also converted into a mosque through the addition of a *mihrab* and mud-brick dome to the pre-existing building, thus changing the axis of the cathedral (Alexander 1988). In summary, W. Y. Adams' (1987:332) point that Qasr Ibrim 'was not simply a continuation of the Christian [occupation]' has to be agreed with, as a clearly defined change between the Christian and Muslim occupations is recognisable in the archaeological evidence. This is in part attributable to the fact that the inhabitants were not Nubians, but a foreign garrison – at least in the initial stages of Muslim occupation.

Elsewhere in Nubia, the continuity remarked on previously is evident, and this is something which is also apparent in aspects of religious practice and social life among different Nubian groups. This subject has been investigated by Kennedy (1978a) with reference to Nubian communities who were relocated in Egypt following the flooding of their lands in association with the building of the dam referred to previously. Funerary practices, for example, indicated aspects of continuity with much earlier traditions, as in the placing of a pottery vessel filled with water or durra (a type of cereal) by the side of the grave, interpreted as 'food for the ghost' and something which can be traced far back in the archaeological record of Nubia (Kennedy 1978b:232). Likewise, Boddy (1989:26) also describes a variety of ways in which continuity is evident in the northern Sudan. Bed burial, interment on an *angarib*, a frame-and-string bed, evident for example in the Meroitic period, continues in a modified form to the present; though rather than the dead being buried on the bed, as previously occurred, the deceased is now only carried to the graveyard on the bed.

Figure 3.7 Castle of *kashef*, Kulubnarti

Other examples exist and are described by Boddy (1989:26). These include the drawing of a cross in antimony sulphide on the forehead of the newborn, the making of ritual ornaments out of fishbones and palm fronds, and the recently discontinued practice of making three vertical cuts on each cheek, described as 'a motif found also on the faces of royalty depicted in Meroitic temple reliefs'. These are all throwbacks to earlier practices, and can be interpreted as ways of identifying with Islam through the inclusion of older elements, and again evocative of the first two phases of Eaton's (1993) model. This might also be further indicated in the practice of incorporating church buildings within mosques. At Qasr Ibrim, the reuse of the cathedral as a mosque might have been for convenience, but elsewhere such an explanation might not be so valid. Zarroug (1991:58–9), for instance, also describes the incorporation of a church into a mosque at al-Kurru, with the apse transformed into a *mihrab*, something which is not a unique instance either.

Space precludes an evaluation of all the sites dating from the Muslim period in Nubia, and selectivity has had to be employed – for besides the major fortified centres of Qasr Ibrim, Faras and Jebel Adda, which are situated above the Batn al-Hajjar in Lower Nubia, numerous other sites with Islamic associations are to be found. Fortunately, W. Y. Adams (1987) has reviewed this evidence and provides a convenient division of the archaeology of Nubia into three sections, with each described as exhibiting its own character. The first is the now flooded Kenzi or Kenzu region in northern Nubia, an area described as of orthodox deeply rooted Islam. South of this, between Kenzi and the Abri-Delgo reach, a zone with little archaeological evidence for Islam, is an area in which the Islamisation of the population was late in date, and where 'it never achieved any significant form of material expression'. Thirdly, and finally, south of Abri is 'the realm of traditional Sudanese Islam' (W. Y. Adams 1987:343) – in other words, as will be described at greater length below, Islam of holy men, saints and Sufism.

South of Qasr Ibrim in the second-to-third-cataract area (Batn el-Hajjar, Abri-Delgo), further fortified sites have been reported. At Kulubnarti, a fortified house or 'castle' (*kourfa*) was recorded on this island in the Nile, interpreted as having been taken over by a small Ottoman garrison who installed themselves in the 'stoutest of the Late Christian fortified houses and turned it into a small castle' (W. Y. Adams 1987:335). It was probably also the base of the local Ottoman administrative official, the *kashef*, when in the district (**figure 3.7**). Kulubnarti is also a site where the only 'overt' evidence for Islam were three ostraca inscribed with Qur'anic verses in Arabic (W. Y. Adams 1977:583), something which led W. Y. and N. K. Adams (1998:93) to remark that 'the archaeological remains at Kulubnarti, like those at Meinarti and Qasr Ibrim, proved incapable of shedding light on either the end of Christianity or the beginning of Islam'.

The fortified houses, one of which was converted at Kulubnarti, date from the thirteenth to eighteenth centuries, thus from both the Christian and Muslim periods. They are built of mud brick or mud brick on lower courses of stone, and vary considerably in size from 15 × 13 m to an average of 9.5 × 8 m, but are always two storeys high and square or nearly square in plan (W. Y. Adams 1994; Adams and Adams 1998). The *kourfa* are described by W. Y. Adams (1987:334) as adaptations of these, literally into small castles, through the addition 'of a walled compound and a bastion tower and parapet'. The presence of these fortified houses along the Nile illustrates the evident preoccupation with defence, certainly a factor in the Dongola reach south of the third cataract, a region beyond Ottoman control (Crawford 1951), and an area of robber barons (Iliffe 1995:56).

A sister garrison to Qasr Ibrim also existed in this area on Sai island, 180 km further south. Here, an Ottoman garrison was stationed between 1585 and 1798, as a result of the formal frontier agreed after the war with the Funj kingdom (discussed below) between 1582 and 1585 (Alexander 1996, 2000). The Ottoman garrison utilised the ruins of an earlier fort, which in turn was built over an Egyptian New Kingdom town dating from 1580–1050 BCE (Geus 1995; Alexander 1997:17). The existing bastions were also strengthened for their cannon. Sai has not been investigated to the same extent as Qasr Ibrim, but the results to date have indicated the existence of houses of 'conventional Islamic type', i.e. courtyard type, which have greater parallels with the architecture of Suakin than that of Qasr Ibrim – features evident in the use of plaster and the cutting of niches in the interior walls. A congregational mosque of about 12 m² was also recorded by the main gate, along with a possible barracks for the Janissaries (Alexander 1997).

Further south was Old Dongola, the capital of the kingdom of Makuria. This has already been mentioned with reference to the installation of Prince Shakanda by the Mamluks. However, 1316 was the turning point in the history of Makuria, as in this year a prince was installed on the throne who was not a Christian but a Muslim. Abdallah Barshambu had converted to Islam while in Cairo (Holt and Daly 1988:23), and his assumption of the throne in Dongola was, according to Hasan (1966:122), 'the hardest blow the Christian faith had suffered until then', and 'marked the end of the kingdom of Christian Nubia'. Al-Qalqashandi notes that this also marked the end of the payment of the *jizyah* or poll tax, as 'their kings had become Muslim' (Vantini 1975:573).

However, not all Nubians instantly became Muslims; the process of conversion to Islam was long drawn out and was still not complete when an Ethiopian monk, Takla-Alfa, visited Dongola in 1596 (Trimingham 1968:23). The 'wholehearted adoption of Islam came', as Trimingham further notes (1968:24), 'after the formation of indigenous clerical families'. Initially, the missionaries of Islam were foreigners, but soon local holy men acted as missionaries in spreading Islam throughout Nubia. The role of the holy man in this region cannot be overstated, and their importance has already been seen elsewhere, as in the Harar region described in the last chapter. As McHugh (1994:10) notes, 'the historical consciousness of Northern Sudanese Muslims is all but dominated by the Muslim holyman or Shaykh, also known as faqih or faki'. This, allied with the introduction of Sufism into the region, ensured the success of the religion, with the whole leading to the development of characteristic Nubian Islam with orthodoxy coexisting alongside 'the belief in saints and miracles' (W. Y. Adams 1977:574), the existence of Sufi orders (see Karrar 1992) and the incorporation of magical elements. This popularisation of religious practice was evident in many ways such as in the Zar possession cult described by Boddy (1989) – a cult dominated by women, and referring 'to a type of spirit, the illness such spirits can cause by possessing humans, and the rituals necessary to their pacification' (Boddy 1989:131). This possession cult, comparable to the Hausa Bori, has been described by Turner (1991:192) as preferable within Islam to the embodiment of spirit power in 'cultic image or object'. Thus these elements of popular Islam in Nubia and the northern Sudan are reminiscent of what has already been charted in Ethiopia and the Horn, and also outlined in chapter 1, and will be further seen across many other parts of the continent south of the Sahara.

In Dongola, the conversion of what appears to have been a church into a mosque was one of the material indicators of the change from a Christian to a Muslim state **(figures 3.8 and 3.9)** – an event which occurred, according to an inscription, in 1317 (Crawford 1951:34), and something which might have taken place for convenience sake, perhaps also for the reasons already described, or as a victory statement by the Muslims **(figure 3.10)**. This structure, which unusually has the remains of a caravanserai on the ground floor, has been investigated. It is situated on the north-eastern edge of the old capital and is built of sun-dried brick with fired brick used in a few decorative contexts. Four entrances were recorded and the building was some 25 m long × 15 m wide (Godlewski and Medeksza 1987). Traces of paintings were also found inside the building. They are somewhat unusual, and it has been debated whether they represent Moses or a Funj king wearing the characteristic Funj horned cap. The latter attribution seems more likely (Crawford 1951:35). Otherwise, little relevant archaeological research has been completed in Old Dongola.

In contrast, Soba, the former capital of Alwa, has been well investigated (Shinnie 1955; Zarroug 1991; Welsby and Daniels 1991; Welsby 1998). Ibn Selim al-Aswani describes a large Muslim community at Soba, which suggests 'substantial trading links with the Arab World' (Welsby and Daniels 1991:9) before Nubia was Muslim. Some evidence for this was found during the excavations, including cut glass from Iran dating from the tenth–eleventh centuries, and a glass assemblage which in general parallelled those from Aidhab, already described, and from Qusayr al-Qadim in Egypt (Morrison 1991:258). However, the Muslim quarter still awaits archaeological investigation, and the

Figure 3.8 Old Dongola church/mosque

Figure 3.9 Interior of Old Dongola church/mosque

circumstances surrounding the disappearance of Alwa are more 'obscure' than those of Makuria (Trimingham 1968:23), though it is known that Soba was in ruins by 1523 when it was visited by David Reubeni (Welsby and Daniels 1991:9).

The Funj

Although the kingdoms of Alwa and Makuria disappeared, their former domains were incorporated within the later Funj kingdom, an entity which provides yet another dimension to the archaeology of Islam within the Nilotic

Figure 3.10 Inscription in Old Dongola church/mosque dated to 13 May 1317

Sudan. The origins of the Funj have been the subject of debate. Arkell (1932, 1947) has suggested that the kingdom was founded by exiles from Bornu in the central Sudan (see chapter 6). This is unlikely, for, as Spaulding (1972:39) notes, 'orthodox Islamic historiography derives the Funj from Umayyad refugees; the more adventurous have proposed Funj origins in Eritrea, Somalia or Bornu'. More recently, Funj origins have been reviewed by Kleppe (2000), who is cautious in approach and not optimistic that they will ever be fully understood. Suffice to say that the Funj might have been a southern Nubian people with their homelands possibly on the White Nile in contemporary Shilluk country (Spaulding 1972). However, it is known that the heartland of the kingdom was at Sennar, from which the Funj rulers controlled a variety of provinces (O'Fahey and Spaulding 1974).

Besides Dongola and Alwa in the north, an area stretching from the Red Sea coast to Kordofan was for a time under Funj control between the sixteenth and eighteenth centuries (Hiskett 1994:69–70). Funj power, nevertheless, was based in the south, the source of the Funj army, with Sennar the linchpin as capital and a renowned trading city inhabited by a variety of foreign merchants from Darfur, Yemen, West Africa and Ethiopia (Spaulding 1985:113). Crawford suggests that, military reasons apart, Sennar was chosen as it was in the centre of the 'region of cultivators directly controlled by the king' (1951:77). It is probable that a royal residence was first built there in the sixteenth century when the permanent capital was established. This was the time of the legendary Funj ruler Amara Dunqas, a Muslim convert from either Christianity or traditional religion, who succeeded in unifying the formerly disparate lands along the Nile (O'Fahey and Spaulding 1974:28).

The archaeology of Funj Sennar has not been investigated in any detail. Crawford (1951:77–81) describes traces of a palace and mosque built of baked brick. The walls of the mosque were then still standing as it was kept in use until 1900, though the palace was only represented by mounds of brick rubble. Fortunately, the palace has been described by various visitors to Sennar, and illustrations which survive show an unusual multi-storey structure **(figure 3.11)**. The whole site is also described as being littered with numerous sherds of 'Funj ware' (Crawford 1951:78) decorated with a 'typical criss-cross pattern, incised, with rows of dots'. The gaps left by the lack of archaeological research are in part filled by historical sources, the most notable of which is the so-called Funj Chronicle (Holt 1999). This was compiled by Katib al-Shuna, the 'clerk of the government granary' who made the original draft before the collapse of the Funj kingdom in 1821 (Holt and Daly 1988:26; McHugh 1994:217). Trade as well as agriculture was important to the Funj economy. The gold trade was at the heart of commerce and was controlled by the government, while the ruler had the 'exclusive right to sponsor caravans to the outside world' (O'Fahey and Spaulding 1974:56). Another of the many items of trade were horses, which were bought by the Suakin caravans and shipped abroad, including to Yemen, where in the late eighteenth century the cavalry were mounted almost entirely on Dongola horses (Crawford 1951:64).

Outside Sennar the power of the provincial lords was also centred around their residences, which have been described as 'smaller, fortified versions of the palace complex of the sultan' (O'Fahey and Spaulding 1974:49). In Dongola the ruler's residence was built of 'unshaped stones', while others were built of mud, rectangular in plan, and employed one or more three- to four-storey towers. In the wetter southern regions where mud architecture would have been less suitable, thorn-fence compounds of thatched huts were built and used (O'Fahey and Spaulding 1974; Crawford 1951). Around the major castles would be quartered

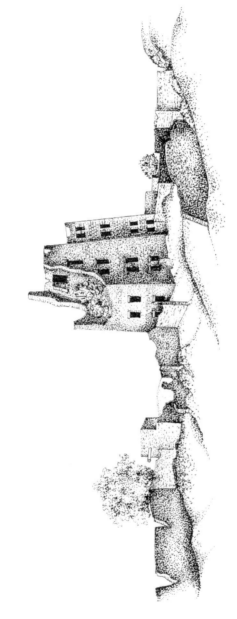

Figure 3.11 View of the palace of the rulers of Sennar

the soldiers – within them if these structures were small. Mixed units of foot-soldiers and horsemen were maintained. These soldiers were frequently well equipped with chain-mail tunics, which were both imported and made locally, as well as spiked iron helmets, while the horses were provided with quilted armour. Swords, javelins and lances were used as weapons, and shields made of elephant, buffalo or giraffe hide for defence (O'Fahey and Spaulding 1974:52–3). The use of cavalry by the Funj rulers in turn provides an analogy with how power was maintained in the central Sudan (see chapter 6), though it is not necessary to argue for any direct connection.

Parallels can also be drawn with elsewhere in sub-Saharan Africa when the Islamisation of the Funj rulers and the outward spread of Islam among the general populace is considered. O'Fahey and Spaulding (1974:32–3) mention that the Funj rulers had converted to Islam by 1523, and suggest the plausible interpretation that this took place 'in order to facilitate trade with neighbouring lands, particularly Egypt'. This is the first of a series of similarities which can be drawn between Islamic conversion here, and in the western Sahel, for example, where facilitating participation in trade was certainly an impetus for conversion to Islam in the first contact situation, as described in general terms in chapter 1 (and see chapter 5). Equally, the spread of Arabic following conversion as a common language of trade and administration has parallels with the situation elsewhere, as does the divine aspect of the Funj ruler to 'make live or make die' (O'Fahey and Spaulding 1974:43), exemplified in the manufacture of amulets in the capital. But as the piety of the kings grew, so they 'lost the aura of sanctity surrounding traditional monarchs' (O'Fahey and Spaulding 1974:87). The divine nature of the Funj rulers was gradually diluted, again mirroring what occurred elsewhere, as in the central Sudan (chapter 6), where divine kingship gradually declined in importance, as Islamisation proceeded or, alternatively, older elements were subsumed within Islamic practice. Features of divine kingship, such as those described in chapter 1 – divinity itself, the ability of the ruler to control nature, i.e. to make rain, taboos in or surrounding the presence of the ruler, such as not looking at them directly, or their speaking through a herald/mouthpiece (Hadfield 1949) – all began to disappear.

Even with the spread of Islam away from the elite, similarities can be seen in the processes apparent in both north-eastern and western Africa. O'Fahey and Spaulding describe Islam in Sennar before the seventeenth century as 'an exotic royal cult', with an unfamiliar language and associated with foreign traders (1974:72), factors which again parallel the situation on the other side of the continent, where initially Islam also appears to have been a royal cult, as seemingly evident in the kingdom of Ghana. Conversion was precipitated on a larger scale by the work of Muslim holy men, analogous to the process already described for Nubia, parts of which fell within the domains of the Funj. McHugh (1994:60–5) also describes how in this early period these holy men made use of a 'pre-existent geography of the spirit'. This was achieved by retreating to hills associated with ancient settlements, leaving sacred trees to grow around their shrines, integrating rain-making and medicinal functions within their ritual practices and even incorporating pre-Islamic symbols within their regalia – items such as the two-horned cap referred to earlier, or the six- or four-legged stool, the *kakar*, instead of a prayer mat at ceremonial occasions (see El-Zein 2000:35 for an illustration of a *kakar*). Through these mechanisms Islam was popularised and converts increased, utilising conversion processes seen to be so successful elsewhere.

Funj society can thus be seen to be a dynamic fusion of multiple sets of beliefs and practices. Yet although Islam spread amongst the Funj, this did not mean that the kingdom was inviolable: it was not, and it too, like its predecessors, declined, and finally disappeared following the Turco-Egyptian occupation of Sennar in 1821 (Holt and Daly 1988; Hiskett 1994). The ultimate result of this occupation was that the ruler of Sennar, once so powerful, became little more than a tax collector for this new administration (Crawford 1951:275).

The southern Sudan

It is possible to think that with the Funj the southern extent of Islamisation in the Nilotic Sudan has been reached, a notion sometimes supported in the literature, as for example by Trimingham (1949), who places the border between Muslims and non-Muslims in the southern Sudan at Banjang, near Renk, on the White Nile. But such a defined boundary is too constricting, and Islamisation today is certainly an ongoing process, exemplified in part by the long-running and none too clear-cut conflict taking place in the Nilotic Sudan between the northern government forces and those of the south. This conflict has its roots, according to Beswick and Spaulding (2000:xiii), in 'the continual transference of wealth from the country's extremely wealthy southern heartlands into the hands of an elite few who reside in the impoverished north'. Similarly, it might seem that an evaluation of Islamisation in the southern Sudan is the realm of the anthropologist, or at best the ethnoarchaeologist; yet the reverse is true, as Islam has a considerable time depth in many areas of the region. This again illustrates that there are few areas in the continent untouched by the religion or its adherents in one form or another.

Among the Nuba, for example, usually cited as wholly non-Muslim, Islamic influence has been present for several centuries, and it would appear that knowledge of the Nuba existed in the Muslim world prior to the first direct contacts. Ibn Hawqal (c.988), for instance, in his *Surat al-Ard*, 'The Picture of the Earth' (Levtzion and Hopkins 1981:43), refers to a 'nation known as the mountain people who are subject to the king of Dongola' (Stevenson 1984:34). As A. P. Davidson (1996:xiv) notes, the Nuba were 'never isolated from the forces shaping the world'. However, besides some data collected on rock paintings and burials, and some ethnoarchaeological research completed in their homelands (see, e.g., Hodder 1982), archaeological work in the Nuba mountains, an area about the size of Scotland, is still in its infancy. Thus Nuba history is somewhat difficult to reconstruct from the available sources (Stevenson 1963, 1984).

One area that was Islamised from a comparatively early date was the Tegali hills in the north-east of the Nuba mountains. Here a kingdom developed from the early sixteenth century, a kingdom described by A. P. Davidson (1996:62) as a 'tributary fiefdom' of Funj Sennar, but which existed in semi-autonomy until the period of the Anglo-Egyptian condominium starting at the end of the nineteenth century (Holt and Daly 1988:9). Islam was introduced to Tegali, according to tradition, by a holy man, Muhammed al-Ja'ali, who came to preach Islam in about 1530, married the chief's daughter and founded a dynasty, thus following the pattern of a legend found across the savannahs (Stevenson 1984:36). Undoubtedly there is an element of myth or at least 'tradition building' evident in this story of the 'wise stranger', but trade certainly meant that Muslim merchants travelled south from towns such as Dongola. They even established settlements in the Nuba mountains, as at Sheibun in the late eighteenth century, a centre used to exploit the goldworkings in nearby Tira (Stevenson 1963:10, 1984:41).

Yet the Nuba were also the subject of extensive slave raids, which led to massive population displacement and retreat into the more inaccessible areas of the hills, to caves and other recesses, 'which can still be seen, for example, in Tegali, in Heiban, or in the Nyimang Hills' (Stevenson 1984:6). These slave raids occurred during the Funj period, and subsequently raids were also launched by the rulers of Darfur who supplanted the Funj as the dominant power in the Nuba mountains in 1790 (A. P. Davidson 1996:66). However, they increased in scale during the earlier Turco-Egyptian period from 1821 to around 1850, when Western pressure caused a decline in slave raids which restarted at the end of the nineteenth century during the subsequent Mahdist period. In fact, Stevenson makes the point that the slave raids were somewhat, perversely, 'a powerful influence in breaking up tribal life and so aided Islam' (1984:51).

The Nuba mountains were the focus of well-organised slave raids as they were one of the Fartit lands. 'Fartit' was, according to O'Fahey (1982:77), 'one of a number of generic and generally pejorative terms used by the savannah Muslims to describe the stateless, non-Muslim and therefore enslaveable peoples of the wetter lands below them'. Besides the Nuba, other Fartit lands included Janakhira below Wadai in the central Sudan, Kirdi below Bagirmi and Bornu in the same area (see chapter 6), and Turuj below Kordofan in the Nilotic Sudan (O'Fahey 1982; Levtzion 1985b). Interestingly, the terms 'mountain people' or 'rock people' were also used to describe these other groups as 'people who live on top of hills or rocks are likely to be pagan and therefore enslaveable' (O'Fahey 1982:77). This description, as will be considered in chapter 7, can also be extended to the Dogon of Mali as well. Certainly, as Reyna (1990:25) notes, these terms were powerful, as with the Bagirmi use of the label *kirdi* 'as a frightful curse, one that classified someone as semihuman'. With regard to the Nuba, a stigma of slavery persists in the defensive location of Nuba villages on the slopes of mountains, and in the term 'Nuba' itself. Both function as reminders of their past role as a source of slaves. These issues of Islamisation and cultural identity are considered among one contemporary Nuba group, the Lafofa Nuba, by Manger (1994:20), who describes how in part because of this stigma, Arabicisation and Islamisation are proceeding as a way of expunging it.

Yet although Manger (1994) presents a picture of cultural subordination among the Lafofa Nuba, of wanting to belong through Arabicising their culture, other scholars indicate that Muslim practice among other Nuba groups amalgamates older practices and beliefs, thereby popularising Islam to suit local needs in ways that are familiar from elsewhere. As A. P. Davidson (1996:115–16) notes, 'Allah may be the One God – few Nuba would bother to dispute this – but this in no way depreciates the universal oneness or connection with nature experienced by the Nuba at a deeper level'. This is a reference to the types of traditional religious practice described by Stevenson (1984:113–17), as, for example, among the Nyimang Nuba who had a belief in a high god, Abradi, the creator, who is rarely addressed in prayer. Instead, intermediaries existed, of the type outlined in chapter 1 and discussed by Mbiti (1975:62). These formed the focus of religious practice, contacted through spirit mediums, and comprised three tiers of spirits, the *kuuni* – spirits of human origin, non-human origin and also minor spirits of features such as rocks and caves. These, along with the hereditary office of the rain-maker, were some of the (admittedly simplified) main features of Nyimang Nuba traditional religion. Elements of these, notably rain-making, might be appropriated by Muslim holy men, and integrated with Islamic practice, in the inclusive process already described, as among the Funj previously.

Elsewhere in the southern Sudan archaeological evidence of relevance to our purposes here is similarly lacking – again, in part, due to a lack of research. As Phillipson (1981:4) notes, prior to the British Institute in Eastern Africa (BIEA) project in the southern Sudan in the 1970s (the last major research in the region, owing to the civil war), only a couple of other sites had been recorded, these being Iron Age occupation mounds around Wau. The BIEA project did not record anything of relevance to our purposes either, but ethnographic and anthropological sources indicate that the influence of Islam is widespread. Jedrej (1995), for instance, in his study of the Ingessana of the Ingessana hills located between the Ethiopian highlands to the east and the grassland plains of the Upper Nile to the west, attests to this. The Ingessana were also the focus of slave raids, being another non-Muslim hill people. But although they remain almost wholly non-Muslim, elements of their ritual practice have been influenced by Islam, as with the identification of their feasts with Muslim ones (Jedrej 1995:34).

Similarly noticeable Muslim influences can be seen among the pastoralist Dinka who live in the savannah of the southern Sudan. Ryle (1982), for example, describes a funerary ceremony among the Panya, a sub-group of the Agar Dinka where an imam was asked to officiate at the funeral, which also incorporated traditional religious and Christian elements. His function included supervising the wives rubbing the corpse with butter oil and wrapping it in a papyrus mat, then leading the mourners to the grave and directing prayers for the Muslims there. These fairly standard elements of Muslim funerary practice (see chapter 1) were integrated with, among other things, the sacrifice of chickens, sheep and bulls, aspects of Dinka traditional religion described by Ray (1976:53) as 'centred upon prophet-led cults of a few major sky-divinities related to the supreme god Nhialic, and upon totemic clan spirits'. Almost certainly a trawl though other ethnographies of the southern Sudan would indicate further Muslim influence in the region, as indeed might also be attested archaeologically once research can resume.

The Mahdi

A further aspect of the archaeology of Islam in the Nilotic Sudan is represented by the residue of the Mahdist era. This is also representative of the wave of Islamic reform which swept across parts of the western, central and eastern savannahs in the nineteenth century (see also chapter 7). The Mahdist state has been described by Hiskett (1994:72) as a 'stark Islamic theocracy, modelled on early Prophetic precedents'. It began as an uprising against Anglo-Egyptian rule, when in 1881 Muhammad Ahmad, an Arab from Dongola, declared himself 'al-Mahdi', the 'divinely guided one' (Holt 1979:23), and an apostle of the Prophet. *Jihad* was preached in this, one of the final shows of Islamic opposition to European (and Egyptian) rule. Initially, the Mahdist base was in Kordofan, and following the morale boosting capture of the provincial capital, El Obeid, in 1883, other victories ensued, including the destruction of an Egyptian force under Hicks Pasha in the same year and the seige of Khartoum and the killing of General Charles Gordon in 1885 (Knight 1989:24). Although the Mahdi died in the same year he was replaced by the Khalifa, Abdullahi, who consolidated and expanded on the Mahdist gains. Ultimately, in 1896, the British reconquest began with the Mahdist forces defeated at the battle of Omdurman in 1898, and the Khalifa killed in November 1899 at Umm Diwaykarat (Knight 1989).

Having stated that the residue of the Mahdist era provides a further dimension to the archaeology of Islam in the region, we must note that this remains to be fully investigated. The most significant site is Omdurman, to which the Mahdist headquarters were transferred as the Mahdi disliked Khartoum (Holt and Daly 1988) **(figure 3.12)**. Holt (1979:249–50) mentions that one of the gateways of the great wall surrounding Omdurman survives. Within the wall were

Figure 3.12 Modern dervish festival, Omdurman

a number of structures including the Mahdi's domed tomb which still survives, as well as the Khalifa's house alongside it. Other buildings in Omdurman included the treasury, arsenal, slave market, prison and, to the west, the main market subdivided by trades and commodities sold – in other words, all the prerequisites of the state. Besides the monuments of Omdurman, various other sites across the region survive from the Mahdist period. Hinkel (1992:290, 293), for example, describes a couple of sites associated with the 'Prince of the East', Osman Digna, the Mahdist leader in Beja territory. These include the remains of an enclosure used for group prayers at Tamai, and Digna's tomb at his former headquarters at Erkowit. In summary, this facet of Islam in the Nilotic Sudan has also left its mark on the archaeological record.

Darfur

The final geographical unit to be considered in this review of the archaeology of Islam in the Nilotic Sudan is Darfur. This is a region in the far west of the country which covers some 190,000 km², and which takes its name from the Fur ethnic group who inhabit the centre of Darfur and are one of the 'oldest' ethnic groups in Darfur (Balfour-Paul 1955:8; Mohammed 1986:9). Although certain elements comparable with those of the central Sudan were isolated when the Funj were considered, such as the extensive use of armoured cavalry, Darfur can be said to be much more central Sudanic in character and thus presents yet another dimension to the archaeology of Islam in the Nilotic Sudan. Largely ethnically divorced from Nubians, Arabs, Beja and the many ethnic groups of the southern Sudan, it forms part of the great sweep of savannah stretching westward as far as Mali (**figure 3.1**). This is a fact not only illustrated environmentally but also demographically, as some of the ethnic groups in Darfur (e.g. Zaghawa, Masalit) extend into neighbouring Chad (Tubiana 1964; Mohammed 1986; Tobert 1988).

Equally, the immigration of both West and central African ethnic groups into Darfur – Hausa, Kotoko, and Fulani, for example – and the existence of the volcanic mountain range, the Jebel Marra, in the centre of the region, have further strengthened its connections with Africa to the west, and served to mark the 'effective limit of Arabization from the east' (O'Fahey 1980:2). It should be noted, however, that Arabicisation is certainly a factor in Darfur today, as among the Berti (Holy 1991), and Arab origins and 'pedigrees' have been claimed by other principal non-Arab ethnic groups of Darfur since they converted to Islam (Balfour-Paul 1955:7). Yet prior to the modern era it is difficult to divorce the archaeology of Islam in Darfur from that of the central Sudan, and it can in many respects be considered as a continuation of the same. However, it is not necessary to go as far as Arkell (1966:213) in suggesting that Darfur was ever a province of Borno to the west. As Mohammed notes (1986:6), such 'diffusionist' approaches cannot be supported. An affinity with the central Sudan is evident in Darfur, but that does not mean that developments such as statehood need be attributed to outside or to the Islamic period. On the contrary, as Holy (1991:17) notes, the 'Darfur sultanate was the heir of earlier pre-Islamic state formations'. It is also worth noting that we are fortunate in that the archaeology of Islam in Darfur is rather better known than that of adjacent countries, and indeed of many of its neighbouring regions in the Nilotic Sudan, as with Kordofan to the east.

When exactly the beginnings of Islamic influence in Darfur can be said to start is not certain. Hiskett (1994:70) describes the area as an 'indeterminate frontier', only faintly Islamised until the early nineteenth century. Mohammed (1986) is more exact: he places the beginning of Islamic influence in Darfur at about 1000, with three phases of Islamisation being apparent. A three-phase system further correlated by Holy (1991) with that developed by Fisher, and discussed in chapter 1. The first phase described by Mohammed (1986) covers the period between 1100 and 1600. This was an era when Darfur was ruled by two different dynasties, the Daju (tenth–late twelfth centuries) and the Tunjur (c.1200–1590), a period when Islam appears to have been of little importance. The non-Muslim character of Darfur at this early date would appear to be supported in the Arabic sources if the identification of the Tajawin with Darfur is correct, for al-Idrisi (d. 1153) describes Tajawa, the capital city of this ethnic group between Kanem and Nubia, as non-Muslim (Mohammed 1986:3).

Archaeological evidence supports this pattern, material remains being non-existent for Islamisation under the Daju, but slightly more informative for the Tunjur (Arkell 1946). At Uri, the first Tunjur capital, a stone mosque, possibly dating from around 1200, was recorded; this, it has been suggested, may be an indicator of the adoption of Islam as the court religion (Balfour-Paul 1955:18). This structure, which was missed in the dense bush by Arkell (1946) during his survey, is of a roughly 30 m-square plan, and according to Balfour-Paul (1954a:140) is unique in 'imperial Fur architecture' in its use of an unroofed central court. The whole settlement is described by the same author as a 'startling city' (1955:11), being surrounded by a stone wall except where natural features made it unnecessary. Within the wall was a further inner citadel of buildings surrounded by their own wall of 2–3 m thickness and 150 m diameter (Arkell 1946:187). This citadel, besides the mosque, contained a ruler's palace and audience platform. A similar platform was found in another structural complex, the upper palace, to which the ruler eventually shifted. Here the audience platform was constructed of stone walls about 5 m in height which enclosed a rock cube and five pillars, which were interpreted as the supports for a wooden floor (Arkell 1946:188). It is possible that the king, of probable divine status (as discussed below), would have appeared to his subjects here.

The face of the peak at Uri was also covered with Tora houses. These Tora houses are one of the unusual and distinguishing features of Fur architecture, and structures which continued to be built under the successive Keira dynasty.

Tora houses were usually built of dry-stone facings and rubble cores and composed of multiples of round huts with flat roofs and surrounded by a ring-wall pierced by two opposite entrances (Mohammed 1986:21). They could vary from three to four interconnected units for a chief to much larger palace complexes for the king, as with the upper palace at Uri (Balfour-Paul 1955; Arkell 1937, 1946). Uri was situated on two important trade routes, the Darb el-Arbain, the forty-day road from the Bahr al-Ghazal to Egypt (Balfour-Paul 1955:1), and another route leading via Gatrun and Murzuk to Tripoli in Libya (Arkell 1946:201) (figure 3.13). A few items obtained via long distance trade were found in a burial ground near Uri, including carnelian beads apparently originating from Cambay (Khambhat) (Arkell 1946:193, and see chapter 5). Whether these graves are of Muslims is unclear. They were lined with masonry and roofed with flat stones, with the bodies oriented north–south, 'apparently facing east' (Arkell 1946:194). Elsewhere in Darfur, Mohammed (1986:71, 209) describes pre-Islamic burials he recorded in the Tagabo range as comprising a cairn superstructure of 1–2 m diameter and 50 cm depth, with the body placed in a pit 2 m long × 80 cm wide in a tightly contracted position. These burials possibly date from the ninth–fourteenth centuries, and are situated in what is traditionally regarded as the original homeland of the Berti ethnic group (Holy 1991:13).

The capital of the last Tunjur ruler, Shau Dorshid, at Ain Farah is a further important site. Here, besides the stone-built round Tora huts, a red-brick 'palace-citadel' and mosque were recorded (Arkell 1936b; de Neufville and Houghton 1965). This mix of traditional and Muslim architectural elements could be interpreted as symbolic, as indicating the adoption of Islam within the context of the court, as could the juxtaposition of the palace on a ridge slightly above the mosque (figure 3.14). The mosque of Ain Farah was more centrally placed than that of Uri, and was 'powerfully constructed of brick and buttressed externally in stone' (Balfour-Paul 1955:13). Here a *diwan* or audience chamber, a structure with glazed windows (Arkell 1936b), was used for affairs of state. This too might indicate the progressive Islamisation of the Tunjur court, with facets of Islamic administration now found, as the *diwan* could indicate. The total settlement covered an area of about1.5 × 1 km, with over 200 stone huts and numerous animal pens also recorded, and was sited there both because of defensive considerations and because of the presence of one of the few springs in the region (de Neufville and Houghton 1965:197).

In the subsequent second phase of Islamisation, i.e. from 1600 to 1800, Darfur was ruled by the Keira (Fur) dynasty, which was certainly Muslim (Mohammed 1986:224). Trade flourished again via the Darb el-Arbain to Egypt and, following the recently established pilgrim route, across the savannahs of the central Sudan to West Africa. The first of the Keira Fur sultans, Sulieman Solong, is generally credited with encouraging the spread of Islam (Balfour-Paul 1955:18). According to local tradition, it is his palace that has been identified in the Jebel Marra, and investigated archaeologically (Arkell 1937). This was

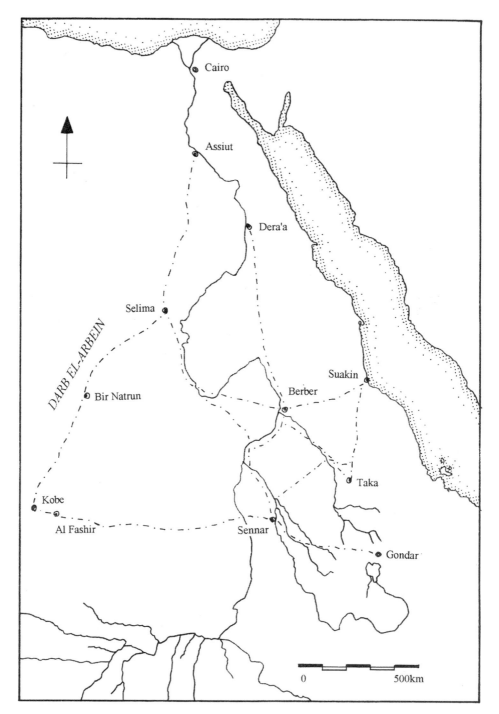

Figure 3.13 Caravan routes to Darfur

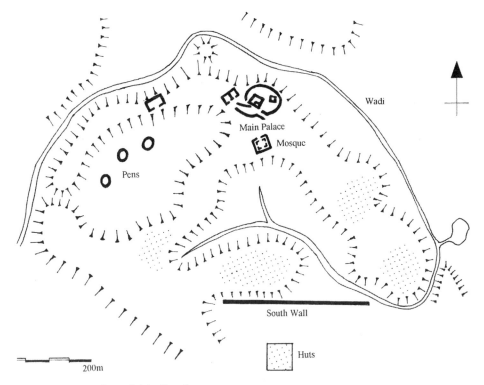

Figure 3.14 Plan of Ain Farah

an impressive construction comprising inner and outer dry-stone compounds,
the whole surrounded by a wall which survived to 3 m in height and which
was in places of equivalent thickness. This palace or *fashir* was one of a number built where needed until a permanent capital was constructed at al-Fashir
in 1791–2 (O'Fahey 1980:24). The layout of these *fasher* have been described
as illustrating 'succinctly the political and spiritual order within the state', as
basically the residence of a divine king, 'to some degree modified by the needs
of the new Islamic order' (O'Fahey and Spaulding 1974:146); in other words, a
further Islamised development from the palaces of the Tunjur rulers just described. It also parallels the type of conceptual notions that underlay some of
the rulers' palaces of the central Sudan, those of tradition and Islam, as perhaps
best exemplified by the palaces of Wadai or Bagirmi (see chapter 6).

Further important Keira sultans' palaces have been recorded at Old Shoba.
Here 'large' and 'small' palaces and a mosque were recorded, with the large
palace attributed to Sultan Teirub (c.1752–87) (Balfour-Paul 1954b; Reed 1994).
This palace complex comprised thirteen ground-floor rooms set around a courtyard measuring 17 m × 25 m. It was set within a maze of stone walls too low
to be defensive and interpreted as designed 'to confuse or impress the visitor, animal or human, and to divide off the women's quarters and the huts of

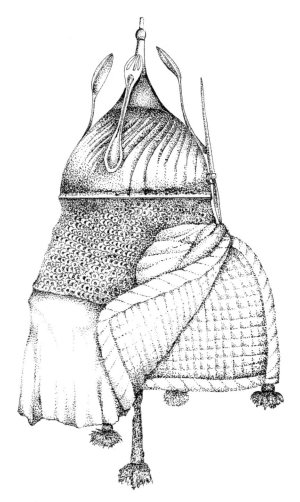

Figure 3.15 Helmet and padded headpiece from Darfur. Note welded
cutlery on top

dependants' (Balfour-Paul 1954b:10). The mosque, at 43 m × 33 m, was the
largest mosque in Darfur and had a two-storeyed partioned area in the south-
east corner functioning as a Qur'an school and bookstore. The size of the structure alone indicates the growing popularity of Islam and its centrality in the
court circle at least. Centralised military power also grew during this period,
with chain mail and sword blades imported, including the latter from Solingen
in Germany (O'Fahey 1980:24) **(figure 3.15)**.

Islam would appear to have taken root in the upper echelons of Fur society,
and, as has been described for elsewhere, its impact began gradually to be felt
outside the court circle. This was largely facilitated by Muslim holy men, who
emerged 'as the key protagonist(s) of Islam' (O'Fahey 1980:115), again replicat-
ing patterns we have noted elsewhere. These were holy men who came from

West Africa, such as Ahmed Abdul Rahman al-Barnawi from Bornu, and also, after the collapse of the Christian kingdoms, from the Nile valley (Mohammed 1986:225). In this respect Darfur differs from much else of the Nilotic Sudan in the lesser importance of Sufis and their associated *tariqahs* as agents of Islamisation (Holy 1991:20). Yet Islamisation by holy men was by no means an instantaneous process. The divine aspect of the Fur rulers was maintained long after Islam was accepted by the ruling class. Balfour-Paul (1955:19), for example, refers to the existence of the *kamnei*, a 'sort of shadow king', who was put to death when the king died, and an office which constitutes a further criterion of divine kingship found elsewhere in the continent. Mohammed (1986:228) notes that the practice of human sacrifice among the Fur rulers was only abolished after the rule of Sultan Solong. Also, the existence of the audience platforms could be linked, as already noted, with divine kingship. It fits with similarly recurring practices such as the wearing of a veil by the divine king, and his speaking through intermediaries. These elements would appear to have declined in importance by the nineteenth century, as O'Fahey records how by this date the 'sultans were encompassed by the full panoply of Islamic orthodoxy, or at least of an orthodoxy as understood in the Sudan' (1980:125). This equates with Mohammed's (1986:223–5) third phase of Islamisation in Darfur, dating from after 1800 and described as one of 'ongoing incorporation and transition'.

Yet although the Fur are Muslims, their religion is still infused with traditional religious elements. Balfour-Paul describes how, in the 1950s, 'you will find on countless hill-tops in Darfur a sacred precinct where offerings of flour and water are splashed and pilgrims crawl round on all fours making prayers to a vague genius loci' (1955:8). O'Fahey (1979:203) also refers to Fur lands being scattered with holy sites associated with spirits, and usually under the custody of old women. The practices just described form part of what Balfour-Paul (1955:8) terms a package of 'animistic cult' features found across the Sudanic belt – taboos on blacksmiths and rain-prophesying ceremonies being other features, with the latter interpreted by Mohammed (1986:228) as reflecting 'the importance of rain in an arid area'. These are all practices broadly paralleled by the Zaghawa as described by Tubiana (1964:198), who refers to sacrifices completed, 'on s'adresse à une montagne, une pierre, un arbre. Ils sont sacrés mais ils ne sont pas eux-mêmes la divinité'. Sacrifices were interpreted by Zahan (1970:26) as 'an offering by which men ask for the return of fecundating water at the end of the dry season, and also for the return of the vegetation indispensable to life'. Similarly, such practices are evident amongst the Berti of Darfur as outlined by Holy (1991). Indeed, it is probably useful to utilise the distinction made by Holy with regard to how the Berti of the Sudan classify these practices, with traditional ones such as sacrificing for rain described as 'custom', and 'religion' referring to Islam (1991:10). This neat categorisation allows for a variety of elements within religious life, and a distinction which can be applicable elsewhere in the continent, as we will see in the next chapter.

Summary and conclusions

Islam within the Nilotic Sudan can be seen to be extremely diverse in character, as is the archaeology of Islam within the region, more so than in many of the other regions which will be considered, but perhaps this is to be expected in such a vast territorial extent. A mosaic of cultures and ethnic groups is represented, and the processes by which Islam has spread have taken many forms and spanned many centuries – ranging from Christian Nubian skirmishes with the first Arab armies to conquer Egypt in the mid-seventh century to the Mahdist state of the late nineteenth century. Here, trade, *jihad* and conquest, and peaceful proselytisation, have all contributed to the spread of Islam. Uniform conversion processes are absent in this region, and models which are suited elsewhere – such as that linking nomads and early Islamic conversion (e.g. Trimingham 1959; Insoll 1996b, and see chapter 1 above) – are here shown to be largely inappropriate, though the correlation between trade and Islamisation as outlined by Levtzion and Fisher (1986) was shown to be of significance on the Red Sea coast as it had been further south in Ethiopia and the Horn. Similarly, the broader phases or processes of conversion to Islam identified by Eaton (1993) in his model were found to be applicable in certain instances – as, for example, in attempting to understand the continuation of pre-Islamic ritual elements in Nubia. The latter is also a model which might help in amplifying the three phases of Islamisation identified by Mohammed (1986) in Darfur.

The Nilotic Sudan is also a region where a pre-existing world religion, Christianity, has disappeared altogether from its former strongholds in Nubia, never having had the geographical defences offered by the Ethiopian highlands where, as we have seen in the last chapter, Christianity continues to thrive. Yet vague traces of earlier traditions persist in Nubia (Kennedy 1978a), as well as an abundant material legacy which has been left behind (W. Y. Adams 1977, 1996). Equally, many variants of Islam are, or have been shown to be, also evident. In Darfur Islam incorporates traditional religious elements, while among the Funj, Islam is equally dynamic but developed its own unique character in part facilitated by the wandering Muslim holy man, the *fuqara*, who served to spread Islam far and wide. In the vast tracts of land bordering the Nile, Islamisation processes again varied, as among the Beja, while in the area of former Christian Nubia, Sufism was of great significance in a landscape dotted with saints' tombs. Even in the south of the Sudan the impact of Islam has been felt, and Islamisation and Arabicisation are ongoing, illustrating that there are few areas of the continent that have remained untouched by Muslims or Islam in one form or another. Equally, the archaeological evidence has allowed a consideration of subjects – pilgrimage, for example – largely precluded in less well-explored regions such as Ethiopia and the Horn of Africa. In summary, the diversity of Islamic archaeology in the Nilotic Sudan is rich, though in many areas it still awaits more detailed study, somewhat in contrast to our next region, the East African coast, a region in which Islamic archaeology has been, perhaps, subject to the most intensive exploration in sub-Saharan Africa.

CHAPTER 4

THE EAST AFRICAN COAST AND OFFSHORE ISLANDS

Introduction

Sites and structure

Below the Horn of Africa lies the East African coast, a region of sub-Saharan Africa from which we have one of the best bodies of archaeological evidence attesting to Islamisation from as early as the mid-eighth century (**figure 4.1**). To give an idea of the amount of data involved, M. Horton (1987a:290) states that 400 Islamic archaeological sites have been recorded in this geographical region (see also Garlake 1966; Allen 1980; T. Wilson 1982 for a more detailed breakdown). This figure is now out of date, as research has moved on considerably even since the mid-1980s. A good example of this is provided by considering how much more is now known about the archaeology of the islands of Pemba and Zanzibar, off the coast of Tanzania, since that point in time. Until recently it was thought that Muslim settlement and evidence for participation in Indian Ocean trade on Pemba 'cannot be placed on present evidence earlier than AD 1100' (Horton and Clark 1985:169). However, it is now known that evidence for the presence of Muslims and/or participation in long-distance trade dates back to at least the ninth century, as indicated by recent finds of Sasanian Islamic pottery of Persian Gulf origin at the Chwaka/Tumbe site complex on this island (LaViolette in press; and see below). Likewise, even the known recorded size of the site chosen as an example, Tumbe, grew from 2 ha to over 30 ha, thanks also to recent research (Fleisher and LaViolette in press; and see Fleisher and LaViolette 1999). Similar examples indicating the growth in archaeological research and thus of available data in the past fifteen to twenty years can be found all along the East African coast (see, e.g., Kessy 1997).

Thus the East African coast is in many ways a privileged region in terms of archaeological research which has been completed within it in comparison to others that have been, or will be, considered. This abundance of data works to our benefit, but equally, as a result of the relatively large quantities of archaeological data we possess, selectivity has had to be employed with regard to the case studies chosen. Needless to say, sites and material that are most relevant to our purposes in exploring the spread and impact of Islam are considered, data which will also be supplemented by ethnographic and historical sources

Figure 4.1 The East African coast

where cogent, again using a multi-source approach. However, it should also be noted that the relative abundance of data from the East African coast does not mean that archaeological research and interpretation in the region is merely a question of fine-tuning. It is not. Some issues and questions are now reasonably well understood, others are not. The East African coast is also a region where new research, often by indigenous rather than expatriate scholars as mentioned in chapter 1, is leading to much questioning of older models. The origins of the Swahili, the impact of Islam away from the coast before the nineteenth century, and pre-Islamic trade are all being re-evaluated, with profound implications for the study of the archaeology of Islam in the area (see, e.g., Chami 1998; Juma 1996b; Chami and Msemwa 1997b).

To make sense of the material chronologically and geographically it has had to be divided into several sections. Firstly, and as with the other chapters, the pre-Islamic background is considered, and current scholarship as regards Swahili origins (the dominant ethnic group on the coast) evaluated. Secondly, the relevant Islamic archaeology is divided into four sections. Initially, a discussion of the archaeology of Islam within the whole region prior to about 1000 CE is provided, and this is followed by three geographical reviews covering the dryer north coast, the lusher south coast, with the border approximately placed on the modern Kenyan–Tanzanian frontier, and finally, the far islands of the Comoros and Madagascar (figure 4.1). Excepting the offshore islands, the coastal division is in broad agreement with the geographical description of the East African coast provided by al-Idrisi (mid-twelfth century), with 'Barbar' north of Mogadishu, and already described, 'Zanj', south of Mogadishu to Pemba island, and 'Sofala', the source of gold, south of this (Hiskett 1994:153). The fourth region of the Arab geographers, 'Waq-Waq', 'a shadowy land' beyond Sofala (Chittick 1977:190) is too rooted in myth to be tied with any certainty to geographical reality here (Freeman-Grenville 1975:120), though it might be linked with Madagascar.

The coast, winds and sea

Geographically, this chapter is largely concerned with the narrow coastal strip that has the Indian Ocean to its east. It is important to stress the importance of seafaring, the sea and Indian Ocean trade, but it should not be thought that the inhabitants of the coast were merely outward looking and removed from their immediate surroundings. The Indian Ocean serves to demarcate the geographical boundary of the coast, but formerly it was thought that there was another border. This was believed to be to the west, and is described by Sheriff (1987:8) as 'a fairly distinct geographical entity...a belt of poor low-rainfall scrub known in Kiswahili as the *nyika* (wilderness)'. This arid zone was defined as progressively narrowing as one moved from north to south, with its existence imposing 'not so much an absolute barrier as a premium on the costs of communication between the coast and the interior' (Sheriff 1987:8). Unfortunately such thinking, of the coast as land-locked by hostile wilderness, did nothing for hypotheses which actually placed the inhabitants of the coastal settlements within their regional setting as part of a complete system evolving from local surroundings, rather than as foreign implants. This is considered in greater depth later, but suffice to say, in the words of Horton and Middleton (2000:97), that 'the old-fashioned notions of the Nyika, a semi-desert 50 or so miles back from the coast, beyond which any contact ceased, is overstated even by modern historians'. In fact the East African coast was not wholly separated and segregated by cultural and environmental differences either from its immediate hinterland or even further into the interior.

Interconnections between coast and hinterland were seamless, and the coast itself also offered varying environmental conditions. In some areas, agricultural potential was good, rice especially could be grown, while in others poor land or intermittent rainfall meant that foodstuffs had to be imported. No one environment predominates on the coast, unsurprising in an area stretching from southern Somalia to southern Mozambique, though formerly, large areas offshore were covered with mangroves – a valuable resource, as will be considered below. Iron ore was also available on parts of the coast, 'mainly in ferruginous concretions (reddish sandstone) in old fossilised sand dunes near to the coast' (Duarte 1993:17), while the sea provided a variety of resources as well – fish and shellfish for consumption and trade, and coral and timber for building. To the mainland coastal strip must also be added the offshore islands, ranging from the near islands of Mafia, Pemba and Zanzibar off the coast of Tanzania (plus numerous smaller ones dotted along the coast), to the four volcanic islands comprising the Comoros, some 300 km from the coast of Africa (Allibert and Verin 1996:461), and of course Madagascar. The latter is the fourth-largest island in the world, 1600 km in length and home to a wide range of environments, from the rainforests of the east coast to the savannah and steppe of the highlands, and the dry, spiny forests of the south (Dewar and Wright 1993:423–4; Middleton 1999:3). Therefore the East African coast (henceforth also including the aforementioned offshore islands without refering to them specifically) must also be seen as an area of diversity, rather than as a homogeneous entity. Yet, having said this, as we will see, remarkable similarities also exist.

Crucial to the development of the Islamised trade centres and settlements on the East African coast were the monsoon cycles **(figure 4.2)**. As Trimingham (1964:2) notes, 'the direction of monsoon-winds from the north-east for four months and from the south-west for a similar period made navigation possible and predictable from the Persian Gulf'. This reference to the Persian Gulf is of importance, as this was the main trading partner of the East African coastal settlements prior to the eleventh century (M. Horton 1996b). The monsoonal seasonal reversal of the winds occurred (and still occurs) with great regularity, culminating in the creation of, in the words of Sheriff (1987:10),

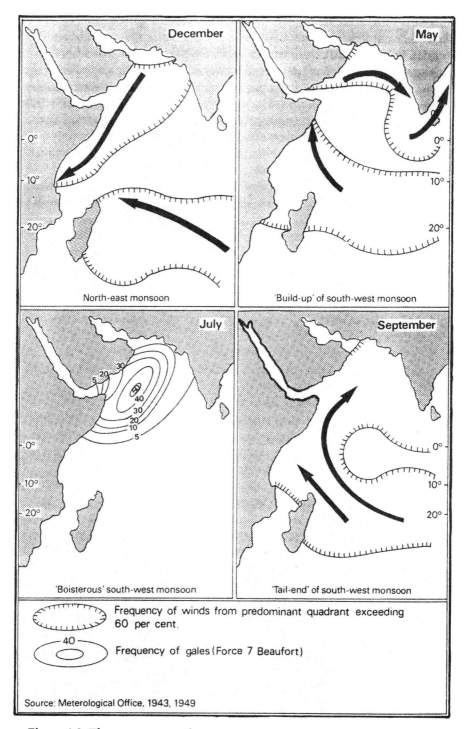

Figure 4.2 The monsoon cycles

'a dynamic system of which the East African coast forms only a fringe'. The monsoons made possible the long-distance seafaring that occurred within the Indian Ocean and which connected with adjacent seas. Yet besides the monsoons themselves, adequate ships were also an obvious requirement, as was adequate nautical knowledge. These vessels and the routes they followed functioned to move cargoes and people around the region, but also served to move ideas, including religious ones (Insoll 1999a), and are thus of great significance for our purpose in many ways.

Little direct evidence for the boats involved in Indian Ocean trade exists, partly because little effort has so far been invested in examining wrecks (Hourani et al. 1995:150). However, on the East African coast, various incised graffiti give an idea of the types of vessel involved. At Kilwa, for example, an important site in southern Tanzania discussed further below, graffito was found scratched on wall plaster inside the building complex known as Husuni Kubwa, and more on the outside of the Great Mosque. These, as Sutton (1990:86) notes, provide 'valuable evidence of the craft of the Western Indian Ocean before the time of the Portuguese'. The reference to the Portuguese is of great significance, for after their arrival in the Indian Ocean at the end of the fifteenth century ship design was fundamentally altered. A key feature of this influence was in the redesign of dhow sterns to the square (transom) type when previously ships had been double ended 'coming to a point at both bow and stern' (Hourani et al. 1995:89). The dhows were one of various classes of boats used in Indian Ocean trade, they were lateen-rigged, and belong broadly, as Sutton (1990:86) remarks, 'to the Arab tradition in the Western Indian Ocean' **(figure 4.3)**. Villiers (1969:395) provides a description of the types of vessel used in the East African and Gulf trade in the 1930s, and it is a distinct possibility that similar classes of vessels were used earlier. These ranged from the *baggala*, the traditional deep-sea dhow of the Persian Gulf to the *bedani*, a smaller craft with one or two masts, and common to the smaller ports of Oman. The ships used in the East African trade varied in size but could be large, large enough to hide a mouse on one vessel which landed at a Dembeni-phase (*c*.ninth–tenth centuries) site on the Comoros, leaving this non-indigenous species behind (Redding and Goodman 1984:53). On the East African coast, *mtepe*-style square-rigged vessels were also found. These were not nailed but sewn together – as indeed were dhows prior, again, to the arrival of Europeans, who precipitated the use of iron fastenings (Hourani et al. 1995:97).

These vessels were sewn together with cords of coir (see Insoll 1993b for a survival of this technology in West Africa). Baumann (1957:11) refers to the production of coir ropes from the fibre of coconut husks on Mafia island at the beginning of the twentieth century. Initially, the husks were buried on the shore at low tide, then dug up after a few months, before the coir was obtained by beating the fibre on a plank with a wooden board. Finally, the coir cords were twisted into rope. The stitching was reinforced and protected with

Figure 4.3 Dhow of type used for long-distance trade

caulking, 'a mixture of pitch or resin and whale oil' (Hourani et al. 1995:97).
Interestingly, the presence of large numbers of turtle bones, some burnt, also
at Dembeni-phase sites in the Comoros was interpreted as possibly indicating
the production of oil for boat maintenance (Redding and Goodman 1984:51).
Timber for boat production was generally not in short supply on the East African
coast, and if not available at the coast itself, it could be sourced in the interior.
Elsewhere, around the Arabian Peninsula for instance, timber was imported
for boat building, especially from India – timber frequently referred to as *saj*
in Arabic, meaning teak but often including other timbers as well. Mangrove
poles, a major export from the East African coast, for example, were sometimes
mistaken for teak, being similarly red in colour and heavy in weight (Chittick
1984:218). India may have supplied ship-building timber, but the East African
coast supplied timber for construction, both mangrove poles and hardwoods.
M. Horton (1986:210) has even put forward the hypothesis that this trade flourished especially during the building of Baghdad and Samarra between the mid-
eighth and mid-ninth centuries. This is an untested, but nonetheless intriguing,
idea.

   Thus, although ships were of crucial significance as the initial agents of
Islamisation, via the individuals they carried to the East African coast, the sum
total of evidence attesting to the centuries of voyaging completed is minimal.
Besides the graffiti, also found at other sites on the coast (Chanudet (1990:63–4),
for instance, refers to a graffito at the site of Mwali Mdjini on Moheli island
in the Comoros discovered in a building actually described as 'la maison au
bateau'), little other evidence has been found. At Kilwa, however, an installation
described as a tapering anchor shank was found (Sutton 1998b:158). Made of
sandstone, some 1.5 m in length, it was sited near the aforementioned Husuni
Kubwa site at the high water line, and had two rectangular holes at its thicker
end for attaching grapnel lines. It provides mute testimony to the extensive sea
trade in which the inhabitants of Kilwa were involved and from which they
prospered, and which is considered in greater detail below.

Indian Ocean trade

Indeed, parallels can be drawn between the role of the camel as an agent in the
introduction of Islam into the western Sahel (see next chapter) and the role of
the ship on the East African coast. However, there was no resultant Sahelian
or Saharan product in the same way that we can talk of products of the Indian
Ocean, be they peoples or items which are somehow suffused, literally, with
the currents of the Indian Ocean. What is meant by this? As will be described
below, the interconnections between the different regions of the Indian Ocean
were profound, leaving a legacy as represented by the bronze lion from the
site of Shanga on the coast of Kenya (Horton and Blurton 1988), or the Siddi
people of African origin in Gujarat in western India (Khalidi 1988). Both these

case studies will be considered in greater detail later. The wide-ranging extent of Indian Ocean contacts is repeatedly indicated in the archaeological record, and is something neatly encapsulated for the purposes of introduction, again by the Dembeni-phase sites of the Comoros. Verin (1994:54) describes how Dembeni villages were situated close to the sea to exploit coastal resources but also to participate in trade. This trade extended to sites such as Siraf and Sohar in the Gulf, to the mainland of Africa and to the neighbouring island of Madagascar, as well as their functioning as a centre of transshipment, for glass from Iran and Egypt, and carnelian beads from western India – all between c.850 and 1000.

Thus it can be seen that Indian Ocean trade and contacts were an indisputable element of life on the East African coast. It is also possible to reconstruct the phases of Indian Ocean trade and other contacts in which the inhabitants of the East African coast participated during the Islamic era (pre-Islamic trade is discussed below). The initial focus upon the Persian Gulf has already been mentioned. This is described by Duarte (1993:22) as a phase of prosperity linked with the Abbasid dynasty and their capital at Baghdad. It is possible that the economic demands of the upper Gulf stimulated a wider trade boom, something already referred to with regard to a possible expansion in the timber trade from East Africa. Regardless of the cause, the existence – and indeed primacy – of contacts with the Persian Gulf is attested in archaeological sites right along the East African coast. Gulf-phase ceramics which attest to this include turquoise glazed jar and bowl fragments frequently referred to as Sasanian Islamic wares. These predominate in assemblages of imported ceramics prior to the eleventh century, as again in Dembeni-phase sites on the Comoros (H. Wright 1984:41), and at Manda on the Kenyan coast (Chittick 1984). Pottery of East African origin is also found in the Gulf, as with sherds of poor-quality earthenwares used as water containers at the site of Ras el-Hadd (Horton and Middleton 2000:78). Coins from the site of Kilwa (otherwise undescribed) have also been recovered from near Salalah in Dhofar, Oman (Lowick 1985:5). Sgraffiato wares also of Gulf origin and dated after about 1000 CE have been widely found at sites on the East African coast (a ware type already described in chapter 2). These can take many forms, but still attest to Persian Gulf contacts with sites such as Siraf in Iran (Whitehouse 1968, 1971).

Thereafter the picture becomes more mixed, and there is a gradual shift in what Duarte (1993:22) defines as the centre of commercial gravity from the Persian Gulf to the Red Sea. This too can be linked with events on the wider world stage, i.e. the primacy of the Fatimids and subsequently the Mamluks in Egypt. Horton and Middleton (2000:78) suggest that Fatimid demands for East African rock crystal, gold and ivory helped in shifting the orbit of East African coastal trade. Fatimid ceramics, however, are not found on the coast, though pottery from Yemen, specifically black-on-yellow wares made outside Aden, are widely found dating from between 1250 and 1350, indicating a possible rise in the importance of Red Sea contacts. This does not mean that Gulf wares completely disappear – they do not – but a different phase in East African trade relations appears to have been entered (with religious implications as well, as discussed below). A third phase of trading relations is also evident in the fifteenth century, when Indian links appear to have been of importance, especially those focused upon Gujarat (Duarte 1993:22).

The pre-Islamic background

Contacts with areas beyond the East African coast substantially pre-date the rise of Islam, and trading voyages along the coast were made – but these remain, as yet, only partially understood. Historical references to the region exist, but these are very limited in number and often confusing and contradictory. The most important pre-Islamic sources are the anonymous *Periplus of the Erythrean Sea*, referred to in chapter 2, and Ptolemy's *Geography* (second century). Kosmas Indikopleustes also briefly mentions the East African coast in the sixth century, an individual 'who sailed from Ethiopia to Ceylon in AD 525' (M. Horton 1996a). Both the *Periplus* and Ptolemy's *Geography* refer to the East African coast as 'Azania' (incidentally the title adopted for the journal published by the British Institute based in the region). Beyond the ports of the Horn described in chapter 2, the *Periplus* also refers to a trade centre called Rhapta, which hints, as Horton notes (1990:99), 'that even pre-Iron Age East Africa was part of a wider world system'. Rhapta was one of only two trade centres mentioned historically prior to 800 CE (Nurse and Spear 1985:3). The other was Qanbalu, described below. In Rhapta there was 'ivory in great quantity, and tortoise-shell', and imports to this centre included 'hatchets and daggers and awls, and various kinds of glass' (Schoff 1995:28). Archaeologists have expended much effort in searching for Rhapta, a none too simple task, as Hourani et al. (1995:137) note, because of 'the inconsistent locations given in the *Geography* of Ptolemy and the *Periplus*'.

Confusing textual mentions aside, archaeologically, few indications of contacts between East Africa and the classical world have been found. However, recent research in the Rufiji delta in Tanzania recovered four Roman glass beads from the site of Mkukutu, dated to around 200–400 CE. These included a segmented gold/silver in glass of about 9 mm in length, a wound light blue and two small dark-blue gadroons. Their presence has been interpreted by the excavator as 'the first archaeological evidence corroborating the *Periplus Maris Erythraei* and Ptolemy's *Geography*', thus meaning that 'the Rufiji region formed a population centre where Rhapta might have flourished' (Chami 1999:240–1). This is a reasonable supposition, but cannot be made any more certain based on the current evidence, for Rhapta could equally be located elsewhere, on Zanzibar or Pemba islands for example, or could now be under water. Loss of sites to the sea would appear to be a recurring problem. Chittick (1964:15), for example, suggests that a third or even half of the site of Kisimani Mafia (see below) might have been lost in this way. Equally, Rhapta, as Hourani et al. (1995:137) suggest, 'may not have been a permanent settlement but rather an ill-defined turning point to conduct trade and await the change in the monsoon'. For the present the location of Rhapta remains unknown.

What is more certain is that the material inventory for contacts between the East African coast and elsewhere prior to the rise of Islam is increasing. Included within this are various pre-Islamic coin finds which have been made on the coast. However, the vast majority of these are of dubious provenance. At Bur Gao in southern Somalia, a site described as a 'possible candidate for Nikon of the *Periplus*' (Hourani et al. 1995:138), a hoard of coins was found. These included various Roman issues of fourth-century date, as well as amphora fragments. This find has been reviewed by Chittick (1969:130), who rightly signals that the accounts of the hoard and its discovery contain 'demonstrable contradictions and innaccuracies'. Equally, a hoard of Parthian, Sasanian, Hellenistic and Roman coin issues found in Zanzibar are also far from reliable. As Freeman-Grenville (1960:33) describes, they 'must be treated with some caution, since they first came to light in an old shoe-box when the Beit al-Amani [Zanzibar] Museum was searched for coins in 1955'. Similar instances are reviewed by M. Horton (1996a:448), who casts equal doubt on various stray coin finds which have been made both on the coast and in the interior of East Africa, such as an antoninianus of Victorinus found in Nairobi.

Less controversially, research by Felix Chami and others in Tanzania has, besides the Mkukutu beads described above, provided further evidence for long-distance pre-Islamic trade or contacts **(figure 4.4)**. At Kivinji, 20 km north of the Rufiji delta, for example, glass was found which has been described as 'comparable to wares observed at the Greco-Roman site of Fayum in Egypt' (Chami and Msemwa 1997b:674–5). Also found was bluey-green alkaline glazed pottery somewhat vaguely described as similar to wares produced from the third century BCE in the Middle East (Chami and Msemwa 1997b). Offshore, on Zanzibar, excavation at the site of Unguja Ukuu, a former harbour situated at the closest point to the African mainland and the best anchorage in this area of the island, recovered wheel-made pottery sherds. These were identified as African red slip-wares produced somewhere in the Mediterranean region in the fifth to early sixth centuries (Juma 1996b). Besides the objects of foreign provenance in East Africa, an item of probable East African origin was recently excavated from a grave at Tell Asmar in Mesopotamia, indicating that the process operated the other way as well. This was a small copal pendant tentatively dated to around 2500 BCE and apparently derived from a tree not found in Mesopotamia but indigenous to East Africa, *Trachylobium* (Meyer et al. 1991, cited in M. Horton 1996a:450).

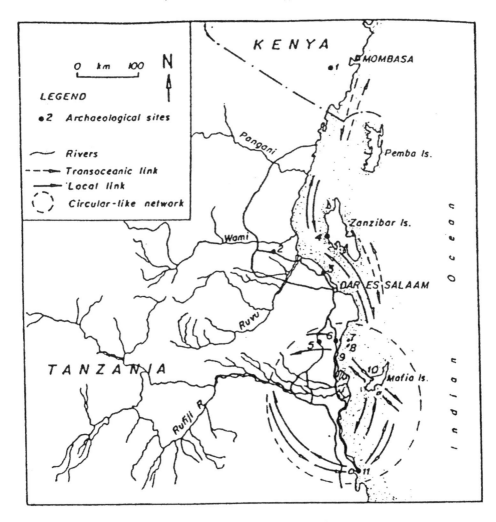

1. Kwale. 2. Kiwangwa. 3. Mpiji. 4. Unguja Ukuu.
5. Limbo. 6. Misasa. 7. Kwale Island. 8. Koma Island.
9. Kivinj. 10. Mafia Island. 11. Kilwa.

Figure 4.4 Possible pre-Islamic trade networks

In summary, archaeological evidence is beginning to accumulate which indicates that the East African coast was involved in some form of long-distance trade, or other contacts, as yet little understood, in the pre-Islamic period. Having discounted coins, this comprises a few sherds of pottery and fragments of glass, material which will undoubtedly grow in quantity as research progresses. But it is material that is of importance, for it has implications for the development of the later Islamised trade centres, as it indicates that these could have had a substantial, but as yet shadowy, ancestry.

Swahili origins

Historiography

These recent discoveries have also had implications for Swahili origins, and a comprehension of these in the light of contemporary scholarship is crucial to understanding the coast during the Muslim period. This is firstly because the date when the Swahili 'cultural package' can be said to have developed has been the subject of much debate. A cultural complex possibly developed in some areas as early as the eighth century (Juma 1996b), though other observers place the full development of the Swahili much later, in the thirteenth century (Hiskett 1994:161). Secondly, as was touched upon in chapter 1, what is also interesting is the manner in which interpretations of Swahili origins have reflected the contemporary political situation and preoccupations. In this respect parallels can again be drawn with the trade centres of the western Sahel, discussed also in chapter 1 and in the next chapter, and the way in which they have been interpreted over time.

Initially, the Swahili settlements were seen as foreign implants, as coral colonies almost, founded by Persian or Arab immigrants. Exemplars of this type of approach were two of the pioneers of East African coastal archaeology, James Kirkman and Neville Chittick. Kirkman (1964:22), for example, sums up such approaches in an oft-cited phrase when he mentions that 'the historical monuments of Africa belong not to the Africans but to the Arabs and Arabized Persians, mixed in blood with the African but in culture utterly apart from the Africans who surround them'. The flaws in such approaches are also encapsulated in Chittick's view (1971:108) that 'these coasts were the most southerly region known to the ancients; consequently in this part only of equatorial Africa do we have any historical knowledge going back to before the fifteenth century'. This is a comment flawed factually, as the discussion of other areas of sub-Saharan Africa in this volume indicates, but also flawed in apparently disregarding oral history in favour of written sources. Chittick also used archaeology to remove the Swahili from their past. Following his excavations at Manda, a town in the Lamu archipelago of Kenya, for example, he states that 'we conclude that the impetus to the creation of this town was due to the settling of immigrants who came from the Arabian/Persian Gulf' (Chittick 1984:217). Further examples abound, and the historiography of the East African coast is well considered by Allen (1993:2–12), who makes the point that the misrepresentation of the Swahili has a long history, stretching back as far as Sir Richard Burton in the mid-nineteenth century – an individual who, again according to Allen, was 'the first to make a serious attempt to alienate the Swahilis from their history' (1993:3).

Type sites such as Kilwa and Manda (already mentioned) and Gede (described in greater detail below) were interpreted as colonial settlements whose stone architecture, way of life and religion – Islam – were brought from overseas. Again to quote Chittick (1971:137), 'we should picture this civilization as a remote outpost of Islam, looking for its spiritual inspiration to the homeland of its religion'. Besides Allen (1993), this 'Asiatic' or 'Arab-colonial' model has been reviewed in detail by various scholars (see also Nurse and Spear 1985; Chami 1998), with a landmark critique of these older views, based upon a re-evaluation of the Manda evidence provided by M. Horton (1986). As Horton indicates, Manda as presented by Chittick is too late, too foreign, and even too permanent. Chittick completely missed seeing the earlier wattle-and-daub structures, a feature of so many coastal settlements (see Fleisher and LaViolette in press, and below), and thus overemphasised the importance of the later, post-thirteenth-century stone architecture. Thus a novel, apparently foreign, civilisation appeared to arise ready formed on the East African coast on the basis of his misreading of the archaeological data.

In many respects, such interpretations can also be seen as a product of their time, of the colonial encounter with Africa. Thus it was easier to justify the position of recent colonists by emphasising that, in this case with regard to the British, modern colonialism was merely a continuation of an age-old process. As Helms (forthcoming) notes, 'the East African coast has long been subjected to the influences of foreign colonial powers. This has resulted in a historical perspective, which in the past has placed undue emphasis on the dominance of external political and economic interests, rather than those of local African communities'. Schmidt (1996:129) further defines coastal research agendas as formerly neglecting 'questions about socio-economic organisation, population size, political organisation, affinities with other settlements, industry or diet'. A similar colonial ethos of justification underlay much of early French archaeological interpretation in the western Sahel, as has already been described in chapter 1 (and see Holl 1996). Yet other scholars working at the same time as Kirkman and Chittick recognised the African origins of these coastal settlements. G. S. P. Freeman-Grenville (1975:122), for instance, states that the Arab geographers before the twelfth century 'make it quite clear that the coast was under the organized control of the Zanj, who were certainly Africans of some sort, with African religious beliefs and practices'. The evidence for this will also be considered later.

Unfortunately, the Arabising of Swahili origins was also undertaken by the Swahili themselves (Sutton 1990). This was in part a reaction to the British colonial portrayal of the Swahili as

inferior on two separate and not entirely compatible grounds: first, because they were 'cross-bred' Arab and African, a 'half-caste' or 'mongrel' race, and it was held that such races must in some sense be inferior to 'pure-bred' ones. Secondly, they were regarded as inferior in so far as the 'superior' Arab blood in their veins had been diluted by that of 'inferior' Africans. (Allen 1993:3)

Thus a claim to purer Arab descent by the Swahili might lead to the dilution of such 'bastardising' tendencies. The British prefered Arabs to Africans, and to claim Arab descent might be useful, as the French preferred the Tuareg over the Africans in some of their West African colonies, such as the French Sudan.

Secondly, it was frequently thought that Arabising/Persianising was equivalent to Islamising origins, and this was a process by no means confined to the Swahili. It is found among various ethnic groups in different parts of sub-Saharan Africa, as has already been discussed in chapter 2, and as will be seen in many other instances in the following chapters. An example of this in an East African context is provided by the claimed descent from Shiraz in Persia, the Shirazi myth, which is recorded in the Kilwa Chronicle (Sutton 1990:77). This was a myth in fact dismantled, according to Allen (1993:5), by Kirkman. Nonetheless its existence could also be interpreted as an attempt at Islamising Swahili origins. Equally, as M. Horton (1996b:3) notes, it could function in an Islamic medium as an African tradition of origin, 'which claimed that many of the Bantu-speaking peoples of coastal East Africa, including the Swahili, came from a single homeland called Shungwaya [see below]. Shiraz was substituted as a supposed origin, on account of its fame as one of the most prosperous cities of the Islamic World' (see also Helms forthcoming).

African origins

Yet when the evidence for supposed Arab or Persian or other immigration to the East African coast is considered, as the archaeological evidence is below, it can be shown to be limited in scale. This is something examined by Allen (1993:243–5), who convincingly illustrates that evidence for a Hadrami or Yemeni influence is not perceptible before 1700. 'Indo-Pakistani' or Persian influence is equally rare, with evidence for the former largely confined to nineteenth-century architecture. In fact, in India, a complete contrast is apparent in many ways, apparently resulting 'from innovations introduced *from* East Africa *to* the Indian sub-continent and not the other way round' (Allen 1993:245, italics added).

India and East Africa

Evidence for contacts between India and East Africa is diverse. One of the most intriguing items found is the Shanga lion, so-called after its find-spot, the site of Shanga in the Lamu archipelago in Kenya (M. Horton 1996b). This is a small (61 mm-high) bronze statuette of a lion dated to around 1100 which parallels figures from the Deccan in west-central India. It could have served various purposes, possibly as an item of royal regalia, a weight, or even as part of a Hindu shrine perhaps dedicated to Durga (Horton and Blurton 1988:18). Whatever its purpose, the source of the metal from which it was cast appears to have been re-melted Chinese coins – 'cash'. Having outlined its Indian parallels, it should also be noted that the origins of the Shanga lion are unclear, and it is best described as 'Indian Ocean' in attribution (Horton and Blurton:22), though the Hindu stylistic affinities place it in the Indian orbit. A further intriguing item of definite Indian origin is a 1 m-long fragment of Gujarati marble found in a tomb at Kilwa dating from about the fourteenth century. This appears to have been originally from a Hindu temple in Gujarat, as indicated by its decorative features, but was subsequently recarved on its upper and lower borders with Qur'anic verses (Sutton 1998b:146). Other items of Indian provenance which have been recovered include fragments of Indian pottery which have been found at Shanga **(figure 4.5)** or, more widely, carnelian beads produced in the Gujarat region of western India. The latter were extensively traded, especially from Khambhat (Cambay), and are found in many regions of sub-Saharan Africa (see chapter 5). On the East African coast they have been recovered from the cemetery of Vohemar in Madagascar, for example (van der Sleen n.d.).

The agate beads also provide a living link to East African–Indian connections. These are provided by the Siddis or Habashis, people of African origin who live in parts of western and central India (see Burton 1998 [1850]; Freeman-Grenville 1988c). Usually, peoples of African origin within India are thought to be there as a result of the slave trade, after which they were extensively employed as guards and soldiers (see, e.g., Bhattacharya 1970; Khalidi 1988). However, it is possible that the Siddis of the Ratanpor district of Gujarat did not arrive in this capacity, but instead are linked with the aforementioned bead trade. The Siddis in the Ratanpor area look after the shrine of Baba Ghor, who was probably killed fighting in Gujarat in the early fifteenth century, and whose shrine stands on the top of a hill at the base of which are some of the best carnelian mines in the region (Francis 1986). These mines are still worked, though the trade to Africa has now virtually disappeared. Near the shrine is Ratanpor village where at least half the inhabitants are African in origin **(figure 4.6)**. This is seemingly inconsequential, but is in fact important evidence for the extensive relations at various levels which have existed between East Africa and India.

Similarly, the presence of Arabic loanwords in Swahili, frequently cited as further evidence for foreign origins, has been shown to be not overly important. As Nurse and Spear (1985:5–6) note, Swahili is an African language, 'closely related to the Bantu languages now spoken along the northern Kenyan and Somali coast, and that it has acquired much of its extensive Arabic vocabulary only

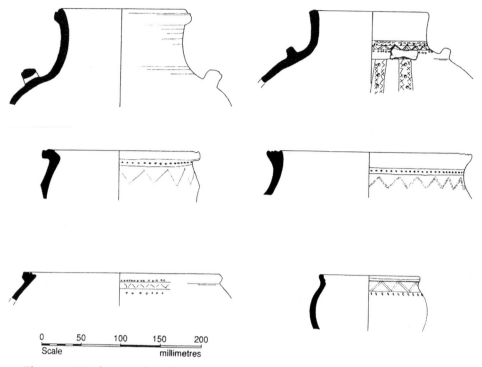

Figure 4.5 Indian unglazed wares from Shanga probably imported as water
containers

in the last few centuries' (see also Nurse 1983; Nurse and Hinnebusch 1993).
Much of the process of Arabic linguistic adoption actually occurred during the
period of nineteenth-century Omani settlement, as M. Horton (1996b:4) remarks, 'especially on Zanzibar, and the subsequent adoption of the Zanzibar
dialect, Ki-Unguja, as standard Swahili'. The Swahili language also includes
about 120 Portuguese words, primarily relating to the sea (Freeman-Grenville
1988b:9) – but equally, this does not mean that the Swahili are Portuguese in
origin.

 Although African origins for the Swahili appear to be convincing these are
still far from universally accepted. Many historians of the Middle East still
posit external Arabian or Persian origins for the Swahili, and indeed Sheriff
(1987:14) makes the point that 'international trade stimulated the growth of
market towns, some of which *may* have been initially established by the indigenous people' (italics added). Judging from the available archaeological evidence, this opinion is unfounded, and echoes earlier sentiments. Yet the details
of the African hypothesis are also the subject of debate. As already noted, one of
the primary revisionists of the Asiatic model in favour of one invoking African
origins was Mark Horton (see for example 1986, 1987a). Based upon his excavations at the site of Shanga in the Lamu archipelago in Kenya (discussed

Figure 4.6 Siddis, people of African descent, Baba Ghor Shrine, Gujarat, India

further below) Horton indicated that the origins of the settlement were indigenous, and that from the second half of the eighth century, the non-Muslim
population came into contact with overseas merchants and gradually converted
to Islam (Horton 1996b). Similar evidence, as already mentioned, is now known
to have been present at Manda (Horton 1986), and also at Pate, likewise in the
Lamu archipelago. In the words of the excavators of the latter site, 'the excavations at Pate and Shanga, and probably all other early sites, are perhaps best
interpreted as African societies in contact with overseas peoples' (Wilson and
Omar 1997:64). This evidence, and that from other early sites which will be
described below, illustrates that later developments such as the stone architectural tradition found all along the coast – and indeed, the very florescence
of Swahili civilisation that accompanied it, especially between the fourteenth
and fifteenth centuries – owe their origins to these indigenous foundations.

Some scholars, notably James Allen (1993) have also been more specific in
their attribution of African origins for the Swahili, claiming a pastoral, possibly Cushitic-speaking, origin. To a lesser extent, Mark Horton has previously
also argued for a pastoralist element, as a significant component among a package of multi-ethnic elements present at Shanga (see Sutton 1994/5 for a convenient summary). The locally produced pottery found in the early levels at
Shanga, the so-called 'Tana tradition' (TT) or 'triangular incised ware' (TIW)
has been interpreted as having pastoralist affinities, 'rather than to Bantu-
speaking agriculturalists' (M. Horton 1996a:454). However, recent research
has indicated that the archaeological evidence 'does not support claims for
the association of TT/TIW with earlier Southern Cushitic agro-pastoralists'
(Helms 2000:282). Rather, early iron-working farming communities speaking a
proto-north-eastern coastal Bantu language emerged on the East African coast
from the late first millennium BCE, with these groups, according to Helms
(2000:293), interacting and integrating with the existing dispersed population
of Southern Cushitic stoneworking hunter-gather communities.

Dietary evidence has also been subject to debate and reinterpretation as to
what it indicates about the specifics of Swahili origins. At Shanga, for example, the differences evident between the three main areas excavated have been
seen as significant. The north-western area of the site has been interpreted as
'significantly less "pastoralist" ' owing to the smaller percentage of cattle and
absence of camel remains, and higher numbers of fish bones, and sheep/goat
and chicken bones found. This contrasted with the south-eastern and south-
western sectors at Shanga, where, for instance, fewer fish bones were recovered
(M. Horton 1996b:392–3). This might be due, according to Horton and Mudida
(1993:682), to the presence of pastoralists who were largely non-fish-eating
and derived their protein from milk and blood. Certainly, ethnographic examples exist of pastoralists avoiding fish, as among the Beja in the Nilotic Sudan
(Simoons 1994:261). But the lesser number of fish remains could equally be due,
as Horton and Mudida (1993:682) also suggest, to a society eating some fish but
getting the bulk of its food from millets and legumes. In general, the available

evidence does not support pastoralist origins for Swahili society, with a multi-ethnic model, perhaps including a pastoralist element, preferable. Indeed, as Wilson and Omar (1997:64) note, the presence of camel bones at Shanga and Pate 'may indicate the proximity of pastoralists about 1075–1150, but do not themselves confirm the influence of camel pastoralists on Swahili origins'.

Whatever the ethnic composition of early Swahili society, its indigenous nature is certainly suggested by the settlement patterning evident at Shanga. Specifically, this can be seen in the posited central enclosure recorded in the primary layout of the settlement, entered through a number of gates and interpreted as reflecting the former existence of a clan system, and mirroring the *kaya* enclosures found among the non-Muslim Mijikenda people of the mainland (M. Horton 1994b, 1996b) **(figure 4.7)**. The Mijikenda are Bantu speaking and comprise nine closely related ethnic groups living in the Kenyan coastal hinterland (Mutoro 1994:134). The *kaya* range from some 5 to 30 ha in size, and are typically formed of a double enclosure set within the forest, with a varying number of gates arranged in east–west or north–south orientation (M. Horton 1991). These are associated with particular clans, and are protected by fingo pots (pots containing prophylactic substances) buried below them. At the centre of the enclosure is a meeting place, the *moro*, for the elders, as well as a repository for insignia of office and ritual items. This is a domed hut set, according to Mutoro (1994:134), between a baobab and a fig tree. The residential part of the *kaya*, the *boma*, housed members of the clan, and parts of the *kaya* were also used for burial, though to qualify for burial, one had to die within the *kaya*, as the dead could not be carried through the gates (Allen 1993:87). Burial areas were marked with *vikango* or grave posts as well as coconut shells and bones left from offerings to the dead (Mutoro 1994:136).

The suggested parallels between the Shanga enclosure and the Mijikenda *kaya* are of interest. The Shanga enclosure was a rectangular area about 100 × 80 m with entrances on its western and eastern sides and 'precisely cardinal north–south in orientation' (M. Horton 1991:103–4). At its centre was a well, with 5 m east of the well a large tree indicated by a burnt stump surrounded by iron slag. This presented evidence of craft activity, but little domestic debris was found in the enclosure and the correlation of tree, well and slag was interpreted as ritually significant, the whole paralleling, as stated, the Mijikenda *kaya*, with the Mijikenda appearing 'to represent the non-Islamicized component of a common society' (M. Horton 1991:105). This is a convincing interpretation, in that what is represented by the presence of the enclosure is the indigenous basis of Swahili society, as well as the incorporation of non-Muslim elements, something reinforced by the fact that the essential demarcated areas of the enclosure and its defined entrances are 'retained through the next six hundred years' (M. Horton 1991:105).

Unfortunately, though, interpretation of the *kaya* phenomena has sometimes been taken too far, with the *kaya* seen as physical indicators of a migration from a mythical homeland of Shungwaya, usually placed in southern Somalia

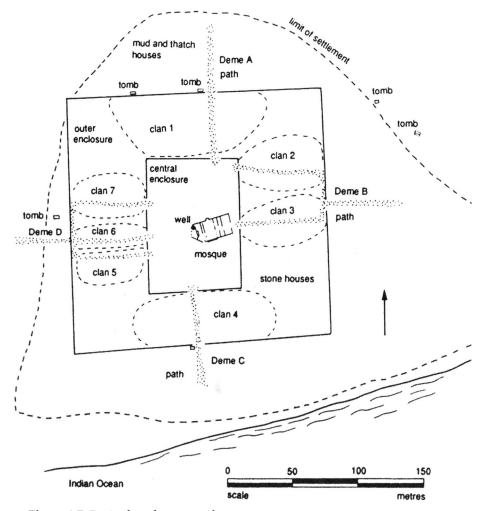

Figure 4.7 Posited enclosure at Shanga

(described, but not agreed with, in Helms forthcoming). However, archaeological research examining settlement in the hinterland surrounding the coastal settlements in Kenya has indicated that 'the *kaya* were not new transplants brought by migrants from a mythical Shungwaya, but rather resulted from the combination of a much longer and continuous process of settlement change and development' (Helms 2000:284). Indeed, the very definition of the *kaya* as 'a timeless distillation of customary essence and identity' (Parkin 1991:43) can – and has been – challenged (J. Willis 1996).

The 'pastoralising' of Swahili origins referred to above has been criticised by Donley-Reid – for example, in suggested interpretations that the central enclosure at Shanga might have been used to stall cattle, something Donley-Reid (1990:123) argues is not supported by the expected presence of cattle dung, which is in fact absent. Equally, Donley-Reid is critical of the explicit African-ising of Swahili origins. Based largely upon a critique of architectural data she suggests that such interpretations have political connotations, as 'this has be-come a politically delicate issue because it is no longer an advantage to claim Arab ancestry in a country governed by Africans' (1990:123). Donley-Reid ar-gues that the founders of Swahili settlements were foreign in origin, 'descended from Arab traders and their African wives' (Donley Reid 1990:117), and that the archaeological data from sites such as Shanga has been misinterpreted. One of her primary concerns is over the interpretation of a sequence of structures un-covered at Shanga as mosques (see below). Donley-Reid's arguments can be faulted in many ways; however, she is correct in emphasising that a political element, consciously or subconsciously, has crept into more recent interpreta-tion – as indeed it existed, as has been shown, in earlier colonial theories.

Having outlined Donley-Reid's criticisms it is pertinent to note that these are flawed and that African origins for the Swahili are correct. It is also likely that these were not pastoralist but multi-ethnic in origin, as described by Helms (2000), and as reflected in the contemporary make-up of the hinterland, with pastoralists in the drier north and agriculturists in southern areas (Nurse and Spear 1985:3). The hinterland peoples were the base from which the Swahili developed, albeit with some foreign influences, as is increasingly being indi-cated by archaeological research. However, whether Swahili origins took place in northern Kenya or elsewhere, for example on the coast of central Tanzania, is also the subject of much debate. The work of Felix Chami has already been referred to and he has argued for an agriculturist Bantu origin for the Swahili in the latter area, with a presence established on the coast by the end of the last century BCE (Chami and Msemwa 1997b:675). Chami argues for a continuity in settlement in central Tanzania from stone-using communities through to those termed early iron working (EIW), and then in turn in the sixth century to those producing the triangular incised ware (TIW) already referred to. Thus a northern Kenyan Swahili origins model linked with Tana tradition pottery does not fit with Chami's (1998:204) interpretation which posits a spread of TIW both north and south from the central Tanzanian coast.

The linchpin of this model is provided by the local ceramics sequence, es-pecially the evolution of the TIW, Tana tradition, or to add more confusion, 'Kitchen' or 'Wenje' ware as it is sometimes also described (**figure 4.8**). Here, the term 'triangular incised ware' is preferred, as it lacks the geographical appella-tion of the other frequently used 'Tana tradition' label, and instead uses a dominant decorative motif as its descriptive referent. The results of Chami's archaeological excavations, such as those on Kwale island (Chami and Msemwa 1997a), are necessitating a review of the regional situation. But as Sutton (1994/5:228) notes, the chronology of the ceramic sequence 'needs to be more satisfactorily established, both inland and on the coast'. However, a correla-tion between early TIW (*c.*sixth to late eighth centuries) and Sasanian Islamic

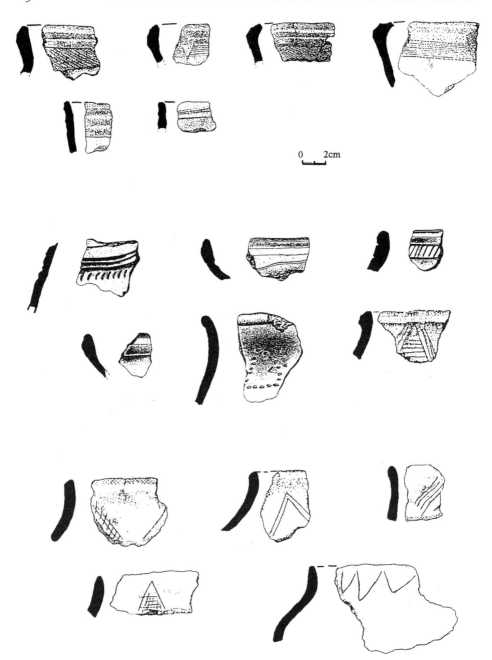

Figure 4.8 Potsherds from the central Tanzanian coast showing the evolution from EIW (top) to TIW (bottom)

turquoise glazed pottery, and later TIW (c.late eighth to tenth centuries) and Islamic white glazed and early sgraffiato wares does appear to exist at certain central Tanzanian sites, adding some support to his suggested chronology (see Chami 1994/5:234). Regardless of refining the dating, Chami is certainly proposing important ideas based on new archaeological material, and although his interpretations and chronology need fine-tuning, and will undoubtedly be revised in the light of future work, he has reopened the debate on Swahili origins in what is a healthy process.

Another factor which has emerged from recent debate over Swahili origins is that early coastal–interior connections are now also being actively considered (see for example Helms 2000; forthcoming). This research has also further and terminally undermined the model of the coastal settlements as outward-looking foreign implants. Instead, they have now been shown to be firmly rooted within their local context. In the coastal hinterland of Kenya for example, Helms (2000) has isolated five phases of cultural development and change dating from prior to 600 CE through to post-1650 CE **(figure 4.9)**. The implications of this research for Swahili origins have already been considered above; they also have a bearing upon the arguments over where, geographically, the development of the Swahili occurred. In this respect Helms (2000:282) points out that the Kenyan evidence does not support Chami's central Tanzanian TIW emergence model. Rather, his evidence from the central and southern coast of Kenya shows similar early emergence, 'and similar evidence would now appear to be emerging from the Upper Tana River Valley, and perhaps along the coast of Mozambique'.

This research also indicates that extensive contacts were maintained between hinterland and coast. Imports obtained from Indian Ocean trade are found at the Kenyan hinterland sites. Prior to 1000 CE at Mgombani and Chombo, for instance, glass beads and fragments of glass were recovered, with Sasanian Islamic pottery recorded at Mgombani, and sherds of Chinese yue stoneware and hatched sgraffiato from Mteza. This evidence has been interpreted as indicative of carefully controlled, high-status exchange (Helms 2000:286). Similarly, after 1000, imports are again found at various hinterland sites including at *kaya* centres. Similar evidence is now being recorded in Tanzania, as at the important site of Dakawa (Haaland 1994/5; Haaland and Msuya in press), a site discussed further in chapter 8. These inland sites could have served as collection points for commodities destined for the coast (Horton 1996b:409). Initially, interregional trade might have taken place in commodities such as iron and grain for fish (Chami and Msemwa 1997b:676), with later, long-distance Indian Ocean trade being added onto this. In many respects this parallels the situation in the western Sahel described in the next chapter, where, as with the Swahili settlements, the trade centres on the fringe of the Sahara in the western Sahel were also within enormous hinterlands with which they were in constant interaction, the details of which are only now beginning to be reconstructed.

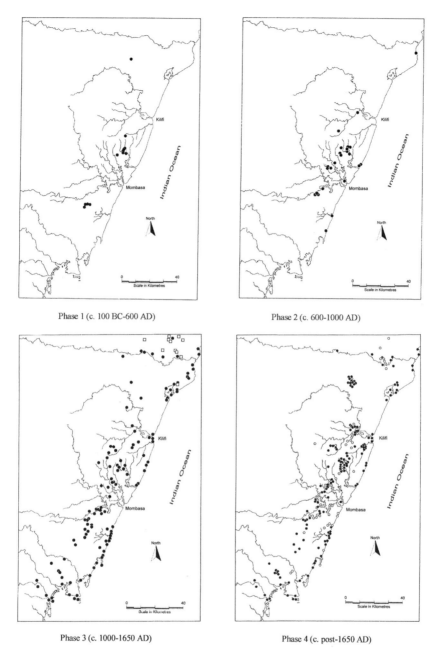

KEY- *Closed circles: iron-working, farming settlements; Open Squares: agro-pastoral settlements*
Open circles: not fully investigated

Figure 4.9 Phases of settlement in the Kenyan coastal hinterland

In summary, the overall African origins of the Swahili are now clear, though the details might be less so and will continue to be argued over. This is in part due to the simple point made by Horton and Middleton (2000:15) that the 'Swahili have now and have had in the past many identities and not just a single one'. They have grown out of an indigenous base, but have adapted to the coast, and have been profoundly influenced by 'their participation in long-distance trade, the adoption of Islam and the development of urban living'. This has fundamental implications for Islamisation and the archaeology of Islam in the region, as it shows, as elsewhere in the continent, that Islam was adapted to fit an indigenous structure, i.e. African foundations, including those of pre-existing religious belief, the archaeological details of which will now be considered.

The archaeology of Islam: pre-1000 CE

With the rise of Islam, trade contacts from the Red Sea, India, Arabia, China and the Persian Gulf increased significantly, as commodities such as gold from southern Africa, ivory, timber and slaves were sought, and in return finished goods such as metalwork, glassware, beads, glazed ceramics and cloth were imported (Duarte 1993; M. Horton 1996b). The phases in trade relations have already been considered, with the Persian Gulf isolated as the primary area in contact with the inhabitants of the East African coast. However, the impact of Islam within this period was not immense. Muslims appear to have been small in number and confined to a few trading centres – some of which, bearing in mind the points already made, they may also have had a hand in establishing. The delay in Islam reaching the East African coast, as compared to the Horn of Africa, has been explained by the fact that land routes were not operating, and it was more problematical to go around the Horn and down the coast than across the Red Sea (Hiskett 1994:151). This would appear to be somewhat simplistic, as the items of foreign origin from pre-Islamic contexts already described (see M. Horton 1996a) indicate that such trading voyages were not always so problematical. However, geographical distances from the central lands of Islam were greater than those from the Nilotic Sudan and the Horn of Africa, and thus contacts with Islam were initially intermittent perhaps for reasons of distance.

One of the earliest centres referred to in the historical sources as occupied by Muslims on the East African coast was the island of Qanbalu. This was supposedly home to a partial Muslim population, 'when the Umayyad caliphate in Damascus gave way to the new Abbasid caliphate in Baghdad' (Hiskett 1994:152), i.e. about 750. Al-Mas'udi (d. 956) records that Qanbalu, 'which is one or two days sail from the coast, has a Muslim population and a royal family' (Freeman-Grenville 1962:17). Perhaps the legendary Qanbalu is to be identified with Pemba (Chittick 1977:192). This is also an identification proposed by Horton and Middleton (2000:66), who suggest that al-Mas'udi was

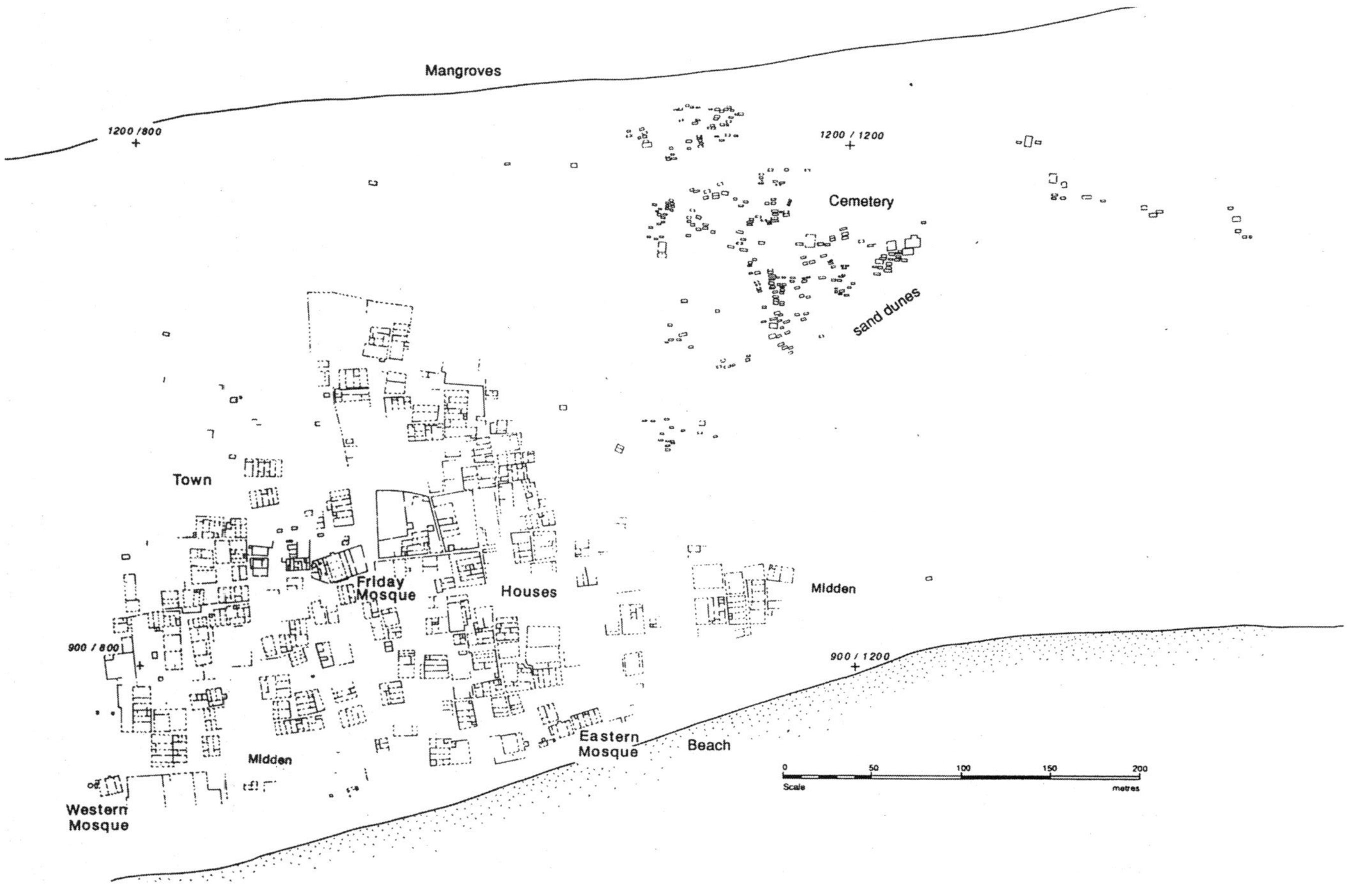

Figure 4.10 Plan of Shanga

referring to the whole island of Pemba rather than a specific point on it. This might be true, but as our knowledge stands at present it is perhaps best to agree with a point made by Hourani et al. (1995:148) that 'in sum, we do not have an archaeologically convincing candidate for the important documented port of Qanbalu'.

Shanga

Less ambiguous than the vague Arabic historical sources is the archaeological data. The earliest archaeological evidence for Islam on the East African coast comes from Shanga, where Muslim burials dated to around 800, and a sequence of one stone and seven timber structures interpreted as mosques were found. The earliest of these structures has been dated to around 750–780. This small rectangular timber structure, 'mosque A', measured 1.64 × 2.59 m, and was built of timber stakes floored with mud collected from the mangrove swamps. The second structure in the sequence, mosque B, was more sizeable at 6.4 × 4 m, but even then could only hold twenty-five or so worshippers. This was interpreted as illustrating that a small Muslim community was living in a predominantly non-Muslim society (M. Horton 1991:105). A gradual growth in the size of the structures is appreciable, with the first stone mosque, H, measuring 5.1 m square, with walls 0.54 m thick. This structure was in turn superseded by a larger congregational mosque (c. 8 × 12m), also built of porites coral, which remained in use until the town was abandoned around 1425 **(figure 4.10)**. The mosque interpretation, which has been questioned (Donley-Reid 1990), was based upon the orientation of the structures, the *qiblah*, as *mihrabs* were absent except for a possible *mihrab* represented by a wooden post in one of the sequence of structures uncovered (mosque F). M. Horton (1996a:442) notes that all the structures were laid out using the dhira or cubit of 518 mm, and that 'they have a consistent *qibla*, albeit some 50 degrees away from the true direction of Mecca'. The deviancy evident in where exactly Mecca was thought to lie was explained by the excavator as representing 'deficient geographical knowledge of the location of Arabia from East Africa' (M. Horton 1996b:229).

Are these actually mosques? This interpretation has been criticised on account of the wrong orientation and lack of *mihrabs* (Donley-Reid 1990:123). However, it is here believed that these structures are mosques, of a primitive kind found elsewhere in the Muslim world as well (see Insoll 1999a:46–9). The initial timber mosques seem to fall within the category of what could be termed 'impermanent' structures – though the lack of permanency in materials used is compensated for, conversely, by permanence of a ritual/religious kind, as indicated by the fact that so many mosques were built in exactly the same spot. More importantly, the first mosque was also built directly over the burnt tree stump, described above, as found within the primary enclosure

(M. Horton 1991:105). This signals an element of religious continuity in a manner which can be found across sub-Saharan Africa. It provides an example of what Eaton (1993) would refer to in a Bengali context as 'inclusion' (see chapter 1) – literally including the old with the new. Furthermore, it can also be suggested that the Shanga mosque sequence, as attested, for example, in its progression towards orthodoxy in the *qiblah* angle employed, physically represents the adoption and integration of Islam within Swahili society as a whole (see below). More prosaically, as the structures grew in size, so must the Muslim community have done. An explanation for the early date for these conversions to Islam can also be sought. This is something which Pouwels (2000:254) suggests was due to the fact that it required 'relatively little intellectual change'. The question can be asked as to why this occurred, and the answer is perhaps because it appears that the possible Eastern Bantu ancestors of the Swahili had a notion of a supreme god, but as is frequently the case elsewhere in sub-Saharan Africa, religious communication was maintained with intermediaries rather than with the supreme god (Pouwels 2000).

The early Muslim burials also illustrate the same initial confusion over orientation, aligned with the early mosques described above, and again something which was corrected over the course of time. Over 500 stone tombs were recorded at Shanga and on the basis of this it was calculated that 2.8 per cent of the population were given stone tombs, allowing for a total population of 3,000 and an annual death rate of 3 per cent. Thus much of the population must have been buried elsewhere, in less ornate tombs. This is a factor of importance and one which relates to Swahili settlements as a whole, i.e. the imbalance in visibility in favour of the stone-built elements (Fleisher and LaViolette in press), as is discussed later. M. Horton (1996b:75) has suggested that the stone tombs might have functioned as markers signalling 'ownership of a particular area'. This is a not unimportant consideration within Swahili society, as will also be considered below with regard to concepts of *waungwana* status. Status concerns might also be reflected in an apparent clustering of tombs in the centre of the settlement, which appeared to underlie the importance of this area to the community (M. Horton 1996b:76). The early occupation levels also contained evidence for timber house structures, which appear to have been the prototypes of over 200 stone houses which were also recorded in later levels (M. Horton 1987a:300) **(figure 4.10)**. As Horton and Middleton (2000:119) note, 'these houses were rebuilt with the same plan, one over another, but using more permanent materials'. They, like the mosques, again illustrate the essentially indigenous development of both Swahili society and its material components.

A variety of archaeological evidence indicated participation by the inhabitants of Shanga in long-distance commerce. These included imported ceramics of Chinese, Persian, Indian and Arabian origin. Over 1,500 glass fragments were also recovered, including fragments from a range of vessels – bowls, flasks, bottles and, from the congregational mosque, pieces of mosque lamp formerly used to light the interior (M. Horton 1996b:317–18). Numerous glass and semi-precious beads were similarly collected, along with a seal ring, inlaid with a disc of black jasper on which was cut an Arabic inscription in reverse (M. Horton 1996b:357). This latter find is of especial significance within this study as it is another personal possession which if found with other categories of material, as at the site of Qasr Ibrim discussed in the last chapter, can indicate the former presence of a Muslim in the archaeological record (as discussed in chapter 1). The seal ring combines both secular and sacred significance, functioning as a sign of both individual and Muslim identity, and an item connected through tradition with the Prophet (Insoll 1999a:116–17).

Various coins were also recovered, including – unusually – silver ones, when copper issues predominate in this region and, much less frequently, gold (Sutton 1997, and discussed below). These included examples minted at Shanga, and others imported from further south on the East African coast – issues from the site of Kilwa and possibly Manda, and the islands of Pemba and Mafia (Brown 1996:369). These latter coins date from around 950–1350, and illustrate the later interconnections that existed along the coast. The silver coins minted in Shanga in the eighth to tenth centuries are of special interest as they bear the inscriptions in Arabic, 'Muhammad/trusts in Allah' and slightly later, 'The Kingdom is Allah's/and in Him trusts Abd Allah'. These were interpreted as being struck by local Muslim leaders, 'and significantly both names are often associated with Muslim converts' (Horton and Middleton 2000:50). These coins, in their proclamation of apparently newly found Muslim faith, function in the same way as tombstones recorded in the city of Gao in the Western Sahel on the other side of Africa, which similarly in their carefully chosen sequence of names also affirm new Muslim identity (see chapter 5). Parallels for the Shanga series are difficult to find, according to Brown (1992), who argues that they most resemble coins struck by the Arab governors of Sind (Pakistan), being approximately the same size, 9 mm, but slightly heavier at about 0.5 g. Brown's Sind comparisons are more convincing than Horton and Middleton's (2000:62) parallels drawn with issues minted by the Zaidi Imams, a Shi'ite group in the ninth century (see below). The Shanga lion, a further unique item of metalwork recovered (Horton and Blurton 1988), has already been described above.

Other mainland sites

Also in the Lamu archipelago, the reinterpretation of the results of excavations at the site of Manda have already been referred to (**figure 4.11**). These allow for an early phase of settlement in wattle-and-daub houses in the ninth to tenth centuries (Horton 1987a:298), rather than the site only being representative of a later Swahili stone town as was previously thought (Chittick 1984). Imports recovered from these early phases of settlement included Sasanian Islamic jar

Figure 4.11 Manda from the air

fragments, Chinese Dusun jar fragments, and sherds of Islamic white-glaze wares – a type of assemblage widely found on coastal sites of this date, and one which indicated that 'Manda was already a flourishing community between 800 and 850 AD' (M. Horton 1986:204). Specific evidence for the presence of Muslims at Manda in these early levels was not found, but Chittick might not have recognised wattle-and-daub mosques if they had been present anyway, as his neglect of domestic structures made of these materials has already been referred to. A similar picture is evident at the site of Pate, again in the Lamu archipelago, as also described above, and where similar early imported ceramics were found, including Sasanian Islamic and Dusun jar sherds dating from the first half of the ninth century (Wilson and Omar 1997). Further south at Kilwa on the Tanzanian coast, settlement began at a similar early date, commencing around 800 (Sutton 1998b). Initial phases of occupation, as at Shanga, were represented by wattle-and-daub housing, and the excavator, Chittick (1974:237), suggested that during the first phase of occupation (ninth to late tenth centuries) the population were followers of traditional religion. This interpretation was based upon the absence of evidence indicating the existence of a Muslim community. However, the presence of a piece of whetstone found in these early levels bearing Arabic graffito 'may suggest the presence of Muslims' (Hourani et al. 1995:147).

The evidence for early Islam at Kilwa might be fairly inconclusive but it is less so even further south, where, at Chibuene in southern Mozambique, four burials, also of ninth-century date, were found. One of these appeared to have been oriented according to Islamic rites (as outlined in chapter 1), and this led the excavator to state that 'if so it could be the earliest known Islamic burial on the East African Coast' (Sinclair 1987:87). The Shanga burials could be earlier, this is unclear, but Chibuene is certainly the southernmost point in the continent in which early Muslim burials have been recorded. It is still a recognised anchorage today, with fresh water available (Sinclair 1982:149), and must have formed a base used by merchants, some presumably Muslim, involved in trade with the southern African interior (see chapter 8). Corroborating evidence for possible contacts with Muslims at this date was provided by the find of sherds of Islamic white-glazed pottery of possible late seventh–early eighth-century date (M. Horton 1996a:445). TIW wares also indicated Swahili connections. Similar supporting evidence was recovered from nearby at Ponta Dundo, and comprised several fragments of ninth-century Sasanian Islamic ware (Sinclair 1982:163).

Although the interpretation of a handful of sherds of imported pottery and a couple of burials cannot be taken too far, the suggestion made by Hourani et al. (1995:149) that the Chibuene area might be Sofala, the source of gold for the Muslim traders, need not be too far-fetched. Investigations at a site actually called Sofala achieved varied results, and no conclusive evidence suggesting an early Muslim or trader presence of any type was found. The material recorded all post-dated the sixteenth century, with the bulk dating from the sixteenth–seventeenth centuries. This included Chinese blue-and-white wares recovered from a trial trench excavated next to Sofala creek, as well as further sherds of Chinese ceramics, including celadons of similar date collected from the main beach (Dickinson 1969:1–2). Besides the Chinese ceramics, various beads were found – opaque Indian red glass cane beads, as well as various other monochrome glass trade beads (Dickinson 1970), and a wound grey-green bead described as similar to one from 'Acropolis A3 at Great Zimbabwe' (Dickinson 1969:5). This might be wishful thinking, or might indicate that this site was one of the coastal contact points for Great Zimbabwe (see chapter 8).

However, the locally made pottery which was recovered could merit a re-examination as within the incised wares there might be found TIW of much earlier date (possibly even represented in the poor-quality drawings attached to the report). This would obviously have important ramifications for Swahili contacts with southern Africa, though it should be stressed that this is merely a hypothesis at present. Yet the area is known to have suffered from severe erosion, the sixteenth-century Portuguese fort having been largely washed away. It is also mentioned by Liesegang (1972:149) that the Portuguese sources indicate that their first fort built in 1505 was not constructed in the existing settlement but between that of the head of the local Muslim community, Yusufu, and another village. Thus other settlements might exist in the area, but it is a distinct possibility that any early Muslim settlement has suffered similarly from coastal erosion, or at best been mixed up with later material.

The offshore islands

Evidence for Islam and Muslim communities on the nearer offshore islands is varied, but is increasing following recent research. This has already been referred to in the introduction to this chapter with regard to Pemba island. Here, various sites have now been recorded with evidence for participation in international trade during the later first millennium. At Chwaka/Tumbe for instance, LaViolette (in press) mentions that TIW and Sasanian Islamic wares dating from the ninth to eleventh centuries were recovered. Similar discoveries of TIW, including below a stone mosque at Pujini, are described by LaViolette and Fleisher (1995). Horton and Middleton (2000:51) also suggest that a mosque dating from the tenth century lies beneath a later stone mosque structure excavated at the site of Ras Mkumbuu. Similar evidence is accumulating on Zanzibar island. The important site of Unguja Ukuu has already been mentioned in the context of pre-Islamic trade (Juma 1996b), and this site continued to be of significance in the early Islamic era, though the results still await publication. Excavations have also been completed at the site of Fukuchani, where middens extend for some 1,200 m along the shoreline of Zanzibar opposite the smaller island of Tumbatu. At this site Gulf-origin earthenware storage jars ascribed a fifth- to eighth-century date range were recorded, along with daub fragments suggest-ing the former presence of timber buildings (Horton and Middleton 2000:44). Thus the patterns on these islands match those on the African mainland – timber buildings, similar trade ceramics and TIW, the probable existence of nascent Muslim communities, with the accompanying implied presence of small mosques and cemeteries.

Further offshore on the Comoros, the inhabitants of the four major islands of Ngazidja (Grand Comoro), Mwali (Moheli), Ndzuwani (Anjouan), and Maore (Mayotte) were certainly involved in long-distance Indian Ocean trade dur-ing the ninth and tenth centuries, as has been remarked upon at the start of this chapter. H. Wright (1984:57) suggests that the islands possibly acted as a transshipment point between Madagascar, Indian Ocean traders and the East African coast. This phase of settlement is referred to as the Dembeni phase, after Dembeni on Maore (Verin 1994:53). Dembeni settlements such as those at M'Bachile, Dzindani, and M'Beni on Ngazidja, are sited near lagoons, are on average about 5 ha in size and are made up of houses of wattle and daub (H. Wright 1984; Allibert et al. 1990). Dembeni-phase imported ceramics are largely from the Gulf/Mesopotamian region and include the ubiquitous Sasanian Islamic wares, and fine opaque white-glazed wares. These sites are actually richer in imported material than those on the mainland, such as Kilwa occupation levels of the same date (H. Wright 1984; Chanudet 1990). Large jars are frequently found, thought to have been used for transporting oils, pitch or date syrup (H. Wright 1984:41).

Although later in date, evidence for an extensive trade in date syrup has been found at source in the Persian Gulf, the area of origin of the Sasanian Islamic jars. An example of this is provided by the thirteenth-century levels in the Islamic fort on Bahrain. Here, the importance of the trade was indicated by the fact that date honey was actually being produced inside the walls of the fort, as indicated by seven structures called *madbasa* used to produce the syrup built within the fort's walls **(figure 4.12)**. The honey was then exported in sealed jars 6–8 kg in weight, examples of which (empty) have also been found (Kervran 1999:50–1). Fragments from glass vessels are also found at Dembeni sites, as are a few glass trade beads.

Local pottery at Dembeni-phase sites includes a plain pottery decorated with shell impressions which 'may result from interaction with Madagascar commu-nitics' (H. Wright 1984:56). Other locally produced wares have been described as resembling, and 'in some cases identical to, contemporary ceramics from Chibuene in southern Mozambique to Manda in northern Kenya' (H. Wright 1992:85). The main industry of these Dembeni villages appears to have been the production of iron, as indicated by furnaces found. The iron was apparently produced for export, as attested by al-Idrisi, for example, who refers to the good-quality iron from East Africa which was exported to India (Verin 1994:54). The diet of the Dembeni villagers also signalled their participation in the Indian

Figure 4.12 *Madbasa*, Bahrain fort

Ocean world, and included goats and millet introduced from Africa, and rice and coconuts introduced from South or South East Asia, as well as a substantial fish component (H. Wright 1984:58; Verin 1994).

The archaeological evidence would also seem to indicate that the majority of Comorians were not Muslims during the Dembeni phase. Certainly no stone mosques have been found, and apparently no other mosques have been recorded, though as Verin (1994:53) notes, this does not mean there were no Muslims, because they could have 'construit un lieu de prière en matériaux végétaux'. Analysis of faunal assemblages from Dembeni sites has also indicated that species were being consumed which are taboo to Muslims. At the site of Dembeni, for instance, the remains of lemurs and tortoises were found in ninth-century levels (Allibert et al. 1990:66), while at M'Bachile a pig tooth was found, which might of course have been an ornament (Redding and Goodman 1984:53). Tenrec remains have also been recovered (Allibert and Verin 1996:465): this small insectivore was classified as a 'kind of pig' by Comorians (Redding 1992:115). Non-Muslim burials have also been recorded dated to the Dembeni phase at a beach site at Ngazidja. The physical anthropology indicated an East African affinity, and the individuals had had their incisors deliberately removed, further supporting this link. This evidence, 'plus the orientation', was interpreted as indicating 'that the people of this hamlet were not Muslims', though 'it is, however, quite possible that other contemporary Comorians could already have accepted Islam' (H. Wright 1992:84).

In fact, funerary evidence indicates that non-Muslims were still present in the population of the Comoros as late as the thirteenth century. At Bagamoyo on Maore, a skull with similarly chipped and pulled teeth was recorded, but this late presence has been interpreted as that of non-Muslim slaves (Allibert and Verin 1996:465). It is also worth repeating that when considering this evidence from early periods of Islamic conversion and Islamisation, and indeed for all points in time thereafter, general factors of non-observance should be considered, as the difference between religious ideals and practice can be substantial (Insoll 1999b). This factor is not only indicated when Islam is considered, but is also a feature of other world religions (Insoll 2001), as recently discussed by Lane (2001) with regard to Christianity, or Hachlili (2001) with regard to Judaism, for example.

In summary, these examples, though not exhaustive, indicate that a similar picture can be seen along the East African coast and on its offshore islands, attesting to the growth of small Muslim communities from the late eighth century onwards. Similar assemblages of trade ceramics indicate participation in Indian Ocean trade by the inhabitants of what were, at this date (the last 250 or so years of the first millennium), small coastal settlements. Broadly similar assemblages of locally produced pottery also indicate the development of a unified cultural tradition, that of the Swahili, as best indicated by the presence of TIW. Building in these settlements was of wattle and daub, and, as we have seen, could include small mosques in the same materials, as well as small numbers of Muslim burials indicating the growth of Muslim communities on the East African littoral. The agent of Islamisation was undoubtedly contacts with Muslims through trade – but trade and Islamisation (as tellingly indicated by the evidence from Shanga) which was negotiated and controlled by local communities and their considerations.

Post-1000 CE: the north coast

The stone towns

Trade increased in importance after 1000, and conversion to Islam on the East African coast proceeded rapidly, with Islam becoming the majority religion in about 1100 among the Swahili (Horton and Middleton 2000). Numerous settlement sites dating from this period are found along the Somali, Kenyan and Tanzanian coastal strip, and on the offshore islands (see, e.g., Horton and Clark 1985; Chittick 1969; Allen 1980). Commonly, evidence for long-distance trade is again present – glazed ceramics from China, Arabia and the Persian Gulf, glass trade beads of Indian, Egyptian and uncertain origin (Davison and Clark 1972), fragments of glass from the Near East – all evidently accompanied by increasing prosperity. This is reflected in the use of elaborate stone architecture, utilising both terrestrial and porites coral, which although found prior to 1000, did not flourish as an architectural form until the thirteenth century (Garlake 1966; M. Horton 1994a:199). In fact, the stone towns were at their most prosperous in the fourteenth–fifteenth centuries.

Muslim congregations had evidently increased in size, reflecting the increased Islamic franchise, and each of the major settlements had a congregational mosque, and often several smaller ward mosques. In this respect, a point made by Horton and Middleton (2000:48) that, 'without exception, every pre-nineteenth century mosque or Muslim tomb known is located within 1000 metres of the sea shore' is of interest, indicating the coastal concentration of the Muslim community. During this period a local Swahili mosque style also evolved, utilising a rectangular prayer hall, with either an even number of columns and a central aisle giving a view of the *mihrab*, or an odd number of rows and no central aisle. These varied greatly in decoration, but the basic plan was derived from small mosques dating from the ninth–tenth centuries which have been found in the Persian Gulf, as at the site of Siraf (M. Horton 1994a:199–200). Thereafter, Muslim elements were adapted in the local context using locally available materials.

Stone houses, palaces and various other structures were also built (Garlake 1966; Chittick 1971). The indigenous origins of structures such as the houses have already been remarked upon as indicated in the sequence of house plans uncovered at Shanga, where timber prototypes were replaced by mud and coral, and finally by all-coral buildings by the early thirteenth century (M. Horton 1996b). Courtyard houses were built, often interlinked into multiples of houses, perhaps representing the extended family structure (see Insoll 1999a:77–9 for further examples). The phases of this can probably be interpreted as 'representing the fission and fusion of family groups over time' (Horton and Middleton 2000:119). However, having stated that the indigenous nature of these structures is evident archaeologically, Islamic influences must also be recognised as a major spatial structuring element, with a presumed growth in possible privacy concerns following conversion to Islam. These points have already been discussed in chapter 1, and are evident in various other examples in sub-Saharan Africa, as in changes in domestic architecture evident in the western Sahel, and considered in the next chapter.

Similar stone houses, tombs and mosques are found along the coast after the thirteenth–fourteenth centuries, from southern Somalia (Sanseverino 1983) to Shanga (M. Horton 1996b) and Pate (Wilson and Omar 1997) in northern Kenya, Gede in central Kenya (Kirkman 1954), Kilwa in Tanzania (Sutton 1998b) and various sites in northern Mozambique (Duarte 1993), as well as offshore, on the Comoros (Verin 1994), or in northern Madagascar (Dewar and Wright 1993). Common elements in the stone architectural form found on the East African coast include features of both design and construction. With construction, the use of two types of coral prevails: finer-grained reef coral for carving and finished work, and coarser coral as a general building material (Garlake 1966). The widespread appearance of coral masonry in the thirteenth century has been suggested (M. Horton 1996b) as reflecting a shift from Persian Gulf to Red Sea contacts, as in the latter area its use is common on the coast (see chapters 2 and 3). Plaster was also applied to all stonework, obtained from burning coral to obtain lime. Mangrove poles were used for ceilings, restricting rooms to between 2 and 3 m in width or multiples thereof after further structural support was provided, usually with octagonal or rectangular columns. Indeed, the use of mangrove poles has been described by Garlake (1966:23) as the limitation governing 'the entire architecture of the coast and it is probably the most important single factor in determining the architectural style'. Other recurring construction elements include the use of dressed coral rain spouts to drain roofs, and red earth or plaster on coral hardcore floors. Commonly occurring design elements include the simple pointed or drop arch used for doorways, *mihrabs* and windows until the eighteenth century and its replacement by the semi-circular arch (Garlake 1966:27).

However, the importance of stone architecture on the East African coast exceeds aesthetic or functional concerns. The existence of status groups within Swahili society was of great significance, with the Swahili conceptualising people as falling into five basic groups. At the apex were the *waungwana*, the oldest and most respected urban families (Nurse and Spear 1985:25), freeborn men and women who were usually wealthy and in positions of authority. Below them were *madada* (female domestic slaves), *wazalia* (locally born slaves), *wa-tumwa* (plantation slaves) and finally, *washenzi* (all other Africans). Within the interrelationships between these groups the domestic structure took on a great importance. To quote Donley-Reid (1990:119), 'the hierarchical relationships among groups of individuals and the interactions between each of these groups centre on the types of houses and where houses were built'. Donley-Reid examined several Swahili coral and clay houses in the Lamu archipelago and on the adjacent mainland of Kenya, all dating from after the early eighteenth century (Donley-Reid 1990, and see Donley 1982, 1987). Who built what, where and when was decided by the *waungwana*, and social progression into and through Swahili society was represented by the progression from the grass round hut into the lower levels of the multi-storey coral house, and finally into the upper levels, and the inner sanctum, the *ndani* (**figure 4.13**). Non-*waungwana* men were excluded from the process of upward mobility altogether, but it was possible for the female descendants of a slave girl taken as a concubine to have a coral house built for them after a couple of generations. Thus in this instance the domestic structure, the traditional Swahili stone house, served as the key to both social mobility and specific gender exclusions.

Therefore it appears that architecture, unsurprisingly, was also interwoven with status concerns and the very structure of Swahili society. But is it possible to project Donley-Reid's specific ethno-historical model back to before the eighteenth century – or, indeed, outside Lamu – to argue that Swahili society was similarly structured on the five-group model, and that architecture functioned in the same way? It appears not – as Nurse and Spear (1985:26) note, such 'generalized model(s)' cannot be projected back in time. They are specific to their own time and place and cannot be used to interpret the social meaning of architecture, for example, in fifteenth-century Gede, or thirteenth-century Shanga. However, we do know that urban Swahili society was probably divided along perhaps similar lines into what Horton and Middleton (2000:127) more broadly define as 'Patricians'' and 'Commoners'' towns – a more feasible description which allows for social differentiation but without the levels of detail and accompanying analogical weakness inherent in applying the more recent *waungwana* model just described.

Within this model both the stone towns and their architecture, its form and function, can be seen to be of social significance. But what exactly is meant by a 'stone town'? An attempt at definition is required. Between about 1100 and 1500 trade expanded on the East African coast, as already noted, which was accompanied by increased building in stone. This was likewise associated with the growth of 'an increasingly wealthy class of merchants... who, by restricting access to wealth, were able to monopolise political power' (Nurse and Spear 1985:85). These were the forerunners of the *waungwana*, the patricians, who invested part of their wealth in building, leading to the development of numerous political centres represented by the stone towns, of which, according to Horton

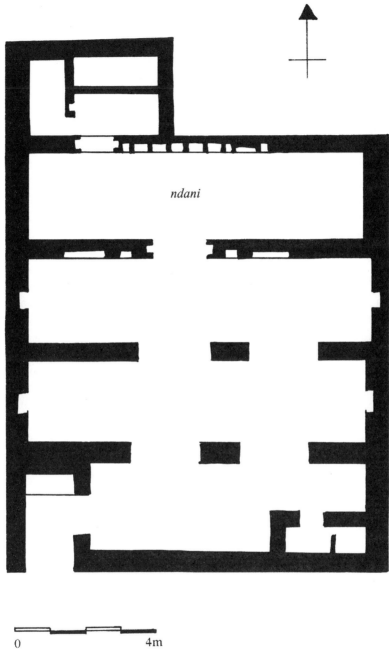

ndani

Figure 4.13 Ground plan of a Swahili house

and Middleton (2000:11), 'no two, are precisely alike either in appearance, lay-out, or ethnic composition'. City-states, or what Nurse and Spear (1985:85) term 'oligarchic republics', were the result, stretching from Mogadishu to Kilwa, as well as offshore. Authority might be invested in the patricians or in a ruling family or the personage of a king. These polities were numerous, and 'such was the fragmented nature of Swahili society that political authority resided within each town or small group of towns' (Horton and Middleton 2000:157).

However, it would be erroneous to assume that the coast was merely an urban society. Urban centres, largely stone towns, were indeed the focal points, but the great majority of people lived in villages, or the non-stone sectors of the stone towns (Nurse and Spear 1985:22). The archaeological balance between the two, stone and non-stone, needs equalising. As Fleisher and LaViolette (in press) rightly note, 'it is becoming increasingly evident, that the richness of the archaeology at stone towns not withstanding, we can only understand the fullness of the Swahili experience by combining the archaeology of the Swahili elite – that minority who lived in stone houses in stone towns – with the archae-ology of the "rest"'. The existence of the non-stone component of stone towns has already been described with regard to Shanga, and increasingly, archaeo-logical research elsewhere is indicating the extent of settlement in wattle-and-daub architecture, both in the stone towns and in the mass of other villages that existed elsewhere. Fleisher and LaViolette (in press), for example, recorded forty-two new sites dating from between the eighth and twentieth centuries during survey and test-pitting of a 200 m-wide strip, 37 km long, between Dar es Salaam and Bagamoyo in Tanzania. Of these sites, many 'were small and had no evidence of stone architecture'. Helms' (2000, forthcoming) relevant research in the coastal hinterland of Kenya, focusing upon a crucial, and until recently missing, element in patterns of coastal settlement, again relating to people living in non-stone architecture, has also already been described.

Examples of these stone towns on the northern part of the coast are numerous. They obviously include Shanga, already well described, as well as other impor-tant Swahili sites in the Lamu archipelago such as Pate, Lamu, Manda and, nearby, Ungwana (Kirkman 1966; Ghaidan 1976). The reinterpretation of the early levels at Manda has already been outlined. The site, like its neighbours, continued to be occupied, flourishing as a stone town – the latter indicated, for example, by the find of a small silver coin dated to around 1000 and issued by a Fatimid mint in Sicily, thus giving an insight into the trade routes that operated, albeit indirectly (Sutton 1990:67). Manda also lays claim, in the ex-cavator's words (Chittick 1984:215), to 'the first detailed analysis made of the fauna from an excavation on the coast'. This indicates how recently archae-ological analysis taken for granted elsewhere has been employed on the East African coast. It also illustrates the difficulty in, at present, assessing important social questions such as the impact of Islam upon diet through archaeological data, owing to a lack of such data. With the Manda faunal data, the absence of dog and porcupine might be due to Islamic proscription. Otherwise, a fairly orthodox dietary picture is presented, of sheep/goat predominating, with cattle not far behind, as well as camel, turtle, dugong, and some fish and wild animal remains present.The presence of large numbers of polished and pierced fish vertebrae was interpreted as evidence of possible use as ornaments such as necklaces and lip/ear plugs (Chittick 1984:215).

In general, a fairly similar picture of Swahili diet is found along the coast, as represented by the Manda and Shanga faunal assemblages. A broadly similar vegetable component is also found – one which has also already been alluded to with regard to the Comoros, with its mixed African (e.g. millet) and South or Southeast Asian (e.g. rice, coconut, bananas) elements (Verin 1994). Rice was a food of special significance, according to Sutton (1998b:122), who refers to it acquiring 'a prestige in Muslim countries as a cosmopolitan food acceptable to travellers and guests'. Freeman-Grenville (1988b:9) also describes subsequent Portuguese additions to the coastal diet, including potatoes, cassava, cucumber, pawpaw, avocado and guava.

Further to the north, into southern Somalia, a continuation of the stone architectural tradition occurs. Numerous stone monuments have been recorded, including a pillar tomb 5 m in height at Ras Kiambone, with a further group of pillar tombs (see below) recorded at Hanassa (Sanseverino 1983). Other monuments described include a mosque at Munghia, various buildings on the Bajun islands and several Muslim tombs at Bur Gao, dating from the twelfth to nineteenth centuries (Chittick 1969). Further south in Kenya is Gede, one of the best known of all the stone towns. Promoted as a tourist site, it was also one of the first coastal towns to be excavated (Kirkman 1954, 1963). The northern part of the site has the greatest density of coral buildings, including a congregational mosque, several smaller mosques and numerous houses. Some of the latter are quite complex structures, such as the so-called 'House of the Porcelain Bowl'. T. Wilson (1982:213) refers to the great 'degree of formal organisation of space' evident at Gede. This is indicated in the house structures and their emphasis upon gradations of privacy, attested by their complex entrances, lack of outward-facing windows (Chittick 1971:133) and sequences of rooms. Perhaps what is evident in the Gede houses is the beginning of the type of spatial structuration described for later centuries by Donley-Reid (1990), the start of the creation of an inner *ndani*-type sanctum, as described previously.

Islam and Swahili identity

What is also apparent in the adaptation and evolution of privacy concerns as rendered in the domestic environment at Gede is the process of the indigenisation of Islam. This, as we saw with the evolution of the Swahili mosque style, was a major factor on the East African coast. Swahili society is a mix of Muslim and indigenous elements, and this is reflected in its material culture, which over the course of the centuries has developed a unique character. Muslim Swahili material culture is integrated with pre-existing elements, in patterns familiar from across sub-Saharan Africa. Various examples can be cited to illustrate this. For example, parallels have been drawn between the *kaya* of the Mijikenda, and the central enclosure at Shanga, and the placing of the first mosque over the burned tree stump. Yet great diversity is also evident on the coast, and the pre-Islamic substratum in one area might not be applicable in another. However, similarities also exist; as Nurse and Spear (1985:98) note, coherence was given to Swahili society through 'common historical experiences, reflected in their traditions, that produce their language and culture'. Nurse and Spear leave out religion – Islam or traditional – in this statement, but Islam is an equal factor in the glue that has created a certain degree of homogeneity in what can be described as Swahili society, and which is evident as such in the archaeological record. This, it is argued here, contradicts Allen's (1993:17) suggestion that 'some Christians have an indisputable claim to be called Swahilis too'. Islam is a major plank of Swahili identity from the very first, as indicated by archaeological evidence, and though undeniably fused with traditional religions, a wholly non-Muslim identity does not equal a Swahili one.

It is also necessary to examine the notion of Swahili Muslim identity in a little more detail in order to place this region within its sub-Saharan African setting. Horton and Middleton (2000:71) make the point that 'there is surprisingly little evidence for non-Muslim religious activities, or even for syncretism of African religious practices with coastal Islam'. This is true to a certain extent, but here, as elsewhere in the continent south of the Sahara, such evidence does exist, albeit, as they rightly point out, in lesser quantities in comparison to other regions – to West Africa, for example. The lack of evidence might in part also be due to a lack of relevant research, something that might in turn have formerly been due to the types of approach to the coast that were once applied – with Islam and Muslims seen as foreign, and peripheral in terms of their relations with the remainder of the Muslim world. In presenting Islam on the East African coast in such a way, the indigenous local basis of conversion to Islam and the integration of older traditional religious or non-Muslim elements was denied or ignored, in the same way that the indigenous basis of Swahili society as a whole was denied by colonial approaches, as discussed above. In reality, a fusion of Islam and non-Muslim practices has occurred, further supporting the picture of indigenous Swahili origins.

The phases of Islamisation are also complex, yet at the same time can be matched with those that have occurred elsewhere in the continent, as have been and will be described. However, there have also been examples of over-complicating the picture of Swahili Muslim identity on the East African coast based upon minimal evidence. Different sects and schools of Islam have been represented on the coast, as they have elsewhere (as with the Ibadis in the western Sahel, described in the next chapter). But the degree to which their presence on the East African coast has been reconstructed is not necessarily always supported by the available evidence. The otherwise excellent work completed at Shanga on early Islam on the coast provides an example of this. Horton and Middleton (2000:62) have suggested, based on the find of the silver coins described above, that it was 'just possible that the early Muslim community at Shanga comprised Zaidite refugees' or 'local Swahili converts who came under Zaidite influence' (the Zaidites were a breakaway Shi'ite group). Coinage similarities between the Shanga and Zaidi issues are invoked as possibly indicating this, though the evidence is slim and contradicts Brown's (1992) more convincing Sind parallels, also referred to previously. Similar identifications for a presence on the East African coast are made for the Carmathians from Bahrain, and the Ibadis. The latter are certainly attested there later (see Sheriff 1992). Yet although the specifics of some of the sectarian interpretations might be too precise based on limited evidence, the general points made by Horton and Middleton (2000:70) can be wholly agreed with: that Islam was 'linked closely to indigenous practice', and though the external sources 'suggest a bewildering range of different conversion and migration processes', the 'situation on the ground may well have been simpler'.

The Shanga evidence can in fact be used in suggesting a reconstruction of the phases of conversion to Islam by the Swahili. Yet here, one has to acknowledge that the applicability of such a phased model over the large area covered by the East African coast is probably limited. Essentially, it can be proposed that building upon the correlation already suggested between the first Shanga mosque, the burnt tree stump, the enclosure and Eaton's (1993) 'inclusion' phase of conversion, we can also see Eaton's subsequent two phases as well. Phase 2, that of 'identification', is possibly indicated by the gradual growth in the Muslim community as represented by the remainder of the Shanga mosque sequence, up to and including the building of the first stone mosque. The third phase, 'replacement', is perhaps indicated by the congregational mosque and, indeed, the stone architectural tradition as a whole found along the coast, a tradition representing Swahili confidence in Islam as their own religion. This would appear to be of importance, as stone architecture, although linked with prosperity, is also, obviously, linked with identity. This includes the indigenisation of Islam and its full absorbtion into the local context. Verin (1994:60) suggests that Islam created an *ummah* (community) between the Swahili, the Comorians and the Madagascar Muslims. We can extend this to the Swahili themselves, and suggest that Islam created an *ummah* among them as well in the first instance, with the notion of community also assisting in reinforcing identity. However, 'replacement' is perhaps not the best term for this phase, as we also see the persistence of non-Muslim – or what might be termed traditional – religious elements.

The latter include visiting the dead and leaving offerings at graves, what Juma (1996a:354) describes as active maintenance of communication with the dead.

This is a common feature of Islam within sub-Saharan Africa and, although rejected by orthodox Islam, it is widely found elsewhere in the Muslim world as well (see Insoll 1999a). Although Juma does not state this, the acquisition of *barakah* might also be an important consideration, as with tomb visiting elsewhere in the Muslim world. Within this context, a striking example of the syncretic mix of Islamic and indigenous features in Swahili society is provided by the pillar tombs of the coast. These are so-called because the deceased is commemorated by a large pillar (up to 6 m), usually made of coral, which was often inset with imported porcelain dishes, frequently subsequently removed by Victorian vandals (see Freeman-Grenville and Martin 1973:99) **(figure 4.14)**. Pillar tombs are found from southern Somalia to Tanzania, and largely date from the fourteenth–seventeenth centuries (Kirkman 1964; Prins 1967; Sanseverino 1983).

A group of these monuments on the northern coast of Kenya was analysed by T. Wilson (1979:33), who found that they seem to have served a variety of functions, beyond merely providing 'a suitable resting place for the earthly remains of worthy or wealthy persons'. These tombs functioned as symbols of ancestry and lineage, of what would later be termed *waungwana* status. But as well as their secular importance to the living, the tombs might also have been imbued with religious significance, and could be used within rituals of ancestor and spirit communication. Their origins might also be linked to pre-Islamic considerations, resembling, for instance, the 'funerary markers or phallic pillars of southern Ethiopia, Somalia or Madagascar' (T. Wilson 1979:41). An example of just such a phallic marker from Mogadishu has already been described in chapter 2.

Abungu (1994) provides various other examples of the types of sacred site found on the East African coast. As well as stone tombs, these include abandoned settlements and their mosques, and caves and rock shelters. The types of offerings left included food, incense and rose-water, and cloth 'flags' hung in large trees. Fleisher and LaViolette (in press) describe an archaeological example of one such site. This comprised a dense scatter of sherds found at the base of a large baobab tree at Pujini on Pemba island. Horton and Middleton (2000:184) also describe the incorporation of *kayara* within Swahili belief, this being 'the offering of food and other objects to remove pollution once acquired', with pollution brought largely by evil spirits, the *mizumu* and *majini* (*djinn*). They also refer (Horton and Middleton 2000:180) to Swahili religion as incorporating *dini* (religion) and *mila* (custom), which is identical to the Berti subdivision of religion and custom described in the last chapter. Nurse and Spear (1985:96) refer to this subdivision as the 'microcosmic' world of the village, and Islam as 'macrocosmic' and associated with the towns – a terminology not agreed with here for reasons described in chapter 1, but indicating the coexistence of Islamic and traditional elements. This is evident in further ways, according to Nurse and Spear (1985): in initiation, through integrating the traditional pattern of ritual

Figure 4.14 Pillar tomb at Takwa

seclusion with the Muslim practices, as well as the use of Qur'anic charms for various purposes.

Possession cults and rituals associated with spirits also existed. Examples are discussed by Caplan (1975) with reference to Mafia island, for instance. All of these are features which can also be found elsewhere in sub-Saharan Africa within other Muslim societies. Furthermore, these examples indicate that extensive evidence for syncretism does exist on the East African coast. However, equally, it does not mean that all Swahili integrated all these practices with their Muslim beliefs, or that such customs are found all along the coast. Many coastal Muslims, as in any other Muslim society in sub-Saharan Africa, or elsewhere, would have followed Islam devoid of any extraneous elements.

Post-1000 CE: the south coast

Swahili rulers, Kilwa and the far south

On the south coast similar processes are apparent, and similar archaeological remains encountered. The site of Kilwa has already been mentioned as an early trade centre, and this site also represents the process of Islamic state development described by Hiskett (1994:154), which occurred on the coast in the twelfth century. He contrasts this process with the previous situation whereby Muslim merchant communities depended on the hospitality of non-Muslim local rulers. Horton and Middleton (2000:177) draw a distinction between two types of ruler on the coast. They suggest that kingship systems which were 'African in character', involving social ranking, importance placed on ancestors and elaborate rituals, are found in areas where the hinterland was most dangerous, i.e. from the Tana delta south. Offshore and in southern Somalia, kingship was more 'Islamic' in nature. Perhaps this was the case – it is difficult to test – but it is certain that similarities can be drawn between the role of Swahili rulers and those elsewhere in sub-Saharan Africa. Nurse and Spear (1985:96) comment that rulers 'had to bridge all worlds of belief', and that their most powerful tool was religion and ritual, 'both African and Islamic'. This precisely parallels what occurred among the rulers of early Kanem-Borno in the central Sudan (chapter 6), or Ghana in the western Sahel (next chapter), for example, usually as Islam was being integrated into society. Parallels also exist in the general trappings of authority – of what are essentially divine kings – the *siwa* or side-blown horns (though these are unique to the coast) **(figure 4.15)**, silk canopies, clothing or palace layout, as in the mid-nineteenth-century palace at Dunga on Zanzibar with its central audience chamber with raised dais (Horton and Middleton 2000:170). The latter feature is reminiscent, for example, of those of the Fur kings described in the last chapter.

The growth of Muslim states, even those that might also have integrated older elements, testifies to the degree of Islamisation on the coast. However, these

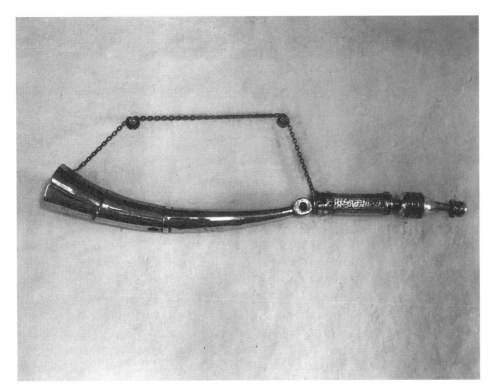

Figure 4.15 Brass *siwa* from Lamu

states, as already noted, varied considerably in size and importance, with Kilwa being of great significance. In historical tradition, the formulation of the Shirazi myth can be attributed to this period of Muslim state growth. The background to the Shirazi myth has already been discussed, and Kilwa is recorded in the Kilwa Chronicle as ruled first by a Shirazi dynasty. The latter document is described by Sutton (1990:77) as 'essentially an oral-historical composition, a version of which was about 1550 AD committed to paper'. The ruler Ali ibn al-Hasan is said to have sailed from Shiraz in Persia to Kilwa, according to the Chronicle. This Shirazi attribution is erroneous, but it is known that Ali ibn al-Hasan founded the Kilwa sultanate some time around 1050 (Sutton 1998b:118), so an element of truth is evident. The Shirazi dynasty was in turn replaced by the Mahdali dynasty (see below) at the end of the thirteenth century. The Mahdalis were still in power when Ibn Battuta visited Kilwa in 1330.

The utility of Ibn Battuta as an unparalleled source on Islam in Africa during the mid-fourteenth century has already been mentioned in chapter 2. His description of Kilwa is extremely useful. He tells us that the 'uppermost virtue' of the inhabitants of this 'great coastal city' was their 'religion and righteousness' (Hamdun and King 1994:22), being believers of the Sunni Shafi'i school (the school that predominates on the coast today). The people of Kilwa also undertook raids against surrounding non-Muslims, and he noted the presence of *sharifs*, holy men, from the Hejaz region of Arabia. Yet traditional practices also persisted, for Ibn Battuta mentions that the people had 'cuttings on their faces', a reference to scarification. The city is described as 'half a month's journey from Sofala', and as built of wood with ceilings of reeds (Hamdun and King 1994).

Trade in gold, copper and ivory from southern Africa generated great riches, and Kilwa testifies to this. It was the most important of the southern Swahili trade centres between the twelfth and fourteenth centuries, but subsequently went through what Sutton (1998b:117) defines as cycles of decline and revival. Stone was used for construction on a substantial scale at Kilwa, especially after the shift to Mahdali rule (Chittick 1974). During this period the Great Mosque was extended and the Husuni Kubwa complex built, both of which are still standing. These monuments both illustrate the wealth of the town, as well as making a statement about Muslim identity as described below. The Great Mosque was originally built in the eleventh century, possibly by Ali ibn al-Hasan, but had an arched and domed extension added to it in the early fourteenth century. This increased the size fourfold from the original one of about 12 × 18 m. This extension collapsed in the mid-fourteenth century, but was rebuilt in the early fifteenth century (Sutton 1998b:135–8).

However, the Great Mosque, difficult as this is to achieve, is somewhat eclipsed by the Husuni Kubwa complex. The latter is a palatial structure sited to command the view of the harbour and to capture cool breezes (Chittick 1974:174). The term 'Husuni' is derived from the Arabic *husn*, and refers, according to Freeman-Grenville (1988a:227), to 'a defended private residence, of greater or lesser complexity according to the personal wealth and needs of the owners'. It is a unique structure, both on the coast and in sub-Saharan Africa, and would appear to have been designed by an architect from the Arabian Peninsula. Its rough dimensions are 70 × 100 m, tapering to about 20 m at the narrowest point above the cliff **(figure 4.16)**. It is a complex made up of various elements, both public and private, such as audience courts and apartments, and mirrors Islamic palace structures elsewhere (Insoll 1999a:68). One of the most intriguing features it contains is an octagonal bathing pool – presumably private – and 8.17 m across, with no visible means of filling it (Chittick 1974:181–2). Filling must have been by hand, and Sutton suggests (1998b:151) that this would have required 50,000 litres of water, indicating a significant control of resources and labour as well. Husuni Kubwa stands as the palace of a wealthy ruler, but east of it is a further structure, Husuni Ndogo. This is a walled rectangular enclosure about 70 × 50 m, which is interpreted by Sutton (1998b:128) as comprising, along with Husuni Kubwa, 'a royal trading emporium and warehouse system with the palace itself'. Architecturally, parallels can be drawn between Husuni Ndogo and the early Islamic desert castles of

Figure 4.16 Husuni Kubwa, Kilwa

Jordan and Syria. This might be to do with a deliberate evocation of images of the early Muslim era, and it should be noted that the use of older plans is not unique to Kilwa but found elsewhere in the Muslim world – as, for example, by the use of a seemingly archaic plan at the Islamic fort in Bahrain referred to previously (see Kervran et al. 1982).

The question can be asked as to why Husuni Kubwa was built and the Great Mosque enlarged. Was this solely because money was available? This appears extremely unlikely, and Sutton (1999) has put forward a convincing hypothesis to account for their construction. He argues that this was linked with the Mahdali dynasty's attempt to stamp Sunni conformism on Kilwa, also indicated by the presence of the Hejazi *sharifs* seen by Ibn Battuta. Supporting evidence for this theory would appear to be lent by the existence of the only issue of gold coins minted at Kilwa. These, though found at Tumbatu island, apparently the Mahdali base prior to the shift to Kilwa, were minted during the reign of al-Hasan ibn Sulaiman (*c.*1310–33), referred to on the coins as 'the Father of Gifts' – a reference to his observance in almsgiving (Brown 1991:4; Sutton 1999:4). He was also a ruler who was, interestingly, a contemporary of Mansa Musa of Mali (Sutton 1997, and see chapter 6 below). In total, the building of Husuni Kubwa, the expansion of the Great Mosque and the pious mottoes on the coins are thought to 'represent a campaign to present Kilwa, politically as well as religiously, as part of the mainstream of orthodox Islam at that time' (Sutton 1999:5). It can be further asked why was this done; it was probably because of the recent change in dynasty, but also because al-Hasan ibn Sulaiman had studied in Aden and been on *hajj* to Mecca, and was aware of prejudices 'in the Islamic heartlands' about places such as Kilwa. Furthermore, his endeavours helped expunge any traces of possible Ibadi or Shi'ite Islam which might have existed previously (Sutton 1998b:129).

Not surprisingly, extensive evidence for both interregional and long-distance trade has also been found at Kilwa. This included Islamic and Far Eastern ceramics, glass vessels and beads and chlorite schist vessels from Madagascar, as well as both imported and locally minted coins (Chittick 1974; Brown 1991). With regard to the latter, besides providing information on Islam, these locally minted coins contain information on the genealogy of the sultans of Kilwa between about 1200 and 1374. Copper coins were the usual issues (though silver was also used; see below), and are of a relatively uniform size of between 20 and 25 mm, and 1.5 and 2.5 g in weight. Although they appear to have no antecedents in the coinage of the Islamic world they are characterised, according to Brown (1991:1), by the rhyme between the two sides: 'the obverse affirms the ruler's faith in Allah... followed by an epithet of Allah chosen to rhyme with the ruler's name, which occupies the reverse'. Their principal function appears to have been to serve the domestic market, as their circulation is fairly limited. Excluding a couple found in Oman, and a single coin at Great Zimbabwe (see chapter 8), they are found in large quantities in the Kilwa region, on Mafia island, and in smaller quantities on Pemba and Zanzibar islands (Brown 1991:1).

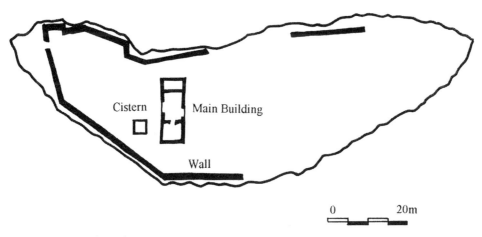

Cistern   Main Building

Wall

0   20m

Figure 4.17 Plan of Somana

Much of the gold obtained from the East African coast came from the Zambezi region in southern Africa (see chapter 8). The rulers of Kilwa prospered through the trade in gold, as Mansa Musa did on the other side of the continent (Sutton 1997). Indeed, both al-Hasan ibn Sulaiman and Mansa Musa were making statements about the power and Islamic identity of their respective African kingdoms at the same time. Further Islamised Swahili settlements existed closer to the gold sources of southern Africa than Kilwa. One of these was the important site of Chibuene, which has already been mentioned, and it is possible that it might have served as the entry point on the far south of the coast for Indian Ocean trade goods, which were then traded onward into the interior in exchange for commodities such as gold and ivory. The recovery of fragments of pink granite and serpentine at the site might indicate contacts with the Zimbabwe plateau (Sinclair 1982:162). Besides the earlier material referred to previously, fragments of eleventh-century Islamic glass were also recovered from Chibuene, indicating the later continuation of trade as well.

Other sites exist on the Mozambique coast, but unfortunately the civil war in Mozambique precluded their serious investigation until recently. Swahili-type stone ruins have been recorded, for example, at Tungi on Cape Delgado, in the Kerimba islands and further south at Somana (Duarte 1993). At the latter, a coral building, a cistern and a length of wall were all surveyed on a small island some 80 m × 40 m and situated a few hundred metres off the coast (**figure 4.17**). It appears that Somana functioned as the base of a rich trader, and the area in which it is located, near the coral reef of Baixo Pinda, is an area rich in 'fish, shellfish, crustaceans and other sea food' (Duarte 1993:80). For instance, the reef at low tide provides an excellent collecting ground for *Cypraea annulus* and *Cypraea moneta* shells. These were extensively used as currency items in parts of sub-Saharan Africa, especially in the western Sahel (Lovejoy 1985, and see next chapter). It can be suggested that the inhabitant of the stone building at Somana prospered through supplying currency shells, perhaps to Kilwa, for onward trade. A specialist function for many of these smaller centres must have existed, with others focusing upon timber, dried fish, slaves, ambergris and iron, as has already been described for the Comoros, or rhino horn and skins for the Far East.

Chinese ceramics

Study of the Far Eastern market is often neglected in favour of trade with Arabia and the Gulf. However, it would appear to have been of some importance, as indicated by the Chinese contacts with eastern and north-eastern Africa which were described in chapter 2. The durable legacy of this trade, besides some coins (as with Sung issues from Zanzibar described by Freeman-Grenville 1960:34), are countless sherds of glazed pottery of Chinese provenance (as well as elsewhere in the Far East) scattered across the beaches and archaeological sites of the East African coast.

The material from the site of Shanga provides a good example of the types of Chinese ceramics found on the East African coast. These are described by M. Horton (1996b:303–10) as falling into four groups – green wares, stonewares, white wares and porcelains. Green wares, sometimes referred to as celadons, are so-called because of their characteristic green glaze and include the widely found Lung Chuan or Longquan green wares. These have an easily recognisable fine pale-grey fabric covered with a green glaze which can range in shade from sea-green to turquoise. The glaze is frequently applied over floral decoration. At Shanga such wares date from the thirteenth century. Stonewares are more coarsely potted, and types found at Shanga include Changsha painted stoneware (ninth century at Shanga), olive green glazed jars which are sometimes called Dusun jars (ninth century at Shanga) and their replacement, Martabani jars. The latter are found in the Shanga sequence from a similar date to the Longquan wares (M. Horton 1996b:305). White wares appear in tenth-century levels at Shanga, but it is in levels dated to the twelfth–thirteenth centuries that a type of white ware widely found on the East African coast is encountered. These are the Qingbai glazed wares, a type of pottery covered in a white glaze with a blue hue. Bowls are the most common forms found, though fragments of jars have also been recovered. Finally, Chinese porcelains are also present on the East African coast. These include blue-on-white porcelain with blue painted decoration and a pale creamy glaze. Such wares were reaching the western Indian Ocean by the fourteenth century (M. Horton 1996b:310).

Much effort had been invested in the building at Somana, a structure whose characteristics, according to Duarte (1993:86), 'strongly suggest that it was a residence, and given its size it was a one family residence'. Carved porites coral floral motifs were found around one door, as well as herringbone motifs, round bosses and carved niches, all characteristic of Swahili architecture of the thirteenth to fourteenth centuries. Duarte (1993:86), quite feasibly, ascribes to Somana a defensive function, but not against attack from the sea. Rather, the defensive wall, which survived to a height of 2.5 m in places, was so placed as to defend against possible threats from the mainland. Somana thus appears to provide an example of a small trading station, for maybe only a single merchant, his family and followers. These were perhaps only resident for brief periods of the year coincident with the monsoon cycles, but were involved in commerce, possibly in shells, yet were also keeping one step removed from the majority of the population living in wattle-and-daub houses on the mainland (as attested by an area of archaeological material of 2–3 ha in extent).

The near offshore islands

Offshore, on the islands of Pemba, Zanzibar and Mafia, extensive evidence for participation in Indian Ocean trade is again found, with Chinese porcelains and Persian Gulf wares indicating a boom in commerce in the twelfth–thirteenth centuries (Horton and Middleton 2000; Insoll in press a). Islam had firmly taken hold, and many Muslim settlements had developed, building upon the foundations described already for the period prior to 1000 CE. At Mtambwe Mkuu, on the lush west coast of Pemba, one of these trading centres was situated on a small triangular islet of about 21 ha (Horton et al. 1986) **(figure 4.18)**. A mosque partially built of coral was uncovered, along with traces of wattle-and-daub structures (author's observations as a student supervisor at this site), mirroring the settlements on the mainland. A cemetery containing twenty burials interred over some 150 years has also been recorded. These, because of their orientation, i.e. set at right angles to the usual Muslim burial orientation (see chapter 1), can, according to Horton and Middleton (2000:51), be 'interpreted as Shi'ite burials, rather than Sunni or Ibadi'. Equally, they could be non-Muslim, for Shi'ah burials do not necessarily differ in their orientation.

Also at Mtambwe Mkuu, a hoard of 2,060 coins were found. All, bar eight gold ones, were silver, and were dated both by the coins themselves and accompanying sgraffiato pottery to around 1100. The gold coins, excluding one surface find, were all from Fatimid mints or copies thereof. The silver coins were locally minted, though made from imported silver, and formed part of the 'local Kilwa-type tradition' (Horton et al. 1986:118). Ten names occur on the coins, starting with Ali ibn al-Hasan, the ruler who established the Kilwa sultanate (Sutton 1998b), already referred to above. Numerous other centres existed on Pemba, as well as scores, 'if not hundreds', of mixed farming and fishing

Figure 4.18 Pottery spread across the beach, Mtambwe Mkuu

Figure 4.19 Inscription, Kizimkazi mosque

villages (LaViolette in press). Although centres such as Mtambwe Mkuu were Islamised, as has been described for Kilwa and Mogadishu, how these smaller centres interacted with their larger counterparts, and the degrees of autonomy they displayed, remains little understood.

Excavations on Zanzibar have shown a similar picture. Tumbatu, a small islet off the north-west coast, provides another good example of a trade centre which flourished in this period. This site also yielded a porites coral inscription dating from about 1100, executed in Kufic script (M. Horton 1994a:200). The inscription, though carved locally, as indicated by the coral used, also illustrated, by the distinctive style of the script, 'that the craftsman had done his schooling and apprenticeship in one of the workshops of Siraf if not of Shiraz itself' (Sutton 1990:80). A similar inscription, bearing a date of 1107, and likewise executed in floriate Kufic, described by Flury (1922:262) as including 'ornamental foliage' with the script, has also been recorded decorating the *qiblah* wall and *mihrab* of the extant Kizimkazi mosque on Zanzibar (figure 4.19). These inscriptions attest to the maintenance of Persian Gulf contacts, as described previously, while the gold Fatimid coins of Mtambwe Mkuu indicate Mediterranean links, and the Chinese pottery – indirectly – Far Eastern ones. In sum, this again reflects the multidirectional commerce of the Indian Ocean.

South of Zanzibar on Mafia island further Kilwa coins, copper issues of Ali ibn al-Hasan, have been recovered at the site of Kisimani Mafia (Horton et al.

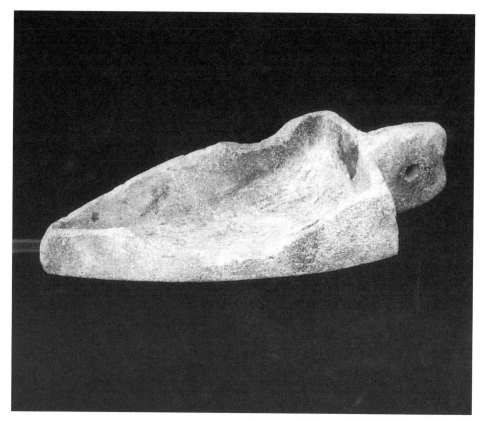

Figure 4.20 Cut stone lamp of similar type to examples from southern
Mauritania on the other side of the continent, found on the beach,
Mafia island

1986:121). These coins, numbering over 600, were discovered in an imported
sgraffiato jar of Persian Gulf origin. Strictly speaking, Mafia is really a group
of islands, but is commonly referred to in the singular after the chief island,
Mafia or Chole island. This is by far the largest island of the group at 434 km^2,
with the other main islands being Juani and Jibondo, as well as various smaller
ones (Baumann 1957:5). The Kilwa Chronicle records that the sons of Ali ibn
al-Hasan settled at Mafia, probably at the site of Kisimani Mafia, according to
Chittick (1961:1). This is a large site, a stone town, with accompanying wattle-
and-daub areas as well. Chittick (1961, 1964) focused his attention initially
on a stone mosque, in which five building phases dating from between 1240
and 1520 were discerned. The remains of other stone structures have also been
recorded at Kua on Juani, and a further mosque on Jibondo (Baumann 1957:16)
(figure 4.20). More recently, Felix Chami (pers. comm.) has been working on
Mafia, and his work will undoubtedly push back the occupation sequence, and
place Mafia within the earlier tradition of Swahili centres as well. In general, the

evidence from sites such as Tumbatu, Kisimani Mafia and Mtambwe Mkuu, as well as the extant Kizimkazi mosque indicate that, although the Shirazi tradition of origins is a myth, strong contacts, as attested by the inscriptions, Gulf ceramics and Kilwa coins, were maintained in the twelfth century between this region of the Gulf and sites associated with the rulers of Kilwa.

Post-1000 CE: the far offshore islands

The Comoros

The possible evidence for early Islam, or rather lack of it, in the Comoros has already been described, and it was in the eleventh–twelfth centuries that the first mosques were built. The central mosques in the harbour towns of Sima and Domoni (Ndzuwani) were, for example, founded at this date. However, they were subsequently reconstructed in the thirteenth century, and again more elaborately in the fourteenth–fifteenth centuries, an era described as the 'classic period' of Comorian culture (H. Wright 1992:126). Intriguingly, in the light of what was said above, the mosque in Domoni was known as the Mkiri wa Shirazi, 'the Shirazian mosque'. Between about 900 and 1400 an accompanying growth in settlement size is evident. Sima grew from 3 to 11 ha, and in the thirteenth century, stone began to be used in building. Initially, according to Verin (1994:59), this was in isolated contexts such as for mosque foundations and *mihrabs*, but by the mid-thirteenth century the first stone house is recorded in Domoni. H. Wright (1992:126) also makes the important point that the growth of congregational mosques such as those in Sima and Domoni might be due to the 'restriction of the central mosque to the townspeople of higher social and political status' – in other words, although he does not suggest this, the growth of the patrician class as defined by Horton and Middleton (2000), and described previously.

Trade-related evidence is again found in the Comoros dating from this period. Verin (1994:59), for instance, draws specific parallels between the types of sgraffiato wares found in both the Comoros and Madagascar, those recovered from the Gulf site of Takht i Sulaiman and Daybul/Banbhore in Pakistan. A further type of unusual sgraffiato ware dating from the eleventh–thirteenth centuries has also been found. This was recovered from the Islamic cemetery at Domoni, and is of interest as it was deliberately selected for funerary use, employing incised designs derived from Arabic calligraphy (H. Wright 1992:105), thus providing a further instance of local adaptation of Islamic material culture to suit a specific cultural context.

This is something that is similarly evident in the Comoros in the 'magico-religious' inscriptions discussed by Blanchy and Said (1990). These perhaps served protective as well as religious purposes, and have been recorded at various sites, including the congregational mosque in Moroni, which was originally founded in the fifteenth century, an undated palace at Ikoni (the capital of the sultanate of Bambao) and in the nineteenth-century town wall at Ntsudjini (Blanchy and Said 1990). Comorian diet also appears to have become more orthodox compared to what was observed in the period before 1000, though Redding (1992:115) again mentions that tenrec remains were found – but not, interestingly, in a sample from a fifteenth-century mosque porch. However, this might be because people do not tend to eat in mosques rather than due to the disappearance of the species from Comorian diet. Interregional contacts are also again evident in this period, as indicated by pottery described by Allibert and Verin (1996:463) as 'Pakistani pottery', or more likely pottery made by the Karana people of Indo-Pakistani origin who live in north-western Madagascar.

Madagascar

The Comoros would therefore appear, as in the period prior to 1000, to still be a point of connection between Madagascar and the African mainland (**figure 4.21**). But thus far, Madagascar has not been mentioned in this discussion, though its Islamic archaeology is also of great interest, and has been recently reviewed by Dewar and Wright (1993). However, it is also important to note that much of Madagascan Islam, and its accompanying material culture, cannot be defined as Swahili (see, e.g., Middleton 1999; Sharp 1999), the material residue for which is really only clustered on the north-western and north-eastern coasts (see Verin 1986). The bulk of the population of Madagascar are a mix of African and Indonesian elements with some Indian and Arab influences, with the Malagasy language likewise being eclectic, and 'judged to be largely Malayo-Polynesian' (Middleton 1999:4). Essentially, the patterns of Islamisation in Madagascar appear to be similar to those on the Comoros. Direct evidence for the presence of Muslims before the eleventh century has not yet been reported, but imported ceramics have been found. An important location is Nosy Mangabe, a small island off the north-eastern coast of Madagascar, where Near Eastern white-glazed wares of ninth–tenth centuries date were found along with sherds of chlorite-schist vessels, slag and local earthenware (Dewar and Wright 1993:430).

Larger quantities of archaeological evidence attesting to participation in Indian Ocean trade as well as the presence of Muslims are found at sites dating from between the eleventh and mid-fourteenth centuries. In the north-west of the island, the most important site dating from this period is located, this being the Islamised port of Mahilaka. Here, some 70 ha of settled area, including both stone and less permanent structures, was enclosed within a wall 2.5 m high and 0.6–0.8 m thick. Substantial mosque foundations (29 × 10 m) were also recorded at this site. Mahilaka appears to have been at the centre of a trade network, a central place, drawing in commodities from the north-east of Madagascar such as chlorite schist, rock crystal and gold, which were then exported. Contacts with sites such as those in the Gorge d'Andavakoera are indicated

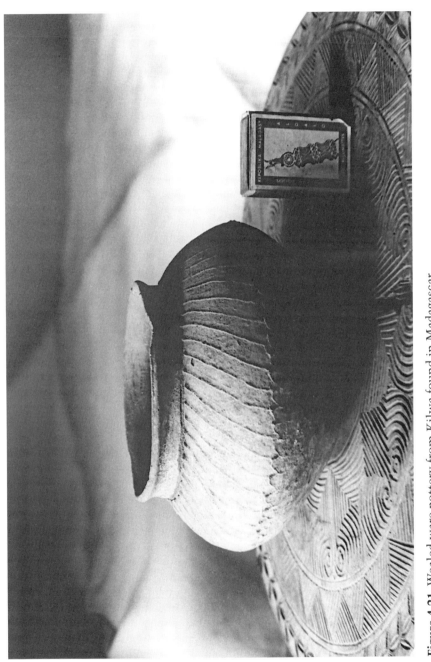

Figure 4.21 Wealed ware pottery from Kilwa found in Madagascar

by local earthenware 'nearly identical' to material from Mahilaka and Irodo, a further important site in the region (Dewar and Wright 1993:431–7). The presence of Muslims in this region is thus attested, as by the mosque at Mahilaka, but trade goods sourced from Indian Ocean trade are found in other areas of Madagascar, which if visited or settled in by Muslim traders, retain no trace. A good example of this is provided by the finds of Song white wares and sgraffiato in the far south of the island, such as at the site of Andranosoa, which 'testify to connections elsewhere' (Dewar and Wright 1993:439), but which do not indicate that Muslims were ever present.

This first generation of entrepôts were largely abandoned by the mid-fourteenth century for reasons little understood, to be replaced by another set, also clustered on the north-western coast, such as Kingany. Muslim communities were not, however, confined only to the north-west. In the north-east Muslims were also present (Verin 1986). At the important site of Vohemar, over 600 tombs have been investigated, and were found to contain a variety of grave-goods of both Madagascan and foreign origin including Chinese porcelain bowls, bronze mirrors, glass vessels, carnelian and glass trade beads, and chlorite-schist vessels and bracelets (Vernier and Millot 1971:17; van der Sleen n.d.:xi). These items were accompanying corpses oriented in the Muslim fashion, east–west (Dewar and Wright 1993:443–5). Adults were buried 1.5–1.2 m deep, with children less so, while all the corpses were wrapped in mats (Vernier and Millot 1971:17). The Vohemar burials provide a further instance of the adaptation of Muslim practices within the sub-Saharan African environment, in this case to the extent that Muslim dogma regarding the prohibition on placing grave-goods with a corpse were being actively flouted. Muslim burial rites were fused 'aux coutumes Malgaches' (Battistini and Verin n.d.:xxxi) **(figure 4.22)**.

The north-east of Madagascar was also the area in which chlorite-schist vessels were produced, with workshops located around Vohemar (Verin 1976). One site at which extensive evidence for chlorite-schist working has been found was at Tafiampatsa in the Irodo region, and Battistini and Verin (n.d.:xxxii) describe chlorite schist as a material worked in this area, 'par les cultures Islamisées ou influencées par elles'. Roughing out was completed at quarries in the interior and final lathe-turning and polishing at coastal sites such as Vohemar (Dewar and Wright 1993:444). Chlorite-schist vessels, especially a three-legged shape with a cover, the so-called 'marmite' (Battistini and Verin n.d.:xxv), were extensively traded throughout the East African coast. Fragments of chlorite-schist vessels have been found at Kilwa and at sites on Pemba island, as well as further north on the coast, as has already been described in the relevant sections above. Interestingly, two of the three-legged vessels were frequently produced out of the same block of stone in a single operation. Three long feet were carved in the middle of the block, which was then cut in two, and the ends hollowed out to produce the bowls (Vernier and Millot 1971). Often chlorite-schist sherds are

Figure 4.22 Muslim tombstone, Madagascar

found showing signs that the original vessels were well curated, being repaired with iron or copper rivets, for example (personal observation), prior to their obvious final deterioration and abandonment. Dewar and Wright (1993:444) suggest that the trade in chlorite schist and the resulting wealth therefrom was possibly responsible for the social differentiation evident in the cemetery at Vohemar, an entirely plausible hypothesis.

Yet Islam in Madagascar is more complex than that illustrated by a succession of trade centres in the north-west and north-east of the island. This is a point well made by Middleton (1999:4), who states that 'of the religious traditions that have shaped contemporary Malagasy cosmologies and social practice, Islamic culture, brought by traders and immigrants since at least the tenth century, has had a profound and lasting impact throughout the island'. This is important, for ethnography shows us that the impact of Islam, as Middleton notes, is widely found in Madagascar, beyond that directly indicated by archaeological evidence. Mack (1995:127) describes the so-called '*Islamises*' of parts of Madagascar as living evidence for the impact of Islam in the island. These are groups such as the Antalaotse, Antambahoaka, and Antaimoro who wear Islamic dress – robes and turbans – and have texts written in Arabic, *soraba*, which are ascribed magical importance (see Gueunier 1994:59 for a description of the latter). Yet as Mack (1995:127) further points out, 'neither Arabic, nor for that matter Swahili, is spoken; the Koran [*sic*] is not known nor studied; there are no mosques'. Elements of Muslim material culture, belief and practice, attesting to the influence of Muslims, or these groups perhaps formerly having been Muslim, exist, yet today these people are not Muslim. Middleton (1999:4) again provides an interesting theory which might help account for this, that 'the Islamic heritage is largely "hidden" because the Islamic elements have become local Malagasy cultural practice'. Other phenomena exist as well. Groups such as the Bemazava of northern Madagascar have no difficulty 'remaining faithful simultaneously to Sakalava religion and the world faiths of Islam or Catholicism' according to Sharp (1999:117). The same author describes this process as not being syncretic, but rather characterised by maintaining Islam and other practices such as spirit possession, 'in separate realms of understanding and experience' (1997:117). Again this is vaguely similar to the division maintained, for example, by the Berti, and indeed described above for the Swahili.

Disruption and revival

The archaeological and other evidence from the East African coast and its offshore islands just described has indicated the diversity of material that exists. However, it is important to note that the mature Swahili trade centres and states did not last forever. Competition appeared on the Indian Ocean at the end of the fifteenth century in the form of the Portuguese. The role of the Portuguese within the Red Sea has already been mentioned in chapter 2, where they along with the Ottomans were described as 'world powers'. This is an apt description, and the overall Portuguese objective was, as Sheriff (1987:15) notes, 'to capture the Indian Ocean trade and divert it from its traditional paths across western Asia to their own maritime artery around the Cape of Good Hope, thus outflanking the Italian-Muslim monopoly over the spice trade'. This had fundamental implications for the Swahili coast. Disruption was brought to Muslim-dominated Indian Ocean trade, and Portuguese naval power led to the decline of many of the Swahili towns and the emergence of other settlements as major trade and political centres. Yet at the same time, Pouwels (2000:251) suggests that this was a period of 'primacy given to religion in the Swahili struggle against Portuguese attacks', a time also when 'Islam and coastal civilisation were making new inroads everywhere in the sixteenth and seventeenth centuries' (Pouwels 2000:259). However, this latter point would not appear to be supported by the archaeological data for the interior (see chapter 8), and similarly on large parts of the coast. In reality, a boom and further spread of Islam actually occurred in the eighteenth–nineteenth centuries after the expulsion of the Portuguese.

On the East African coast the Portuguese focused upon the two major trade centres of Mombasa and Kilwa. As a result, Kilwa was cut off from Sofala, and Fort Jesus was built at Mombasa in the late sixteenth century after the Portuguese had previously twice razed the city in 1505 and 1528 (Sheriff 1987:16). The fort was built to protect the trade routes to India, and to stop the Ottomans preying on the African–Indian trade (Kirkman 1974:3). The Fort Jesus site was investigated by James Kirkman between 1958 and 1969. The fortress was designed by an Italian architect, Giovanni Battista Cairata, who incorporated various features of Italian fortress design, such as the quadrilateral plan with wide bastions at each corner, and the rectangular projection between the two seaward towers **(figure 4.23)**. Construction was begun in 1593, and supposedly completed three years later, a date which according to Kirkman (1974:9) has been much disputed. Whatever the date of its eventual completion, Fort Jesus subsequently suffered a chequered history, notably in two major events: firstly, the Portuguese garrison and their families were massacred in 1631, with the fort re-taken by the Portuguese in the following year; and secondly, in the three-year siege by the Omanis of the fortress between 1696 and 1698 (Sheriff 1987:17). Although the Ottomans had been considered the enemy, ultimately, the Portuguese were to lose control of the coast to the Omanis – an action which was completed with the fall of Fort Jesus, after which Portuguese influence was confined to the coast south of the River Rovuma in Mozambique (Trimingham 1964:20).

One of the reasons for the fall of Fort Jesus was probably that it was undermanned. Kirkman (1974:8) describes how there were no more than fifty professional soldiers present at the start of the great siege in 1596. Although the impact of the Portuguese at many places on the coast was profound in disrupting previous trade patterns, and diverting them for their own purposes, overall the material residue of their presence is not extensive, reflecting this lack of physical presence. Fort Jesus is obviously very substantial, but it should be remembered that this was subsequently remodelled in parts both by the

Figure 4.23 Fort Jesus, Mombasa

Omanis and the British, the latter using it as a prison. Elsewhere, Horton and Clark (1985:170) describe two Portuguese factories. Both were on Zanzibar, with one at the Zanzibar fort or *gereza*, and another at Fukuchani. The latter was possibly a place where tobacco was dried, as reconstructed from the

Swahili *fukusha*, meaning 'place of fumigation', with tobacco a crop introduced by the Portuguese in the seventeenth century (Horton and Clark 1985). Other Portuguese introductions, both in crops and in loanwords to Swahili, have already been described. Further material remains of the Portuguese presence on the East African coast are considered by Freeman-Grenville (1988b). These are scattered up and down the coast, and include, by way of example, the remains of a chapel at Shela near Lamu, and a *padrao* or cross brought by Vasco da Gama to Malindi in 1498. Traces of the Portuguese presence thus remain, but outside Mozambique, which remained a Portuguese colony until the early 1970s, these are none too substantial.

This stands in contrast to that of the Omanis, who, as we have seen, expelled the Portuguese from the coast at the end of the seventeenth century. Following this event, the Swahili towns of the coast appear to have entered a period of revival and prosperity, 'under the impetus of Omani-dominated trade and accompanied by markedly greater Arab influences' (Nurse and Spear 1985:81). Such influences are manifest in architecture, such as in the heavy carved Zanzibar doors, for example, which are copies of Omani ones, or in a greater number of Arabic words entering Swahili. But these influences were also made more marked by a substantial immigration of Arabs into the East African coast for the first time. Previously, there had been immigration, but this was probably only a trickle, perhaps intermittent, and without a great impact demographically, contrary to the colonial hypotheses regarding Swahili origins discussed at the start of this chapter, which saw the Swahili as largely Arab derived. The boom evident in the eighteenth and nineteenth centuries was largely due to the integration of East Africa into what Sheriff (1987:33) terms 'the world capitalist system from the last third of the eighteenth century onwards [which] distinguishes the modern history of East Africa from the preceding eras'. New markets for slaves (prior to European abolitionary efforts – **figure 4.24**), ivory, and, importantly, spices were opened up in Europe and the Americas. Trade patterns and political identity during the Omani period on the coast differed markedly from that of the earlier 'medieval' centres, but the East African coast was once again fully integrated in Indian Ocean trade networks – networks which in turn connected with wider trade routes beyond.

Zanzibar, a major focus of Omani settlement, provides an interesting case study to consider the material impact of the Omanis. Plantations were established on the island, and to a lesser extent on Pemba, and Zanzibar became a base for traders venturing into the interior (see chapter 8). Initially, Zanzibar town started as a humble fishing village founded in the twelfth century on the Shangani peninsula, but experienced rapid growth from the mid-seventeenth century, hand in hand with new Arab settlement and the economic revival just described (Sheriff 1995). In Zanzibar town, the primary monument attesting to the Omanis is the Zanzibar fort, whose Swahili name, meaning prison, *gereza*, is actually taken from the Portuguese for church, *igreja*, indicating also that it

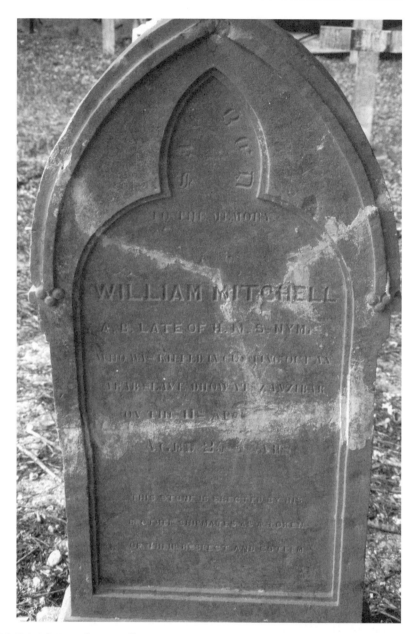

Figure 4.24 British Royal Navy dhow-runner's grave, Grave island, Zanzibar

was built, in part, over a Portuguese church (Freeman-Grenville 1988b). Various palaces were also constructed by Omani rulers on Zanzibar, especially after the transference of the al-Busaidi from Oman to Zanzibar in the 1820s (Pouwels 2000:262). Examples include the palaces built by Said ibn Sultan at Mtoni, or by Barghash ibn Said (1870–88) at Maruhubi (Horton and Clark 1985:171).

Figure 4.25 View of Zanzibar stone town

Zanzibar town rapidly grew into the premier entrepôt on the coast in the nine-teenth century (**figure 4.25**), and the new arrivals inevitably created another layer of Muslim material culture in parts of the coast. This was the case with the Omanis, who were largely followers of Ibadi doctrines (as defined in chapter 1). This in itself raises interesting issues – notably, how might one recognise differ-ent Muslim sects through archaeological evidence; a subject further explored, also with regard to the Ibadis, in the next chapter.

However, on Zanzibar the study of architectural evidence has shown to be ef-fective in recognising the Ibadi presence. A wide-ranging study of the mosques of Zanzibar stone town (Sheriff 1992) has illustrated how the various differ-ences between the mosque architecture of the Sunni and Ibadi communities living there was manifest. This is something that could also, theoretically, be archaeologically visible (Insoll 1999a:45). Various features indicated the Ibadi presence. Their egalitarian ethos was manifest in the absence of a congrega-tional mosque until recently, as none of the Omani rulers wanted to be elected to the imamate; an elected imam being a requirement of Friday prayers. This meant, firstly, there was an absence of *minbars* (see chapter 1 for definition). Secondly, this egalitarian and austere ethos was further reflected in the shallow plain *mihrab*, a feature interpreted by Sheriff (1992:13) as because 'their dogmas disapprove of their prayer leaders being isolated in the niche away from their followers'. Interior decoration was also lacking in Ibadi mosques so that it did not distract the worshippers. Furthermore, the minority status of the Ibadis led to concealment. This was achieved through, for example, the non-protrusion of the *mihrab* niche, in direct contrast to the Sunni community, and build-ing a raised floor to the prayer hall so their rituals could not be observed, and thus attention be drawn to them. Finally, their mosques tended to be broad and shallow so worshippers could obtain greater spiritual reward by being closer to the *qiblah*, and grand minarets were also absent. Simple staircase minarets were used instead (Sheriff (1992:13). The latter feature is certainly comparable to those also identified in the western Sahel (Schacht 1954, 1957b, and see next chapter). In summary, this example indicates that the diverse layering of the material culture of Islam on the East African coast, a process noted in the mosque sequence at Shanga one thousand years before, was still continuing in the nineteenth century and, indeed, is still ongoing.

Summary and conclusions

At first glance, Islam on the East African coast does not appear to exhibit the diversity seen in the Nilotic Sudan or the great time-depth of Ethiopia and the Horn of Africa. However, this is only a surface appearance. In reality, patterns are much more complex than that seemingly presented by what appears to be a uniform urban-based Muslim civilisation which began to develop from the late eighth century onwards. Urbanism, for example, only represents a small part of the settlement patterns evident on the coast; numerous other fishing and agricultural villages existed, indicating much more diverse patterns of settlement. Moreover, settlements, be they villages or stone towns, interacted with, and were reliant upon, a vast hinterland, as recent research is increasingly showing.

Similarly, with Islam, conversion patterns are complex. Experimentation with the new religion occurred, as did the integration of older elements, and the presence of different sects and schools are also all attested archaeologically and historically. This diversity inherent in coastal Islam was also indicated when an attempt was made to apply Eaton's (1993) phased conversion model to conversion patterns on the coast. This model is of great utility in understanding processes of Islamic conversion elsewhere in the continent south of the Sahara, but has limited applicability here. This is again for the reason that the coast is as dissimilar as it is similar, and the application of a single model to this vast stretch of coastline and its offshore islands is not feasible. It might work in a site-specific context, such as when applied to Shanga, and appear more universally applicable after the development of the stone-town tradition from the thirteenth century onwards, but even with regard to this latter phase, when material culture seems more uniform, great variety is still evident on the coast.

It can also be seen that the illusion of unity in much of the archaeology of Islam on the East African coast does not correlate with a blandness of material culture, or in some form of mimicry of the Islam of Arabia or the Persian Gulf. Local interpretation of Islam, and adaptation of Islamic material culture, occurred, as our case studies indicated, and Islam on the East African coast continues to exhibit its own distinctive character today. The dynamism of coastal Islam and its associated material culture is similarly a recurring feature, from the pillar tombs and houses discussed to the Ottoman glass tulip vases imported in the nineteenth century and described by Allen (1993:248). These were designed for a specific purpose, to hold a single bloom, but were adapted to suit the local context, fitted with perforated metal caps and thereafter used as rosewater sprinklers. Equally, the coastal towns, whether oligarchic republics, city-states, kingdoms or whatever their political constitution, were not all in continual harmony. Polities came and went and competition was rife, as changing fortunes in the Muslim world exerted their influence upon the East African coast, as the reconstructed phases of trade indicate. The point was also made that the archaeology of the coast is currently undergoing a resurgence in new research. Old theories have been dismantled and discarded, and new more convincing ones proposed, illustrating the dynamism of the settlements on the East African coast, their African origins and their place within regional systems. These are discussed further in chapter 8, but it is important to note that this is an exciting time for the archaeology of the coast. New data is being collected at a rapid pace, and here, perhaps more than in any of the other regions considered in this volume, a rewrite of the archaeology of Islam will again soon be required.

CHAPTER 5

THE WESTERN SAHEL

Introduction

On the opposite side of the continent from the trade centres of the Swahili coast a group of entrepôts, which in many ways were analogous to their East African counterparts, were located in the western Sahel (**figure 5.1**). Similarities exist in their geographical situation, for example. The Swahili centres hug the coast of the Indian Ocean in the same way as the West African entrepôts were scattered on the outer fringe of the Sahel, the semi-desertic fringe of the Sahara. In fact, the Sahel has been described as functioning in the same way to the Sahara as the East African coast does to the Indian Ocean. This is described by Nehemia Levtzion (1973:10) thus: '*Sahil* is the Arabic word for "shore", which is well understood if the desert is compared to a sea of sand, and the camel to a ship. Hence, the towns which developed in the Sahel – Takrur, Ghana and Gao – may be regarded as ports'. This is a useful analogy, and the Sahara should not be considered as the sort of total block to contacts and trade as it has sometimes been portrayed, but obviously it also has to be borne in mind that the Sahara is not as conducive to trade and the spread of ideas, including religious ones, as a true littoral.

However, certain parallels are also evident in the trade patterns that operated on the Swahili coast and in the western Sahel. The dominant pattern was one of raw materials exported in return for manufactured goods, frequently of what could be termed luxury categories – items such as the ubiquitous glazed ceramics, which in East Africa and also the Horn were both from China and the Muslim world, but in the western Sahel were predominantly from North Africa, Islamic Spain and the Near East (Levtzion 1973; M. Horton 1996b; Insoll 1996b, 2000). The triumvirate of gold, slaves and ivory was shipped north across the Sahara in exchange for – besides glazed ceramics – glasswares, beads, items of metalwork, cloth, paper and, most importantly for this study, and albeit indirectly, Islam (Levtzion 2000). Trade can thus again be seen to be of especial significance in the initial introduction of Islam into the western Sahel, as it was on the East African coast. The contemporaneity of the two groups of trade centres is also striking, a factor linked with the expansion of trade in the Muslim world from the early ninth century and the accompanying upsurge in demand for raw materials (Lapidus 1988).

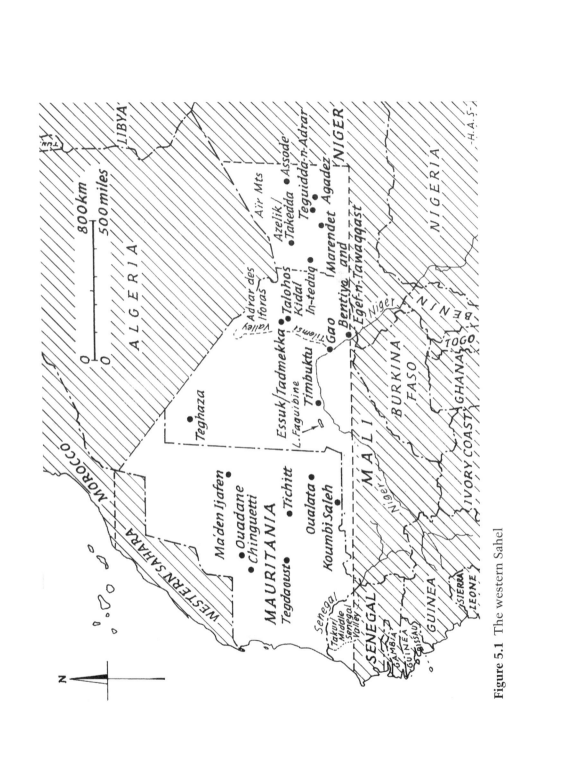

Figure 5.1 The western Sahel

Moreover, it would be wrong to extend the comparison as far as suggesting that a comparable cultural phenomenon to the Swahili existed in the western Sahel. It did not; the degree of unity evident in the Swahili trade centres (although its extent is subject to some discussion, as we have seen) never existed in this region. As has already been noted, the origins of the Swahili still remain the subject of heated debate, and something must have differed as regards the circumstances surrounding the growth and operation of the trade centres in the western Sahel. What this factor, or more probably factors, were remains uncertain, but archaeology, as we shall see, indicates marked differences between the trade centres west of the Niger Bend and those to the east, which nullifies an analogous concept of cultural unity to that which existed, at least in the stone towns, on the Swahili coast. One reason for this might have been the existence of large indigenous polities in the western Sahel such as the kingdoms of Ghana and Songhai (see Levtzion 1973, 1985a; Hunwick 1985b), with comparable entities absent on the East African coast, as can be seen from the discussion in the previous chapter. Another may have been the mosaic of ethnic groups that existed in the western Sahel, but even this does not seem too convincing as an explanatory device, as the coast and hinterland of East Africa equally displays great ethnic heterogeneity, though perhaps not to the same degree.

Yet to deny that ethnic diversity was of importance for the establishment of the major trade centres and a significant factor in the progress of Islamisation in the western Sahel would be foolhardy. Although it is dangerous to project contemporary observations regarding this back into the past, supporting evidence, such as the significant body of historical documents written in Arabic which exists (see Levtzion and Hopkins 1981) and oral tradition (see, e.g., Rouch 1953), indicates that some of the ethnic patterns observable today are at least partly valid for well over a thousand years ago. Pastoralism would have dominated in the more arid regions away from the major bodies of water such as the Rivers Niger and Senegal, with the ancestors of the nomadic Tuareg, Moors and Fulani herding sheep, goats, cattle and camels in the semi-desert, perhaps with limited agriculture confined to oases (Nicolaisen 1963; Swift 1975; Brett and Fentress 1996). Alongside the river – and in certain other privileged contexts – agriculture was viable, and settled communities would have been established, today represented by groups such as the Songhai, Soninke, Bambara, and Wolof (Rouch 1954; Zahan 1960; R. J. McIntosh 1998). The rivers and other large bodies of water might have been exploited by specialised groups, as parts of the River Niger are by the Bozo and Sorko today (Rouch 1950; Ligers 1964).

It can be seen that economic activities and the environment are intimately connected. In this respect, it is apparent that the climate in this region has not been fixed: it has changed over the course of the millennia (Goudie 1996; Shaw 1985; Nicholson 1996; S. K. and R. J. McIntosh 1988). Today, the Sahel is classified as a transitional zone between the Sahara, the true desert and the more thickly wooded Sudanic savannah. Cram-cram grass, acacia-type thorn trees and doum palms are the characteristic vegetation of the Sahel (Trimingham 1959:2–3). The typical fauna include gazelle, various other species of antelope, buffalo, giraffe, elephant and lion, and in the major watercourses such as the River Niger, hippopotamus and crocodile (S. E. Smith 1980:468). This is significant for, as was discussed in chapter 1, economic occupation, whether pastoralist, town-dweller, or sedentary agriculturalist, may have been of importance in influencing when and why conversion to Islam took place in parts of sub-Saharan Africa. Within the western Sahel this seems to have been so, and this can be charted in part through archaeological data, as will be discussed in detail below. Thus archaeology, Islam, economy, ethnicity and, ultimately, climate and environment (as the dominant structuring variable) are all interconnected, and though this is obviously the case in other areas of sub-Saharan Africa, it would seem to be especially so in this region.

The pre-Islamic background

Chariot routes and Romans

As with elsewhere in the continent south of the Sahara, Islam was adapted to pre-existing culture, which in the western Sahel had already undergone a considerable development process, contrary to earlier opinions which saw phenomena such as urbanism accompanying foreign Muslim traders, with no, or limited, indigenous input (see, e.g., Mauny 1961). This is similar to the situation already described for the East African coast, and indeed for other areas of the continent, as was discussed in chapter 1. Contacts with North Africa prior to the arrival of Muslim traders in the late eighth century were limited. However, archaeological evidence appears to contradict this and to indicate that extensive travel took place in the Sahara, and, by inference, north–south contacts, in the second half of the first millennium BCE. These are supposedly attested by, for example, numerous rock-engravings and paintings, many of which depict chariots, sometimes harnessed to horses, either crudely engraved or painted, so-called, 'flying gallop chariots' (Muzzolini 1997:349). These are grouped in two relatively narrow bands running across the desert. One leads from southern Morocco through the Adrar of Mauritania and along the Tichitt–Walata escarpment to the area west of Timbuktu **(figure 5.2)**. The second runs from the Gulf of Syrtis in Libya to the Niger Bend, near Gao in Mali, with an offshoot to the Aïr mountains (Camps 1974; Mauny 1978; Lhote 1982:15–44; Muzzolini 1986). Owing to these narrow groupings, they have been interpreted as 'chariot tracks', or even, to quote Lhote (1960:129), 'a great highway, cutting through the whole of the Sahara from Phazania [the Fezzan], to the Niger'.

Further supporting evidence for trans-Saharan contacts prior to the start of Muslim-controlled trade in the ninth century would appear to be lent by various historical documents which also record contacts, albeit limited in number, over

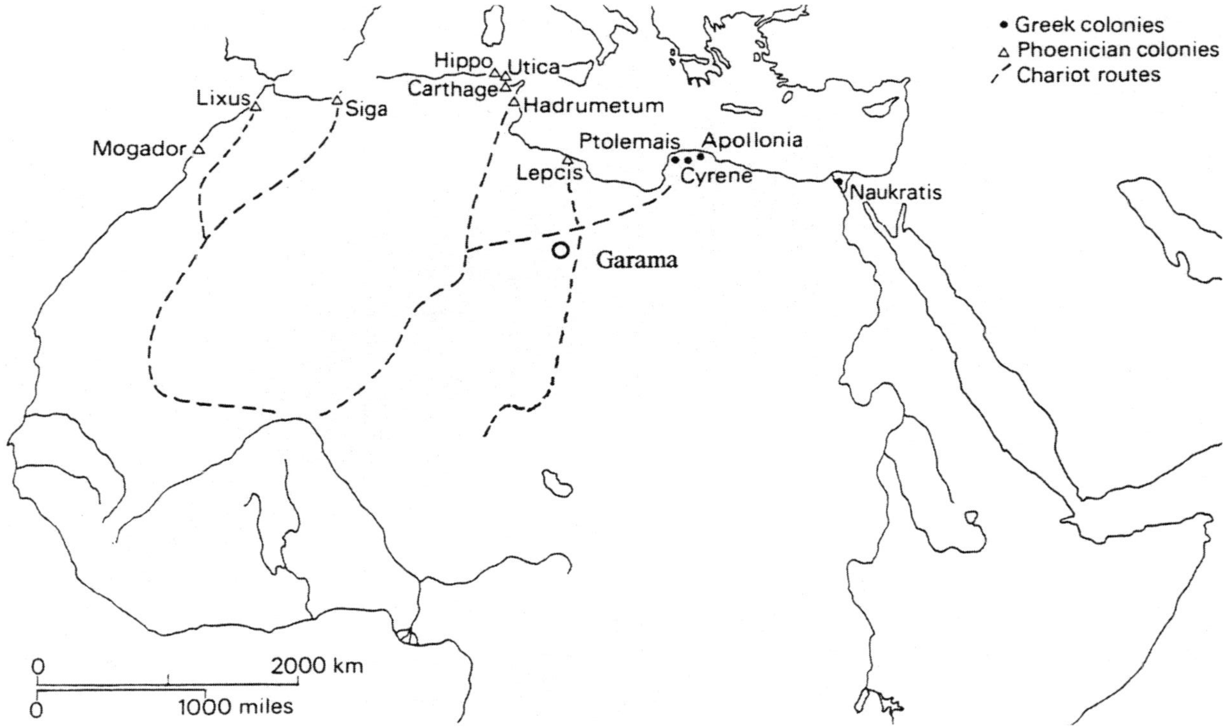
Greek colonies
Phoenician colonies
Chariot routes
Hippo
Utica
Carthage
Hadrumetum
Lixus
Siga
Mogador
Ptolemais
Apollonia
Lepcis
Cyrene
Naukratis
Garama
0
2000 km
0
1000 miles

Figure 5.2 The chariot routes

time. Perhaps one of the best known is the mention by Pliny the Elder of a punitive expedition led by the Roman proconsul Cornelius Balbus against the Garamantes in 19 CE. As well as capturing the Garamantian capital Garama, situated in the central Fezzan, Balbus' expedition reached several rivers, one of which was named the Dasibari, which has been interpreted as the River Niger, possibly in the vicinity of Gao. This identification was based upon a connection formed between the name 'Dasibari' and the Songhai word 'Isabari', from 'Isa' (river) and 'Bari' (big), with 'Das' meaning 'masters of the river'. This became 'Da Isa Bari', and was possibly the river recorded by Pliny and reached by Balbus (Lhote 1960:131–2).

At first glance it would seem that a convincing case for pre-Islamic trans-Saharan contacts between the western Sahel and North Africa can be constructed, but when this evidence is examined in any detail it can be seen to be flawed. The distribution of the chariot rock-engravings and paintings, for instance, as Connah (1987:119) points out, need not follow routes but merely distributions of rock outcrops. Equally, the utility of the very means of transport illustrated can also be questioned when the chariots themselves are examined (see, e.g., Lhote 1982:79–82; Roset 1986:136–7; Muzzolini 1986). It appears that the chariots shown are predominantly light vehicles not really suitable for commercial transport, such as hauling loads of ivory or gold, but more suited to hunting and warfare (J. Wright 1989:6; Brett and Fentress 1996:20–1). It has even been suggested that the chariots were used as *engins de prestige* to raid central Saharan groups, and, to the south, these groups painted on rocks the vehicles they knew and feared and which came from the north (R. J. McIntosh, pers. comm.). Furthermore, the dating of the chariot engravings is far from secure, and thus their identification with the 'Libyans', or whoever, is uncertain (see Muzzolini 1994, 1996:64, for recent chronological reinterpretations). Secondly, the historical records can also be questioned – the expedition of Cornelius Balbus and the identification of the Dasibari with the Niger for example (Lhote 1960). Although the punitive expedition against the Garamantes no doubt took place, the trip to the banks of the Niger has no evidence to support it. There is at present a total lack of archaeological evidence on the Niger Bend, or elsewhere in the western Sahel, attesting to a Roman or other pre-Arab Mediterranean presence, however fleeting (Dawa 1985; Insoll 1996b). Furthermore, the factual basis of the historical data can also be queried, as Balbus was only proconsul for a year, severely limiting what he could do (Salama 1990:288).

Evidence for international trade comparable to that which existed in Ethiopia and the Horn or in the Nilotic Sudan prior to the arrival of Muslim merchants is lacking in the western Sahel. Such evidence is largely confined to the Sahara (see, e.g., Brett and Fentress 1996), though an exception is provided by beads recovered from the site of Jenne-Jeno in Mali (see S. K. and R. J. McIntosh 1980; S. K. McIntosh 1995 and chapter 7 below). Here, at least one bead dated to between 250 BCE and 50 CE, a small blue glass specimen of the 'potash-silica type' (Brill 1995:252), would appear to be of Indian, East Asian or South East Asian origin. Two further beads dated to between about 300 and 800 CE have a 'composition consistent with Roman origins' (Brill 1995:256). However, as stated, it is in the Sahara that the bulk of material attesting to pre-Islamic international trade and other contacts is found (see also chapter 6 for a discussion of the Garamantes and their connections with the central Sudan). A notable example of such a site is provided by the tomb of Tin Hinan, the legendary Berber queen, who according to tradition gave birth to a daughter, Kella, from whom are descended the Kel Rela Tuareg (Brett and Fentress 1996:208). The tomb of Tin Hinan is located near the oasis of Abalessa in the Hoggar mountains. This is a site described by Brett and Fentress (1996:208) as 'the most famous archaeological site of the desert', and where excavation uncovered the remains of a tall woman laid on a bed. Interred with this woman, presumably Tin Hinan, were a number of Roman items of fifth-century date, including gold leaf bearing coin imprints of Constantine I, fragments of glass and a Roman lamp (Reygasse 1950; Law 1967:194).

The archaeological evidence also appears to indicate that the camel, with all its obvious advantages over the horse or ox in trans-Saharan travel, might have been available in the western Sahel before Muslim-organised trade began. However, it was not utilised to maintain international contacts until the growth of the aforementioned trade in the ninth century. Yet, having stated this, it is as well to note that the introduction of the camel into the western Sahel is far from clear. As research stands it is generally regarded as having had a polyglot diffusion westwards from the centre of domestication in the Arabian Peninsula into North Africa and the Sahara and subsequently into West Africa at a date which remains unclear (Bulliet 1975; R. T. Wilson 1984; Clutton-Brock 1993).

Indigenous origins of social complexity

Although evidence for trans-Saharan contacts prior to the development of Muslim-controlled trans-Saharan commerce in the ninth century might be lacking, both political complexity and urban centres had long since developed in the region (see S. K. and R. J. McIntosh 1984; R. J. McIntosh 1998). The settlement of Jenne-Jeno again provides an example of this. It was founded by iron-using people, and shows a steady growth in size from 300 BCE, leading to full urbanism by 500 CE, with by 800 CE the settlement covering an area of some 33 ha, and surrounded by a city wall of 2 km circumference (S. K. and R. J. McIntosh 1980; S. K. McIntosh 1995). Similar, though slightly later, developments were occurring at other urban centres in the region. At Gao on the Niger Bend in Mali, for example, occupation has now been dated back to the sixth century (Insoll 1997b, 2000b:4), while at Koumbi Saleh and Tegdaoust in Mauritania (Thomassey and Mauny 1951, 1956; Berthier 1997) similar evidence has been recorded. Yet at these latter two sites, early settlement evidence was for some time unnoticed until reinterpreted by S. K. and R. J. McIntosh (1984:91), who came to the conclusion that the presence of 2 m of what are termed pre-urban levels probably indicated nothing of the sort, but rather was a reflection of the difficulty of recognising mud or banco architecture archaeologically. Thus settlement at these major trade centres also appears to pre-date the development of Muslim trans-Saharan trade, with these settlements possibly occupied from the seventh century, or even before.

Sahelian-centred polities such as the kingdom of Ghana, the first of the great kingdoms of this region, are now also known to be indigenous in origin, with significant developments occurring from the mid-first millennium (see R. J. McIntosh 1998 for a discussion of this). These developments in turn were ultimately to lead to the apogee of Ghana between the ninth and eleventh centuries (Levtzion 1973). Archaeological data collected in various parts of the region is substantiating this picture. In the Méma area of Mali, for example, survey has recorded the presence of over 100 sites dating from the fourth to the fourteenth centuries and varying in size from 1 ha to nearly 80 ha, as well as many other sites dating from the Late Stone Age (Togola 1996:101). This is an area which, along with various less feasible candidates, could be the hinterland, or alternatively even the original progenitor, of the kingdom of Ghana (R. J. McIntosh 1998:257). Similar early evidence attesting to the indigenous origins of social complexity in the region has been recorded in northern Mauritania at the Dhar Tichitt escarpment (Levtzion 1973; Munson 1980; Holl 1985; Togola 1996). Here, the ceramics, architecture and settlement patterns all indicate the development of an indigenous cultural complex flourishing between 1500 and 500 BCE. The civilisation included villages covering 90 ha at this early date, as at the site of Dakhlet el Atrouss, and a cultural complex which has been interpreted as functioning as a 'pristine chiefdom' (MacDonald 1997:396). Thus, when the Muslim merchants first arrived in the urban centres of the western Sahel they encountered a thriving local culture and economy built upon already longstanding foundations. In fact, it can be argued that it was the prosperity of the western Sahel, which was already in place, that served to attract the Muslim Arab and Berber traders from North Africa, and led to the initial introduction of Islam to the region.

Early Muslim contacts (ninth century)

Ibadi and other traders

The Muslim conquest of North Africa began, according to Lapidus (1988:368), 'with scattered raids from Egypt' (the conquest of which has already been considered in chapter 3). By about 679 Qayrawan ('caravan' – 'a halt at the head of the desert road from Egypt' (Brett and Fentress 1996:84)) had been founded as a centre for further Arab operations and headquarters for the conqueror of the region 'Uqba ibn Nafi, and Tunisia was occupied. This was followed by the Arabs reaching both Morocco and Spain by 711, though their overall numbers were still fairly limited. Gradually the indigenous inhabitants of North Africa converted to Islam, with nomadic Berbers tending to convert prior to their sedentary counterparts, who initially remained Christian. Even then, again as Lapidus (1988:368) notes, 'while many Berbers threw in their lot with the Arabs, many others adopted Kharijism, which allowed them to accept the new religion but to oppose Arab domination'. In totality, the conversion of the population of North Africa and the Saharan regions to Islam was not really complete until the thirteenth century; but once achieved, a degree of unity was lent to the region which had previously not existed. The key to this unity was Islam, and the existence of a contiguous *dar al-Islam* stretching far into the Sahara served to facilitate trade and other contacts over long distances.

According to the Arabic historical sources the first Muslim contacts with the western Sahel were undertaken by Kharijites, namely, Ibadi merchants (Lewicki 1960, 1962, 1964, 1971). Among the earliest recorded contacts are those between the Ibadi Imamate of Tahert (in modern Algeria) and Gao, soon after the foundation of Tahert in the late eighth century. Between the mid-ninth and early tenth centuries there are various other references to trade relations between Tahert and the western Sahel. For example, Ibn as-Saghir, the chronicler of Tahert, wrote at the beginning of the tenth century that a notable of the city, Muhammad ibn 'Arfa, stayed for a period at the court of a king of the Sudan (a reference to the western Sahel region). During his stay he acted as an ambassador for an Ibadi Rostemid Imam of Tahert who ruled between 823 and 872. Although this Sudanese ruler is not mentioned by name, Lewicki (1971:119) makes the point that it is conceivable that this envoy was sent to the ruler of either Ghana or Gao. Similarly, Ibadi sources also refer to trade with Tadmekka (Lewicki 1971:117), probably to be identified with the site of Essuk in Mali (Farias 1990, and see below).

Kharijite tenets were described in chapter 1, where it was noted that they differ in certain respects from those of other Muslim groups, including the prevalent Sunni Maliki Islam of both northern and western Africa. Ibadi communities were formerly widely found across North Africa from 'Jabal Nafusa in Tripolitania, across the Djarid in southern Tunisia to Tahert in Algeria' (Levtzion 1973:136). Small communities still exist in parts of North Africa, as for example in the Mzab area of Algeria (Roche 1970), but all traces of Ibadi beliefs in West Africa have disappeared. Equally elusive is material evidence for these first Muslim trans-Saharan journeys to the western Sahel. The absence of archaeological evidence attesting to these contacts is probably a reflection of the fact that they were only on a small scale. At the majority of the urban centres in the western Sahel known to have been occupied at this date, material indicating contacts with the Muslim world is lacking: glazed pottery and glass, mosques, Muslim burials, inscriptions and coins. Both direct and indirect evidence is absent. The exception is provided by a few sherds of rather poorly described glazed pottery given a Tunisian (Ifriqiyan) provenance from the Mauritanian site of Tegdaoust (in all certainty to be identified with the Awdaghust of the Arabic sources). These sherds are described as coming from levels dating from 'undoubtedly earlier than 900', and were found along with various precious and semi-precious stones, likewise lacking further details (Devisse 1992:197).

Similarly in Gao such evidence is rare (Insoll 1996b:61–2). Archaeological evidence such as trade goods from Ibadi areas has not yet been found. The sole possible link is in the use of brown glaze on three sherds of imported pottery recovered from contexts dated to the eleventh–twelfth centuries in the traders' town of Gao Ancien (and thus later than the period being considered), brown glaze being a decorative technique known to have been used in Tahert (Marcais and Dessum-Lamarre 1946:57). Otherwise, parallels are not found between the material from Gao and that from any of the successive major centres of Ibadi occupation. These included Tahert – as described – abandoned in 909, Wargala and Sedrata – founded shortly thereafter – or those in the Mzab, the rocky plateau on the threshold of the Sahara in southern Algeria where Ibadi communities are found to this day, and where occupation was established after Sedrata also had to be abandoned owing to religious persecution (Mercier 1922:5; Marguerite van Berchem 1953:165, 1954:157; Levtzion 1973:137). Likewise at Koumbi Saleh, perhaps to be identified with the merchant town attached to the as yet unlocated capital of the kingdom of Ghana in Mauritania, evidence for these early Muslim contacts (pre-*c*.900) is absent (Thomassey and Mauny 1951, 1956; Berthier 1997). Equally, to the west of the region in Senegal, such indications are absent, with the so-called northern tumuli linked to events in the early second millennium and polities such as Takrur (S. K. and R. J. McIntosh 1993:105, and see below).

Yet it should be noted that this absence may partly also be due to the fact that attention has been focused in the wrong place. Essuk/Tadmekka in the Adrar des Iforas mountains was a very important early Berber- or Tuareg-controlled trade centre, and still awaits detailed archaeological investigation which may yield evidence for contacts and Islamisation before the start of the tenth century. Its position, literally on the Saharan fringe to the north of Gao, might have been of especial importance; certainly its Muslim significance is obvious: as al-Bakri recorded in the second half of the eleventh century, 'its name means "the Mecca-like"' (Levtzion and Hopkins 1981:85). Levtzion (1978:650) has suggested that Tadmekka and Tegdaoust were so placed as they were considered to be within the *dar al-Islam*, and thus an important distinction was being made, with centres further south such as Koumbi Saleh and Gao not then considered as such. This is an interesting point, but the evidence from Tegdaoust to indicate a Muslim presence in these early levels is lacking, whilst Essuk/Tadmekka awaits investigation. It is also possible, as Levtzion further suggests (1973:45), that Tadmekka was initially Ibadi in outlook owing to its links with Tahert, and that this was eradicated following a joint campaign between 1083 and 1084 launched against its inhabitants by forces from the kingdom of Ghana, and those of the southern Almoravids, a reforming Berber movement (Farias 1990:93).

Thus far only preliminary observations on this important site have been made. However, the presence of two mosques, including a congregational mosque measuring 23.5 × 15.5 m, and divided into five rows parallel to the *mihrab*, has been reported (Cressier 1992:71–3). Muslim cemeteries, pre-Islamic tombs, Arabic inscriptions and the remains of a settlement have also all been variously recorded (de Gironcourt 1920; Mauny 1951a; Farias 1990; Cressier 1992). These indicate the considerable antiquity of settlement at Essuk/Tadmekka. The inscriptions recovered are of especial significance, and over 188 were recorded by de Gironcourt (1920) at the start of the twentieth century. Some of these have recently been investigated by Farias (1990, 1999, forthcoming), including 'the oldest dated epigraph so far reported from the Adrar or anywhere else in West Africa' (1990:95). This inscription, described as a graffito on a rock face, dates from the period between 13 July 1013 and 2 July 1014. Furthermore, another inscription from Essuk ('the market') conclusively supports the identification of the site with that of Tadmekka or Tadmakkat of the Arabic historical sources. This inscription refers to 'a market in conformity to (or: a longing for) Bekka (or: Mecca)' (Farias 1999:109). This identification with Mecca has been interpreted by Farias (1999:107) as functioning as part of a process whereby 'expatriate Muslims coming to live in the periphery of the world known to them who first strove to find there simulacra of the city that was most central to their religion'.

Besides the lack of archaeological evidence, one further possible indicator of former Ibadi contacts with, and presence in, the western Sahel does appear to exist: certain features in the so-called Sudanese style of architecture, which have parallels with the architecture of the Mzab and other Ibadi areas of North Africa. The possible existence of these features has been the subject of some debate. Mercier (1928) suggested that the minarets of the region have their prototypes in the Mzab. Certainly, similarities can sometimes be seen – as between the now destroyed mosque in El-Ateuf, the first Ibadi town founded in the Mzab in 1012 (Bisson 1962:215; Roche 1970:25), and the mosque and tomb of Askia Muhammad, a Songhai emperor who reigned in the late fifteenth and early sixteenth centuries. These similarities include features such as the three-tier structure and the staircase minaret **(figure 5.3)** (Mauny 1950; Insoll 1996b:55). These ideas of architectural parallels were expanded upon by Schacht (1954, 1957b, 1961), who proposed that the archaic type of staircase minaret found in some areas of West Africa can also be seen in Ibadi areas of North Africa – for example, Sousse and Djerba island in Tunisia. The staircase minaret is an Ibadi architectural feature already mentioned in the last chapter with reference

Figure 5.3 The mosque and tomb of Askia Muhammad, Gao

to Zanzibar. Although there may be some utility in discussing such residual Ibadi architectural influences in the western Sahel, it should also be borne in mind that these similarities might be partly dictated by the same construction materials being used in both areas: banco (liquid mud) and palmwood. Such factors can limit both architectural expression and building technology, and certainly the question deserves further investigation.

Nomads

Thus far, emphasis in the discussion has been upon a North African Muslim perspective – namely, the evidence for their presence in the western Sahel up to the start of the tenth century. But equally, an attempt should be made to consider the acceptance of Islam within the local context by the indigenous population; and here, as elsewhere in the continent, this was not an instantaneous process. It was spread over several centuries – but, as was noted at the start of this chapter, it would appear that in the western Sahel the pace of conversion to Islam can in part be correlated with different socio-economic groups (Insoll 1996b). Yet, having said this, it is not possible to shoehorn the evidence to fit models such as R. Horton's (1971, 1975) or Fisher's (1973a, 1985) phased models of Islamic conversion described in chapter 1. Rather, elements drawn from a variety of approaches can be drawn together in an attempt to reconstruct Islamisation in the region, thus following the pioneering work of scholars such as Levtzion (1985b, 1986b).

Within parts of the western Sahel, it would seem that among the first converts to Islam were members of the nomadic population, for reasons already suggested in chapter 1. These included, to recap, the ease of worship which Islam enjoys (no formal clergy etc.), and through nomads' exposure to Muslim-dominated trade, as guides for instance (Trimingham 1959), or because Islam acted in nomad societies as a means 'towards tribal cohesion and solidarity' (Trimingham 1968:40). Although the relevant archaeological work to support this admittedly general statement is still in its infancy, the suggestion that nomads were among the first to be Islamised might help in explaining the site patterning evident in some areas.

An example of this is provided by a map of Muslim cemeteries in the Niger Bend area of Mali prepared by de Gironcourt (1920:161) **(figure 5.4)**. It is apparent from this map that the majority of the cemeteries containing Muslim inscriptions are to be found clustered along the River Niger, predominantly along the left bank (Songhai – *Awsa* or *Hawsa* (Hunwick 1994:11)), as well as along the Tilemsi valley running north from Gao, and to a lesser extent the paleo-tributaries of the Niger (Insoll 1996b:13). This cemetery patterning would appear to be of interest, as it follows the main axes of communication and of trade. It is unlikely to be unduly influenced by de Gironcourt's survey methodology, as his coverage of the area was very thorough, and could, perhaps,

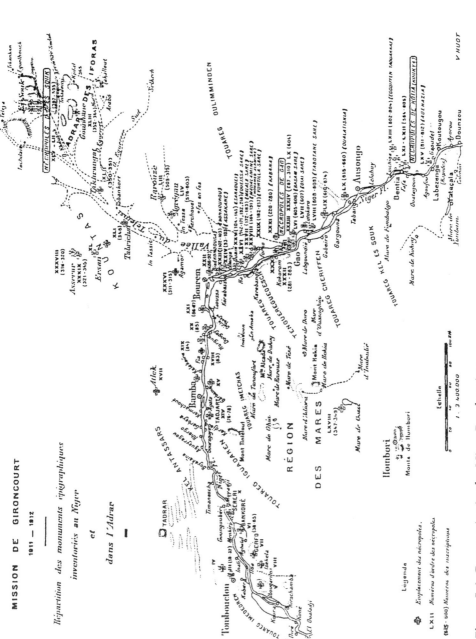

Figure 5.4 Cemeteries in the Niger Bend region

indicate, besides testifying to mortality rates among merchants and other Muslim travellers, that nomads were among the first to convert to Islam in this region, as many of the cemeteries cluster in their current territories. Yet this remains, at present, merely a hypothesis, as the data presented in the map is 'raw' data, a mix of early and more recent material. The full potential of the data will not be realised until all the inscriptions have been established and a cemetery chronology established, something which is ongoing (Farias forthcoming). Nevertheless, this map and the corpus of inscriptions it represents is of great significance to the study of Islamisation processes in the western Sahel, as Max van Berchem (1920:355–6) noted over eighty years ago:

Il est donc certain que les matériaux rapportés par M. de Gironcourt constituent une source précieuse et entièrement nouvelle pour l'histoire de l'Islam au Niger... Il sera possible sans doute, par l'examen comparé des dates mortuaires, de retracer la marche de l'invasion musulmane du Sahara vers le golfe de Guineé et d'en fixer peut-être l'époque approximative.

The spread of Islam (tenth–thirteenth centuries)

Traders and trade centres

Beginning in the tenth century there is an increase in archaeological evidence attesting to contacts with the Muslim world. Items such as glazed pottery, glass vessels, glass beads and brass metalwork are all found at sites such as Gao (Insoll 1996b, 2000b). Secondly, the first direct evidence for the presence of Muslims in the western Sahel is found – evidence already discussed in chapter 1, such as mosques, Muslim burials and the remains of domestic structures which might have been arranged according to Muslim social requirements. It is also conceivable to begin to further develop the model of Islamisation in the region, for besides a possible correlation between the nomadic population and early conversion to Islam, a further group of initial converts to Islam in the western Sahel may have been the North African merchants' local partners in trade.

The role of trade in encouraging the spread of Islam has already been signalled in chapter 1, where Levtzion's theories (1986a) on this subject were discussed. Being a Muslim might have conferred advantages in trade, certainly as regards trade in North African centres. Equally, perceptions of the western Sahel may have been of importance. For example, within Indian Ocean trade, considered in the last chapter, tax rules were less stringent in areas considered as being within the *dar al-Islam* (Tampoe 1989:128–9). Issues of trust might have been similarly easier when dealing with one's coreligionists. Brett (1983:440) describes how a *fatwa* (a religious edict) mentions that an overseer or 'watchman' was appointed with authority over the Muslim communities in the *bilad al-Sudan* (a reference to the wider region of which the western Sahel formed a part). Perhaps this individual had a similar status to the 'Representative of Merchants' (Tampoe 1989:128), found in the major Indian Ocean trading centres on the other side of the continent, a role that had been instituted to look after the interests of Muslim merchants who had died or who had encountered difficulties.

Nevertheless, the relations between Muslim merchants and the local elites in the major centres of the western Sahel should not be thought of as purely amicable and trusting from the start. On the contrary, they appear to have been somewhat cautious, and this is represented by the dual settlements that developed across the region (Levtzion 1973). Koumbi Saleh, the merchant town attached to the capital of the kingdom of Ghana, as yet undiscovered, has already been mentioned (and is described more fully below). But this was by no means an isolated instance. At Gao, which was later to develop into the capital of the Songhai empire, the last and biggest of the 'medieval' West African polities that flourished between the mid-fifteenth and late sixteenth centuries (Hunwick 1985b), dual settlements existed. The settlement structure within Gao is described in detail by the Arab historians and geographers, beginning with al-Muhallabi in the late tenth century who recorded that the king of Kawkaw, or Gao, 'has a town on the Nile (Niger), on the eastern bank, which is called Sarnah, where there are markets and trading houses and to which there is continuous traffic from all parts. He has another town to the west of the Nile where he and his men and those who have his confidence live. There is a mosque there where he prays but the communal prayer ground is between the two towns' (Levtzion and Hopkins 1981:174). The existence of twin settlements at Gao is also recorded by al-Bakri in the mid-eleventh century, but not by al-Idrisi writing in the mid-twelfth century (Levtzion and Hopkins 1981). Archaeology testifies to Gao being a large, prosperous settlement consisting of two components, the citadel of Gao Ancien (Old Gao) and the attached 'suburb' of Gadei, within the area of the modern city, and Gao-Saney, a large tell 7 km to the north-east of the city (Insoll 1997b). However, when the archaeological evidence is considered in detail (see below), it can be seen that although broadly agreeing with the historical sources, the picture of settlement structure at Gao is much more complex than the Arab historians describe – and, indeed, as has been promoted by historians subsequently (see, e.g., Lange 1991, 1994).

Other dual settlements existed in the western Sahel. The Do royal town, for instance, was separated from the Muslim commercial centre of Yaresna by the Upper River Senegal (Levtzion 1973:188). Farias (1990:105) has also suggested that these patterns are found south of Gao on the River Niger, with the relationship between an unnamed site located near the dune of Egef-n-Tawaqqast and the village of Bentiya being similarly representative of the dual settlement phenomenon, and the site near Egef-n-Tawaqqast being the Muslim centre (an area recently re-surveyed by Arazi (1999)). The existence of dual settlements has also been noted elsewhere in the continent, as was described for Ethiopia in chapter 2, where it was also mentioned that they were a characteristic feature of 'early urban development' in eastern and northern Europe as evident in dual Slav and Viking settlements (Dolukhanov 1996:189). Thus their existence is far from unique to the western Sahel.

Restrictions were certainly maintained in this first contact situation upon where the Muslim merchants could travel (Devisse 1992:204), and these might not have been relaxed until conversion to Islam had spread beyond mercantile and perhaps nomad contexts. There are references in the Arabic historical sources which imply that the movement of Arab and Berber merchants was restricted. Yaqut (d. 1229), in the context of describing the inhabitants of an unspecified area where gold was extracted, makes the point that 'this is how their manners are reported though those people never allow a merchant to see them' (Levtzion and Hopkins 1981:170). But certainly by the time Ibn Battuta visited the western Sahel in the mid-fourteenth century, intercourse between foreign merchants and the indigenous population was common, and no restrictions appear to have been placed upon his travels (Hamdun and King 1994).

Thus at first, relations were cautious on both sides while relationships were formed, with what could be termed two levels of inter-site spatial relationship evident over time. Initially these were long distance, as referred to previously with reference to Levtzion's (1978:640) description of this arrangement, as represented by the relationship between Tegdaoust and the capital of Ghana, several hundred kilometres apart. Yet over time distances shrank, as between Koumbi Saleh and the as yet undiscovered local settlement (if indeed it is to be found within the vicinity of Koumbi Saleh), which was adjacent to the sacred grove, *al-ghaba* (Levtzion 1973:25). Similarly, to the east, there was a further long-distance inter-site relationship between Tadmekka and Gao (Levtzion 1978), later collapsed to that between Gao Ancien and Gao-Saney (Insoll 1997b).

Certainly, the archaeological evidence indicates a growth in trade contacts with the Muslim world after about 1000. At Tegdaoust, as has already been mentioned, the earliest evidence found indicating these trade contacts, Ifriqiyan glazed pottery and semi-precious stones, dates from the ninth century. However, the main period of occupation dates from the late ninth to early fourteenth centuries, when Muslim-dominated trade was in full flow (D. Robert 1970a, 1970b; Vanacker 1979; Robert-Chaleix 1989). Tegdaoust covers some 12 ha, and consists of two principal components, a town and a necropolis (D. Robert 1970b:64) (figure 5.5). The necropolis, which is aligned north–south over about 700 m, is of some interest owing to the differing orientation of the skeletal remains within it, and the distinct types of graves found, some with *mihrabs*. Corpse orientation varied from being buried north–south with the face to the east in one group of interments (north central) to others facing south with heads to the west (northern group) (D. Robert 1970b:65). This variation has been interpreted by the excavators as indicating different phases of Islamisation. This matter remains to be investigated in detail, but is according to one of the

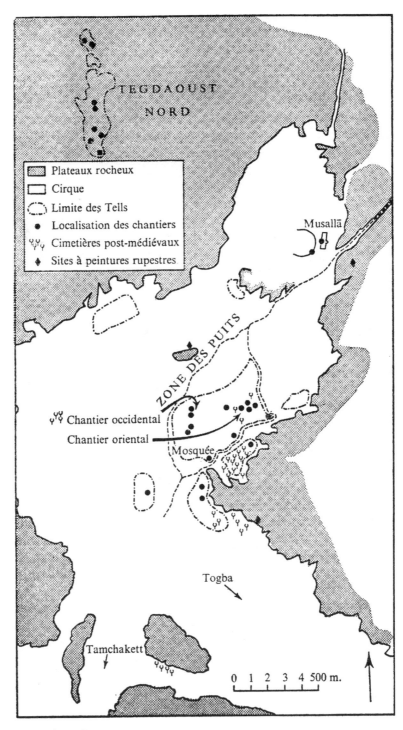

Figure 5.5 Plan of Tegdaoust

investigators, S. Robert, 'sans doute beaucoup plus complexe que les textes Arabes ne laissient apparaître' (1970:275). Alternatively, it might equally indicate coexisting religious traditions. Without a more precise idea of cemetery chronology this will continue to remain unclear.

A more concrete assertion of Muslim identity is provided by a large stone-built mosque which was also uncovered (precise dimensions unclear). This was oriented south–south-east, interpreted as possibly indicating Maghrebi or Andalusian (Spanish) influences (D. Robert 1970b:66). Al-Bakri (c.1068) refers to the main mosque at Awdaghust in his description of the town: 'In Awdaghust there is one cathedral mosque and many smaller ones, all well attended...The people of Awdaghust enjoy extensive benefits and huge wealth...There are handsome buildings and fine houses' (Levtzion and Hopkins 1981:68). Well-constructed houses were another feature recorded at Tegdaoust (Polet 1985). These are structures that appear to exhibit an emphasis upon privacy, and in the early phases of occupation were built of dressed stone to a courtyard plan. Subsequently, sun-dried brick replaced stone or was used in conjunction with it to build houses of a similar plan, now decorated with coloured red or white plaster. Finally, stone-built architecture was again used but the houses were smaller and contained a variety of triangular and rectangular niches in their walls (D. Robert 1970b:65–6), presumably for storage and broadly comparable to those described for Harar in chapter 2. Items obtained via trans-Saharan trade were also recovered, including white-slipped pottery in levels dated to the tenth century, as well as numerous sherds of green-glazed wares (D. Robert 1970b; Robert-Chaleix 1983). Source areas of this material included Ifriqiya, the Maghreb and al-Andalus. These sources were supplemented by glass fragments said to resemble material from Fustat in Egypt (Vanacker 1979:166–8, 1983:522).

Rulers and townspeople (Takrur and Ghana)

The historical records indicate that Islam was not long confined to nomad and mercantile contexts. By the late tenth and early eleventh centuries they record a new phenomenon – that conversions, not of traders but of local rulers, were beginning to take place for reasons already described in chapter 1, and which will be further outlined below. In Takrur on the River Senegal, for example, al-Bakri notes that 'the inhabitants are Sudan [blacks], who were previously, like all the other Sudan, pagans and worshipped idols until Warjabi b. Rabis became their ruler. He embraced Islam, introduced among them Muslim religious law and compelled them to observe it' (Levtzion and Hopkins 1981:77). This occurred about 1040–1. The nature of Islam in Takrur also appears to have differed from that of Gao and Ghana. It has been described as more 'zealous' by Levtzion (1973:183), with Takruris spreading Islam beyond their borders, to the neighbouring kingdom of Silla for example. Takruri Islam is identified by Levtzion

(1973) as characteristic of a second trend in the development of Islam in West Africa in contrast to that of Gao with its symbiosis of Islam and traditional religions (see below). Takrur 'aimed at the imposition of the new religion in all its vigorousness, forcing the subjects to adopt Islam, introducing the Islamic law, carrying the propagation of Islam among neighbours and waging the holy war against infidels' (1973:184). Eaton (1993) would define it as a phase of 'displacement' – though here in Takrur the previous two phases do not appear to have been passed through. What occurred in Takrur is also reminiscent of the wave of reform that spread through the region in the eighteenth–nineteenth centuries.

However, although evidence for involvement in trans-Saharan trade is found in the region formerly controlled by the Takrur polity dating from this period (S. K. and R. J. McIntosh 1993; S. K. McIntosh 1995), direct evidence for Islam itself (mosques, burials) is lacking. A similar picture is evident at the site of Sincu Bara in the Middle Senegal Valley, which has been suggested as possibly being linked with the Silla polity (Thilmans and Ravisé 1980). Excavations at this site uncovered a wealth of material including elephant ivory, locally produced pottery, a single sherd of North African glazed pottery, a dozen cowries and thousands of copper artefacts such as small bells and cylinders. This site was originally dated to between the fifth and eleventh centuries, and interpreted as resulting from a single, long-lasting occupation phase (Thilmans and Ravisé 1980). More recent excavations have shown the sequence at Sincu Bara to be much more complex (McIntosh and Bocoum 1998, 2000). Multiple occupation deposits were uncovered dating from the whole of the first millennium. The trade evidence was also re-evaluated, and most of the artefacts recovered were made from locally available raw materials, though the marine shells and copper were interpreted as archaeological manifestations 'of a more extensive trade that included, if the Arab sources have it right, staples, slaves, and probably salt' (McIntosh and Bocoum 2000:36). Otherwise, any direct evidence for the presence of Muslims was not found.

Also documented in the Arabic sources are both the pre-Islamic religion and the conversion of the ruler of Ghana to Islam, and this provides a further variant of Islamisation in the western Sahel, described by Levtzion as 'that of Muslims who live under the auspices of pagan rulers' (1973:186). The Arabic historical sources record that the official religion in Ghana was one based on a divine king, and unlike the ruler of Takrur, or Kawkaw (Gao, discussed below), the King of Ghana had not even nominally converted to Islam by the mid-eleventh century. The detailed and oft-cited description by al-Bakri of the capital of Ghana gives an insight into the religious practices there in the mid-eleventh century. The city consisted of twin settlements, as already noted, one Muslim and possessing twelve mosques, the other the residence of the king, and described as surrounded by 'domed buildings and groves and thickets where the sorcerers of these people, men in charge of the religious cult, live. In them too are their idols and the tombs of their kings' (Levtzion and Hopkins 1981:79–80). The king and his heir are also described as the only people allowed to wear sewn clothes, and the king sat in audience in a domed pavilion surrounded by the trappings of state, to which petitioners came, fell to their knees and sprinkled dust on their heads. Sacrifices were also made to the dead, and idols worshipped (Levtzion and Hopkins 1981).

Thus many of the elements of divine kingship which have been remarked upon in general contexts, as well as for parts of the Nilotic Sudan in chapter 3, can again be seen to be apparent in the western Sahel. The question can be posed as to why then the ruler of Ghana tolerated Muslims, apparently in large numbers, at his capital. One suggested reason has been that administration was improved through the use of Arabic (in what were pre-literate contexts) as well as through using Muslim officials (Dramani-Issifou 1992:57). This would appear to be supported by the historical sources, as al-Bakri also recorded that 'the King's interpreters, the official in charge of his treasury and the majority of his ministers are Muslims' (Levtzion and Hopkins 1981:80). These are also reasons as to why the non-Muslim Asante rulers allowed a substantial Muslim presence in their capital (see chapter 7). Equally, it could be asked why a ruler might convert to Islam when he had a divine status, or was what Mbiti (1975:161) describes as 'God's earthly representative'. Numerous suggestions can be made to account for this – genuine belief, or the addition it could make to the panoply of ritual, perhaps. Levtzion (1979b:214) makes the point in this respect that among Muslims with little or no Islamic education, 'the ritual rather than the legal aspects of Islam were of greater importance'.

Trade considerations might also have been important, as already noted above. Nevertheless, rulers such as those of Gao or Ghana could also be cautious and assume a middle position 'between Islam and the traditional religion, so that most of them were neither real Muslims nor complete pagans' (Levtzion 1985a:162). Conversion to Islam could also be used as a means of gaining ascendancy over rivals or enemies, as was described for the end of the Christian kingdom of Makuria in chapter 3. Besides maintaining or obtaining positions of power, it could prove possible to enslave one's enemies if they were non-Muslims. Within the Qur'an slavery is regarded as a recognised institution, and guidance is provided for who may and may not be enslaved (see Fisher and Fisher 1970; J. R. Willis 1985b). Those enslaved were frequently regarded, as Farias (1985:38) notes, as 'barbarians outside civilised life if not outside humanity'.

Equally, as rulers converted it is possible that Muslim communities in the western Sahel could have been enlarged by conversions to Islam among town-dwellers within centres such as Gao and the capital of Ghana. For as I. M. Lewis (1980a:37) notes, Islam cannot be made to serve the needs of a divine ruler for long as 'by its very nature, Islam cannot in the long run be constrained to serve the interests, or be applied to the exclusive benefit, of particular kings, aristocracies, or peoples'. It is inevitable that here in the western Sahel, as elsewhere in sub-Saharan Africa, Islam would have gradually spread. However, the utility of suggesting why in the urban context Islam might prove popular, as was outlined in chapter 1 with reference to Trimingham's (1959) ideas on this subject, can be questioned. A certain degree of cohesiveness of ethnic groups might be achieved under the banner of Islam, but equally, no cohesiveness can exist at all after conversion to Islam (see Miner 1953 for a revealing study of Islam and ethnicity in this region).

The gold trade of Ghana

The empire of Ghana prospered through trade, especially the gold trade. Al-Idrisi, writing in the mid-twelfth century, describes the King of Ghana tethering his horse to a 'brick of gold' (Levtzion and Hopkins 1981:110). The brick grew in weight from some thirty pounds in al-Idrisi's day to a ton in weight when Ibn Khaldun reported its later sale in the fourteenth century (Bovill 1968:81). Even allowing for dramatic licence, it is undeniable that large quantities of gold were available in West Africa at this time. The court of the King of Ghana was described in detail by al-Bakri in the mid-eleventh century, and the wealth of gold available is evident in his description: the king wore a golden headdress, the pages carried gold-hilted swords, the horses had gold trappings, and even the dogs guarding the royal pavilion wore collars with bells of silver and gold. In view of the amount of gold in circulation, steps had to be taken to ensure its continuing value: this was achieved by making all nuggets the property of the king, and only gold dust available for trade (Bovill 1968:81–2).

Some detail on how the gold was obtained is also provided by the Arabic sources. The gold, extracted from shallow surface workings, was mined not in the Sahel but further south in the savannahs of the western Sudan (see chapter 7). Two of the most important sources were at Bambuk and Bure, where gold was extracted in a process shrouded in mystery to which Yaqut (d. 1229) alludes when he records that, to quote, 'this is how their manners are reported though those people never allow a merchant to see them' (Levtzion and Hopkins 1981:170). Once, one of the gold miners was captured by a group of traders in an attempt to discover the exact source of the gold. This was unsuccessful, as Bovill (1968:82) records in somewhat dated language: 'He pined to death without saying a word, and it was three years before the negroes would resume the trade, and then only because they had no other way of satisfying their craving for salt.' Thus the gold-miners were left largely to their own devices.

Salt was one of the main commodities exchanged for gold – again according to the Arabic sources, sometimes weight for weight. The actual process of exchange was one that has been described as 'silent trade'. This is also described in detail by al-'Umari (d. 1349), who reports that 'some of the remote peoples of the Sudan do not show themselves. When the salt merchants come they put the salt down and then withdraw. Then the Sudan put down the gold. When the merchants have taken the gold the Sudan take the salt' (Levtzion and Hopkins 1981:273). However, whether such a silent trade actually ever took place is unproven. To this day some gold-working exists in the savannah regions of Mali, but on a much reduced scale to that of the medieval period (S. Berthe, pers. comm.).

Thus far, as already noted, only the merchant town Koumbi Saleh has been identified as part of the settlement complex possibly associated with the capital of Ghana. Therefore we are limited in what we can say about overall Islamisation processes based upon archaeological evidence, as only the Muslim settlement has been investigated. As at Tegdaoust, Koumbi Saleh was organised on a reasonably regular plan, and was made up of multi-storey houses **(figure 5.6)**. Various other structures were also recorded, including a large congregational mosque, measuring 46 m east–west × 23 m north–south, and which was revealed by a succession of *mihrabs* to have been rebuilt three times between the tenth and fifteenth centuries, probably as the Muslim congregation grew in size (but see below). Beside the stone houses lay a suburb of earthen houses, and also two cemeteries containing numerous Muslim burials, various funerary enclosures, and what appears to be a monumental *qubba* tomb measuring 5 m² and 2 m in height (Bonnel de Mézières 1923; Thomassey and Mauny 1951, 1956; Devisse and Diallo 1993; Berthier 1997). The whole settlement was bisected by a broad main avenue running east–west and up to some 12 m width in front of the mosque. In total the population of Koumbi Saleh has been estimated at between 15,000 and 20,000 (Levtzion 1973:24; and see Berthier 1997).

A variety of items sourced from or inspired by objects obtained via trans-Saharan trade were also recovered from Koumbi Saleh. These included several sherds of slipped wares produced locally but which resembled ceramic water filters of types made in Egypt (Thomassey and Mauny 1956:124). Five sherds of what seem to be lustre-decorated ceramics were also recovered during more recent excavations, as well as blue, green and yellow glass trade beads of types found across the continent (see Berthier 1997:92). In total thirty-eight fragments of glass, mostly dating from the eleventh century, were also recorded during excavations conducted in the habitation quarter (Berthier 1997). To these can be added seven described glass fragments recovered during earlier excavations. The imported material found, however, is in much smaller quantities than might perhaps be expected at so important a trade centre, in contrast to Tegdaoust, where much larger quantities of imported materials were found (see above and Devisse 1983). In conclusion, a rather standard trade centre was excavated

Figure 5.6 Interior of a house at Koumbi Saleh

which sheds little light on the central issue of the conversion to Islam of the ruler and people of Ghana.

This, the conversion to Islam of the inhabitants of Ghana, is an issue which has been the subject of much debate and misinterpretation. Formerly, it was widely held, based upon readings of the Arabic historical sources, that conversion was forcible (see Trimingham 1962; Bovill 1968; Levtzion 1973, 1985a; B. Davidson 1990). For example, al-Zuhri (c.1137–54) in a manuscript referred to as the 'Book of Geography' recorded that the people of Ghana turned Muslim in 1076–7 due to the actions of the Almoravids (Levtzion and Hopkins 1981:98), a reforming puritanical movement which drew its support from the Sanhaja nomads of the western Sahara (Levtzion 1985a:138). Also, Ibn Khaldun (d. 1406) in his *Kitab al-'Ibar* relates that 'the veiled people' (also a reference to the Almoravids) 'extended their domination over the Sudan, and pillaged, imposed tribute and poll-tax, and converted many of them to Islam' (Levtzion and Hopkins 1981:333). Little supporting evidence has been found for these claims, yet for a long time it was believed that zealous hordes of Almoravid desert warriors, supported by soldiers from the Muslim kingdom of Takrur in Senegal, destroyed the pagan (*sic*) empire of Ghana and forcibly converted the inhabitants to Islam in 1076–7.

A re-evaluation of both the Arabic and local oral sources by the historians David Conrad and Humphrey Fisher (1982, 1983) has convincingly shown that Ghana was not conquered by the Almoravids. Similarly, the archaeological evidence does not support the conquest hypothesis. The evidence for the accompanying destruction that supposedly went hand in hand with the conquest is not conclusive at Koumbi Saleh. The evidence for destruction was reported as being found at a depth of 5 m, though it was also admitted that this hardly constituted conclusive proof for an Almoravid raid (Devisse 1992a:186). Remember that this was after all a town whose population has been estimated at between 15,000 and 20,000, and bisected by an avenue up to 12 m in width (see above), so a lot of evidence for destruction might be expected. In fact, the only other noticeable change of any relevance is that the mosque dimensions altered at the end of the eleventh century, as already noted above. But rather than suggesting that this was a result of Almoravid destruction, it probably reflects rebuilding to accommodate a larger sized congregation – a sizeable congregation certainly being implied by the estimated population size. One can also ask why, being Muslims, would the Almoravids destroy a mosque? – though this has been proposed (Devisse 1992a:186). Moreover, the interpretation that the mosque was rebuilt to serve a larger congregation suggests the presence of Muslims in Koumbi Saleh before the supposed conquest and forced conversion (see Insoll 1994).

An alternative possible interpretation to explain the change in the mosque dimensions at Koumbi Saleh is that rebuilding was undertaken to eradicate traces of Ibadism, perhaps paralleling what has been described for Essuk/Tadmekka already. In fact, Hrbek and El-Fasi (1992:40) suggest that the whole episode of the supposed forced conversion of the people of Ghana to Islam can be better understood as 'merely an imposition of orthodox Malikite Islam on a previously Ibadite community'. It is possible that a decline in Ibadi Islam and a desire to expunge the material traces of this sect could have led to the mosque being rebuilt, though this interpretation is not as convincing as one invoking a growth in the Muslim congregation overall (a largely Sunni one) as an explanatory device. However, it is also worth noting that until the royal capital is located and investigated, which might not be anywhere near Koumbi Saleh, the whole issue of any Almoravid involvement in the conversion of the ruler and people of Ghana will remain unresolved.

The context of the Arabic sources in the historiography of the western Sahel

An overreliance upon, or misinterpretation of, the Arabic historical sources in interpreting the past of the western Sahel and Sudan was relatively common, especially in the colonial period. This was touched upon in examining the history of research on Islam in sub-Saharan Africa in chapter 1, and the result of this approach was that the past of these regions often tended to be viewed through what could be euphemistically termed 'North African-tinted spectacles'. Although a critical analysis of African historiography in general has been undertaken (Fage 1989; Curtin 1989; Levtzion 1992; Masonen 1994; Masonen and Fisher 1995), little attempt has been made to assess the validity of the Arabic sources in relation to the historical archaeology of the western Sahel and Sudan. The Arabic historical sources were all too often lent an unwarranted importance without any due regard as to their biases and shortcomings – biases which can be attributed to a variety of factors (Masonen 1994; Masonen and Fisher 1995). Firstly, the geographical context in which these sources were written was a factor of importance, as the majority were written north of the Sahara, in areas geographically removed from those they were describing. Levtzion (1992:1) makes the relevant point that 'the history of the Western Sudan is unfolding from north to south, from the Maghreb, across the Sahara to the Sahel and the Savanna'. Thus the authors were based in the urban centres of North Africa, Spain and Egypt, which bore little resemblance to the population centres of the western Sahel or Sudan.

Secondly, these sources were often written by Arab merchants, historians or geographers, who had little in common with the peoples and customs they were writing about. They were from a relatively restricted circle and, as Dramani-Issifou (1992:59) has pointed out, were not predisposed to become enlightened historians of the African past or even sympathetic observers of the life of non-Muslim societies. The social and environmental context of the authors of the Arabic sources inevitably coloured what they wrote. These men were looking at societies vastly different to their own, which were predominantly non-Muslim, rural and, most importantly, black. This point is of fundamental importance, as the western Sudan and, to a lesser extent the western Sahel, were the source of the slaves who supplied the homes, fields and workshops of North Africa and the wider

Islamic world with labour. E. W. Bovill (1968:93) made the point about the famous fourteenth-century Moroccan traveller Ibn Battuta that 'he had hardly arrived [in the western Sudan] before he was regretting having come, merely because he was disgusted at finding Negroes, whom hitherto he had known only as slaves, behaving as masters in their own country'.

Thirdly, the writers were all Muslims, often very devout Muslims, whose lives and way of thinking were structured by Islam. Their writings represent the Islamic ideology, as the oral traditions usually represent the non-Islamic ideology (Levtzion 1973:209). Furthermore, many of the sources, especially the later ones, were compiled from second- or third-hand accounts, often without much thought as to the value of the original sources or their date (Trimingham 1962:2).

The inherent racial bias that is present in many of the writings (and, as was discussed in chapter 1, also to be found in other sources such as Victorian explorers' accounts) must be remembered when these sources are being used as an aid in interpretation and reconstruction. Reading the Arabic historical sources in terms of 'black-and-white' facts is inappropriate – more shades of grey are called for, as the historian Paulo Farias has noted with reference to the Arabic historical sources elsewhere (1974:480). If they are used carefully they can be an aid to archaeological interpretation, but facts must be sorted from fictions and embellishments, as with all good historical research.

Gao: a case study

A further early centre of Islam in the western Sahel was Gao, a city already mentioned briefly, and one which serves as a useful case study to focus upon for three main reasons. Firstly, because it was one of the earliest centres of Islam in the western Sahel. Secondly, because of its importance, politically and economically, which was ultimately manifest as its role as the capital of the Songhai empire, the last of the West African medieval empires. Thirdly, because Gao has been the focus of recent detailed archaeological investigation which has provided much information on Islam in the region (Insoll 1996b, 2000b). This evidence can be considered in conjunction with the relevant historical sources, bearing in mind the points already made about the cautionary approach to their use that has to be employed.

The historical evidence

Gao figures prominently in the historical sources, and the first historical reference to the acceptance of Islam in the city is by al-Muhallabi (c.975–85), who records that 'their King pretends before them to be a Muslim and most of them pretend to be Muslims too' (Levtzion and Hopkins 1981:174). This suggests that Islamisation was not very profound. Al-Bakri provides further information over half a century later when he mentions that the king (and only a Muslim could rule) received a signet ring, a sword and a copy of the Qur'an from the 'Commander of the Faithful' (Levtzion and Hopkins 1981:87), which is possibly a reference to the Umayyad ruler of Muslim Spain (Flight n.d.:2). Besides the reference to Muslim symbols of identity being received, al-Bakri also records that the majority of the people worshipped idols 'as do the other Sudan', and that when the king was eating, women danced and none could go about their business until he had finished. This suggests, as examples elsewhere have shown, that divine kingship was in operation and that the majority of the population were still not Muslim. The next major source of information is al-Idrisi (mid-twelfth century), who states that the king of Kawkaw had the Friday sermon delivered in his own name (Levtzion and Hopkins 1981:113). This illustrates the independent status, as well as the Muslim identity, of the ruler of Gao in the mid-twelfth century. Besides this source, there is a lack of historical evidence to illustrate the progression of Islam in Gao between the mid-twelfth and mid-fifteenth centuries (Hunwick 1985a:10).

The archaeological evidence

The archaeological evidence does not as yet allow the levels of precision required to answer the specific questions raised by the Arabic historical sources as to the precise date at which a ruler of Kawkaw first converted to Islam, and the identity of this ruler (Insoll 1996b:89). However, the general processes are apparent, and the archaeological evidence is in broad agreement with the Arabic sources (excluding the Ibadi ones discussed earlier). This extends to the facts that the presence in Gao of a Muslim community does not appear to predate the tenth century, and that evidence for contacts with the Muslim world increases in the eleventh–twelfth centuries.

Settlement, epigraphy and Islam

Settlement, as described above, was in two centres, at Gao Ancien and Gao-Saney during the 'first contact' situation (**figure 5.7**). Initially this separation was probably due to religious differences, but the continued existence of dual settlements after Islam had spread to the inhabitants of Gao Ancien in the late eleventh–twelfth centuries was possibly due to security concerns – keeping nomads at a distance from Gao Ancien (Insoll 1996b:48), something which was a recurring concern owing to nomad raids. At Gao-Saney, the primary Muslim mercantile centre, the site complex, comprising a tell and associated Muslim cemeteries and tombs, has not been as intensively investigated as Gao Ancien (Flight 1975, 1978, 1979). However, the first direct evidence for the presence of

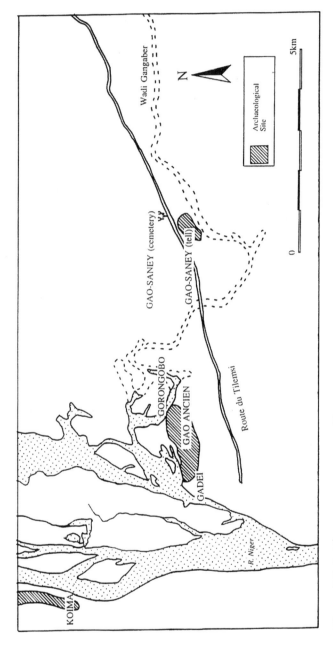

Figure 5.7 Settlement structure at Gao

Muslims in this region was found there, and this consists of various inscribed
Muslim tombstones (stelae) which date from between about 1100 and 1300.
Five of the stelae found at Gao-Saney were even imported ready carved, bearing
name and date, in the early twelfth century, and appear based upon the marble
that used to be from the vicinity of Almeria in Muslim Spain (Sauvaget 1950;
Vire 1958; Farias 1990; Insoll 1993a).

Besides providing further evidence for the operation of trans-Saharan trade,
these imported stelae have a much greater significance. Their very presence in
the Gao region meant that the Almoravid dynasty then controlling al-Andalus
had overcome its scruples about using commemorative funerary stelae in providing these items for export. Farias (1990:76) has suggested that the religious
austerity of the southern Almoravids evident in their home territories of the
western Sahara was transferred north, hence the dearth of funerary inscriptions
dating from their period of control of Spain (1056–1147). But a desire for such
commemorative devices obviously existed at Gao, and this was fulfilled as the
Almoravid appetite for the commodities which could be sourced from this region was stronger than their religious scruples. Through the presence of these
inscriptions at Gao-Saney much more information can be gained than merely
learning that 'person A was buried here in year B', and that they were Muslim.
It would also appear that the funerary stelae at Gao were used for purposes
other than commemorating the dead, for they seem also to have been used to
proclaim the new-found faith of Islam, mirroring processes already described
for the East African coast (see chapter 4). Three of the kings commemorated on
stelae in the cemetery at Gao-Saney, including two on the imported Spanish
examples dating from the early twelfth century, were recent converts to Islam.
Their new identity, and indeed their piety, were clearly shown by successively
adopting the name of the Prophet, and of the first two caliphs, Abu Bakr and
'Umar (Flight n.d.:1). The stelae bearing the names Muhammad and Abu Bakr
were among the imported Spanish examples.

Stelae were not confined to Gao-Saney. Gao Ancien was also ringed with
Muslim cemeteries, and the inscriptions recovered from these have also provided information on Islamisation processes within the region. At one of the
cemeteries, Gorongobo, to the north-west of the trade centre of Gao Ancien,
several Muslim tombstones inscribed in Arabic and dating from between 1130
and 1306 were recorded. One tombstone, dated to 1210, appears to bear the
female Songhai names of either Waybiya or Buwy, depending on the reading
(figure 5.8). This is of significance as it is first and foremost a Muslim tombstone, bearing a local name – and female as well – conclusive proof for local
conversion to Islam by the early thirteenth century. Previously, direct clues as
to the ethnicity of the individuals buried were not forthcoming. For example,
the person commemorated on another stele dating from 1130 was named Taha,
a common Arabic name derived from the enigmatic letters at the beginning of
the Qur'an (*surah* 20), a name anyone could use (Farias 2000).

Figure 5.8 Muslim tombstone from Gorongobo bearing a date of 1210

The concentration of funerary epigraphy in the east of the region is also of interest, as its rarity at more westerly sites such as Tegdaoust and Koumbi Saleh has been interpreted as a reflection of specific Muslim Maliki treatises, which say a tomb should not have an inscription (Farias 1990:69). In the east, at centres such as Gao, this restriction was flouted as the Tuareg tradition of epigraphy in their own script, Tifinagh, had given way to a precedent for inscriptions in Arabic. Although Muslim cemeteries are found across the region, as in the Lake Faguibine area (Raimbault 1991:208–9), funerary inscriptions are comparatively rare or absent at these more westerly sites, perhaps for these reasons. What might be apparent here is what has been noted elsewhere in the continent, the adaptation of Muslim practice and material culture to suit the local context.

However, a recent discovery of several epigraphs (painted in reddish-brown haematite pigment) in Arabic (and Tifinagh) in the rock-shelter of Aïre Soroba near Lake Debo in Mali indicates that epigraphy was used for other purposes. Erosion made it difficult to decipher all the Arabic, but various words were isolated, and Mecca figured prominently, being repeated nearly fifteen times (and thus reminiscent of what was noted at Essuk/Tadmekka referred to previously). There was also a reference to a traveller, Ibn al-Fazar, who had returned from Mecca. A similar dedication also bore an early date of 1075 (Marchi 1997:80), and an epitaph interpreted as that made by a merchant from Arabia or Egypt sheltering in the cave, rather than that of a local pilgrim (Marchi 1997:81). Whether this interpretation is correct is unclear, for it could well be by a local hand, and might perhaps even be a reference to the town of Tadmekka rather than Mecca itself.

What is apparent from these few examples from the western Sahel is the many dimensions that can be apparent in Islamic epigraphy above and beyond commemorating the deceased. Inscriptions, including funerary ones, are used for many purposes. This could be to signal gender, social status, occupation, religious piety, and for claiming origins and ethnicity, ownership or use of something or somewhere through descent, to express religious beliefs, and even to 'indigenise' Islam, bridging the gap between Islamic and non-Muslim practice (Insoll 1999a:187). Similarly, though epigraphy has largely yet to be studied in the same way as Farias (1990) has done for the western Sahel, such information might be derived from elsewhere in sub-Saharan Africa. Parts of the Nilotic Sudan, Ethiopia and the Horn, and indeed the East African coast, offer great potential for such study.

Life, diet, architecture and Islam

The funerary inscriptions might provide direct evidence for the presence of Muslims in the western Sahel. Other categories of material were recovered from Gao which do not function as such Muslim 'type fossils', but are also significant. Within this category are the personal possessions a Muslim might own, such as a large wooden bead from a set of prayer beads, or what is sometimes erroneously referred to as a Muslim 'rosary'. This was recovered from excavations in Gadei, the quarter adjacent to mercantile Gao Ancien, in contexts dated to between the mid-eleventh and fourteenth centuries (Roy 2000:106) **(figure 5.9)**.

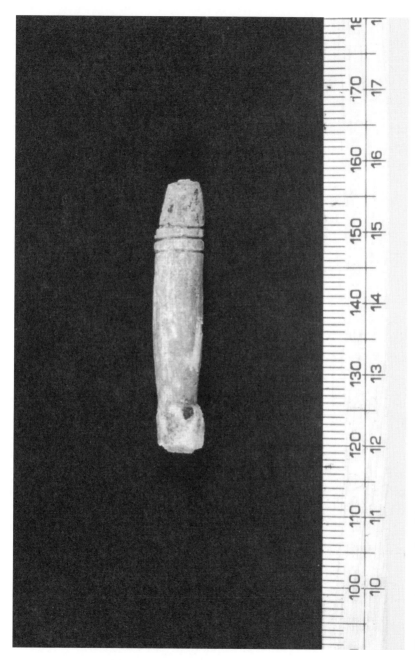

Figure 5.9 Prayer bead from Gadei

Similarly, and also from Gadei, the remains of what appear to have been an amulet cover were found – a copper casing containing the remains of fibrous matter which might have been the prayer or invocation (Insoll 2000b:134). This object is reminiscent of the types of amulets described from Qasr Ibrim in the Nilotic Sudan (see chapter 3).

Diet, as we have seen, can also be a further significant indicator of the presence of a Muslim community. Foodstuffs were certainly an important item of interregional trade throughout the western Sahel, especially with the drier regions to the north where food supplies were more limited (Insoll 1996b:80). Al-Bakri, for example, records that at Tadmekka 'sorghum and other grains are imported for them from the land of the Sudan' (Levtzion and Hopkins 1981:85). Other Arabic sources refer to the growth of wheat, rice and barley at Gao (see Lewicki 1974). The excavations in Gadei and Gao Ancien provided, largely from the later occupation levels, evidence for rice, dates, local fruits such as the jujube, pearl millet, watermelon and cotton (Fuller 2000). The latter, cotton, is generally regarded as an introduction in the Islamic period, i.e. after the tenth century (Watson 1983, cited in Fuller 2000:33).

Extensive faunal assemblages were also recovered from all the excavations in Gao. These initially indicated that the diet in Gao was fairly conservative (Hutton MacDonald and MacDonald 1996), compared to other sites of comparable date in the western Sahel (and Sudan) from which faunal remains have been analysed. At Tegdaoust, for example, cattle, sheep and camel remains were found, but these were supplemented, at least in lower levels dated to between the ninth and eleventh centuries, by oryx and dog. The latter is represented by isolated fragments rather than complete skeletons, suggesting butchery for dietary use (Bouchud 1983:361). However, the Arabic sources again contain some information on livestock in Gao. Ibn Battuta, for example, refers to many chickens and fish in the city, while cattle and sheep are mentioned by other sources (Lewicki 1974:80, 84, 90). A variety of species are certainly represented in the archaeological remains. These included fish, shellfish, mammals and birds, and indicated that a variety of environments were exploited. Fish and shellfish were obtained from streams, from main channels of the River Niger, pools on the flood plain, fast- and slow-flowing water, and swampy and reed-filled environments (Milner 2000; Cook 2000).

A similarly varied picture of resource exploitation was indicated by the faunal remains from Gadei, with both wild and domesticated species present. Of especial interest was the presence of dog remains in contexts dated to between the early/mid-eleventh–late sixteenth centuries, i.e. certainly after Islam was the majority religion in the city. This was interpreted as food refuse owing to the context in which they were found (Stangroome 2000:56), thus similar to Tegdaoust, and suggests that a mixed community was resident in the Gadei quarter of Gao, both Muslim and non-Muslim or, alternatively, Muslims who continued to eat species forbidden under Islamic dietary law (see chapter 1). By contrast, dog remains were lacking in Gao Ancien, perhaps to be expected in this evidently more Islamised quarter. Otherwise, the patterns evident in the species present are broadly comparable to those at Gadei, with both wild and domestic found, though it appears, according to Barrett-Jolley (2000:54), that there was an increase in reliance on domesticates after 1000.

Differences in the character of the various quarters of Gao were apparent. Gao Ancien provided extensive evidence for trans-Saharan trade and Gao-Saney for manufacturing, with Gadei differing in appearing more 'domestic'. This latter characteristic is indicated by the large quantities of faunal and botanical remains recovered, as well as by associated cooking equipment such as utilitarian pottery, stove fragments and strainers. From this evidence it has been possible to reconstruct something of the resultant cuisine, and it appears that many of the bones were subjected to 'heavy' chopping, possibly indicating boiling as a cooking method. This concurs with MacLean's (2000:77) suggestion that a 'wet' cuisine was in use in Gao, and that kitchen mobility, a characteristic of Songhai cooking today, was also a factor several hundred years ago (MacLean and Insoll 1999); in other words, the maintenance of traditional African cuisine, though diet was largely structured by Islamic law.

The architecture was further representative of these distinctions, domestic Gadei as opposed to cosmopolitan Gao Ancien. In the former, part of a round-house built of liquid mud or banco was uncovered dating from the eleventh–fourteenth centuries (Insoll 2000b:15–17). This type of structure is so far absent in Gao Ancien where buildings universally employed the right angle and are of fired brick, stone and mud-brick (Insoll 1996b). Whether the presence of the roundhouse can be associated with the persistence of traditional religion in this quarter is unclear. But such a question can be posited, as in many areas of sub-Saharan Africa there appears to be a correlation between roundhouses and traditional religion, and square or rectangular houses and Islam. However, although the correlation occurs frequently enough in the archaeological record to suggest that it is of some significance, and that there can be a switch in how space becomes ordered following conversion to Islam in certain areas (Insoll 1999a:77), to say that it is uniform without assessing each particular set of circumstances is flawed. This is because Islamised groups can live in roundhouses and vice versa (see Engestrom 1959:65; Sanogo 1991:152), and also because the reasons underlying a change in house form can be much more complex than such a simple correlation allows.

Yet the architecture in Gao Ancien differed considerably, and in style (but not materials) was much more reminiscent of the type of structures encountered at other trade centres such as Tegdaoust and Koumbi Saleh (Devisse 1983; Polet 1985; Berthier 1997). A large mosque with a fired-brick *mihrab* has been recorded, measuring 43.4 m north–south and 27 m east–west (Mauny 1951b). More recent excavations have uncovered part of a palace or rich merchant's house also built of fired brick, elements (an aisle) of what might have been another mosque and the remains of a substantial stone-built wall and gate-house which would have once encircled the central citadel, all dating from the twelfth–thirteenth centuries (Insoll 1996b, 2000b) (**figure 5.10**). Thus a variety of architectural forms was evident in Gao, of varying degrees of permanency, and again broadly similar in this mix to what is evident in the East African coastal centres.

Trade and Islam

The trade and Islam connection discussed previously as a significant factor in the Islamisation of the western Sahel appeared again in the Gao evidence. In Gao Ancien abundant evidence was found testifying to long-distance contacts. This consisted of items destined for export across the Sahara, and imports received via trans-Saharan trade which have helped in reconstructing the areas of the Muslim world the inhabitants of Gao were in contact with (Insoll and Bhan 2001). However, it should be noted that the picture of trans-Saharan trade in both directions is skewed in favour of more durable items. Many trade commodities are known to us only from the Arabic sources – paper, cloth, spices and salt, for example (Levtzion and Hopkins 1981) (**figure 5.11**), though sometimes evidence can exist at source to indicate the former trade in less archaeologically durable commodities. The salt trade, for example, is well represented by the salt-mining centre of Teghaza which remains as its testimony. Survey at this site, the Tatantal of the Arabic sources, found that the houses and even the mosque were built of blocks of rock salt (Terrasse 1938; Monod 1938, 1940), indicating the extent of the exploitation of this commodity and by inference the trade itself.

At Gao, possibly the most spectacular evidence for the export trade was a cache of over fifty hippopotamus tusks (**figure 5.12**). These were uncovered in a context dated to the mid-ninth century in Gao Ancien. The hypothesis has been advanced that these tusks represent a consignment of ivory placed on beams within the pit in which they were found and were awaiting shipment to the ivory workshops of North Africa, but were never sent for reasons which remain unclear (Insoll 1995). A substantial ivory trade between West and North Africa certainly existed, but is little mentioned in the Arabic sources, possibly because it was frowned upon by more orthodox Muslims, like the use of feathers, horns, hoofs or tusks derived from animals which were not ritually slaughtered (Levtzion and Hopkins 1981:55). The North African jurist Ibn Abi Zayd al-Qayrawani (d. 996) specifically mentions that the use of elephant tusk is expressly disapproved of (Hunwick 1994:11). But large quantities of ivory were certainly used in the workshops of the Maghreb, Islamic Spain and Egypt. The workshops of Islamic Spain are justly famous for the inlaid and carved caskets and ivory encrusted mosque furniture which were produced in cities such as Madinat as-Zahra in the tenth century, and in other centres during subsequent

Figure 5.10 Wall and gatehouse unearthed at Gao

Figure 5.11 Contemporary salt trader at Mopti

Almoravid, Almohad and Nasrid rule (Pinder-Wilson 1960). Ivory cubes, often along with blocks of ebony and other woods, were used to create inlaid patterns, and it is for this work that hippopotamus ivory would have been most suited, being whiter, denser and less prone to splitting than elephant ivory (Penniman 1952; Krzyszkowska 1990).

Figure 5.12 Cache of hippo tusks from Gao

Evidence for the extensive gold trade recorded in the Arabic historical sources is more elusive, which is not surprising considering its ease of recyclability as a material and its enduring value. In Gadei a small gold bead was found, while the discovery on the surface at Gao Ancien of a gold *mithqal* coin of North African origin dating from 952–75 has been reported (Latruffe 1953). The bead has recently been analysed, and it was found that the gold used precisely matched that of coins struck in Sijilmasa by the Almoravids (Guerra 2000). This further indicates the strength of the connections between the Almoravids and the Gao region, as attested by the funerary inscriptions discussed previously. Other evidence possibly indicative of a former trade in gold are two fragments of glass weights which could have been used for weighing gold dust recovered from Gao-Saney and Gao Ancien (Thomassey and Mauny 1956:138–9). This is the sum total of the evidence for the gold trade found at Gao. Equally, evidence for the slave trade is lacking, though the remains of large burial pits on the outskirts of Gao Ancien have been recorded (P. Farias, pers. comm.). These might have been used for the disposal of slaves, for they appear to contain human skeletal remains and display no consistency with regard to the orientation or placement of the bodies with which they were filled.

Much more abundantly testified are items sourced from North Africa, the Near East, and in certain instances, even further afield. A large assemblage of imported glazed pottery and glass was recovered from Gao Ancien dating primarily from the eleventh to twelfth centuries (Insoll 1996b:63–6) **(figure 5.13)**. This assemblage is important, as it is of good quality, and not solely made up of export-quality wares, such as those that have been described for the East African and Red Sea coasts. The ubiquitous Chinese celadons and sgraffiato wares are lacking, and a completely different range of material is found, indicating that the North African and Egyptian contacts were maintained, rather than Persian Gulf, Arabian or Indian Ocean ones. Spanish, Egyptian and Ifriqiyan pottery has all been identified. These include lustre wares comparable to twelfth-century material from Malaga in Spain (see Jenkins 1980:339), as well as *cuerda seca* or dry-cord wares similar to eleventh-century Ifriqiyan material (R. Ward, pers. comm.). Noteworthy is the fact that all glazed pottery found in the western Sahel (and throughout West Africa and the central Sudan) was imported; it was not produced in these regions until the modern era. The glass recovered was also obtained from North Africa and the Near East, cut glass similar to material from Qayrawan, marvered glass comparable to Egyptian material, and a range of plain glass from various sources (see Hasson 1979; Marcais and Poinssot 1952:393; Insoll 1998c).

Objects, namely beads and cowrie shells (see below), in all probability obtained via Indian Ocean origin, were also found. But, rather than through direct participation in these trade cycles, the goods would have been obtained by the merchants in Gao via a series of stages – probably via the Red Sea and Egypt.

Figure 5.13 Imported Islamic pottery and glass from Gao, including Spanish lustre wares, top row

Notable among these are beads of red carnelian. The vast majority of carnelian beads appear to have been produced in the western Sahel and possibly in the central Sudan – the former indicated, for example, by evidence from the site of Gao-Hydrocarbure, a proto-historic and 'medieval' site where complete carnelian beads were found (Gaussen and Gaussen 1988, cited in Holl 1995:23). Carnelian-bead production in the western Sahel is also attested in the Arabic historical sources, for example by al-Bakri, who refers to a 'mine of stone called *tasi-n-nasamt*, which resembles agate (aqiq)' (Levtzion and Hopkins 1981:86, cited in Holl 1995:24). Al-Bakri also describes this stone as being polished and pierced in the western Sahel. However, it is possible that some carnelian beads were imported and these could have been obtained from Gujarat in India, possibly from Cambay (see Trivedi 1964; Kenoyer et al. 1991; Karanth 1992) **(figure 5.14)**, a region already mentioned with reference to the African presence in India in the last chapter. This source of beads is known to have supplied the Sudan and East Africa, for example (Arkell 1936a). At present this remains unsubstantiated, pending the results of source analysis of West African samples currently being completed and compared with Indian carnelian samples (Insoll in press b).

Equally, some of the vast quantities of coloured-glass 'seed' beads found in Gao might be of Indian origin (Insoll and Shaw 1997), and these are again identical to those already described, as for the East African coast, for example. With regard to the glass trade beads, it is a distinct possibility that Gao served a 'wholesaler' function in these items, trading them as far afield as Igbo-Ukwu in eastern Nigeria, as discussed in chapter 7. A single glass bead from Gao recently analysed by Peter Robertshaw (pers. comm., 25 Oct. 2001) was found to be 'remarkably similar' to beads analysed previously from Igbo-Ukwu.

Metalwork, some of which must have been imported, was also recovered from Gao Ancien. This also provides another useful marker for trans-Saharan trade in the form of brass, which was not produced south of the Sahara until the nineteenth century (Craddock 1985; Craddock and Picton 1986). Brass objects, including ingots and a bracelet fragment, were found in the same import-rich layers underlying the palace and possible mosque in the central citadel (Insoll 1996b:69, 2000b:138–40). Some of this could have been sourced via the copper-working centre of Marendet (perhaps to be identified with medieval Maranda) or, less likely, Azelik (likewise perhaps to be identified with medieval Takedda) in northern Niger. At Marendet, for example, over 40,000 crucibles and mould fragments were found dated to between the sixth and eleventh centuries (Lhote 1972:450–3). Also from here, Lhote describes a mould fragment which could easily have been used to cast the types of ingots found in Gao, being almost identical in shape. A gold coin from Egypt was also found, dating from the Mamluk period (Bernus and Cressier 1991). Unfortunately, evidence for early Islam was not found at either of these copper-working sites, all the more

Figure 5.14 Carnelian mine, Ratanpor, Gujarat, India

surprising considering they figure in early Arabic historical sources (Levtzion and Hopkins 1981), and hence must have been exposed to Islamic influences from an early date. This stands in contrast to the In Gall-Tegidda-n-Tesemt area, also in Niger, where over ten sites were test excavated with a variety of evidence recovered indicating early contacts with the Muslim world, including numerous coins dating from the ninth to tenth centuries (Bernus and Cressier 1991).

However, the trade in brass, and its scale, is best attested by a unique find in Mauritania, where at the 'lost caravan' site in the Ijafen dunes several thousand cowrie shells once in sacks, along with 2,085 bars of brass, were found (Monod 1969). These items, dating from the twelfth century, had been buried for safe-keeping by a caravan crossing the desert to the western Sahel and never recovered. This find also provides what appears to be the sole reported instance of the archaeological survival of a camel caravan. This is surprising considering the extent of the trade, which was regularised leaving nothing to chance, and we are fortunate that al-Idrisi gives us an insight into how Saharan travel was organised in the autumn caravan season. To quote:

They travel in the following manner: they load their camels at late dawn, and march until the sun has risen, its light has become bright in the air, and the heat on the ground has become severe. Then they put their loads down, hobble their camels, unfasten their baggage and stretch awnings to give some shade from the scorching heat and the hot winds of midday . . . When the sun begins to decline and sink in the west, they set off. They march for the rest of the day, and keep going till nightfall when they encamp at whatever place they have reached. (Levtzion and Hopkins 1981:118)

The presence of the cowrie shells at the 'lost caravan' site is also significant, as they were one of the various currencies that were used in the western Sahel (and Sudan). Ibn Battuta, for example, recorded their use at Gao in the mid-fourteenth century, in noting that 'the transactions of its people in buying and selling are carried out by means of cowries' (Hamdun and King 1994:66). Cowrie shells have been recovered from Gao (Milner 2000), and are reported in early second-millennium contexts from Koumbi Saleh (Thomassey and Mauny 1951:451), Tegdaoust (Devisse 1992b:208), Azelik in Niger (Hogendorn and Johnson 1986:104) and from south of Gao on the River Niger in the Dallol Bosso valley (de Beauchene 1969:54). They also provide another indicator of north–south contacts before the start of the second millennium. Though rare at this date, their discovery has been reported by Togola (1996:107) in a burial (number unspecified) at the site of Akumbu in the Méma dated to between 780 and 1010. The Méma, to recap, is a region which has been suggested as the hinterland of the kingdom of Ghana. They also provide another link with East Africa, as the most popular variety, *Cyprea moneta*, were imported from the Maldive islands in the Indian Ocean, via the markets of North Africa (Lovejoy 1985:669). Indeed, the possible existence of a shell-collecting function for the

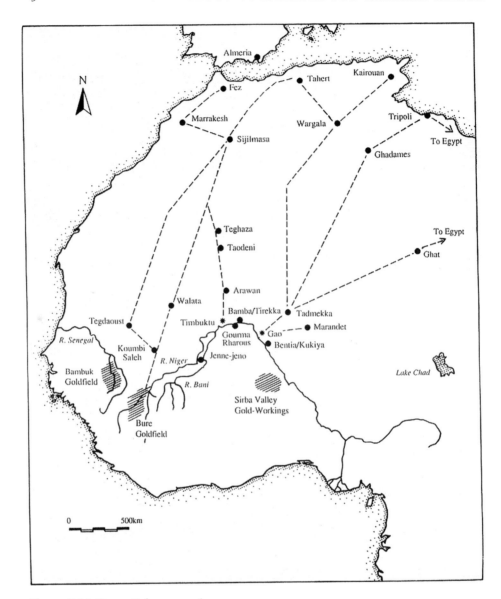

Figure 5.15 Trans-Saharan trade routes

site of Somana on the coast of Mozambique (Duarte 1993) has already been suggested, archaeological testimony to this trade. Cowrie shells again indicate the long-distance links that were maintained. The western Sahel was tied by tentacles of commerce to the rest of the Muslim world **(figure 5.15)**, and to other regions of sub-Saharan Africa, again indicating the interconnections that existed.

Islam: adaptation and percolation (post-thirteenth century)

Sedentary farmers and Muslim conversion

The focus upon the Gao case study has illustrated something of the types of information that can be obtained on Islam, Islamisation and related processes through archaeological evidence. Unfortunately, little is yet known from archaeology about Islam in the succeeding period – that is, from the start of the fourteenth century onwards. However, it is apparent that Islam was not solely confined to the cosmopolitan, urban, mercantile environments of the western Sahel – or, indeed, to the nomadic population (Insoll 1996b:92). A large swathe of the population has been neglected thus far, the sedentary agriculturists who formed much of the population alongside the Rivers Niger and Senegal. They appear to have been the final group to convert (as much as the broad model proposed here seems to indicate). Numerous reasons have been proposed to account for why this might have been so, and these were touched upon in chapter 1, where the general utility of these models as explanatory devices was questioned.

Yet in the western Sahel and also in the West African Sudan and forest as well (see chapter 7), the persistence of the sedentary agriculturist population as among the final groups to convert to Islam seems a reasonably persuasive observation. The reasons for the long-drawn-out nature of this process were various. According to Trimingham (1959:25), the integrated structure of the farmer's life turning around crops, livestock and children was well furnished by traditional religions, and initially at least, Islam could not provide an adequate substitute. This relates to a point made by Zahan (1970:155) about the agriculturists' 'profound attachment to the soil' and being 'riveted' to it 'to the point of not being able to freely separate himself from it'. Traditional religions were linked to this notion of relationships, 'whether with other living people, or with the spirits of the dead, or with animals, or with cleared land, or with the bush' (Ranger 1991:109).

These relationships were negotiated and built up through traditional religious practices and beliefs as evident in what Ranger (1991) terms 'cults', cults of the land for example. Breaking with or altering this balance through conversion to Islam might be difficult, as Dramani-Issifou (1992:55) and Bravmann (1974) have noted. Although this interpretation might not work in other areas of sub-Saharan Africa, it does seem applicable in parts of West Africa. Furthermore, although relevant archaeological data is still sparse for the western Sahel from the fourteenth century onwards, it would appear that large-scale conversion among sedentary agriculturists was limited until more recently. In some instances it occurred only after the collapse of the great states. As Levtzion (1986b:15) notes, when the great states disappeared and the urban foundation of the religion crumbled in the seventeenth and eighteenth centuries this meant that Muslims moved into the countryside, 'and won adherents among peasants and fishermen, who had hardly been influenced by Islam before'. Obviously, prior to this point, wandering holy men had had little impact, unlike in other parts of the continent.

South of Gao, for example, were various settlements which served to send various commodities up the River Niger. Among the most important of these was gold obtained from the Sirba valley in Niger (see Devisse 1993a). Close to here an Islamic 'frontier' appears to have existed (Hunwick 1985a). This would seem to be indicated by the sites of Bentiya (Kukiya) and Egef-n-Tawaqqast, which were referred to earlier as representative of the dual-settlement phenomena. These are also sites where Arabic funerary inscriptions (thirteenth–fifteenth centuries) have been recorded (Farias 1990:105–6; Arazi 1999:38–9). Further south of this point, evidence for Islam dating from before the fifteenth century – both direct evidence, such as mosques and burials, and indirect evidence, such as trade goods sourced from the Muslim world – is so far lacking (Insoll 1996b). Even close to Gao, an early centre of Islam as we have seen, mosques, Muslim burials – rectangular architecture, even – are rare according to survey evidence, or where found are late in date (Dawa 1985; Insoll 1996b:11–15; Arazi 1999:36). This is a pattern that appears to be repeated elsewhere, but the absence of archaeological research outside the main urban centres limits what can be inferred from this source of evidence at present.

Yet the Muslim identity of the inhabitants of a Songhai, Soninke or other sedentary agriculturist village in the western Sahel is usually obvious today, attested not least by the presence of a mosque or prayer area (Rouch 1954; Stoller and Olkes 1987). Equally, origin myths and traditions can be thoroughly Islamised through claiming an early Muslim or Arab genealogy (Gado 1986: 199), a pattern which has been shown to exist among various ethnic groups in sub-Saharan Africa, as in parts of Ethiopia in chapter 2 for example. Conversion and Islamisation has occurred, as both the recent archaeological evidence and ethnographies indicate, but for this to succeed Islam has been adapted to suit the types of requirements listed above, either through linkage to the agricultural cycle, to the landscape or to older beliefs. There is also the success of Muslim traders and holy men in spreading Islam in the rural environment of the western Sahel in the type of process referred to by Levtzion (1986a) and mentioned above. Other mechanisms existed. These included *jihad*, a very important agent, especially in the later eighteenth century and the nineteenth century (see chapters 6 and 7), and also through the spread of Sufi *tariqah*, or brotherhoods. This is similar to the role of Sufism as already described for Nubia and other parts of the Nilotic Sudan in chapter 3.

Sufism

Unfortunately, archaeological indications of Sufism in the western Sahel or elsewhere in sub-Saharan Africa are rare (hence its neglect thus far in this volume), but the existence of Sufism has been suggested at the site of In-Teduq in the north of Niger. At this site, intimately connected to Gao through the Azawagh valley, clusters of stone-built tombs, places of prayer and houses or shops were recorded grouped around a mosque (pre-sixteenth century, but otherwise undated) (Paris et al. 1999). These have been interpreted as indicative of the site being centred around the monumentalisation of the *qiblah*, in turn interpreted by the investigator, Cressier (1992:75–7), as 'peut-être interprété comme la manifestation architecturale de l'élan vers Dieu du fidèle Sufi'. Of significance perhaps as a material manifestation of Sufi ritual (see box on Sufism), In-Teduq is one among a number of important sites with Islamic archaeological remains in northern Niger. Similar Sufi centres existed elsewhere in the Azawagh and Aïr regions, but still await archaeological exploration (Norris 1990:xvii). At Assode in the centre of the Aïr massif, for example, a 'great mosque' similar to the extant mosque in Agadez (founded mid-fifteenth–early sixteenth century) has been noted (Cressier and Bernus 1984:39; Cressier 1989:155). Yet at Saharan locations such as In-Teduq the linkage would have been with a largely nomadic rather than sedentary population. Archaeological evidence for Sufism further south in this region has yet to be reported, though architectural, historical and ethnographic information indicates its popularity in places.

Among the most popular of the Sufi orders, or *tariqah*, in the western Sahel are the Qadiriyya and the Tijaniyya. The Qadiriyya was founded in the twelfth century and, according to Arnold (1935:328), was introduced into West Africa, to Walata in Mauritania, in the fifteenth century. This date, however, would appear too early, and Vikor (2000:444) suggests a date of the seventeenth to eighteenth centuries for the full 'realization of a Qadiri identity'. By contrast, the Tijaniyya was a much later foundation, founded in Algiers in the late eighteenth century (Arnold 1935). Missionary activity associated with this order was initiated in the western Sahel in the early nineteenth century. Other orders of significance in the region include the Fadiliyya and the Muhtariyya (see Vikor 2000). Nevertheless, as Trimingham (1959:91) notes, the influence of the *tariqah* in this region is modest in comparison to the situation in the Nilotic Sudan for example, though pockets of especial popularity are found, as in parts of Senegal.

Sufism

Mystical Islam in various forms is a popular manifestation of Muslim practice. Sufism is an element of this. The word Sufism is derived from *suf*, Arabic for wool, 'to denote the practice of wearing a woollen robe – hence the act of devoting oneself to the mystic life' (Gibb and Kramers 1961:579). Prior to the ninth–tenth centuries, the mystical tradition within Islam was represented either by individuals who retreated from worldly concerns, or perhaps by a teacher and his circle of pupils. After this, as Islam spread, more organised communities of mystics began to form in lodges, with at their head a religious master (*shaykh* or *pir*), surrounded by a group of disciples. These *tariqahs* (meaning path or way) took the form of brotherhoods or orders which were usually male, but occasionally female, and followed sets of rules which laid out behaviour, litanies and etiquette, the path to spiritual understanding (Schimmel 1975). At the heart of Sufi teaching is the 'truth of the Divine Unity' (Nasr 1991:3), and the spiritual 'path' for the initiate is in a variety of stages, whose number and sequence vary between orders. Fundamental among Sufi rituals is the *dhikr*, 'the repeated vocal invocation or silent remembrance of the name, Allah' (Waines 1995:140), and whose basic practice varies little between the orthodox orders. Music, poetry and dance can also be used to attain the ecstatic trance-like state that the *dhikr* can bring on. Numerous *tariqahs* have existed or continue to be found throughout the Muslim world, most named after their founders. The *Shorter Encyclopaedia of Islam* lists over 180, and that is not including the branches within the main fraternities (Gibb and Kramers 1961:575–8; and see Trimingham 1971b). However, all are united in their adherence to the mystical path and in their basic similarities of practice (Insoll 1999a:22). The material indication of the *tariqah* is frequently the *zawiyah*, a religious centre usually comprising accommodation for the Sufi *shaykh* or *muqaddam*, his family, disciples and pilgrims possibly attracted by the tomb that could form the focus of the complex, a mosque, and perhaps a school (Trimingham 1971b).

Muslim scholarship and teaching: the example of Timbuktu

Further to the west, another dimension in the development of Islam in the western Sahel is represented by Timbuktu. This is very much a city of mystery in popular imagination (see Herbert 1980), and took over from Gao the role of premier entrepôt in the region following the decline of the latter in the late sixteenth century. The new dimension that Timbuktu adds to the region is that of Muslim scholarship and teaching, as Timbuktu was what could be termed a university town, though without drawing 'facile comparisons' (Hunwick 1999:lviii) with European institutions. This parallels Harar, the other great sub-Saharan centre of Muslim learning to the east, described in chapter 2. This educational role was assumed by Timbuktu from its western neighbour Walata, following the latter's decline in the late thirteenth century (Hunwick 1985a:16). However, besides Walata, a tradition of Muslim scholarship had existed in other towns in the region prior to the rise to pre-eminence of Timbuktu. These are discussed by Reichmuth (2000:425–6) and Hunwick (1999:lvii), who single out

Tadmekka, and the towns of Kabara and Dia to the west of Djenne, as further important scholarly centres in the region. Hunwick (1999:lvii) describes the latter two as 'early centres of learning that produced scholars deeply versed in the literature of the Maliki *madh'hab* from which Timbuktu profited'. It is undeniable that Timbuktu did profit from the influx of scholars such as Muhammad Baghayogho al-Wangari, and soon Islamic texts and sciences were studied and copied at various places in Timbuktu. Celebrated among these was the Sankore mosque complex.

The Sankore mosque stands to this day, and is one of the structures that contributes to the World Heritage status conferred upon the city by UNESCO (Insoll 1998a) **(Figure 5.16)**. Although rebuilt, it was originally founded some time during the period of Mande or Malian control of the city between 1325 and 1433. Built of mud brick, but also utilising Timbuktu stone (a type of hard clay or limestone), it covers an area of approximately 31 m^2, with an inner courtyard of 13 m^2 (Mauny 1952; Insoll 1999c). Sankore was the abode of the most prominent scholars where students were taught the Qur'an, *hadith* and Islamic law and sciences, with the core of the teaching process 'the receiving of a text, which was handed down through a chain of transmitters from the author to the student' (Hunwick 1999:lviii). From Timbuktu scholars travelled to other great centres of Muslim learning such as Cairo and Mecca, and visitors were likewise received. Many private libraries were also established within the city, the noted scholar Ahmed Baba is reputed to have had 1,600 volumes at the time of the Moroccan conquest of Timbuktu in 1591, following their defeat of Songhai forces at the battle of Tondibi (Saad 1983:79).

According to the Arabic sources, Timbuktu was a relatively late foundation, as a seasonal pastoralist camp, in about the eleventh century. It then prospered through the trans-Saharan trade in salt and gold, especially during its 'high period' (*c.* 1350–1600) (Pefontan 1922; Herbert 1980). Possibly more than any other urban centre in the western Sahel, it suffered the vicissitudes of numerous different rulers, a fact which often impinged directly upon the practice of Islam within the city (see Bovill 1968; Hunwick 1985b). This contrast in Islamic practice is well illustrated by comparing the situation under Sonni authority, and under subsequent Askia authority, both Songhai dynasties. Timbuktu was captured by the Songhai ruler Sonni Ali in 1468, and the city incorporated into the Songhai empire. However, Sonni Ali was castigated in the local seventeenth-century chronicle the *Tarikh al-Sudan*, for not being a good Muslim (Es-Sa'di 1900:103; Hunwick 1999), and was condemned for making sacrifices, consulting soothsayers, and for persecuting the Muslim scholars of Timbuktu. Yet at the same time, as Hunwick (1985b:340) notes, he adhered to certain Muslim practices such as saying his prayers, and thus 'trod' the thin line 'between Islam and ancestral religion'. But as we have seen this is not exceptional either in Africa or, as was discussed in chapter 1, in other parts of the Muslim

Figure 5.16 The Sankore mosque, Timbuktu

world, and Sonni Ali was probably castigated more for political reasons. However, following his death and replacement by Askia Muhammad in 1493, a new
era of Islamic revival began in both Timbuktu and Gao. Muslim scholarship
flourished, the Songhai empire prospered, and Askia Muhammad went on pilgrimage to Mecca, both to fulfil his religious duty and also to 'establish firmly'
his image 'as a Muslim ruler' (Hunwick 1985b:342).

Unfortunately, archaeology tells us little about this period, primarily because
of an absence of relevant research (Insoll 1998a, 2000a), and it is to the historical
sources that we must turn. The most notable of these are the aforementioned
seventeenth-century *Tarikh al-Sudan* and its companion history, the *Tarikh
al-Fettach* (Es-Sa'di 1900; Kati 1913; Hunwick 1999). Although this absence
of archaeological evidence is a reflection of the lack of relevant research, it is
perhaps also in part due to a change in the nature of Timbuktu and Gao during
the period of the Songhai empire. At Gao it was recorded that the Moroccans
were severely disappointed upon entering the city in the late sixteenth century,
finding uninspiring architecture and none of the indications of wealth they
had anticipated. As Bovill (1968:175–6) notes, 'they found only the mud-and-
thatch huts typical of the Sudan and no signs of the great wealth they had
expected'. At present such a picture is borne out by the archaeology, as indicated
by a general paucity of material dating from this period in Gao, compared to
the preceding high period of trans-Saharan trade (Insoll 1996b, 2000, and see
above). 'Type fossils' of this period such as tobacco pipes, which appear after
the introduction of tobacco via European trade to the West African coast in the
late sixteenth century, are as yet lacking in Gao. The exception to this pattern is
provided by the extant tomb of Askia Muhammad (Mauny 1950). At Timbuktu,
the situation appears to have differed, with more evidence for later periods
of settlement (see below), but to be certain further archaeological research is
necessary.

This absence of archaeological research is surprising considering the fame of
Timbuktu. The surrounding region has been surveyed (S. K. and R. J. McIntosh
1986), and the standing monuments have been recorded (Mauny 1952), but
only limited and ongoing exploratory work has been completed within the city
itself (Insoll 1998a, 2000a) **(figure 5.17)**. Other indicators of the importance
of Timbuktu still stand, for besides the Sankore, two other mosques dating
from the 'medieval' period are extant, though these too have been rebuilt over
the centuries. These are the Djinguereber, possibly thirteenth century in origin, and the Sidi Yahya, founded in about 1440 (Mauny 1952:901–11; Insoll
1999c). The importance of these monuments appears to lie not only in their
early foundation dates, but also in their locations, if a hypothesis advanced by
Saad (1983:109–10) is to be supported. He suggests that Timbuktu was representative of a further dual settlement, with the mosques as material indicators of this. Djinguereber was the black settlement, Sankore the white,
and Sidi Yahya, 'halfway in the middle along the Sankore–Jingerebir axis,

Figure 5.17 Archaeological excavation in progress in Timbuktu

[was] a crucial step in integrating the two main centres of populations' (Saad 1983:110).

Archaeological evidence for the existence of dual settlements at Timbuktu is inconclusive **(figure 5.18)**. Possible areas of early settlement have been suggested by survey evidence from the vicinity of the Sankore and Djinguereber mosques. These include a fragment of a glass bracelet similar to material dated

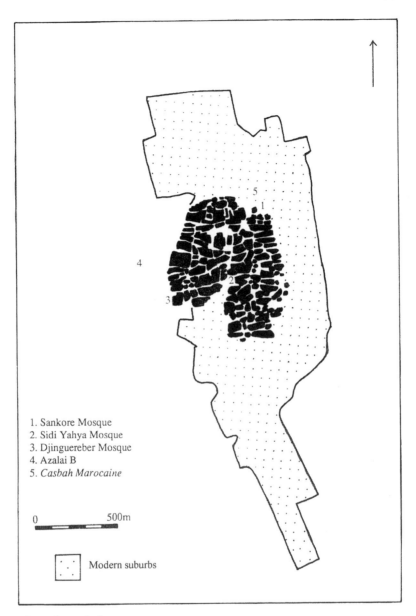

1. Sankore Mosque
2. Sidi Yahya Mosque
3. Djinguereber Mosque
4. Azalai B
5. *Casbah Marocaine*

0   500m

Modern suburbs

Figure 5.18 Plan of Timbuktu

to the fourteenth century at the site of Qusayr al-Qadim in Egypt (Whitcomb
1983:106–7), and also paralleling material from the salt-mining site of Teghaza
in the Malian Sahara (Monod 1975:717), as well as a possible sherd of southern Chinese celadon dated to the late eleventh–early twelfth centuries (Insoll
1998d). Yet recent excavation did not confirm the survey evidence, with only
material dating from the late eighteenth century onwards being recovered

(Insoll 2000a), though it is probable that earlier deposits remain to be excavated. Both the radiocarbon dates and the presence of tobacco pipes confirm the late date of the occupation sequences investigated. So do the shells that were found, which have been tied to a precise historical event by Milner (forthcoming). These finds of koroni or marginella shells were clustered in specific levels, and are linked with the substitution of koroni shells for cowrie shells as a currency item for a short period in the 1780s–90s. However, in 1795 the Timbuktu authorities ordered that all koroni shells be buried on account of rampant inflation and only cowries henceforth be used (Hogendorn and Johnson 1986). This would appear to be what is indicated by the Timbuktu koroni hoards (Milner forthcoming).

If the archaeology at present remains somewhat uninformative, the historical sources help to fill in some of the gaps, and it is known that the Moroccan occupation of Timbuktu in the late sixteenth century had a significant impact on the city. Bovill (1968:186–7) relates how many scholars were exiled to Morocco, being sent along with 'their books and other possessions, across the desert to Marrakech'. This had a serious effect on the role of Timbuktu as a centre of Muslim scholarship, just as the plundering of the city's wealth affected the well-being of Timbuktu as a whole (see Hunwick 1999:lxii). But the Moroccan occupation also had an impact upon local systems of authority. This is something of interest, for it provides a rare (perhaps sole) case of the direct transference of North African administrative systems into the western Sahel, in this instance through the use of the offices of a pasha and amins as agencies of government by the Moroccans in Timbuktu. The city became, as Hiskett (1994:96) notes, 'a *pashalik* of the Moroccan Sharifian empire'. This is something of consequence, for outside a few contexts such as parts of Nubia or the Red Sea coast controlled by the Ottomans, it stands in direct contrast to the examples already discussed in preceding chapters. To recap, Muslim administrative offices might be instituted, as in Mogadishu (as recorded by Ibn Battuta and related in chapter 2), but these were offices locally chosen, not subject to foreign imposition. The Moroccan invasion of the western Sahel, and subsequent collapse of the Songhai empire, also marked the end of the great states of the region. Many of the places mentioned, however, were to fall within the domains of other polities which arose in the *jihad* era of the latter eighteenth and nineteenth centuries, the archaeology of which is discussed in chapter 7.

Summary and conclusions

The western Sahel was the first point of Muslim contact in West Africa, and it can be seen, as on the Red Sea and East African coasts, that the archaeology of Islam in this region is again initially trade related in origins and development.

From the late eighth century intermittent contacts occurred through the agency of trans-Saharan trade, which took a couple of centuries to develop into anything sizeable. Yet it was also evident that conversion to Islam was by no means instantaneous, and it proved possible to advance a general model to account for this process in this region, charting the spread of Islam through various socio-economic groups – traders, nomads, rulers, urban dwellers and agriculturists. In this instance the types of generalised model critiqued in chapter 1 would appear to work, as the historical, and currently available, archaeological data seem to support such a model. However, it was also stated that no single model, such as those developed by Fisher (1973a, 1985) or R. Horton (1971, 1975), is suitable, for it has to be acknowledged that a strictly linear progression in conversion is highly unlikely, and numerous exceptions to such patterns would have occurred. More useful was Levtzion's (1986a, 1986b) type of approach, linking a variety of elements such as the actions of merchants and holy men as agents of Islamic conversion in the region. Further archaeological research should help in either refuting or supporting the model that has been advanced here, though such research should also be concentrated away from the major trade centres, the focus of the bulk of research to date.

Besides the trade connection, of significance both in the first contact situation and subsequently with the onward diffusion of Islam throughout the western Sahel and into the savannah and forest zones, other factors and mechanisms for the spread of Islam must be admitted. Complexity is the key, as was outlined in chapter 1. The development of Sufism was described as a means by which Islam was popularised (Vikor 2000), especially in the last couple of hundred years. The role of Muslim scholarship and education was also of significance (Hunwick 1999; Reichmuth 2000). Of further consequence was the related dimension of Muslim literacy and its magical or powerful importance; these subjects are considered in detail in chapter 7. Similarly, genuine belief can be related to all of the above – and the difficulties in assessing this as a factor behind religious conversion have to be acknowledged, especially when the evidence for conversion is archaeological (see Insoll 1999b). The western Sahel is, however, a region for which there is one of the most extensive corpora of historical sources in sub-Saharan Africa, both foreign and indigenous (as evidenced by Levtzion and Hopkins' (1981) volume), and these can greatly illuminate the archaeological data. Yet it must be remembered that the sources are subject to their own shortcomings, as was described, and these must be allowed for before they can be utilised effectively.

Comparisons were also drawn between the trade centres of the western Sahel and those on the East African coast, but differences also exist, both in the other areas of the Muslim world with which they were in contact and in their respective political and social development. Although the western Sahel witnessed the kingdoms and empires of Ghana and Songhai (Mali is discussed in chapter 7), no comparable phenomenon to the largely culturally unified Swahili developed in the west, and the degree of Islamic conversion away from the trade centres in the east was much less than in the western Sahel. These factors again illustrate that the continent is not a homogenous and monolithic entity. At face value the archaeology of Islam might look the same – mosques, burials, trade goods, as described in chapter 1 – but look deeper, and great differences emerge.

800 – first Muslims in Sahel
1000 – Muslims widely dispersed but vast majority remain in tribal religions
1200–1300 – full Islamization

CHAPTER 6

THE CENTRAL SUDAN

Introduction

Neighbouring the western Sahel on its eastern border is the central Sudan, a vast region which forms the link between the Nilotic Sudan and the western Sahel and Sudan (**figure 6.1**). It is also a continuation of the same environmental zones, with, below the Sahara, the Sahel shading into the savannahs, both grassland and wooded, before the forest regions of central Africa are reached (Adams et al. 1996). However, unlike in the west, there is no defined geographical entity, the 'central Sahel'; rather, it is incorporated within the general term the central Sudan, and is treated as such here. Dotted across the north of the region are also various mountainous regions. These include the Tibesti mountains in the south-eastern corner of the Sahara on the Libyan–Chad border, and, further to the south-east, the Ennedi massif (Cline 1950). Within the middle of this region is the most prominent lake in West Africa, Lake Chad. This landlocked lake, which receives its water from surrounding river systems such as the Chari–Logone, is only a shallow remnant of its former self, traces of which manifest themselves as fossil lake shorelines far from the contemporary lake. However Lake Chad continues to be of great importance within the region, providing a range of environments and supporting a variety of wildlife, as well as extensive human settlement on its shores and islands (Grove 1978; Connah 1981).

As in the west of the continent, the savannah regions that stretch in a continuous band almost from the Atlantic to the Red Sea support a wide range of animal and plant resources, as does the Sahel to a lesser extent. These include, as Connah (1981:14) notes, 'ancestors of the cultivated sorghums, millets, West African rice and fonio', resources which are all important food crops to this day. In fact, Graham Connah has made the relevant point that 'it is probable that the African savanna is for Man the most important single biome in the continent and has long been so' (1981:13). Agricultural productivity is obviously linked to rainfall, which can vary considerably. This variation is indicated, for example, in Hausaland, a region defined by the presence of its dominant ethnic group, the Hausa (see below), and an area that encompasses large areas of northern and central Nigeria as well as parts of Niger. Here, annual rainfall ranges from about 1.2 m in the south to about 40 cm around Sokoto in the north

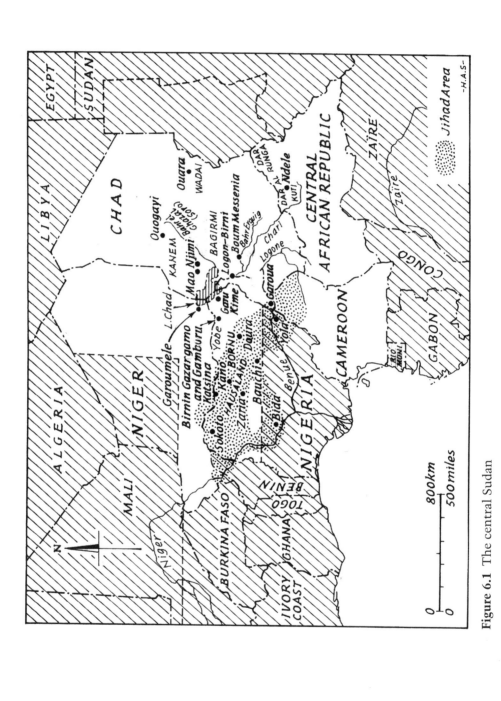

Figure 6.1 The central Sudan

(Moughtin 1964:21). A considerable difference is thus evident. Where agricultural potential is good, much of the Sudanic belt has been turned into what Grove (1978:149) terms 'farmed parkland'. This is defined as consisting of mature trees, usually of useful species such as, for instance, the shea-butter tree, a source of vegetable butter for cooking and lighting, and the baobab, whose leaves and bark are also used for various purposes, interspersed with fields. Mineral resources such as iron ore, natron and salt are also all present in the central Sudan. Salt is obtained both from desert salines such as those at Bilma near the Kawar oasis (see below), and other production sites further south in the Sahel. Natron, also a salt, but with 'higher concentrations of sulphates and carbonates' (Lovejoy 1986:15), which is often used as a cattle-lick, is extracted from the north-eastern shore of Lake Chad, as well as from Saharan sources (Grove 1978:152).

Although the central Sudanic belt should not be portrayed as some sort of idyll, it is indisputable that conditions were eminently suited to supporting life, and as in the Nilotic Sudan and western Sahel, an equally diverse ethnic composition is evident. There were Muslim pastoralist groups in the north, such as the Teda-Tebu and Tuareg (Cline 1950), and mixed Muslim pastoral and sedentary communities in the sahel–savannah borders: Kanuri, Fulani, Hausa and Shuwa (Cohen 1967; Joffé and Day-Viaud 1995). Further to the south the great Islamised emirates and city-states, with their diverse populations, intermingled with scattered pockets of non-Muslims, while the latter predominate in the forest zone. This, as with its neighbours already discussed, was also a region of early state development and of urbanism. However, many of these processes as they pertain to the Islamic period are as yet little understood because of a large-scale lack of relevant archaeological research in many parts of the central Sudan. Though certain areas are well investigated, as Gronenborn (1998:230) notes when he refers to the Chad basin being 'one of the most intensively examined regions in sub-Saharan Africa', others are less so. This is a point supported by Kalck's (1993) assertion that, for instance, the Central African Republic was not investigated systematically until the 1960s. In general, the central Sudan, for all its importance, could still be described as remaining one of the last great blank archaeological areas of sub-Saharan Africa for the archaeology of Islam.

Yet this is not an undue hinderance for our purposes here, as the archaeological evidence can be supplemented by historical records – although also comparatively meagre as regards earlier, Arabic, sources – and also by the accounts of the first European visitors to the region. Writings were left by individuals such as Heinrich Barth (1890), a polymath, who has left an immensely detailed record of his travels in west-central Africa in the 1850s. His account is also not subject to the same prejudices that many of his co-explorers, such as Richard Burton, suffered from. Thus a variety of sources of evidence, besides archaeological, will be utilised to supplement our understanding of the archaeology of Islam in the central Sudan. This is a region of paramount importance within this study, for to paraphrase Cohen (1967:1), it is a region of emirates, sultanates, kingdoms and empires, with Songhai in the west giving way to the Hausa kingdoms, Kanem-Borno, Bagirmi, Wadai and, in the east, Darfur in the Nilotic Sudan. To these can be added the frontier state of Dar al-Kuti, and the Kotoko principalities. Excluding Songhai and Darfur, which have already been considered in chapters 3 and 5, each of these polities will be examined to assess the archaeology of Islam in the region and to evaluate what can be learnt about the nature of Islam through the material remains and accompanying historical sources. Furthermore, these polities, which were gradually Islamised over time, were often in conflict with each other. This was also the region par excellence for cavalry (R. S. Smith 1989; Reyna 1990; Spring 1993), utilised both in military campaigns and slave raiding, and provides material for one of the case studies to be considered in this chapter. The central Sudan also provides an opportunity to consider *jihad*, warfare in general and slavery – institutions that were frequently interlinked in a bloody cycle which had repercussions deep into the heart of Africa, as will become apparent. Thus this region is critical within the archaeology of Islam in sub-Saharan Africa, as a cross-continental link and powerbase.

The pre-Islamic background

Pre-Islamic trade

Contact between the central Sudan and North Africa via Trans-Saharan trade routes running from the Fezzan to the Lake Chad region appears to pre-date the arrival of Muslim traders from perhaps as early as the late ninth century, but the details of the trade and contacts that existed is unclear. In part this was probably due to the existence of the Garamantes, who were referred to in the last chapter, and whose homelands were in the Fezzan (El-Rashedy 1986). Moreover, the position of the Garamantian heartlands implies contacts more with the central Sahara and Sudan rather than with regions further west such as the western Sahel. Slaves and ivory could have been obtained in the central Sahara and Sudan, and the so-called Ethiopian slaves pursued by the Garamantes might have been ancestors of peoples such as the Teda-Tebu or other groups further south (see Cline 1950). However, archaeological evidence indicating the existence of such trade and other possible contacts is elusive, and items of North African origin before the Arab trade have yet to be conclusively proven south of the Garamantian homelands. Survey of the oases of Kawar in northern Chad, for example, a strategic location on any such trade route, failed to find any evidence for this pre-Islamic trade even though similarities have been suggested between the name 'Agisymba', placed south of the Garamantes country by Ptolemy, and 'al-Qasaba' (the citadel), one of the principal Kawar settlements (Lange and Berthoud 1977:33, and see below) **(figure 6.2)**. Lewicki's (1971:114) statement

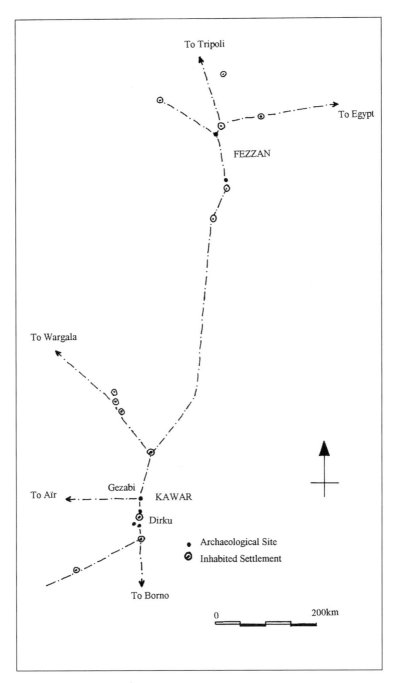

To Tripoli

To Egypt

FEZZAN

To Wargala

To Aïr

Gezabi

KAWAR

Dirku

● Archaeological Site

◎ Inhabited Settlement

To Borno

0 200km

Figure 6.2 Central Saharan trade route

regarding the Mediterranean coast, that it was an area 'where since times im-
memorial there had been numerous Phoenician and Grecian trading-posts and
emporia; their presence and affluence were largely a result of trans-Saharan
trade' is not, at present at least, supported by the archaeological evidence.

It is also probable that the requirements that did exist for sub-Saharan
African products during the Carthaginian and Roman periods were met by
the Garamantes. However, as Daniels (1970:43) notes, 'no ancient authority
actually states that caravan trade either from or via the Garamantes existed'.
Furthermore, until recently, little archaeological research had been undertaken
in the Fezzan, the Garamantian heartlands (for exceptions see Daniels 1970,
1989; El-Rashedy 1986). The Garamantes appear to have been secretive in their
trade and sources of materials, and the only known commodity obtained from
them are carbuncles, possibly aggry beads, though this, too, is far from sure.
Imported Roman 'South Gaulish' wares dating from the first and second centuries CE have been found in the Garama region, along with 'fine red wares and
glass' of the fourth century (Daniels 1989). More recent excavations at the site
of Aghram Nadharif at the southern end of the Wadi Tanezzuft have provided
further evidence for northern imports in the Garamantian heartlands. These
included two types of Roman amphorae, Tripolitania 1 of the first century CE
and Tripolitania 3 of the third to early fourth centuries (Liverani 2000:36).

This is a picture reinforced by other excavations in the Wadi el-Agial, a
roughly 180-km linear depression running east–west across the Fezzan, and
in which the former Garamantian capital, Garama, was sited (Mattingly et al.
1997; Mattingly et al. 1998; Edwards et al. 1999). Some sherds of imported
pottery are described which were found during the recent excavations and
surveys in the Wadi el-Agial. These include, for example, African red slip-
ware and Tripolitanian red slip-ware of the first to fourth centuries CE along
with amphora sherds of Tripolitanian type and similarly dated (Mattingly et al.
1998:136), but this appears to be as far south as such types of ceramics are found
(excluding of course, the sherds of African red slip-ware found much further to
the south-east on Zanzibar, described in chapter 4, which is wholly unconnected with what is being discussed here). The imported pottery testifies to
Garamantian–Mediterranean contacts, but the Garamantes, it can tentatively
be suggested, acted as a form of buffer perhaps, or filter, to direct contacts between the Mediterranean and the central Sudan during the Carthaginian and
Roman periods. That this might be a feasible interpretation would appear to be
further supported by the fact that the Garamantes were apparently protective
of both their trade and their independence. This in turn galled the Roman authorities and led to various skirmishes, as well as punitive expeditions heading
south into Garamantian territory, including the one led by Balbus (Lhote 1960)
that was referred to in the last chapter.

Perhaps, then, the central Sudan was the source of some of the commodities
traded by the Garamantes. This would appear logical but remains unclear. Also

logical is the existence of a trade route linking up the Sudanic belt from west to east from an early date, but this too appears not to have existed until comparatively late (see, e.g., Works 1976; Birks 1978). The utility of travelling through the relatively amenable savannahs from the Nile to the Niger is obvious in comparison to travelling north through the Sahara, and then down the Nile. In fact, Sutton (1991:145) has recently speculated that the Christian kingdoms of the Nile could have been reached by travelling 'eastward from the Lake Chad region' rather than across the Sahara to North Africa. This, he further suggests, was possibly the route used to obtain the large quantities of imported multi-coloured glass beads found at the site of Igbo-Ukwu in eastern Nigeria, in contexts dating from the ninth–tenth centuries (Shaw 1970, 1977, and see chapter 8 below). Although an attractive scenario, the existence of east–west contacts can be disputed for such an early date – and indeed for several centuries subsequently (see Insoll and Shaw 1997). The reason for this is, as Birks (1978:12) notes, that 'it was not until the 1750s, when Sultan Teyrab annexed Kordofan, that Muslim governments held sway from Lake Chad to the Red Sea'. Conversion to Islam obviously preceded this date among large segments of the population in much of the central Sudan, but the cohesiveness provided by a common religion across the whole region was lacking, a factor already shown to have been of importance in the western Sahel. Even if it had existed, it is likely that an unhindered passage across the savannah would have been difficult on account of the intermittent inter-state warfare that existed both between Muslim polities and Muslim and non-Muslim polities alike.

Early Islam: Kanem-Borno and its influence

The origins of complex society, the Zaghawa and the Ibadis

Primary among the early polities in the central Sudan, and ultimately a conduit for the spread of Islam in the region, was the kingdom of Kanem, sometimes referred to as Kanem-Borno. Borno is a reference to its later reincarnation following the geographical shift of the kingdom from east to west of Lake Chad (see below) (figure 6.3). The origins of Kanem are somewhat obscure, and the early Arabic geographers refer to the kingdom by the name Zaghawa rather than Kanem, with the earliest reference being that of Wahb ibn Munabbih around 730 (Lange 1992:220). It is only in the ninth century, as Lange (1993:263) notes, that al-Ya'qubi 'links the two notions by providing the important information that the Zaghawa were living in Kanem'. The Zaghawa, who were referred to in chapter 3, are described by Levtzion (2000:80) as 'nomads of the Central Sahara', and Lange (1992:220) has suggested a plausible theory to account for why they were instrumental in the origins of Kanem, some distance from their Saharan homelands. This, he suggests, was due to their possessing iron weapons and horses, by means of which they gradually brought under their sway 'the

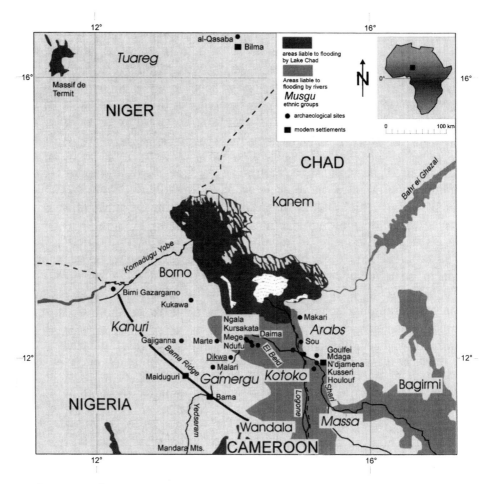

Figure 6.3 The Kanem-Borno region

agriculturalist and pastoralist peoples living in the region south east of Kawar, between Lake Chad and the Bahr al-Ghazal – the region later to be known as Kanem'. Their possession of iron weapons has been linked with the Haddad, or so-called 'blacksmith culture', which flourished between the fourth and eighth centuries, as exemplified by material recovered from Koto Toro between Lake Chad and Tibesti (Lange 1992:216).

As elsewhere in the continent, archaeology again indicates that the origins of metallurgy and complex society pre-date the arrival of Muslim traders in the central Sudan. In the Kanem-Borno area, or more specifically the Borno area of northern Nigeria, for example, archaeological research has indicated the indigenous development of urbanism. Connah's (1981) excavations at Daima uncovered an occupation sequence dating from about 550 BCE to 1500 CE. A similar antiquity for settlement in the region was indicated at the site of Kursakata, where occupation begins between 1200 and 800 BCE. This site has also been the focus of recent reinvestigation (Gronenborn 1996, 1998), with a complex occupation and architectural sequence uncovered, including the remains of circular buildings utilising potsherd pavements. These pavements were literally constructed of potsherds set in mud mortar. Other aspects of what is sometimes referred to as the Sao culture are discussed below.

Besides the possible technological advantages enjoyed by the Zaghawa being a factor in the growth of Kanem, trade was also of certain importance in its foundation. As Connah (1981:222) notes, Kanem was ideally situated close to Lake Chad at the southern end of any feasible trade route running via Kawar and the Fezzan to North Africa. This location was 'doubtless no accident' (Lange 1984:247). The Kawar oasis has already been referred to in the context of pre-Islamic trade, and is in reality a group of oases, running north–south for some 75 km on the main trade route between the central Sudan and the Fezzan. The Kawar oasis has been surveyed and a series of large archaeological sites recorded (Lange and Berthoud 1977) **(figure 6.2)**. These are, as yet, unexcavated, but represent the remains of former settlements, which were in turn divided into two main groups with the northern sites catering to travellers and the southern ones to the salt trade. An example of one of the settlement sites which was recorded is provided by Gezabi, a mound measuring 470 m north–south and 300 m wide, which was covered with sherds of pottery and 'de bijoux étrangers à la région et des tapis originaires du nord et l'on distingue les traces de nombreuses habitations' (Lange and Berthoud 1977:21).

Similarly, extensive remains were found in the salines at the southern end of the oasis. An example of such a site is provided by Dirku, where to the south-west of the salt workings were discovered the remains of the old town which had been extensively robbed for building materials, but which was still partly walled in the mid-1970s. An old mosque was also reported at Bilma (Lange and Berthoud 1977:27), one of the most important of these desert salines. Lovejoy (1986:59) mentions that the earliest historical reference to salt production at Kawar is by al-Idrisi in the mid-twelfth century. However, it is quite possible that sites such as Bilma were worked from an earlier period. Al-Ya'qubi refers to the Bilma trail as a slave-trading route at the end of the ninth century (Reyna 1990:28), though no mention is made of salt. Lovejoy (1986:56–7) also describes the techniques used to extract salt from the Kawar sites, and these differ from the mines to the north of Timbuktu, such as the site of Teghaza described in the last chapter (and see Monod 1938, 1940). At Bilma, for example, salt and natron were extracted by breaking off the crust that forms on top of the salines through evaporation. This salt crust was then further broken up into moulds to form both flat cakes and cones of salt which would then be transported by camel caravan to the markets of the south.

From the south, ivory, slaves and animal products were exported north, while – above all – horses (for reasons that will become apparent later), along with weapons, books, cloth and beads, and salt from the workings at Bilma, would have been exported south (Lange and Berthoud 1977; Lange 1984, 1992). This again replicates the patterns noted elsewhere in the continent, predominantly one of raw materials being exported and finished goods imported, as has already been described for the western Sahel in the last chapter. However, these patterns are reconstructed from what is known about Muslim-controlled trade in the central Sudan; as noted earlier, trade patterns, routes and commodities are still largely unclear. As Liverani (2000:43) notes, overall there is a difficulty in determining 'whether trans-Saharan trade prior to Islamic times was a negligible affair – as maintained by the current scholarship [sic] – or was already regularly and relevantly organised'.

Muslim contacts with the central Sudan, as with the western Sahel, appear to have been initiated by followers of Kharijite Ibadi tenets in the first instance. Similarities between the two areas can be extended further in that all traces of Ibadism have likewise disappeared in the central Sudan, being replaced by Sunni Malikism (Hiskett 1994), as they have in the western Sahel. Historical references to Ibadi trade exist and have been reviewed by Lewicki (1971). He suggests that the first Ibadi 'merchant-missionaries' (1971:127) probably travelled from the kingdom of Zawila through Kawar to the central Sudan as early as the mid-eighth century. Lewicki further notes that no clear evidence attesting to local converts to Ibadi Islam in the central Sudan exists in the Arabic sources. But it is possible that a part of the local population might have converted to Ibadi Islam in Kanem, as probably also occurred in Gao and elsewhere in the western Sahel, as has been described previously.

Besides the historical references to Ibadi trade, material traces of a possible Ibadi presence in the central Sudan are elusive. However, Schacht (1954) has suggested, as was also described in the last chapter, that elements of the mosque architecture in the region might signal remnant Ibadi influences. These include the staircase minaret found in Fulani mosques in the central Sudan. Architectural similarities are also cited by Lange and Berthoud (1977:35) as indicating traces of an Ibadi presence in the Kawar oasis. Quite what this evidence is, is unclear though they suggest 'le nom de Djado lui-même semble provenir du nom tout à fait identique de la principale ville de Djebel Nefusa'. Yet this evidence in totality is somewhat inconclusive, though it is fair to surmise that contacts between Kanem and the Muslim world could have existed as early as the mid-eighth century. Equally, it is as well to reiterate, in the words of Lange (1992:222) that 'Islam played no part in the founding of Kanem or in the early stages of its development'. In summary, although Trimingham's various volumes might now be somewhat outdated, he is still correct when he states (1962:108) that the early history of the central Sudan and the origins of Islamisation 'are even more obscure than those of the Western Sudan and we have to rely far more than is wise upon historical myth, distorted by reflection through a thousand mirrors'.

Kanem and the Saifawa

The haze clears somewhat following a dynastic change in Kanem. This appears to have occurred when, around 1075, the Zaghawa were pushed 'eastwards into a region where they are still to be found today' (Lange 1992:220), i.e. on the borders of the Nilotic Sudan (thus their inclusion in chapter 3). This was achieved by the new Saifawa or Sefuwa dynasty of Kanem. This new dynasty traced its ancestry to Saif ibn Dhi Yazan, 'a pre-Islamic leader in the Yemen' (Brenner 1973:9), and in itself is reminiscent of the Arabising of origins remarked upon previously elsewhere in the continent (see, e.g., chapter 2). Furthermore, it has often been erroneously assumed that the assumption of power by the Saifawa equated with the simultaneous conversion of Kanem to Islam, through the acceptance of Islam by Hummay, the first Saifawa ruler. This 'hey-presto tale of the arrival of Islam' (Hiskett 1994:105) has now been shown to be incorrect. Notwithstanding the possible pre-existing Ibadi history just described, Lange (1992:225) relates that the first Muslim ruler of Kanem was one Hu or Hawwa, who was possibly even a woman, and that his/her conversion to Islam occurred around 1067–71. Hu was followed by another Muslim ruler *prior* to the reign of Hummay of the Saifawa. Thus genealogical differences might be evident, but the Saifawa cannot be credited with the origins of Islamisation in Kanem.

Kanem was, as noted previously, at this time centred east of Lake Chad (in modern Chad). Here, the existence of towns in the region is first mentioned in the twelfth century by al-Idrisi, who refers to Manan and Anjimi (Connah 1981). Birni Njimi, the Kanem capital, has never been satisfactorily located, with attempts to find it stretching back to those of Heinrich Barth in the mid-nineteenth century (Barth 1890; Bivar and Shinnie 1962:7). In part, it can be suggested, its archaeological elusiveness might be due to the fact that it could have been largely composed of structures built of impermanent materials (Gronenborn 2001:104). Barkindo (1992:504), for example, refers to Kanuri compounds in Borno being predominantly formed of roundhouses with mud or wooden framework walls, surrounded by matting. Cohen (1967:19) also suggests that it was possibly a 'city of tents' in its original incarnation. Nevertheless, archaeological visibility aside, it has to be acknowledged that only limited surveys of the original Kanem area in Chad have been conducted. These recovered little informative evidence: a possible mosque at Tié, a site described by Bivar and Shinnie (1962:9) which 'in no way fulfils the requirements of the capital of Njimi', as well as undated buildings and enclosures between Mao, Moussoro, and the Chadian Bahr al-Ghazal (Bivar and Shinnie 1962; A. M. D. Lebeuf 1962).

Thus the ruler of Kanem had converted to Islam in the mid-eleventh century. The reasons behind this, it is assumed, are similar to those already described as those underpinning to conversion to Islam by other rulers in sub-Saharan Africa. To recap, they could include all or some of the following – prestige, genuine belief, access to trade, the benefits brought to administration through the use of Muslim officials and Arabic and the enhancement of magical and secular power. Following this, conversions to Islam among the general populace increased, following patterns described for elsewhere, and Levtzion (2000:80) argues that it was the majority religion in Kanem by the thirteenth century. However, as Lange (1984:253) notes, owing to the need for slaves to supply the trans-Saharan and local markets it was 'not in the interests of the kings of Kanem to facilitate the expansion of Islam beyond certain limits'. The enslavement of Muslims was not permitted (see below).

This increasing Islamisation of Kanem is evident in various events. An example of this is provided by a pilgrimage to Mecca made by a ruler of Kanem in the mid-thirteenth century, as recounted by Maqrizi (Levtzion and Hopkins 1981:353). It is similarly evident in a further symbolic act by another king of Kanem shortly afterwards, the opening of the 'mune' by the ruler Dunama. What exactly the mune was is unclear; Lange (1984:254) suggests it 'was probably the focal element of a royal cult handed down from pre-Islamic times' – possibly even, he has later proposed (1993:266–7), a statue of Amun originally obtained from Meroë in the Nilotic Sudan. Whatever its physical form it was obviously a powerful link with older religious traditions and could have functioned, as R. S. Smith (1989:33) argues, as a source of power in war. In this instance a link with the past was being severed as Islamisation increased, rather than the alternative process of incorporating the old with the new. The latter mechanism has already been described as taking place in numerous other contexts in sub-Saharan Africa.

The Bulala and Borno

The act of unwrapping the mune, and thus the symbolic destruction of its mystique and the sapping of its power, was to have profound consequences both for the Saifawa dynasty and for Kanem as a whole. For this action, according to Levtzion (2000:80), 'alienated the Bulala clan, of more traditionalist disposition', leading to the breakup of Kanem and the shift of the Saifawa to Borno, west of Lake Chad. This move, following conflict between the Bulala and the Saifawa, occurred during the reign of the Kanembu ruler Mai Umar Idrismi (c.1394–8). But it was not until the reign of Ali Dunamami (c.1472–1504) that a new capital, Birni Ngazargamo, was built, 'the first permanent home a Saifawa Mai had enjoyed in a century' (Brenner 1973:10).

Various settlements associated with Borno have been investigated. At Garoumele in eastern Niger, a possible former capital of Borno (Connah 1981:227), a variety of structures have been recorded. These included a number of rooms made of fired red brick (Zakari 1985:46–7). These structures were set within a rectangular enclosing wall roughly 200 × 100 m, in turn set within a further enclosing wall built of tubali, or moulded egg-shaped mud bricks (Bivar and Shinnie 1962:4). This latter enclosure measured some 3 km in diameter and was entered by four gates (Binet 1956; Zakari 1985), with the outer area possibly functioning as the section occupied by the general populace – perhaps living in less permanent structures such as reed huts – while the inner enclosure was used by the royal family. Gronenborn (2001:106) has even suggested that Garoumele might be associated with the Saifawa as well as Borno. Further sites associated with Borno which have been examined include Garu Kime, and Birni Ngazargamo, the permanent capital established in 1470, which survived until it was sacked by Fulani soldiers in the early nineteenth century, and was in turn supplanted by the town of Kukawa as capital (Cohen 1967:17; Brenner 1973). Birni Ngazargamo was similarly defended, but by an earthern rampart up to 7 m in height with five entrances, the whole enclosing a defended area some 2 km across (Bivar and Shinnie 1962:3) **(figures 6.4 and 6.5)**. Within this wall a number of buildings were recorded built of well-fired red moulded bricks, an introduction of disputed origins to the region (Gronenborn 2001:114), and mortar. These included a central complex, the ruler's palace and a number of other buildings scattered across the internal area, the latter interpreted as the residences of other leading people (Connah 1981:229).

Again the majority of the population would appear to have lived in wooden, reed or grass huts, or houses built of sun-dried rather than fired brick, thus being less visible archaeologically (Bivar and Shinnie 1962). The nature of Kanuri compounds and the possible tented aspect of the Kanem capital has already been mentioned, and other descriptions of the use of more ephemeral building materials in this region exist. Heinrich Barth (1890:325), for example, describes the reed governors' palaces he found in Borno, such as that of the governor of the province of Mashena who lived in a reed house with an attached reedwork audience hall. Gronenborn's (1996) excavation of circular earthen-walled buildings at Kursakata has also already been referred to, a further example of a more archaeologically transient building type. This probable use of less durable or less visible materials would also help in explaining the large open areas evident in many of the published plans of walled sites in this region, for the gaps almost certainly do not denote a lack of settlement but rather a lack of surface visibility **(figure 6.5)**. Thus this is similar to the imbalance evident in the way Swahili settlements have been portrayed until fairly recently, in the case of the East African coast with a cluster of – in this instance – stone buildings, surrounded by large open areas frequently being portrayed, as was discussed in chapter 4.

The increasing Islamisation of the population of Kanem has also been referred to, a process which appears ultimately to have led to the geographical shift of the centre of authority following the conflict over the *mune*. Within Borno the Muslim identity of both the ruler and people was firmly established, as indicated by the titles 'sultan' and 'emir' being used in historical sources (Gronenborn 2001:110), as well as the traditional title *mai*. Barkindo (1992) describes how Borno became a centre of scholarship and attracted Muslim scholars from elsewhere in the region. These scholars were of two types – those

Figure 6.4 Birni Ngazargamo

Figure 6.5 Birni Ngazargamo from the air. Note the wall and apparently empty interior

who assisted the ruler in the maintenance of good government, and those in rural areas, 'where they taught and spread the religion' (Barkindo 1992:508). With the latter group parallels are thus evoked with the holy men of the Funj, who spread far and wide disseminating Islam (see chapter 3). Indeed, the importance of Islam is signalled, as Cohen (1967:22) notes, in the title given to the chief judge and religious leader in early Borno, *talba*, an individual who is referred to in the traditions as 'second to the king'. Yet the emphasis upon the divine aspect of the king, the *mai*, appears not to have wholly disappeared, or even to have reappeared, for many of the manifestations of divine rule seem to have coexisted alongside features of Islam. These are by now familiar, and include seclusion of the ruler, people prostrating themselves before him, his being spoken to through intermediaries, and his being seated in a special cage – the equivalent of the types of royal platform referred to elsewhere, as in Darfur (Cohen 1967; Barkindo 1992; Levtzion 2000).

Later Islam: the influence of Kanem-Borno

The Sao and ethnicity

Elements of divine rule aside, the existence of a large, increasingly Islamised polity such as Kanem – and subsequently Borno – obviously had implications for its neighbours. The apparent restriction of Islamic conversion, because of its impact upon slavery, has already been referred to, and these effects appear in many instances to have been profound, leading to wholesale population replacement or disappearance, usually as a result of procuring slaves. However, to reduce the relationships between polities such as Kanem-Borno and its neighbours to the level of slave-raiding and conflict alone is flawed. For as MacEachern (1993:250) notes, much research completed 'often seems to be the history of states expanding against an undifferentiated mass of "peripheral" peoples', when in reality the picture is frequently more complex.

These varying relations can sometimes be traced archaeologically, and a good example of this is provided by considering the indigenous inhabitants of the area west and south of Lake Chad. These are peoples often referred to as the So or Sao, the precise meaning of which has been the subject of some debate (Lebeuf et al. 1980:7; Lange 1989, 1992). Lange (1989:210) states that Sao most likely means 'city' or 'city-dweller'. This was a reference to the inhabitants of the walled villages and towns located on the flood plains encountered by the Kanembu, the inhabitants of Kanem, as they moved into the region following the move from Kanem. A more general interpretation of the use of the term Sao, also posited by Lange (1992:218), is that 'the same term recurs in every region in which the Kanem peoples have superseded earlier populations and was used to denote the indigenous populations who were unable to resist assimilation'.

These processes of assimilation are in part recognisable archaeologically, but are also recorded historically. The first historical references to the Sao appear in the fourteenth century, about the same time as the large-scale campaigns against the Sao began, but the bulk are from the account of Ibn Fartua, or Furtu, written in 1576 at Birni Ngazargamo (Lange 1989). This chronicle recounts the contemporary military expeditions of *Mai* Idris Aloma, and thus campaigns against the Sao are recorded (see Palmer 1967). One settlement mentioned is Amchaka, a site which has never been investigated archaeologically (Gronenborn 2001:118). Interestingly, once the Sao were suppressed during these campaigns, the term is no longer used, except 'as the name of a legendary people ancestral to Kanuri and non-Kanuri groups alike' (Lange 1989:210).

Gronenborn (2001:118) suggests that this 'increasing dominance of Kanem-Borno can be observed in changes in pottery styles'. This is indicated by the appearance of pottery bearing twisted-strip roulette decoration found at sites such as Daima, pottery previously well known in fifteenth century contexts at, for example, Birni Ngazargamo. Cultural change is also apparent in the burial evidence recorded at Sao sites on the Chadian plains, with three phases evident in the Kotoko-Logone region, for example (Trimingham 1962:105). Firstly, burial of the corpse simply stretched out full length in the ground was evident (c. late twelfth century); during the second phase of burial, corpses were placed in a foetal position within large pots (c. late fifteenth century); and thirdly, corpses were again placed at full length and jar burials disappear. According to Jansen and Gauthier (1973:9), 'this change in the funeral customs betrays the influence of Islam, taking root in the Sao country'. Jansen and Gauthier (1973:9) also suggest that the virtually concomitant disappearance of Sao bronze working and degeneration in art forms indicates that 'the Sao no longer existed as a people' by the late sixteenth century **(figure 6.6)**. Whether the Sao ever actually existed as a people is, however, debatable; the term might merely be, as noted above, a reference to their patterns of settlement. What is important is that the concepts of ethnicity in this region have altered considerably over time. Connah, for example, has suggested that some of the Sao 'probably became Kanuri' (1981:240).

The Kanuri are one of the major ethnic groups in the region linked with Borno. Yet their origins are also unclear; the term does not appear, according to Gronenborn (1998), until the nineteenth century, though Lange (1993:275) has argued that Kanuri origins can be charted back to the foundation of Borno following the move from Kanem. In general, as Levtzion (1985b:184) notes, where areas were becoming more closely politically associated with Borno, both 'the beginning of Kanurization and Islamization' were evident. The notion of what constitutes identity is complex, and identity can be adapted or changed for various purposes, as has recently been discussed by S. Jones (1997). Furthermore, it should not be thought that this Sao–Kanuri ethnic change was an isolated instance. Heinrich Barth (1890) also recorded changes in ethnicity taking place in parts of the central Sudan in the mid-nineteenth century, as among the Marghi. This was (and is) occurring across the continent to suit myriad purposes, as with the issue of Swahili identity discussed in chapter 4, or that of Arabisation in the Nilotic Sudan in chapter 3. Other Sao, for instance, became Kotoko, another ethnic group found in Cameroon, and referred to below. Kotoko could also become Kanuri, something Gronenborn (1998) suggests is evident archaeologically, as at the mound site of Mege in northern Nigeria. Here, he has interpreted the appearance of sgrafitto pottery decoration in contexts dating to the late nineteenth–early twentieth centuries as indicating 'ethnic change from Kotoko to Kanuri taking place within the area during the last 100 years' (Gronenborn 1998:238). This is also evident at other sites in the

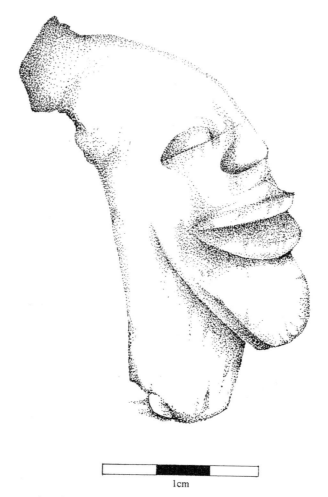

1cm

Figure 6.6 Sao head from the settlement mound at Amja, Borno

region (see Gronenborn and Magnavita 2000), and not confined to sub-Saharan Africa either. Ménage (1979:53), for example, refers to the change in ethnicity and/or population replacement that occurred in Anatolia – in the eleventh century the bulk of the population was 'predominantly Greek-speaking and Christian; in the early sixteenth century it was predominantly Turkish-speaking and about 90 percent Muslim'.

Within this context the Sao pot burials of the second phase, described previously, could be interpreted as a final reaction, a cultural statement, before the inevitable occurred and the Sao were overrun. It is also interesting to note that some of these pot burials contained grave-goods including glass and carnelian beads, which appears to suggest that the Sao were in other forms of contact, besides violent ones, with their more powerful neighbours who were importing these items via trans-Saharan trade. Gronenborn (1998:247) also remarks on the presence of 'elaborate and exotic goods' in the Sao region before Borno advances into the former in the fifteenth and sixteenth centuries. At the mound site of Mdaga, for instance, 14 km north of N'Djamena in Chad, various blue glass beads were found in burials at this Sao site (Lebeuf et al. 1980:11). Mdaga is a site from which interesting evidence for contacts with Muslims was found. Although Islamisation of the inhabitants is placed between the seventeenth and nineteenth centuries by the investigators (Lebeuf et al. 1980:15), four footed bowls were found in levels dated to about the fifteenth century. These bowls bear Qur'anic inscriptions in Arabic, 'ces textes sont inscrits en rond, en partant du bord vers le fond: répétes plusieurs fois, ils sont tracés de manière à recouvrir toute la surface interne du récipient' (Lebeuf et al. 1980:132). These bowls probably served a protective purpose, perhaps for drinking from, with the potency of the Qur'anic text serving to cure or protect. There is possibly also significance in the choices of Qur'anic text chosen, though what this might be is unclear. An example of the text is provided by that contained on bowl 1093:

Line 1: The Address. 'In the name of God, our Lord Muhammad'.
Line 2: Surah 91. 'The Sun', verses 4 and 5.
Line 3: Surah 91, verse 14.
Line 4: 'The house that preserved them from hunger and sheltered them'.
Line 5: Surah 106. 'The Quraysh', verse 3.

Similarly, both glass and carnelian beads were recovered from the mound site of Houlouf on the Chadian plain in northern Cameroon (Holl 1994). The later Iron Age levels, i.e. those dating from between about 700–800 and 1200 CE, were, in the words of the excavators, 'characterised by the presence of exotic goods such as carnelian beads and the development of copper and brass metallurgy' (Holl et al. 1991:17). Although the notion of a brass industry at such an early date can be questioned (see chapter 5), the presence of carnelian beads several centuries before Kanurisation and Islamisation is interesting. Furthermore, a change in architecture was also noted with the appearance of quadrangular houses 'built with flat roofs and sun-dried mudbricks' (Holl et al. 1991:22; and see Holl 1988) in contexts post-dating the thirteenth century, but again unconnected with Islamisation. This type of evidence, if recorded elsewhere in the continent – as in northern Ghana (see chapter 7) – might be interpreted as concomitant with conversion to Islam or the arrival of Muslims, but here such a case cannot, apparently, be made.

Quite why the Sao were overcome can be assessed. Barth (1890:413) makes the observation that 'pagans' (non-Muslim followers of traditional religion) in the regions through which he was travelling 'in general' did not live in distinct villages or towns 'where the dwellings stand together, but in single farms and hamlets, or clusters of huts, each of which contains an entire family, spreading over a wide expanse of country'. This lack of a cohesive settlement pattern

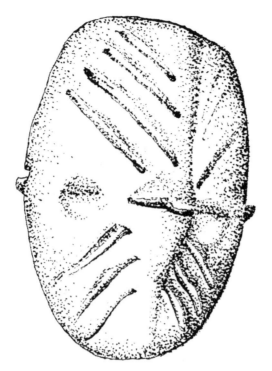

Figure 6.7 Unprovenanced Sao 'mask' from Chad

was a distinct disadvantage when it came to defensive considerations, and thus they were easy prey for slavers. Yet Sao settlements appear not to have been similarly structured. Mound sites are common, some surrounded by ramparts (Jansen and Gauthier 1973:8), indicating agglomerated rather than dispersed settlement. In part this was due to the environment, flooding during the rainy season restricting suitable area for settlement (Gronenborn 1996:34); but equally, the Sao were not people lacking political centralisation. Holl and Levy describe, for example, the Sao ancestors of the Kotoko of northern Cameroon as developing from around 1000 what is defined as 'a small-scale Sultanate or complex chiefdom' (1993:171). Similar interpretations are presented by Gronenborn (1998:247) based upon his research at various mound sites south of Lake Chad, also associated with the Sao, where the burials with grave-goods dating from before Borno advances into the region in the fifteenth–sixteenth centuries have already been described **(figure 6.7)**. This evidence again suggests that complex societies were already emerging in this region, from at least the fourteenth century. In summary, it appears that a mix of circumstances account for the disappearance of the Sao in the face of Borno expansion. Thus MacEachern's (1993) comment quoted at the start of this section can be seen to be of great relevance, for the relations that existed cannot simply be classified as a process of great states overcoming the unorganised and uncentralised.

The Kotoko and ancestry

The notion of ethnic change has been considered, and a further manifestation of this process appears to be represented by the Kotoko. This is an ethnonym which appears for the first time as a description of the Chadic-speaking peoples of the plains south of Lake Chad, according to Gronenborn and Magnavita (2000:39), after the conquests of Idris Aloma. Furthermore, Gronenborn (1998:253) has suggested that the Kotoko city-states emerged from the Sao polities, thus building upon the legacy described previously. The effect of the Borno conquests was not the development of political centralisation and complex societies, but the start of the process of Islamisation – and although Muslims today, the Kotoko remain, as Lebeuf and Lebeuf note, 'loyal to the past' (1973:66). This is especially evident in the Logone-Birni palace, the capital of a Kotoko polity in northern Cameroon (A. M. D. Lebeuf 1969). Here the ruler is recorded as having converted to Islam about 1800 (Trimingham 1962:212). However, a blending of Islam and traditional religious belief is evident both in the architectural layout of the palace complex and that of the whole settlement.

This settlement layout has been described by Lebeuf and Lebeuf as providing an 'image of the world' (1973:62), as conceptualised by the Kotoko. To achieve this the town is divided into two parts, Halaka (north) and Alagué (south), separated by a median zone, the boundary, in which the king's residence is situated. The palace has what can be defined as a mediating role, both in traditional religion and in Islam. The latter is indicated in traditional Kotoko settlements by the juxtaposition of mosque and ruler's palace, with the settlement patterning centred on the ruler's palace, a feature evident throughout the 'hierarchy of sultans' residences' (Holl and Levy 1993:175–6). The Logone-Birni palace itself served as a residence and thus contained all the prerequisites such a function entailed – accommodation, stores, guardhouse etc. – but it also served an important religious role. According to Lebeuf and Lebeuf (1973), two symbolic structures within the complex indicate this, structures which were erected 'for an essentially religious purpose', that of guaranteeing 'universal order' (Lebeuf and Lebeuf 1973:63).

One of these structures was the *tukuri*, meaning 'full or 'homogeneous'. This consisted of 'two symmetrical parallelpipedical earthen blocks' inside the living quarters of the king (figure 6.8). These blocks were separated by a narrow passage above which were a pair of living rooms inhabited by the ruler after the enthroning ceremony and during Ramadan. Consequently, Muslim and traditional elements were interlinked, drawing on the power of the ancestors – indicated, for example, by the *tukuri* being attributed, along with the town walls, to the Sao. Thus one of the elements of African traditional religions discussed in chapter 1 is again apparent, that of mediation, the use of intermediaries, and of possession of land and authority through ritual and ancestry (Mbiti 1975; Ranger 1991). Ancestry is further indicated through the function of the *tukuri*,

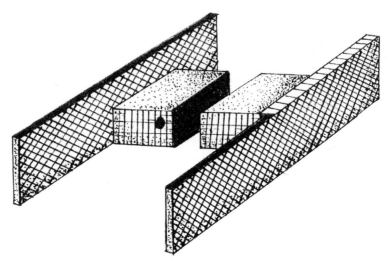

Figure 6.8 The *tukuri*

as also described by the Lebeufs (1973:67) as revealing the world's duality, symbolised by the *tukuri* supporting the 'two primordial twins, ancestors of the human race' – the northern male, the other female – as well as functioning as the rulers' primordial ancestor.

Although the Kotoko-Logone palace cannot be classed as a Muslim monument, Muslim elements are evident, as in its use at Ramadan. Syncretism is again found; the process of 'composite origins' and ongoing 'synthesis and erasure' (Shaw and Stewart 1994:7) apparent elsewhere in the continent therefore exists here as well. Indeed, Mosse (1994) follows on to note that the 'composite origins' – or, in this instance – nature of religion is found everywhere. Here, as in Darfur, Funj, Kanem or Ghana, the rulers' authority and strength is in part contingent upon aspects of pre-Islamic traditions and beliefs. These older traditions were not expunged following the conquests and subsequent ethnic, religious and cultural influences of Borno.

The Shuwa, Wandala and 'ripple factors'

Influences from Borno, and effects upon the Sao, were also felt by and from the Shuwa. The Shuwa are one among a number of Arab groups who were dispersed from Egypt following campaigns launched against them by the Mamluks (see chapter 3). Other groups similarly dispersed included the Tayy, Bali, and Djuhayna (Holl and Levy 1993:174). The Shuwa, however, ultimately ended up in the Chad basin, and their presence is first recorded in a letter dating from 1391–2 which was sent by Uthman ibn Idris, then ruler of Borno, to a Mamluk sultan. Within this letter the Shuwa are described as the Judham, which is of importance, as the Banu Judham 'were one of the important tribes of Yemen at the end of the seventh century' (Holl and Levy 1993:174). This would appear to indicate that here we have a viable ancestral tradition of Arab origins – rather than the usual spurious ones. The Judham were also among the first Arab groups to settle in Egypt following the arrival of the newly Islamised Muslim armies there. Reports as to how the Shuwa interacted with their neighbours following their arrival in the vicinity of Lake Chad vary. The letter from the Bornoan sultan, referred to previously, reputedly denounced the Shuwa for raiding their coreligionists in Borno, while Holl and Levy (1993:175) suggest that their relations with their neighbours were largely peaceful and that they were always dominated by the Kotoko.

The former scenario that inter-ethnic relations varied, is probably more realistic. Barth (1890) refers to the Shuwa raiding for slaves, and also records that they numbered between 200,000 and 250,000, having fields during the rainy season but otherwise wandering 'about with their cattle' (Barth 1890:403). Lyons (1996:355) similarly describes the Shuwa raiding the northern borders of Wandala, a minor vassal of Borno in northern Cameroon, and a state which became Muslim in the early eighteenth century. In turn the Wandala condemned the Shuwa as committing 'serious sins against Islam', such as drinking (Lyons 1996:355). Indeed the Shuwa, if this is correct, are hardly unique, because drinking, as was noted in chapter 3, is found among both Muslim and non-Muslim groups alike, though usually practised more covertly in the former. In fact, much of this should be looked at in the light of nomad–sedentary relations across the continent in general, relations which were often acrimonious. Among the Fulani, for example, another major ethnic group in the region, de St Croix (1945:14) describes how 'the settled Fulani scorn the nomadic types for their laxity in their religious outlook'.

The maintenance of distinctions and differences between these various ethnic groups is also something that has recently been investigated through material culture, particularly using ethnoarchaeological and architectural studies. Lyons (1996:359), for example, has looked at house plans in the predominantly Wandala town of Déla in northern Cameroon. She found that both the distribution of rectilinear structures within the community and the use of different construction materials varied, functioning as 'one means of maintaining economic and social differences between ethnic communities (Wandala, Shuwa, Mura, and Urza) and between individual men within each community'. Related research has also been completed by Holl and Levy (1993), while MacEachern (1993) has considered relations between the Wandala and their non-Muslim 'kirdi' or montagnard neighbours from a historical and archaeological perspective, especially between the late sixteenth and nineteenth centuries. Interestingly, the non-Muslim groups were literally 'selling the iron for their shackles' (MacEachern 1993:257), through trading iron for essential commodities which they needed in their mountainous, inselberg retreats, notably salt and protein-rich foods. Wandala, in contrast, profited from proximity to Borno, expanding prior to conversion by its ruler to Islam in the eighteenth century, and growing through trade with its powerful neighbour. Conversely, the absence of evidence for long-distance trade at sites not associated with Wandala was also attested archaeologically, as at the site of Mehé Djiddere, east of Wandala, where only one 'tin-glazed faience bead introduced through external trade' was found (MacEachern 1993:265).

In effect, this mosaic of polities and ethnic groups were constantly interacting with each other in different ways as religious and other identities were renegotiated and hierarchies altered. This can certainly be charted archaeologically, via the 'ripples' from supra-polities such as Kanem-Borno, and effects which recur throughout the history of the central Sudan (see Acri and Bitiyong 1983). It is further indicated, for example, by Darling's (1985:7) reference to a 'wave pattern' which similarly occurred during the later *jihad* period of the late eighteenth to nineteenth centuries in the central Sudan, whereby 'thousands of settlements built walls, shifted locally, migrated great distances or were conquered and became deserted'.

Bagirmi and sacrifice

A further state that was also affected by its neighbour to the west, i.e. Kanem, and subsequently by the Bulala, was Bagirmi. However, Bagirmi still awaits detailed archaeological investigation (Reyna 1990:168), but has been studied, in part, ethnographically and historically (see for example, A. M. D. Lebeuf 1967; Paques 1977). Bagirmi arose on the right bank of the Shari river, southeast of Lake Chad, in an area formerly raided for slaves (Levtzion 1985b:183). The early inhabitants of the region appear to have been culturally related to the Sao, 'if linguistically distinct' (Lavers 1983:30). A similar pattern of raised village settlements to avoid flooding along the banks of the Shari and its tributaries is found, with a number of city-states – Maffaling, Busso, Matiya and Damye, for example – having developed by the fifteenth century, perhaps even earlier. Lavers (1983:30–1) also records that subsequent traditions mention that these city-states were gradually incorporated into one state, which, along with the nomadic population, gave rise, 'it is said, to the name Bagirmi that is *bagar miya* or "cattle, one hundred"'. This occurred in the 1520s and during the reign of the ruler or *mbang*, Abdullah (c.1568–1608), a Muslim convert, the court was Islamised and Bagirmi became what could be classified as a Muslim state.

In the first instance, in a pattern by now familiar, conversion to Islam was largely restricted to the court circle, and Trimingham (1962:137) makes the point that the administrative and military systems were modelled on those of Borno. Also of interest, and contrary to the usually described patterns, Lavers

(1983:31) suggests that Abdullah actually *introduced* many of the features of divine rule to boost prestige, including 'seclusion of the ruler, food restrictions and other factors calculated to enhance the status of the monarchy'. The divine nature of the Bagirmi ruler functioned within a cosmological framework, as Reyna (1990:1) notes that the inhabitants of Bagirmi 'associate their sovereign, the *mbang*, with the sun and his officials, *maladonoge*, with planets'. It was not until the reign of *Mbang* Muhammad al-Amin (c.1751–85) that Islam spread more widely among the general populace. Even then, the practice of Islam among the bulk of the population in Bagirmi appears to have been paralleled with the continuation of belief in elements of traditional religion. Cordell (1985:41) mentions how Fulani clerics, who might have entered Bagirmi as early as the fifteenth century, condemned the Bagirmi rulers for 'trying to reconcile the demands of orthodox Islam with the traditional beliefs of many of their subjects'. Levtzion (1985b:183) further notes how Barth remarked on the bulk of the population of Bagirmi still being non-Muslim during the time of his visit in the mid-nineteenth century – that is, several centuries after *Mbang* Abdullah's conversion. Thus, in this respect, it is similar to the patterns of Islamisation noted in parts of the western Sahel, as evident in the time-lag in conversion by many sedentary agriculturists.

The persistence of traditional religions is reflected, as in the Kotoko Logone-Birni palace, in the capital of Bagirmi, Boum Massenia. This was occupied from the foundation of the kingdom in the early sixteenth century through to its abandonment in 1898 (A. M. D. Lebeuf 1967:215). Elaborate spatial symbolism underlay the plan and construction, not only of the city, but also of the ruler's palace. The walled city, an oval shape some 6.5 km in length, was the seat of government and of the *mbang*, and was divided into several quarters (mainly made up of impermanent structures), with the palace complex, the *ger*, at its heart (**figure 6.9**). Barma (Bagirmi) cosmology was reflected in the town plan, which symbolised the head and four limbs of a sacrificial animal, while the ramparts were thought to represent a serpent biting its tail (Paques 1977:22). The *ger*, which included a mosque, indicating the recurrent juxtaposition of Islam and traditional religion, was equally highly spatially structured (A. M. D. Lebeuf 1967:224–5), but 'l'orientation est inverse de celle de la ville, rappelle ainsi l'opposition des chemins du soleil et de la lune' (Paques 1977:196). The whole came together, again in the words of Paques (1977:22), to create 'une figuration du cosmos après le sacrifice primordial'. This meaning emphasises another of the recurring elements of African traditional religions – sacrifice – which, to repeat B. C. Ray's (1976:17) definition, functions as 'a re-creation of the group's solidarity', the 'supreme prayer', as described by Zahan (1970:33). This interlinking of sacrifice, cosmology and spatial layout was of similar significance among the next ethnic group to be considered, the Hausa.

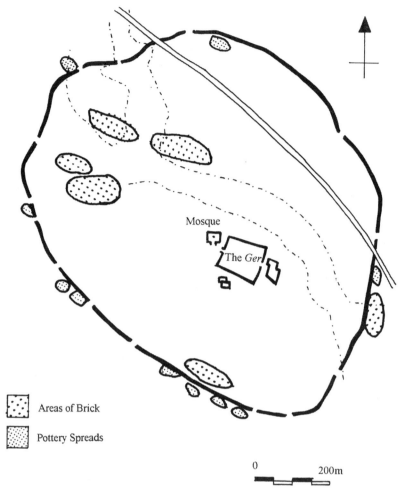

Figure 6.9 Boum Massenia

In summary, the central Sudan can be seen to be filled with various polities of differing size, the inhabitants of which interpreted Islam in similarly
varying ways. Kanem-Borno might be regarded as the most Islamised, but even
here facets of traditional religious expression and authority remained unaltered,
such as the elements of divine rule described. The adaptation of religion to local context and requirements was earlier described as a universal (Mosse 1994),
and no reason to disagree with this statement has been isolated so far. Within
the central Sudan, as throughout sub-Saharan Africa, adaptation of Islam has
occurred with the incorporation of traditional religious elements as an adjunct
to those of the new religion. This, as we have seen, might take place for a
variety of reasons, notably the perpetuation of systems of authority through

integrating the old and the new. The blending of 'heterogeneous beliefs and practices' (van der Veer 1994:208) and amalgamation are key concepts here in the central Sudan – and, indeed, throughout the continent south of the Sahara. Yet a reaction to these processes, what could be termed 'anti-syncretism' or 'denial' (Shaw and Stewart 1994:12), was to occur across the central Sudan and throughout West Africa. This will be discussed later, but it is now necessary to look at what were, besides Kanem-Borno, the other most significant Islamised polities in the central Sudan, the Hausa kingdoms.

The Hausa kingdoms

Origins and early Islam

Even within the Hausa kingdoms the influence of Kanem-Borno was felt as the latter acted as one of the conduits for the spread of Islam into Hausaland. The Hausa are one of the dominant ethnic groups in the central Sudan (and beyond), and the term Hausa 'properly refers to the Hausa language and by extension to those who speak Hausa as a mother tongue' (Works 1976:vii). Although indisputably a people indigenous to the region, previously it was believed that the Hausa kingdoms owed their origins to outside influences, an interpretative process reminiscent of those described elsewhere in the continent. Logan (1929:402), for example, describes the Hausa ancestors as 'originally from wandering Arab tribes who had crossed the Red Sea and gradually worked across the desert'.

Such origin theories are in part interwoven with Hausa origin traditions, like that concerning Bayajida who travelled from Borno, Kanem or Baghdad, 'who slew the snake that controlled the well of Daura, and of his son Bawo and further offspring who supposedly established the seven original kingdoms' (Sutton 1979:179; and see M. G. Smith 1964:340–1; Fugelstad 1978). This is a reference to the Hausa *bokwoi*, the seven original city-states of Daura, Zaria or Zazzau, Biram, Kano, Rano, Katsina and Gobir. The list always numbers seven, but is sometimes subject to some variation as to composition (Sutton 1979:195). This list is possibly also in part subdivided according to city function – as indicated, for example, by Kano sometimes being referred to as 'king of indigo' or Zaria as 'king of slaves' (Adamu 1984:270). *Bokwoi* refers to the original city-states, though frequently the term *birane* (sing. *birni*) is also used to refer to the old Hausa capitals as well as 'those of new emirates of the *jihad* period, notably Bauchi' (Sutton 1976:1). The other term commonly used to describe Hausa settlements is *garuruwa* (sing. *gari*) which refers to villages and small towns (Sutton 1976).

As noted, influence from Kanem-Borno to the east was felt in Hausaland; but equally, Islamic influences were also exerted by Muslim Mande and Songhai

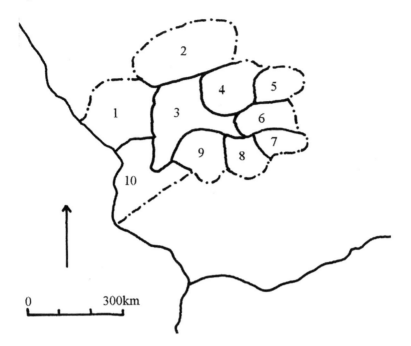

1. Kebbi. 2. Gobir. 3. Zamfara. 4. Katsina. 5. Daura. 6. Kano. 7. Rano. 8. Zaria.
9. Gwari. 10. Yawri

Figure 6.10 The Hausa states *c.*1400 according to Davidson

missionaries from the west (**figure 6.10**, and see chapter 7). Interestingly, trade
does not appear to have been the dominant reason for the introduction of
Islam, or the mechanism by which it was dispersed in Hausaland (Trimingham
1968:18). The foreign merchant element of such significance in the western
Sahel, for example, here appears of little importance. In contrast, the role of
the *mallams*, the local holy men, was of fundamental importance in spreading Islam (Greenberg 1946:69–70). Levtzion (2000:83) makes the point that
the first Muslim clerics came from Mali, i.e. Mande, but that the coming of
Islam to Kano 'coincided with the shift of the Saifawa dynasty from Kanem
to Bornu'. This, therefore, gives a date of the late fourteenth century or there-
abouts. Initially, conversion was on a limited scale, and the influence of Islam was again restricted to the court circle, with elements of *shari'ah*, and
administration using Arabic, being introduced, while the bulk of the population remained non-Muslim and were thus barely affected (Hiskett 1994:108–9).
From the sixteenth century, Griffeth (1981:156) argues that Islam provided the
dominant cultural orientation for the populations of the cities in Hausaland,
but traditional religion (see below) in the countryside or in the smaller states
'was never entirely displaced by Islam'.

As in many of the regions considered in this study, an impetus provided by Islam, or Muslims, was equally not responsible for the origins of urbanism, i.e. for the formation of the Hausa towns. These pre-date the arrival of Islam in the region, and they grew large and then attracted international attention (Griffeth 1981:152). However, it is also necessary to record that their origins remain largely unclear, as little archaeological research has been done in the Hausa *bokwoi*, or in the 'Bastard Seven', a further group of related non-Hausa states, some of which were Islamised over time (but see Haour 1999). Having said this, various elements can be seen to have been of significance in the foundation of the Hausa cities. At Zaria, for example, Acri and Bitiyong (1983:2) suggest that the increased production of iron tools in the seventh century meant that agricultural output was accordingly expanded and craft specialisation could be better supported. This facilitated the development of urbanism in Hausaland, which in turn was assisted by the fact that the Hausa city-states were located in a region of relatively fertile soils and good rainfall (Griffeth 1981:176).

Initially, naturally defensible areas such as rock features or inselbergs were often utilised, as at Kano and Zaria (Darling n.d.a:6), until population expansion meant that man-made fortifications were built and settlements grew and expanded across their surrounding plains. The inselbergs served a variety of purposes – as defensive refuges, possibly important in the face of slave raiding, but also as potential sources of iron-rich laterite as at Kano (Nast 1996:49). The inselbergs also served the purpose of storing groundwater, as 'large well-jointed granite masses are capable of storing considerable quantities of water through percolation' (Mortimore 1970:106). The water can be released as springs at the base of these prominent hills. The recurrence of including inselbergs in early Hausa settlements is a feature frequently referred to (Sutton 1976; Griffeth 1981; Mortimore 1970). Kano encloses two (**figure 6.11**), the 162-ha enclosed site of Burumburum envelops several (Darling n.d.b:4), while Moughtin (1985:10) makes the point that 'some smaller settlements stand at the foot of other similar formations, while inselbergs not associated with settlements today show evidence of earlier occupation'.

The evidence for settlement to which Moughtin (1985) refers is varied and is as yet little studied. Mortimore (1970:107) describes various features and artefacts recorded at inselberg sites. These include stone walls, grinding hollows, hollows used for the local game *ayo*, portable stone pestles and mortars, polished stone axes, pottery (including types interpreted at one site, Turunku, as being specifically used for storing and transporting water (Effah-Gyamyi 1986:129)), and a group of terracotta figurines from an inselberg north-west of Zaria (otherwise unspecified, though Darling (n.d.a:6) refers to 2,000-year-old terracottas being found at Kwartakwashi, perhaps the location being referred to). Sutton (1977) also investigated the remains of a settlement site on the lower forward spur of the inselberg of Kufena, near Zaria, and recorded a similar range

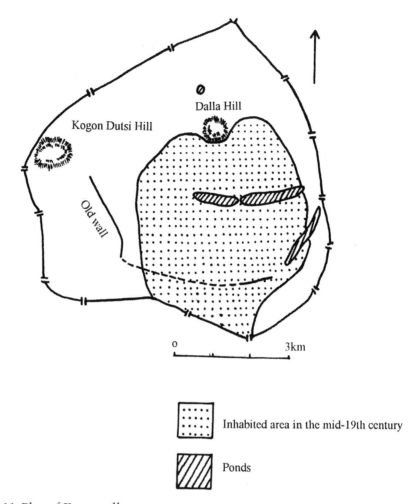

Figure 6.11 Plan of Kano walls

of material at this site and in its surrounding area – hut bases, stone axes and grinding stones, 'altars' (possibly a type of stone seat), grinding hollows, and at the base of the inselberg, a burial site 'marked by pots laid horizontally in line' (Sutton 1977:13). Botanical remains also appear to attest to the antiquity of settlement at inselberg sites, for Mortimore (1970) also mentions finding *Ensete gilletii*, the male banana, and possibly the 'vestige of an ancient crop complex, now almost vanished from West Africa'. Furthermore, as settlements grew, agricultural land was frequently included within the walls as well, as with the deep rich *fadama* soils included within the walls at the site of Turunku (Effah-Gyamyi 1986:122).

Yet thus far, besides the reference to the figurines, interpretations as to the significance of settlement on inselbergs or their later enclosure within larger settlements has focused upon purely functional reasons. Of equal – if not greater – importance was the ritual meaning of the inselbergs. Oral tradition suggests that proximity to the traditional Hausa nature spirits was also a factor in the original foundation of several of the Hausa settlements (Griffeth 1981:154). The Dalla hill at Kano functioned in this capacity, as an abode of spirits (A. Smith 1970:340), and where 'lived Barbushe, the priest of a spirit who dwelt in a sacred tree and received sacrifices of goats, fowls and dogs from his worshippers' (M. G. Smith 1964:341). The Kano Chronicle records that Barbushe lived on Dalla hill some time before the tenth century, and Last (1979) has argued that this settlement system centred on Dalla hill came into prominence between the twelfth and fourteenth centuries, with it 'defeating and dispersing' (Nast 1996:49) the neighbouring settlements of Santolo and Fangwai. Interestingly, the fourteenth century was when Islamic influences also began in Kano, perhaps a factor in the pre-eminence of Dalla hill – though it must also be added that Islam in Kano is not recognised as being 'firmly established' (Nast 1996:53) in the Kano Chronicle and oral tradition until the reign of King Rumfa (1463–99).

Hausa traditional religion

The inselbergs as dwelling places of the *iskoki*, or spirits, was obviously of significance and within traditional Hausa religion the *iskoki* functioned as the arbiters of daily human affairs, with above them the high god Ubangiji. The system of Hausa traditional religion thus in many respects parallels the general patterns defined in chapter 1, Ubangiji being remote and not interfering in day-to-day affairs (Moughtin 1985:22), and the *iskoki* resembling the intermediary spirits, the focus of ritual practice whose existence has been identified elsewhere in this study. Moughtin (1985) describes how relationships were maintained with the *iskoki* – through a ritual specialist, the *mai-gida*, in each compound, the *sarkin-noma* for agricultural rituals, and through the king on behalf of the state. To these could be added a priest class, or *bokaye*, 'skilled in contacting the spirits (Bori in this condition), who would speak through them'. Bori is the name of a spirit possession cult very similar to the Zar cult of the Nilotic Sudan described in chapter 3. Bori continues to this day, and has been described as 'a kind of unofficial religion that predates Islam and provides an alternative source of help in times of trouble' (Callaway 1987:84). It is especially popular among women (Onwuejeogwu 1972; Callaway and Creevey 1994).

Yet it would be incorrect to say that the Bori cult represents the sole survival of pre-Islamic traditional Hausa religion. The Maguzawa, or non-Muslim Hausa, allow further insight into traditional religious practice. However, to refer to them as non-Muslim is slightly misleading in itself, for they now 'freely admit that Allah is the ultimate control of the universe' (Greenberg 1946:27). Practices and devotions might be addressed to the *iskoki*, but the high god would appear to have been Islamised, and thus this is further reminiscent of processes of religious change noted elsewhere, as among the Nuba in chapter 3. Although decreasing in number and found in rural areas only, Maguzawa ritual practices include making sacrifices to the *iskoki* at their specific locales – notably, to Kure, the son of Inna who is the mother of all the spirits, and whose favourite habitat is the *dasi* tree, one of which is found in most Maguzawa compounds, and at the base of which offerings of guinea corn and blood sacrifices are made (Greenberg 1946).

Sacred trees and trees as archaeological indicators

The almost universal importance of sacred trees in sub-Saharan African traditional religion is a feature worth commenting on (see, e.g., Mbiti 1970:111–12). Zahan (1970:27) has interpreted their importance as being due to their offering 'complete material bases for conceptualizations, since all of nature seems to bond together to accomplish those syntheses which, in their eyes [followers of African traditional religions], vegetable species represent'. Although this interpretation is subject to debate, the existence of trees, sacred or otherwise, can have more than theoretical or theological importance to the archaeologist. The baobab tree, for example, a species unique to Africa, can be of especial significance to the archaeologist, as Sutton (1977:14) notes, in refering to the baobab as 'so commonly an indicator of former settlement'. Practical examples of their role as indicators of sites of historical importance abound. Within the central Sudan, Effah-Gyamyi (1986), for instance, mentions the presence of baobab trees at the site of Turunku, which, according to tradition, was the ancestral seat of Zaria, and where the baobabs, probably of more secular than sacred importance, attest to the antiquity of settlement. Similarly on the East African coast, baobab trees are an invaluable indicator of former settlements; as LaViolette and Fleisher (1995:62) note, 'baobab trees, native to the savanna and not the littoral, are usually a sign of habitation sites on the coast, and are often associated with Swahili settlements'.

Issa (1995:67–70) also describes a useful purpose served by the jujube (rhemnus) tree on Zanzibar. The leaves of this tree were used for washing the dead, as they become soapy in water. Thus the tree acts as a marker for graveyards, 'even in areas where tombs have been demolished' (Issa 1995:70). Trees have served other purposes in historical reconstruction as well. On the opposite side of the continent, in Zimbabwe and Botswana, for example, Guy (1967) has utilised baobabs as a source of evidence in reconstructing the routes used by European explorers, individuals such as David Livingstone, in traversing this region. This was achieved through comparing sketches of baobabs in the European explorers' accounts with trees still flourishing, and through the records of initials carved on some of these trees.

Elements of Hausa traditional religion might also become incorporated within Muslim practice, though frequently they were also diluted. Moughtin (1985:24) relates how *bokaye* came to share power with *mallams*, and how *iskoki* might be demoted to the category of harmless *jinn*, types of spirits found across the Muslim world. Similarly, traditional Hausa settlement structure and orientation 'governed by an ancient cosmology which regulates numerous facets of daily life' (Moughtin 1985:34) could sit side by side with Islam, or could disappear. In fact, the happy coincidence of Hausa orientation to Mecca being to the east, correlating with the traditional Hausa emphasis on the east as direction of birth and sacrifice, for example, means the traditional orientation frequently continues (see Nicolas 1966). This is something which has also been considered by Darling (1985:7) with reference to the alignment of archaeological sites, and he makes the point that alignments vary widely. In certain instances, however, realignment to face Mecca can be picked up, as at the site of Avyo, where the northern wall of one of two 75-ha overlapping rectangular enclosures had been realigned to face Mecca (Darling n.d.b:5). Thus continuity, acknowledged or unacknowledged – or, equally, an abrupt break with older traditions – could exist. An example of the latter is provided by King Rumfa's construction of his palace outside the walled city at Kano, an action interpreted by Nast (1996:54) as 'the symbolic and physical distancing of the aristocracy from pre-Islamic practices in the city'.

The city-states

Once founded, the Hausa settlements grew to incorporate all the elements of urban life that might be expected: markets, mosques, areas of industry and of housing – the latter being the mud-walled compound or *gida* reflecting Hausa social structure, as exemplified by wife seclusion, and the 'hierarchical organisation' of polygamous family life (Griffeth 1981:156). Although archaeological evidence might be sparse, a variety of information on various aspects of the developed Hausa settlement can be gained from recent studies of the Hausa towns, and also from observations made since Europeans, such as Heinrich Barth (1890), first travelled through the region from the mid-nineteenth century onwards. Barth, for instance, provides a vivid picture of towns such as Katsina and Kano. The inhabited areas of Kano are described as never 'filling up' the immense space comprised within the walls' (1890:297), with the quarters within largely divided according to ethnic composition, and Dalá or Dalla 'the most ancient quarter'. Housing was a mix of clay houses and thatched huts, with the clay houses of 'Arab' style built 'with no other purpose than that of obtaining the greatest possible privacy for domestic life, without any attempt to provide for the influx of fresh air and light' (Barth 1890:299). A further comment by Barth also agrees with the functional label ascribed to Kano and referred to previously, in that weaving and dyeing are described as the most important industries.

However, the proviso must also be added that much of what was observed by travellers such as Barth was not a 'fossilised' reflection of the city-state period but post-dates the period of Fulani conquest. The Fulani, as a reaction against their perception of the impurity of Islam in the region, which led to the *jihad* being started in the early nineteenth century (see below and Johnston 1967), deliberately destroyed many of the pre-*jihad* monuments and historical documents (Schacht 1954), the so-called *habe* legacy. Thus besides the walls of various settlements, certain standing monuments belong to the initial period of Islamisation in the *bokwoi*, but these are few in number. At Katsina, the core of the Gobirau 'tower' or minaret is said to be 300 years old, while the Masallaci Juma'a mosque in Zaria apparently also predates the *jihad* period (Dmochowski 1990a:2.10, 2.15, 5.17). A tower comparable to that at Katsina also survived at Bauchi (Moughtin 1972:155). Also, as was described with regard to a possible Ibadi presence in Kanem-Borno and the western Sahel, remnant Ibadi influences have similarly been argued for in some of the mosques of Hausaland (Schacht 1954). Yet in general the material legacy, above ground, of the pre-Fulani era is small, and much of that below ground still awaits investigation.

Where archaeological investigations have been completed the results have been very encouraging, as with research completed in western Hausaland. Here, excavations at the site of Leka (sometimes referred to as Malah or Mali, a name of obvious interest in indicating possible contacts with the Mande) uncovered three occupation levels represented by three floors. The lowest two were paved with potsherds laid flat on the concave side (Obayemi 1977:81), and are reminiscent of the Bornoan floors described previously. Evidence for participation in long-distance trade was also recorded including a 'gastropod-shell currency' (Obayemi 1977:81), multi-coloured glass bracelet fragments and white and multi-coloured glass beads. The shells are described as being identical to ones from Timbuktu, Djenne and Tichitt, where they were 'used as a currency during periods of short supply of cowries and in the Gao–Tumbuktu–Djenne area this could well have been during the seventeenth century' (Obayemi 1977:80). This must be a reference to the use of the koroni currency which was briefly employed in Timbuktu, evidence for which has been found archaeologically, and which was described in the last chapter. Certainly, on the basis of the material present, Obayemi (1977) would appear to be right in ascribing a post-1500 date to Leka.

Thus at this site various facts are indicated by the archaeological evidence, most notably long-distance trade, which was almost certainly directed, for one, to the Niger Bend region, as indicated by the possible koroni currency and also the site nomenclature. Direct evidence for Islam such as mosques or Muslim burials is not described, though an 'ablutions' pot roughly 5.5 cm in diameter and 11.4 cm height, and which 'carries black inscriptions in Arabic characters on the inside' (Obayemi 1977:75), was found by a villager digging for building materials. Yet the small size of this vessel precludes its posited interpretation as an ablutions pot. A more convincing interpretation is that it served a magical or protective role. Similar pots found elsewhere in this region, and elsewhere in sub-Saharan Africa, are usually filled with water, and the water drunk for its protective, healing or magical properties acquired through coming into contact with the inscription (see Owusu-Ansah 2000 for other examples of similar amuletic powers, and Insoll 1999a:125 for general background). However, for this interpretation to be proven, the inscription needs reading.

Other relevant archaeological research which has been completed in Hausaland has primarily been achieved through archaeological survey rather than excavation, and this is described in the next section. In summary, Griffeth (1981:145) is correct in emphasising that, with a few exceptions aside, much of the research completed has neglected the formative period of the Hausa city-states, 'as an era of unrelieved internal competition and warfare'. However, competition and conflict between the Hausa kingdoms was intense, and vivid testimony for this exists in the form of the elaborate fortifications that usually surrounded the major population centres, and in what can be reconstructed of the military strategies and forces that were developed, equipped and employed.

Warfare

The fundamental and surviving legacy of inter-Hausa conflict is provided by the town walls of the region. However, a general preoccupation with defence was not confined to Hausaland alone, but is found across the central Sudan (R. S. Smith 1989; Spring 1993). As Darling (1985:3) notes, Barth recorded over 200 'walled, moated or stockaded settlements' in what is now Nigeria. Also, as has been described, this total is supplemented by others in neighbouring countries – Niger or Chad, for instance. The walls of the central Sudan could take many forms, and in Hausaland were regularly made of *tubali*, 'pear-shaped sun-dried mud bricks embedded in mud mortar' (Darling n.d.b:6), though they could also be of stone or fired brick, or composed of simple earthen ramparts (see also Sutton 1976:2–3). However, the general pattern, as R. S. Smith (1989:104) notes, is that built ramparts predominate in the savannah, while dump ramparts are found in the forest zone.

Frequently, it is possible to reconstruct the chronology of wall building. At Zaria, for example, various stages of wall building have been isolated as the settlement grew (Sutton 1976, 1977). The initial walls, a sequence named the Kufena, Madarkaci and Tukur-Tukur walls, and possibly dating from as early as the tenth–eleventh centuries, were replaced under Queen Amina (c.1492–1522) by a new wall 24 km in circumference. This was in part a response to the earlier defeat of the Zaria armies by forces from Kano who were using horses and chain mail, then unknown in Zaria (Acri and Bitiyong 1983:3). A similar response to further tactical developments was necessitated around 1700 when the Amina wall was reduced in size to 15.8 km. The height of the wall was also increased, with gates incorporated allowing the defenders to fire on attacking forces, and a thorn hedge included as a first line of defence. A preoccupation with defence also appears to pre-date the period of the mature Hausa city-states, as indicated, for example, by Haour's (1999) work in Niger. Here, at the site of Kufan Kanawa, which according to oral tradition was 'the original location of Kano' (Haour 1999:44), a roughly trapezoidal area of about 200 m × 900 m × 1500 m was enclosed by a wall constructed upon a grass embankment. This, if tradition is to be believed, is thus earlier than the defensive works at its successor, Kano.

Thus the defensive preoccupation in Hausa settlements would appear to have a long history, and it is important to reiterate that these walls were amorphous entities, constantly adapted as circumstances necessitated. The adaptations at Zaria attest to this, and similarly at Kano, where Moody (1967:23–24) suggests there were three phases of wall building. The first dates from the twelfth century, the second from the fifteenth century and the third from the seventeenth century. Unfortunately, severe deterioration of many of these walls, allied with an absence of archaeological information, means that little is known of their morphology over time. Yet these structures could be complex pieces of military engineering. Logan (1929:402), who fortunately observed the Kano walls before they had suffered the depredations of the remainder of the twentieth century, describes how they were built in two great terraces, 'leading up to a fighting platform protected by a continuous battlement'. This first terrace was used by horsemen 'to gallop around and reinforce threatened points' (Logan 1929:402). Besides the permanent walls surrounding the main settlements, various other types of fortifications were used in the central Sudan. Ibn Fartua, for example, refers to fortified or stockaded camps being used during the campaigns of *Mai Idris Aloma* of Kanem-Borno (R. S. Smith 1989:107). This type of temporary camp continued to be used in the later Fulani *jihad* period as well (see below).

Obviously, the elaborate fortifications surrounding both the Hausa cities and many of the other settlements of the central Sudan were not built without reason. Defence against cavalry was one of the primary reasons for their construction, and in this region more than anywhere else in the continent south of the Sahara the use of cavalry appears to have been of central importance. Humphrey Fisher (1973b:362) succinctly encapsulates this in noting that 'the two themes, of cavalry power and walled towns, march hand in hand through early Hausa history'. Why cavalry became of such consequence in Hausaland and throughout the central Sudan could be due to a variety of reasons. One of the most important of these must have been the nature of the terrain. Wide, flat vistas of savannah are ideal country for the use of cavalry, in comparison to the forest zone to the south where horses would have been largely ineffective in dense tree cover, if the tsetse fly had not precluded their keeping anyway (R. S. Smith 1989:90). Tactical and psychological advantages would have been other factors. These are well indicated by MacEachern's (1993:260) point concerning non-Muslim mountain dwellers' views of horsemen in Cameroon: 'Muslims are horsemen and slavers, and the acquisition of horses and conversion to Islam are intimately tied to the beginning of slave-raiding.' The heyday of cavalry in the region lasted from the thirteenth–fourteenth centuries through to the latter part of the nineteenth century. According to R. S. Smith (1989:48), these two dates were probably concurrent, initially with the introduction of larger breeds of horse from North Africa, along with better saddles and stirrups, and latterly with the widespread use of firearms – which rendered cavalry largely redundant.

Yet to make the use of cavalry effective a supply of horses was needed, along with good equipment. It appears, based on Arabic-derived Hausa terminology for saddle, bit and stirrup, that 'horse accoutrement was introduced into West Africa during early Islamic times' (R. S. Smith 1989:78). This might be correct, but it is indisputable that the introduction of the horse into the region pre-dates any Muslim contacts. Within West Africa archaeological evidence for its introduction is not particularly informative (see Fisher 1972, 1973b; Law 1980). Blench (1993:88) has put forward the hypothesis that the domestic horse was present in West Africa as early as 500 BCE. However, this level of precision is unsupported, though in general the point made by Fisher (1972:377), that 'we may accept, then, that the arrival of the horse in the Sudan preceded the arrival of Islam there', can be agreed with. Two major types of horse are found in the central Sudan, the smaller breeds of the southern savannah and the larger horses of North African origin found in Hausa and Kanem-Borno (Spring 1993:44). The supply of new blood that was required for breeding was achieved, according to Fisher (1972:381), by importing horses from across the Sahara. Borno horses were among the best known, though horses were also bred in non-Muslim areas such as the Mandara mountains of northern Cameroon. Their use was similarly not confined to states, but their effective military employment by what are defined as non-Muslim 'stateless' peoples was not usual as they lacked the 'good harness and equipment' (Fisher 1973b:378), and more powerful larger breeds required for their large-scale and efficient use.

The employment of cavalry was almost cyclical in purpose, and conflict was of two types, raiding and warring, distinguished from each other by the size of the military units involved, objectives, timescales and the like (Reyna 1990:144). With the former – raiding – mounted forces could be used to pursue and capture slaves directly, or indirectly slaves could be acquired through success in larger-scale warfare, in which cavalry obviously played a significant role. These slaves could then be used to acquire more horses through being sent north across the Sahara, with horses coming south in return; to quote Griffeth, 'thus completing the circle of economic interconnectedness that linked slave-raiding to the overall military situation' (1981:172). Slaves could also be used to feed soldiers through the produce they grew, therefore further adding to this interconnected chain. At Zaria, for example, slave farms were established for this purpose, with the food produced used 'to feed the palace and the stables'

Figure 6.12 Hausa horsemen, northern Nigeria

(Acri and Bitiyong 1983:6). Similarly, in Zaria, slave soldiers were utilised to supplement military forces. In fact, Goody (1971b) has argued that states in this region were set apart from smaller-scale societies through their extensive use of cavalry in the savannahs, and firearms in the forest zones.

In Hausaland and throughout the central Sudan both light and heavy cavalry were employed. The Shuwa were regarded as the 'most accomplished of mounted spearmen', while the Kanuri held the accolade for the footsoldier equivalent (Spring 1993:44). For, again as Fisher (1973b:362) notes, 'military effectiveness of horses lay not in cavalry alone, but in the intelligent combination of infantry and cavalry'. Both infantry and heavy and light cavalry were utilised in Hausaland. The cavalry forces could be very well equipped, with both horse and rider provided with armour in some of the Hausa states. This would be made of cloth padded with kapok, and was frequently brightly coloured, as is still evident today in the cavalry reviews or pageants which form a part of ceremony in areas of northern Nigeria (**figure 6.12**). Chain mail was also used, though Spring (1993:36) argues that this was not made in the central Sudan but imported from the Nilotic Sudan where it was produced until the 1940s, or from Egypt and elsewhere in North Africa. Metal headgear might also be used, but more frequently basketry was employed, reinforced with cloth and covered with a turban (R. S. Smith 1989:78). Weapons were also varied. These included javelins for light cavalry, and swords and lances for heavy cavalry. Bows and arrows were used but largely as an infantry weapon (Reyna 1990:142), while sword blades were often imported via North Africa from European centres of production such as Marseilles and Bordeaux in France, and later, Solingen in Germany. These would be fitted with a handle and scabbard in the central Sudan, and sometimes also with a talismanic Arabic inscription etched on the blade (Spring 1993:32).

The use of firearms is first mentioned in the central Sudan in the late sixteenth century. This is a reference to Turkish musketeers being employed by *Mai* Idris Aloma (R. S. Smith 1989:82). However, they did not come into common use until the latter part of the nineteenth century. This hiatus between their introduction and wide-scale use stands in contrast to the situation regarding firearms in the interior of south-central and east-central Africa, where the pursuit of firearms could lead rulers to sell their own people (see chapter 8). Initially, firearms, and importantly, the people who could use them, were acquired from North Africa, and the subsequent sequence of their spread in the central Sudan has been charted by Fisher and Rowland (1971:216): 'Bornu first, through trans-Saharan contacts; Hausaland next, probably from Bornu; Darfur later, trading with Egypt; and finally Wadai'. The introduction of firearms was also, ultimately, to seal the fate of walls as an effective form of defence, for gunpowder allowed them to be more easily breached, as occurred in 1870 at Massenia in Bagirmi when a 'copper-coated basket full of powder' (Fisher and Rowland 1971:226) was buried under the wall and detonated. Likewise, the ubiquity of firearms rendered cavalry obsolete, ending this chapter in the military history of the central Sudan.

The Fulani jihad

Yet a new one was to be emerge, and it has already been mentioned how the Fulani *jihads* of the early nineteenth century in part arose as a response to the perceived lax Islam of the Hausa city-states. *Jihad*, or holy war, 'the spread of Islam by arms', and often the subject of fear and stereotypes in the West, is, according to Gibb and Kramers, 'a religious duty upon Muslims in general' (1961:89), and the only type of war authorised and regulated by Islamic law (Peters 1977:3). As noted previously, according to orthodox Muslim doctrine two major domains exist in the world: the *dar al-harb*, the land or abode of war; and the *dar al-Islam*, the land of Islam. Within the latter, Muslim rule is established, Islamic law is in place and non-Muslim peoples have submitted to Muslim control. The creation of the latter is the object of *jihad* (Insoll 1999a). The Fulani *jihads* could be described in their aims as 'anti-syncretic', as described by Shaw and Stewart (1994:7). Yet the notion of anti-syncretism, if we are to use this as a definition for the ethos underpinning the *jihads*, must also be considered, for it is not value free. It too is a construct with its associated claims of 'authenticity' and 'purity', and with it frequently acting, as Shaw and Stewart (1994:12) also note, as a 'dominant reading in discourses of nationalist, ethnic or regional identity'. Essentially, the Fulani *jihads* might equate with what Eaton (1993) would define as a phase of 'displacement', yet they too served a purpose wider than merely eradicating what was perceived as lax Islam and practices integrated from traditional religions.

The Fulani

The Fulani are one of the major ethnic groups of West Africa and the central Sudan, and are dispersed over a vast area of some 3,000 km stretching from Senegal in the west to beyond Lake Chad in the east. They are known by different names according to where they are found. These include Fula, Fulani (actually a Hausa term), Peul, Felaata, or Fulbe. The latter is the term actually used by the Fulani, along with the singular, Pullo (Stenning 1959:2). The origins of the Fulani have been much debated – Near Eastern, Ethiopian and Arabian origins have all been posited – but in reality they are a people indigenous to West Africa. Subdivision of the Fulani is in part based upon subsistence mode and, contrary to frequent misconceptions which see the Fulani as wholly composed of pastoral nomads, settled Fulani communities are also found, as represented by the Khassonke of Kayes in Mali for instance (Stenning 1959:4–9). Owing to their initiatory role in the *jihads* of the late eighteenth and nineteenth centuries in West

Africa and the central Sudan, the Fulani are frequently also portrayed as zealously and totally Muslim. Again this is not wholly the case. De St Croix (1945), though acknowledging that almost all Fulani are Muslims, describes the range of spirits that exist in traditional Fulani religion, the *hendu* or *keni*, as well as a variety of practices connected with spirit possession and magic.

Other factors that underlay this 'new broom' of Islamic revival which swept across the central and western Sudan included the endemic competition between the nomadic (largely Fulani) and sedentary populations over land, and the general political state of the region. Thus a bundle of circumstances contributed to the start of the *jihads*. Although the original *jihad* state was in Futa Djallon (see chapter 7), in Hausaland initially a preaching – rather than military – *jihad* was started under the leadership of Uthman dan Fodio in 1804. Uthman was a Fulani of Degel in Gobir and a preacher who 'was at pains to point out the errors and shortcomings of the Hausa' (Stenning 1959:15). This, however, was largely unsuccessful and, following a battle with the son of the king of Gobir, Yunfa, at Kwotto Lake in June 1804, a battle which Uthman won, he was declared 'Commander of the Faithful' and a holy war was declared. Between 1804 and 1832 Uthman dan Fodio, along with his sons, rapidly 'created a vast empire' (R. S. Smith 1989:32), on the ruins of Hausa and other states. Kano, Katsina, Zaria and Daura were taken by 1810, Sokoto was established as a base, Fulani dynasties were also established in Nupe and Ilorin, and new Fulani kingdoms were established, as at Adamawa (Kirk-Greene 1958; Hogben and Kirk-Greene 1966; Johnston 1967). Borno was also affected by the Fulani *jihad*. Birni Ngazargamo was sacked by Fulani armies in 1808, but help was received from Kanem via a Kanembu chief or *shehu*, Laminu (Cohen 1967:17). Further assistance was provided to Borno from the same source in 1811–12, but the final outcome was that the *shehu* took over real power in Borno and established a capital at Kukawa, leaving only a titular Sefuwa dynasty in place (Brenner 1973). Gronenborn (2001:119) provides a summary of the historical descriptions of Kukawa, and also makes the point that besides two brief surveys undertaken in the early 1990s, no detailed archaeological research has yet been completed in the city.

The social, political and religious effects of the Fulani *jihads* were manifold. Militarily, the resultant wave pattern of fortifications, as outlined by Darling (1985:7), has already been described. Fortification building was encouraged by the *jihad* leaders, as a means of frontier defence (Bonfiglioli 1988:64), and a new form of fortified structure appeared, the *ribat*. This has been described as 'a base from which to prosecute Holy war' (Hillenbrand 1994:331), and analogous, in effect, to a type of 'fortified monastery' which is found on many of the frontiers of the Muslim world (Insoll 1999a:139). However, what might start as merely a territorial defence element could in turn develop into a sizeable settlement, as soldiers were joined by other officials, and mosques, markets and houses for camp followers and dependants were built beside the military installation (Bonfiglioli 1988). The *ribats* serve also as a material manifestation of the break with the past, indicated both in their orientation and layout. This is something commented upon by Darling (n.d.b:6), who makes the point that they 'were rectilinear and orientated at about 75° to face Mecca: they were usually sited away from the hills where *iskoki* were thought to dwell'. The latter point is of interest, for depending on how one reads the question of location, it could either indicate revulsion for the old beliefs, as might be expected, or alternatively, the continuation of a certain guarded respect for them.

In general, many possibilities still exist for archaeological research on sites associated with the *jihad* period. However, a variety of architectural information exists, and various post-*jihad* monuments in the region are described, for example, by Dmochowski (1990a, 1990b). These include both Hausa and Fulani structures, which differ in character, with rectangular architecture characteristic of the former, and circular of the latter. A further characteristic of Fulani architecture is the use of impermanent materials in religious, military and domestic structures. Barth (1890:428) refers to a mosque he visited in the Fulani settlement of úba in Adamawa as a quadrangular building 'consisting entirely of halls built of mats and stalks'. This is very similar to a standing structure, also in Adamawa, at Gurin, described by Dmochowski (1990a:2.40) as open in plan, and built of cornstalks, grass and wood. Brick and earthen structures were also built. Barth (1890:461) again refers to the governor's house at Yola being built of clay. Uthman dan Fodio's tomb in Sokoto was also built of more permanent materials and is described by Schacht as an 'unadorned structure of brick, with a square ground plan' (1957a:135–6). The central tomb is surrounded by the tombs of Uthman's descendants. Interestingly, it has also become the object of pilgrimage, leading to a full circle being turned, for, as Schacht remarks, the Fulani sought to eradicate such customs, as 'contrary to pure Islam', but 'gave rise, in turn, to the same customs' (1957a:136).

Yet it is also indisputable that one of the effects of the Fulani *jihad* was to mark the turning point in greatly increasing Islamic conversion among the Hausa, certainly in the rural environment (see, e.g., Greenberg 1946). However, Griffeth goes as far as to suggest that the construction of large central mosques in the Hausa cities did not occur until the period of Fulani rule in the nineteenth century. Prior to this, he argues, the ruler's palace and market were 'more significant physical landmarks' than the mosques (1981:156). Yet such an interpretation would appear flawed, as both architectural and historical evidence suggests that congregational mosques existed well before the Fulani period within the Hausa urban environment. This is indicated, for instance, by records that King Rumfa built a congregational mosque and minaret over a traditional religious site in Kano in the latter half of the fifteenth century (Nast 1996:54). Sutton (1976:9) equally refers to a 'reputed' site of a 'Friday mosque of pre-Fulani times' in Zaria. Instead, based upon parallels drawn from patterns already considered elsewhere, as in the western Sahel in the last chapter, it can be suggested that both the twin pillars of Islam and traditional religion supported authority prior to the *jihad* era. Following the *jihads*, traditional religions declined or were further interwoven with Islam as recorded by Greenberg (1946), Moughtin (1985) or Callaway (1987).

Dar al-Kuti

Other polities existed in the central Sudan which were largely unaffected by the Fulani *jihad*. One of these was Wadai and its satellites such as the Dar al-Kuti sultanate, established south of the Aouk river (in the present-day Central African Republic) in the nineteenth century. Dar al-Kuti can be considered as the true frontier between Islam and traditional religions in central Africa, and in discussing it the very heart of the continent is reached **(See figure 6.1)**. It was here that Arab slavers and traders, travelling north-west from Zanzibar, made inroads into the Ulele-Ubangi basin in search of slaves and ivory in the nineteenth century (Levtzion 1985b, and see chapter 8 below). Slaving missions were also made into this region by Muslim Fulani from Ngaoundere, vassals of the sultan of Yola to the west, and from Wadai, Bagirmi and the Chadian borderlands of Dar Runga in the north (Cordell 1985; Kalck 1993). Slavery was endemic in this region and has thus had a great influence upon both the practice and perceptions of Islam and Muslims in this area, where neither Muslim dress nor Arabic as a language is 'a reliable index of belief' (Cordell 1985:96).

Dar al-Kuti prospered through participation in the slave and ivory trade, though it would be incorrect to assume that from its inception in the 1820s the trade in these commodities was wholly controlled by foreign Muslim traders. Cordell (1985) makes the important point that the first Muslims to enter the region were small groups of traders who exchanged cloth predominantly for ivory, with slaves only later becoming of primary importance as a trade item. Significantly, local people in many instances were responsible for exchanging captives taken from their neighbours for the goods offered by the northern traders. Gradually these traders put down permanent roots and the scale of slave raiding increased with more direct participation by the foreign traders. The second phase could be said to have begun in the 1870s with the development of centralised authority in Dar al-Kuti under Muslim control. Three main settlements developed in this region: Sha, Mongo-Kuti and Kali. Political events accelerated after this, with in 1890 the deposition of the local ruler, Kobur, from his capital at Kali by the Sudanese adventurer Rabih, and the installation of a new ruler in Dar al-Kuti, al-Sanusi (Cordell 1986).

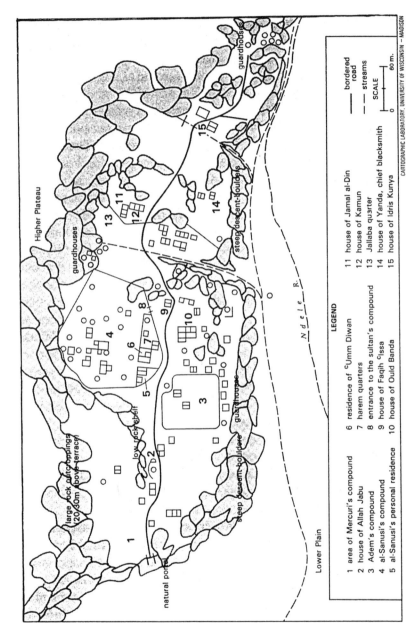

Figure 6.13 Plan of Ndele

LEGEND

1 area of Mercuri's compound
2 house of Allah Jabu
3 Adem's compound
4 al-Sanusi's compound
5 al-Sanusi's personal residence

6 residence of ʿUmm Diwan
7 harem quarters
8 entrance to the sultan's compound
9 house of Faqih ʿIssa
10 house of Ould Banda

11 house of Jamal al-Din
12 house of Kamun
13 Jallaba quarter
14 house of Yanda, chief blacksmith
15 house of Idris Kunya

bordered road

streams

SCALE

0   60 m.

CARTOGRAPHIC LABORATORY, UNIVERSITY OF WISCONSIN – MADISON

Rabih

Rabih is a character who looms large in the history of Islam in the central and Nilotic Sudan in the late nineteenth century. A slave raider and adventurer, his influence extended over a vast region from Darfur to Borno (Works 1976:28). Besides being instrumental in replacing the leader of Dar al-Kuti with one of his own lieutenants, al-Sanusi, he also sacked Kukawa and drove the traditional ruler of Dikwa out of power before assuming authority personally. Rabih followed this by having a fortified palace built for himself and his two sons in the centre of Dikwa, to the east of the traditional meeting place, the *dendal*. This palace contained all the elements necessary for rule, and besides his personal quarters also contained a barracks, stable and harem. Rabih was killed in 1900 and his palace partly ransacked before being taken over as a base for the German colonial authorities (Gronenborn and Magnavita 2000). A test excavation has been completed near Rabih's palace which uncovered various burnt layers possibly associated with the French campaign at the beginning of the twentieth century. Pottery familiar in other areas bearing sgraffito and twisted-strip roulette decoration was also found dated to the late nineteenth century, and indicative of a change in 'ethnic self-identification' and the adoption of the Kanuri language (Gronenborn 2001:124). In other words this signalled Kanurisation once again, a process already described.

As Works (1976:29) notes, al-Sanusi owed 'his prosperity and independence from Dar Runga and Wadai to Rabih'. He quickly gathered around him Muslim advisers from Tripoli, Darfur and even Zanzibar as a means of stabilising his authority, and in the early 1890s founded a new capital, Ndele. The remains of Ndele have been surveyed (Cordell 1985, 1986), and an initial factor in its location appears to have been defence. The nucleus of the city, the royal citadel, was placed on a 'high, well-watered platform', which the city gradually outgrew, spreading onto the plains below (Cordell 1985:83). Initially, straw and earthen architecture was used, but as wealth grew through slave raiding a pentagonal stone-and-earthen central complex was built on the flank of this high plateau covering an area of about 800 m east–west and 250 m at its widest point. This comprised the ruler's living quarters and audience area, a harem and, importantly, the only congregational mosque and Qur'an school in the settlement **(figure 6.13)**. The restriction of these elements to the ruler's quarters is a reflection of the intertwining of religious and secular power, and something often present in early Islamic settlements (Insoll 1999a), with perhaps an allusion to this being made here.

But besides Islam providing 'the ideological underpinnings of the city and the state' (Cordell 1985:79), Cordell (1986:347) also makes the point that al-Sanusi attempted to incorporate 'local earth chiefs and non-Muslim rituals' into his activities in an attempt 'to institutionalize his rule'. This is reminiscent of processes described already for many other areas of the continent. In fact, Trimingham (1962:219) has described Dar al-Kuti as a vague religious borderland where 'chiefs and trading villages received an Islamic orientation'. He further describes the region as covered with a Muslim veneer which was apparent among certain individuals, and outwardly visible through Muslim dress, Arabic names and the use of appellations such as sultan or sultanate. It is unlikely that this is a wholly accurate description, for, as we have seen, interpretations of Islam vary greatly not only in sub-Saharan Africa but across the Muslim world. However, the threat of slave raids might have led some individuals to adopt the trappings of Islam, without the accompanying beliefs.

Slave trading provided the funds, as noted, for the development of Ndele, and the scale of slave raiding increased once firearms were common in both Dar al-Kuti and across the central Sudan in the late nineteenth century. Yet not everyone could be enslaved. The prescriptions and rules applying to slavery from a Muslim perspective were touched upon in the last chapter, where it was noted that within the Qur'an, slavery is regarded as a recognised institution. People were quantified according to who was enslavable. J. R. Willis (1985a:18) describes how, for example, the Muslim scholar Ahmed Baba 'points a contrast between those lands known to have come over to Islam, such as Bornu, Kano, Mali, Songhai, Gobir, Katsina, and Gao, and those which remained under the threat of *jihad*, such as Mossi, Gurma, Bobo, Busa, Dogon, and Yoruba'. The latter groups within the *dar al-harb* were thus fair game for the focus of slave raids, for, as Hunwick (1992:11) notes, 'it became commonly accepted that since the peoples of the *Dar al-Harb* were non-Muslims and hence liable to be attacked in a *jihad*, they were also all potential slaves'.

However, it is as well to remember, as Fisher and Fisher (1970:7) sensibly state, that sometimes 'it is difficult to draw a sharp line between characteristics of African slavery which were survivals of pre-Muslim practice, and those which were imported later'. Yet although a degree of complexity in rules pertaining to slavery has to be recognised, it is also true that economic motivation sometimes did not encourage the propagation of Islam, as sources of slaves would then dry up, owing to prohibitions (not always observed) on enslaving fellow Muslims. As Fisher and Fisher (1970:23) again note, the German explorer Gustav Nachtigal, when travelling through parts of Africa between 1869 and 1874, observed that the inhabitants of Bagirmi 'made no effort to share the blessings of Islam with their pagan neighbours' for just such reasons.

The material correlates of slavery vary considerably, and are often ephemeral, as has already been described in chapter 5. In Dar al-Kuti and its surrounding region, *zaribas* (temporary fortified enclosures) and *dems* (depots) were often used as holding pens and forward camps by slaving missions. These could become quite substantial settlements, as with Dem Zubayr, the capital of al-Zubayr, an ally of the Zande kings, whose depot was established in the Bahr al-Ghazal region of the Nilotic Sudan (Kalck 1993). In the 1860s region was thick with slave-raiding depots, which were placed at intervals of every 30 km or so (Cordell 1986:340). Thus they were ubiquitous, and also inevitably played a role in the spread of Islam in the region – for the *zaribas* also served, as Levtzion (1985b:187) notes, to introduce 'a permanent and continuous presence of Muslims in the area', albeit one associated with violence. The slave raiders were subsequently often joined by Muslim holy men, who served to further propagate Islam.

Many of the *zaribas* which were constructed were undoubtedly temporary, with a brushwood palisade and structures built of impermanent materials, but other more lasting structures existed. Cordell (1986:353), for instance, refers to the settlement built by the Kresh warlord Sa'id Baldas on the borders of what is today the Central African Republic and the Nilotic Sudan. When this was visited by the French traveller Prins in 1901 it was home to over 4,000 people, and comprised a core fortified village defended by a clay wall, 5 m thick at the base and topped with bamboo spikes, inhabited by Baldas, other Muslim converts, and his riflemen. Interestingly, the term *zariba* has also been applied to certain of the settlements associated with pilgrim and trader communities in parts of the central Sudan. Works (1976:43), for instance, describes the *zariba* of the Hausa at Abéché, formerly part of Wadai (see below) in Chad. Initially, this was a small settlement surrounded by a thorn fence, which grew more permanent, the thorn fence being replaced by thick earthen walls pierced by two gates and containing mosques, compounds and industries such as tanneries inside. *Zariba* was perhaps an apt term applied by the Wadaians to describe its formative stages, though more frequently such settlements are referred to as *zongo* or 'strangers' quarter' (Birks 1978:144).

Further permanent reminders of the last gasp of the trans-Saharan slave trade directed from areas such as Dar al-Kuti via Wadai are found in the Saharan regions of northern Chad and southern Libya. Here a large number of sites has been recorded, some of which appear to have been associated with the slave trade operating in the eighteenth–nineteenth centuries (see H. Wright 1992 for historical background). At Ouagayi in Chad, for example, a complex of fired-brick structures was recorded, of which two groups of buildings and three courtyards were uncovered (Huard and Bacquié 1964). It is situated between Tripoli and Ouara, the capital of Wadai, and a role in the slave trade is strongly implied as the investigators suggest, and linked with 'une autorité Arabe ou Turque du Fezzan ou de la Tripolitanie comme lieu de groupement de caravanes amenant des esclaves du Ouadai' (Huard and Bacquié 1964:18). Other comparable sites in the Chadian Sahara include Goz Calmai, Kerenegui and Callagodei. It should also be noted that some of these might be associated with the Senusi movement, a religious brotherhood founded around 1843 which established centres in Tibesti, Borku and Wadai (A. M. D. Lebeuf 1962; Cline 1950:19; J. Wright 1989:81).

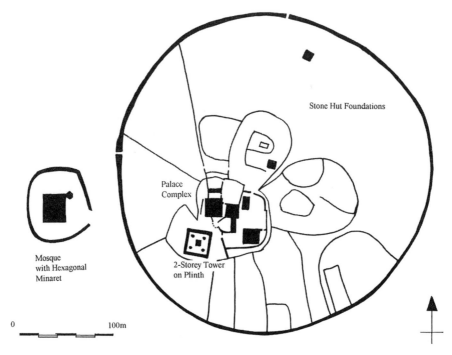

Figure 6.14 Plan of Ouara

Wadai

The final of the polities to be considered here is Wadai, which has already been mentioned in the context of the slave trade, and a state to which Dar al-Kuti periodically owed allegiance. Wadai also forms the eastern extremity of the central Sudan as defined here and is contiguous with Darfur in the Nilotic Sudan, indicating the inappropriateness, in many instances, to the material of the boundaries that have had to be applied. Wadai was even ruled by the Tunjur, the same dynasty that controlled Darfur (see chapter 3), until driven out in a so-called *jihad* by Abd el Karim in the early seventeenth century. The archaeological evidence for Islamisation in Darfur under the Tunjur has already been considered in chapter 3, where the emphasis upon divine kingship was noted (Arkell 1946; Mohammed 1986). Equally, the spread of Islam away from the court circle during the subsequent Keira (Fur) dynasty was also remarked on. Similar patterns are evident in Wadai, where Islam only began to be spread more widely after the campaigns of Abd el Karim, and a process in part achieved through the proselytising activities of Funj holy men (Trimingham 1962:39).

Abd el Karim also founded a capital in Wadai, in around 1640, at Ouara, some 400 km west of Shoba in Darfur. This site has been investigated by a number of scholars (Balfour-Paul 1954b; de Neufville and Houghton 1965; Lebeuf and Kirsch 1989). The main feature recorded was a central complex of fired-brick buildings set within an enclosing wall **(figure 6.14)**. Thus a preoccupation with

Figure 6.15 Central buildings at Ouara

defence is again evident, with about 10 ha enclosed behind a wall nearly 7 m high and 2.5 m thick. It was a massive construction, rightly interpreted as 'a token of the power of the rulers of Wara' (de Neufville and Houghton 1965:202) **(figure 6.15)**. Intriguingly, the fired-brick mosque, which had a hexagonal-sided minaret, was placed outside the enclosing walls indicating that the type of mosque/palace association of importance at, for example, Ndele was not thought of such significance, for whatever reason, here. The whole complex was abandoned about 1850, and Balfour-Paul (1954b:16), based upon uncertain evidence, suggests that most of the buildings still standing date from the early nineteenth century.

The concern for defence certainly ties Ouara into the chain of similar such sites already described both in the central Sudan and neighbouring Darfur, and other similarities exist. These include the remains of a raised wooden dais, 'suggestive of audience chambers' utilised by the ruler (Balfour-Paul 1954b:15) which has been recorded, paralleling the types of structure described for Darfur. Similarly suggestive of divine kingship is another building which Balfour-Paul (1954b) describes as a plinth some 25 m² and 4 m in height, built of brick and surmounted by a small square tower with windows facing all four points of the compass which allowed the sultan 'to observe what went on in all four corners of his capital'. Next to this were placed four roundhouses interpreted as accommodation for choice members of the harem. Although a direct connection cannot be postulated, perhaps the logic underlying this structure was similar to that of the Logone-Birni palace described earlier (Lebeuf and Lebeuf 1973), i.e. as a point of set-aside and reflection, though obviously the ancestral symbolism of the *tukuri* is not of significance here. Likewise, the existence of a platform on top of Thorega hill to the west of Ouara is suggested by de Neufville and Houghton (1965:203) as having functioned as the ceremonial centre used for the investiture of each new sultan. This again is suggestive of the types of sacred precinct also already described as having existed in Darfur (Balfour-Paul 1955, and see chapter 3). Thus at Ouara, as at numerous other sites both across the central Sudan and neighbouring regions, we again see the juxtaposition of Muslim – the mosque – and traditional elements – here, the tower, dais and possible sacred precinct, a pattern seemingly characteristic of the pillars of authority in this region, as indicated archaeologically, and recorded historically (see, e.g., Levtzion and Hopkins 1981).

Summary and conclusions

At first glance the initial conversions to Islam in the central Sudan appear to be more recent in date than in the other regions discussed so far. These seem to have taken place in Kanem-Borno in the eleventh century. Yet it is almost certain that this is incorrect; hints of Ibadi contacts and of a much greater time-depth for Muslim contacts exist, perhaps as early as the mid-eighth century, but the lack of archaeological research focused on sites with Islamic associations hinders our understanding of these processes. What is apparent is that although pan-Sudanic trade routes did not develop until comparatively late, the central Sudan functioned as a form of bridge across the continent, linking up Darfur in the east to Songhai in the west, with both areas sometimes exerting direct influence upon the central Sudan, as has been noted for Hausa in the west and Wadai in the east. But it is also evident that interpretations and manifestations of Islam and Islamic practice vary across the central Sudan, something which is reflected in the archaeological record – from Islamised Kanem-Borno (Cohen 1967) to the syncretism of Bagirmi (Lavers 1983), or the complexity represented by the traditional religious elements evident in the Kotoko Logone-Birni palace (Lebeuf and Lebeuf 1973).

It is also apparent that the initial converts to Islam across the central Sudan were the rulers of the many different polities that existed, for reasons which have already been described in detail. Yet other aspects of a processual conversion model such as that applied to aspects of the data in the western Sahel as discussed in the last chapter do not work in this region. The trade connection so evident elsewhere also appears to be lacking; imported goods from the Muslim world are largely absent. Although in part this is inevitably a reflection of the absence of archaeological research undertaken, the question can also be posed as to whether this patterning also indicates different relationships between the inhabitants of this region of sub-Saharan Africa and their neighbours. Similarly, is this patterning a possible representation of the different conversion processes which it can be asked might have existed in the central Sudan? As yet the answer is still unclear.

Although the paucity of archaeological research looking at the Islamic period limits our understanding of the impact of Islam on certain social processes – on diet for instance – a multi-source approach has provided a point of entry, as outlined in chapter 1, into looking at other institutional systems and associated changes. Changes in identity and ethnicity, for example, seem to have been a key feature in parts of this region, more so than in many of the other regions considered, but it has also been shown that the central Sudan exhibits both similarities and differences with its neighbours. Common patterns also occur, the aforementioned juxtaposition of Islam and traditional religions, for example, as evident in pre-*jihad* Hausaland (Moughtin 1985), and to a certain extent afterwards (Greenberg 1946), or in Wadai (Balfour-Paul 1954b). This lends weight to the notion of deep similarities existing across the continent in the way Islamic practice has developed, especially with regard to popular religious practice – bearing in mind the problems outlined in chapter 1 in attempting to define this too narrowly. Yet features unique to the central Sudan are also apparent. The role of military power, of cavalry and of fortifications to protect against them appear to have been of especial significance in this region (R. S. Smith 1989; Reyna 1990). At times it seems that warfare was endemic, but such perceptions should not mean that the region ought to be dismissed as one racked with perpetual warfare. The available archaeological and historical information indicates this to be untrue; cultural and social developments equalled those of supposedly more peaceful regions of the continent. Yet the interconnected nature of states, military power and slavery were also shown to be exceptional in this region, apparently more so than elsewhere, culminating, it could be suggested, in the Fulani *jihad*, which was also to be of great significance in the next region to be considered, the West African Sudan and forest.

800 - early limited missionizing by Ibadis
1000 - Kanem islamization & Borno, Hausa 1300-1400 firmly established 1450
1700 - Kotoko "
1750-1800 - Bagirmi "

CHAPTER 7

THE WEST AFRICAN SUDAN AND FOREST

Introduction

The second zone of Islamic penetration in West Africa was the western Sudan (**figure 7.1**). This region lies below the western Sahel and is being treated separately, for it differs both in terms of environment – Sahel/desert as opposed to forest/savannah – and in the processes and factors that influenced Islamic conversion and Islamisation, i.e. trade directed north across the Sahara in the western Sahel which was, initially at least, in external Arab and Berber hands, in contrast to indigenous largely Mande-derived/controlled processes in the West African Sudan and forest. The Sudan as an environmental zone has already been outlined in the last chapter, being well settled, characterised by 'strongly seasonal rainfall', predominantly between June and September, and frequently described as resembling 'farmed parkland' (Grove 1978:148). Further to the south the tree cover thickens as what is termed the Guinean Savannah is encountered. Here, rainfall increases from the 400–1,000 mm annual average of the northern savannahs to over 1,000 mm. The Guinean Savannah is also dotted with various ranges of hills; the Futa Djallon, the Jos plateau and the Guinean Dorsal for example, described by Grove (1978:149) as 'old crystalline rocks' rising to over 1,500 m and a 'source of gold, tin ore, manganese and diamonds'. Finally, in the far south of the region, as the Atlantic coast is approached, the rainforest zone is reached. This, though formerly extensive, is now much reduced in size, being confined to the seaward slopes of the highlands and the lowlands nearer the coast.

The forest zone is also being considered in this chapter, as it was via traders from the western Sudan that Islam was initially transmitted to the forest, thus forming a useful continuum between the two. These environmental zones shade into each other, and contacts were maintained across great distances – usually for the purposes of trade. As Trimingham notes, 'West Africa is essentially a climatic region, for no physical barriers separate it from the Sahara in the north and equatorial regions in the south' (1959:1). R. S. Smith (1988:5) encapsulates how these interconnections existed when he makes the point that 'the forest products travelled across the lagoons, up the river highways and along intricate tracks through the bush until they reached the Sudan, and not only the Sudan, since, through the markets of Kano, Timbuktu, and lesser centres, they

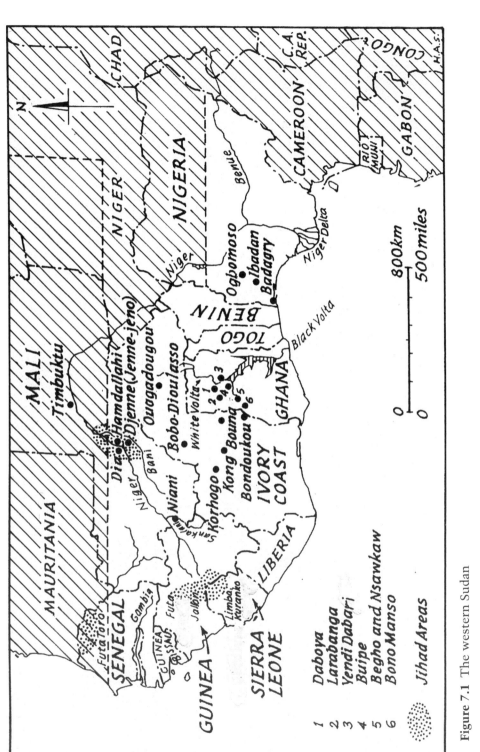

Figure 7.1 The western Sudan

1 Daboya
2 Larabanga
3 Yendi Dabari
4 Buipe
5 Begho and Nsawkaw
6 Bono Manso

Jihad Areas

were brought across the desert to Barbary and the Mediterranean'. As the forest products travelled north, so goods from the western Sahel and Sudan travelled south, along with ideas, including religious ones.

The West African Sudan and forest zones also provide further examples showing how Islam has been popularised. This slow process began following the initial introduction of Islam to various ethnic groups via, primarily, the agency of traders (Levtzion 1986b). These traders were subsequently followed by or travelled with holy men (Levtzion 1986a:28), in processes now familiar from other areas of the continent already discussed. In this respect the similarities evident in the conversion processes found in the West African Sudan and forest are frequently strikingly similar to those recorded and reconstructed for earlier periods elsewhere in sub-Saharan Africa, as will become apparent. Notable among these traders were the Mande, who moved south across the savannahs to the forest fringe of northern Ghana and the Ivory Coast from their homelands in the vicinity of the inland Niger delta and other areas to the west on the River Niger in Mali. These movements were precipitated by a search for commodities such as gold and kola nuts (Vansina et al. 1964). This occurred possibly as early as the fourteenth century, though it was mainly in the fifteenth to early sixteenth centuries. Further to the east, Hausa and Borno traders entered the Volta country (Burkina Faso) stimulated by similar motives, though apparently at a later date, that is, from the sixteenth century (Hiskett 1994:106).

The net result of this is that the West African Sudan and forest regions are rich in Islamic traditions. These are also diverse in character, and encompass many different elements. They range from those associated with one of the great 'medieval' empires of West Africa, Mali – as recorded by our now familiar source, Ibn Battuta (Hamdun and King 1994) – to those just remarked upon and associated with the activities and influences of the Mande (Posnansky 1987). This region was also influenced by the (again, largely Fulani) Islamic revivalist movements of the nineteenth century which have already been seen to be of great significance in the central Sudan (Barth 1890). To these can be added many other dimensions: the impact of the Muslim community in Kumasi upon their hosts, the Asante (Wilks 1980), or the processes of Islamic conversion among the Nupe (Nadel 1954), and subsequently among the Yoruba (Ryan 1978). There is thus a variety of peoples, circumstances, processes and results to consider.

However, as with the other regions discussed thus far, it is necessary to employ a multi-source approach, for two reasons. Firstly, this is because the degree of archaeological coverage across the region varies considerably. Certain areas – northern Ghana or parts of the inland Niger delta area of Mali, for example – have been reasonably well studied, but elsewhere, in Burkina Faso, Benin or Sierra Leone, for instance – and even in Nigeria, one of the most populous and potentially richest countries in the region – very little relevant archaeological research has been completed. But secondly, it is because we are fortunate in the fact that a wide range of other sources of evidence is available: ethnographic, art-historical, anthropological and historical. Together these allow a detailed consideration of features such as the syncretism between Islamic and local traditions that has occurred. This, for example, will be discussed with reference to the role of masking traditions, including its persistence among certain Muslim groups in the region. This further adds to the dimensions of syncretism already considered.

The pre-Islamic background

Contacts between some of the inhabitants of the West African savannahs and other areas, such as North Africa, certainly existed prior to the rise of Muslim-dominated trade. However, this statement has to be justified with the proviso that these were limited in extent and confined, almost wholly, to the northernmost areas of this region. Possibly the best example, and certainly the only unambiguous evidence found of such contacts, is provided by material already described in chapter 5 as being recovered from the site of Jenne-Jeno. This, to recap, comprised two Hellenistic beads which were found in levels dated to the late first millennium BCE (S. K. and R. J. McIntosh 1988:124; Brill 1995:256). These are unlikely to have been delivered by merchants from North Africa or elsewhere in the classical world, but do provide evidence for the filtering of items from the Mediterranean world to West Africa long before the rise of the later 'medieval' trans-Saharan trade which has also already been extensively described. Further evidence for such contacts is lacking both in the western Sudan and forest. However, Garrard (1988:3) has suggested, based upon numismatic evidence, that West African gold began to be exploited on a systematic basis as early as the fifth or sixth century. These sources, he suggests, were those at Bambuk and Bure (see chapter 5) rather than the forest gold sources such as those in the Akan lands. Nevertheless, if correct, the existence of such early gold trade might imply that further evidence for pre-Islamic trade could be found in the region.

Similarly, as in the western Sahel, the origins of social complexity in the western Sudan and forest pre-date the rise of Muslim-dominated commerce or any contacts with Muslims or the more northerly regions which were in earlier contact with the Muslim world. The relevant evidence to support this statement will be outlined as this chapter proceeds, yet it is worthwhile noting that archaeology is increasingly indicating the scale and early date of developments in this region. Darling (1997:114), for instance, makes the point 'that there was substantial state formation in the rainforest at roughly the same time as in the savannah over much of sub-Saharan Africa'. This point refers to evidence associated with the Yoruba town of Ijebu-Ode in south-western Nigeria (described below), but is equally applicable to developments at Ife (Garlake 1978), or the startling finds at Igbo-Ukwu (Shaw 1977), both also in Nigeria, or among the

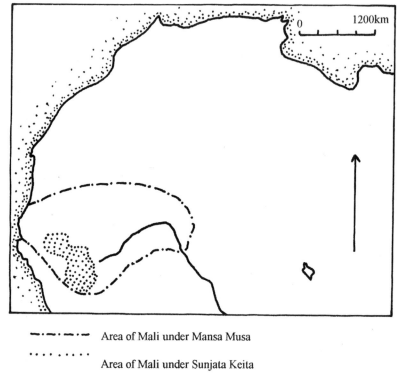

‑‑‑‑‑‑‑‑‑‑ Area of Mali under Mansa Musa

. . . . Area of Mali under Sunjata Keita

Figure 7.2 The borders of Mali

Asante in Ghana (Shinnie and Shinnie 1995). Again, all this material is further described below.

The empire of Mali

Myth and religion

Away from the forest and its fringes, evidence for the development of social and political complexity and its material correlates has also been found. Perhaps the most important of the polities that developed in the region was the empire of Mali, the second great West African empire, successor to Ghana and predecessor to Songhai (see chapter 5). Mali filled the vacuum left by the collapse of the empire of Ghana (see chapter 5), and reached its peak in the early fourteenth century. Furthermore, unlike Ghana and Songhai, which were both Sahelian-founded polities, Mali was centred geographically in the western Sudan (figure 7.2). This was perhaps due to environmental degradation of the Sahelian epicentre of Ghana leaving a gap which was rapidly exploited by 'proto-Mali'. Mali grew from humble beginnings in the eleventh–twelfth centuries among the Mande peoples on the modern Mali–Guinea border. It was established following epic battles between Sunjata, the ancestor of the Malian royal lineage, and the blacksmith Sumanguru (Levtzion 1973; Conrad 1994).

According to oral tradition (Niane 1986), Sunjata drew upon various sources of power, or what R. J. McIntosh (1998:262) terms 'the invention of a new legitimation tradition out of older traditions of hunters' authority, supernatural powers of Wangara and of the *nyamakalaw* (blacksmiths), and out of inventing a claim to the imperial tradition of Ghana'. He utilised sources of power associated with what Levtzion (2000:66) defines as 'the particularistic spirit of the nation'. Equally, though Sunjata was possibly only what Levtzion (1973:191) calls 'a nominal Muslim', he was not slow in realising that power might be gained from Islam as well as from traditional religion and magic. This is seemingly indicated by his utilisation of 'filled power bundles called *boli* brought back from Mecca by his lieutenant N'Fatigi' (R. J. McIntosh 1998:263). Sunjata's Islamic links are also evident in his ancestry which was traced back to Bilal, the first *muezzin*, who is seen as the 'ancestor of the Keitas' (Niane 1986:2), the princes of Mali. This again provides a further instance of the Islamising of origins seen elsewhere in sub-Saharan Africa. In contrast, Sumanguru, the King of Sosso, who was ultimately defeated at the battle of Krina by Sunjata, was descended from a line of smiths. Sumanguru kept his 'artefacts' of power in a room in his palace, including a giant serpent, skulls of defeated leaders, a balafon (a type of musical instrument) and various three-edged weapons (McNaughton 1988:61–2). This juxtaposition is of importance, for the smiths in their knowledge of transforming ore into iron were simultaneously feared, respected and despised, and said to be great sorcerers (Niane 1986:38). To this day smiths are still much respected in Mande society (and indeed in many other societies in sub-Saharan Africa), where they function also as woodcarvers, healers, diviners and sorcerers (McNaughton 1988; LaViolette 1995).

Although traditions record that the kings of Mali were early converts to Islam in the twelfth century (Levtzion 1985a:162), it appears that prior to the mid-thirteenth century, Islam within Mali was weak. This was altered to a certain extent following the pilgrimage to Mecca completed by the Malian ruler Mansa Ulli between 1260 and 1277, for in the process he legitimised himself as a Muslim ruler in the wider Muslim world. This is not something unique to Mali; as Hiskett (1994:94) notes, pilgrimage served as a means of gaining recognition for the state from external Muslim powers, a mechanism also utilised by the rulers of Songhai and Borno, as we have seen. A further and more spectacular pilgrimage was made by Mansa Musa, possibly the most famous of the rulers of Mali. Mansa Musa set out on *hajj* in 1324 accompanied by numerous followers, including 500 slaves, 'each carrying a staff of gold', and 80–100 camel loads of gold of some 300 pounds each (Bovill 1968:87). This gold was spent so prodigiously by Mansa Musa and his entourage that when al-'Umari was in Cairo twelve years later he found the townspeople still singing the praises

of Mansa Musa (Bovill 1968:87). Equally, gold was still devalued as a result
of Mansa Musa's visit and his profligate spending (Levtzion and Hopkins 1981).

The pilgrimage of Mansa Musa was also to start one of the enduring myths
of West African history. This involved Mansa Musa supposedly being accompanied on his return by the Andalusian poet and sometime architect al-Saheli.
This individual is in turn credited with bringing fired-brick architecture to
the western Sahel and Sudan, and with the construction of the main mosques
in Gao and Timbuktu (Aradeon 1989:99–100). Needless to say, the al-Saheli
story has been shown to be a myth. As Aradeon (1989:99) states, 'the myth was
founded on ignorance of the qualities of African traditional architecture combined with ethnocentric values and a belief that some aspects of North African
architecture must have been imported into the Western Sudan'. Although
al-Saheli definitely existed and apparently visited the western Sudan, attributing the development of formal architecture to this individual has been shown
to be erroneous through a re-evaluation of the historical, architectural (Aradeon
1989) and archaeological evidence (Insoll 1996b). In fact, al-Saheli did more than
visit West Africa – he died there, for Ibn Battuta records the existence of a grave
of Abu Ishaq al-Sahili of Granada during his visit to Timbuktu (Hamdun and
King 1994:63). But regardless of the role of al-Saheli, it is correct to emphasise,
as Levtzion (1985a) has done, that it was during the reign of Mansa Musa that
Mali could be said to have resembled a true Muslim empire.

Archaeology and history

Yet for all its large size and historical importance, the empire of Mali remains very little investigated archaeologically; our main sources of evidence
are largely historical. An exception – also, it could be argued, imbued with
mythic qualities – is provided by archaeological research that has been undertaken in an attempt to try and identify the former capital of Mali, a subject of
much discussion (see Hunwick 1973; Conrad 1994). The focus of this research
was at the site of Niani, just across the border from Mali inside the Republic
of Guinea. The location was chosen because it 'was on the edge of the forest,
a source of gold, kola nuts and palm oil, where Malinke traders came to sell
cotton and copper goods' (Niane 1984:136). Overall, the area of archaeological
remains has been estimated as stretching for some 25 km from Niani to Sidikila,
with three quarters identified at Niani itself: the 'Arab quarter', *Larabou-so*;
the fortified royal quarter, Niani-Kaba; and the eastern quarter inhabited by
the local population. Three phases of occupation were reconstructed, the first
encompassing the sixth–ninth centuries, the second the tenth–thirteenth and
the third the thirteenth–seventeenth, when Niani was 'le principal centre
politique, économique et administratif du Mali' (Filipowiak 1981:71). However, this chronology has been questioned (Conrad 1994:369), with an apparent
clustering of radiocarbon dates in the sixth–tenth and sixteenth–seventeenth

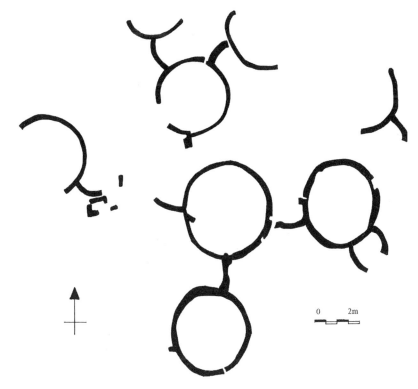

Figure 7.3 The 'royal' quarter at Niani

centuries, rather than a fourteenth-century zenith, as might be expected. Specific structures and features which were recorded included stone-house platforms **(figure 7.3)**, the *mihrab* of a mosque, tells, a metal-working area, burials (including tumulus and house burials) and an audience chamber (Filipowiak 1979; Niane 1984:144–5). Based upon this evidence, an enthusiastic, but not altogether successful, attempt was made to match the archaeological finds with the historical description of the capital of Mali provided by Ibn Battuta in the mid-fourteenth century.

For example, Ibn Battuta describes an audience chamber used by the ruler of Mali, then Mansa Suleyman, thus: 'a chamber with three wooden arches, the woodwork is covered with sheets of beaten silver and beneath these, three more covered with beaten gold, or, rather, it is silver covered with gilt' (Hamdun and King 1994:46–7). Excavations at Niani revealed a building measuring 20 m² and built of banco and on two levels. This, it was suggested, was the audience chamber described by Ibn Battuta. Close by this structure the remains of a roundhouse were recorded which in turn was suggested as being 'most probably the palace' (Filipowiak 1978:32). A mosque was recorded between the main residential area and the palace. This was indicated by stone foundations

including those of a minaret measuring some 4×5 m and a prayer hall of approximately 16×12 m (Filipowiak 1981:77). These discoveries were said to 'fully
prove Niani to be the medieval capital of the Mali empire' (Filipowiak 1978:32).
Although the mosque identification seems secure, other aspects of this interpretation, that Niani was the capital of Mali, cannot be substantiated based
upon the available evidence. Besides the shoehorning of the structural evidence to fit Ibn Battuta's description, as Conrad (1994:368) notes, matching
'sixteenth–seventeenth century archaeological evidence with Arabic documen-
tation of a fourteenth century city', there is an absence of imported material
such as glass, glazed pottery, beads etc. These are all types of artefact which
might be expected from so important a site, if parallels with other capitals such
as Gao are drawn. However, very little of such material was found besides a
few fragments of 'faience importe' (Filipowiak 1981:77).

Furthermore, as Conrad (1994:377) notes, the capital of Mali might have been
organised in a wholly different way to that imagined by the investigators, and
could have shifted 'more than once during its imperial period from the twelfth
century to the sixteenth century'. Conrad also persuasively argues that Niani
might have functioned as a political capital in the sixteenth century, which does
concur with part of the occupation sequence at the site, with earlier capitals
located in the vicinity of Dakajalan in contemporary Mali. However, no archaeological work has yet been completed at Dakajalan, again as Conrad (1994:376)
notes, for it is a sacred place 'and it appears to have been protected as such'.
In summary, it is safe to conclude that the capital of Mansa Musa and Mansa
Suleyman awaits the archaeologists' attention, and is not to be identified with
Niani. Both the archaeology and its comparison with the historical description
provided by Ibn Battuta make the Niani identification highly unlikely.

Yet the evidence from Niani, confusing as it is, cannot be wholly disregarded;
for if the chronology of the site is correct, and there is no reason to dispute the
earlier chronology, the finds of cabbage and lentil seeds in layers dating from
the tenth century are exciting. These are, as Filipowiak claims, 'indicative of
early relations of Niani with Islam, most probably with North-West Africa'
(1978:33). This statement is substantiated by Lewicki (1974:61), who mentions
that the cultivation of cabbage was introduced into Mali from Morocco and
al-Andalus. The links between the introduction of the cabbage and trans-
Saharan contacts are further indicated by its name in local languages: for example, in Songhai, cabbage is *kurombu*, derived from the Arabic *kuranb* or *kurunb*
(Lewicki 1974:169). Such information is of great significance in reconstructing
all the facets of the archaeology of Islam in sub-Saharan Africa, as discussed in
chapter 1.

Ibn Battuta also provides information on Islamic practice at the court of the
ruler of Mali, and it is apparent from his description that Islam had been blended
with elements of traditional religion and ceremonial. However, there had been
a shift away from the predominance of traditional religion evident in Sunjata's

time, 'as the small Malinke kingdom turned into a vast multi-ethnic empirc' (Levtzion 1973:191). Mansa Suleyman was evidently a good Muslim, as was much of the population of his capital, as evidenced by the Qur'an readings, prayers and Muslim festivals Ibn Battuta was present for. In fact, he was impressed by the way the times of prayer were meticulously observed, and how the mosque was well attended. But he was less impressed by other features, including the consumption of meat from animals not ritually slaughtered, of dogs and donkeys, and by a ceremony he observed which included some very non-Islamic elements (Hamdun and King 1994). At this ceremony prayers were held, an event at which Mansa Suleyman was present, to signal either the feast of rejoicing following the end of Ramadan ('*id al-fitr*) or the feast of sacrifice ('*id al-adha*), which is unclear (Bravmann 1974:48). During the course of this ceremony griots (poets) appeared, wearing masks like birds' heads and costumes made of feathers; they recited poetry, and upon enquiring about this Ibn Battuta was informed 'that this performance is old amongst them; they continued it from before Islam' (Hamdun and King 1994:54).

What appears to be evident here is the popularising of religion, which, though unappealing to Ibn Battuta, indicates the comfortable coexistence of the two elements, Muslim and traditional; in other words, the adaptation of belief to suit the local context and requirements. It is also reminiscent of the types of process discussed in chapter 1, especially that described by Eaton (1993) as having occurred during conversion to Islam in Bengal. Here, to recap, he identified three phases in the process of Islamisation: inclusion, identification and displacement. Although not directly comparable, it can be suggested that what Ibn Battuta was observing was both inclusion and identification, the fusion of the old with the new, but as yet the older traditions had not been displaced. This subject has also been examined by Rene Bravmann (1974:6), who emphasises that the expansion of Islam in the western Sudan was characterised 'by tolerance and a highly pragmatic approach to the problems associated with culture contact and change'. Furthermore, he discusses the example of the masked dance witnessed by Ibn Battuta and describes how a similar dance was witnessed by the explorer Binger in 1888 at Dafina, 'a nerve centre of Islam' (Bravmann 1974:51) in the Voltaic region. Displacement had still evidently not occurred, and again had not taken place by the 1960s, the time period from which the third example Bravmann introduces is drawn. This is the involvement of Muslim Mande in – or at least their acceptance of the existence of – masking associations such as the Bedu, Gbain and Do in west-central Ghana and the Cercle de Bondoukou in the Ivory Coast. In effect, the development of popular Islamic traditions incorporating masking traditions in parts of this region has a heritage stretching back to the time of the empire of Mali, and is an element which has thus far not been displaced. It indicates 'not only the flexibility with which Muslims have adapted themselves to local cultural situations but also the tenacity of indigenous art traditions' (Bravmann 1974:58).

This resembles the situation elsewhere. The component parts might vary, but the concept of syncretism, and the popularising of Islam as evident here, is found right across sub-Saharan Africa, as we have seen.

Popular Islam in Sierra Leone

As in many parts of the West African Sudan and forest the Mande were responsible for the introduction of Islam into what is today known as Sierra Leone. The date at which this first occurred could be as early as about 1450–1500. Initially, traders, missionaries and 'refugees from war' (D. E. Skinner 1978:32) were the agents of Islamisation, but the major spread of Islam among the local population only took place after the eighteenth century (D. E. Skinner 1997). Again, the parallels with processes which had taken place several centuries earlier – in the kingdom of Ghana, for example – are striking. Traders established bases in Sierra Leone, Arabic was influential linguistically, Muslim charms became popular, and Muslim holy men acted in advisory capacities to local rulers. A synthesis, by now familiar, also often happened between traditional religious elements and Islamic ones, as in the Temne identification of their main deity, Kuru, with Allah (D. E. Skinner 1978:59). Popular Muslim practice could also incorporate masking traditions, as in the *sande* initiation society of the female Mende, the female equivalent of the widely found male *poro* society. Ferme (1994:31) describes how in his study area 'blackened helmet masks' were used, dropped for a while following pressure from a local imam, and then reincorporated. Whether the persistence of these traditions can be accounted for by masking being 'deeply embedded in African culture' (Mack 1994:36) is open to debate.

Archaeological indicators of popular religious traditions have also been found. DeCorse (1989) looked at various sites in north-eastern Sierra Leone which were associated with three ethnic groups, the Yalunka and Kuranko, Mande groups, and the Limba, who are related to the aforementioned Temne. He found that, for example, although 90 per cent of the Yalunka consider themselves Muslim, their prayer areas are frequently next to traditional shrines, 'indicating the syncretic nature of religious beliefs' (1989:135). These shrines could be ephemeral in nature, such as that associated with the founder of the Yalunka town of Musaia, where a virgin had been sacrificed and buried under a young orange tree. Nothing denoted 'the special significance of the tree except that the fruit-laden branches remain unpicked' (DeCorse 1989:135). Mosques and prayer grounds tended to be more substantially built, as with the unusual round mosque at Sokoria **(figure 7.4)**. In parts of the country such as the capital, Freetown, however, permanency of mosque construction is apparently a fairly recent phenomenon, according to Proudfoot (1959:405).

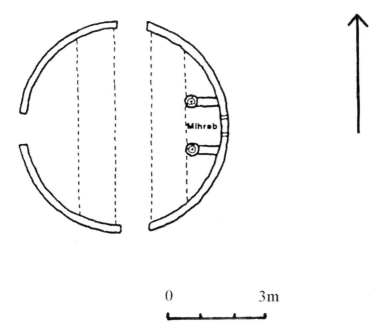

Figure 7.4 Yalunka round mosque

The inland Niger delta

Besides the development of syncretic traditions it is also important to recognise that Islam could (and can) coexist alongside traditional religions and non-Muslim practices without obliterating or assimilating them. This can also be manifest archaeologically and is evident in the inland Niger delta area of Mali. This is a vast alluvial plain, around 450 km in length and up to 220 km in width which is inundated each year by the waters of the Rivers Bani and Niger, 'following their being flooded by waters from the source of the Niger in the Fouta Djallon' (Hunwick 1999:xxiii–iv). At the site of Toguere Doupwil near Mopti-Sevare, for example, non-Islamic burial practices were found dating from the fifteenth century. This involved the corpse being placed in a large 'coffin-jar' in a contracted position accompanied by grave-goods such as iron bracelets and ankle-rings (Bedaux 1976:41). The existence of these burial practices led the excavator to conclude, quite correctly, that 'Islamic influence did not penetrate far beyond the well-known centres' (Bedaux 1979:34). Similar coffin-jar burials were found at the neighbouring site of Toguere Galia, a mound on the right bank of the River Bani, some 12 km east of Djenne (Bedaux 1978, 1991). These were of similar date, and persisted a long time 'après l'Islamisation de la région de Djenne' (Bedaux 1991:97).

A further feature which indicates the coexistence of Islam and traditional religions in the inland Niger delta region are the numerous terracotta figurines that have been found. Although there are no specific early pronouncements by

Figure 7.5 An example of a figurative terracotta found near Bamako

the Prophet Muhammad on figural arts, the Qur'an states that Allah is the true fashioner (*Surah* 59:24), and a *hadith* codified the opposition to representational art (Ettinghausen 1992:62). Representational art is, however, frequently found in many areas of the Muslim world (see Insoll 1999a:136–7), as has already been described with reference to the masks utilised by certain Muslim groups. Yet objects such as the terracotta figurines of the middle Niger differ, and cannot really be said to be indicative of either Islamic beliefs or syncretic processes. They also appear in contexts after people had converted to Islam in the region.

The production of anthropomorphic terracotta figurines first appears in the inland Niger delta in the eleventh century, and expands dramatically between the twelfth and fifteenth centuries (S. K. McIntosh, pers. comm.) **(figure 7.5)**. At Jenne-Jeno over seventy animal or human representations have been found, the majority rather crude, and it is possible that these cruder examples might have functioned as toys. However, other figurines appear to have served ritual purposes. This latter category of figurines are comparatively frequent until about 1200–1350. The contexts of these figurines vary and include a pair of kneeling, probably male and female, figurines, discovered in a wall foundation, possibly fulfilling a protective role (S. K. McIntosh 1995:214). Another statuette fulfilled a similar role, a single kneeling figure with arms crossed over its torso, possibly associated with local legend 'to ensure that the mud-brick houses of the city would remain standing' (R. J. and S. K. McIntosh 1979:53), or alternatively associated with 'ancestor worship' (R. J. and S. K. McIntosh 1979:53). The latter activity continued in Djenne as late as 1910. Other terracotta figurines interpreted as ritually significant were found associated with funerary urns and what are termed 'rain-making altars' (R. J. and S. K. McIntosh 1988:156; R. J. McIntosh 1989). Unfortunately, the vast majority of the figurines known are without context, having come from looted sites (see R. J. McIntosh et al. 1995; Schmidt and McIntosh 1996). Thus the material from Jenne-Jeno is of great importance and the presence of the figurines at the site has been interpreted by Rod McIntosh as possibly marking 'a retrenchment or revitalization of traditional practices in the face of growing conversions to an Islam intolerant of representations of the human form' (1998:212). This latter point can be debated, for as already noted the repertoire of Islamic art does not necessarily preclude representational forms; however, other evidence from Jenne-Jeno suggests that as yet not fully understood changes possibly occurred with conversion to Islam.

Jenne-Jeno

The site of Jenne-Jeno in the inland Niger delta area of Mali, though not directly associated with Islam, needs to be briefly mentioned for its importance to West African archaeology. It was one of the first sites in the region to be excavated using modern methods and has yielded a variety of important information since work began there in the mid-1970s (S. K. and R. J. McIntosh 1980; S. K. McIntosh 1995). One of the earliest urban foundations in sub-Saharan Africa, Jenne-Jeno grew from a village founded around 250 BCE to a full urban centre by 300 CE, and expanded to a maximum size of 33 ha by 900 CE. The estimated population for the site and its outlying suburbs at its peak has been reconstructed at about 27,000 people. It was also enclosed during its mature urban phase by a wall some 2 km in length and 3.6 m in width. Decline of the site began between 1100 and 1200, and it was finally abandoned around 1400 (see main text). The subsistence evidence found indicated a picture of 'stability through time' (S. K. McIntosh 1995:390), with the population utilising a variety of resources: fish, turtle, millet, rice, sheep/goat and cattle. Complex ritual/religious practices are indicated by the terracotta statuettes which have been recovered, along with the burial practices recorded. The latter include interment in large urns both in residential areas and dedicated cemeteries (R. J. McIntosh 1998:202) **(figure 7.6)**.

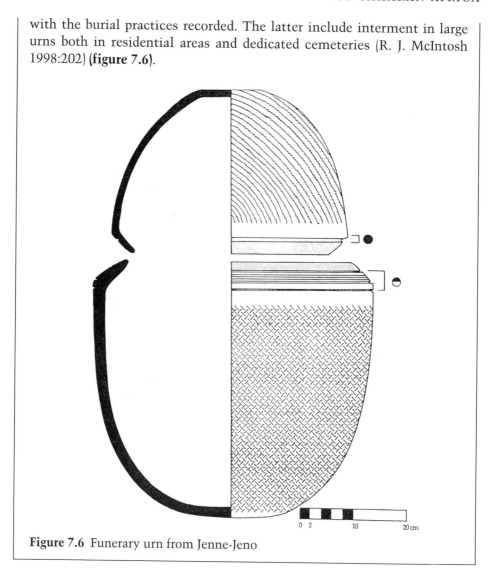

Figure 7.6 Funerary urn from Jenne-Jeno

One of these changes appears to have been linked with changes in settlement occupation. Initially, it was suggested that Jenne-Jeno was abandoned (around 1400) in favour of neighbouring Djenne, the currently occupied town, as it was considered too tainted by non-Muslim practices by the newly Islamised population (S. K. and R. J. McIntosh 1980; S. K. McIntosh 1995). Prior to this, and beginning around 1100–1200, Jenne-Jeno had gone through a period of decline. This coincided with the appearance of material suggestive of North African influences, such as rectilinear house plans, and spindle whorls (discussed further below), apparently indicating that conversion to Islam was a gradual process culminating in the 'triumph of Islam' at approximately the same time as Jenne-Jeno was abandoned (R. J. and S. K. McIntosh 1988:156). However, R. J. McIntosh (1998:202–3) has recently re-evaluated the evidence and suggests that rather than the two settlements being successive, decline might have been more gradual than previously thought.

Although the penultimate relationship between Djenne and Jenne-Jeno might not be fully understood it is evident that Djenne rapidly became a centre of Islamic learning, a status it enjoys to this day. Yet if the *Tarikh al-Sudan* is to be believed (see chapter 5), even in Djenne, the process of transition to Islamic orthodoxy was not instantaneous. 'Pre-Islamic customs' persisted in the city until the late fifteenth century, when 'a pious Juula came to Jenne from the south and destroyed the house of idols that the people continued to worship' (Levtzion 2000:75). Djenne is also of significance as the location of one of the most architecturally important mosques in West Africa **(figure 7.7)**. Rebuilt in 1909, it is frequently cited as the culmination of the vernacular earthen architectural traditions of the region. However, the authenticity of its architectural style has been the subject of debate, with some scholars arguing that it is 'clearly indigenous' (LaViolette 1994:94; and see Bourgeois 1987), and others that it was built by local builders but with French assistance, and based on the 'French military Residence at Segou' (Prussin 1994:186). Architectural legitimacy aside, the significance of the inland Niger delta to Islamic scholarship is further reinforced by the northern neighbour of Djenne, Dia, another important centre of Muslim learning in the region. This is a town described by Hunwick (1999:xxviii) as 'a point of dispersion for teachers and preachers of Islam who became known as Diakhanke' (see also Sanneh 1979).

Hence the data from the inland Niger delta is of interest for the patterning evident. In the urban context traditional religions and rituals, as represented by the terracotta figurines, were earlier replaced by Islam, while in the rural environment traditional practices continued for some time after conversion to Islam had occurred in the urban centres. This is therefore similar to processes already identified for the western Sahel (see chapter 5). Its persistence in the urban environment is indicated, for instance, by the burial evidence already described. This once again supports the notion of varying acceptance of Islam over time, as outlined in chapter 1 with reference to the phased conversion models developed by Fisher (1973a, 1985), R. Horton (1971, 1975) and Eaton (1993). Furthermore, though not directly comparable in circumstances, general support is also lent to the model presented in the last chapter whereby interlinks between different conversion rates and socio-economic groups were proposed.

Thus, while the varied and staggered nature of conversion is indicated archaeologically here in the inland Niger delta, it is also attested historically. Izard and Ki-Zerbo (1992), based upon historical reconstruction, for example, describe how the initial exposure of the Bambara to Islam, again through the actions of

Figure 7.7 Djenne mosque

traders and accompanying holy men, caused them to reconsider their structures of belief, in a manner by now familiar to us. A direct consequence of increasing exposure to Islam was, for the Bambara, 'to stress once again the Supreme God, *Maa Ngala*, the sovereign above the spirits honoured by particular cults' (Izard and Ki-Zerbo 1992:363). Robin Horton's contact model as outlined in chapter 1 would thus appear to be of relevance here, with the growth of the 'macrocosm' important in the face of Islamic contact. This, following the reconstructed sequence of events, also paved the way for the Bambara rulers of the kingdoms of Segu and Kaarta to begin to consult 'the ministers of this Great God through the persons of the marabouts while remaining faithful to their own cults' (Izard and Ki-Zerbo 1992:363). However, without doubting the steps that were followed in the process of Islamic conversion among the Bambara, again paralleling Eaton's (1993) 'inclusion' and 'identification' stages, one can question other aspects of the aforementioned reconstruction – namely, whether the supposed growth of the Ngala macrocosm is in fact a reflection of what Zahan (1974:1) defines as the emphasis in studies of Bambara religion on 'the ground roots, and not in its highest forms of expression'. This means, as frequently used to be the case in studies of African tradional religions, that the high god was omitted altogether, or given a much reduced role, and that, consciously or subconciously, world religion was given an overblown status in African spiritual 'development'.

The forest fringe: the Mande

Trade patterns and goods

Djenne, along with other centres on the middle Niger, was also home to the Mande, something of major significance – for, as already mentioned, the Mande were possibly the most successful agents in spreading Islam away from the urban centres and throughout the West African Sudan and forest zones. Great traders, they also succeeded in establishing what Levtzion (1986b:12) has defined as 'lines of communication', Islamic learning networks which linked the main centres 'to the remotest rural Muslim'. It is also important to note that 'Mande' is just one name by which this influential group is known. To quote Audouin and Deniel (1978:13), 'ils sont appelés Diula chez les Malinké du Haut-Niger, Marka chez les Bambara de Ségou et de Djenné, Dafing dans la région de la Volta Supérieure, Yarsé chez les peuples parlant les langues du groupe Voltaïque, Wangara par les auteurs Arabes anciens ainsi chez les Peul et les Hausa'. The Mande, as they will be referred to for convenience here, established links between the termini of the trans-Saharan trade routes in the Sahel, and the savannah and forest zones (**figure 7.8**). Two main routes linked forest to desert, Teghaza to Timbuktu, 'and from Jenne to the forest' (Levtzion 1968:5). They also settled in separate merchant quarters alongside the peoples

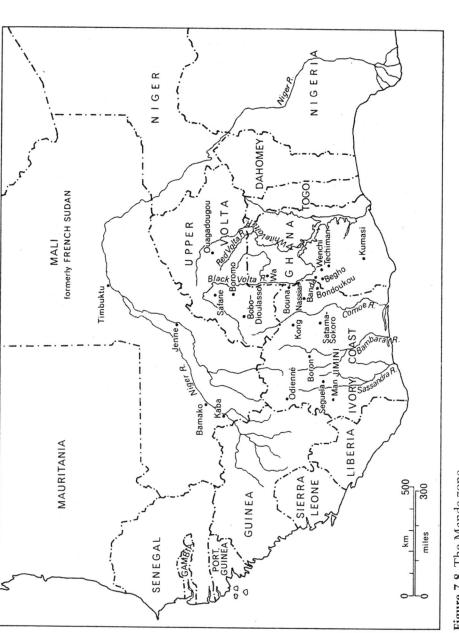

Figure 7.8 The Mande zone

of the southern forest and savannah areas in the same way as the Berber and Arab merchants had settled in centres such as Koumbi Saleh and Gao-Saney 500 years earlier (see chapter 5).

Parallels between the earlier Sahelian mercantile activities and those of the Mande can also be extended further – to the patterns of trade, for example. These traders dealt in a variety of commodities, gold and kola nuts being among the most important, exchanging a variety of items in return – including finished goods, cloth, metalwork and books, for instance – as well as salt and horses (Vansina et al. 1964; Goody 1968b). Trade rather than missionary zeal appears to have been the initial motive behind why the Mande travelled south from their homelands on the middle Niger – though, as Wilks (2000:94) notes, 'although the communities of the Juula [Mande] diaspora originated as parts of a trade network, not all Juula traded all the time, and some did not trade at all'. Gold was a major incentive, and Garrard (1988:4) makes the important point that the established gold sources in the western Sudan (Bambuk and Bure) appear to have declined in the latter part of the fourteenth century, to be replaced by new supplies from the forest. To what degree the Mande ventured south at this date is unclear. The fifteenth–early sixteenth centuries seem more likely, as recorded, for example, in traditions relating to Gonja in Ghana, which note that armed horsemen came south from Mali in the late fifteenth–early sixteenth centuries to investigate a hold-up in the flow of gold (Shinnie 1981:66). These horsemen stayed rather than returning north.

In contrast to the sources in the Sudan, the gold in the forest was more dispersed (Posnansky 1973), but dispersed throughout the forest. Concentrated alluvial gold-working existed along certain forest streams, however, with a major area of production being the Akan region (Garrard 1988). The growth in the forest gold trade from the later fourteenth century had consequences in the region, as Garrard notes, and 'a number of small villages along the northern fringe of the Akan region began to develop into prosperous gold-trading towns' (1988:4). These included the important trade centres of Begho and Bono Manso. The northern fringes of the forest were, however, the main area in which the Mande traders established a presence; as Goody notes (1968b:200), the White Volta forms the rough boundary for the 'Sudanese style of mosque-building...the flat-roofed compound, the secret society and the xylophone, all Mande traits'. An important reason for this loose geographical restriction to the forest fringe is the presence of sleeping sickness in the forest, meaning that pack animals could not be utilised. This was a problem further compounded by the dense vegetation which made animal transport in the forest ineffective and human porterage the preferred option (Stahl 1994:84). However, this did not mean that Muslim traders and missionaries were solely confined to the forest fringes; they were not, as the evidence from Asante indicates (see below).

Begho

The archaeological evidence testifying to the former presence of these pioneers of Islam varies in quantity and quality, and among the most notable of these trade centres was Begho, which was occupied between about the thirteenth and eighteenth centuries (see Posnansky 1973, 1987). It was a trading entrepôt where Akan gold from the forest 'was exchanged for northern commodities – salt, cloth, and copper alloys' (Stahl 1994:84). Unfortunately, this important site still awaits full publication, but the existing reports indicate that Begho was composed of some 1,500 mounds, probably the remains of collapsed compounds, which appeared to be clustered in four areas representing the former quarters of the town. These, when partially excavated, showed that differences existed between their respective inhabitants. The earliest quarter was Nyarko, where occupation pre-dated the arrival of the Mande traders by 200–300 years, traders who 'probably came into contact with people already resident in the area who were exploiting locally available gold resources' (Stahl 1994:86). The Mande themselves occupied the Kramo quarter, a term, according to Posnansky (1987:17), which means 'people of the book', and is thus an obvious indicator of a former Muslim presence. Anquandah (1993:645) also makes the important point that this was 'where presumably a mosque(s) built of mud must have stood', though none has yet been reported. The third quarter, Dwinfour, was the artisanal area, while the largest quarter, Brong, was interpreted as the centre of the town's ritual life.

A variety of evidence was recovered from the excavations supporting the existence of functional differentiation between the four quarters at Begho and, more importantly, seemingly attesting to a Muslim presence in the Kramo quarter. Two burials were recorded in the Kramo quarter, with the skeletons extended on their backs north–south and oriented (in what direction is unclear). This was a type of burial differing from those found elsewhere at Begho, as in Brong and Dwinfour, where burials were 'flexed on their sides' (Posnansky 1987:19), and followed no consistent orientation. These could conceivably be Muslim burials. Other possible categories of evidence indicating a Muslim presence in Kramo included the absence of grass-cutter remains – in contrast to Brong, where they were abundant, and absent 'perhaps because of Muslim dietary restrictions' (Posnansky 1987:19). Similarly, the presence of ceramic drainpipes was interpreted as evidence for the former use of flat-roofed architecture at Begho (Posnansky 1973). This was an imported architectural form resembling the architecture of more northern areas, such as the Mande homelands where less rain fell and flat roofs were more useful.

Such architecture is not, however, restricted to Begho but is also found at various sites in northern Ghana, and apparently sometimes was even multistoreyed and could have an added tower – the so-called 'Gonja tower-houses' (Anquandah 1982:77). The growth of the settlement as a whole over time also appears to have been meaningful, as the Brong and Kramo quarters were initially well separated but gradually grew towards each other. Again in this respect the parallels with the archaeology of the earlier trade centres far to the north in the Sahel are obvious, where initially Muslims often occupied one distinctive quarter or settlement until greater conversions to Islam among the local population meant that such a division was rendered unneccessary (see chapter 5). However, it is also worth noting that the patterning of sites with Mande associations varies considerably. At Begho the four quarters were isolated, while at New Buipe, three high mounds parallel to the river were found, and at Daboya (both also in Ghana), a single large mound 'with several peaks scattered across it' was recorded (Shinnie and Kense 1989:230).

Begho flourished between the fifteenth/sixteenth and eighteenth centuries, described by Stahl (1994:86) as 'a period of intensified contact with societies of the Middle Niger'. Yet the absence of much evidence for participation in trade or for these long-distance contacts is surprising, but might also be a reflection of the fact that much of the site still awaits investigation. Indirect evidence for such influences and contacts is, however, found. This included spindle whorls recovered from both the Brong and Kramo quarters which were identical to both those in use today in the Begho region, and to spindle whorls from Djenne. Posnansky also makes the point that spindle whorls were made by 'Muslim, Mande-speaking men' (1987:17–18), and that technology transfer between the two regions, via the medium of the Mande, was supported by similarities in the loom forms found. The importance of cloth and clothing, and the link to modesty within Islam, have been mentioned previously. Moreover, cloth also frequently served as a form of currency, further encouraging its manufacture and trade. Esther and Jack Goody (1996:78), for example, refer to the former use of narrow strips of cloth in Gonja for currency purposes. These strips ranged between 3 and 30 cm in width.

Another 'northern influence' (Stahl 1994:87) is indicated by the find of a brass foundry in the Dwinfour quarter at Begho. The importance of brass as an indicator of long-distance Muslim contacts in the Sahelian trade centres has already been described (chapter 5), and in Begho it would appear to be indicative of Mande links. Besides indications of the technology of brass casting itself, various brass vessels have been recorded in this region which were imported from the Islamic world. For example, six bowls of 'Syro-Egyptian' (Mamluk) origin and dating from the mid-fourteenth–mid-fifteenth centuries are still in existence in the Brong Ahafo and Ashanti regions of Ghana (Posnansky 1980; R. A. Silverman 1982). These were originally used for ritual ablution purposes by Muslim traders, but eventually they found their way into non-Muslim Akan hands. Interestingly, Silverman, in his description of this material, mentions that most of the villages in which they were found 'maintain strong historical traditions of having been involved in trade with the north and/or Muslims' (1982:15), providing additional evidence for Mande contacts and enterprise.

Similar brass vessels have been recorded elsewhere in the western Sudan. Goody (1968a), for instance, refers to a three-legged vessel with 'Moorish' design at Afré-Boka in the northern Ivory Coast.

According to Garrard (1988:4), the first supplies of North African brass received by the Akan were in the form of brass bowls and perhaps also ingots. As well as receiving raw material from the north, the Akan might also have received inspiration, as Garrard (1972a:7) also suggests that the *kuduo* ritual vessels used by them 'are known to be derived from Islamic prototypes'. However, from the late fifteenth–early sixteenth centuries, this northern trade in brass appears to have declined as brass was increasingly obtained from European traders on the West African coast who imported large quantities of the metal both in the form of vessels and as ingots or manillas (Ozanne 1971:62). Garrard records the astounding figure of 10,000 tons of brass having been imported in total by European traders to the Gold Coast (Ghana) by the nineteenth century, in comparison to the 2 or 3 tons a year 'traded into the Akan area by the trans-Saharan routes' (1988:5). Other imports to the West African coast included firearms, gunflints, cloth, glassware and pottery. Some of this material found its way into the interior, though the majority has been recovered during excavation of the European trade centres or 'castles' themselves (Lawrence 1963; DeCorse 1992, 1993).

A further practical benefit introduced to the peoples of the West African forest and its fringe through contacts with the Muslim Mande included accurate systems of weights and measures. At Begho 'chipped, shaped potsherds' (Stahl 1994:87) were found which conform closely to the Islamic *mithqal* and *wakia* standards. The gold dinar or *mithqal*, which was derived from the Roman denarius, was used for weighing gold, and had a standard ranging between 4.3 and 4.7 g. The *wakia* or *uqiya*, which was derived from the Greek and Phoenician drachm, was used for weighing both silver and other commodities, and had a standard ranging between 26 and 30 g (Garrard 1972a:1). The introduction of these weights has been extensively studied by Timothy Garrard (1972a, 1972b, 1973a, 1973b, 1988), who notes that they were diffused throughout the western Sudan and into the forest by the Mande (1972a:2–5). Similar pottery weights found at Jenne-Jeno support this assertion, including a rounded potsherd, which 'falls convincingly within the Islamic weight standard' (S. K. and R. J. McIntosh 1980:161). At Begho and Jenne-Jeno the weights found might be fairly crude potsherds, but the Akan also produced weights of Muslim standards of great aesthetic value. Following their initial adoption (perhaps from as early as around 1400), these were produced in simple geometric forms, but by the seventeenth century elaborate figurative weights were being made (Garrard 1988). These figurative weights depict a variety of subjects including animals, religious acts, everyday events and images of power such as firearms (McLeod 1981:126–8) **(figure 7.9)**.

Figure 7.9 Nineteenth-century Asante goldweight possibly depicting a northern warrior on horseback

Other centres

Begho was certainly not an isolated settlement. Other towns with Mande quarters and associations existed across the region – Daboya, Bono Manso and Buipe, for example **(figure 7.10)**. It is also important to note that the Mande were not the only Muslim traders operating in the region. Traders from Borno and Hausa were also recorded as settling there. The Kano Chronicle mentions that routes were opened from Borno to Gonja in the mid-fifteenth century (Garrard 1972a:5), while Salaga in Gonja was known to be an important commercial centre for trade to Hausaland (Shinnie 1981:68), with a trade route from Salaga running to Borgu (Levtzion 1968:24). It was not only traders from Hausaland who travelled. Wilks (1965:89), for example, describes how a Hausa holy man, Mallam Mahama, was said to have moved close to Yendi Dabari in Dagomba (Ghana) at an unspecified point in time. The holy man was accompanied by numerous followers – weavers, butchers, well diggers and blacksmiths – 'a complete civilisation to Dagomba'. This move theoretically has implications

Figure 7.10 Mosque with Mande associations, Bande Nkwanta

for the archaeological record in differentiating Hausa as opposed to possible Mande influences.

A further important site with Mande associations which has been investigated in northern Ghana is Daboya, one of the trade centres associated with the Gonja polity which flourished between the sixteenth and nineteenth centuries. It has already been mentioned how horsemen from Mali came south to Gonja, and according to both oral tradition and an eighteenth-century historical source, the *Kitab Ghanja*, Gonja was supposedly founded by these mounted soldiers from the north, the *gbanya*, in the late fifteenth–early sixteenth centuries (Shinnie 1981:66; Stahl 1994:90). This would appear to be a possible signifier of Mande influence, but the archaeology does not appear to confirm the sudden arrival of an immigrant group, though it is still possible that the Mande influenced state formation in this area. On the contrary, the usually presented evidence for Mande influence from the north, a type of red-painted pottery of the so-called Silima tradition, though present at Daboya, was found to pre-date the arrival of the northern invaders by some three hundred years. This led the investigators, Shinnie and Kense (1989:130), to suggest that the red-painted pottery 'was originally a Sahelian development; perhaps from the time of the Ghana and Mali empires, and it became a regionalized tradition within a number of savanna societies'. They further suggest (1989:240) that its distribution 'could have been the result of the spread of Islamic communities through West Africa'.

Hence, although the linkage with the northern 'founders' of Gonja is disproved, earlier connections between the forest fringe and the Sahel and savannah appear to have also existed, as indicated by the red-painted pottery. However, as Posnansky (1987:17) notes, it is not possible 'to assign a single place and time' for its derivation. This Silima (Buipe) tradition pottery is described by Anquandah (1976:30) as being 'painted and slipped, calciform, trunco-conical and carafe wares which are highly reminiscent of the medieval Sudan traditions'. Less technically, Ozanne (1971:48) refers to the forms as comprising wide-rimmed jars, hemispherical bowls and pedestalled dishes. The decoration, painting on slip, is described as being composed of lines and various motifs such as triangles filled with diamond cross-hatching, which are painted in red, or red and black (York 1973; Posnansky 1987; Shinnie and Kense 1989).

The only evidence for the arrival of the *gbanya* at Daboya is in fact indirect, if it indeed can be interpreted as indicating such an event. This comprised horse bones dated 'just prior to AD 1600', evidence which was interpreted as lending support to 'the oral and written traditions of the area, which suggest that the *Gbanya* horseman arrived at Daboya at approximately the same time' (Shinnie and Kense 1989:225). Similarly, evidence for long-distance trade and for the impact of Islam on the local population at Daboya was also rare. Evidence for orthodox Muslim burial was lacking, with the local claim to bury both sexes facing east not supported by the archaeological evidence. Some pig bones were also found, and in general the point made by Shinnie and Kense that Islam 'remained restricted to only a segment of the population' (1989:235) would seem a viable interpretation of the evidence. This is especially so when we recall similar material from other areas in the continent.

Elsewhere in the former territories of Gonja, an undated mosque at Buipe has been reported, reputedly associated with the early Islamisation of the region (Shinnie 1981:69), while excavations at New Buipe showed that architectural change accompanied the introduction of Islam. This was the appearance of rectangular flat-roofed architecture utilising projecting drainpipes (13–18 cm in diameter and 30–45 cm in length), similar to those mentioned previously, and described by York (1973:160) as 'a concomitant of Islam'. These structures differed from preceding architectural styles, and were established by the sixteenth century, or Period 4a in the sequence at Buipe. Interestingly, from the end of Period 4a burials are not found in habitation areas, a feature interpreted by York as being due to the adoption of Islam, for 'Muslims normally make use of cemeteries some distance away from the settlement'. The architectural change at New Buipe is also similar to evidence already described at Begho, and indeed, a similar change in architecture was noted at Old Wiae, including a shift from circular to rectangular house plans occurring in the mid-sixteenth century (Agorsah 1986:29).

As already noted, other polities besides Gonja existed in northern Ghana, and these are conveniently and concisely described by Stahl (1994:89). They included the Akan state of Bono Manso, and the states of Dagomba and Mamprussi. Overall, the extent of Mande input into state formation in the region can be debated. Wilks (2000:94) notes various Mande settlement patterns including, most commonly, settlement among 'stateless' peoples such as the Bobo, Gurensi or Lobi. Secondly, there is settlement in older centralised kingdoms such as Dagomba, and thirdly, their role as catalysts in the process of state formation as in Gonja, already discussed. Within Bono Manso, a foreigners' settlement was also present; known as Kramokrom, it was located about 4 km west of the capital (Effah-Gyamyi 1985:23). It appears that here, unlike at Begho, where as we have seen the Muslim and other quarters grew together over time, the foreign traders at Bono Manso were more scrupulous in maintaining their separation, a reaction to a fear 'that they might be sacrificed to the local gods' according to claims noted by Effah-Gyamyi (1979:178). Thus again, parallels with patterns recorded elsewhere are apparent.

Three phases of occupation were defined at Bono Manso, spanning the thirteenth–fifteenth, mid-sixteenth–mid-seventeenth and late seventeenth–eighteenth centuries (Anquandah 1993:650). Trade items were lacking at Bono Manso, though well-defined horse trails were recorded as converging on the capital (Posnansky 1987:19), providing indirect and unusual evidence for trade. The settlement was located to benefit from trade on the Djenne–Begho route, as well as north-east to Hausaland (Effah-Gyamyi 1979:180). Although trade evidence was largely absent, evidence for craft production, weaving, brass-casting and iron working was found. Stahl (1994:89) also notes that the carinated vessels that were recovered 'were interpreted as imitations of brass vessels', providing further possibly indirect evidence for trade and Mande contacts.

The site of Yendi Dabari (ruined Yendi) (Shinnie and Ozanne 1962:90), which was the capital of Dagomba, has also been investigated. Of interest are a variety of structures recorded, which might possibly be the remains of structural complexes similar to caravanserai (a hostel for travellers common in the Islamic world, as has already been described with reference to the *wakala* at Suakin in chapter 3). However, to the author's knowledge, these structures in Yendi Dabari are unique in this region. One building complex is described as 160 m long, divided into a series of rectangular enclosures both by high walls and rows of rooms, some of which were once two or three storeyed. This led the excavator to conclude that, 'since buildings other than of circular plan are foreign to Dagomba, and houses of more than one storey rare, it is likely that this was a strangers' complex of warehouses and paddocks for pack animals' (Ozanne 1971:55–6). This provides further evidence for the flourishing commerce that linked this region to elsewhere in West Africa.

The Mossi

The Mossi are described by E. P. Skinner (1980:174) as developing as an ethnic group in the Upper Volta (Burkina Faso) region as a result of the northward expansion of the Dagomba of Ghana, 'who conquered and partially assimilated the autochthonous peoples such as the Ninisi, Foulse, and Habe', thus giving rise to the Mossi. Four major kingdoms were developed by the Mossi, all under rulers called *naba*. Today the Mossi are the majority ethnic group in Burkina Faso, and are agriculturists. Mossi traditional religion was centred on *keema*, ancestor veneration, propitiated by means of animal sacrifice. A supreme deity, Winnam, was also acknowledged, who was usually associated with another deity, Tenga, materially manifest by features such as sacred groves, rivers and mountains (E. P. Skinner 1964, 1980:174–5). Mossi religious beliefs were also manifest in the house form, described by Zahan (1970:70) as representing 'the divinity conceived as a four-faceted being that is doubly male and female. But it also symbolises the world and, more precisely, the "stomach of the world"'. Islam is increasingly gaining ground in Mossi society (see main text).

The Yarse and the Dyula

The noticeable emphasis on Ghana evident in the discussion thus far does not reflect personal preference but the archaeological research completed to date. Mande and other Muslim trader settlements existed elsewhere in the region, as trade routes criss-crossed the savannah and forest. Mande trade centres were also established from the sixteenth century along the major caravan trails in the area covered by modern Burkina Faso, but these still await archaeological investigation. However, as in modern Ghana, the trade routes further east also served to spread Islam among various ethnic groups in the region, most notably the Mossi (Levtzion 1968; E. P. Skinner 1980). The point about the differing nomenclature applied to the Mande according to geographical context has already been made, and in the Mossi lands they were known as Yarse. These are described by Levtzion (1968:165) as people of Mande origin, but assimilated with the Mossi to the extent that they speak their language, More. Settlements in which the Yarse stayed included Kaya, Rakaye, Patenga and, later in the eighteenth century, Ouagadougou, where they had their own quarter (Audouin and Deniel 1978:17).

In general, the spread of Islam was dependent on the goodwill of the Mossi kings, something which was not always forthcoming. This was, in part, because the relations between the Mossi and Muslims had not always been good. E. P. Skinner (1980:176–7) records how, for example, the Mossi of Yatenga sacked Timbuktu some time between 1328 and 1333, and that conflict with Muslims continued until the late fifteenth century. Ultimately, in 1498, the Songhai ruler Askia Muhammad (see chapter 5) launched a *jihad* against the Mossi to make them convert to Islam. This was largely unsuccessful, as 'the Mossi rulers felt they had to retain their ritual connections with their royal ancestors' (E. P. Skinner 1980:177). More successful was a compromising attitude as adopted by the Yarse traders which, according to Levtzion (1968:108), served three purposes. Firstly, it created favourable conditions for the growth of Muslim communities. Secondly, it secured the position of Muslims in rulers' courts. Thirdly, it infused Muslim elements into the rulers' ceremonies and customs. It was obviously successful, as evident in *Naba* Mogho, a ruler of Ouagadougou (1796–1825), becoming a Muslim and building a mosque (though also remaining true to the old ways). Izard and Ki-Zerbo (1992:365) rightly interpret this as indicating the 'aristocratic' character of Islam among the Mossi; a point, as we have seen, which has been relevant to many of the examples considered, concerning the first converts to Islam, from the Fur sultans, to those of Borno, to the rulers of Mali.

Similar Mande settlements were located in the Ivory Coast, with Kong, in the north of the country, a particularly important centre (Bernus 1960), and described by Captain Binger (1892) as having five mosques in the latter part of the nineteenth century. Kong was a major regional trade entrepôt but also became a centre of Islamic learning. Here, the Mande were referred to as Dyula, and Dyula Muslim influences in this region from the late fifteenth–early sixteenth century have been considered by Green (1986). The first elements of Dyula culture which were accepted by non-Muslims in the Kong region were textiles and 'Islamic supernatural aids', and the second was the power of writing by the non-literate (Green 1986:108–9). Another successful mechanism used to further conversions to Islam was the combination of pre-Islamic ritual with Muslim elements. In sum these elements led, as Green (1986:122) notes, to the further spread of Islam, 'by introducing its propogators, the Dyula, into the remote villages of the trade routes as traders, teachers and specialists of the supernatural'.

Once again, the pragmatic approach can be seen to be successful. Among the Mossi, Eaton's (1993) processes of 'inclusion' and 'identification' were much more successful than the sword. Similarly, in the Kong region, force was not a useful mechanism for encouraging conversion to Islam among the local populace. Rather, as in ancient Ghana 500 years earlier, the power of Arabic literacy was used, especially for supernatural purposes in enhancing and supporting power. These similarities with processes both in the western Sahel and elsewhere in sub-Saharan Africa indicate the commonalities in the conversion process that exist. Others which have been isolated in this consideration of the role of the Mande include those seen through archaeology, such as the changing nature of settlement patterns evident at sites such as Begho, literally reflecting the acceptance of Islam over time. In summary, the tentacles of Muslim commerce – but commerce also associated with the transfer of religion and, as we have seen, technology – served to link desert to savannah, and, as will now be illustrated, to forest as well.

The forest: the Akan/Asante

The role of literacy and Muslim supernatural aids such as amulets as primary mechanisms for attracting attention to Islam has been seen to be of significance in the Kong region of the Ivory Coast, and elsewhere, as among the Funj of the Nilotic Sudan (see chapter 3). A similar instance can be seen among the Akan of central and southern Ghana and the eastern Ivory Coast, but, ultimately, with different outcomes. The Akan are what could be termed a confederation of peoples including the Asante, Baule and Brong (Garrard 1988:1). They were involved in the gold trade, which has already been described, and were the southern suppliers of gold to the Muslim merchants in the more northerly trade centres such as Begho. However, the input of the Akan into their relations with the savannahs to the north was not always necessarily docile. Besides having a hand in founding states in the region, such as Bono Manso, and assuming hegemony over others (Kense 1987), the Asante, upon whom this case study will focus, were responsible in the eighteenth century for sacking Begho. This was one of a number of factors which led to the gradual decline of the site and its eventual abandonment, probably later in the same century (Posnansky 1973). Allied with this was the shift in Mediterranean-focused commerce (indirectly) via Djenne and Timbuktu, to one based on the Atlantic and European trading stations on the West African coast (see DeCorse 1992, 1993). The Asante benefited from this shift, and the Asante state has been described as 'a forest state that dominated the Ghanaian scene from the terminal seventeenth through the nineteenth centuries' (Stahl 1994:88).

The origins and early history of the Asante are difficult to trace, as 'little forest archaeology has been carried out' (McLeod 1981:11), and the Asante oral traditions 'are contradictory about their own earliest existence' (McLeod 1981:11). However, it is important to note that 'the Akan world of the forest developed in the second and third quarters of the second millennium AD quite independently from the areas on the northern fringe' (Posnansky 1987:21). Thus here, neither Muslims nor northern contacts were responsible for the development of social and political complexity as evidenced by the Asante. Peter and Ama Shinnie's research (1995, and see Shinnie 1996) indicates the indigenous developments that occurred among the Asante. One site investigated, Asantemanso, provided dates ranging from 1000 BCE to the present. The earlier part of the sequence cannot be linked with the Asante as defined today, but does indicate occupation in the region. The later archaeological evidence, however, i.e. from the tenth century CE, comprising house floors, faunal remains, slag and pottery, can be considered as linked with 'ancestors of the Asantes' (Shinnie and Shinnie 1995:7–8). Asantemanso is also of great significance as it is a site 'where it is claimed, the Asante people came out from a hole in the ground' (Shinnie and Shinnie 1995:6).

At this juncture it should be noted that Asante cannot be regarded as a Muslim state or even a Muslim-dominated state in the manner of many of the other polities described in this study thus far. It was not, but the presence of Muslims in its capital, Kumasi, is indisputable, and included believers from Gonja and Dagomba, Hausa 'and even traders and mendicant Holymen from as far away as the Maghreb, Egypt, and Baghdad' (Bravmann and Silverman 1987:94). In fact, there was a Muslim community numbering some 1,000 individuals in Kumasi. The Muslims controlled the cattle industry as well as a large portion of the distribution of gold, slaves, kola and salt, through their links to the Muslim-dominated long-distance trade routes (Wilks 1980:153).

Little evidence for northern contacts was found during the course of the Asante Research Project, though one possible remnant of such contacts is provided by various tobacco pipes recovered which were decorated with elaborate incised bowls similar to ones found on the River Niger (Shinnie and Shinnie 1995:12). The issue of the introduction of tobacco smoking to West Africa is a vexing one but it is quite possible, as Ozanne (1971:55) notes, that it was diffused from the Senegambia via the western Sudan to northern Ghana in the early seventeenth century. Alternatively, tobacco smoking might have been diffused via Timbuktu from North Africa at the same date (Ozanne 1969). The elaborate incised bowls referred to previously are a recurring feature of pipes from Timbuktu (Clague 2000). Thus tobacco smoking might be derived from northern, Muslim influences. Moreover, it should also be noted that plainer

European 'kaolin clay pipes' were also found during the Asante Research Project (Shinnie and Shinnie 1995:12). Ozanne (1971:55) accounts for such material by allowing for an independent introduction, via Europeans, into southerly areas such as Accra.

The main facet of Asante material culture which was influenced by Islam was, however, in the domain of magical protection. Although the Asante did not convert – possibly for the reasons Levtzion (1968:188) suggests, that to militarily powerful forest states 'Islam did not represent a serious challenge to their religion' – they did take in elements which increased religious power, such as Muslim amulets and prayers. In general, a deep concern with magic is apparent in many areas of the Muslim world; magic for protection, fulfilling desires, health, potency in love or war, myriad dimensions are especially manifest. As R. Silverman (1991:19) notes, 'orthodox Islam denies the efficacy of amulets and other magico-religious devices, but these traditions have always been a vital aspect of popular Islam, just as they have played a significant role in the belief systems of many people throughout history'. Numerous media can be employed to protect, curse or destroy – paper, metals, water, textiles, leather – but a common element is the efficacy of the Qur'an, as a supremely powerful agent. Besides verses from the Qur'an, notably the *Bismallah* and the *Fatihah*, cabbalistic signs, magical formulae, the beautiful names of God, numerical representations and various substances can all be used for magical and protective purposes (Insoll 1999a). Within the western Sudan, the amulet-covered war coats formerly used by soldiers provide a material, archaeologically visible manifestation of this **(figure 7.11)**, such as, for example, Posnansky's (1973) reference to a small flat rectangular piece of glass which might have come from 'an amulet of the type stitched into jackets' found at Begho.

Within Asante amulets for various purposes were popular, especially in Kumasi, where Owusu-Ansah (1983:100) notes, 'amulets were in demand everywhere – from the Asante palace to the slave's hut'. The Asante palace was visited by the British consul Joseph Dupuis in 1820, who found the ruler, Asantehene Osei Bonsu, wearing a white cloth covered in Arabic writing (Bravmann and Silverman 1987:94). Similarly, another ruler, Kofi Kakari, who reigned later in the nineteenth century, had the soles of his sandals covered in Islamic talismans, 'traces of Arabic writing and Islamic magical squares drawn in sepia ink upon the soles' (Bravmann and Silverman 1987:99). The Asante kings, though fiercely protective of their traditional beliefs and practices, were utilising elements of Muslim ritual and practice which they thought might benefit them. According to Owusu-Ansah (1983:112), Asante traditional religion focuses on Nyame, the supreme being; *nsamanfo*, ancestors; *abasom*, lesser gods; *nsuman*, charms; *abayifo*, witches; and *sasa*, individual spiritual powers of animals and humans. The *abasom* are often housed in special shrines, or *abasomfie* (Swithenbank 1969:15). When Dupuis met Osei Bonsu he had been involved in a traditional sacrifice, feeding the stools of his ancestors, and his

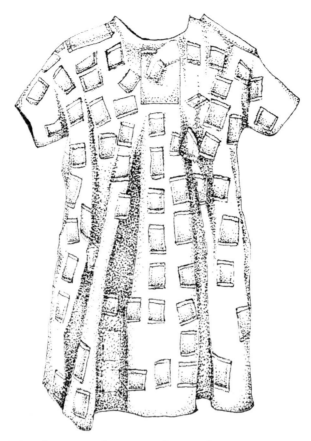

Figure 7.11 Amulet-covered war smock worn by Asante senior commanders

forehead was still smeared with a streak of blood. In total, as Bravmann and
Silverman (1987:99) describe, 'covered with his Arabic inscribed cloth suffused
with the blood of the *Awukudae* sacrifices upon his skin, the Asantehene succeeded fully in proclaiming his closeness to Allah and his own ancestors'.

The power of Arabic literacy and associated magical protection, as we have
seen, can hardly be said to be unique either in West Africa or indeed in sub-
Saharan Africa. The explorer Mungo Park, though not a Muslim, in part earned
his passage across the western Sudan through writing charms, and noted that
'all the natives of this part of Africa consider the art of writing as bordering on
magic: and it is not in the doctrines of the Prophet, but in the arts of the magician, that their confidence is placed' (1807:57). Park might have been over-
emphasising the situation somewhat, but the point about the importance of
writing – of literacy – is interesting. As has been noted with regard to the western Sahel, having Muslim officials to assist in running the court was important in ancient Ghana, for example (chapter 5). Administration was facilitated
through literacy in Arabic, and its possible magical import in a first-contact

situation is also easy to understand. As Goody notes, writing 'as a means of communication with the supernatural powers' was recognised among all aspects of society in the region – non-Muslims, Muslims, non-literate and literate (1968b:202). Magical and practical (the two are equally interlinked) benefits could be derived from literacy, and as Sanneh (1994) argues, non-Muslim populations often appropriated Arabic phrases before converting to Islam. The Asante rulers apparently recognised the benefits and according to Owusu-Ansah (1983:111), 'the king also consulted the Muslims at his court for political and spiritual advice on many occasions when the interests of the nation were concerned'. Furthermore, Wilks (1980:158) makes the important point that 'the king, and all his idolatrous subjects believed in it [the Qur'an] too'.

Perhaps then, the question can be posited, left to its own devices, the king and court of Asante might eventually have become Muslim, continuing the age-old process witnessed elsewhere in the continent. This, however, did not occur. Indeed, Wilks (1980:160) mentions how one Asante ruler, Osei Kwame (1777–c.1801) was 'dethroned by his chiefs' for becoming too close to Islam. Within Asante, it was all right to take elements from Islam, but the final steps, Eaton's (1993) 'identification' and 'displacement', did not occur.

The forest: Igbo and Yoruba

Igbo-Ukwu

Among the Asante the impact of contacts with the Islamic world might have been direct, through the presence of a Muslim community in Kumasi. But evidence for indirect contacts with the Muslim world can also be found in areas removed from direct contacts with Islam. This will be seen to be of especial consequence in the next chapter when interior eastern and southern Africa is considered, but is also found in the West African savannahs and forest.

At the site of Igbo-Ukwu in eastern Nigeria, for example, over 165,000 glass and carnelian beads were found, the majority of which would have been imported by Muslim-controlled long-distance trade, possibly via the city of Gao (Insoll and Shaw 1997). Although the inhabitants of Igbo-Ukwu (as with the Asante state) were not Muslim, they were obtaining prestige items, beads, via Muslim-dominated trade, with most of the beads also originating in the Muslim world, such as Egypt, and parts of western India, for example (Insoll and Shaw 1997). But unlike among the Asante, also non-Muslim as noted, there was no Muslim community resident at Igbo-Ukwu. The date of the Igbo-Ukwu material, if anything, precludes the presence of a Muslim community so far south, although the dating has been subject to some debate (Shaw 1970, 1977, 1978). Recent re-evaluation and correction of radiocarbon samples from the site has provided a date range of between the eighth and eleventh centuries (Bowman et al. 1990; Shaw 1995a, 1995b). In fact it is erroneous to talk of one site. Rather, the Igbo-Ukwu material represents a site complex. This was interpreted as comprising a regalia store known as Igbo-Isaiah; a burial chamber once lined with wooden planks and floored with matting, Igbo-Richard; and a pit used for the deliberate disposal of ritual and ceremonial objects following the razing of a shrine house, called Igbo-Jonah (Shaw 1970). Besides the beads, a remarkable array of bronzes cast by the lost-wax process were also recovered, along with several complete pots, and the decayed remains of six individuals (Shaw 1977).

This material cannot be interpreted as being associated with Muslim or even syncretic contexts. The presence of the material was instead interpreted as being connected with the *eze Nri* title-taking system (Shaw 1977), an interpretation which has been more fully expanded by K. Ray (1987). He suggests (1987:68) that Igbo-Isaiah, for example, was an *obu* or lineage temple, where elders and title-holders met to discuss affairs, and store 'collective wealth and prestige items'. Ray (1987:70) also agrees that Igbo-Richard represents a burial of an *eze Nri*, as well as possibly a shrine. The *eze Nri* was the pivot of the *Nri* ritual system, 'and had to observe the strictest safeguards of his ritual purity'. Analogy with ethnographic records of *eze Nri* burial in the 1930s, as well as the fact that many of the Igbo-Ukwu items bore the hallmarks of being connected with *Nri* symbolism and imagery, makes this interpretation convincing. Of the latter, the depiction of *ichi* facial scarification markings on bronze representations of human heads was good evidence in support of this interpretation. These are described by G. I. Jones (1984:36) as consisting of 'an unbroken series of diagonal gashes which covered the upper part of the face like a mask'. Today the Igbo are converting to Islam, and in the process many of the shrines, and much of the ritual paraphernalia, such as that associated with the *eze* lineages, is being destroyed. Interestingly, however this is not being done by the Igbo converts themselves, at least in the instance Ottenberg (1971:242) describes, but rather by 'northern' Muslims – perhaps Hausa, though this is unspecified – requested to do so by the Igbo Muslim converts.

Nupe and Yoruba

The relevant evidence from elsewhere in the region could be said to be dull in comparison to the spectacular and unique finds made at Igbo-Ukwu. However, it is not, and another important ethnic group who have been influenced by Islam both through direct and indirect contacts with Muslims are the Yoruba. The Yoruba today number some 15 million, and live in the 'rich forest and farmland of south-western Nigeria' (R. S. Smith 1988:6–7). Contacts between the Yoruba and Muslims from Hausaland and Borno began possibly as early as the fifteenth–sixteenth centuries, but certainly by the seventeenth century. Another conduit for Islamic contacts among the Yoruba could have been via the Nupe (Ryan 1978:104–5). The Nupe are another ethnic group in Nigeria inhabiting the savannahs, who, Nadel (1954:232) suggests, appear to have been influenced by Islam from the late seventeenth century. By the late eighteenth–early nineteenth centuries Muslim communities of varying size were recorded in many of the large market towns or ports in Yorubaland, including Badagry, Lagos, Oyo and Ketu. These were commercial centres in which 'Islam could easily thrive' (Gbadamosi 1978:5–6; see also Parrinder 1953). They were also all centres associated with the Yoruba Oyo kingdom, meaning that Islam was permeated by Oyo custom. Gbadamosi (1978:3–4), in his study of Islam among the Yoruba, makes the important point that the complexity of Yoruba traditional religion was in fact 'an obstacle to the progress of Islam'. How is unclear, and it is difficult to guess at, though it is known that Yoruba traditional religion is and was homogeneous, and centred on Olurun (Oludomare), 'and in a panoply of "gods" (*orisa*) such as *Esu, Ogun, Orisala* and the like' (Gbadamosi 1978:3; and see Fabunmi 1969; McClelland 1982).

Facets of Yoruba traditional religion have been revealed through archaeology, especially during excavations in Ile-Ife, the traditional capital of the Yoruba, and their 'spiritual centre' (R. S. Smith 1988:7). One important site, which was excavated by Peter Garlake (1978), was Obalara Land. Here, a potsherd pavement, similar to those already described for Borno in chapter 6, was uncovered, of sherds set on edge. Also recorded was the remains of what appeared to have been a small timber shrine as indicated by an abundance of iron nails found. At the centre of this postulated shrine had been carefully placed a stack of broken terracotta statuary along with a group of forty human skulls. These appear not to have been sacrificial victims, but rather were 'probably brought together after the corpses had decayed' (Garlake 1978:133). The date of this complex was around the fourteenth century. Ife was renowned both for the terracotta statuary just mentioned and also for bronze heads and figurines. In one of the royal houses of Ife alone, the Wunmonije compound, seventeen bronze heads were found (R. S. Smith 1988:19). These, as an art style, have been dated by radiocarbon and thermoluminescence (TL) to between the twelfth and early fifteenth centuries, and at all the sites where they have been recorded they have been associated with potsherd pavements (Eyo 1977:120–2).

The major heads have been interpreted as representing Yoruba rulers or *oni* and leading members of the court, while smaller statuettes were produced for shrines perhaps in commemoration of sacrificial victims (R. S. Smith 1988). Besides Ife, the spiritual centre, Oyo appears to have been the major political capital, but in total there were, according to one list, over 1,000 minor and major Yoruba rulers (R. S. Smith 1988:6–7). Urban centres were common, but only a few have been examined through archaeology. An example of one that has is provided by the rainforest town of Ipole-Ijesa, capital of a Yoruba polity, and a site where house remains, ramparts and a shrine were all recorded. These apparently date from the town's high point, the sixteenth century. Several cowrie shells were also collected, including one *Cypraea moneta* and several *Cypraea annulus*. The latter variety is indigenous to the Indian Ocean and introduced by Portuguese traders in the seventeenth century (Ogundiran 1994:7). These kingdoms were sometimes demarcated by earthworks (Agbaje-Williams 1990), and one of these has recently been investigated by Darling (1997). It is called Sungbo's Eredo, after a wealthy widow who supposedly had it built, and is an earth rampart 160 km long which surrounds the Yoruba town of Ijebu-Ode, and was built about 1,000 years ago. Ijebu-Ode has been surveyed, and various remains, including churches, mosques, cemeteries, houses and shrines, were recorded. Islam is here described as 'the first of the foreign religions to be introduced' (Momin 1989:42), and apparently Muslims, Christians and followers of traditional religions all coexisted. The latter are attested by various spirit groves, including the Oro grove, dedicated to the god Oro, to the south-west of the town.

However, relations with Muslims, Yoruba and foreign, were, as with the Mossi, not always good. This is best exemplified by the *jihad* launched from Ilorin, which was checked by Yoruba forces in 1840 at the battle of Osogbo. This was a turning point, and thereafter 'the picture of Islam among the Yoruba was largely a dismal one' (Gbadamosi 1978:12); not too dismal though, as Picton (1995a:76) notes that some 50 per cent of the Yoruba were reckoned to be Muslim by the 1960s. Yet Yoruba Islam is also characterised by syncretic tendencies. This includes consulting oracles, and sacrificing and participating in traditional festivals, as well as, in certain areas, the use of masks to proclaim the successful return from *hajj* by a family member (Omosade Awolalu 1979:194–5; Picton 1995a:94; Abimbola 1991:53–4).

The activities of the initial Muslim missionaries in Yorubaland would appear to have been reasonably successful, as by the end of the eighteenth century the Yoruba themselves were propagating Islam in neighbouring Togo and Benin (ex-Dahomey). Andre describes the Muslim community in Benin as existing 'au milieu de la grande majorité des Animistes, les Islamisés, venus de l'étranger pour la plupart, formaient un petit îlot' (1924:116). The parallels with the situation recorded elsewhere are striking and go further, as the Muslims had a chief/leader appointed amongst themselves to act as an intermediary with 'le roi fétichiste' (Andre 1924:116). This is reminiscent of though not exactly paralleling, the function of the representative of the merchants which existed several hundred years earlier on the East African coast and in the western Sahel, as described in chapters 4 and 5. The Muslim community in southern Nigeria and Benin was also supplemented by returning slaves from the mid-nineteenth century, including the Aguda, Yoruba repatriates from Brazil (Picton 1995a:78). Among the huge numbers exported in the Atlantic slave trade were Muslims; Fulani, Songhai, Mande, Yoruba, all ethnic groups could be included with people captured in war or sold into slavery for various offences, real or imagined. The Aguda also introduced the Yoruba-Brazilian style of mosque architecture which is found in both southern Nigeria and Benin. Mosques built in this style are often mistaken for churches owing to the use of a front elevation made up of a central pediment flanked by two towers, thus creating, in effect, a European Baroque design. This was transmitted through the Portuguese to Bahia in Brazil and then brought to West Africa (Khan 1994:254–5) **(figure 7.12)**.

Figure 7.12 Bahian-influenced mosque in Abomey, Benin

Jihad and the Islamic revivalist movements

A striking contrast to the weaker Islam of the forest zone is provided by the final case study to be considered in this chapter, the *jihads* that swept much of the western Sudan in the nineteenth century. The Fulani *jihad* of Uthman dan Fodio has already been discussed (chapter 6), and similar militant Islamic reform movements were initiated for various reasons, almost contemporaneously, in the western Sudan and forest zones. Their characteristic achievement was the creation of 'centralized Islamic polities forged either out of the autonomous

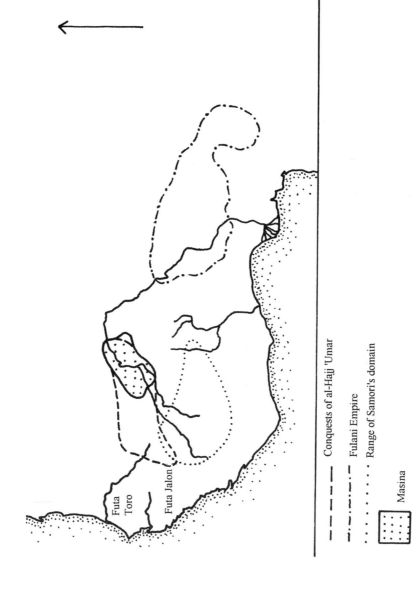

Futa
Toro

Futa Jalon

Conquests of al-Hajj 'Umar

Fulani Empire

Range of Samori's domain

Masina

Figure 7.13 *Jihad* areas in West Africa

principalities of half-hearted Muslim chiefs prone to mixing or out of the fragmented pieces of the medieval empires of the Sahel' (Hiskett 1994:114). First among the *jihad* movements of this region was that started in the Futa Djallon, a mountainous area of Guinea in the late eighteenth century (Viellard 1940) **(figure 7.13)**. As with the movements further east, this too was Fulani inspired.

The history of these reform movements is recounted by Robinson (2000), who describes how a second reform movement grew in another Fulani area, the Futa Toro, i.e. the middle valley of the Senegal river. Initially small in scope, this region was ultimately to provide one of the greatest *jihad* leaders in the region. This was al-Hajj 'Umar Tal, who was born in Futa Toro in the late eighteenth century, and studied in Futa Djallon, where he became a practitioner of the Tijaniyya Sufi movement. A *hajji*, as his title indicates, he travelled widely through the western Sudan as well, and in 1852 launched a *jihad* against the Bambara kingdoms of Segu and Kaarta (following a foray against another smaller kingdom, Tamba). This was successful, with his forces taking Nioro, the Kaarta capital in 1855, and Segu in 1861, where he 'staged a public ceremony of destruction of fetishes from the palace' (Robinson 2000:141). 'Umar also attacked the Fulani capital of Masina, Hamdallahi, for what he regarded as their apostasy in supporting Segu, and, though initially victorious, was himself killed in 1864.

Unfortunately, archaeological sites associated both with these movements and with the *jihadi* period in general have still largely to be investigated, though one aspect of material culture which has been recorded is the Fulani mosque architecture of the Futa Djallon and Futa Toro regions. Viellard (1940), for instance, describes the unique mosques of Futa Djallon with their thatched outer coverings, usually circular, placed over the internal square or rectangular prayer hall. The congregational mosque of Medina Maunde at Timbi is a notable example. However, more work has been done on the mosques of Futa Toro by Bourdier (1993). Interestingly, he notes that the earthen mosques built in the first years of reform in the region consciously follow the plan of the Prophet's dwelling in Medina, as with the mosque of Seno Palel, built some time before 1776. This is indicated, for example, by the square plan with multiple entrances. The square plan is important 'because of its association with the sacred form of the central monument' (Bourdier 1993:34). The central monument referred to is the Ka'bah, the focal point of all mosques (see chapter 1). In so doing, and in light of the link with the reform movement, it can be suggested that a conscious effort was being made to reach back to the perceived purity of early Islam through the plan of these mosques. We have seen this feature elsewhere, often associated with religious reform or renewal.

Hamdallahi

One site which has been investigated archaeologically is Hamdallahi, the capital of the Fulani caliphate of Masina, mentioned previously as being captured by

Figure 7.14 The inner wall at Hamdallahi

al-Hajj 'Umar. The city, Hamdallahi, meaning 'Praise be to God', was founded in 1818–20 by Sekou Amadou, who himself had started a successful *jihad* in the early nineteenth century aimed at Segu, and the abhorent Muslim practices he saw in Djenne as a student there (Robinson 2000:139). A further aim was to 'control and convert the still "wild" Fulani', thus he decreed that it was an 'obligation of all pastoralists to have a permanent village in the *seno-bourgou* lands of the floodplain' (R. J. McIntosh 1998:300). This would also create military reserves which he could draw upon as needed, as well as making it easier to keep an eye on dissenters (Mayor 1997:41).

Hamdallahi, the remains of which are still standing 21 km south-east of Mopti in Mali, has been partially excavated (Gallay et al. 1990). The plan of the city revealed that it was fortified with a wall of sun-dried brick, pentagonal in shape and measuring 2 km north–south, and 1.9 km east–west **(figure 7.14)**. At the heart of the city were the congregational mosque and Amadou's palace, side by side – thus again, it can be suggested, returning to early Islamic metaphors in illustrating the lack of differentiation between the secular and sacred aspects of life in Islam. This was a recurring feature of early Islamic settlements, as indicated, for example, by the Round City at Baghdad (Lassner 1970). Hamdallahi is also reminiscent of the large fortified urban centres of the central Sudan described in the last chapter, sites such as Garoumele, and Birni Ngazargamo, for instance (Bivar and Shinnie 1962). Between the outer enclosing wall and the palace complex and congregational mosque at the centre were numerous other structures: houses, shops, courtyards containing tents and other nomad shelters (Gallay et al. 1990). One of these structures was excavated uncovering a large courtyard, roughly 25 m × 15 m, with a single entrance and two buildings inside. The disproportionate size of the courtyard to the structures suggested that straw huts were constructed on the inside, and that cattle were also kept in the courtyard (Mayor 1997:49, 57). A Fulani attribution thus seems likely, an interpretation supported by the results of the pottery analysis which found that 75 per cent of the pottery from Hamdallahi could be attributed 'à la tradition Peule' (Mayor 1997:55), vessels used for storing water, or for cooking dietary staples such as couscous.

The nomadic origins of this Fulani-led *jihad* are also evident in another site investigated close to Hamdallahi, Modjodjé. This was a temporary site occupied by Sekou Amadou while Hamdallahi was being constructed (Mayor 1997). A variety of dry-stone structures were recorded at Modjodjé including the possible remains of a mosque, the residence of Sekou Amadou, and the house of his family. Also significant, in view of Sekou Amadou's sedentarisation policies, was 'le remplacement progressif des constructions de paille, habituelles aux Peuls nomades, par une architecture plus durable' (Mayor 1997:41). However, of equal interest was the fact that Modjodjé was built at the foot of hills occupied by Dogon.

The Dogon

The Dogon are a people who occupy the Bandiagara cliffs, the sandstone plateau at its summit, and the sandy Seno plain at its base. They have been studied since the beginning of the twentieth century by anthropologists, most notably Marcel Griaule (1965), and increasingly by archaeologists (see, e.g., Bedaux 1972, 1978). The first recognisable group known in the proto-historical cultural sequence of the Bandiagara region are the Toloy, represented by about forty granaries made of stacked mud coils in the Sanga area, and dating from the third to second centuries BCE. By the eleventh century the Toloy had been succeeded by the Tellem, according to Bedaux (1988:38), with no sign of occupation in the intervening period. However, recent research is questioning this model (E. Huysecom, pers. comm.). Where the Tellem emerged from is unclear, possibly they were displaced from elsewhere by the decline of the empire of Ghana. The Tellem are better known than the Toloy through archaeology, but largely through the caves they used for burial. Burial was with grave-goods, many of which have survived, providing information on Tellem lifeways. These include textiles, pottery, iron and leather objects, as well as ritual items such as wooden statuettes (Bedaux 1988:39; Bolland 1991). The interchange between the Tellem and the Dogon is the subject of further debate. Bedaux (1988:41) suggests that some of the Tellem were incorporated by the Dogon, others were taken in slave raids, while others died of disease. Whatever the cause, a group called the Dogon, also of uncertain origins, were the occupiers of the Bandiagara escarpment by the late sixteenth century. Again, it is highly likely that the reconstruction just presented will be fundamentally altered in the light of ongoing archaeological research (E. Huysecom, pers. comm.).

Dogon religion is complex, and is summarised by van Beek (1988). The head of the Dogon triumvirate is Ama or Amma, the sky god, the others being Nomo, the water god, and Lewe or Lebe, the earth god. Sacrifices and rituals are primarily directed toward Ama, though carved figurines are also produced, which are 'representations of the living' (van Beek 1988:60). However, these too serve as mediators with Ama – in helping in solving problems, for instance. Divination is also a key feature of Dogon religion, as are masked dances (figure 7.15). The complex Dogon cosmology is made materially manifest in village and house form. The Dogon house, for example, is described by Zahan (1970:71) as representing 'a human being stretched out on his right, his procreative side, a position which is equally that of the man on the conjugal bed and of the corpse in the tomb'. Increasingly, the Dogon are converting to Islam and mosques are now a feature of many Dogon villages.

Figure 7.15 Masked Dogon dancer, Ende village

The presence of the Muslim settlement had an effect upon the nearest Dogon village, Bona, in several ways which could be charted in the 'transformations matérielles' (Mayor 1997:57). These included the abandonment of the traditional collective tombs in favour of a cemetery for individual burial, the shift

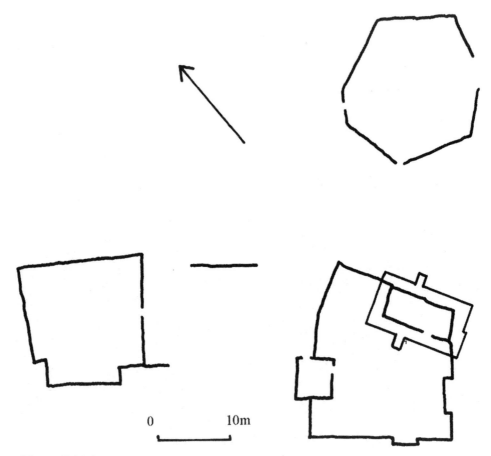

0   10m

Figure 7.16 Stone structures at Modjodjé

in location of the village after the 1860s (Hamdallahi being destroyed in this decade), and its final desertion in favour of Modjodjé by 1900 **(figure 7.16)**. A further effect was the abandonment of the traditional painted circumcision place. Essentially, what was being charted in the material remains and oral tradition was the progress of Islamisation. This is an explicit instance of Islamisation, but the remainder of the Dogon in their highland retreat, the Bandiagara escarpment, were not untouched by the currents of Islam swirling around them. Goody (1971a:457), for example, suggests that the wearing of clothing by the Dogon was the result of Muslim influence. Thus ethnic groups such as the Dogon, frequently cited as bastions of traditional religions and practices, were not immune from Islamic influences. An example of the frequently perceived 'pristine' state of the Dogon is provided by de Heusch (1985:1) who states, referring to the work of Marcel Griaule, that, 'beginning in 1931, these expeditions led, after the Second World War, to the discovery of the extraordinary complexity of those ancient West African civilisations which *had not been penetrated* *by Islam'* (emphasis added). Rather, the reverse is true, reinforcing the picture that Muslim influence was felt across almost the whole of the continent in varying degrees.

The Dogon also appear to have played a more direct role in the *jihads*, casting further light on the pragmatics of Muslim–non-Muslim relations in the area. At Hamdallahi, three corpses were uncovered which had been left in a heap in the road and had not been accorded funerary rites according to Muslim or, apparently, any other tradition. Rather than casualties of war, i.e. attacking forces, their presence, and the fact that they were robust individuals wearing earrings, was interpreted as representing 'les mercenaires Dogons engagés par El Hadj Omar lors des derniers combats' (Mayor 1997:40). This is a plausible interpretation considering the context of the discovery, and the final throes of Hamdallahi.

Summary and conclusions

Conversion to Islam in the western Sudan and forest zones can be seen to be comparatively late in date, starting with the nominal Islamisation of the rulers of Mali in the twelfth century. Moving south, it gets progressively later, and remains very much an ongoing process in many areas. A further important feature of Islam in the region which was isolated is the unity lent to much of the Islamisation process and the resultant material culture legacy through the actions of the Mande. Their energetic and, it must be remembered, essentially peaceful trading activities served to spread Islam far from their savannah homelands to the forest fringe between the fifteenth and eighteenth centuries. The impact of this indigenous merchant group was substantial, and it has also proved possible to isolate various parallels with processes apparent in the western Sahel several centuries earlier, namely, in the establishment of separate quarters or settlements as at Begho or Bono Manso (Posnansky 1973; Effah-Gyamyi 1985), paralleling the situation at Gao for example (Insoll 2000b, and see chapter 5). Differences do also exist in, for example, the indigenous nature of conversion processes via the Mande in the West African Sudan and forest as opposed to the North African Arab and Berber element in the western Sahel.

A further, and repeat, theme of this chapter has been how Islam has been popularised, evident in many ways – through, for instance, the incorporation of masking traditions in certain areas (Bravmann 1974). Pragmatism and conciliation have also been seen to be key elements in how Islam was spread through the savannah and forest zones. Among the Mossi or the Yoruba, the sword was unsuccessful; instead, effective and beneficial elements of Muslim practice, such as Islamic supernatural aids, Arabic literacy or Muslim courtly advisers were used to promote the religion (Ryan 1978; E. P. Skinner 1980). Facets of these are recognisable through archaeological evidence, and as relevant archaeological research continues these processes will be better documented through material culture. However, to obtain a fuller picture of the impact of Islam, a multi-source approach will still be required, for reasons already described. The coexistence of different religious traditions was also well attested through archaeological evidence, as with the continuation of urn burial or the proliferation of terracotta figurines in the inland Niger delta (Bedaux 1978; R. J. McIntosh 1998). A further and less peaceful dimension to this analysis was added by the *jihads* of the eighteenth and nineteenth centuries. These, as just described, swept through much of the region and served to spread Islam much further, deep into the forests, increasing conversions in the process. Finally, the far-reaching effects of Islam in sub-Saharan Africa were again indicated, through the influences felt among the Dogon, for example. It is this latter theme that will become even more evident as we now move on to consider the archaeology of Islam in the heart of interior eastern and southern Africa in the final regional chapter.

CHAPTER 8

THE AFRICAN INTERIOR: EASTERN, CENTRAL AND SOUTHERN AFRICA

Introduction

The inhabitants of the interior of eastern, central, and southern Africa were the last to be exposed to Islam in sub-Saharan Africa (**figure 8.1**). It is also worth noting that the geographical area covered by this chapter is vast, and a wide range of environments is found. These include the humid coastal forest found slightly inland, largely in the more northerly stretches, i.e. from central Mozambique north (Alpers 1975:5), as well as great tracts of savannah grasslands and woodland savannah encountered further into the interior. The latter is an ecozone which predominates across many parts of eastern-central and southern Africa (as well as elsewhere in the continent, as we have seen). These savannahs have provided an environment for a variety of states. Good examples of these are provided by the kingdoms that developed in the savannah regions north of the Zambezi and south of the equatorial forest, where, among others, the Kongo, Luba, Kazembe and Lozi kingdoms all flourished (Vansina 1966). This is also a region of great lakes – Malawi, Tanganyika and Victoria – as well as many smaller ones and, in certain areas, of navigable stretches of river. The River Rovuma, for instance (Alpers 1975:5), or, in the rainforest, the Zaire/Congo river.

The term 'rainforest' just used is, as Vansina (1990:39) notes, 'a general term to designate low altitude forests exposed to high rainfall, with stable temperatures in the 25 to 27 degrees Centigrade range, characterized by closed canopies, often disposed on several layers, and by evergreen or semi-deciduous trees'. However, as Vansina also rightly points out (1990:44–5), the term 'rainforest' equally does not allow for the range of environmental diversity encompassed within the equatorial forests usually designated thus. This is understandable, as approximately 15 million hectares of land stretching some 3,400 km in length is included within this defined rainforest belt, parts of which fall within our concern here. Other environments which will come within the discussion include the Zimbabwe plateau, in which Great Zimbabwe and over fifty other stone ruins or *madzimbahwe* were situated (Hall 1987:92), as well as the southern edge of the Makgadikgadi pans in Botswana, an important place for ivory working (Reid and Segobye 2000). These are all further areas which also form part of the archaeology of Islam in sub-Saharan Africa.

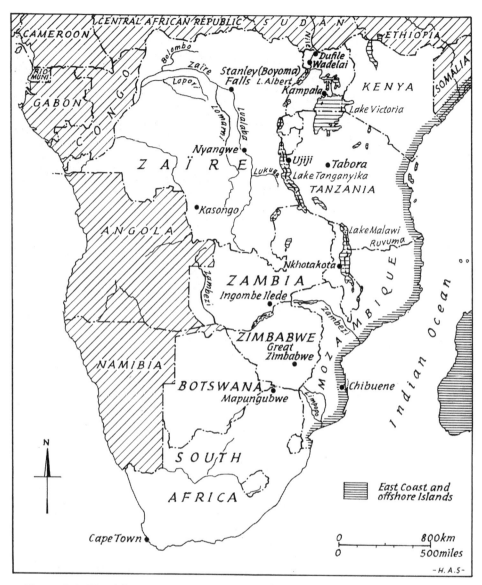

Figure 8.1 The African interior: east, central and southern Africa

This huge territory also abuts many of the other regions which have already been discussed, and in many cases interlinks with events occurring elsewhere. Northern Uganda was thus connected with the Nilotic Sudan, Dar al-Kuti bordered the termini of the East African Swahili and Arab traders and slavers, and the East African coast was intimately connected with events in much of southern and eastern-central Africa. Yet to what degree the inhabitants of this immense area had exposure to Islam prior to the commencement of activities by Muslim Arab and Swahili traders who entered the interior in the nineteenth century in search of ivory and slaves (Alpers 1975) is subject to debate. Opinions vary as to the impact and even presence of Muslim traders in the interior prior to this point in time. Within southern Africa, for example, Fagan (1972:7) suggests that Arab traders first ventured into the interior from the eleventh century. However, Hiskett (1994:158) is more cautious and says that Muslim merchants were established in the Zambezi area, such as at Sena and Tete, by the early sixteenth century. In eastern-central Africa, Kagabo (1988:16) mentions that 'les commerçants d'Afrique orientale aient cherché à établir des relations commerciales avec le Rwanda' from as early as the seventeenth century.

Hiskett might be correct in dating limited contacts in the Zambezi area to the early sixteenth century, but elsewhere it is unlikely that Muslim merchants, slavers, or whoever, maintained any sustained contacts with the interior until the nineteenth century. However, having made this point, it is also necessary to note that trade goods obtained from the coast, items such as coloured glass beads and marine shell, have been found at various sites in the interior dating from the late first millennium onwards. These range from various locations in Zimbabwe (Swan 1994) to the Upemba depression in Zaire/Congo (de Maret 1999) and around Lake Victoria in Uganda (Robertshaw 1997) (see below). Yet the recovery of this material need not be interpreted as implying its delivery by coastal merchants. Rather, it is more likely that these types of item were gradually traded through local trade networks and in this manner worked their way inland.

It is also relevant to note that in this chapter it is unnecessary to speak of the pre-Islamic background in a distinct section, as has been done in the other chapters. This is because there was no 'Islamic' period as such. Similarly, the diversity evident in the multiplicity of kingdoms and other polities found across this region renders their summary to a couple of paragraphs meaningless. Instead, the relevant material will be described as we proceed. A further point which should also be made is that as with the other chapters, a multi-source approach will again be adopted. This is in part necessitated by a lack of archaeological research in many areas, something Vansina (1966:11) remarks upon in stating that 'very few archaeological excavations dealing with Iron Age sites have been carried out so far, however, and it will take many more before the archaeological picture becomes even reasonably detailed'. This point was made nearly forty years ago in reference to the savannah regions of eastern-central Africa, notably Zaire/Congo, where unfortunately, little further research has been able to take place owing to political events in the area. Exceptions will be discussed later, but in other areas archaeological research has proceeded greatly – in parts of East Africa (Sutton 1990), or Zimbabwe (Hall 1987), for example. Thus the archaeological evidence will be supplemented by other sources, again following the pattern established in the preceding chapters. In this respect anthropology contributes much, but of especial use are historical sources – notably, allowing for bias, the writings of the first European explorers, missionaries and soldiers to enter the region. These individuals often observed, or came into conflict with, the Arab and Swahili traders and their allies from the mid-nineteenth century onwards (see, e.g., Burton 1993 [1860]; Hinde 1897).

In effect, we have reached the other end of the timescale, far removed geographically and temporally from the early Muslim contacts with the Horn of Africa discussed in chapter 2. But the question can be posed as to whether we have reached the end of the line as regards historical process, or come full circle. Concerning direct parallels with events on the Red Sea over 1,200 years previously, it is obvious that these are few, but neither has the 'end of the line' been reached. Conversion to Islam continues and the processes of Islamisation, as among the Yao of Malawi (Thorold 1987) are remarkably similar to those described in previous chapters for over a millennium ago, as will become apparent. However, it is also true that in reaching the heart of the continent we have come full circle.

Southern Africa

Coastal–interior trade

The existence of trade between the interior and the lower reaches of the East African coast was touched upon in chapter 4, where it was mentioned that this was not accompanied by local conversions to Islam. The first archaeological evidence for trade goods obtained from the coast and Indian Ocean trading networks reported from the region, in Zimbabwe and Zambia, is described by Swan (1994:72–3). This includes two dozen glass beads and a conus shell from the East African coast found at the Gokomere tunnel site dated to 570–90 cal CE, as well as two white and a single red-on-green glass bead from Mabveni dated to 600–15 cal CE. Both these sites are in Zimbabwe, but cowrie shells have also been found in mound sites on the Batoka plateau of southern Zambia dated to the mid-sixth century. The shells are not of particular significance as, though indicative of coast–interior contacts, they are not necessarily proof of international trade. In contrast, the beads are of interest, as these were almost certainly imported from further than the eastern or southern African coast and, if the dates are correct, they would be from pre-Islamic trade networks, the existence of which was discussed in chapters 2 and 4.

Why such coastal–interior trade patterns were established could be due to a variety of reasons, such as the desire to obtain prestige items (see below), economic imperatives, scarcity or surpluses. Precise reasoning is largely uncertain, though it is certain that it was 'indigenous forces which moulded the pattern of international trade' (Alpers 1975:29). Indigenous forces such as the rarity of cake salt were a major factor, as Fagan (1972:5) states, in the 'development of complex but informal barter networks among the farming communities of Southern Africa over a thousand years ago'. In the same way as described for the development of trans-Saharan trade in the western Sahel (see chapter 5), long-distance trade routes were added onto already well-established local ones which were used to move foodstuffs, metals and the like.

After the ninth century the numbers of beads found on archaeological sites in southern Africa increase, as exemplified by the forty-one dark-blue snapped-cane glass beads recovered from Boggie's Hill in Zimbabwe. This evidence leads Swan (1994:76) to suggest that 'there seems to have been far more external-exchange activity during this period'. This certainly seems correct, and a likely channel for this material would have been the coastal site of Chibuene in southern Mozambique described in chapter 4 (and see Sinclair 1987). Another area of southern Africa integrated into the network of Indian Ocean trade at this time appears to have been the Limpopo basin. Pwiti (1991:52–3) reports that glass beads dating from the early ninth century were recovered from Schroda, a site where thirty-six carnivore skulls were found, material which was interpreted as evidence for a trade in leopard skins. Ivory shavings and bangle fragments were also found at Schroda, and similarly at K2 (Hall 1987:79). The latter site immediately post-dates Schroda and also appears to have been an ivory-working centre, as indicated by the tusk fragments and ivory chips found.

This pattern of ivory working has been interpreted by Reid and Segobye (2000) as possibly indicating that the Indian Ocean trade centres were supplied with finished ivory items rather than the raw material itself. Their excavations at the site of Mosu 1, located on the southern boundary of the Makgadikgadi pan in Botswana, found a cache of ivory bangles, apparently once placed in a sack, and dated to the tenth century. This evidence, along with ivory-working debris found at Bosutwe and Taukome, also in Botswana, could signal that items such as finished ivory bangles were destined for centres such as Schroda and K2 for onward trade to the coast (Reid and Segobye:329). This postulated finished-ivory trade is perhaps explained by a large market for African ivory in India where it was consumed for ornaments in Hindu wedding rituals (Fagan 1972:6). This trade was necessitated by the fact that African ivory is much easier to work than the more brittle Indian ivory. In return, beads and other commodities were received, beads being durable and also surviving at Mosu 1 and at K2.

Items such as the glass beads found at many of these sites appear not to have been sterile trinkets. They also seem to have functioned in more profound ways, as markers of status and prestige. This would certainly appear to be the case at Mapungubwe (Voight 1983), again in the same Limpopo–Shashe region. Here, the inhabitants appear to have 'grasped the opportunity of obtaining rare and exotic goods' (Hall 1987:79). These included monochrome glass seed beads, some of which have been sourced, using plasma mass spectroscopy, to Fustat near Cairo in Egypt. The identification was made possible as the 'alkali agent used to make the glass is specific to seawater and its derivatives, as found on the desert coasts of Egypt' (Saitowitz et al. 1996:101). Other glass beads were probably manufactured at the coastal trade centres them-selves. Besides glass beads being imported, Swan (1994:78) also reports that two sherds of Sung celadon were found at Mapungubwe, along with cowrie shells. In return, animal skins and ivory might have been exported. However, ivory-working debris is absent at Mapungubwe (Reid and Segobye 2000:330), though bone working – producing points, tubes and spatulas, for example – took place (Hall 1987:81).

It is also undeniable that Mapungubwe represents a more complex politi-cal entity than its predecessors such as Schroda and K2. As Pwiti (1991:54) notes, 'it was probably the centre of the region's first state system, develop-ing from the eleventh century AD and collapsing sometime during the early part of the thirteenth century'. Although, as Hall (1987) remarks, it is unsat-isfactory to invoke participation in Indian Ocean trade as a causal mechanism for state development here, it is also undeniable that it was of significance in providing items used in negotiating political relationships in the area. For 'cattle, military service and other forms of tribute would have flowed inwards to the major centres of power, while beads, cloth and other valued signifiers of status would have moved outwards to regional centres and to local chiefs who acknowledged the suzerainty of the Mapungubwe kings' (Hall 1987:90). Thus although it can be seen that it is wrong to attribute social and politi-cal developments, in this instance, to stimuli derived from Muslim-dominated Indian Ocean trade, equally it can be seen that the opportunity of obtaining new prestige items was rapidly capitalised upon by local rulers in keeping and increasing power. Parallels can again be drawn with other regions, with Borno for example (see chapter 6), where prestige items were also obtained via long-distance Muslim-controlled trans-Saharan trade. But the essential difference in southern Africa is that unlike in Borno, there was no allied religious impact whatsoever.

By the mid-to late twelfth century circumstances appear to have changed, pre-cipitated by the rise in demand for gold which led to a shift in coastal–interior trade northwards, centred on the Zimbabwe plateau (Hall 1987). This shift was probably linked with the more abundant gold deposits found in the Zimbabwe plateau as opposed to the Limpopo valley (Pwiti 1991:55). As Horton and Middleton (2000:102) note, 'rather than trade routes moving further down the coast, it appears that the earliest ones are the most southerly, based on the Limpopo, and that successor states developed routes based on the Save and Zambezi Rivers'. This is also a period which sees the rise of a successor state to Mapungubwe, centred upon Great Zimbabwe, the rulers of which were also involved in coastal trade. The newly important gold trade was capitalised upon by the inhabitants of Great Zimbabwe, and although there is no evidence to link the occupants of the stone buildings with actual mining, evidence for gold smelting and manufacture was found, activities which were possibly controlled by the elites (Swan 1994:122). In total some 200 ounces of gold has been found at Great Zimbabwe during the various excavations completed at the site (see box). Although apparently valued no higher than copper or bronze, it was used for a variety of purposes – to produce wire, as sheets fixed to wooden backing with gold pins, and cast into beads of spherical, cuboidal, barrel and biconical shapes (Garlake 1973:115–16).

Great Zimbabwe

Great Zimbabwe is one of the most famous archaeological sites in sub-Saharan Africa, and for this reason has been much discussed (Garlake 1973; Hall 1987). It has also suffered an extremely chequered history in terms of research conducted at the site and the resulting interpretations that have been proposed. These varying approaches to Great Zimbabwe have been extensively documented by Hall (1987, 1990). The first European to examine the site, Carl Mauch in 1871, started the process of misinterpretation when he 'believed that the stonework, incorporating Lebanese cedarwood, was built at the instruction of the Queen of Sheba' (Hall 1987:103). Alternative interpretations have included attributing the stone ruins to South Arabians or ancient Egyptians – in other words, anyone but the indigenous population. However, these misinterpretations have been rectified by the attentions of professional archaeologists, scholars such as Gertrude Caton-Thompson (1931), Peter Garlake (1973) and Thomas Huffman (1996). The site is now incontrovertibly known to be an indigenous foundation associated with a major kingdom which developed on the Zimbabwe plateau and which derived its wealth from control of cattle, local trade, and trade, including that in gold, to the coast.

Great Zimbabwe covers approximately 700 ha and might have had a population as high as 18,000 people during its heyday between the mid-thirteenth and mid-fifteenth centuries. The site is dominated by a large stone-built hill complex with the acropolis or Hill Ruin at the top (**figure 8.2**). The lower slopes of this hill were covered with several hut terraces, the base of which was partly surrounded by the inner perimeter wall. A further outer perimeter wall encloses the hill and several structures in the lower valley and ridge complex including the Great Enclosure (Huffman 1996:125). Further residential zones are found beyond the central settlement. The central palace area functioned to seclude the sacred leader, the divine king, while lesser leaders lived in smaller palaces on the outskirts, and the bulk of the population below and beyond the hill (Huffman 1996:154). It is also important to note that Great Zimbabwe was at the apex of a settlement hierarchy, with over fifty other *madzimbahwe* known. These have been interpreted as 'provincial courts' (Garlake 1973:197), which might have housed other elites linked with the Zimbabwe state within their stone enclosing walls – regional centres, in effect. How-ever, as Hall (1987:93) notes, 'much, and perhaps the majority, of the popula-tion of early Zimbabwe lived away from the *madzimbahwe*'. These village sites might lack the stonework of the Zimbabwe sites, but also formed part of the Zimbabwe polity (Sinclair 1984). Great Zimbabwe has provided ex-tensive evidence indicating participation in coastal–interior trade (see main text), but as Swan (1994:78) notes, glass trade beads, for example, are found at many other Zimbabwe tradition sites such as Chiwona, Cornucopia, Vuhwa and Ruanga.

The most significant find indicating the type of material which was received at Great Zimbabwe in return for the gold from the coastal traders was a hoard within the Renders Ruin. The material within this hoard was diverse in ori-gin and is well described by Garlake (1973:124, 132–3). The component of the hoard derived from the coast primarily consisted of thousands of glass beads, monochrome spheres, oblates and cylinders – in other words, the type of trade beads found across the continent. A small glazed pot inscribed in glazed relief in Arabic in the Naskhi script (see chapter 1) was also found. This appears to be of Persian provenance and of fourteenth-century date, a date in turn ascribed to the complete hoard. A fragment of a glass vessel was also found, probably manu-factured in one of the major Near Eastern glass centres such as Damascus, Cairo or Aleppo. Chinese pottery was also present, 'sherds of no more than about 13 vessels' (Garlake 1973:129). These included sherds from a Ming celadon vessel (1368–1644), as well as a single sherd of possible earlier Sung date (960–1279). Cowrie shells and a quantity of brass wire, along with items of wider African and more local production were also recovered. The latter include iron wire, hoes, axes, three iron gongs and a soapstone dish.

The significance of the hoard has been the subject of varying interpretations which have important ramifications for whether it actually signals the presence of a coastal merchant at Great Zimbabwe. R. N. Hall, the original excavator, interpreted the cache as the contents of 'an Arab trading centre of medieval times' (Garlake 1973:132). Garlake (1973:133) rightly notes that it 'shows that Great Zimbabwe about the fourteenth century had ultimately far-flung trading contacts and that it was probably in direct contact with the coastal cities'. Obvi-ously, there is a major difference in interpreting the hoard as indicating coastal contacts as opposed to the physical presence of coastal, Muslim merchants at Great Zimbabwe. Although the occasional visit of Arab or Swahili traders to the interior cannot be discounted, it is probable that the coast–interior trade was largely in the hands of locally appointed intermediaries who travelled to the coast. Archaeological evidence for the presence of Muslim communities in the interior of Southern Africa is thus far lacking prior to those established follow-ing Dutch colonisation of the Cape from the mid-seventeenth century onwards

Figure 8.2 The acropolis, Great Zimbabwe

(see below). Some scholars, however, argue that Arabs, Swahili or Islamised local groups were 'well-established until the arrival of the Portuguese' (Alpers 2000:304) on the Zimbabwe plateau, with these communities numbering as many as 2000 individuals in total. However, the evidence for their presence is inconclusive, yet the Lemba, 'whose clan names indicate Arab influence' (Alpers 2000:305), might, at a pinch, be their descendants.

At present the archaeological evidence does not suggest that Muslims were present at Great Zimbabwe. Thus it is highly unlikely that the hoard is a cache of their trade goods dating from the fourteenth century. Rather, when the composition of the hoard is looked at in more detail, a more convincing alternative can be proposed, as indeed has been done by Huffman (1996). He suggests that the presence of kingly insignia such as the three iron gongs and two bronze spearheads indicate that the hoard was found in the residence of the *vahozi*, 'the only person with the right and duty to keep the king's possessions, especially his spears and axes, no one else could have lived here' (Huffman 1996:143). Therefore, the hoard obviously indicates coastal contacts, but its presence signals something more complicated than merely a cache of trade goods left by an Arab merchant. It also signals prestige in the range of goods kept by the *vahozi* for the sacred leader. Gold, abundant in the local context, was not especially prestigious or valuable at Great Zimbabwe, whereas at the coast its value was great. Likewise, beads and glazed pottery were abundant at the coast, as we have seen in chapter 4, and their prestige value increased significantly in the interior as their rarity concomitantly increased (Hall 1987:102).

The hoard further functions within the complex ritual meaning that underlay Great Zimbabwe. This extends through the settlement and architectural layout, the patterning of the material found, and the material itself. In fact, Garlake (1973:184) has interpreted the function of Great Zimbabwe firstly as controlling long-distance trade, and secondly as 'a major religious centre'. The religious function of Great Zimbabwe is probably indicated, most famously, by the soapstone birds that have been found **(figure 8.3)**. Seven complete examples and one fragment of these birds have been recorded; all stood about 1 m in height, and appear to represent a generic rather than specific type of bird. More common are the soapstone monoliths that have been recovered. These are the same height and shape as the birds and were distributed in areas of 'sacred character' – along the tops of walls, grouped on low earthen platforms, set in altars, or set in groups in the ground. These might have functioned as 'reminders or "tallies" of the individual dead' (Garlake 1973:122). In sum, Huffman (1996:132) suggests that the monoliths, stone towers and features such as vertical grooves cut in doorways represented 'the two dominant responsibilities of sacred leadership – justice and defence together with agricultural bounty and human fertility'.

Trade was not only with the coast. Iron, copper, salt, cloth and various other commodities were probably traded with communities to the north as 'typified

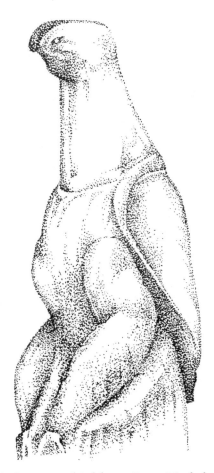

Figure 8.3 Soapstone bird from Great Zimbabwe

by Ingombe Ilede' (Garlake 1973:194). Ingombe Ilede, meaning 'the place where the cow lies down' (Fagan 1972:8), is situated some 5 km from the River Zambezi in southern Zambia. The occupants of the site appear to have participated in the ivory trade, as indicated by the presence of elephant limb bones in all the levels. Two phases of occupation were recorded, with the site first occupied in the seventh century, abandoned for a while, then reoccupied for a short period around 1400. It is this latter period that is of importance here, as forty-six burials dating from the fourteenth to fifteenth centuries were excavated. Some of these contained a variety of grave goods, including eleven richer burials with items from the coast. These latter coastal items, rather than being obtained directly from the coastal trade centres, were possibly obtained via local trade networks running through Great Zimbabwe, with copper being traded for iron produced in Great Zimbabwe (Hall 1987:98). Objects ultimately derived from Indian Ocean trade included fragments of textile which had been

Figure 8.4 Burial at Ingombe Ilede

preserved where they had come into contact with copper arm and leg bangles **(figure 8.4)**. These were tentatively identified as possibly Indian in origin. The by-now-ubiquitous glass trade beads were also present – strings of blue, yellow, red and turquoise glass beads, again probably of Indian origin (Fagan 1972:16).

The richer burials are described by Brian Fagan as 'gold burials', and interpreted as belonging to the heyday of the Karanga kingdom (1972:30). The possible ritual authority enjoyed by the occupants of the richer burials was indicated by other grave-goods present. These included ceremonial iron hoes, and iron flange welded bells. These form part of the repertoire of paraphernalia associated with leadership across many areas of southern and eastern-central Africa. The role of similar items in the West African Sudan was also described in the last chapter, where the importance of blacksmithing was recorded. Besides hoes and bells, iron gongs such as those described for Great Zimbabwe, or hammers, anvils, spears and knives could serve similar purposes (Herbert 1993:135; De Maret 1999). To these could be added perishable items such as drums, which rarely survive in the archaeological record. In total, these items served two purposes, in the words of Sassoon (1983:95): firstly, to show that the king had the authority to rule; and secondly, they were used in the 'performance of religious ceremonies designed to benefit the state'.

Cruciform copper ingots averaging 3.62 kg in weight were also present, perhaps the type of raw material that was traded onwards to Great Zimbabwe. Intriguingly, one skeleton also had an amulet attached around its wrist. This consisted of a conus shell and copper razor joined by a cord to two wooden amulets, thought 'to have Islamic associations' (Fagan 1972:16). It is highly unlikely that the individual interred was a Muslim. The burial position, comprising an extended corpse, with some individuals having their hands clasped over the belly, as well as the grave-goods, largely precludes this (see chapter 1). However, it is possibly indicative of the processes described in the last chapter, as seen, for example, among the Asante: namely, the recognition of the protective, powerful and prestige qualities of Islamic magic and literacy among pre-literate peoples. Whether it also signals incipient Islamisation processes brought to a halt for an unknown reason, we can only guess at.

Thus far only vague allusions have been made to coastal trade centres and although direct correlations should not be drawn, events in the interior were in part paralleled on the coast or vice versa. Hall (1987:99), for instance, notes that the growth in the gold trade at Great Zimbabwe was apparently linked with events at Kilwa, a process beginning initially in the late twelfth century. Similar links can be suggested for the fourteenth century when Husuni Kubwa was built. Indeed, as was noted in chapter 4, a coin from Kilwa was found at Great Zimbabwe, indicating these links. Prosperity at the coast, and as we have seen, events in the interior, were often linked. Kilwa acted, as has been described, as the major trade centre on the southern end of the East African coast. It is also possible that more southerly coastal centres such as Sofala served to move goods and commodities, such as finished ivory products (Reid and Segobye 2000), gold, skins etc., to Kilwa. These centres probably also served as distribution nodes for goods received from Kilwa. Items such as beads, Chinese pottery and cloth were then traded into the interior from these southerly coastal trading hubs from which they would have been further distributed outwards from major centres such as Great Zimbabwe. Certainly the reach of Kilwa was great in later centuries. Vansina (1966:235), for instance, says that in the mid-eighteenth century 'the hinterland of Kilwa reached as far as Lake Nyasa' (Malawi). With Kilwa exerting an influence at this time upon the Yao (Thorold 1987, and see below), Sutton (1999:11) describes this time as offering 'renewed commercial opportunities' for Kilwa.

Therefore within this region it can be seen that evidence for Islamisation is non-existent, besides the amulet found at Ingombe Ilede. This pattern stands in contrast to those recorded in many other areas of the continent south of the Sahara, where as we have seen elements of Muslim material culture or ritual might be adopted even if conversion to Islam did not take place. Furthermore, trade contacts with the coast were maintained from possibly as early as the second half of the first millennium, but the physical presence of Muslims within most of the region also seems unlikely. This would appear to be the major difference from other regions of sub-Saharan Africa where the establishment of small Muslim communities or the movements of individual Muslim merchants and holy men served to spread Islam (see, e.g., Levtzion 1986a). The necessary personal touch in this region was missing, hence conversions to Islam did not occur.

The Dutch and Islam

Elsewhere in southern Africa, Muslim communities were established on a more permanent basis, though at a later date, and although it might seem like a strange concept, the Dutch were directly responsible for bringing Islam to the far south of the continent. This occurred in 1652 when the Dutch East India Company 'established a refreshment station at the southern tip of Africa, the southwestern peninsula of what is now South Africa' (Tayob 1999:21). The introduction of Islam was achieved by the settlers bringing with them Muslim slaves, labourers and convicts from their colonies in the East Indies – Javanese and Malays, people later somewhat offensively termed 'Cape Coloureds' (Hiskett 1994:174). In fact, this emphasis on race is apparent in much of the earlier research into this community, exemplified in the series title in which one of the first studies of the Cape Malays (now called Cape Muslims) was published: 'Publication Number 1 in the Race Relations Series of the Sub-Department of Coloured Affairs' (du Plessis and Lückhoff 1953). The stated aims of the series further indicate the racial slant to the research. These were to 'correlate facts about the coloured people of South Africa, to draw conclusions from these facts and to publish work which will lead to a better understanding of this group' (du Plessis and Lückhoff 1953: frontispiece). I. D. du Plessis, one of the 'experts' on the 'Cape Malays', who 'contributed heavily to the redefinition of "Malay" as an ethnic designation in terms of the larger racialist scheme of apartheid', was a member of the Afrikaner Broederbond, a secret society involved in propping up the apartheid regime (Chidester 1992:167; see also du Plessis 1972). Thus the racial preoccupation formerly evident in South African society is reflected in much of the research completed on the South African Muslim community. Equally, it has largely focused on the Cape Muslims, and other parts of the Muslim community in South Africa have been neglected until recently – the Indians, and African converts, for example (but see Chidester 1992).

The first leader of the small number of Muslims in South Africa is usually considered to be an Indonesian religious leader, Sheikh Yusuf, sent to exile in South Africa by the Dutch in the late seventeenth century. His crime was to have supported Sultan Ageng in the 1650s in his attempts to break the Dutch trade monopoly in Indonesia (Chidester 1992:158). Sheikh Yusuf was a leader of the Khalwatiyya Sufi order, and attracted many followers to his place of exile, Zandvliet farm. Following his death, his tomb became a *karamat* or holy place among the Cape Muslim community, one among five *karamats* encircling Cape Town in an Islamic 'sacred geography' (Chidester 1992:159). This tomb at Faure, along with the other *karamats*, is described in some detail by du Plessis and Lückhoff (1953:35–7). They depict a fairly conventional structure commemorating Sheikh Yusuf: domed with four pillars, topped with a crescent, and inside a stone slab, covered with 'quilts of silk and satin, brightly coloured and exquisitely worked' (du Plessis and Lückhoff 1953:37), under which Yusuf was buried. Immediately outside, four of his followers were also buried. This tomb rapidly became a place of pilgrimage, and is analogous in its function to other structures already described, Uthman dan Fodio's tomb in Sokoto (chapter 6), or the tomb of Sheikh Hammali in Massawa (chapter 2). The fact that it became a place of pilgrimage is also of interest because, according to Chidester (1992:159), Sheikh Yusuf, though interred at Faure in 1699, was repatriated to Indonesia six years later. Thus his tomb is apparently empty, something obviously of no importance, as it is a place still imbued with sanctity, exuding *barakah* or blessings.

Initially, quarries were used as places of prayer by the nascent Muslim community (du Plessis and Lückhoff 1953:11). This was because the Cape was under a 'single dominant regime' in the eighteenth century, the Dutch Reformed Church, which meant that Roman Catholics and Muslims were forbidden from public worship (Chidester 1996:70). Converted houses were also used for prayers, and in 1798 the first mosque in South Africa was founded, the Auwal mosque in Cape Town (Bradlow and Cairns 1978). The founder of this mosque was Tuan Guru, who Chidester (1992:161) describes as usually being credited as the 'founder of Islam in South Africa'. This was because he was the organiser of the first Muslim community, as opposed to a Sufi *tariqah*, thus differing from Sheikh Yusuf. Tuan Guru was also an Indonesian exile, a convict, whose tomb, again paralleling that of Yusuf, became a *karamat* following his death in 1807.

Outside Cape Town small Muslim communities also existed, on what Chidester (1996:93) refers to as the 'eastern Cape frontier' where otherwise undescribed inscribed Muslim tombstones have been recorded. Similarly, at Port Elizabeth, the largely Indonesian community built a mosque in 1855. This structure was partly financed by the Ottoman Turkish government, and has been described as the 'first ascertainable reference to a mosque with dome and minaret' in South Africa (Bradlow 1978:18). Subsequently, the initial South African Muslim community, of largely South East Asian origin, was enriched by the arrival of immigrants from the Indian subcontinent, who contributed to the spread and character of Islam throughout the region. In Botswana, for example, Indian Muslims from South Africa were one of the main agents in introducing and spreading Islam (Parratt 1989). Similar processes were completed by Indian Muslim communities introduced by the British as indentured labourers, for example, in interior Kenya, Tanzania, Uganda and Malawi (Oded 1974).

Eastern interior and central Africa

It is to these interior regions that we now turn as Muslim Swahili and Arab traders penetrated deep into eastern and central Africa in search of slaves and ivory in the nineteenth century. These interior trade missions were given a significant boost – according to Ceulemans (1966:188) as a result of Sultan Sayyid Majid of Zanzibar's economic policies in the latter half of the nineteenth century, when, following his encouragement, Arab traders moved beyond Lake Tanganyika and occupied the Maniema region of the Congo. A web of routes stretched from the Swahili coast, from towns such as Bagamoyo and Kilwa Kivinje, via inland trade centres, such as Tabora and Ujiji. Trade routes then skirted around the Great Lakes to the interlacustrine kingdoms, or west deep into the heart of Africa to Arab outposts such as Kasongo and Nyangwe in Maniema on the Lualaba river in the Congo (Levtzion 1985b:192).

A party of coastal traders also succeeded in crossing the continent from east to west. Ibn Habib, accompanied by two companions and forty other followers, set out from the coast in 1850, travelling via Tabora, Ujiji and Kazembe, and came out on the west coast at Benguella in 1852 (Rangeley 1963:23; Vansina 1966:235). Soon after this, Arabs began to settle in central Africa, as with Muhammad ibn Saleh at Kazembe (Vansina 1966:236). Obviously their religion, Islam, accompanied the traders, but the effects of Islam were by no means uniform. The primary interest of the Arab and Swahili traders was mercantile, not proselytisation (Ceulemans 1966:189). In some areas people did convert to Islam. These include specific groups such as slaves, and chiefs in Maniema, for example (Levtzion 1985b:192), or all groups, as among the Yao of Malawi

(Thorold 1987). In other areas conversions were limited or non-existent, and the effects of Islam were negligible, even if those of the traders were not (see Vansina 1966:235–41). Local circumstances had a considerable impact, but it is also true to say that had not European involvement in the region severely disrupted most areas of life from the late nineteenth century, the numbers of Muslims today would undoubtedly be substantially greater.

Coastal–interior trade before the nineteenth century: Tanzania/Uganda and the Congo

Prior to looking at the developments in the nineteenth century in greater detail it is first necessary to look at the earlier, archaeological evidence for possible coastal–interior trade links. One item stands out above all others as a possible indicator of such trade, by now familar here: glass trade beads. Within nineteenth-century trade these are known to have been a significant item; Sir Richard Burton (1993 [1860]) describes a variety of trade goods carried into the interior – cloth, brass 'and other wires' and beads, carried in long narrow bags, while A.Wilson (1972:583) makes the point that 'until about 1860 the trade goods going up country from the east coast consisted almost entirely of cloth and beads'. Burton also bemoaned the fact that although a trade in beads had lasted for centuries the material remains of this trade were elusive. To quote, 'beads...are yearly imported into East Africa by the ton – in quantities which excite the traveller's surprise that so little is seen of them' (1993 [1860]:527). In fact, he is wrong, for as has been described for southern Africa prior to the nineteenth century, glass beads also survive on archaeological sites in eastern-central Africa and attest to some form of coastal–interior contacts.

Beads have been recovered from various archaeological sites across the region. Their totals are added to all the time as archaeological research in the interior of countries such as Kenya, Tanzania and Uganda proceeds. At Munsa earthworks in western Uganda, for example, Robertshaw uncovered a few blue-green glass beads in burials dating from between 900 and 1200 (1997:13–14). These were individual burials of adults or sub-adults, with the corpse oriented with the head to the west and feet to the east. Besides the glass beads, other grave-goods included iron and copper bracelets and iron beads. The presence of the beads and jewellery was interpreted as possibly indicating that at least some of these burials were of people of elite status. Although Robertshaw acknowledges that the dating at the site needs refining, these bead finds seem secure, as they are not isolated occurrences. At Ntusi, a major settlement of cattle-keepers, also in south-western Uganda, a further seventeen glass beads, as well as two cowrie shells, were found in various contexts dated to the thirteenth–fourteenth centuries (Reid 1991:2). This site also provided evidence for ivory working, though how widely traded it was is unclear (Sutton 1998c:51). Similarly, at Engaruka, a complex of irrigation terraces and village sites in northern Tanzania, three glass beads were found in levels dating from the late fifteenth to mid-seventeenth centuries (Sassoon 1966:88; Robertshaw 1986:17). Sutton (1998a) also reports that waterpipe or 'hubble-bubble' pipe-bowl fragments were found. These have been interpreted as used to smoke cannabis, and 'evidence of cultural connections in a broad sense – but not necessarily direct commercial contact – with the coast and the Indian Ocean' (Sutton 1998a:25).

Even further into the interior, glass beads and cowrie shells have been reported from the Zaire/Congo area (De Maret 1979). These are from the Upemba depression, 1,500 km from the nearest coast and the heartland of the Luba kingdom. In Upemba, fifty or so archaeological sites have been documented and six excavated (de Maret 1999). Within these, about 300 graves have been uncovered. Settlement sites have also been recorded but lacked 'significant structures' (de Maret 1999:152), owing to poor preservation and re-use of the best occupation sites. The total Upemba sequence uncovered runs from the Kamilambian of the seventh century through to recent Luba dated to after 1700 (de Maret 1979). Of interest here is the period known as the Classic Kisalian dating from the tenth to twelfth centuries, when cowrie shells appear in graves, and the subsequent Kabambian A (thirteenth–fifteenth centuries), when both cowrie shells and glass beads are found in graves. These are unlikely, as in Great Zimbabwe, to represent trade goods delivered by Muslim traders; rather, they represent local exchange networks operating in various stages to the coast. This pattern of glass beads being used in burials continues into the recent Luba period when, in the nineteenth century, the Luba state expanded, 'in step with that of long-distance trade with the Arabs' (de Maret 1999:159). The use of glass beads and other trade goods is attested in ethnographic literature as well among the Luba. W. F. P. Burton (1961:35), for instance, describes the burial of a Luba woman, in which the grave-goods included 'a basket of charms and beads, and a gourd of oil' placed at her head.

The savannah kingdoms

The Luba polity comprises one of the savannah kingdoms described by Jan Vansina (1966) in a book of the same name. This group of polities were to be found in the savannah regions between the Zambezi and the equatorial forest, an area where almost all peoples 'have developed kingdoms or chiefdoms' whereas 'in the surrounding area most populations are stateless' (Vansina 1966:4). Examples of states include Luba, as already mentioned, as well as those of Kongo, Lunda, Kazembe and Lozi. The similarities between these polities extend in many ways. They were indigenously founded, but were variously influenced in the east by Arabs in the nineteenth century, and in the west, from the early sixteenth century, by the Portuguese. Subsistence methods are also similar, primarily based on shifting cultivation utilising the so-called 'American complex' involving manioc, sweet potatoes, maize and groundnuts. Religion also exhibits great similarities, which 'is true to such an extent that even the terms used are often related' (Vansina 1966:30). Common features include a belief in a high god, and prominence in the worship of the 'shades', defined as the recently dead, whom 'the worshipper has known during his life' (Vansina 1966:31). Such spiritual relationships are set apart from those of natural spirits (rarer in the savannah kingdoms), a separation described by Mbiti (1975:70) thus: 'Whereas nature spirits have no direct physical kinship with people, human spirits are those that were once ordinary men, women and children.' Ritual practices also exhibit great similarities – in sacrifice, divination and the like, as well as in linking religion and 'social values' (Vansina 1966:32) through the personage of the divine king.

Archaeological investigation of these polities, as was noted in the introduction to this chapter, is still in its infancy, primarily because of the recurring political problems in much of the region. However, archaeological research could contribute much, as, for example, to our understanding of the foundation dates of the kingdoms and the processes involved in their foundation. Where archaeological research has been carried out, as in the Luba heartlands (see main text), the results have been very useful (de Maret 1979, 1999). They have cast light on trade networks linking coast and interior, albeit indirectly, from the beginning of the second millennium, as well as indicating the complexity inherent in ethnicity and in defining just what these polities were in the past. This is a point made by de Maret (1999:161) with regard to the Luba but which could equally apply to the other savannah kingdoms as well, when he states that, 'in recent years, "Luba" has been shown to be a most ambiguous category, covering many different territories and identities, and ethonyms more significant at the periphery than in the centre'. Archaeology is indicating that the 'timeless' African past which has often been presented, and is rightly critiqued by Alpers (1975:1), is in reality much more fluid, active and changeable – as represented by the fluidity of the Luba kingdom.

Trade goods such as glass beads and cowrie shells were probably moved from the coast into the interior over a number of stages, and recently a possible inland centre closer to the coast which might have been involved in these networks has been investigated. This is the site of Dakawa, located 200 km inland from the Tanzanian coast and situated where a small seasonal stream runs into the River Wami. It is a site which appears to have been a 'point of agglomeration of inland products transported to the coastal area' (Haaland and Msuya in press). Radiocarbon dates have indicated that this site was occupied between about 650 and 880. Importantly, the pottery bridges 'the gap in pottery sequences between the EIA (Kwale) tradition with the later Tana tradition' (Haaland and Msuya in press; and see Haaland 1994/5). The debate over Tana pottery/TIW (triangular incised ware) has already been covered in chapter 4, and the evidence from Dakawa appears to support Felix Chami's (1998) hypothesis that TIW originated on the central Tanzanian coast and was then spread via rivers into the interior. TIW-type pottery has now been found as far inland as Kirando on the shores of Lake Tanganyika, 900 km from the coast (Mapunda 1995:326). As we have seen in chapter 4, however, TIW development is also apparent on the Kenyan coast, making such a precise attribution very unlikely.

In effect, what is being indicated by the increasing archaeological evidence is a picture of complexity in coastal–interior networks. These networks were rooted in local Iron Age traditions, devoid of Muslim participation until the nineteenth century. In summary, the point made by Robertshaw (1997:18) that 'the view prevailing hitherto that extra-African trade goods did not reach Uganda until very recent centuries looks increasingly untenable' can be extended much further than Uganda. As further archaeological investigations are completed, undoubtedly additional evidence for trade goods of coastal origin will be found in the interior. Helms' (2000) research in the coastal hinterland of Kenya, for example (see chapter 4), is showing that what appeared anomalous only a few years ago is now looking a lot more routine. However, what is also being indicated is more than just trade, as 'cultural traditions' (Haaland and Msuya in press) flowed across the region as well. These also apparently substantially pre-date the period of Muslim control of the coast, if the indications of items of coastal origin such as marine shells appearing in Neolithic (late Stone Age) levels in parts of the interior are correct (P. Robertshaw, pers. comm.).

The trade routes and settlements after the nineteenth century

Tanzania

Thus the complexities of coastal–interior trade networks and processes before the nineteenth century are still being unravelled. After this point in time, our knowledge improves somewhat, as written historical sources exist, though archaeology contributes as well. This is because some of the settlements associated with the early European explorers in the region, as well as with the interior trade networks, have begun to be investigated archaeologically (Lane 1993; Insoll 1997d). Recently, for example, an archaeological survey of a small fort visited by Burton and Speke in 1857 close to the coast was completed (Lane 1993). This fort, at Tongwe, some 30 km from Pangani in Tanzania, was built on the orders of Sultan Sayyid Said of Zanzibar around 1833 as a visible statement of his 'authority over the area' (Lane 1993:136). A small structure some 4.6 m² and 3.5 m high, with walls 50 cm thick, it was built of uncoursed stone rubble bonded with mortar and finished with plaster **(figure 8.5)**. The wall was

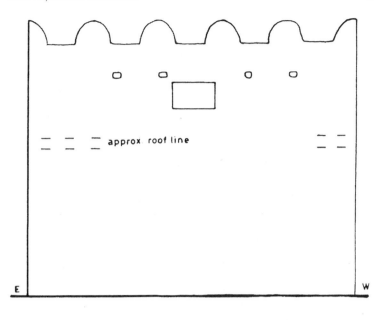

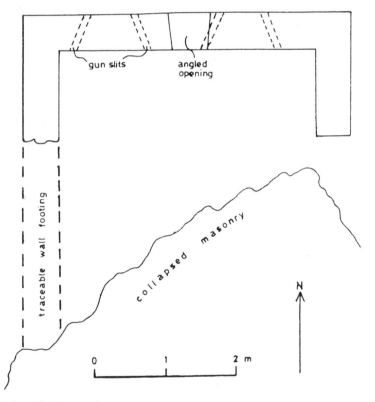

Figure 8.5 Plan of Tongwe fort

topped with rounded crenellations and inset with four angled rifle-slits and two hatch-covered gun ports. Although damaged by being hit by a fallen tree, this structure survived, as it was built of durable materials. This is unlike many of the structures associated with the Arab trade, which were built of less archaeologically durable materials such as wood and thatch. An example is provided by Sultan Sayyid's fort at Chogwe, which had a wooden pallisade and earth-and-thatch houses inside. Lane (1993:140) similarly examined a caravan halt a few miles north of Tongwe at Kwa Fungo, but few traces of it survived because it was built of these less permanent materials.

A similar archaeological survey has also been completed of sites associated with John Hanning Speke's visit to Buganda. During the course of this survey, two Muslim trading sites were identified, both described by Speke (Insoll 1997d). The first of these sites, Ngandu, was described by Speke (1863:265) as 'the farthest trading depot of the Zanzibari ivory merchants'. The second, Ngambezi, was under the control of one of the uncles of the Bugandan ruler Mutesa I (see below). Both sites are located just south of the Ugandan border in Tanzania on the far side of Lake Victoria. Owing to the climate, and the use of reed, straw and mud as building materials, very little survived at the site that was visited, Ngambezi, other than a stone which was used for cleaning the feet prior to entering the mosque. This pattern of non-survival is repeated throughout this region.

Further into the interior we are more reliant upon documentary sources for descriptions of relevant sites, as archaeological research has yet to be carried out. One useful source, after the racial stereotyping is taken into account, are the writings of Richard Burton (1993 [1860]). The information he provides on the Nyamwezi of western Tanzania, for example, is useful. These were a people actively involved in commerce with the coast, with networks extending as far west as Katanga in the Congo. Levtzion (1985b:190) underlines the extent of the importance of coastal trade to the Nyamwezi when he relates that 'it is estimated that at the end of the nineteenth century about a third of the male population of Unyamwezi went to the coast each year as traders and porters'. Various Arab trading stations and halts were also established in Nyamwezi territory. Foremost among these was Kazeh, described by Burton (1993 [1860]:211) as the 'capital village of the Omani Arabs'. This was home to a fluctuating Arab population of between four and twenty-five individuals, and a settlement which was first occupied about 1852, the events preceding which having already been described above (see Vansina 1966:236). Situated in Unyanyembe, the central province of Nyamwezi, the Arab and Swahili merchants lived a comfortable life in single-storey mud-built defensible houses with a verandah, and a 'portcullis-like door' leading into a vestibule for guests (figure 8.6). From this guest-room a characteristic angled passageway, 'to baffle the stranger's curiosity', gave access to the domestic quarters of the house. These were a series of rooms for the merchant and his wives leading onto a central courtyard and lacking outward-facing

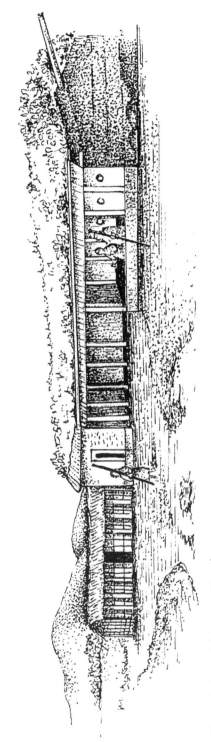

Figure 8.6 Arab house at Kazeh

doors or windows (R. Burton 1993 [1860]:216–17). The structuring elements of a traditional Muslim domestic environment as outlined in chapter 1 can be seen to be again evident (and see Campo 1991; Insoll 1999a). In this respect it is similar to concepts already described for Muslim domestic structures across sub-Saharan Africa.

Around the Arab and Swahili settlements local housing would grow, in a region, according to Burton, devoid of towns but containing villages and hamlets. Thus the core of Muslim-type housing would be surrounded by African domestic structures, and it can be suggested that this differentiation, theoretically at least, would be archaeologically visible. Another element of material culture which set the Arab and Swahili traders apart was the use of burial according to Muslim rites. This is described by Burton (1993 [1860]:38) as being 'usually cleared ovals, with outlines of rough stone and a strew of smooth pebbles'. A piece of wood was used to indicate the correct orientation (see chapter 1). This was clearly different to local funerary customs, which among the Nyamwezi – until the arrival of Muslim traders – did not involve burial. Formerly, corpses had been left in the bush to be devoured by scavengers, and the Muslim merchants had to be persuasive in their requirements for burial, as the Nyamwezi objected 'for fear of pollution' (R. Burton 1993 [1860]:286–7). Yet ultimately the Muslim merchants were successful.

In this instance, although exposed to Islam both through extensive contacts with the coast and the presence of small numbers of Muslim merchants in their territory, the Nyamwezi did not convert to Islam in any substantial numbers. As Levtzion (1985b:190) notes, 'in West Africa [this] would have brought about the spread of Islam'; not so here, though people did adopt the customs of the coast and spoke Swahili – 'Swahilization without Islamization' (Levtzion 1985b:191). This does indeed contrast strongly with the West African Sudan and forest, for example, where the presence of the Mande would have have led to more than merely acculturation (see chapter 7 and Levtzion 1968; Wilks 2000). Levtzion (1985b:191) suggests that the uniformity/communication tools necessary for successful trade, and supplied by Islam in West Africa, were here supplied by the diffusion of other mechanisms, such as Swahili possession cults (see chapter 4), hence the difference between the two regions. However, some of the Nyamwezi must have become more than acculturated by coastal custom, and actually converted to Islam as well. For among the groups Kubai (1992:34) names as being influential in the early Muslim community of Nairobi (late nineteenth–early twentieth centuries) are the Nyamwezi, indicating that stereotyping many groups as wholly non-Muslim might actually be flawed.

Congo

Trade centres were also to be found on the other side of Lake Tanganyika. Again, historical accounts are a useful source of information on the Arab and Swahili settlements in the Congo region. This was also an area in which many of the famous names of nineteenth-century east-central African exploration appear – Stanley, and Tippu Tip (see box), for example. The penetration of this region by Muslim traders probably began in the 1840s, soon after the establishment of a base at Ujiji (Hinde 1897). Initially the Maniema region of north-eastern Congo was the focus of operations, but by the early 1880s the Stanley Falls had been reached (Ceulemans 1966:188). Relations between the Arab and Swahili traders and the local peoples varied according to the power of the latter. Young (1969) makes the important point that two states which were encountered in the south of the region, Msiri and Lunda, possessed firearms. Hence here 'Swahili contacts in these zones were carefully restricted to trade, which left behind no Islamic legacy', while a different situation prevailed where 'weak, disorganized, segmentary societies were found' (Young 1969:251).

Although some positive contributions might have been made by the Swahili and Arab traders in the north of this region (though this is debatable), within the south 'there was nothing constructive about their presence' (Vansina 1966:241). Here the traders and their local allies, such as the Luba under Kasongo Kalambo in the 1860s, and the Bemba, wrought havoc in their search for slaves and ivory. The significance of firearms in this region should not be underrated. As Rangeley (1963:24) notes, 'the flint lock gun and the cap gun were to no small extent responsible for the ease with which Arabs penetrated to the interior'. Guns became part of a vicious circular trade, being used to obtain ivory and slaves, commodities which could in turn be traded for more firearms, especially from the 1860s – a trade which meant that some rulers began to sell their own people to obtain more guns (A. Wilson 1972:585). The reason behind this was, according to Horton and Middleton (2000:104), royal internecine struggles which 'meant that when guns, ammunition and gun-powder became available from the eighteenth century they were eagerly seized upon as not only desirable but also politically essential commodities'. This is a situation in contrast to that described for the role of firearms in the central Sudan in chapter 6, where the availability of guns from the late sixteenth century did not lead to their use on a large scale until the latter part of the nineteenth century (Fisher and Rowland 1971).

Tippu Tip

The exploits of Tippu Tip in the heart of Africa appear almost fictional. Born in Zanzibar in 1840, Tippu Tip was a Swahili of mixed African and Arab origins, his grandfather having been an Omani. Tippu Tip, or Hamed bin Muhammad al Murjebi (de Maret and Legros 1993:378), to give him his full name, was introduced to the coastal–interior trade at an early age by his father, who was a pioneer of the trade routes (Young 1969:253). According to Vansina (1966:236), Tippu Tip's first expedition in the late 1850s–early 1860s was on a small scale, a trading expedition to Mulongo Tambwe accompanied by twenty men. This expedition has been confirmed by oral traditions collected by a Belgian administrator (Congo having been a Belgian colony), which indicate that he did indeed travel to the lands of the Luba of Mulongo, north of the Upemba Depression (de Maret and Legros 1993). By the end of the 1860s Tippu Tip's expeditions had changed massively in scale, 'with four thousand men in his caravan' recorded (Vansina 1966:236). Tippu Tip was now state building (see main text) and perhaps earned his name at this time, 'Tippu Tip' being suggested as based on the sounds of the muskets of his followers (Young 1969). Finally, between 1887 and 1890, Tippu Tip became governor of the Stanley Falls district for the Congo Independent State, prior to finally leaving the Congo (Vansina 1966:239). De Thier (1963) provides a rough plan of the camps established in the Stanley Falls area, including Tippu Tip's (figure 8.7).

Although Swahili and Arab traders were the agents for the spread of Islam it should be recognised that they differed greatly from, for example, the Mande, who were essentially peaceful in outlook in spreading Islam through the West African Sudan and forest zones (see chapter 7). However, as noted above, the impact of the Arab and Swahili merchants within the Congo varied from region to region depending upon the individual involved and the types of society encountered. Levtzion (1985b:191) makes the point that Arab and Swahili traders had to create 'some kind of political order'. Altering rather than creating political order might be a better way of putting it. Thus Tippu Tip assumed political authority, and 'everywhere in the region between Lomami and Lualaba, north of the Luba kingdom of Kasongo, he replaced chiefs or confirmed them in office, as a paramount would' (Vansina 1966:238). The impact of Islam was also marginal in this region. Some conversion to Islam did take place among the local population, but it should be remembered, as noted previously, that the primary reason for the traders' presence far from their homelands was trade and not the encouragement of conversion. Yet Young (1969:258) notes that the socially dislocated, primarily the Batetela-Bakusu, who settled around the Swahili and Arab centres such as Kasongo and Nyangwe, did 'emulate a way of life accepted as superior... One of the patterns copied, along with coastal dress and Swahili language, was the basic external ritual of Islam'. Once again parallels with elsewhere can be drawn, notably with Dar al-Kuti to the north, where the surface at least became Islamised (see chapter 6 and Cordell 1985). But true conversion, often downplayed, also occurred, as evidenced, for instance, by the Muslim community that still exists in parts of the Congo today (see Ceulemans 1966).

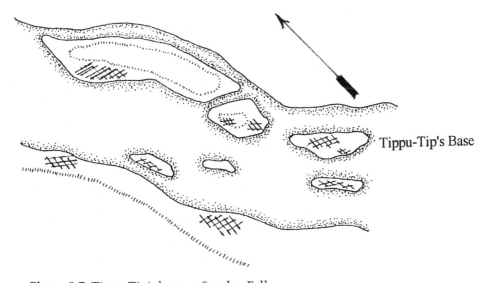

Tippu-Tip's Base

Figure 8.7 Tippu Tip's base at Stanley Falls

The presence of the Swahili and Arab traders and their followers also had a material impact, but this has largely yet to be investigated. Settlements were established and plantations laid out in which crops such as sugar cane, rice and maize were grown (Young 1969:252). In fact, Ceulemans (1966:190) makes the point that it was in agriculture that the contribution of the Muslim traders was most marked. This resembled what also occurred in Buganda (see below). Reasonably detailed accounts of some of these settlements exist. One such account is provided by S. L. Hinde (1897), a British medical officer who accompanied the Belgian-led forces of the Congo Free or Independent state during their campaigns against the Arab and Swahili traders between 1892 and 1895. This was a conflict which broke out for a variety of reasons – mistrust on both sides, and for the suppression of the slave trade – but 'by 1895, Swahili power had been totally broken' (Young 1969:254).

Hinde (1897) describes Kasongo (which, as already mentioned, along with Nyangwe on the Lualaba river, was one of the two principal Muslim centres) as a rich settlement. Prior to the military campaigns it was home to up to 30,000 inhabitants, the bulk of whom would not have been Arabs or Swahili, but slaves and followers of the former. Some of the latter could become quite powerful, Ngongolutete, the lieutenant of Tippu Tip (Young 1969:254–5) providing a good example. Kasongo was situated 'in the corner of a virgin forest, and for miles round all the brushwood and great trees had been cleared away' (Hinde 1897:187). Oranges, guavas, pineapples and pomegranates were all grown in the resulting plantations, and granaries were well stocked with coffee, rice and maize. Hinde was also impressed with the houses and their contents. One or more bathrooms were found in the principal houses in Kasongo and Nyangwe, with showers formed from a suspended canoe or hollowed-out log with a hole drilled in the bottom. Waste water was channelled away by further hollowed-out logs (Hinde 1897:201). As in Buganda, soap making by mixing potash with palm oil was introduced with the Muslim traders, and Hinde (1897:201) remarks that 'every house or hut, however small, had an enclosure attached to it containing the same arrangements for cleanliness, with the exception only of the shower-bath'.

Hinde also provides important information on the fortifications used by the Arab and Swahili traders while on the march. These are probably very similar to the *zaribas* used by the Muslim slave raiders of the central Sudan described in chapter 6. Indeed, these two groups operated very close to each other, emphasising the point that the heart of the continent had been reached. As Levtzion (1985b:188) notes, 'in the Nile–Congo divide, in the interior of Africa, Arab slave raiders from the north encountered the advanced parties of Arab slave raiders from the east'. Sudanese raiding parties met their counterparts from Zanzibar here, though the former withdrew during the Mahdist period, and the latter's power was broken by Congo Independent State forces in the early 1890s (Vansina 1990:240). The construction of the fortified enclosures used by the Arab and Swahili traders in the Congo was an ingenious affair. Slaves were employed to carry timber while on the move, and when a halt was reached two circles of timber would be erected, the inner one some 50 m in diameter, for the 'chiefs and officers', and an outer one 300–400 m in diameter in which the remainder of the caravan stayed. Against these timber circles would be placed an earth bank inset with banana stalks, which, once removed, upon drying, would leave ready-made loopholes. The inside of the inner enclosure would be filled with huts which were semi-subterranean, and roofed with timber and earth; further palisades could also be used to subdivide the enclosures, meaning that if they were breached the defenders could retreat to another area within (Hinde 1897:101–2). Similar very substantial fortifications were known to have been used by Arab and Swahili traders on Lake Malawi in the late nineteenth century (see below). Terry (1965b) describes one of these stockades, *kopa-kopa*, as having a solid mud wall 2 m in height, pierced with loopholes and topped with a further pole stockade intertwined with thorns, the whole reaching 5 m in height. Many of these structures must have been built, clustered along the caravan routes, and whether any have survived is a question which awaits investigation.

Buganda and Rwanda

The relationship between the Swahili and Arab traders and the peoples of the Congo region, where they lacked firearms, might have been one largely of exploitation, but this was not always the case in the interior of eastern and central Africa. The Nyamwezi benefited from trade, as has been described, and even more astute were the rulers of Buganda. This is a kingdom in Uganda, which encompasses the contemporary capital, Kampala, and stretches along the northern shore of Lake Victoria for about 300 km as well as some distance inland (Kigongo Mugerwa 1991; Insoll 1997c:179). Here, the rulers, the *kabakas*, played off the representatives of Islam and Christianity (and with regard to the latter, the subdivisions within), in order to get what they wanted. This was both prestige and trade goods, the two frequently being interlinked in ways already described. In Rwanda, a further pattern was evident. The Rwandan kings wanted trade goods, cloth and guns for instance, and even created a special section of the treasury, 'the surplus', to control access to these goods, but they did not want coastal traders in their lands. Certain traders tried to gain access – Muhammad ibn Khalfa, also known as 'Rumaliza' (the Exterminator), for example – but he did not succeed on account of the prowess of the Rwandan military forces (Kagabo 1988:17–18).

Within Buganda, an exclusion process was not practised, though trade and other relations with coastal traders were dictated on Bagandan (the inhabitants of Buganda) terms. Contacts with Muslim traders were initially established in the 1840s, and the first recorded visit by an Arab trader to Buganda was in 1844, by Shaykh Ahmed ibn Ibrahim, a Wahabi (Gray 1947). The route the Muslim merchants followed went inland from Tabora, then north around the western shore of Lake Victoria (Marissal 1978). Although some contacts were maintained from the 1840s, it was during the reign of the Bugandan *kabaka* Mutesa I (c.1856–84) that the first noticeable effects of both the presence of the Arab and Swahili traders and of Islam were seen in Buganda. Mutesa converted to Islam, yet continued to practise his traditional religion as well. This is described by Low (1971:18) as being focused on 'a pantheon of instrumental gods – of war, of health, of thunder and so on' (see also Roscoe 1911; Kigongo Mugerwa 1991). Thus again we seem to be seeing what Eaton (1993) has defined as 'inclusion', of the older traditional beliefs and practices with the new, Islam. This would appear to be reinforced by a point made by Oded (1974:305), that adherence to Islam during the reign of Mutesa was mainly expressed by imitating the traders' ceremonials.

Besides religious ones, the effects of contacts with Muslim traders in Buganda were various. These were primarily felt in the capital, the court circle and the trade centres. They included the building of mosques, the introduction of soap and woven grass-mat manufacture, and of certain crops and vegetables, such as wheat, tomatoes, pomegranates and pawpaws, alongside the adoption of the robe and turban, the introduction of reading and writing in Arabic, and changes in royal burial customs (Oded 1974:72–96; Soghayroun 1984:145–9). The latter, for example, were altered fundamentally. Previously, the king's jawbone had been removed during the mourning period, decorated, and placed separately in a jawbone shrine for worship (Kigongo Mugerwa 1991:3). This practice was forbidden following an edict from Mutesa I, perhaps as a direct result of the teachings of the coastal merchants. However, Mutesa was also buried according to other aspects of tradition. According to Sassoon (1983:98), he was the first ruler to be buried in the Kasubi tombs, with three ritual anvils among his ritual insignia displayed in front of his tomb – a blacksmith king as well.

In general, it can be seen that the impact of Islam and the influence of the Muslim traders waxed and waned according to the perceptions of its usefulness by the ruler. This is attested, for example, by the decline in enthusiasm for Islam by Mutesa I in the mid-1870s in the face of what he perceived to be a threat to his authority from the new religion (Twaddle 1993:25). This again replicates patterns seen elsewhere, though here other factors intervened, such as the rise in influence of Christian European missionaries, meaning that the top-down process of Islamisation was largely arrested. This is unlike other areas of the continent, where Islamisation might have been temporarily, but not permanently, halted.

The material remains of this period largely await investigation, and what little is known is predominantly gleaned from historical sources. An exception is provided by a recent study of mosque architecture in Buganda (Insoll 1997c). This found that the traditional wattle-and-daub structures are rapidly being replaced by concrete mosques built according to a perceived 'universal' plan with minarets and domes. The earliest mosque recorded in Kampala was adjacent to the traditional tombs of the *kabakas*, the Kasubi tombs (figure 8.8), indicating an interesting juxtaposition of the two traditions, and perhaps not unexpected in the light of the Muslim–*kabaka* relationship just described. This mosque, according to oral tradition, was built in the late nineteenth century, though it was subsequently partially rebuilt (Insoll 1997c:182–3). The influence of the East African coast, several hundred kilometres distant, is, however, evident in the architecture of the traditional wattle-and-daub mosques, now only found outside Kampala, which resemble the type of house found in rural Swahili communities (see Prins 1967:77–8) (figure 8.9).

The use of the rectangular mosque plan was also a radical innovation in this region in the nineteenth century (J. E. G. Sutton, pers. comm.). The Buganda roundhouse, the traditional indigenous habitation structure, is built from different materials in a very different manner, obviously to a circular plan. In these, work is begun from the top of the structure once the initial framework of stakes has been erected. A thick reedwork roof is then added which extends down to the ground, except at the doorways (Roscoe 1911:369–76). Therefore, in summary, it can be seen that the result of the presence of the Swahili and Arab traders in Buganda differed from that in the Congo. In Buganda the relationship was not merely exploitative, but negotiated on Bagandan terms, and beneficial, primarily to the *kabakas* and their court, as a source of trade goods, new ideas and technologies. Yet here, unlike, for instance, in Gao, the conversion process did not proceed beyond the inclusion phase.

Figure 8.8 Kasubi tombs, Kampala. An example of the thatched style of construction

Figure 8.9 Older-style Bugandan mosque

Malawi: the Yao

The situation in Buganda stands in contrast to the final case study to be considered, that of the Yao, a people who gradually converted to Islam in large numbers. The original homeland of the Yao was in northern Mozambique, described by Alpers (1975:15) as 'one of the prominent peaks that dot the region', though Price (1964:12) prefers a broader definition for the Yao heartland as 'a tract of grassy upland, diversified by prominent named peaks and ridges, some 20 miles from north to south and apparently not much less from east to west'. Whatever the precise location of their homeland, the Yao began to move into southern Malawi in the mid-eighteenth century (Thorold 1987), where today they are the most important source of Islam in the country (Bone 1982:130). Trade between the Yao and the coast in commodities such as tobacco and skins, which were exchanged for salt, cloth and beads, was established by the seventeenth century (Mitchell 1956:23). Kilwa looms large as an important coastal trade partner, again emphasising its longevity and supremacy. A major incentive for Yao trade with the coast was prestige – not only that obtained from owning rare goods sourced from the coast, but also prestige in terms of political importance. As Thorold (1987:20) notes, 'the prestige and regard in which those Yao who had been to the coast were held by their fellows provided a possibility of gaining wider leadership within Yao society'. Coastal contacts also profoundly influenced the structure of Yao society, again as Thorold (1987:20) relates, precipitating 'an enlargement of the Yao political process from the village structured around a matrilineal sorority-group under the authority of a headman, to the territorial chiefdoms based on trade links and military strength'.

The Arab and Swahili 'sultanates'

Besides the Yao, a Muslim presence was also established in Malawi when a group of Arab and Swahili traders attempted to set up small sultanates on the shores of Lake Malawi in the mid-nineteenth century. One of these was founded near Nkhotakota on the central-western shore by Salim ibn Abdullah in 1840, who eventually usurped the local chiefs and started the line known as the Jumbes of Nkhotakota. The last of the Jumbes was displaced by the British in 1895 (Bone 1982:127). A further Arab and Swahili centre was established at Mpata near Karongo at the northern end of Lake Malawi, by an individual named Mlozi (Msiska 1995:51). Mlozi was to become embroiled in conflict with the British in the so-called 'Arab war on Lake Nyasa' (Terry 1965a, 1965b). This flared up in 1887, primarily over the suppression of the slave trade, and included the first use of a steamer on Lake Malawi, the *Ilala*. It was a conflict which lasted until Mlozi was eventually captured and hanged in 1895.

Conversion to Islam did not, however, take place on any scale for nearly another 200 years after inaugural Yao contacts with the coast were established. The explorer David Livingstone noted coastal influences on architecture and dress at the Yao capital, Mwembe, in 1866, which was 'designed deliberately to resemble a coastal town' (Thorold 1987:22). Yet according to Bone (1982:128) it was not until the 1870s that the first conversions began. Prior to this point, in processes now familiar, the Yao chiefs made use of Muslim scribes and advisers, and it was these chiefs who were the first to convert to Islam. Rangeley (1963:23) is somewhat more simplistic in his interpretation as to why this occurred, arguing that the Yao only converted to Islam after the Arab traders came to the Yao settlements, because Islam then became fashionable among the Yao chiefs who 'desired more contact with the wealthy and admired Arabs who had formerly remained aloof in their seaports'. Among the first chiefly converts was Makanjira III, who converted in about 1870. Msiska (1995:56) provides a more complex and convincing interpretation of why this occurs, in relating that the chiefs converted 'for political and ritual legitimization and the desire for the regularisation of their economic ties with Zanzibar and *the advantages offered to this end by the attainment of literacy in Arabic script*' (emphasis added). This description could equally apply to parts of the West African Sudan and forest 300 years earlier, Borno 600 years earlier, or the western Sahel nearly 1,000 years earlier. The mechanisms of conversion are also the same – initially traders, or traders accompanied or followed by Muslim holy men and missionaries, who spread Islam to other chiefs, and then down through society (Levtzion 1985b:189).

Msiska (1995:70) also makes the point that the success of the spread of Islam among the Yao was in part due to the fact that it 'merely modified or made slight changes to some of the local customs'. In fact, a three-phase model has been proposed to explain Yao conversion to Islam. This involves a phase of 'visibility' – in dress, food regulations and prayers; a second phase of 'mixing'; and a third phase of 'consolidation' (Thorold 1987:25). This model builds upon those discussed in chapter 1, and though using different terminology essentially fits well with the conversion framework developed by Eaton (1993) which is preferred here. In the first phase, for example, the Qur'an has been described as functioning 'as a sort of fetish, a source of power rather than doctrine' (Thorold 1993:84). The second phase included the continuation of traditional initiation rites such as the boys' *lupanda* and the girls' *ciputu*, rites which became blended with or replaced by the coastal rites of *jandu* and *nsondo* (Mitchell 1956:82). This could be interpreted as functioning within the third phase of consolidation, or Eaton's (1993) third phase of displacement.

Materially, the Yao have yet to be investigated archaeologically, though conversion to Islam has made itself felt in material culture in the types of categories as outlined in chapter 1. Mosques have been built, of brick in the villages of the most important chiefs, mud and thatch elsewhere (Mitchell 1956:64). Islam has also affected Yao diet with a refusal to eat pork and carrion, and an insistence that meat must be properly slaughtered. Muslim burial rites have also been adopted, but with certain differences to orthodox procedure, such as the Yao practice of cutting a hole in the neck of the corpse through which to squeeze the intestine empty (Bone 1982:132). Among the Yao, conversion to Islam, albeit with the subsequent adaptation of certain practices to suit local requirements, and over a reasonably lengthy period of time, has occurred. Thus a further variant of Islamisation process is provided in this region of sub-Saharan Africa.

Summary and conclusions

Within this chapter the end of the line has been reached chronologically in terms of the material that will be covered. However, many of the processes that have been charted for the nineteenth century have been shown to be similar to those described for other areas of the continent much earlier. In terms of trade, similarities are evident, as Swahili and Arab traders entered the interior to obtain commodities familiar from across sub-Saharan Africa, such as ivory, slaves, and, in the south, gold. In return, categories of finished goods also now well known from the preceding chapters were brought – notably beads, cloth, glazed pottery, glass and, with more profound consequences, firearms. Thus, what could almost be called a 'customary' trading pattern, largely of commodities for finished goods, is again noticeable. Similarities are also evident in terms of the Islamisation processes that have been described. The Yao, for example, could almost be considered a textbook case as regards the types of process that have been repeatedly seen across sub-Saharan Africa. It is exemplified by the initial appeal of Islam seen in the power of Arabic literacy, the prestige associated with the new religion in terms of increasing power and in the top-down process of conversion, as well as the agents of conversion themselves – traders, missionaries and holy men. Among the Yao, the three-phase conversion model as developed by Fisher (1973a, 1985) or Trimingham (1968), and refined by Thorold (1987) to be applicable to the Yao, seems to work, further emphasising the similarities with elsewhere.

Yet this region has also shown great differences in comparison with other areas of sub-Saharan Africa. The trade that appears to have existed between large areas of southern and eastern-central Africa and the coast from at least the end of the first millennium, as attested by archaeological evidence, was not, apparently, accompanied by any religious influence – of any lasting significance, at least. Such trade was channelled through, and helped to perhaps create – and certainly sustain – centres such as Great Zimbabwe and its predecessors, as well as those lesser known centres of the Upemba depression, for example. Conversion to Islam might not have taken place for various reasons, but one overriding difference with other regions is that Arab and Swahili merchants appear not to have travelled into the interior until the nineteenth century, and this might have been of significance. As was stated earlier, the required personal touch, seen to be of such importance elsewhere, in Funj or Darfur in the Nilotic Sudan, for example, was lacking. However, there are glimmers that some degree of Islamic influence on the interior might have existed, the intriguing amulet from Ingombe Ilede providing the evidence found thus far. This is easily discounted as an unusual trinket devoid of religious significance, but possibly, and alternatively, it is testimony to the first flickerings of Eaton's (1993) 'inclusion' phase in southern Africa.

When the Arab and Swahili merchants did strike into the interior from the mid-nineteenth century, their impact varied but was frequently devastating. Overall, it was seen that conversion to Islam – in the Congo, for instance – was limited. The closest parallels that can be drawn for this situation are with parts of the central Sudan, where in chapter 6, the paramountcy of slavery was shown to also be of importance. This was because, theoretically at least, one should not enslave a Muslim, so it is possible that conversion to Islam was restricted for this reason. Similarities also exist between the two areas in the veneer of Islamisation that sometimes existed, as in Dar al-Kuti (Cordell 1985), or in Nyamwezi, or among the dispossessed surrounding the Muslim traders and raiders in the Congo. In part, these similarities are explained by the fact that the northern area of the Congo region is where the centre of our circle is reached, the area where northern Muslim traders met eastern ones, as in Azande.

In other ways this region is unique, as attested by the Dutch role, albeit not deliberate, in introducing Muslims to the far south of the continent, or the political astuteness of the *kabakas* of Buganda in their dealings with Muslim merchants. The latter is similar, yet also very dissimilar, to the types of relationship enjoyed by the Asante rulers and Muslim merchants outlined in the last chapter. In summary, it was stated at the beginning of this chapter that events in this region were far removed geographically and temporally from the first Muslim contacts across the Red Sea with Ethiopia and the Horn. As regards direct parallels this can of course be said to be true, but indirectly it has been possible to chart a continuous process around the continent, with at its core the relationship between Islam and the peoples of Africa, in all its many dimensions, something which will now be explored further by way of conclusion in the last chapter.

CHAPTER 9

CONCLUSIONS

The aims of the study

The aim of the study was to depict the richness and diversity of Islamic material culture in sub-Saharan Africa. Much research has recently been done on the archaeology of many regions of Africa in the last 1000–1500 years. This book is the first synthesis of such research in which the material culture of Islam provides a point of entry. This is because Islam swept across the continent, if in irregular pulses, and with far from uniform results. Although some peoples resisted conversion, Islam is surely the leitmotiv of African archaeology and history over the last millennium. Furthermore, although this book is a synthesis of archaeological investigations, it also discusses, to a limited but necessary extent, the process of conversion to Islam and also the role of Islam in the lives of Africans over the centuries. The very diversity of Islamic traditions in Africa must also be traced to the diverse pre-Islamic cultures and their own histories of spiritual development. Consequently, this book has portrayed the context in the various regions of sub-Saharan Africa in which Islam, to a greater or lesser extent, became established. One of the key issues that has recurred throughout this study is therefore the recognition of diversity – regional diversity, as is re-summarised below, but also diversity in why people converted to Islam, thereby creating the rich archaeological record that we have considered across almost the whole of the continent south of the Sahara. The application of a checklist – that a mosque or Muslim burial is present, and thus the presence of a Muslim or Muslim community can be inferred – only takes us so far (see Insoll 1999a). Archaeology has been the focus of this study, but a multi-source approach has allowed the archaeological evidence to be supplemented in considering issues of conversion, for instance.

Possible reasons for conversion

It is possible to attempt to consider why people converted to Islam in Africa south of the Sahara. A key factor is force, usually allied with *jihad*, but although of great significance in some regions of sub-Saharan Africa, in the Nilotic Sudan today for instance (Beswick and Spaulding 2000), and possibly in Nubia previously (Hasan 1966), or in parts of West Africa and the central Sudan (Reyna

1990), elsewhere it was of little importance. Rather, what *jihad* seems to have been primarily used for is what Pouwels (2000:251) describes – that is, as an instrument of 'enforcement'. It more frequently functioned as a tool of reform, as in the Fulani-led *jihads* of the central or West African Sudan (Robinson 2000), or as a mechanism whereby people were kept in line in practising what was perceived as orthodox Islam. *Jihad* might also be conducted without any intention of encouraging conversion. In fact the opposite might be true, and campaigns might be completed for profit – to obtain slaves, for example. This was the case in parts of the central Sudan, as for example among the kings of Kanem, as it was not in their interests to encourage the spread of Islam beyond certain limits (Lange 1984:253), in case it restricted the supply of slaves. This was because, theoretically at least, one is not meant to enslave a fellow Muslim (Willis 1985a).

Thus force was not usually the key; rather, people converted to Islam for a variety of reasons. Islam provided the language and commonality in which alliances could be made, not only among Africans, but could also provide or extend connections to the world outside sub-Saharan Africa. People also converted as they were in some instances already predisposed to the existence of a High God (Ray 1976; I. M. Lewis 1980a), however remote and perhaps not directly communicated with. This has been shown to be the case among the Bambara (Zahan 1974) and the Somali (I. M. Lewis 1980a, 1994), for instance, yet it is not necessarily a uniform element of African traditional religions. However, in this respect it is worth noting that although African traditional religions are complex phenomena and subject to differing historical development, as was described in chapter 1, certain similarities in both beliefs and practices are found across the continent, as in initiation rites or the role of sacrifice in particular (Ray 1976), as has also been discussed.

People converted for many reasons. Conversion might also take place for reasons of religious prestige, as was described among the Yao of Malawi (Thorold 1987). Equally, it could be for more prosaic reasons of trade-related prestige, in obtaining prestige items from trading networks controlled by Muslims, as might have been one of the factors underlying conversions to Islam in the kingdom of Ghana (Levtzion 1973). It is also undeniable that in many areas of sub-Saharan Africa the development of long-distance trade and conversion to Islam went hand in hand, and underpinning this was access to trade goods and services brought by this trade (Levtzion 1979a). However, broadening economic horizons do not correlate with broadening religious ones, and caution is required in not applying a simple reductionism by invoking long-distance trade as equating to conversion to Islam in all cases. In part this is because there exists archaeological evidence for pre-Islamic long-distance trade in many regions of sub-Saharan Africa, though generally it was not on the scale evident in the subsequent Islamic era. However, examples of exceptions to this lack of comparable scale in the pre-Islamic and Islamic periods do exist, and would include the

Sudanese kingdoms on the Nile, such as Meroë and its predecessors (Edwards 1996; Wildung 1997), or Aksum in the Ethiopian highlands (Phillipson 1998; Pankhurst 1998), also as described. Yet in the western Sahel or the central Sudan, for instance, a comparable scale of long-distance trade (excluding the extensive interregional networks that operated) appears not to have existed until the Islamic era (Insoll 1996b; Liverani 2000).

A range of benefits beyond purely religious ones might then be accrued from converting to Islam, especially for a ruler. These might also include improving secular administration using Islamic administrative systems, as was seen by Ibn Battuta in Mogadishu, for example (Hamdun and King 1994:16–21), as well as literacy using Arabic (Levtzion 1986b; Sanneh 1994). Yet elsewhere such a rationale is not so persuasive. In parts of southern Africa, as at Great Zimbabwe (Garlake 1973), or in the Asante kingdoms of the West African forest (Wilks 1980), rulers did not convert, though they had access to trade goods from Muslim-controlled networks, and certainly in the case of the latter, to ideas and services from Muslims present in their capitals (Owusu-Ansah 1983). To this package of reasons for conversion could be added factors such as increasing magical power through converting to Islam, or gaining ascendancy over one's rivals or enemies. A variety of reasons for conversion to Islam therefore exists.

The processes of conversion

It has also proven possible to consider the processes of conversion, and it was seen that catch-all models which invoke similarities from one end of the continent to the other are largely unsuccessful (see, e.g., Trimingham 1968). However, certain similarities are evident, and the best framework for examining these was provided by Eaton's (1993) three-phase model – developed, as noted, for understanding Islamic conversion processes in Bengal. This was successful in comparison to the other models that have been considered, because though tailored to a specific geographical area, the notion of the phases of inclusion, identification and displacement fits well with some of the sub-Saharan African data. These concepts provide a useful framework to allow an examination of the processes by which Islam spread in some areas of sub-Saharan Africa, as was argued for the East African coast, for example. Yet it would be naive to imply that these three phases always exist, and always follow in strict linear progression. This is a factor remarked upon in a general context by Ryan (1978:304), who makes the point that the different stages of Islamisation can 'coexist and even interpenetrate. This holds true not only within one ethnic group, but also within one family, and sometimes, indeed, even within the experience of one individual.'

However, in some areas a seemingly more linear conversion sequence can be found – in the Western Sahel, for example, where a nomad, merchant, ruler, townspeople, sedentary agriculturist-type sequence seems more applicable (Insoll 1996b). Yet it is possible that as new data becomes available this tidy sequence might need revision or dismantling. Similarly, to extend this model beyond the western Sahel is also difficult. The universal paradigm that nomads equal early conversion to Islam and orthodoxy as might seemingly be indicated in the western Sahel, or by the Fulani-inspired *jihads* in various parts of the continent (R. S. Smith 1989; Robinson 2000), or even outside sub-Saharan Africa, as with the early spread of Islam among the nomadic population of parts of the Arabian Peninsula (Hitti 1974), can be seen to be flawed. The case studies considered from Ethiopia and the Horn of Africa, for instance, where practicality or existing tradition might impinge upon perceptions of orthodox Muslim behaviour, such as the absence of veiling among nomadic Somali women (I. M. Lewis 1994), indicates this to be so. Exceptions can of course be found to undermine all such models, for as well as societies we are dealing with individuals, and therefore individual decision making influencing group identity as well. Ultimately, it has to be acknowledged that all of these conversion process models are flawed, owing to the range of factors involved. Yet they provide a useful start in understanding the complexity inherent in approaching processes such as religious conversion as evident in archaeological data, in this case pertaining to Islam in sub-Saharan Africa.

A return to the nature of Islam in sub-Saharan Africa

A key recurring feature of Islam in sub-Saharan Africa is the notion of continuity, how the pre-Islamic foundations and religious heritage have been incorporated in a syncretic process, a process defined as 'basic not only to religion and ritual but to the "predicament of culture" in general' (Shaw and Stewart 1994:1). As well as syncretism, coexistence of traditional beliefs might exist, with a literal separation perhaps employed with Islam defined as religion, and traditional beliefs and practices as custom, as seen among the Berti of the Nilotic Sudan (Holy 1991), or as evident archaeologically in the inland Niger delta area of Mali – as attested by the growth in terracotta figurine production (R. J. McIntosh 1998), or the persistence of urn burial (Bedaux 1979) – after conversions to Islam had begun in parts of the region. African traditional religions frequently appear to have meshed with Islam rather than acting as agents of confrontation with it. The history and archaeology of Africa show that various traditions and religions could coexist. Today, however, there are many tensions precisely along these lines. Nations created by colonial powers – the Nilotic Sudan, for instance (Beswick and Spaulding 2000) – are now embroiled precisely in religious and other ethnic conflicts.

The rarer alternative is that besides coexistence or syncretism, previous religious traditions could be expunged or displaced, or driven underground by *jihad* or other reform processes. This is also something that can be evident archaeologically – in, for instance, allusions being made through the use of material culture to the early days of Islam, and thus to perceptions of early Islamic purity, as indicated by the earthen mosques of Futa Toro and their references to the Prophet Muhammad's house in Medina (Bourdier 1993). In general though, the archaeology of Islam in sub-Saharan Africa indicates, largely, not processes of foreign imposition but intra-African dynamics. This is accounted for by the simple fact that the archaeology of Islam in sub-Saharan Africa is also a continuation of African Iron Age archaeology, where the material previously interpreted during the colonial era as that of foreign imposition has been reconsidered; in the western Sahel (Holl 1996; Insoll 1996b), or on the East African coast (M. Horton 1986; Helms 2000), for example, the supposed foreign foundations have been shown to be false, and the result of more recent political considerations.

The 'real cases' of foreign imposition are comparatively rare, the Moroccan invasion of Songhai providing an example (Bovill 1968), but even here the majority of the Songhai were already Muslim, and the Moroccan campaigns cannot be classified as religious in intent. Similarly with the Ottoman occupation of parts of the Red Sea coasts of Africa (Tedeschi 1969), or the Omani one of the East African coast (Sheriff 1987), a religious motive is lacking. Where the impact did come was in the devastating slave raids launched across many parts of the continent, but again these were predominantly by Africans against Africans, though exceptions do occur, as with the Arab slavers in interior eastern-central Africa (Levtzion 1985b), or with some of the slavers operating in the Nilotic Sudan and eastern parts of the central Sudan (Cordell 1985). Moreover, these slavers' motivation was once again more often than not led by profit rather than religious fervour and a desire to promote conversion to Islam.

Regional identities

Distinct regional identities have developed within Islam in sub-Saharan Africa. In Ethiopia and the Horn of Africa, important factors which were identified as significant were the continued existence of another world religion, Christianity, and the extensive legacy of pre-Islamic contacts with the Arabian side of the Red Sea that had occurred. The latter contacts were of especial importance in the formative years of Islam, for they attested to the close relationship enjoyed between the inhabitants of the two shores of the Red Sea, as indicated by the asylum given to members of the early Muslim community by the Ethiopian ruler (Lapidus 1988; Pankhurst 1998). The cult of saints was also identified as important in parts of Ethiopia and the Horn, notably in Harar (Foucher 1994), as was the role of holy men. Both of these functioned as agents of great relevance in popularising, spreading and moulding the character of Islam in

Ethiopia and the Horn of Africa, and similarly in the Nilotic Sudan. Sudanese Islam, at least in Nubia and the Nile valley, was further dominated by the holy man (McHugh 1994), and these holy men served to spread Islam in the region – for example, among the Funj (O'Fahey and Spaulding 1974). To these elements can be added Sufism as another major element of Nilotic Sudanese Islamic identity (Karrar 1992).

Within the western Sahel and also on the East African coast regional identities again differ. Important entrepôts were situated in both these areas, and broad parallels can be drawn, unlikely as this might initially seem, between these two regions – in their chronological contemporaneity, their respective geographical (coastal–Sahara and Indian Ocean) situations (Levtzion 1973; M. Horton 1996b; Insoll 1996b) and in the role of trade as an agent of Islamisation – but significant differences are also evident. The reasons for this are various, and could include factors such as the absence of the degree of cultural unity in the western Sahel that was evident on the East African, largely Swahili, coast; however, when this seeming unity is looked at in detail it too can be seen to be deceptive. This was because in reality the polities on the East African coast were as dissimilar as they were similar, and, as in the western Sahel, traces of experimentation with different sects and schools of Islam exist (Horton and Middleton 2000), other than those that prevail on the coast today.

Southern Africa and east-central Africa differ again. Trade goods originating in the Islamic world are found in parts of the region, as with the range of material from Great Zimbabwe (Garlake 1973), or the finds of glass beads in parts of Uganda (Robertshaw 1997), or in the Upemba depression (de Maret 1979). However, it is noticeable that Muslims themselves, aside from small bands of Arab and Swahili traders and slavers, were largely absent prior to the arrival of Europeans – colonists who were accompanied by Indonesian Muslims in South Africa (Chidester 1992), or later by Muslims of South Asian origin in Uganda, for instance (Oded 1974). Thus, until comparatively recently conversion to Islam was apparently completely non-existent among the vast majority of the population of southern and interior east-central Africa. This stands in contrast to the West African Sudan and forest where the actions of traders, notably the Mande, served to spread Islam through the region in what was essentially a peaceful process (Levtzion 1986b). In contrast, within the central Sudan, holy men and, to a lesser extent, traders appear to have served in spreading Islam (Hiskett 1994; Levtzion 2000). This was also a region in which important empires, kingdoms, city-states and emirates flourished and disappeared. These contributed significantly to the character of Islam in the region, and to the existence of warfare and *jihad*, which here, more than in any of the other regions of sub-Saharan Africa considered, seem to have been of particular importance and longevity (R. S. Smith 1989; Reyna 1990), as attested by a rash of fortified towns and cities scattered across the central Sudan.

The archaeology of Islam in sub-Saharan Africa today

The archaeology of Islam in sub-Saharan Africa can be seen to be the residue of dynamic processes, and in many instances the monuments and sites described play an important role today. Islam is a point of pride to many governments, and measures have been taken to preserve ancient monuments. However, this entails a certain commodification of the archaeological record. In East Africa, for instance, now a major tourist destination, monuments play a significant role in many areas as a source of tourist revenue. The monuments of Zanzibar island provide such an example, and especially those in the old stone town of Zanzibar itself, where much effort and money has been invested in restoring and presenting sites such as the Omani fort built upon the remains of the Portuguese church, or in conserving the traders' mansions built in the nineteenth century (**figure 9.1**) (Sheriff 1995). Similarly, on the mainland coastal strip of East Africa numerous sites now form part of tourist itineraries: Kilwa is presented, rightly, as a major site of historical importance (Sutton 1998b), as is Fort Jesus at Mombasa in Kenya. The coastal or Swahili element of many package tours to East Africa, combined with a few days at the beach, are now considered as important as the safari element. A similar role for monuments is found in the interior of the region as well. The Kasubi tombs in Kampala, the ancestral tombs of the *kabakas* of Buganda (Kigongo Mugerwa 1991), for example, are now firmly placed on the itineraries of the developing tourist industry in Uganda.

Outside the main centres of sub-Saharan African tourism, i.e. eastern and southern Africa, heritage presentation might not be so well developed, but the sites are of no lesser importance. Timbuktu has been gazetted as one of Mali's UNESCO World Heritage sites and is increasingly drawing well-heeled tourists, including day-trippers who fly in to visit the Sankore and Djinguereber mosques (Ali Ould Sidi, pers. comm.). Similarly, on the Dahlak islands, a Saudi-financed leisure development has been planned (Dowden 1996). An awareness of the significance of archaeological sites extends beyond the few examples chosen here, including in areas which as yet receive few visitors, which is something positive as it means that sites and monuments stand a better chance of being protected if they can be seen by local people as a possible source of revenue (E. Toure, pers. comm.). Yet a more negative element may also be evident as well, and this is something remarked upon with regard to the East African coast by Horton and Middleton (2000:198) which they describe, rightly or wrongly, as suffering from the effects of 'vast numbers of culturally illiterate foreigners staying in the many hotels built in the last decades by foreign and local elite entrepreneurs selling Swahili culture and the Swahili landscape'.

Besides functioning as possible sources of tourist revenue, sites and monuments can also act as sources of national or ethnic pride, as well as continuing to have religious significance. An example of this is provided by the mosque

Figure 9.1 Zanzibar Fort

and tomb of Askia Muhammad in Gao in Mali (Mauny 1950), which is the tomb of the greatest of the Songhai emperors, as well as a functioning mosque and one of the focal points of both Songhai and Muslim identity within Gao. Besides these roles it is also an important historical monument, respected and maintained as such and presented with pride to the few tourists and travellers who visit the city. This monument, as with many others in sub-Saharan Africa, functions in multiple ways; the past is used, reinterpreted and of great importance in the present. The mosque and tomb of Askia Muhammad is actively assimilated within contemporary historical traditions, legends, myths and everyday economic and religious life.

Future directions in the archaeology of Islam in sub-Saharan Africa

This book is a provisional synthesis of archaeological research. Some subjects, such as the role of women within Islam in sub-Saharan Africa, have been archaeologically neglected to date, in part because there has been little research on the subject. Indeed, there is much work to do on many aspects of Islamic archaeology in sub-Saharan Africa, from environmental and economic work to a more sophisticated use of historical materials. Further future priorities in the archaeology of Islam in sub-Saharan Africa include rectifying the imbalance evident in archaeological research in some areas of the continent, as in Ethiopia for example, where the privileging of Christian and Aksumite archaeology to the detriment of research on Islam was noted as an issue that needed redressing (H. Ahmed 1992). Equally, the development of co-operative research projects with, and the provision of training and study opportunities for, African scholars by their European and North American colleagues should also be a priority. An excellent example of what can be achieved through such programmes is provided by the co-operative outcomes of the Swedish-funded (SAREC) Urban Origins project in Eastern and Southern Africa (see, e.g., the bulletin *Mvita*, produced by the regional archaeology centre for the study of archaeology in eastern and southern Africa which was established in 1990 as part of the overall SAREC project). Finally, in pointing out these possible future research priorities it should be noted that this does not mean that this study ends on a negative note: on the contrary, it ends positively in indicating that this is a point of entry into many interesting research problems. In conclusion, it is hoped that this volume will succeed in encouraging other scholars to fill in these many gaps and to remove the flaws in this study.

REFERENCES

Abdi, M. 1992. *Histoire des croyances en Somalie*. Paris: Diffusion des Belles Lettres.

Abimbola, W. 1991. The Place of African Traditional Religion in Contemporary Africa. In Olupone, J. K. (ed.), *African Traditional Religions in Contemporary Society*. New York: Paragon House, pp. 51–8.

Abu-Lughod, J. L. 1987. The Islamic City – Historic Myth, Islamic Essence, and Contemporary Relevance. *International Journal of Middle Eastern Studies* 19: 155–76.

Abungu, G. 1994. Islam on the Kenyan Coast: An Overview of Kenyan Coastal Sacred Sites. In Carmichael, D., Hubert, J., Reeves, B. and Schanche, A. (eds.), *Sacred Sites, Sacred Places*. London: Routledge, pp. 152–62.

Acri, B. and Bitiyong, Y. 1983. Warfare as a Factor of Urban Growth in Hausaland – the Case of Birnin Zaria, *c*.1400–1808 AD. Unpublished paper, Ninth Pan-African Congress of Prehistory and Related Studies, Jos, Nigeria.

Adams, N. K. 1990. Life in Ottoman Times at Qasr Ibrim. In Bonnet, C. H. (ed.), *Papers of the Seventh International Conference for Nubian Studies*. Geneva: University of Geneva, pp. 1–16.

Adams, W. M., Goudie, A. S. and Orme, A. R. (eds.). 1996. *The Physical Geography of Africa*. Oxford: Oxford University Press.

Adams, W. Y. 1977. *Nubia. Corridor to Africa*. London: Allen Lane.
    1987. Islamic Archaeology in Nubia: An Introductory Survey. In Hagg, T. (ed.), *Nubian Culture Past and Present*. Stockholm: Almqvist & Wiksell, pp. 327–61.
    1994. *Kulubnarti I. The Architectural Remains*. Lexington: University of Kentucky Press.
    1996. *Qasr Ibrim. The Late Medieval Period*. London: Egypt Exploration Society.

Adams, W. Y. and Adams, N. K. 1998. *Kulubnarti II. The Artifactural Remains*. London: Sudan Archaeological Research Society.

Adamu, M. 1984. The Hausa and their Neighbours in the Central Sudan. In Niane, D. T. (ed.), *Africa from the Twelfth to the Sixteenth Century*. London: Heinemann, pp. 266–300.

Afolayan, F. 1998. Zanj Slave Revolts (c.689–883). In Rodriguez, J. P. (ed.), *The Historical Encyclopedia of World Slavery*. Santa Barbara (Calif.): ABC Clio, p. 713.

Agbaje-Williams, B. 1990. Oyo Ruins of Northwestern Yorubaland, Nigeria. *Journal of Field Archaeology* 17: 367–73.

Agorsah, E. 1986. House Forms in the Northern Volta Basin, Ghana: Evolution, Internal Spatial Organisation and the Social Relationships Depicted. *West African Journal of Archaeology* 16: 25–51.

Ahmed, A. M. 1990. A Survey of the Harar Djugel (Wall) and its Gates. *Journal of Ethiopian Studies* 23: 321–34.

Ahmed, Akbar. 1988. *Discovering Islam, Making Sense of Muslim History and Society*. London: Routledge.

Ahmed, H. 1992. The Historiography of Islam in Ethiopia. *Journal of Islamic Studies* 3: 15–46.

1993. Trends and Issues in the History of Islam in Ethiopia. In Alkali, N. (ed.), *Islam in Africa*. Ibadan: Spectrum Books, pp. 205–20.

Akyeampong, E. K. 1991. *Drink, Power and Cultural Change. A Social History of Alcohol in Ghana*. Oxford: James Currey.

Alexander, J. 1988. The Saharan Divide in the Nile Valley: The Evidence from Qasr Ibrim. *African Archaeological Review* 6: 73–90.

1994. Islamic Archaeology: The Ottoman Frontier on the Middle Nile. *Sudan Archaeological Research Society Newsletter* 7: 20–6.

1996. The Turks on the Middle Nile. *Archéologie du Nil Moyen* 7: 15–36.

1997. Qalat Sai, the Most Southerly Ottoman Fortress in Africa. *Sudan and Nubia* 1: 16–20.

2000. The Archaeology and History of the Ottoman Frontier in the Middle Nile Valley 910–1233 AH/1504–1820 AD. *Adumatu* 1: 47–61.

Alexander, J. and Driskell, B. 1985. Qasr Ibrim 1984. *Journal of Egyptian Archaeology* 71: 12–26.

Allen, J. de V. 1980. Settlement Patterns on the East African Coast, *c*.AD 800–1900. In Leakey, R. E. and Ogot, B. A. (eds.), *Proceedings of the Eighth Pan-African Congress for Prehistory*. Nairobi: Louis Leakey Memorial Institute for African Prehistory, pp. 361–3.

1993. *Swahili Origins*. London: James Currey.

Allibert, C., Argant, A., and Argant, J. 1990. Le Site de Dembeni (Mayotte, Archipel des Comores). Mission 1984. *Etudes Océans Indiens* 11: 63–172.

Allibert, C. and Verin, P. 1996. The Early Pre-Islamic History of the Comores Islands: Links with Madagascar and Africa. In Reade, J. (ed.), *The Indian Ocean in Antiquity*. London: Kegan Paul, pp. 461–70.

Alpers, E. A. 1975. *Ivory and Slaves in East Central Africa*. London: Heinemann. East Central Africa. In Levtzion and Pouwels 2000, pp. 303–25.

Amiji, H. M. 1969. The Asian Communities. In Kritzeck and Lewis 1969, pp. 141–81.

Andre, P. J. 1924. *L'Islam noir*. Paris: Paul Geuthner.

Andrzejewski, B. W. 1986. The Literary Culture of the Somali People. In Loughran, K. S. et al. (eds.), *Somalia in Word and Image*. Bloomington: Indiana University Press, pp. 33–45.

Anfray, F. 1967. Matara. *Annales d'Ethiopie* 7: 33–88.

1968. Aspects de l'archéologie éthiopienne. *Journal of African History* 9: 345–66.

1972. Fouilles de Yeha. *Annales d'Ethiopie* 9: 45–64.

1973. Les Fouilles de Yeha, Mai–Juin 1973. *Documents pour Servir à l'Histoire des Civilisations Ethiopiennes* 4: 35–8.

1990. *Les Anciens Ethiopiens*. Paris: Armand Colin.

Anquandah, J. 1976. The Rise of Civilisation in the West African Sudan. *Sankofa* 2: 23–32.

1982. *Rediscovering Ghana's Past*. Harlow: Longman.

1993. Urbanization and State Formation in Ghana during the Iron Age. In Shaw, T., Sinclair, P., Andah, B. and Okpoko, A. (eds.), *The Archaeology of Africa. Food, Metals and Towns*. London: Routledge, pp. 642–51.

Aradeon, S. B. 1989. Al-Sahili. The Historian's Myth of Architectural Technology Transfer from North Africa. *Journal des Africanistes* 59: 99–131.

Arazi, N. 1999. An Archaeological Survey in the Songhay Heartland of Mali. *Nyame Akuma* 52: 25–43.

Arkell, A. J. 1932. Fung Origins. *Sudan Notes and Records* 15: 201–50.

1936a. Cambay and the Bead Trade. *Antiquity* 10: 292–305.

1936b. Darfur Antiquities I. Ain Farah. *Sudan Notes and Records* 19: 301–11.

1937. Darfur Antiquities II. The Tora Palaces in Turra at the North End of Jebel Marra. *Sudan Notes and Records* 20: 91–105.

1946. Darfur Antiquities III. The Ruined Town of Uri in Northern Darfur. *Sudan Notes and Records* 27: 185–202.

1947. More about Fung Origins. *Sudan Notes and Records* 27: 87–97.

1966. *A History of the Sudan from the Earliest Times to 1821*. London: Athlone Press.

Arnold, T. W. 1935. *The Preaching of Islam*. London: Luzac.

Arnoldi, M. J. 1986. The Artistic Heritage of Somalia. In Loughran, K. S. et al. (eds.), *Somalia in Word and Image*. Bloomington: Indiana University Press, pp. 17–25.

Audouin, J. and Deniel, R. 1978. *L'Islam en Haute-Volta à l'époque coloniale*. Paris: Harmattan.

Azaïs, R. P. and Chambard, R. 1931. *Cinq années de recherches archéologiques en Ethiopie*. Paris: Paul Geuthner.

al-Azzawi, S. H. 1969. Oriental Houses in Iraq. In Oliver, P. (ed.), *Shelter and Society*. London: Barrie & Jenkins, pp. 91–102.

Balfour-Paul, H. G. 1954a. Islam at Uri. *Sudan Notes and Records* 35: 139–40.

1954b. Sultan's Palaces in Darfur and Wadai. *Kush* 2: 5–18.

1955. History and Antiquities of Darfur. *Museum Pamphlet* 5. Khartoum: National Museum.

Banning, E. B. and Köhler-Rollefson, I. 1992. Ethnographic Lessons for the Pastoral Past: Camp Remains near Beidha, Southern Jordan. In Bar-Yosef, O. and Khazanov, A. (eds.), *Pastoralism in the Levant. Archaeological Materials in Anthropological Perspectives*. Madison: Prehistory Press, pp. 181–201.

Barkindo, K. M. 1992. Kanem-Borno: Its Relations with the Mediterranean Sea, Bagirmi and Other States in the Chad Basin. In Ogot, B. A. (ed.), *UNESCO General History of Africa*, vol. V: *Africa from the Sixteenth to Eighteenth Centuries*. London: Heinemann, pp. 492–513.

Barrett-Jolley, S. 2000. The Faunal Remains from Gao Ancien. In Insoll 2000b, pp. 45–55.

Barth, H. 1890. *Travels and Discoveries in Northern and Central Africa*. London: Ward, Lock & Co.

Bassat, R. 1893. Les Inscriptions de l'Ile de Dahlak. *Journal Asiatique* 9: 77–111.

Battistini, R. and Verin, P. n.d. Irodo et la tradition vohémarienne. In *Arabes et Islamisés à Madagascar et dans l'Océan Indien*. Antananarivo: Centre d'Archéologie de la Faculté des Lettres, pp. xvii–xxxii.

Baumann, D. 1957. Mafia Island. *Tanganyika Notes and Records* 46: 4–24.

Bedaux, R. 1972. Tellem, reconnaissance archéologique d'une culture de l'Ouest Africain au moyen-âge: recherches architectoniques. *Journal de la Société des Africanistes* 42: 103–85.

1976. Mali (Note on Excavations at Togueres Doupwil and Galia). *Nyame Akuma* 8: 40–3.

1978. Recherches archéologiques dans le delta intérieur du Niger (Mali). *Paleohistoria* 20: 92–220.

1979. Archaeological Research in the Bani–Niger Region (Mali). *Nyame Akuma* 14: 34–5.

1988. Tellem and Dogon Material Culture. *African Arts* 21(4): 38–45.

1991. Des Tellem aux Dogon: recherches archéologiques dans la boucle du Niger (Mali). *Dall' Archeologìa all' arte tradizionale Africana*. Rome: Centro Studio Archeologìa Africana.

Bernus, E. 1960. Kong et sa région. *Etudes Eburnéenes* 8: 241–324.

Bernus, E. and Cressier, P. (eds.). 1991. *Azelik-Takadda et l'implantation médiévale*. Paris: Karthala.

Berthier, S. 1997. *Koumbi Saleh*. BAR S680. Oxford: Archaeopress.

Beswick, S. and Spaulding, J. 2000. Introduction. White Nile, Black Blood. Historical Perspectives on Africa's Longest Civil War and the Forced Transfer of Southern Sudanese Wealth to Khartoum (1820–1994). In Spaulding, J. and Beswick, S. (eds.), *White Nile, Black Blood. War, Leadership and Ethnicity from Khartoum to Kampala*. Trenton: Red Sea Press, pp. xiii–xxviii.

Bhattacharya, D. K. 1970. Indians of African Origin. *Cahiers d'Etudes Africaines* 10: 579–82.

Binet, Capitaine. 1956. Notes sur les ruines de Garoumele (Niger). *Notes Africaines* 53: 1–2.

Binger, Capitaine. 1892. *Du Niger au Golfe de Guinée*. Paris: Hachette.

Birks, J. S. 1978. *Across the Savannas to Mecca. The Overland Pilgrimage Route from West Africa*. London: Hurst.

Bisson, G. 1962. Destruction d'une ancienne mosquée à El-Ateuf (Mzab). *Travaux de l'Institut de Recherches Sahariennes* 21: 215–17.

Bivar, A. D. H. and Shinnie, P. 1962. Old Kanuri Capitals. *Journal of African History* 3: 1–10.

Blanchy, S. and Said, M. 1990. Inscriptions religieuses et magico-religieuse sur les monuments historiques à Ngazidja (Grand Comore). Le Sceau de Salomon. *Etudes Océan Indien* 11: 7–62.

Blench, R. 1993. Ethnographic and Linguistic Evidence for the Prehistory of African Ruminant Livestock, Horses and Ponies. In Shaw, T., Sinclair, P., Andah, B. and Okpoko, A. (eds.), *The Archaeology of Africa. Food, Metals and Towns*. London: Routledge, pp. 71–103.

Bloom, J. 1989. *Minaret, Symbol of Islam*. Oxford Studies in Islamic Art 7. Oxford: Oxford University Press.

Bloss, J. F. E. 1936. The Story of Suakin. *Sudan Notes and Records* 14: 272–300.

Boddy, J. 1989. *Wombs and Alien Spirits. Women, Men and the Zar Cult in Northern Sudan*. Madison: University of Wisconsin Press.

Bolland, R. 1991. *Tellem Textiles*. Amsterdam: Royal Tropical Institute.

Bone, D. 1982. Islam in Malawi. *Journal of Religion in Africa* 13: 126–38.

Bonfiglioli, A. M. 1988. *Dudal. Histoire de famille et histoire de troupeau chez un groupe de Wodaabe du Niger*. Cambridge: Cambridge University Press.

Bonine, M. E. 1977. From Uruk to Casablanca. Perspectives on the Urban Experience of the Middle East. *Journal of Urban History* 3: 141–80.

Bonnel de Mézières, M. 1923. Recherche de l'emplacement de Ghana. *Mémoire de l'Académie Inscriptions et Belles-Lettres* 13: 227–64.

Bouchud, J. 1983. Paleofaune de Tegdaoust. In Devisse 1983, pp. 355–63.

Bourdier, J. P. 1993. The Rural Mosques of Futa Toro. *African Arts* 26: 32–45.

Bourgeois, J.-L. 1987. The History of the Great Mosques of Djenne. *African Arts* 20: 54–62, 90–2.

Bovill, E. W. 1968. *The Golden Trade of the Moors*. London: Oxford University Press.

Bowman, S., Ambers, J. and Leese, M. 1990. Re-evaluation of British Museum Radiocarbon Dates Issued between 1980 and 1984. *Radiocarbon* 32: 59–80.

Bradlow, F. R. 1978. The First Mosque in Cape Town. In Bradlow and Cairns 1978, pp. 9–39.

Bradlow, F. R. and Cairns, M. (eds.). 1978. *The Early Cape Muslims. A Study of their Mosques, Genealogy and Origins*. Cape Town: Balkema.

Braukämper, U. 1984a. On Food Avoidances in Southern Ethiopia: Religious Manifestation and Socio-Economic Relevance. In Rubenson, S. (ed.), *Proceedings of the Seventh International Conference of Ethiopian Studies*. Uppsala: Scandinavian Institute of African Studies, pp. 429–45.

  1984b. Notes on the Islamicization and the Muslim Shrines of the Harar Plateau. In Labahn, T. (ed.), *Proceedings of the Second International Congress of Somali Studies*, vol. II. Hamburg: Helmut Buske Verlag, pp. 145–74.

  1997. A Vanishing Socio-Religious System: Fandano of the Hadiya. In Fukui, K., Kurimoto, E. and Shigeta, M. (eds.), *Ethiopia in Broader Perspective: Papers of the Thirteenth International Conference of Ethiopian Studies*, vol. II. Kyoto: Shokado Book Sellers, pp. 314–26.

Bravmann, R. 1974. *Islam and Tribal Art in West Africa*. Cambridge: Cambridge University Press.

  1995. Sahel and Savanna. In Phillips 1995, pp. 479–533.

Bravmann, R. and Silverman, R. A. 1987. Painted Incantations: The Closeness of Allah and Kings in Nineteenth Century Asante. In Schildkrout, E. (ed.), *The Golden Stool: Studies of the Asante Center and Periphery*. New York: American Museum of Natural History, pp. 93–107.

Brenner, L. 1973. *The Shehus of Kukawa*. Oxford: Clarendon Press.

  1993a. Constructing Muslim Identities in Mali. In Brenner 1993c, pp. 59–78.

  1993b. Introduction: Muslim Representations of Unity and Difference in the African Discourse. In Brenner 1993c, pp. 1–20.

Brenner, L. (ed.). 1993c. *Muslim Identity and Social Change in sub-Saharan Africa*. London: Hurst.

Brett, M. 1983. Islam and Trade in the Bilad al-Sudan, 10th–11th Century AD. *Journal of African History* 24: 431–40.

Brett, M. and Fentress, E. 1996. *The Berbers*. Oxford: Blackwell.

Brill, R. H. 1995. Chemical Analysis of some Glasses from Jenne-Jeno. In McIntosh, S. K. 1995, pp. 252–6.

Broberg, A. 1995. New Aspects of the Medieval Towns of Benadir in Southern Somalia. In Ådahl, K. and Sahlstrom, B. (eds.), *Islamic Art and Culture in Sub-Saharan Africa*. Uppsala: Acta Universitatis, pp. 111–22.

Brown, H. 1991. Three Kilwa Gold Coins. *Azania* 26: 1–4.

  1992. Early Muslim Coinage in East Africa: The Evidence from Shanga. *Numismatic Chronicle* 152: 83–7.

  1996. The Coins. In Horton, M. 1996b, pp. 368–77.

Bruce, J. 1964 [1790]. *Travels to Discover the Source of the Nile*. Edinburgh: Edinburgh University Press.

Bruce, S. 1995. *Religion in Modern Britain*. Oxford: Oxford University Press.

Bulliet, R. W. 1975. *The Camel and the Wheel.* Cambridge (Mass.): Harvard
    University Press.
    1979. Conversion to Islam and the Emergence of a Muslim Society in Iran. In
    Levtzion 1979a, pp. 30–51.
Burton, R. 1864. *A Mission to Gelele. King of Dahome.* London: Tinsley Brothers.
    1964 [1893]. *Personal Narrative of a Piligrimage to al-Madinah and Meccah,*
    vol. I. New York: Dover.
    1987 [1894]. *First Footsteps in East Africa. Or, An Exploration of Harar.* New
    York: Dover.
    1993 [1860]. *The Source of the Nile. The Lake Regions of Central Africa.*
    London: Folio Society.
    1998 [1850]. *Sindh, and the Races that Inhabit the Valley of the Indus.* Delhi:
    Munshiram Manoharlal.
Burton, W. F. P. 1961. *Luba Religion and Magic in Custom and Belief.* Tervuren:
    Musée Royal de l'Afrique Centrale.
Buxton, D. 1947. The Christian Antiquities of Northern Ethiopia. *Archaeologia*
    92: 1–42.
    1971. The Rock-Hewn and Other Medieval Churches of Tigre Province,
    Ethiopia. *Archaeologia* 103: 33–100.
Cailliaud, F. 1823. *Voyage à Meroe.* Paris: L'Imprimerie Royale.
Callaway, B. J. 1987. *Muslim Hausa Women in Nigeria.* Syracuse: Syracuse
    University Press.
Callaway, B. J. and Creevey, L. 1994. *The Heritage of Islam. Women, Religion, and
    Politics in West Africa.* London: Lynne Riener.
Campo, J. E. 1991. *The Other Sides of Paradise. Explorations into the Religious
    Meanings of Domestic Space in Paradise.* Columbia: University of South
    Carolina Press.
Camps, G. 1974. *Les Civilisations préhistoriques de l'Afrique du Nord et du
    Sahara.* Paris: Doin Editeurs.
Caplan, A. P. 1975. *Choice and Constraint in a Swahili Community.* London:
    International African Institute.
Cassanelli, L. 1986. Society and Culture in the Riverine Region of Southern
    Somalia. In Loughran, K. S. et al. (eds.), *Somalia in Word and Image.*
    Bloomington: Indiana University Press, pp. 67–74.
Castiglione, A. and Castiglione, A. 1998. *Berenice Panchrysos (Deraheib).* Varese:
    Centro Ricerche sul Deserte Orientale.
Castiglione, A., Castiglione, A. and Vercoutter, J. 1998. *L'Eldorado dei faraóni
    alla scopèrta di Berenice Pancrisia.* Novara: Istituto Geografico DeAgostini.
Caton-Thompson, G. 1931. *The Zimbabwe Culture. Ruins and Reactions.*
    Oxford: Clarendon Press.
Ceulemans, P. 1966. Introduction de l'Islam au Congo. In Lewis, I. M. 1996,
    pp. 174–92.
Chailley, M., Bourlon, A., Bichon, B., Amon d'Aby, F. and Quesnot, F. 1962. *Notes
    et études sur l'Islam en Afrique noire.* Paris: Peyronnet.
Chakrabarti, D. K. 1997. *Colonial Indology: Sociopolitics of the Ancient Indian
    Past.* Delhi: Munshiram Manoharlal.
Chami, F. 1994/5. The First Millennium AD on the East Coast: A New Look at
    the Cultural Sequence and Interactions. *Azania* 29–30: 232–7.
    1998. A Review of Swahili Archaeology. *African Archaeological Review* 15:
    199–218.

1999. Roman Beads from the Rufiji Delta, Tanzania: First Incontrovertible Archaeological Link with the Periplus. *Current Anthropology* 40: 237–41.

Chami, F. and Msemwa, P. 1997a. The Excavation at Kwale Island, South of Dar es Salaam, Tanzania. *Nyame Akuma* 48: 45–56.

1997b. A New Look at Culture and Trade on the Azanian Coast. *Current Anthropology* 38: 673–7.

Chanudet, C. 1990. Un Site majeur de Moheli: Mwala Mdjini. *Etudes Océan Indien* 12: 9–123.

Chaudhuri, R. A. 1982. *Mosque. Its Importance in the Life of a Muslim*. London: London Mosque.

Chidester, D. 1992. *Religions of South Africa*. London: Routledge.

1996. *Savage Systems. Colonialism and Comparative Religion in Southern Africa*. Charlottesville: University Press of Virginia.

Chittick, N. 1961. *Kisimani Mafia. Excavations at an Islamic Settlement on the East African Coast*. Tanganyika Ministry of Education, Antiquities Division, Occasional Paper 1. Dar es Salaam: Tanganyika Government.

1964. Appendix 1. Report on Excavations at Kisimani Mafia and Kua. *Annual Report of the Antiquities Department*. Dar es Salaam: Tanzanian Government.

1969. An Archaeological Reconnaissance of the Southern Somali Coast. *Azania* 4: 115–30.

1971. The Coast of East Africa. In Shinnie, P. (ed.), *The African Iron Age*. Oxford: Clarendon Press, pp. 108–41.

1974. *Kilwa. An Islamic Trading City on the East African Coast*. Nairobi: British Institute in Eastern Africa.

1976. An Archaeological Reconnaissance in the Horn: The British–Somali Expedition 1975. *Azania* 11: 117–33.

1977. The East Coast, Madagascar and the Indian Ocean. In Fage, J. D. and Oliver, R. (eds.), *The Cambridge History of Africa*, vol. III. Cambridge: Cambridge University Press, pp. 183–232.

1981. A Cistern at Suakin, and Some Remarks on Burnt Bricks. *Azania* 16: 181–3.

1982. Medieval Mogadishu. *Paideuma* 28: 45–62.

1984. *Manda, Excavations at an Island Port on the Kenya Coast*. Nairobi: British Institute in Eastern Africa.

Clague, A. 2000. An Analysis of Clay Tobacco Pipes from Timbuktu: Origins and Social Use. BA Honours dissertation, University of Manchester.

Clarke, P. 1989. Islam in Tropical Africa in the Twentieth Century. In Clarke, P. (ed.), *Islam*. London: Routledge, pp. 180–91.

1991. Introduction to Traditional Religions. In Sutherland, S. and Clarke, P. (eds.), *The Study of Religion, Traditional and New Religion*. London: Routledge, pp. 63–6.

Cline, W. 1950. *The Teda of Tibesti, Borku, and Kawar in the Eastern Sahara*. Menasha (Wis.): George Banta.

Clutton-Brock, J. 1993. The Spread of Domesticated Animals in Africa. In Shaw, T., Sinclair, P., Andah, B. and Okpoko, A. (eds.), *The Archaeology of Africa. Food, Metals and Towns*. London: Routledge, pp. 61–70.

Cohen, R. 1967. *The Kanuri of Bornu*. New York: Holt, Rinehart & Winston.

Cole, D. P. 1975. *Nomads of the Nomads. The Al Murrah Bedouin of the Empty Quarter*. Chicago: Aldine.

Connah, G. 1981. *Three Thousand Years in Africa. Man and his Environment in the Lake Chad Region of Nigeria.* Cambridge: Cambridge University Press.
    1987. *African Civilisations.* Cambridge: Cambridge University Press.
Conrad, D. C. 1994. A Town Called Dakajalan: The Sunjata Tradition and the Question of Ancient Mali's Capital. *Journal of African History* 35: 355–77.
Conrad, D. C. and Fisher, H. 1982. 'The Conquest that Never Was: Ghana and the Almoravids, 1076', Part 1: The External Arabic Sources. *History in Africa* 9: 21–59.
    1983. 'The Conquest that Never Was: Ghana and the Almoravids, 1076', Part 2: The Local Oral Sources. *History in Africa* 10: 53–78.
Cook, H. 2000. The Fish Bones from Gadei. In Insoll 2000b, pp. 38–44.
Cordell, D. 1985. *Dar al-Kuti and the Last Years of the Trans-Saharan Slave Trade.* Madison: University of Wisconsin Press.
    1986. Warlords and Enslavement: A Sample of Slave Raiders from Eastern Ubangi-Shari, 1870–1920. In Lovejoy, P. (ed.), *Africans in Bondage. Studies in Slavery and the Slave Trade.* Madison: University of Wisconsin Press, pp. 335–65.
Coulon, C. 1983. *Les Musulmans et le pouvoir en Afrique noire.* Paris: Karthala.
Craddock, P. T. 1985. Medieval Copper Alloy Production and West African Bronze Analyses – Part 1. *Archaeometry* 27: 17–41.
Craddock, P. T. and Picton, J. 1986. Medieval Copper Alloy Production and West African Bronze Analyses – Part 2. *Archaeometry* 28: 3–32.
Crawford, O. G. S. 1951. *The Fung Kingdom of Sennar.* Gloucester: John Bellows.
Cressier, P. 1989. La Grande Mosquée d'Assode. *Journal des Africanistes* 59: 133–62.
    1992. Archéologie de la devotion Soufi. *Journal des Africanistes* 62: 69–90.
Cressier, P. and Bernus, P. 1984. La Grande Mosquée d'Agadez: architecture et histoire. *Journal des Africanistes* 54: 5–39.
Cresti, F. 1994. La Mosquée de Sayh Hammali. In Lepage, C. (ed.), *Etudes Ethiopiennes*, vol. I. Paris: Société Française pour les Etudes Ethiopiennes, pp. 303–15.
Cribb, R. 1991. *Nomads in Archaeology.* Cambridge: Cambridge University Press.
Crowfoot, J. W. 1911. Some Red Sea Ports in the Anglo-Egyptian Sudan. *Geographical Journal* 37: 523–50.
    1922. A Note on the Date of the Towers. *Sudan Notes and Records* 5: 83–7.
Cuoq, J. M. 1975a. *Les Musulmans en Afrique.* Paris: Maisonneuve & Larose.
    1975b. *Recueil des sources arabes concernant l'Afrique occidentale.* Paris: Editions du Centre Nationale de la Recherche Scientifique.
Curle, A. T. 1937. The Ruined Towns of Somaliland. *Antiquity* 11: 315–27.
Curtin, P. D. 1989. Recent Trends in African Historiography and their Contribution to History in General. In Ki-Zerbo, J. (ed.), *UNESCO General History of Africa*, vol. I: *Methodology and African Prehistory.* London: James Currey, pp. 23–8.
Daniels, C. 1970. *The Garamantes of Southern Libya.* North Harrow: Oleander Press.
    1989. Excavation and Fieldwork amongst the Garamantes. *Libyan Studies* 20: 45–61.
Darling, P. J. 1985. Walled, Moated and Stockaded Settlements in Nigeria. Unpublished seminar paper, Department of History, Bayero University, Nigeria.

1997. Sungbo's Eredo: Africa's Largest Monument. *The Nigerian Field* 62: 113–29.

n.d.a. Aerial Archaeology in Africa. The Challenge of a Continent. Unpublished paper, African Legacy, Bournemouth.

n.d.b. Discovering Africa's Ancient Earthworks – Known and Unknown Quantities. Unpublished paper, African Legacy, Bournemouth.

Daum, W. (ed.). 1987. *Yemen. 3000 Years of Art and Civilisation in Arabia Felix.* Innsbruck: Pinguin Verlag.

Davidson, A. P. 1996. *In the Shadow of History.* London: Transaction Publishers.

Davidson, B. 1990. *A History of West Africa, 1000–1800.* Harlow: Longmans.

Davison, C. C. and Clark, J. D. 1972. Trade Wind Beads: An Interim Report of Chemical Studies. *Azania* 9: 75–86.

Dawa, S. 1985. *Inventaire des sites archéologiques dans le cercle de Gao.* Mémoire de Fin d'Etudes (unpublished dissertation). Bamako: Ecole Normale Supérieure.

de Barros, P. 1990. Changing Paradigms, Goals and Methods in the Archaeology of Francophone West Africa. In Robertshaw, P. (ed.), *A History of African Archaeology.* London: James Currey, pp. 155–72.

de Beauchene, G. 1969. Recherches archéologiques au Niger en 1966. *Actes du 1er Colloque International d'Archéologie Africaine, 1966. Fort Lamy.* Fort Lamy: Institut National Tchadien pour les Sciences Humaines, pp. 50–61.

DeCorse, C. 1989. Material Aspects of Limba, Yalunka and Kuranko Ethnicity: Archaeological Research in North Eastern Sierra Leone. In Shennan, S. J. (ed.), *Archaeological Approaches to Cultural Identity.* London: Unwin Hyman, pp. 125–40.

1992. Culture Contact, Continuity, and Change on the Gold Coast, AD 1400–1900. *African Archaeological Review* 10: 159–92.

1993. The Danes on the Gold Coast: Culture Change and the European Presence. *African Archaeological Review* 11: 149–73.

de Gironcourt, G. R. 1920. *Missions de Gironcourt en Afrique occidentale, 1908–1909, 1911–1912.* Paris, Société de Géographie.

de Heusch, L. 1985. *Sacrifice in Africa.* Manchester: Manchester University Press.

de Maret, P. 1979. Luba Roots: The First Complete Iron Age Sequence in Zaire. *Current Anthropology* 20: 233–5.

1994. Archaeology and other Prehistoric Evidence of Traditional African Religious Expression. In Blakely, T., van Beek, W. and Thomson, D. (eds.), *Religion in Africa. Experience and Expression.* London: James Currey, pp. 182–95.

1999. The Power of Symbols and the Symbols of Power through Time: Probing the Luba Past. In McIntosh, S. K. (ed.), *Beyond Chiefdoms. Pathways to Complexity in Africa.* Cambridge: Cambridge University Press, pp. 151–65.

de Maret, P. and Legros, H. 1993. Tippo Tip à Mulongo. Nouvelles données sur le début de la pénétration arabo-swahili au Shaba. *Civilisations* 41: 377–401.

de Neufville, R. L. and Houghton, A. 1965. A Description of Ain Farah and of Wara. *Kush* 13: 195–204.

de St Croix, F. W. 1945. *The Fulani of Northern Nigeria.* Lagos: Government Printer.

de Thier, F. M. 1963. Singhitini, la Stanleyville musulmane. *Correspondance d'Orient* 6.

Delafosse, M. 1922. *Les Noirs de l'Afrique.* Paris: Payot.

Devisse, J. (ed.). 1983. *Tegdaoust III*. Paris: Association Diffusion Pensée Français.

  1992a. The Almoravids. In Hrbek, I. (ed.), *UNESCO General History of Africa*, vol. III: *Africa from the Seventh to the Eleventh Century* (abridged edn). London: James Currey, pp. 176–89.

  1992b. Trade and Trade Routes in West Africa. In Hrbek, I. (ed.), *UNESCO General History of Africa*, vol. III: *Africa From the Seventh to the Eleventh Century*. (abridged edn). London: James Currey, pp. 190–215.

  1993a. L'Or. In Devisse 1993b, pp. 344–57.

  (ed.). 1993b. *Vallées du Niger*. Paris: Editions de la Réunions des Musées Nationaux.

Devisse, J. and Diallo, B. 1993. Le Seuil du Wagadu. In Devisse 1993b, pp. 103–15.

Dewar, R. E. and Wright, H. T. 1993. The Culture History of Madagascar. *Journal of World Prehistory* 7: 417–66.

Dickie, J. 1978. Allah and Eternity: Mosques, Madrasas and Tombs. In Michell, G. (ed.), *Architecture of the Islamic World*. London: Thames & Hudson, pp. 15–47.

Dickinson, R. W. 1969. Report on Sofala Investigations. MS on file, British Institute in Eastern Africa, Nairobi.

  1970. Report on Sofala Investigations. MS on file, British Institute in Eastern Africa, Nairobi.

Dieterlen, G. 1951. *Essai sur la religion Bambara*. Paris: Presses Universitaires de France.

Dmochowski, Z. R. 1990a. *An Introduction to Nigerian Traditional Architecture*. vol. I: *Northern Nigeria*. London: Ethnographica.

  1990b. *An Introduction to Nigerian Traditional Architecture*, vol. II: *South-Western and Central Nigeria*. London: Ethnographica.

Doe, B. 1971. *Southern Arabia*. London: Thames & Hudson.

Dolukhanov, P. M. 1996. *The Early Slavs*. Harlow: Longman.

Donley, L. 1982. House Power: Swahili Space and Symbolic Markers. In Hodder, I. (ed.), *Symbolic and Structural Archaeology*. Cambridge: Cambridge University Press, pp. 63–73.

  1987. Life in the Swahili Town House Reveals the Symbolic Meaning of Spaces and Artefact Assemblages. *African Archaeological Review* 5: 181–92.

Donley-Reid, L. 1990. A Structuring Structure: The Swahili House. In Kent, S. (ed.), *Domestic Architecture and the Use of Space*. Cambridge: Cambridge University Press, pp. 114–26.

Dowden, R. 1996. Eritrea Beckons Fun-Loving Saudi Men. *Independent on Sunday*, 14 January.

Dramani-Issifou, Z. 1992. Islam as a Social System in Africa since the Seventh Century. In Hrbek, I. (ed.), *UNESCO General History of Africa*, vol. III: *Africa from the Seventh to the Eleventh Century* (abridged edn). London: James Currey, pp. 50–62.

Duarte, R. T. 1993. *Northern Mozambique in the Swahili World*. Uppsala: Uppsala University.

du Plessis, I. D. 1972. *The Cape Malays*. Cape Town: Balkema.

du Plessis, I. D. and Lückhoff, C. A. 1953. *The Malay Quarter and its People*. Cape Town: Balkema.

Duyvendak, J. L. L. 1949. *China's Discovery of Africa*. London: Arthur Probsthain.

Eaton, R. M. 1993. *The Rise of Islam and the Bengal Frontier, 1204–1760*. Berkeley: University of California Press.

Edwards, D. N. 1996. *The Archaeology of the Meroitic State*. BAR S640. Oxford: Tempus Reparatum.

1999. Christianity and Islam in the Middle Nile: Towards a Study of Religion and Social Change in the Long Term. In Insoll 1999b, pp. 94–104.

Edwards, D. N., Hawthorne, J., Dore, J. and Mattingly, D. J. 1999. The Garamantes of Fezzan Revisited: Publishing the C. M. Daniels Archive. *Libyan Studies* 30: 109–27.

Effah-Gyamyi, E. 1979. Bono Manso Archaeological Research Project. *West African Journal of Archaeology* 9: 173–86.

1985. *Bono Manso: An Archaeological Investigation into Early Akan Urbanism*. Calgary: University of Calgary Press.

1986. Ancient Urban Sites in Hausaland. *West African Journal of Archaeology* 16: 117–34.

Elisséeff, N. and El Hakim, R. 1981. *Mission soudano-française dans la province de Mer Rouge (Soudan)*. Lyons: Maison de l'Orient Méditerranéen.

El-Rashedy, F. 1986. Garamantian Burial Customs: Their Relation to Those of Other Peoples of North Africa. *Libya Antiqua*. Paris: UNESCO, pp. 77–105.

El-Zein, I. S. 2000. The Archaeology of the Early Islamic Period in the Republic of the Sudan. *Sudan and Nubia* 4: 32–36.

Engestrom, T. 1959. Origin of Pre-Islamic Architecture in West Africa. *Ethnos* 24: 64–9.

Erlich, H. 1994. *Ethiopia and the Middle East*. London: Lynne Riener.

Es-Sa'di, A. 1900. *Tarikh es-Soudan* (Houdas, O. trans). Paris: Ernest Leroux.

Ettinghausen, R. 1992. The Man-Made Setting. In Lewis, B. (ed.), *The World of Islam*. London: Thames & Hudson, pp. 57–72.

Evans-Pritchard, E. E. 1956. *Nuer Religion*. Oxford: Clarendon Press.

1971. Sources with Particular Reference to the Southern Sudan. *Cahiers d'Etudes Africaines* 11 (41):144–5.

Eyo, E. 1977. *Two Thousand Years of Nigerian Art*. Lagos: Federal Department of Antiquities.

Fabunmi, M. A. 1969. *Ife Shrines*. Ife: University of Ife Press.

Faegre, T. 1979. *Tents. Architecture of the Nomads*. London: John Murray.

Fagan, B. 1972. Ingombe Ilede: Early Trade in South Central Africa. *Addison Wesley Modular Publications* 19: 1–34.

Fage, J. 1989. The Development of African Historiography. In Ki-Zerbo, J. (ed.), *UNESCO General History of Africa*, vol. I: *Methodology and African Prehistory*. London: James Currey, pp. 10–15.

Farias, P. F. de Moraes. 1974. Review Article. Great States Revisited. *Journal of African History* 15: 479–88.

1985. Models of the World and Categorial Models: The 'Enslavable Barbarian' as a Mobile Classificatory Label. In Willis, J. R. (ed.), *Slaves and Slavery in Muslim Africa*, vol. II: *The Servile Estate*. London: Frank Cass, pp. 27–46.

1990. The Oldest Extant Writing in West Africa. *Journal des Africanistes* 60: 65–113.

1999. Tadmakkat and the Image of Mecca: Epigraphic Records of the Work of the Imagination in 11th Century West Africa. In Insoll 1999b, pp.105–15.

2000. Appendix 2. The Inscriptions from Gorongobo. In Insoll 2000b, pp. 156–9.

forthcoming. *Medieval Arabic Epigraphy in the West African Sahel*. London: British Academy.

Fattovich, R. 2000. Review of *Ancient Ethiopia*. *African Archaeological Review* 17: 90–4.

Feilberg, C. C. 1944. *La Tente noire*. Copenhagen: National Museum of Ethnography.

Ferme, M. 1994. What 'Alhaji Airplane' Saw in Mecca, and What Happenned When he Came Home. In Stewart, C. and Shaw, R. (eds.), *Syncretism/Anti Syncretism. The Politics of Religious Synthesis*. London: Routledge, pp. 27–44.

Filesi, T. 1972. *China and Africa in the Middle Ages*. London: Frank Cass.

Filipowiak, W. 1978. Results of Archaeological Research at Niani. *Nyame Akuma* 10: 32–3.

   1979. *Etudes archéologiques sur la capitale médiévale du Mali*. Szczecin: Muzeum Narodowe.

   1981. Le Complexe du palais royale du Mali. In *Le Sol, la parole et l'écrit. Mélanges en hommage à Raymond Mauny*. Paris: Société Française d'Histoire d'Outre-Mer, pp. 71–89.

Fisher, A. and Fisher, H. 1970. *Slavery and Muslim Society in Africa*. London: Hurst.

Fisher, H. J. 1972. 'He Swalloweth the Ground with Fierceness and Rage': The Horse in the Central Sudan, 1. Its Introduction. *Journal of African History* 13: 369–88.

   1973a. Conversion Reconsidered: Some Historical Aspects of Religious Conversion in Black Africa. *Africa* 43: 27–40.

   1973b. 'He Swalloweth the Ground with Fierceness and Rage': The Horse in the Central Sudan, 2. Its Use. *Journal of African History* 14: 239–56.

   1985. The Juggernaut's Apologia: Conversion to Islam in Black Africa. *Africa* 55(2): 153–73.

Fisher, H. J. and Rowland, V. 1971. Firearms in the Central Sudan. *Journal of African History* 12: 215–39.

Fleisher, J. and LaViolette, A. 1999. The Recovery of Swahili Settlements in the Absence of Stone Architecture: Two Preliminary Surveys from Pemba Island, Tanzania. *Nyame Akuma* 52: 64–78.

   in press. Elusive Wattle and Daub: Finding the Silent Majority in the Archaeology of the Swahili. *Azania* 34.

Flight, C. 1975. Gao 1972: First Interim Report: A Preliminary Investigation of the Cemetery at Sané. *West African Journal of Archaeology* 5: 81–90.

   1978. Gao 1974: Second Interim Report. Excavations in the Cemetery at Sané. MS on file, Centre of West African Studies, University of Birmingham.

   1979. Gao 1978: Third Interim Report: Further Excavations at Sané. MS on file, Centre of West African Studies, University of Birmingham.

   n.d. Thoughts on the Cemetery at Sané. Unpublished paper, Centre of West African Studies, University of Birmingham.

Flury, S. 1922. The Kufic Inscriptions of Kizimkazi Mosque, Zanzibar, 500H (AD 1107). *Journal of the Royal Asiatic Society*: 257–64.

Foucher, E. 1994. The Cult of Muslim Saints in Harar: Religious Dimension. In Zewde, B., Pankhurst, Richard and Beyne, T. (eds.), *Proceedings of the Eleventh International Conference of Ethiopian Studies*, vol. II. Addis Ababa: Institute of Ethiopian Studies, pp. 71–9.

Francis, P. Jr. 1986. Baba Ghor and the Ratanpor Rakshisha. *Journal of the Economic and Social History of the Orient* 29: 198–205.

Freeman-Grenville, G. S. P. 1960. East African Coin Finds and their Historical Significance. *Journal of African History* 1: 31–43.

    1962. *The East African Coast. Select Documents from the First to the Earlier Nineteenth Century*. Oxford: Clarendon Press.

    1963. Coins from Mogadishu, c.1300 to c.1700. *Numismatic Chronicle* 3: 179–200.

    1975. The Arab Geographers and the East African Coast. In Chittick, N. and Rotberg, R. I. (eds.), *East Africa and the Orient*. New York: Africana Publishing Company, pp. 115–46.

    1988a. Husuni. In Freeman-Grenville, G. S. P., *The Swahili Coast. Second to Nineteenth Centuries*. London: Variorum, chap. 16.

    1988b. The Portuguese on the Swahili Coast: Buildings and Language. In Freeman-Grenville, G. S. P., *The Swahili Coast. Second to Nineteenth Centuries*. London: Variorum, chap. 11.

    1988c. The Sidi and the Swahili. In Freeman-Grenville, G. S. P., *The Swahili Coast. Second to Nineteenth Centuries*. London: Variorum, chap. 17.

Freeman-Grenville, G. S. P. and Martin, B. G. 1973. A Preliminary Handlist of the Arabic Inscriptions of the Eastern African Coast. *Journal of the Royal Asiatic Society* 2: 98–122.

Frend, W. H. C. 1996. *The Archaeology of Early Christianity*. London: Geoffrey Chapman.

Frishman, M. and Khan, H.-U. (eds.). 1994. *The Mosque*. London: Thames & Hudson.

Fritz, J. 1978. Paleopsychology Today: Ideational Systems and Human Adaptation in Prehistory. In Redman, C. (ed.), *Social Archaeology: Beyond Subsistence and Dating*. New York: Academic Press, pp. 37–60.

Froelich, J. C. 1962. *Les Musulmans d'Afrique noire*. Paris: Editions de l'Orante.

Fugelstad, F. 1978. A Reconsideration of Hausa History before the Jihad. *Journal of African History* 19: 319–39.

Fuller, D. 2000. The Botanical Remains. In Insoll 2000b, pp. 28–35.

Gado, B. 1986. Possible Contacts between the Central Valley of the Nile and the River Niger Area. *Libya Antiqua*. Paris: UNESCO, pp. 187–234.

Gallay, A., Huysecom, E., Honegger, M. and Mayor, A. 1990. *Hamdallahi*. Stuttgart: Franz Steiner.

Garlake, P. 1966. *The Early Islamic Architecture of the East African Coast*. London: British Institute in Eastern Africa.

    1973. *Great Zimbabwe*. London: Thames & Hudson.

    1978. *The Kingdoms of Africa*. Oxford: Elsevier Phaidon.

Garrard, T. F. 1972a. Studies in Akan Goldweights (I). The Origin of the Goldweight System. *Transactions of the Historical Society of Ghana* 13: 1–20.

    1972b. Studies in Akan Goldweights (II). The Weight Standards. *Transactions of the Historical Society of Ghana* 13: 149–62.

    1973a. Studies in Akan Goldweights (III). The Weight Names. *Transactions of the Historical Society of Ghana* 14: 1–16.

    1973b. Studies in Akan Goldweights (IV). The Dating of Akan Goldweights. *Transactions of the Historical Society of Ghana* 14: 149–68.

    1988. The Historical Background to Akan Gold-Weights. In Fox, C. (ed.), *Asante Brass Casting*. Cambridge: African Studies Centre, pp. 1–13.

Gaussen, J. and Gaussen, M. 1988. *Le Tilemsi préhistorique et ses abords: Sahara et Sahel maliens*. Paris: Editions du CNRS.

Gbadamosi, T. G. O. 1978. *The Growth of Islam among the Yoruba, 1841–1908*. London: Longman.

Geertz, C. 1960. *The Religion of Java*. Glencoe: Free Press.

   1968. *Islam Observed. Religious Development in Morocco and Indonesia*. New Haven: Yale University Press.

Gellner, E. 1981. *Muslim Society*. Cambridge: Cambridge University Press.

Geus, F. 1995. Archaeology and History of Sai Island. *Sudan Archaeological Research Society Newsletter* 8: 27–34.

Ghaidan, U. 1976. *Lamu. A Study in Conservation*. Nairobi: East African Literature Bureau.

Gibb, H. A. R. (trans.) 1993. *The Travels of Ibn Battuta*. Delhi: Munshiram Manoharlal.

Gibb, H. A. R. and Kramers, J. H. (eds.). 1961. *The Shorter Encyclopedia of Islam*. Leiden: Brill.

Gilat, A., Shirav, M., Bogoch, R., Halicz, L., Avner, U. and Hahlieli, D. 1993. Significance of Gold Exploitation in the Early Islamic Period, Israel. *Journal of Archaeological Science* 20: 429–37.

Godlewski, W. and Medeksza, S. 1987. The So-Called Mosque Building in Old Dongola (Sudan). A Structural Analysis. *Archéologie du Nil Moyen* 2: 185–205.

Goody, E. and Goody, J. 1996. The Naked and the Clothed. In Hunwick, J. and Lawler, N. (eds.), *The Cloth of Many Colored Silks*. Evanston: Northwestern University Press, pp. 67–89.

Goody, J. 1968a. Archaeological Sites in the Northern Ivory Coast. *West African Archaeological Newsletter* 9: 59.

   1968b. Restricted Literacy in Northern Ghana. In Goody, J. (ed.), *Literacy in Traditional Societies*. Cambridge: Cambridge University Press, pp. 199–246.

   1971a. The Impact of Islamic Writing on the Oral Cultures of West Africa. *Cahiers d'Etudes Africaines* 11: 455–66.

   1971b. *Technology, Tradition and the State in Africa*. London: Oxford University Press.

Goudie, A. S. 1996. Climate: Past and Present. In Adams et al. 1996, pp. 34–59.

Gray, Sir J. 1947. Ahmed bin Ibrahim: The First Arab to Reach Buganda. *Uganda Journal* 11: 80–97.

Green, K. L. 1986. Dyula and Sonongui Roles in the Islamization of the Region of Kong. *Asian and African Studies* 20: 103–23.

Greenberg, J. 1946. *The Influence of Islam on a Sudanese Religion*. Seattle: University of Washington Press.

Greenlaw, J. P. 1995. *The Coral Buildings of Suakin. Islamic Architecture, Planning, Design and Domestic Arrangements in a Red Sea Port*. London: Kegan Paul.

Griaule, M. 1965. *Conversations with Ogotemeli. An Introduction to Dogon Religion*. London: Oxford University Press.

Gridden, H. 1954. The Khor Nubt Tombstone. *Kush* 2: 63–5.

Griffeth, R. 1981. The Hausa City-States from 1450 to 1804. In Griffeth, R. and Thomas, C. (eds.), *The City-State in Five Cultures*. Oxford: ABC Clio, pp. 143–80.

Gronenborn, D. 1996. Beyond Daima: Recent Excavations in the Kala-Balge Region of Borno State. *Nigerian Heritage* 5: 34–46.

1998. Archaeological and Ethnohistorical Investigations along the Southern Fringes of Lake Chad, 1993–1996. *African Archaeological Review* 15: 225–59.

2001. A Brief Summary of the History and Archaeology of an Empire in the Central *Bilad al-Sudan*. In DeCorse, C. (ed.), *West Africa during the Atlantic Slave Trade: Archaeological Perspectives*. Leicester: Leicester University Press, pp. 101–30.

Gronenborn, D. and Magnavita, C. 2000. Imperial Expansion, Ethnic Change, and Ceramic Traditions in the Southern Chad Basin: A Terminal Nineteenth Century Pottery Assemblage from Dikwa, Borno State, Nigeria. *International Journal of Historical Archaeology* 4: 35–70.

Grove, A. T. 1978. *Africa*. Oxford: Oxford University Press.

Gueunier, N. J. 1994. *Les Chemins de l'Islam à Madagascar*. Paris: L'Harmattan.

Guerra, M. F. 2000. A Report on the Composition of a Gold Bead from Gao (GAD 96 A 13). In Insoll 2000b, pp. 153–5.

Guillaume, A. 1954. *Islam*. London: Penguin.

Guy, G. L. 1967. Notes on Some Historic Baobabs. *Rhodesiana* 16: 17–26.

Haaland, R. 1994/5. Dakawa: An Early Iron Age Site in the Tanzania Hinterland. *Azania* 29–30: 238–47.

Haaland, R. and Msuya, S. C. in press. Iron Working and Trade: More than Archaeological Material can Tell. The Case of Dakawa (Central Tanzania). *Azania*.

Hachlili, R. 2001. The Archaeology of Judaism. In Insoll, T. (ed.), *Archaeology and World Religion*. London: Routledge, pp. 96–122.

Hackett, R. 1996. *Art and Religion in Africa*. London: Cassell.

Hadfield, P. 1949. *Traits of Divine Kingship in Africa*. London: Watts & Company.

Hall, M. 1987. *The Changing Past. Farmers, Kings and Traders in Southern Africa. 200–1860*. Cape Town: David Philip.

1990. 'Hidden History': Iron Age Archaeology in Southern Africa. In Robertshaw, P. (ed.), *A History of African Archaeology*. London: James Currey, pp. 59–77.

Halm, H. 1991. *Shiism*. Edinburgh: Edinburgh University Press.

Hamdun, S. and King, N. 1994. *Ibn Battuta in Black Africa*. Princeton: Markus Wiener.

Haneda, M. and Miura, T. (eds.). 1994. *Islamic Urban Studies. Historical Review and Perspectives*. London: Kegan Paul International.

Haour, A. 1999. Blank Page in Niger. *Nyame Akuma* 52: 44–49.

Hasan, Y. F. 1966. The Penetration of Islam in the Eastern Sudan. In Lewis, I. M. (ed.), 1966, pp. 112–23.

al-Hassan, A. Y. and Hill, D. R. 1992. *Islamic Technology. An Illustrated History*. Cambridge: Cambridge University Press.

Hasson, R. 1979. *Early Islamic Glass*. Jerusalem: L. A. Mayer Memorial Institute for Islamic Art.

Hastings, J. 1911. *Encyclopedia of Religion and Ethics*. Edinburgh: T. & T. Clark.

Hattox, R. S. 1991. *Coffee and Coffeehouses. The Origins of a Social Beverage in the Medieval Near East*. Seattle: University of Washington Press.

Hebbert, H. E. 1935. El-Rih – A Red Sea Island. *Sudan Notes and Records* 18: 308–13.

Hecht, E.-D. 1982. The City of Harar and the Traditional Harar House. *Journal of Ethiopian Studies* 15: 56–78.

Harar and Lamu – A Comparison of Two East African Muslim Societies. *Transafrican Journal of History* 16: 1–23.

Helms, R. M. 2000. Conflicting Histories: The Archaeology of the Iron-Working, Farming Communities in the Central and Southern Coast Region of Kenya. Ph.D. thesis, University of Bristol.

forthcoming. Re-Evaluating Traditional Histories in Coastal East Africa. An Archaeological Perspective. In Lane, P. and Reid, A. (eds.), *African Historical Archaeologies*. New York: Plenum Press.

Herbert, E. 1980. Timbuktu: A Case Study of the Role of Legend in History. In Swarz, B. and Dumett, R. E. (eds.), *West African Culture Dynamics*. The Hague: Mouton, pp. 431–54.

1993. *Iron, Gender, and Power*. Bloomington: Indiana University Press.

Hillenbrand, R. 1994. *Islamic Architecture. Form, Function and Meaning*. Edinburgh: Edinburgh University Press.

Hinde, S. L. 1897. *The Fall of the Congo Arabs*. London: Methuen.

Hinds, M. and Menage, V. 1991. *Qasr Ibrim in the Ottoman Period. Turkish and Further Arabic Documents*. London: Egypt Exploration Society.

Hinds, M. and Sukkout, H. 1986. *Arabic Documents from the Ottoman Period at Qasr Ibrim*. London: Egypt Exploration Society.

Hinkel, F. W. 1992. *The Archaeological Map of the Sudan VI. The Area of the Red Sea Coast and Northern Ethiopia Frontier*. Berlin: Akademie Verlag.

Hinnells, J. (ed.). 1995. *The Penguin Dictionary of Religions*. London: Penguin.

Hiskett, M. 1994. *The Course of Islam in Africa*. Edinburgh: Edinburgh University Press.

Hitti, P. 1974. *History of the Arabs*. London: Macmillan.

Hodder, I. 1982. *The Present Past*. London: Batsford.

Hogben, S. J. and Kirk-Greene, A. H. M. 1966. *The Emirates of Northern Nigeria*. London: Oxford University Press.

Hogendorn, J. and Johnson, M. 1986. *The Shell Money of the Slave Trade*. Cambridge: Cambridge University Press.

Holl, A. 1985. Background to the Ghana Empire: Archaeological Investigations on the Transition to Statehood in the Dhar Tichitt Region (Mauritania). *Journal of Anthropological Archaeology* 4: 73–115.

1988. *Houlouf 1: Archéologie des Sociétés Protohistoriques du Nord-Cameroun*. Oxford: British Archaeological Reports.

1990. West African Archaeology: Colonialism and Negritude. In Robertshaw, P. (ed.), *A History of African Archaeology*. London: James Currey, pp. 296–308.

1994. The Cemetery of Houlouf in Northern Cameroon (AD 1500–1600): Fragments of a Past Social System. *African Archaeological Review* 12: 133–70.

1995. Réseaux d'échanges préhistoriques dans la plaine tchadienne. *Sahara* 7: 17–28.

1996. African History: Past, Present, and Future. In Schmidt, P. and Patterson, T. (eds.), *Making Alternative Histories*. Santa Fe: School of American Research Press, pp. 119–47.

Holl, A. and Levy, T. 1993. From the Nile Valley to the Chad Basin: Ethnoarchaeology of Shuwa Arab Settlements. *Biblical Archaeologist* 56: 166–79.

Holl, A., Levy, T., Lechevallier, C. and Bridault, A. 1991. Of Men, Mounds and Cattle: Archaeology and Ethnoarchaeology in the Houlouf Region (Northern Cameroon). *West African Journal of Archaeology* 21: 7–36.

Holt, P. M. 1979. *The Mahdist State in the Sudan. 1881–1898*. London: Oxford University Press.

1999. *The Sudan of the Three Niles: The Funj Chronicle, 910–1288/1504–1871.* Leiden: Brill.

Holt, P. M. and Daly, M. W. 1988. *A History of the Sudan.* Harlow: Longman.

Holy, L. 1991. *Religion and Custom in a Muslim Society.* Cambridge: Cambridge University Press.

Horton, M. 1986. Asiatic Colonisation of the East African Coast: The Manda Evidence. *Journal of the Royal Asiatic Society* 201–13.

1987a. Early Muslim Trading Settlements on the East African Coast. *Antiquaries Journal* 67: 290–323.

1987b. The Human Settlement of the Red Sea. In Edwards, A. J. and Head, S. M. (eds.), *Key Environments. Red Sea.* Oxford: Pergamon Press, pp. 339–62.

1990. The Periplus and East Africa. *Azania* 25: 95–9.

1991. Primitive Islam and Architecture in East Africa. *Muqarnas* 8: 103–16.

1994a. East Africa. In Frishman and Khan 1994, pp. 194–207.

1994b. Swahili Architecture, Space and Social Structure. In Parker Pearson, M. and Richards, C. (eds.), *Architecture and Order. Approaches to Social Space.* London: Routledge, pp. 147–69.

1996a. Early Maritime Trade and Settlement along the Coasts of East Africa. In Reade, J. (ed.), *The Indian Ocean in Antiquity.* London: Kegan Paul, pp. 439–59.

(ed.). 1996b. *Shanga.* London: British Institute in Eastern Africa.

Horton, M. and Blurton, T. R. 1988. 'Indian' Metalwork in East Africa: The Bronze Lion Statuette from Shanga. *Antiquity* 62: 11–23.

Horton, M., Brown, H. and Oddy, W. 1986. The Mtambwe Hoard. *Azania* 21:115–23.

Horton, M. and Clark, C. 1985. Archaeological Survey of Zanzibar. *Azania* 20: 167–71.

Horton, M. and Middleton, J. 2000. *The Swahili.* Oxford: Blackwell.

Horton, M. and Mudida, N. 1993. Exploitation of Marine Resources: Evidence for the Origin of the Swahili Communities of East Africa. In Shaw, T., Sinclair, P., Andah, B. and Okpoko, A. (eds.), *The Archaeology of Africa. Food, Metals and Towns.* London: Routledge, pp. 673–93.

Horton, R. 1971. African Conversion. *Africa* 41: 85–108.

1975. On the Rationality of Conversion. *Africa* 45: 219–35.

1993. *Patterns of Thought in Africa and the West: Essays on Magic, Religion.* Cambridge: Cambridge University Press.

Hourani, G. F. 1995. *Arab Seafaring* (expanded and rev. edn by J. C. Carswell, with additional notes from H. Frost, M. Horton, D. King, G. King, P. Morgan, G. Scanlon and H. Wright). Princeton: Princeton University Press.

Hrbek, I. and El-Fasi, M. 1992. Stages in the Development of Islam and its Dissemination in Africa. In Hrbek, I. (ed.), *UNESCO General History of Africa,* vol. III: *Africa from the Seventh to the Eleventh Century* (abridged edn). London: Heinemann, pp. 31–49.

Huard, P. and Bacquie, Capt. 1964. Un Etablissement islamique dans le désert tchadien. *Bulletin de l'Institut Français d'Afrique Noire (B)* 26: 1–20.

Huffman, T. 1996. *Snakes and Crocodiles. Power and Symbolism in Ancient Zimbabwe.* Johannesburg: Witwatersrand University Press.

Huntingford, G. W. B. 1955. Arabic Inscriptions in Southern Ethiopia. *Antiquity* 29: 230–3.

Hunwick, J. 1973. The Mid-Fourteenth Century Capital of Mali. *Journal of African History* 14: 195–206.

1985a. *Shari'a in Songhay: The Replies of al-Maghili to the Questions of Askia al-Hajj Muhammad*. London: Oxford University Press.

1985b. Songhay, Borno and the Hausa States, 1450–1600. In Ajayi, J. F. A. and Crowder, M. (eds.), *The History of West Africa*, vol. I. Harlow: Longman, pp. 323–71.

1989. Islam in Tropical Africa to c.1900. In Clarke, P. (ed.), *Islam*. London: Routledge, pp. 164–79.

1992. Black Africans in the Mediterranean World: Introduction to a Neglected Aspect of the African Diaspora. In Savage, E. (ed.), *The Human Commodity. Perspectives on the Trans-Saharan Slave Trade*. London: Frank Cass, pp. 5–38.

1994. Comment by John Hunwick. *Saharan Studies Association Newsletter*. 2: 11.

1999. *Timbuktu and the Songhay Empire*. Leiden: Brill.

Hunwick, J. and O'Fahey, R. S. 1994. *Arabic Literature of Africa*, vol. I: *The Writings of Eastern Sudanic Africa*. Leiden: Brill.

1995. *Arabic Literature of Africa*, vol. II: *The Writings of Central Sudanic Africa*. Leiden: Brill.

1998. *Arabic Literature of Africa*, vol. III: *The Writings of the Muslim Peoples of Eastern Africa*. Leiden: Brill.

Hutton MacDonald, R. and MacDonald, K. 1996. A Preliminary Report on the Faunal Remains Recovered from Gao Ancien and Gao-Saney (1993 Season). In Insoll 1996b, pp. 124–5.

Idowu, E. B. 1962. *Olódùmarè: God in Yoruba Belief*. London: Longman.

Iliffe, J. 1995. *Africans. The History of a Continent*. Cambridge: Cambridge University Press.

Insoll, T. 1993a. Looting the Antiquities of Mali: The Story Continues at Gao. *Antiquity* 67: 628–32.

1993b. A Note on a Sewn Canoe in Use at Gao, the Republic of Mali. *International Journal of Nautical Archaeology* 22: 345–50.

1994. The External Creation of the Western Sahel's Past: The Use and Abuse of the Arabic Sources. *Archaeological Review from Cambridge* 13 (1): 39–49.

1995. A Cache of Hippopotamus Ivory at Gao, Mali; and a Hypothesis of its Use. *Antiquity* 69: 327–36.

1996a. The Archaeology of Islam in Sub-Saharan Africa: A Review. *Journal of World Prehistory* 10: 439–504.

1996b. *Islam, Archaeology and History, A Complex Relationship: The Gao Region (Mali). Ca AD 900–1250*. Cambridge Monographs in African Archaeology 39. BAR International Series 647. Oxford: Tempus Reparatum.

1996c. A Report on an Archaeological Reconnaissance made to the Dahlak Islands. Unpublished paper, University of Cambridge.

1997a. An Archaeological Reconnaissance made to Dahlak Kebir, the Dahlak Islands, Eritrea: Preliminary Observations. In Fukui, K., Kurimoto, E. and Shigeta, M. (eds.), *Ethiopia in Broader Perspective: Papers of the Thirteenth International Conference of Ethiopian Studies*, vol. I. Kyoto: Shokado Book Sellers, pp. 382–8.

1997b. Iron Age Gao: An Archaeological Contribution. *Journal of African History* 38 (1): 1–30.

1997c. Mosque Architecture in Buganda, Uganda. *Muqarnas* 14: 179–88.

1997d. Ngandu and Ngambezi, Two Sites in North-Western Tanzania Associated with the Expedition of John Hanning Speke 1861–1863. *Azania* 32: 109–12.

1998a. Archaeological Research in Timbuktu, Mali. *Antiquity* 72: 413–17.

1998b. East Africa. In Rodriguez, J. P. (ed.), *The Historical Encyclopedia of World Slavery*. Santa Barbara (Calif.): ABC Clio, pp. 239–40.

1998c. Islamic Glass from Gao, Mali. *Journal of Glass Studies* 40: 77–88.

1998d. A Note on a Late Eleventh–Early Twelfth Century Sherd of Southern Chinese Celadon Found at Timbuktu, the Republic of Mali, West Africa. *The Oriental Ceramic Society Newsletter* 6: 18–19.

1998e. Review of *The Coral Buildings of Suakin. Islamic Architecture, Planning, Design and Domestic Arrangements in a Red Sea Port*, by J.-P. Greenlaw. *African Archaeological Review* 15: 81–4.

1999a. *The Archaeology of Islam*. Oxford: Blackwell.

(ed.). 1999b. *Case Studies in Archaeology and World Religions. The Proceedings of the Cambridge Conference*. BAR International Series 755. Oxford: Archaeopress.

1999c. Mud Mosques of Timbuktu. In Scarre, C. (ed.), *Great Builders of the Past*. London: Thames & Hudson, pp. 143–6.

2000a. The Origins of Timbuktu. *Antiquity* 74: 483–4.

2000b. *Urbanism, Archaeology and Trade. Further Observations on the Gao Region (Mali). The 1996 Fieldseason Results*. BAR S829. Oxford: British Archaeological Reports.

2001. Introduction. The Archaeology of World Religion. In Insoll, T. (ed.), *Archaeology and World Religion*. London: Routledge, pp. 1–32.

in press a. An Analysis of the Chinese Pottery from the Settlements of Mtambwe Mkuu and Ras Mkumbuu on Pemba Island, and Tumbatu and Mkokotoni on Zanzibar Island. In Horton, M. (ed.), *The Zanzibar and Pemba Excavations*. Nairobi: British Institute in Eastern Africa.

in press b. Timbuktu and Europe: Trade, Cities, and Islam in 'Medieval' West Africa. In Linehan, P. and Nelson, J. (eds.), *The Medieval World*. London: Routledge.

forthcoming. *Archaeology and Religion*. London: Routledge.

Insoll, T. and Bhan, K. 2001. Carnelian Mines in Gujarat. *Antiquity* 75: 495–6.

Insoll, T. and Shaw, T. 1997. Gao and Igbo-Ukwu: Beads, Inter-Regional Trade and Beyond. *African Archaeological Review* 14: 9–23.

Issa, A. 1995. The Burial of the Elite in Nineteenth Century Zanzibar Stone Town. In Sheriff, A. (ed.), *The History and Conservation of Zanzibar Stone Town*. London: James Currey, pp. 67–80.

Izard, M. and Ki-Zerbo, J. 1992. From the Niger to the Volta. In Ogot, B. A. (ed.), *UNESCO General History of Africa*, vol. V: *Africa from the Sixteenth to Eighteenth Centuries*. London: Heinemann, pp. 327–67.

Jacob, P. 1997. La Communauté Afar et l'Islam. In Fukui, K., Kurimoto, E. and Shigeta, M. (eds.), *Ethiopia in Broader Perspective: Papers of the Thirteenth International Conference of Ethiopian Studies*. vol. III. Kyoto: Shokado Book Sellers, pp.175–88.

Jama, A. D. 1990. Urban Origins on the Southern Somali Coast with Special Reference to Mogadishu. AD 1000–1600. In Sinclair, P. (ed.), *Urban Origins in East Africa. Proceedings of the 1990 Workshop*. Stockholm: Central Board of Arts, pp. 106–8.

Jansen, G. and Gauthier, J.-G. 1973. *Ancient Art of the Northern Cameroons: Sao and Fali*. Oosterhout: Anthropological Publications.

Jedrej, M. C. 1995. *Ingessana. The Religious Institutions of a People of the Sudan–Ethiopia Borderland*. Leiden: Brill.

Jedrej, M. C. and Shaw, R. 1992. *Dreaming, Religion and Society in Africa*. Leiden: Brill.

Jenkins, M. 1980. Medieval Maghribi Lustre-Painted Pottery. In *La Céramique médiévale en méditerranée occidentale*. Paris: Editions du CNRS, pp. 335–42.

Joffé, G. and Day-Viaud, V. 1995. *Chad*. World Bibilography Series 177. Oxford: Clio.

Johanson, D. C. and Edey, M. A. 1990. *Lucy. The Beginnings of Humankind*. London: Penguin.

Johnston, H. A. S. 1967. *The Fulani Empire of Sokoto*. London: Oxford University Press.

Jones, G. I. 1984. *The Art of Eastern Nigeria*. Cambridge: Cambridge University Press.

Jones, S. 1997. *The Archaeology of Ethnicity: Constructing Identities in the Past and Present*. London: Routledge.

Joussaume, R. 1980. *Le Mégalithisme en Ethiopie*. Addis Ababa: Addis Ababa University.

Juma, A. M. 1996a. Muslim Burial Customs on the East African Coast. *Tor* 28: 349–55.

　1996b. The Swahili and the Mediterranean World: Pottery of the Late Roman Period from Zanzibar. *Antiquity* 70: 148–54.

Kagabo, J. H. 1988. *L'Islam et les 'Swahili' au Rwanda*. Paris: Editions de L'Ecole des Hautes Etudes en Sciences Sociales.

Kalck, P. 1993. *Central African Republic*. World Bibliography Series 152. Oxford: Clio.

Karanth, R. V. 1992. The Ancient Gem Industry in Cambay. *Man and Environment* 17: 61–70.

Karrar, A. S. 1992. *The Sufi Brotherhoods in the Sudan*. London: Hurst.

Kati, M. 1913. *Tarikh el-Fettach* (Houdas, O. and Delafosse, M. ed. and trans.). Paris: Ernest Leroux.

Kawatoko, M. 1993a. Preliminary Survey of Aydhab and Badi Sites. *Kush* 16: 203–25.

　1993b. On the Tombstones found at the Badi Site, the al-Rih Island. *Kush* 16: 186–224.

Kennedy, J. G. (ed.). 1978a. *Nubian Ceremonial Life. Studies in Islamic Syncretism and Cultural Change*. Berkeley: UCLA Press.

　1978b. Nubian Death Ceremonies. In Kennedy 1978a, pp. 224–44.

Kenoyer, J. M., Vidale, M. and Bhan, K. K. 1991. Contemporary Stone Bead Making in Khambhat, India: Patterns of Craft Specialisation and Organisation of Production as Reflected in the Archaeological Record. *World Archaeology* 23: 44–63.

Kense, F. J. 1987. The Impact of Asante on the Trade Patterns of Northern Ghana and Ivory Coast. In Schildkrout, E. (ed.), *The Golden Stool: Studies of the Asante Center and Periphery*. New York: American Museum of Natural History, pp. 29–35.

　1990. Archaeology in Anglophone West Africa. In Robertshaw, P. (ed.), *A History of African Archaeology*. London: James Currey, pp. 135–54.

Kervran, M. 1999. Le Commerce maritime au moyen âge. *Dossiers d'Archéologie* June: 46–53.

Kervran, M., Negre, A. and Pirazzoli t'Sertsevens, M. 1982. *Excavation of Qal'at al-Bahrain*. Bahrain: Ministry of Information.

Kessy, E. T. 1997. Archaeological Sites Survey from Kisiju to Dar es Salaam. *Nyame Akuma* 48: 57–69.

Khalidi, O. 1988. African Diaspora in India: The Case of the Habashis of the Dakan. *Hamdard Islamicus* 11(4): 3–22.

Khan, H.-U. 1994. An Overview of Contemporary Mosques. In Frishman and Khan 1994, pp. 247–72.

Kidane, G. and Wilding, R. 1976. *The Ethiopian Cultural Heritage*. Addis Ababa: University of Addis Ababa.

Kigongo Mugerwa, R. 1991. *Kasubi Tombs*. Kampala: R. M. K. Associates.

Kirby, J. P. 1994. Cultural Change and Religious Conversion in Africa. In van Beek, W. E. A. and Blakely, T. (eds.), *Religion in Africa. Experience and Expression*. London: James Currey, pp. 57–71.

Kirk-Greene, A. H. M. 1958. *Adamawa Past and Present*. London: Oxford University Press.

Kirkman, J. 1954. *The Arab City of Gedi: Excavations at the Great Mosque, Architecture and Finds*. Oxford: Oxford University Press.

   1963. *Gedi, the Palace*. The Hague: Mouton.

   1964. *Men and Monuments on the East African Coast*. London: Lutterworth Press.

   1966. *Ungwana on the Tana*. The Hague: Mouton.

   1974. *Fort Jesus. A Portuguese Fortress on the East African Coast*. Oxford: Clarendon Press.

Kleppe, E. J. 2000. The Funj Problem in Archaeological Perspective. In Spaulding, J. and Beswick, S. (eds.), *White Nile, Black Blood. War, Leadership and Ethnicity from Khartoum to Kampala*. Trenton: Red Sea Press, pp. 237–61.

Knight, I. 1989. *Queen Victoria's Enemies 2. Northern Africa*. London: Osprey.

Kohl, P. and Fawcett, C. 1995. *Nationalism, Politics and the Practice of Archaeology*. Cambridge: Cambridge University Press.

Kratz, E. 1989. Islam in Indonesia. In Clarke, P. (ed.), *Islam*. London: Routledge, pp. 119–49.

Kritzeck, J. and Lewis, W. H. (eds.). 1969. *Islam in Africa*. New York: Van Nostrand-Reinhold.

Krzyszkowska, O. 1990. *Ivory and Related Materials. An Illustrated Guide*. London: Institute of Classical Studies.

Kubai, A. 1992. The Early Muslim Communities of Nairobi. *Islam et Sociétés au Sud du Sahara* 6: 33–44.

Kuban, D. 1974. *Muslim Religious Architecture*. Leiden: Brill.

Lane, P. 1993. Tongwe Fort. *Azania* 28: 133–41.

   2001. The Archaeology of Christianity in Global Perspective. In Insoll, T. (ed.), *Archaeology and World Religion*. London: Routledge, pp. 148–81.

Lange, D. 1984. The Kingdoms and Peoples of Chad. In Niane, D. T. (ed.), *UNESCO General History of Africa*, vol. IV: *Africa from the Twelfth to Sixteenth Centuries*. London: Heinemann, pp. 238–65.

   1989. Preliminaires pour une histoire des Sao. *Journal of African History* 30: 189–210.

   1991. Les Rois de Gao-Sané et les Almoravides. *Journal of African History* 32: 251–76.

1992. The Chad Region as a Crossroads. In Hrbek, I. (ed.), *UNESCO General History of Africa*, vol. III: *Africa from the Seventh to the Eleventh Century* (abridged edn). London: James Currey, pp. 216–25.

1993. Ethnogenesis from within the Chadic State. *Paideuma* 39: 261–77.

1994. From Mande to Songhay: Towards a Political and Ethnic History of Medieval Gao. *Journal of African History* 35: 275–301.

Lange, D. and Berthoud, S. 1977. Al-Qasaba et d'autres villes de la route centrale du Sahara. *Paideuma* 23: 19–40.

Lapidus, I. M. 1988. *A History of Islamic Societies*. Cambridge: Cambridge University Press.

Lassner, J. 1970. *The Topography of Baghdad in the Early Middle Ages*. Detroit: Wayne State University Press.

Last, M. 1979. Early Kano: The Santolo-Fangwai Settlement System. *Kano Studies* 1: 7–23.

Latruffe, J. 1953. Au Sujet d'une pièce d'or millénaire trouvée à Gao. *Notes Africaines* 60: 102–3.

Lavers, J. E. 1983. An Introduction to the History of Bagirmi. *C*.1500–1800. *Annals of Borno* 1: 29–44.

LaViolette, A. 1994. Masons of Mali: A Millennium of Design and Technology in Earthen Materials. In Childs, S. T. (ed.), *Society, Culture, and Technology in Africa*. MASCA Research Papers in Science and Archaeology 11, pp. 87–97.

1995. Women Craft Specialists in Jenne. In Conrad, D. C. and Frank, B. E. (eds.), *Status and Identity in West Africa. Nyamakalaw of Mande*. Bloomington: Indiana University Press, pp. 170–81.

in press. Swahili Archaeology on Pemba Island, Tanzania: Pujini, Bandari ya Faraji and Chwaka. *Nyame Akuma* 53.

LaViolette, A. and Fleisher, J. 1995. Reconnaissance of Sites Bearing Triangular Incised (Tana Tradition) Ware on Pemba Island, Tanzania. *Nyame Akuma* 44: 59–65.

Law, R. 1967. The Garamantes and Trans-Saharan Enterprise in Classical times. *Journal of African History* 8: 181–200.

1980. *The Horse in West African History*. Oxford: Oxford University Press.

Lawrence, A. W. 1963. *Trade Castles and Forts of West Africa*. London: Jonathan Cape.

Leary, A. 1978. West Africa. In Mitchell, G. (ed.), *Architecture of the Islamic World*. London: Thames & Hudson, pp. 274–7.

Lebeuf, A. M. D. 1962. Enceintes de briques de la région tchadienne. In Mortelmans, G. and Nenquin, J. (eds.), *Actes du IVe Panafricain Congres de Préhistoire et de l'Etude du Quaternaire*. Tervuren: Musée Royal de l'Afrique Centrale, pp. 437–43.

1967. Boum Massenia. Capitale de l'Ancien Royaume du Baguirmi. *Journal des Africanistes* 37: 214–44.

1969. *Les Principautés Kotoko: Essai sur le caractère sacré de l'autorité*. Paris: CNRS.

Lebeuf, A. M. D. and Lebeuf, J. P. 1973. Symbolic Monuments of the Logone-Birni Royal Palace (Northern Cameroons). In Alexandre, P. (ed.), *French Perspectives in African Studies*. London: Oxford University Press, pp. 62–72.

Lebeuf, J. P. and Kirsch, J. H. I. 1989. *Ouara, ville perdue (Tchad)*. Paris: Editions Recherches sur les Civilisations.

Lebeuf, J. P., Treinen-Claustre, F. and Courtin, J. 1980. *Le Gisement Sao de Mdaga*. Paris: Société d'Ethnographie.

Levtzion, N. 1968. *Muslims and Chiefs in West Africa*. Oxford: Clarendon Press.

1973. *Ancient Ghana and Mali*. London: Methuen.

1978. The Sahara and the Sudan from the Arab Conquest of the Maghrib to the Rise of the Almoravids. In Fage, J. D. (ed.), *The Cambridge History of Africa*, vol. II. Cambridge: Cambridge University Press, pp. 637–80.

(ed.). 1979a. *Conversion to Islam*. New York: Holmes & Meier.

1979b. Patterns of Islamization. In Levtzion 1979a, pp. 207–16.

1979c. Toward a Comparative Study of Islamization. In Levtzion 1979a, pp.1–23.

1985a. The Early States of the Western Sudan to 1500. In Ajayi, J. and Crowder, M. (eds.), *History of West Africa*, vol. I. Harlow: Longman, pp. 129–66.

1985b. Slavery and Islamization in Africa: A Comparative Study. In Willis 1985b, pp. 182–98.

1986a. Merchants vs. Scholars and Clerics in West Africa: Differential and Complementary Roles. *Asian and African Studies* 20: 27–43.

1986b. Rural and Urban Islam in West Africa. An Introductory Essay. *Asian and African Studies* 20: 7–26.

1992. Berber Nomads and Sudanese States: The Historiography of the Desert–Sahel Interface. Unpublished paper, International Conference on Manding Studies. Bamako, Mali.

2000. Islam in the Bilad al-Sudan to 1800. In Levtzion and Pouwels 2000, pp. 63–91.

Levtzion, N. and Fisher, H. (eds.). 1986. Rural and Urban Islam in West Africa. *Asian and African Studies* 20.

Levtzion, N. and Hopkins, J. F. P. 1981. *Corpus of Early Arabic Sources for West African History*. Cambridge: Cambridge University Press.

Levtzion, N. and Pouwels, R. (eds.). 2000. *The History of Islam in Africa*. Oxford: James Currey.

Lewicki, T. 1960. Quelques extraits inédits relatifs aux voyages des commerçants et des missionaires ibadites nord-africains au pays du Soudan occidental et central au moyen âge. *Folia Orientalia* 2: 1–12, 1–27.

1962. L'Etat nord-africain de Tahert et ses relations avec le Soudan occidental à la fin du VIIIe et au IXe siècle. *Cahiers d'Etudes Africaines* 8: 513–35.

1964. Traits d'histoire du commerce transsaharien, marchands et missionaires ibadites en Soudan occidental et central au cours des VIIIe–XIIe siècles. *Etnografia Polska* 8: 291–311.

1971. The Ibadites in Arabia and Africa. *Cahiers d'Histoire Mondiale* 13: 3–130.

1974. *West African Food in the Middle Ages*. Cambridge: Cambridge University Press.

Lewis, H. S. 1966. The Origins of the Galla and Somali. *Journal of African History* 7: 27–46.

Lewis, I. M. (ed.). 1966. *Islam in Tropical Africa*. London: Oxford University Press.

1980a. Introduction. In Lewis, I. M. 1980b, pp. 4–98.

(ed.). 1980b. *Islam in Tropical Africa* (2nd edn). London: Hutchinson.

1980c. Preface. In Lewis, I. M. 1980b, pp. vii–ix.

1986. Islam in Somalia. In Loughran, K. S. et al. (eds.), *Somalia in Word and Image*. Bloomington: Indiana University Press, pp. 139–42.

1994. *Peoples of the Horn of Africa* (repr.). Asmara: Red Sea Press.

Lewis, N. 1938. *Sand and Sea in Arabia.* London: Headley Brothers.

Lhote, H. 1960. *The Search for the Tassili Frescoes.* London: Readers Union Hutchinson.

1972. Recherches sur Takedda, ville decrité par le voyageur arabe Ibn Battouta et située en Air. *Bulletin de l'Institut Fondamental d'Afrique Noire (B)* 34: 429–70.

1982. *Les Chars rupestres sahariens.* Paris: Editions des Hespérides.

Liesegang, G. 1972. Archaeological Sites on the Bay of Sofala. *Azania* 7: 147–59.

Ligers, Z. 1964. *Les Sorko (Bozo). Maîtres du Niger.* Paris: Librarie des Cinq Continents.

Liverani, M. 2000. Looking for the Southern Frontier of the Garamantes. *Sahara* 12: 31–44.

Logan, P. N. 1929. The Walled City of Kano. *Journal of the Royal Institute of British Architects* 36: 402–6.

Lovejoy, P. E. 1983. *Transformations in Slavery. A History of Slavery in Africa.* Cambridge: Cambridge University Press.

1985. The Internal Trade of West Africa before 1800. In Ajayi, J. and Crowder, M. (eds.), *History of West Africa*, vol. I. Harlow: Longman, pp. 648–90.

1986. *Salt of the Desert Sun.* Cambridge: Cambridge University Press.

Low, D. A. 1971. *Buganda in Modern History.* Berkeley: University of California Press.

Lowick, N. 1985. Islamic Coins and Weights from Julfar. In Hansman, J. (ed.), *Julfar, an Arabian Port: Its Settlement and Far Eastern Ceramic Trade from the Fourteenth to the Eighteenth Centuries.* London: Royal Asiatic Society, pp. 1–9.

Lyons, D. 1996. The Politics of House Shape: Round vs Rectilinear Domestic Structures in Déla Compounds, Northern Cameroon. *Antiquity* 70: 351–67.

MacDonald, K. 1995. Why Chickens? The Centrality of the Domestic Fowl in West African Ritual and Magic. In Ryan, K. and Crabtree, P. J. (eds.), *The Symbolic Role of Animals in Archaeology.* Philadelphia: University of Pennsylvania Museum of Archaeology and Anthropology, pp. 51–6.

1997. The Late Stone Age and Neolithic Cultures of West Africa and the Sahara. In Vogel, J. (ed.), *Encyclopedia of Precolonial Africa.* Walnut Creek: Altamira, pp. 394–8.

MacEachern, S. 1993. Selling the Iron for their Shackles: Wandala–Montagnard Interactions in Northern Cameroon. *Journal of African History* 34: 247–70.

Mack, J. 1994. *African Masking.* In Mack, J. (ed.), *Masks. The Art of Expression.* London: British Museum Press, pp. 33–55.

1995. Islamic Influences: The View from Madagascar. In Ådahl, K. and Sahlstrom, B. (eds.), *Islamic Art and Culture in Sub-Saharan Africa.* Uppsala: Acta Universitatis, pp. 123–37.

MacLean, M. R. 2000. The Locally Manufactured Pottery. In Insoll 2000b, pp. 62–97.

MacLean, M. R. and Insoll, T. 1999. The Social Context of Food Technology in Iron Age Gao, Mali. *World Archaeology* 31: 78–92.

Madigan, C. T. 1922. A Description of Some Old Towers in the Red Sea Province, North of Port Sudan. *Sudan Notes and Records* 5: 78–82.

Manger, L. O. 1994. *From the Mountains to the Plains.* Uppsala: Scandinavian Institute of African Studies.

Mapunda, B. 1995. An Archaeological View of the History and Variation of Ironworking in Southwestern Tanzania. Ph.D. thesis, University of Florida, Gainesville.

Marcais, G. and Dessum-Lamarre, A. 1946. Tihert-Tagdemt. *Revue Africaine* 90: 24–57.

Marcais, G. and Poinssot, L. 1952. *Objets kairouanais. IXe au XIIIe siècle. Reliures, verreries, cuivres et bronzes, bijoux.* Tunis: Direction des Antiquités et Arts.

Marchi, S. 1997. Les Peintures rupestres d'Aïré Soroba au Mali. In Sottas, B., Hammer, T., Roost Vischer, L. and Mayor, A. (eds.), *Afrikanische Studien Band 11.* Hamburg: Lit Verlag, pp. 75–87.

Marissal, J. 1978. Le Commerce zanzibarite dans l'Afrique des Grands Lacs au XIXe siècle. *Revue Française d'Histoire d'Outre-Mer* 65: 212–55.

Marty, P. 1917. *Etudes de l'Islam au Sénégal.* Paris: Leroux.

Masonen, P. 1994. *Ancient Ghana in European Thought.* Unpublished paper, African history seminar, School of Oriental and African Studies, London.

Masonen, P., and Fisher, H. 1995. Not Quite Venus from the Waves. The Almoravid Conquest of Ghana in West African Historiography. Unpublished paper, International Conference on Mande Studies, Leiden.

Mathew, G. 1956. Chinese Pottery in East Africa and on the Coast of Southern Arabia. *Oriental Art* 2: 50–5.

Matthews, D. H. 1953. The Red Sea Style. *Kush* 1: 60–87.

Mattingly, D., al-Mashai, M., Aburgheba, H., Balcombe, P., Eastaugh, E., Gillings, M., Leone, A., McLaren, S., Owen, P., Pelling, R., Reynolds, T., Stirling, L., Thomas, D., Watson, D., Wilson, A. and White, K. 1997. The Fezzan Project 1997: Methodologies and Results of the First Season. *Libyan Studies* 28: 11–25.

Mattingly, D., al-Mashai, M., Chapman, S., Coddington, H., Davison, J., Kenyon, D., Wilson, A. and Witcher, R. 1998. The Fezzan Project 1998. Preliminary Report on the Second Season of Work. *Libyan Studies* 29: 115–44.

Mauny, R. 1950. La Tour et la mosquée de l'Askia Mohammed à Gao. *Notes Africaines* 47: 66–7.

  1951a. Sur l'emplacement de la ville de Tademekka, antique capitale des Berbères soudanais. *Notes Africaines* 51: 65–9.

  1951b. Notes d'archéologie au Sujet de Gao. *Bulletin de l'Institut Français d'Afrique Noire (B)* 13: 837–52.

  1952. Notes d'archéologie sur Tombouctou, *Bulletin de l'Institut Français d'Afrique Noire (B)* 14: 899–918.

  1961. *Tableau géographique de l'Ouest Africain au moyen âge.* Dakar: Institut Français de l'Afrique Noire.

  1978. Trans-Saharan Contacts and the Iron Age in West Africa. In Fage, J. D. (ed.), *The Cambridge History of Africa,* vol. II: *From c.500 BC to AD 1050.* Cambridge: Cambridge University Press, pp. 272–341.

Mayor, A. 1997. Les Rapports entre la Diina Peule du Maasina et les populations du delta intérieur du Niger, vus au travers des traditions historiques et des fouilles archéologiques. In de Bruijn, M. and van Dijk, H. (eds), *Peuls et Mandingues.* Paris: Karthala, pp. 35–60.

Mbiti, J. S. 1970. *Concepts of God in Africa.* London: SPCK.

  1975. *Introduction to African Religion.* London: Heinemann.

McClelland, E. M. 1982. *The Cult of Ifa among the Yoruba*. London: Ethnographica.

McHugh, N. 1994. *Holymen of the Blue Nile*. Evanston: Northwestern University Press.

McIntosh, R. J. 1989. Middle Niger Terracottas Before the Sympleglades Gateway. *African Arts* 22(2): 74–83.

  1998. *The Peoples of the Middle Niger*. Oxford: Blackwell.

McIntosh, R. J. and McIntosh, S. K. 1979. Terracotta Statuettes from Mali. *African Arts* 12(2): 51–3.

  1988. From Siècles Obscurs to Revolutionary Centuries in the Middle Niger. *World Archaeology* 20: 141–65.

McIntosh, R. J., Togola, T. and Keech McIntosh, S. 1995. The Good Collector and the Premise of Mutual Respect among Nations. *African Arts* (Autumn): 60–9.

McIntosh, S. K. (ed.). 1995. *Excavations at Jenne-jeno, Hambarketolo, and Kaniana (Inland Niger Delta, Mali), the 1981 Season*. Los Angeles: University of California Press.

McIntosh, S. K. and Bocoum, H. 1998. An 800-year Cultural Sequence at Sincu Bara: Evaluating the Implications. Unpublished Paper presented at the SAFA Conference, Syracuse, New York, May 1998.

  2000. New Perspectives on Sincu Bara, a First Millennium Site in the Senegal Valley. *African Archaeological Review* 17: 1–43.

McIntosh, S. K. and McIntosh, R. J. 1980. *Prehistoric Investigations in the Region of Jenne, Mali*. Cambridge Monographs in African Archaeology 2. Oxford: British Archaeological Reports.

  1984. The Early City in West Africa: Towards an Understanding. *The African Archaeological Review* 2: 73–98.

  1986. Archaeological Reconnaissance in the Region of Timbuktu, Mali. *National Geographic Research* 2: 302–19.

  1988. From Stone to Metal: New Perspectives on the Later Prehistory of West Africa. *Journal of World Prehistory* 2: 89–133.

  1993. Field Survey in the Tumulus Zone of Senegal. *African Archaeological Review* 11: 73–107.

McLeod, M. D. 1981. *The Asante*. London: British Museum Press.

McNaughton, P. 1988. *The Mande Blacksmiths*. Bloomington: Indiana University Press.

Ménage, V. L. 1979. The Islamization of Anatolia. In Levtzion 1979a, pp. 52–67.

Mercier, M. 1922. *La Civilisation urbaine au Mzab*. Algiers: University of Algiers.

  1928. Notes sur une architecture berbère saharienne. *Hesperis* 8: 413–29.

Meyer, C., Todd, J. M., and Beck, C. W. 1991. From Zanzibar to Zagros: A Copal Pendant from Eshnunna. *Journal of Near Eastern Studies* 50: 289–98.

Middleton, K. 1999. Introduction. In Middleton, K. (ed.), *Ancestors, Power and History in Madagascar*. Leiden: Brill, pp. 1–36.

Miles, G. C. 1952: Mihrab and Anazah: A Study in Early Islamic Iconography. In Miles, G. C. (ed.), *Archaeologica Orientalia in Memoriam Ernst Herzfeld*. New York: J. J. Augustin, pp. 156–71.

Milner, N. 2000. The Marine and Freshwater Molluscs. In Insoll 2000b, pp. 36–8.

  forthcoming. The Shell Money of Timbuktu. In Insoll, T. *Recent Archaeological Research in Timbuktu* (working title).

Miner, H. 1953. *The Primitive City of Timbuctoo*. Princeton: Princeton University Press.

Mitchell, J. C. 1956. *The Yao Village*. Manchester: Manchester University Press.

Mohammed, I. M. 1986. *The Archaeology of Central Darfur (Sudan) in the First Millennium AD*. Cambridge Monographs in African Archaeology 14. Oxford: British Archaeological Reports.

Momen, M. 1985. *An Introduction to Shi'i Islam. The History and Doctrines of Twelver Shi'ism*. Oxford: George Ronald.

Momin, K. N. 1989. Urban Ijedu Ode. An Archaeological, Topographical, Toponymical Perspective. *West African Journal of Archaeology* 19: 37–49.

Monod, T. 1938. Teghaza, la ville en Sel Gemme (Sahara occidental). *La Nature* (15 May): 289–96.

1940. Nouvelles Remarques sur Teghaza (Sahara occidental). *Bulletin de l'Institut Français d'Afrique Noire* 2: 248–54.

1969. Le 'Ma'den Ijafen: une epave caravanière ancienne dans la Majabat al-Koubra. *Actes du 1er Colloque International d'Archéologie Africaine, 1966. Fort Lamy*. Fort Lamy: Institut National Tchadien pour les Sciences Humaines, pp. 286–320.

1975. A Propos des bracelets de verre sahariens. *Bulletin de l'Institut Fondamental d'Afrique Noire (B)* 37: 702–18.

Monteil, V. 1964. *L'Islam noir: une religion à la conquête de l'Afrique*. Paris: Seuil.

Moody, H. 1967. The Walls of Kano City. *Nigeria Magazine* 92: 19–38.

Mordini, A. 1957. Un Tissu musulman du moyen âge provenant du couvent de Dabra Dammo (Tigrai, Ethiopie). *Annales d'Ethiopie* 2: 75–7.

Morris, B. 1987. *Anthropological Studies of Religion*. Cambridge: Cambridge University Press.

Morrison, H. M. 1989a. The Beads. In Munro-Hay 1989, pp. 168–78.

1989b. The Glass. In Munro-Hay 1989, pp. 188–209.

1991. Vessels of Glass. In Welsby and Daniels 1991, pp. 246–59.

Mortimore, M. 1970. Settlement, Evolution and Land Use. In Mortimore, M. (ed.), *Zaria and its Region – A Nigerian Savanna City and its Environs*. Zaria: Ahmadu Bello University Department of Geography Occasional Paper 4: 102–22.

Mosse, D. 1994. The Politics of Religious Synthesis: Roman Catholicism and Hindu Village Society in Tamil Nadu, India. In Stewart, C. and Shaw, R. (eds.), *Syncretism/Anti Syncretism. The Politics of Religious Synthesis*. London: Routledge, pp. 85–107.

Moughtin, J. C. 1964. The Traditional Settlements of the Hausa People. *The Town Planning Review* 35: 21–34.

1972. The Friday Mosque, Zaria City. *Savanna* 1: 143–63.

1985. *Hausa Architecture*. London: Ethnographica.

Msiska, A. W. C. 1995. The Spread of Islam in Malawi and its Impact on Yao Rites of Passage. *The Society of Malawi Journal* 48: 49–86.

Munro-Hay, S. (ed.). 1989. *Excavations at Aksum*. London: British Institute in Eastern Africa.

1991. *Aksum. An African Civilisation of Late Antiquity*. Edinburgh: Edinburgh University Press.

1996. Aksumite Overseas Interests. In Reade, J. (ed.), *The Indian Ocean in Antiquity*. London: Kegan Paul, pp. 403–16.

Munson, P. 1980. Archaeology and the Prehistoric Origins of the Ghana Empire. *Journal of African History* 21: 457–66.

Mutoro, H. W. 1994. The Mijikenda *Kaya* as a Sacred Site. In Carmichael, D., Hubert, J., Reeves, B. and Schanche, A. (eds.), *Sacred Sites, Sacred Places*. London: Routledge, pp. 132–9.

Muzzolini, A. 1986. *L'Art rupestre préhistorique des massifs centraux sahariens*. BAR S318. Oxford: British Archaeological Reports.

1994. Les Chars au Sahara et en Egypte. Les Chars des 'Peuples de la Mer' et la 'Vague Orientalisante' en Afrique. *Revue d'Egyptologie* 45: 207–34.

1996. Northern Africa: Some Advances in Rock Art Studies. In Bahn, P. and Fossati, A. (eds.), *Rock Art Studies, News of the World I*. Oxford: Oxbow, pp. 59–70.

1997. Saharan Rock Art. In Vogel, J. (ed.), *Encyclopedia of Precolonial Africa*. Walnut Creek: Altamira, pp. 347–52.

Nadel, S. F. 1954. *Nupe Religion*. London: Routledge & Kegan Paul.

Nasr, S. H. 1991. *Islamic Spirituality. vol. II: Manifestations*. London: SCM Press.

Nast, H. 1996. Islam, Gender, and Slavery in West Africa c.1500: A Spatial Archaeology of the Kano Palace, Northern Nigeria. *Annals of the Association of American Geographers* 86: 44–77.

Nawata, H. 1997. An Exported Item from Badi on the Western Red Sea Coast in the Eighth Century. Historical and Ethnographical Studies on Operculum as Incense and Perfume. In Fukui, K., Kurimoto, E. and Shigeta, M. (eds.), *Ethiopia in Broader Perspective: Papers of the Thirteenth International Conference of Ethiopian Studies*, vol. I. Kyoto: Shokado Book Sellers, pp. 307–25.

Nesbitt, L. M. 1955. *Desert and Forest*. London: Penguin.

Newbold, D. N. n.d. Archive papers (Beja). Griffith Institute, Ashmolean Museum, Oxford.

Niane, D. T. 1984. Mali and the Second Mandingo Expansion. In Niane, D. T. (ed.), *UNESCO General History of Africa*, vol. IV: *Africa from the Twelfth to Sixteenth Centuries*. London: Heinemann, pp. 117–71.

1986. *Sundiata. An Epic of Old Mali*. Harlow: Longman.

Nicholson, S. E. 1996. Environmental Change within the Historical period. In Adams et al. 1996, pp. 60–87.

Nicolaisen, J. 1963. *Ecology and Culture of the Pastoral Tuareg*. Copenhagen: National Museum.

Nicolas, G. 1966. Essai sur les structures fondamentals de l'espace dans la cosmologie Hausa. *Journal de la Société des Africanistes* 36: 65–107.

Nicolle, D. 1995. *The Janissaries*. London: Osprey.

Nizami, F. A. 1989. Islam in the Indian Subcontinent. In Clarke, P. (ed.), *Islam*. London: Routledge, pp. 62–83.

Norris, H. T. 1990. *Sufi Mystics of the Niger Desert*. Oxford: Oxford University Press.

Norton, J. D. 1989. The Turks and Islam. In Clarke, P. (ed.), *Islam*. London: Routledge, pp. 84–101.

Nurse, D. 1983. A Linguistic Reconstruction of Swahili Origins. *Azania* 18: 127–50.

Nurse, D. and Hinnesbusch, T. J. 1993. *Swahili and Sabaki: A Linguistic History*. Berkeley: University of California Press.

Nurse, D. and Spear, T. 1985. *The Swahili. Reconstructing the History and Language of an African Society, 800–1500*. Philadelphia: University of Pennsylvania Press.

Obayemi, A. M. 1977. Archaeology and the History of Western Hausaland: An Introductory Contribution. *Ahmadu Bello University. Northern History Research Scheme. Fourth Interim Report. 1971–1976*. Zaria: Ahmadu Bello University, pp. 72–82.

Oded, A. 1974. *Islam in Uganda. Islamization through a Centralized State in Pre-Colonial Africa*. New York: John Wiley.

O'Fahey, R. S. 1979. Islam, State, and Society in Dar Fur. In Levtzion 1979a, pp. 189–206.

   1980. *State and Society in Dar Fur*. London: Hurst & Co.

   1982. Fur and Fartit. The History of a Frontier. In Mack, J. and Robertshaw, P. (eds.), *Culture History in the Southern Sudan. Archaeology, Linguistics and Ethnohistory*. Nairobi: British Institute in Eastern Africa, pp. 75–87.

O'Fahey, R. S. and Spaulding, J. 1974. *Kingdoms of the Sudan*. London: Methuen.

Ogundiran, A. 1994. Archaeological Survey at Ipole-Ijesa, Southwestern Nigeria. A Preliminary Report. *Nyame Akuma* 42: 7–13.

Oliver, P. 1987. *Dwellings. The House Across the World*. Oxford: Phaidon.

Oman, G. 1974. The Islamic Necropolis of Dahlak Kebir in the Red Sea. Report on a Preliminary Survey Carried out in April 1972. *East and West* 24: 249–95.

Omosade Awolalu, J. 1979. *Yoruba Beliefs and Sacrificial Rites*. Harlow: Longman.

Onwuejeogwu, M. 1972. The Cult of the Bori Spirits among the Hausa. In Douglas, M. and Kaberry, P. M. (eds.), *Man in Africa*. London: Tavistock, pp. 279–305.

Ottenberg, S. 1971. A Moslem Igbo Village. *Cahiers d'Etudes Africaines* 11: 231–60.

Otto, R. 1950. *The Idea of the Holy*. Oxford: Oxford University Press.

Owusu-Ansah, D. 1983. Islamic Influence in a Forest Kingdom: The Role of Protective Amulets in Early Nineteenth Century Asante. *TransAfrican Journal of History* 12: 100–33.

   2000. Prayer, Amulets and Healing. In Levtzion and Pouwels 2000, pp. 477–88.

Ozanne, P. 1969. The Diffusion of Smoking in West Africa. *Odu. Journal of Yoruba Studies* 2: 29–42.

   1971. Ghana. In Shinnie, P. L. (ed.), *The African Iron Age*. Oxford: Clarendon Press, pp. 36–65.

Palmer, H. R. 1967. *Sudanese Memoirs*. London: Frank Cass.

Pankhurst, Richard 1975. Some Notes on the Historical and Economic Geography of the Mesewa Area. *Journal of Ethiopian Studies* 8: 91–116.

   1979. Ethiopian Medieval and Post-Medieval Capitals: Their Development and Principal Features. *Azania* 14: 1–19.

   1985. *History of Ethiopian Towns from the Middle Ages to the Early Nineteenth Century*. Wiesbaden: Franz Steiner Verlag.

   1988. Muslim Commercial Towns, Villages and Markets of Christian Ethiopia Prior to the Rise of Tewodros. In Uhlig, S. and Tayla, B. (eds.), *Collectanea Aethiopica*. Stuttgart: Franz Steiner Verlag, pp. 111–30.

   1998. *The Ethiopians*. Oxford: Blackwell.

Pankhurst, Rita. 1997. The Coffee Ceremony and the History of Coffee Consumption in Ethiopia. In Fukui, K., Kurimoto, E. and Shigeta, M. (eds.),

Ethiopia in Broader Perspective: Papers of the Thirteenth International Conference of Ethiopian Studies, vol. II. Kyoto: Shokado Book Sellers, pp. 516–39.

Paques, V. 1977. *Le Roi pêcheur et le roi chasseur*. Strasbourg: University of Strasbourg.

Paribeni, R. 1907. Ricerche nel luògo dell'antica Adulis. *Monumenti Antichi, Reale Accademia del Lincei* 18: 438–572.

Paris, F., Bernus, E. and Cressier, P. (eds.). 1999. *Vallée de l'Azawagh (Sahara du Niger)*. Paris: SEPIA.

Park, M. 1807. *Travels in the Interior Districts of Africa. 1795, 1796, and 1797*. London: W. Bulmer & Co.

Parkin, D. 1991. *Sacred Void. Spatial Images of Work and Ritual among the Giriama of Kenya*. Cambridge: Cambridge University Press.

Parratt, S. N. 1989. Muslims in Botswana. *African Studies* 48: 71–81.

Parrinder, G. 1953. *Religion in an African City*. London: Oxford University Press.
    1976. *African Traditional Religion*. Westport: Greenwood Press.

Paul, A. 1952. Ancient Tombs in Kassala Province. *Sudan Notes and Records* 33: 54–7.
    1954. *A History of the Beja Tribes of the Sudan*. Cambridge: Cambridge University Press.
    1955. Aidhab: A Medieval Red Sea Port. *Sudan Notes and Records* 36: 64–70.

Pefontan, Lieutenant. 1922. Histoire de Tombouctou de sa Fondation à l'occupation française (XIIe siècle–1893). *Bulletin du Comité d'Etudes Historiques et Scientifiques de l'Afrique Occidentale Française* (1922): 81–113.

Pellat, C. 1971. Hayawan. *Encyclopedia of Islam* (2nd edn), vol. III. Leiden: Brill, pp. 304–9.

Pels, P. 1997. The Anthropology of Colonialism: Culture, History and the Emergence of Western Governmentality. *Annual Review of Anthropology* 26: 163–83.

Penniman, T. K. 1952. *Pictures of Ivory and other Animal Teeth*. Oxford: Pitt-Rivers Museum.

Peters, F. E. 1994. *The Hajj. The Muslim Pilgrimage to Mecca and the Holy Places*. Princeton: Princeton University Press.

Peters, R. 1977. *Jihad in Medieval and Modern Islam*. Leiden: Brill.

Petersen, A. 1994. The Archaeology of the Syrian and Iraqi Hajj Routes. *World Archaeology* 26: 47–56.

Petherbridge, G. T. 1978. The House and Society. In Michell, G. (ed.), *Architecture of the Islamic World*. London: Thames & Hudson, pp. 193–208.

Phillips, J. 1997. Punt and Aksum: Egypt and the Horn of Africa. *Journal of African History* 38: 423–57.

Phillips, T. (ed.). 1995. *Africa. The Art of a Continent*. London: Royal Academy of Arts.

Phillipson, D. 1981. A Preliminary Archaeological Reconnaissance of the Southern Sudan, 1977–8. *Azania* 16: 1–6.
    1985. *African Archaeology* (2nd edn). Cambridge: Cambridge University Press.
    1995. Excavations at Aksum, Ethiopia, 1993–4. *Antiquaries Journal* 75: 1–41.
    (ed.). 1997. *The Monuments of Aksum*. Addis Ababa: Addis Ababa University Press.
    1998. *Ancient Ethiopia*. London: British Museum.

Phillipson, D. and Reynolds, A. 1996. BIEA Excavations at Aksum, Northern Ethiopia, 1995. *Azania* 31: 99–147.

Philon, H. 1980. *Early Islamic Ceramics*. Athens: Benaki Museum.

Picton, J. 1995a. Islam, Artifact and Identity in Southwestern Nigeria. In Ådahl, K. and Sahlstrom, B. (eds.), *Islamic Art and Culture in Sub-Saharan Africa*. Uppsala: Acta Universitatis, pp. 71–98.

    1995b. West Africa and the Guinea Coast. In Phillips 1995, pp. 327–477.

Pinder-Wilson, R. H. 1960. *ADJ*, Ivory. In *The Encyclopedia of Islam*, vol. I. Leiden: Brill, pp. 200–3.

Plumley, J. M. 1970. Qasr Ibrim 1969. *Journal of Egyptian Archaeology* 56: 12–18.

Polet, J. 1985. *Tegdaoust IV. Fouillé d'un quartier de Tegdaoust*. Paris: Editions Recherche sur les Civilisations.

Posnansky, M. 1973. The Early Development of Trade in West Africa: Some Archaeological Considerations. *Ghana Social Science Journal* 2: 87–100.

    1980. Trade and the Development of the State and Town in Iron Age West Africa. In Leakey, R. and Ogot, B. A. (eds.), *Proceedings of the Eighth Pan-African Congress*. Nairobi: Louis Leakey Memorial Institute for African Prehistory, pp. 373–5.

    1987. Prelude to Akan Civilisation. In Schildkrout, E. (ed.), *The Golden Stool: Studies of the Asante Center and Periphery*. New York: American Museum of Natural History, pp. 14–22.

Pouwels, R. 2000. The East African Coast. *c*.790 to 1900 CE. In Levtzion and Pouwels 2000, pp. 251–71.

Price, T. 1964. Yao Origins. *The Nyasaland Journal* 17(2): 11–16.

Prins, A. H. J. 1967. *The Swahili-Speaking Peoples of the East African Coast*. London: International African Institute.

Proudfoot, L. 1959. Mosque Building and Tribal Separatism in Freetown East. *Africa* 29: 405–16.

Prussin, L. 1994. Sub-Saharan West Africa. In Frishman and Khan 1994, pp. 181–93.

Puglisi, G. 1969. Alcuni vestigi dell'Isola di Dahlac Chebir e la leggènda dei Furs, *Proceedings of the Third International Conference of Ethiopian Studies*. Addis Ababa: Institute of Ethiopian Studies, pp. 35–47.

Pwiti, G. 1991. Trade and Economics in Southern Africa. *c*.AD 700–1200. *Zimbabwea* 3: 51–6.

Raimbault, M. 1991. Prospection dans les Daounas et environs (Juin 1986). In Raimbault, M. and Sanogo, K. (eds.), *Recherches archéologiques au Mali*. Paris: Karthala, pp. 203–14.

Rangeley, W. H. J. 1963. The Arabs. *Nyasaland Journal* 16: 11–25.

Ranger, T. 1991. African Traditional Religions. In Sutherland, S. and Clarke, P. (eds), *The Study of Religion, Traditional and New Religion*. London: Routledge, pp. 106–14.

Ravaisse, P. 1931. Appendice 1: Stèles et inscriptions arabes du Harar. In Azaïs and Chambard 1931, pp. 283–309.

Ray, B. C. 1976. *African Religions*. Englewood Cliffs: Prentice Hall.

Ray, K. 1987. Material Metaphor, Social Interaction and Historical Reconstruction: Exploring Patterns of Association and Symbolism in the Igbo-Ukwu Corpus. In Hodder, I. (ed.), *The Archaeology of Contextual Meanings*. Cambridge: Cambridge University Press, pp. 66–77.

Redding, R. W. 1992. The Vertebrate Remains. pp.113–17 in Wright, H., Early Islam, Oceanic Trade and Town Development on Nzwani: The Comorian Archipelago in the IIth–XVth Centuries AD. *Azania* 27: 81–128.

Redding, R. W. and Goodman, S. 1984. Reptile, Bird and Mammal Remains. pp. 51–54 in Wright, H., Early Seafarers of the Comoro Islands: The Dembeni Phase of the IXth–Xth Centuries AD. *Azania* 19: 13–59.

Reed, G. 1994. Archaeological Remains in the Kebkebiya Area of Northern Darfur. *Sudan Archaeological Research Society Newsletter* 7: 5–19.

Reichmuth, S. 2000. Islamic Education and Scholarship in Sub-Saharan Africa. In Levtzion and Pouwels 2000, pp. 419–40.

Reid, D. A. M. 1991. Evidence for Ivory Bead Manufacture and other Beads from Excavations at Ntusi, Southern Uganda. *Bead Study Trust Newsletter* 18: 1–2.

Reid, D. A. M. and Segobye, A. 2000. An Ivory Cache from Botswana. *Antiquity* 74: 326–31.

Reygasse, M. 1950. *Monuments funéraires préislamiques de l'Afrique du nord*. Paris: Arts et Métiers Graphiques.

Reyna, S. P. 1990. *Wars Without End*. Hanover: University Press of New England.

Ricklefs, M. C. 1979. Six Centuries of Islamization in Java. In Levtzion 1979a, pp. 100–28.

Robert, D. 1970a. Les Fouilles de Tegdaoust. *Journal of African History* 11: 471–93.

1970b. Report on the Excavations at Tegdaoust. *West African Archaeological Newsletter* 12: 64–8.

Robert, S. 1970. Fouilles archéologiques sur le site présumé d'Aoudaghost (1961–1968). *Folia Orientalia* 12: 261–78.

Robert-Chaleix, D. 1983. Céramiques découvertes à Tegdaoust. In Devisse 1983, pp. 245–94.

1989. *Tegdaoust V*. Paris: Editions Recherche sur les Civilisations.

Robertshaw, P. 1986. Engaruka Revisited: Excavations of 1982. *Azania* 21: 1–26.

1990. The Development of Archaeology in Eastern Africa. In Robertshaw, P. (ed.), *A History of African Archaeology*. London: James Currey, pp. 78–94.

1997. Munsa Earthworks: A Preliminary Report on Recent Excavations. *Azania* 32: 1–20.

Robinson, D. 2000. Revolutions in the Western Sudan. In Levtzion and Pouwels 2000, pp. 131–52.

Roche, M. 1970. *Le M'zab. Architecture ibadite en Algerie*. Paris: Arthaud.

Rogers, M. 1976. *The Spread of Islam*. Oxford: Elsevier.

Roman, S. 1990. *The Development of Islamic Library Collections in Western Europe and North America*. London: Mansell.

Rosander, E. E. 1997. Introduction. The Islamization of 'Tradition' and 'Modernity'. In Rosander and Westerlund 1997, pp. 1–27.

Rosander, E. E. and Westerlund, D. (eds.). 1997. *African Islam and Islam in Africa*. London: Hurst.

Roscoe, J. 1911. *The Baganda*. London: Macmillan.

Rose, P. J. n.d. *Report on the Pottery from Berenike Pancrysos 1997*. Unpublished paper, McDonald Institute, Cambridge.

Roset, J. P. 1986. Iwelen – An Archaeological Site of the Chariot Period in Northern Aïr, Niger. *Libya Antiqua*. Paris: UNESCO, pp. 113–46.

Ross, E. S. in press. Africa in Islam. What the Afrocentric Perspective can Contribute to the Study of Islam. *International Journal of Islamic and Arabic Studies*.

Rouch, J. 1950. The Sorkawa, Nomad Fishermen of the Middle Niger. *Farm and Forest* 10: 36–53.

1953. *Contribution à l'histoire des Songhay*. Dakar: Institut Français de l'Afrique Noire.

1954. *Les Songhay*. Paris: Presses Universitaires de France.

Rowley-Conwy, P. 1989. Nubia AD 0–550 and the 'Islamic' Agricultural Revolution: Preliminary Botanical Evidence from Qasr Ibrim. *Archéologie du Nil Moyen* 3: 131–8.

Roy, B. 2000. The Beads. In Insoll 2000b, pp. 98–126.

Ryan, P. J. 1978. *Imale: Yoruba Participation in the Muslim Tradition*. Harvard: Scholars Press.

Ryle, J. 1982. *Warriors of the White Nile: The Dinka*. Amsterdam: Time-Life Books.

Saad, E. N. 1983. *Social History of Timbuktu. The Role of Muslim Scholars and Notables 1400–1900*. Cambridge: Cambridge University Press.

Sadr, K., Castiglione, A. and Castiglione, A. 1993. *Interim Report on the Eastern Desert Research Centre's (CeRDO) Archaeological Activities 1989/93*. Varese: Centro Ricerche sul Deserto Orientale.

Saitowitz, S. J., Reid, D. L. and van der Merwe, N. J. 1996. Glass Bead Trade from Islamic Egypt to South Africa *c*.AD 900–1250. *South African Journal of Science* 92:101–4.

Salama, P. 1990. The Sahara in Classical Antiquity. In Mokhtar, G. (ed.), *General History of Africa* (abridged edn), vol. II: *Ancient Civilisations of Africa*. London: James Currey, pp. 286–95.

Salt, H. 1967 [1814]. *A Voyage to Abyssinia*. London: Frank Cass.

Sanneh, L. 1979. *The Jakhanke*. London: International African Institute.

1994. Translatability in Islam and Christianity in Africa. In Blakely, T., van Beek, W. and Thomson, D. (eds.), *Religion in Africa. Experience and Expression*. London: James Currey, pp. 23–45.

1997. *The Crown and the Turban*. Oxford: Westview.

Sanogo, K. 1991. La Mission d'inventaire dans la zone de retenue du barrage de Manantali. In Raimbault, M. and Sanogo, K. (eds.), *Recherches archéologiques au Mali*. Paris: Karthala, pp. 151–63.

Sanseverino, H. 1983. Archaeological Remains on the Southern Somali Coast. *Azania* 18: 151–64.

Sassoon, H. 1966. Engaruka. Excavations during 1964. *Azania* 1: 79–99.

Sassoon, H. 1983. Kings, Cattle and Blacksmiths: Royal Insignia and Religious Symbolism in the Interlacustrine States. *Azania* 18: 93–106.

Sauvaget, J. 1950. Les Epitaphes royales de Gao. *Bulletin de l'Institut Français de l'Afrique Noire* 12: 418–40.

Schacht, J. 1954. Sur la diffusion des formes d'architecture religieuse musulmane à travers le Sahara. *Travaux de l'Institut de Recherches Sahariennes* 11: 11–27.

1957a. Islam in Northern Nigeria. *Studia Islamica* 8: 123–46.

1957b. Notes Mozabites. *Al-Andalus* 22: 1–20.

1961. Further Notes on the Staircase Minaret. *Ars Orientalis* 4: 137–41.

1964. *An Introduction to Islamic Law*. Oxford: Clarendon Press.

1970. *Islamic Calligraphy*. Leiden: Brill.

1975. *Mystical Dimensions of Islam*. Chapel Hill: University of North Carolina Press.

1990. *Calligraphy and Islamic Culture*. London: I. B. Tauris.

Schmidt, P. 1996. Using Archaeology to Remake History in Africa. In Schmidt, P. and Patterson, T. (eds.), *Making Alternative Histories*. Santa Fe: School of American Research Press, pp. 119–47.

Schmidt, P. and McIntosh, R. J. 1996. *Plundering Africa's Past*. Oxford: James Currey.

Schneider, M. 1967. Stèles funéraires arabes de Quiha. *Annales d'Ethiopie* 7: 107–18.

1970. Stèles funéraires musulmanes de la province du Choa. *Annales d'Ethiopie* 8: 73–8.

Schoff, W. H. 1995 *The Periplus of the Erythraean Sea* (repr.). Delhi: Munshiram Manoharlal.

Serjeant, R. B. 1966. South Arabia and Ethiopia – African Elements in the South Arabian Population. *Proceedings of the Third International Conference of Ethiopian Studies*. Addis Ababa: Institute of Ethiopian Studies, pp. 25–33.

Sharp, L. 1999. Royal Difficulties: The Anxieties of Succession in an Urbanized Sakalava Kingdom. In Middleton, K. (ed.), *Ancestors, Power and History in Madagascar*. Leiden: Brill, pp. 103–43.

Sharpe, E. J. 1986. *Comparative Religion. A History*. London: Duckworth.

Shaw, R. and Stewart, C. 1994. Introduction: Problematizing Syncretism. In Stewart, C. and Shaw, R. (eds.), *Syncretism/Anti Syncretism. The Politics of Religious Synthesis*. London: Routledge, pp. 1–26.

Shaw, T. 1970. *Igbo-Ukwu, an Account of Archaeological Discoveries in Eastern Nigeria*. London: Faber & Faber.

1977. *Unearthing Igbo-Ukwu*. Ibadan: Oxford University Press.

1978. *Nigeria, its Archaeology and Early History*. London: Thames & Hudson.

1985. The Prehistory of West Africa. In Ajayi, J. and Crowder, M. (eds.), *History of West Africa*, vol. I. Harlow: Longman, pp. 48–86.

1995a. Further Light on Igbo-Ukwu, Including New Radiocarbon Dates. In Andah, B., de Maret, P. and Soper, R. (eds.), *Proceedings of the Ninth Pan-African Congress on Prehistory and Related Studies*. Ibadan: Rex Charles, pp. 79–83.

1995b. Those Igbo-Ukwu Dates Again. *Nyame Akuma* 44: 43.

Sheriff, A. 1987. *Slaves, Spices and Ivory in Zanzibar*. London: James Currey.

1992. Mosques, Merchants and Landowners in Zanzibar Stone Town. *Azania* 27: 1–20.

1995. An Outline History of Zanzibar Stone Town. In Sheriff, A. (ed.), *The History and Conservation of Zanzibar Stone Town*. London: James Currey, pp. 8–29.

Shinnie, P. 1955. Excavations at Soba. Sudan Antiquities Service Occasional Papers 3. Khartoum: Sudan Antiquities Service.

1981. Archaeology in Gonja, Ghana. In *Le Sol, la parole et l'écrit. Mélanges en hommage à Raymond Mauny*. Paris: Société Française d'Histoire d'Outre-Mer, pp. 65–70.

1996. Early Asante: Is Wilks Right? In Hunwick, J., and Lawler, N. (eds.), *The Cloth of Many Colored Silks*. Evanston: Northwestern University Press, pp. 195–203.

Shinnie, P. and Kense, F. J. 1989. *Archaeology of Gonja, Ghana. Excavations at Daboya.* Calgary: University of Calgary Press.

Shinnie, P. and Ozanne, P. 1962. Excavations at Yendi Dabari. *Transactions of the Historical Society of Ghana* 6: 87–118.

Shinnie, P. and Shinnie, A. 1995. *Early Asante.* Calgary: University of Calgary Press.

Sidebotham, S. E. and Wendrich, W. Z. 1998. Berenike: Archaeological Fieldwork at a Ptolemaic–Roman Port on the Red Sea Coast of Egypt: 1994–1998. *Sahara* 10: 85–96.

Silverman, R. 1991. Arabic Writing and the Occult. In Fisher, C. G. (ed.), *Brocade of the Pen. The Art of Islamic Writing.* Michigan: Michigan State University, pp. 19–30.

Silverman, R. A. 1982. 14th–15th century Syrio-Egyptian Brassware in Ghana. *Nyame Akuma* 20: 13–16.

Simoons, F. J. 1981. *Eat Not This Flesh.* Westport: Greenwood.

    1994. *Eat Not This Flesh* (2nd edn). Madison: University of Wisconsin Press.

Simpson, St J. 1995. Death and Burial in the Late Islamic Near East: Some Insights from Archaeology and Ethnography. In Campbell, S. and Green, A. (eds.), *The Archaeology of Death in the Ancient Near East.* Oxford: Oxbow Books, pp. 240–51.

Sims, E. 1978. Markets and Caravanserais. In Michell, G. (ed.), *Architecture of the Islamic World.* London: Thames & Hudson, pp. 97–111.

Sinclair, P. 1982. Chibuene. An Early Trading Site in Southern Mozambique. *Paideuma* 28: 149–64.

    1984. Some Aspects of the Economic Level of the Zimbabwe State. *Zimbabwea* 1(1): 48–53.

    1987. *Space, Time and Social Formation.* Uppsala: Uppsala University.

Skinner, D. E. 1978. Mande Settlement and the Development of Islamic Institutions in Sierra Leone. *International Journal of African Historical Studies* 11: 32–62.

    1997. Islam in the Northern Hinterland and its Influence on the Development of the Sierra Leone Colony. In Jalloh, A. and Skinner, D. E. (eds.), *Islam and Trade in Sierra Leone.* Trenton: Africa World Press.

Skinner, E. P. 1964. *The Mossi of the Upper Volta.* Stanford: Stanford University Press.

    1980. Islam in Mossi Society. In Lewis, I. M. 1980b, pp. 173–93.

Smith, A. 1970. Some Considerations Relating to the Formation of States in Hausaland. *Journal of the Historical Society of Nigeria* 5: 329–46.

Smith, M. C. and Wright, H. T. 1988. The Ceramics from Ras Hafun in Somalia: Notes on a Classical Maritime Site. *Azania* 23: 115–41.

Smith, M. G. 1964. The Beginnings of Hausa Society. In Vansina, J., Mauny, R. and Thomas, L. V. (eds.), *The Historian in Tropical Africa.* London: Oxford University Press, pp. 339–54.

Smith, R. S. 1988. *Kingdoms of the Yoruba.* London: James Currey.

    1989. *Warfare and Diplomacy in Pre-Colonial West Africa.* London: James Currey.

Smith, S. E. 1980. The Environmental Adaptation of Nomads in the West African Sahel: A Key to Understanding Prehistoric Pastoralism. In Williams, M. A. J. and Faure, H. (eds.), *The Sahara and the Nile.* Rotterdam: Balkema, pp. 467–87.

Snow, P. 1988. *The Star Raft. China's Encounter with Africa*. London: Weidenfeld & Nicolson.

Soghayroun, I. Z. 1984. *The Omani and South Arabian Muslim Factor in East Africa: The Role of the Zanzibari and Swahili Traders in the Spread of Islam in Uganda*. Riyadh: Dar al-'Ulum.

Spaulding, J. 1972. The Funj: A Reconsideration. *Journal of African History* 13: 39–53.

   1985. *The Heroic Age in Sinnar*. East Lansing: African Studies Centre.

   2000. Precolonial Islam in the Eastern Sudan. In Levtzion and Pouwels 2000, pp. 117–29.

Speke, J. H. 1863. *Journal of the Discovery of the Source of the Nile*. London: Blackwood.

Spring, C. 1993. *African Arms and Armour*. London: British Museum.

Stahl, A. B. 1994. Innovation, Diffusion, and Culture Contact: The Holocene Archaeology of Ghana. *Journal of World Prehistory* 8: 51–112.

Stangroome, C. 2000. The Faunal Remains from Gadei. In Insoll 2000b, pp. 56–61.

Stenning, D. J. 1959. *Savannah Nomads*. London: Oxford University Press.

Stern, E. 1987. Early Roman Glass from Heis on the North Somali Coast. *Annales du 10e Congrès pour l'Histoire du Verre. Madrid 1985*. Amsterdam: L'Association, pp. 23–26.

Stevenson, R. C. 1963. Some Aspects of the Spread of Islam in the Nuba Mountains. *Sudan Notes and Records* 44: 9–20.

   1984. *The Nuba People of Kordofan Province*. Khartoum: University of Khartoum.

Stoller, P. and Olkes, C. 1987. *In Sorcery's Shadow: A Memoir of Apprenticeship among the Songhay of Niger*. Chicago: Chicago University Press.

Stone, P. G. and Molyneaux, B. L. 1994. *The Presented Past: Heritage, Museums and Education*. London: Routledge.

Sutherland, S. 1991. The Study of Religion and Religions. In Sutherland, S. and Clarke, P. (eds.), *The Study of Religion, Traditional and New Religion*. London: Routledge, pp. 29–40.

Sutton, J. E. G. 1976. The Walls of Zaria and Kufena. Zaria Archaeology Paper 11 (mimeo).

   1977. Kufena and its Archaeology. Zaria Archaeology Paper 15 (mimeo).

   1979. Towards a Less Orthodox History of Hausaland. *Journal of African History* 20: 179–201.

   1989. Aksum, the Erythraean Sea, and the World of Late Antiquity: A Foreword. In Munro-Hay 1989, pp. 1–6.

   1990. *A Thousand Years of East Africa*. Nairobi: British Institute in Eastern Africa.

   1991. The International Factor at Igbo-Ukwu. *The African Archaeological Review* 9: 145–60.

   1994/5. East Africa: Interior and Coast. *Azania* 29–30: 227–31.

   1997. The African Lords of the Intercontinental Gold Trade before the Black Death: Al-Hasan bin Sulaiman of Kilwa and Mansa Musa of Mali. *Antiquaries Journal* 77: 221–42.

   1998a. Engaruka: An Irrigation Agriculture Community in Northern Tanzania Before the Maasai. *Azania* 33: 1–37.

   1998b. Kilwa. *Azania* 33: 113–69.

1998c. Ntusi and Bigo: Farmers, Cattle-Herders and Rulers in Western Uganda, AD 1000–1500. *Azania* 33: 39–72.

1999. Kilwa in the Early Fourteenth Century. Unpublished paper, Islam in East Africa Conference, Rome.

Swan, L. 1994. *Early Gold Mining on the Zimbabwe Plateau*. Uppsala: University of Uppsala.

Swift, J. 1975. Pastoral Nomadism as a Form of Land-Use: The Tuareg of the Adrar-n-Iforas. In Monod, T. (ed.), *Pastoralism in Tropical Africa*. London: International African Institute, pp. 443–54.

Swithenbank, M. 1969. *Ashanti Fetish Houses*. Accra: Ghana Universities Press.

Talbot Rice, D. 1971. *Islamic Painting. A Survey*. Edinburgh: Edinburgh University Press.

1993. *Islamic Art*. London: Thames & Hudson.

Tampoe, M. 1989. *Maritime Trade between China and the West*. BAR S555. Oxford: British Archaeological Reports.

Tarekegn, A. 1998. The Mortuary Practices of Aksumite Ethiopia with Particular Reference to the Gudit Stelae Field (GSF) Site. Ph.D. thesis, University of Cambridge.

Tayob, A. 1999. *Islam in South Africa*. Gainesville: University Press of Florida.

Tedeschi, S. 1969. Note Storiche Sulle Isole Dahlak, *Proceedings of the Third International Conference of Ethiopian Studies*. Addis Ababa: Institute of Ethiopian Studies, pp. 49–74.

Terrasse, H. 1938. Sur des tessons de poterie vernisée et peinte trouvés à Teghasa. *Bulletin du Comite d'Etudes Historique et Scientifique Afrique Occidentale Français* 21: 520–2.

Terry, P. T. 1965a. The Arab War on Lake Nyasa. Part 1. *The Society of Malawi Journal* 18(1): 55–77.

1965b. The Arab War on Lake Nyasa. Part 2. *The Society of Malawi Journal* 18(2): 13–52.

Thesiger, W. 1935. The Awash River and the Aussa Sultanate. *The Geographical Journal* 85: 1–23.

1998. *The Danakil Diary*. London: Flamingo.

Thilmans, G. and Ravisé, A. 1980. *Protohistoire du Sénégal II: Sinthiou Bara et les sites du fleuve. Mémoire de l'IFAN 91*. Dakar: Institut Fondamental de l'Afrique Noire.

Thomassey, P. and Mauny, R. 1951. Campagne de fouilles à Koumbi Saleh. *Bulletin de l'Institut Français de l'Afrique Noire (B)* 13: 438–62.

1956. Campagne de fouilles de 1950 à Koumbi Saleh. *Bulletin de l'Institut Français de l'Afrique Noire (B)* 18: 117–40.

Thorold, A. 1987. Yao Conversion to Islam. *Cambridge Anthropology* 12: 18–28.

1993. Metamorphoses of the Yao Muslims. In Brenner 1993c, pp. 79–90.

Tilahun, C. 1990. Traces of Islamic Material Culture in Northeastern Shoa. *Journal of Ethiopian Studies* 23: 303–20.

Tobert, N. 1988. *The Ethnoarchaeology of the Zaghawa of Darfur (Sudan)*. BAR S445. Oxford: British Archaeological Reports.

Togola, T. 1996. Iron Age Occupation in the Méma Region, Mali. *African Archaeological Review* 13: 91–110.

Török, L. 1997. *The Kingdom of Kush. Handbook of the Napatan–Meroitic Civilisation*. Leiden: Brill.

Trigger, B. 1989. *A History of Archaeological Thought.* Cambridge: Cambridge University Press.

Trimingham, J. S. 1949. *Islam in the Sudan.* London: Oxford University Press.
  1952. *Islam in Ethiopia.* London: Oxford University Press.
  1959. *Islam in West Africa.* Oxford: Clarendon Press.
  1962. *A History of Islam in West Africa.* London: Oxford University Press.
  1964. *Islam in East Africa.* Oxford: Clarendon Press.
  1968. *The Influence of Islam upon Africa.* London: Longman.
  1971a. Habash. In *The Encyclopedia of Islam* (2nd edn), vol. III. Leiden: Brill, pp. 5–6.
  1971b. *The Sufi Orders in Islam.* London: Oxford University Press.

Trivedi, R. K. 1964. *Agate Industry of Cambay. Census of India 5.* Delhi: Government of India.

Tubiana, M.-J. 1964. *Survivances préislamiques en pays Zaghawa.* Paris: Institut d'Ethnologie Musée de l'Homme.

Turner, H. W. 1991. Africa. In Sutherland, S. and Clarke, P. (eds.), *The Study of Religion, Traditional and New Religion.* London: Routledge, pp. 187–94.

Twaddle, M. 1993. *Kakungulu and the Creation of Uganda.* London: James Currey.

Ullendorff, E. 1956. Hebraic–Jewish Elements in Abyssinian Monophysite Christianity. *Journal of Semitic Studies* 1: 216–56.

Vanacker, C. 1979. *Tegdaoust II. Recherches sur Aoudaghost. Fouillé d'un quartier artisanal.* Nouakchott: Institut Mauritanien de la Recherche Scientifique.
  1983. Verres à décor géométrique à Tegdaoust. In Devisse 1983, pp. 515–22.

van Beek, W. 1988. Functions of Sculpture in Dogon Religion. *African Arts* 21(4): 58–65.

van Beek, W. and Blakely, T. 1994. Introduction. In Blakely, T., van Beek, W. and Thomson, D. (eds.), *Religion in Africa. Experience and Expression.* London: James Currey, pp. 1–20.

van Berchem, Marguerite. 1953. Uncovering a Lost City of the Sahara: Excavating Sedrata, the Thousand-Year-Old Capital of the Ibadites in Southern Algeria. *The Illustrated London News* 222: 165.
  1954. Un Chapitre nouveau de l'histoire de l'art musulmane, campagnes 1951 et 1952. *Ars Orientalis* 1: 157–72.

van Berchem, Max. 1920. Note sur les inscriptions lithiques rapportées par le mission de Gironcourt. In de Gironcourt 1920, pp. 355–6.

van der Sleen, W. G. N. n.d. Perles de Madagascar et de l'Afrique orientale. In *Arabes et Islamises à Madagascar et dans l'Océan Indien.* Antananarivo: Centre d'Archéologie de la Faculté des Lettres, pp. xi–xv.

Van der Veer, P. 1994. Syncretism, Multiculturalism and the Discourse of Tolerance. In Stewart, C. and Shaw, R. (eds.), *Syncretism/Anti Syncretism. The Politics of Religious Synthesis.* London: Routledge, pp. 196–211.

van Donzel, E. 1994. *Islamic Desk Reference* Leiden: Brill.

Vansina, J. 1966. *Kingdoms of the Savanna.* Madison: University of Wisconsin Press.
  1990. *Paths in the Rainforest.* London: James Currey.

Vansina, J., Mauny, R. and Thomas, L. V. 1964. The Influence of the Mande in West Africa. In Vansina, J., Mauny, R. and Thomas, L. V. (eds.), *The Historian in Tropical Africa.* London: Oxford University Press, pp. 91–3.

Vantini, G., Fr. 1975. *Oriental Sources Concerning Nubia*. Warsaw: Polish Academy of Sciences.

Verin, P. 1976. The African Element in Madagascar. *Azania* 11: 135–51.
    1986. *The History of Civilisation in North Madagascar*. Rotterdam: Balkema.
    1994. *Les Comores*. Paris: Karthala.

Vernier, E. and Millot, J. 1971. *Archéologie malgache*. Paris: Musée de l'Homme.

Viellard, G. 1940. Notes sur les Peuls du Fouta-Djallon. *Bulletin de l'Institut Français de l'Afrique Noire (B)* 2: 85–210.

Vikor, K. 2000. Sufi Brotherhoods in Africa. In Levtzion and Pouwels 2000, pp. 441–76.

Villiers, A. 1969. *Sons of Sinbad*. New York: Charles Scribner.

Vire, M. M. 1958: Notes sur trois épitaphes royales de Gao. *Bulletin de l'Institut Français de l'Afrique Noire (B)* 20: 368–76.

Voight, E. A. 1983. *Mapungubwe: An Archaeo-Zoological Interpretation of an Iron Age Community*. Pretoria: Transvaal Museum.

Waines, D. 1995. *An Introduction to Islam*. Cambridge: Cambridge University Press.

Watson, A. M. 1983. *Agricultural Innovation in the Early Islamic World*. Cambridge: Cambridge University Press.

Weir, S. 1985. *Qat in Yemen. Consumption and Social Change*. London: British Museum.

Welsby, D. 1996. *The Kingdom of Kush*. London: British Museum.
    1998. *Renewed Excavations within the Metropolis of the Kingdom of Alwa in Central Sudan*. London: British Museum Press.

Welsby, D. and Daniels, C. (eds.). 1991. *Soba. Archaeological Research at a Medieval Capital on the Blue Nile*. Nairobi: British Institute in Eastern Africa.

Wheatley, P. 1975a. Analecta Sino-Africana Recensa. In Chittick, N. and Rotberg, R. (eds.), *East Africa and the Orient*. New York: Africana, pp. 76–114.
    1975b. Appendix 2. Notes on Chinese Texts Containing References to East Africa. In Chittick, N. and Rotberg, R. (eds.), *East Africa and the Orient*. New York: Africana, pp. 284–90.

Whitcomb, D. 1983. Islamic Glass from al-Qadim, Egypt. *Journal of Glass Studies* 25: 101–8.
    1988. *Aqaba. Port of Palestine on the China Sea*. Chicago: Oriental Institute.

Whitehouse, D. 1968. Excavations at Siraf, First Interim Report. *Iran* 6: 1–22.
    1971. Excavations at Siraf, Fourth Interim Report. *Iran* 9: 1–18.

Wiet, G. 1951. Roitelets de Dahlak. *Bulletin d'Institut de l'Egypte* 34: 89–95.

Wilding, R. 1976. Harari Domestic Architecture. *Art and Archaeology Research Papers* 9: 31–7.
    1980. The Desert Trade of Eastern Ethiopia. In Leakey, R. E. and Ogot, B. A. (eds.), *Proceedings of the Eighth Pan-African Congress for Prehistory*. Nairobi: Louis Leakey Memorial Institute for African Prehistory, pp. 379–80.

Wildung, D. 1997. *Sudan. Ancient Kingdoms of the Nile*. Paris: Flammarion.

Wilks, I. 1965. A Note on the Early Spread of Islam in Dagomba. *Transactions of the Historical Society of Ghana* 8: 87–98.
    1980. The Position of Muslims in Metropolitan Ashanti. In Lewis I. M. 1980b, pp. 144–65.
    2000. The Juula and the Expansion of Islam into the Forest. In Levtzion and Pouwels 2000, pp. 93–115.

Willis, J. 1996. The Northern *Kayas* of the Mijikenda: A Gazetteer, and an Historical Reassessment. *Azania* 31: 75–98.

Willis, J. R. 1985a. Jihad and the Ideology of Enslavement. In Willis 1985b, pp. 16–26.

    (ed.). 1985. *Slaves and Slavery in Muslim Africa*, vol. I, *Islam and the Ideology of Enslavement*. London: Frank Cass.

Wilson, A. 1972. Long Distance Trade and the Luba Lomani Empire. *Journal of African History* 13: 575–89.

Wilson, R. T. 1984. *The Camel*. Harlow: Longman.

Wilson, T. 1979. Swahili Funerary Architecture of the Northern Kenya Coast. *Art and Archaeology Research Papers* (Dec.): 33–46.

    1982. Spatial Analysis and Settlement Patterns on the East African Coast. *Paideuma* 28: 201–19.

Wilson, T. and Omar, A. 1997. Archaeological Investigations at Pate. *Azania* 32: 31–76.

Works, J. A. 1976. *Pilgrims in a Strange Land. Hausa Communities in Chad*. New York: Columbia University Press.

Wright, G. R. H. 1987. Mud Building in Yemen. *Archäologische Berichte aus dem Yemen IV*. Mainz: Verlag Phillip von Zabern, pp. 203–17.

Wright, H. 1984. Early Seafarers of the Comoro Islands: The Dembeni Phase of the IXth–Xth Centuries AD. *Azania* 19: 13–59.

    1992. Early Islam, Oceanic Trade and Town Development on Nzwani: The Comorian Archipelago in the IIth–XVth Centuries AD. *Azania* 27: 81–128.

Wright, J. 1989. *Libya, Chad and the Central Sahara*. London: Hurst & Co.

    1992. The Wadai–Benghazi Slave Route. In Savage, E. (ed.), *The Human Commodity. Perspectives on the Trans-Saharan Slave Trade*. London: Frank Cass, pp. 174–84.

York, R. N. 1973. Excavations at New Buipe. *West African Journal of Archaeology* 3: 1–189.

Young, C. 1969. The Congo. In Kritzeck and Lewis 1969, pp. 250–69.

Zahan, D. 1960. *Société d'initiation Bambara*. Paris: Mouton.

    1970. *The Religion, Spirituality, and Thought of Traditional Africa*. Chicago: University of Chicago Press.

    1974. *The Bambara*. Leiden: Brill.

Zakari, M. 1985. Contribution à l'histoire des populations du sud-Est Nigérie. *Etudes Nigeriennes* 53. Niamey: Institut de Recherches en Sciences Humaines.

Zarins, J. and al-Badr, H. 1986. Archaeological Investigation in the Southern Tihama Plain II. *Atlal* 10: 36–57.

Zarins, J., Murad, A. and al-Yish, K. 1981. The Comprehensive Archaeological Survey Programme. The Second Preliminary Report on the Southwest Province. *Atlal* 5: 9–42.

Zarroug, M. 1991. *The Kingdom of Alwa. African Occasional Papers 5*. Calgary: University of Calgary Press.

Zekaria, A. 1991. Harari Coins. A Preliminary Survey. *Journal of Ethiopian Studies* 24: 23–46.

Zuesse, E. M. 1991. Perseverance and Transmutation in African Traditional Religions. In Olupone, J. K. (ed.), *African Traditional Religions in Contemporary Society*. New York: Paragon House, pp. 167–84.

INDEX